Canadian Political Party Systems

Canadian Political Party Systems:

A Reader

edited by R.K.Carty

broadview press

Canadian Cataloguing in Publication Data

Carty, R. Kenneth, 1944-

Canadian Political Party Systems: A Reader

ISBN 0-921149-90-5

1 - Political parties - Canada. 2. Canada - Politics and government. I. Title.

JL195.C37 1992   324.271   C92-093423-4

Broadview Press gratefully acknowledges the support of the Canada Council, the Ontario Arts Council and the Ontario Government

This book is for my teacher John Meisel at Queen's University and for my students at the University of British Columbia

Contents

Introduction Canadian Party Systems

This is a book about Canada's national political parties. It examines the how and why of their organization and operation, over three distinct periods in the country's political life. Not only are each of these periods important and interesting in their own right but I believe it is difficult to understand contemporary parties without an appreciation of their past. There is nothing here on the pre-Confederation period but for those interested I recommend Gordon Stewart's *The Origins of Canadian Politics* for a brief but brilliant introduction.

The readings are organized in terms of each of the three Canadian party systems. The first, a period of two-party national competition, stretched from Confederation until the first world war. It was followed by the second system, a period of Liberal dominance and brokerage that lasted to the late 1950s and the Diefenbaker realignment. By contrast, the contemporary system has been highly competitive with more political uncertainty and minority governments than any other time in our history. In each of these periods the electoral system has had a considerable impact on the parties. In an important essay Alan Cairns (*C.J.P.S.* vol. 1, #1) revealed how it shaped the second party system. Students will find it interesting to extend his analysis back into the first period, or forward to the contemporary one, to discover its impact on these quite different systems.

Each of the sections on the party systems has readings that discuss the political environment, the structure and organization of the parties, leadership, finance and the critical relationship between the media and the parties. This makes it possible to see each system as an operating whole. It also makes it possible to follow how any one of these aspects of Canadian party life changed over the three systems. In each of the sections on the first two systems I have deliberately included some readings written by contemporaries (e.g. Siegfried, Williams) who observed and studied the systems at first hand. There are also pieces by practicing politicians (Ames, Power and Walker) of each era. In their voices one can hear something of the rhythms of their parties and their times.

The other section of readings has several pieces that look at the three party systems from differing, but complementary, perspectives. Smith, Johnston et al., and Carty, who explore party governance, electoral appeals and coalitions, and party organization and practice respectively, all see the same three party systems. Together they make a powerful argument for interpreting Canadian party history in this way.

This set of readings was first put together for students in a course on Canadian political parties at the University of British Columbia. I want to thank those students. It continues to be a stimulating privilege to teach them. By listening, but then questioning, they ensure I do not get too fixed in my thinking. They also raise more issues that need to be researched if we are to understand this country. Research is fun at UBC, in large part because of a set of sparkling and encouraging colleagues. Among them I must particularly thank Don Blake, Alan Cairns, Dave Elkins, Richard Johnston, Paul Tennant and Lynda Erickson (now across town at Simon Fraser University) all who have listened to me talk about Canadian parties and applied appropriate correctives. Finally, I want to acknoweledge John Meisel who first got me interested in Canadian parties when I was a student at Queen's University many years ago. I know I was one of many but I treasure the experience no less for that. For me this book is a way of sharing that with my students.

Contributors

Herbert B. Ames Member of Parliament (for a Montreal riding) 1904-20, Financial Director of the League of Nations 1919-26, sociologist of working-class Montreal, businessman, civic reformer. He died in Montreal in 1954 in his 91st year.

Keith Archer teaches at the University of Calgary. Archer is one of the leading students of the NDP in Canada and recently published a book on it entitled *Political Choices and Electoral Consequences*.

Andre Blais is a political scientist at the University of Montreal. He has extraordinarily wide interests and has published in a number of areas of the discipline. Most recently he directed a survey for the Royal Commission on Electoral Reform and Party Financing on Canadians' attitudes towards electoral reform.

Henry Brady is a member of the National Election Survey team. He is currently a member of the Department of Political Science in the University of California at Berkeley and is widely regarded as one of the discipline's most innovative methodologists and students of electoral behaviour.

E. Donald Briggs teaches at the University of Windsor and is part of a group of scholars there interested in the role of the modern media.

R.K. Carty is an Associate Professor at the University of British Columbia currently finishing a study of constituency level party organization and activity. He recently published (with Don Blake & Lynda Erickson) *Grassroots Politicians: Party Activists in British Columbia.*

John Courtney is a senior member of the political science department at the University of Saskatchewan. His book, *The Selection of National Party Leaders in Canada,* remains one of the most definitive studies of party leadership. His interest in representation has led him to serve on the Federal Electoral Boundaries Commission in Saskatchewan.

John Crete is a well known political scientist at Laval University. He has published widely on Quebec electoral behaviour and was part of the 1988 national election study team.

John English teaches history at the University of Waterloo. He is the author of *The Decline of Politics* which looks at the Conservative Party in the first two decades of this century. At present he is working on the biography of Lester Pearson, Canada's 14th prime minister.

Lawrence Hanson is a graduate of the University of Saskatchewan. He did the research for the paper that appears in this reader while a graduate student at the University of British Columbia.

E.E. Harrill completed a PhD on the *Structure of Organization and Power in Canadian Political Parties* at the University of North Carolina in 1958. The piece used here is an excerpt from that work.

Richard Johnston is one of Canada's leading students of voting behaviour. He teaches political science at the University of British Columbia which was the host institution for the 1988 national election survey. The path-breaking work done by his group is reported in *Letting the People Decide* published by McGill-Queen's University Press.

John Meisel, a Queen's political scientist, Meisel is recognized as the founder of electoral behaviour research in Canada and as one of the country's most influential students, teachers and interpreters of its party politics.

Leslie Pal is a University of Calgary political scientist. Best known for his work on public policy he also edited an interesting book on Canadian political leadership *Prime Ministers & Premiers* from which the essay reprinted here is drawn.

K.Z. Paltiel The late K.Z. Paltiel was for long Canada's leading scholar of political finance. His work as research director for the Barbeau Committee on Election Expenses in the 1960s laid the groundwork for many of the reforms of the following decade.

C.G. (Chubby) Power Member of Parliament (1917-55) and subsequently Senator, Power was one of the Liberal Party's leading organizers in Quebec over the life of the second party system. His memoir *A Party Politician* still makes fascinating reading for anyone interested in the period.

Walter Romanow teaches at the University of Windsor and is part of a group of scholars there interested in the role of the modern media.

Royal Commission on Electoral Reform and Party Financing was created in November 1969 to conduct a sweeping review of the workings of Canadian elections. Its 1991 report *Reforming Electoral Democracy* sets an agenda for modernization and change. The Commission consisted of Pierre Lortie (Chairman), Pierre Fortier, William Knight, Robert Gabor and Lucie Pepin. The publications of its research programme, under the direction of Peter Aucoin, will provide a valuable resource for students of Canadian parties and elections.

Paul Rutherford is a historian at the University of Toronto. The piece used here is from his interesting book on the daily press in 19th century Canada entitled *A Victorian Authority*.

André Siegfried was a distinguished French academic who contributed to many fields and made especially important contributions to electoral geography. In Canada, however, he is remembered for his book *The Race Question in Canada*, first published in 1906 but still considered one of the most insightful interpretations of this country. All students of Canadian history and politics should read it.

David Smith is a political scientist at the University of Saskatchewan. Smith has written a number of important books on western politics including *The Regional Decline of a National Party*.

Walter Soderlund teaches at the University of Windsor and is part of a group of scholars there interested in the role of the modern media.

Gordon Stewart is a Scot who teaches Canadian history to Americans at Michigan State University. He is the author of an important book on 19th century Canada entitled *The Origins of Canadian Politics*.

Brian Tanguay teaches Canadian politics at Wilfrid Laurier University. His past research has focused of political economy and Quebec politics.

Ronald Wagenberg teaches at the University of Windsor and is part of a group of scholars there interested in the role of the modern media.

Peter Waite is one of the country's leading historians. He has had an especial interest in the Maritimes and is the author of a wonderful biography of Sir John Thompson, Canada's 4th prime minister.

David Walker has been a political scientist at the University of Winnipeg, an associate of Angus Reid (the pollster), and in 1988 was elected the Liberal MP for Winnipeg North-Centre defeating the NDP in what had long been their safest seat in the country.

Joseph Wearing teaches political science at Trent University. Wearing has combined an active role in the Liberal party with his academic interest in Canadian parties. Among other work he is the author of *The L-Shaped Party*.

Reginald Whitaker is the author of *The Government Party*, an extraordinarily rich study of the Liberal party during the second party system. He is currently a member of the political science department at York University.

John R. Williams is an American political scientist who wrote an important study of the Conservative party over the period 1920-49.

Jeremy Wilson teaches politics at the University of Victoria in British Columbia. His current research deals with environmental policy making.

Walter Young The late Walter Young was a political scientist at the University of British Columbia and later the University of Victoria. He published widely on Canadian politics but is perhaps best known for his *Anatomy of a Party,* a biography of the CCF.

PART 1 The First Party System

The readings in this section deal with the character of Canadian parties during the first party system (from Confederation to World War I) and reveal the distinctive flavour of this period. The first is taken from André Siegfried's *The Race Question in Canada,* first published in 1907 and still thought by many to be one of the best books ever written about Canadian politics. Siegfried was so perceptive about the essence of Canadian life that it seems hard to believe that he wrote this ninety years ago. More than one student, on discovering the book, has instinctively compared Siegfried to that other great French interpreter of North American life, Alexis de Tocqueville. We have only a short excerpt from *The Race Question* here, but the whole book is a must for students of early Canada.

The second and third readings, from historians Gordon Stewart and Peter Waite, focus on the centrality of patronage to all aspects of politics and party-building in this first party system. Stewart demonstrates just how the party leaders of the period systematically used patronage to build and sustain the parties that were vital to the initial rounds of Canadian state-building. In a stimulating little book, *The Origins of Canadian Politics,* Stewart demonstrates how these patronage parties were an integral part of the political culture of the day. The brief excerpt from Waite is a miniature case study. In it we see John Thompson, Minister of Justice and a future Prime Minister, struggling on a daily basis with the demands of constituents. Though carrying a huge work load as a senior minister, he spent much of his time receiving and firing off telegrams to insistent constituents in Antigonish; that was the basis of party life and electoral survival in the small scale, localistic politics of the period.

Herbert Ames, whose one paragraph biography in the *Canadian Encyclopaedia* suggests an amazing Canadian life, was an amateur political scientist as well as a professional politician in turn-of-the-century Canada. In this brief piece, written for a now defunct magazine, Ames laid out just how elections were fought in Montreal where he was elected as a Tory MP from 1904-20. His prescriptions would make sense to a modern constituency strategist. But a contemporary, unnamed, politician obviously thought Ames had rather delicately skipped over the question of political money and so we have his gentle corrective to remind us of how at least one other first party system politician saw these problems.

Siegfried tells us that Canadian political competition was quite unusual for its focus on leadership even in this early period. The focus on party leaders is not a new preoccupation in Canada; they were extraordinarily important to all aspects of party organization and activity from the very beginning. In the piece by John Courtney we discover what kind of individuals came to party leadership, how they did so, and what demands the parties put on them. In the process Courtney reveals much about the nature of the closed, caucus-based parties that were pre-eminent political institutions of this era.

Financing parties was an ongoing problem in the first system; politics then was probably more expensive than it has been since. Any research on party politics in this period soon stumbles over the seemingly endless scandals that characterized it (see for instance Jeffrey Simpson's book, *The Spoils of Power*) and is reminded of the prevalence of patronage which had the effect of transferring some of the costs of party politics to the public service. The late Professor K.Z. Paltiel knew more about the history of Canadian party finance than anyone and in a short excerpt from one of his books we have a succinct portrait of the essence of early practice.

All politicians are preoccupied with getting their message out to the electorate. In the years of the first Canadian party system the media was still dominated by a partisan press, but by the end of the period politicians began to face the specter of an independent press they couldn't manipulate. As Paul Rutherford demonstrates, the press was no neutral communication channel in these years; it was an active participant in the party wars. And as in so much of what went on in the period, patronage was the glue that drove the system.

After fifty years this stable, well integrated party system came crashing down. Everything changed: the character of organization, the nature and process of leadership, the patterns of finance, the shape of party-media relationships, the latent functions performed for the wider political system. There is no better account of the final years of the first party system than John English's *The Decline of Politics*, from which our last reading is taken. In this selection English brings the story to an end and helps us understand how civil service reform spelled the end of the era of the great old parties. His description of Meighen's new inability to satisfy his constituents' demands stands in sharp contrast to Waite's portrait of Thompson's efforts in Antigonish. In it we see the essence of the change, and the end of the first party system.

André Siegfried Party Politics in Canada

The Role of Parties in Canadian Politics

Political activity in Canada is carried on, according to the rules of the parliamentary system, by two rival political parties which, turn by turn, succeed each other in power. In this chapter we shall study their character and role.

Constituted on the British model, Canadian parties have not escaped the American contagion which more and more tends to penetrate the Dominion. From the metropolitan power they derive their names (Liberal and Conservative), their respect for British forms, certain of their traditions. From the United States, the tone of their polemics, their eye for material advantages, above all their shrewd working of the constituencies. It is a curious fact that the French influence in this field is totally non-existent. Not only do the English-speaking population not submit to it, which is natural, but the French Canadians have a fashion of conducting politics which in no way recalls our spirit or methods. They seem to have forgotten our jealous individualism, our impatience of disciplined action. Anglo-Saxon practices have become familiar to them and they have adapted themselves with an ease which would be inexplicable did not one recall that they come in great numbers from French provinces that were historically friends of hierarchical rule and were, like Normandy, akin to southern England.

Originally formed to subserve a political idea, the parties are often induced, especially when they have partially attained their goal, to place themselves above the principles that were the reason for their birth. On these occasions the pure and simple continuation of their own existence becomes their principal preoccupation and the measure of their ideals. Such is the dangerous slope on to which, as elsewhere and to a much greater degree than elsewhere, Canadian parties constantly allow themselves to be swept. Even without a programme they continue to live, still more to prosper. As the carrying out of their practical activity perverts their true nature, they tend to become chiefly agencies for the conquests of power. As for doctrines or reforms, these are put aside, distorted or transfigured according to the needs of the moment. And they frequently end by appearing to be no more than weapons, blunt or sharp, which may be taken up indifferently by either of the adversaries facing one another. During this time the organization, held in admirable marching order by skilful managers, continues its regular activity, capable of functioning without ideas, like a well-mounted piece of machinery. This is exactly where danger reveals itself. The natural form of the political party risks being corrupted into an unwholesome caricature, a machine for winning elections.

The fact that in the Dominion parties exist apart from their programmes, or even without a programme at all, frequently deprives the electoral consultations of the people of their true meaning. In the absence of ideas or doctrines to divide the voters, there remain only questions of material interest, collective or individual. Against their pressure the candidate cannot maintain his integrity, for he knows that his opponent will not show the same self-restraint. The result is that the same promises are made on both sides, following an absolutely identical conception of the meaning of power. Posed in this way, the issue of an election manifestly changes. Whoever may be the winner, everyone knows that the country will be administered in the same way, or almost the same. The only difference will be in the personnel of the government. This is the prevailing conception of politics—except when some great wave of opinion sweeps over the whole country, covering under its waters all the political pygmies. In the intervals between these crises, which are violent no doubt but at bottom healthy, even the most naive can hardly help but see that it is not the party which is at the service of the idea but the idea which is at the service of the party.

Canadian statesmen—and each generation regularly produces its crop of them—undoubtedly take higher views. However, they seem to fear great movements of opinion, and they devote themselves to weakening such movements rather than encouraging them or availing themselves of them. Thus, deliberately and not from narrowness of mind, they also help to confirm the state of things which we have just described.

The reason for this attitude is easy to understand. Canada, we know, is a country of violent oppositions. English and French, Protestant and Catholic, are jealous of each other and fear each other. The lack of ideas, programmes, convictions, is only apparent. Let a question of race or religion be raised, and you will immediately see most of the sordid preoccupations of patronage or connection disappear below the surface. The elections will become struggles of political principle, sincere and passionate. Now this is exactly what is feared by the prudent and far-sighted men who have been given the responsibility of maintaining the national equilibrium. Aware of the sharpness of certain rivalries, they know that if these are let loose without any counter-balance, the unity of the Dominion may be endangered. That is why they persistently apply themselves to prevent the formation of homogeneous parties, divided according to race, religion or class—a French party, for instance, or a Catholic party, or a Labour party. The clarity of political life suffers from this, but perhaps the existence of the federation can be preserved only at this price.

In this sense the existing parties are entirely harmless. The Liberals and the Conservatives differ very little really in their opinions upon crucial questions, and their conception of power seems almost identical. Both parties are made up of heterogeneous elements: employers and labourers, townsmen and farmers, French and English, Catholics and Protestants, are to be found alike in both. In these conditions any attempt to assume an explicit attitude towards burning questions would shatter them into atoms, and they are able to preserve their unity only by dint of extraordinary compromises. In this way they have come to regard each other without alarm: they know each other too well, and resemble each other too closely for that.

This conception of politics is no doubt prudent. One must record, however, that it indisputably tends to lower the general level of political life. In the deliberate absence of programmes, questions of material interest, of public works, take too important a place. There are certainly more burning issues; people are always thinking of these, but the leaders prefer that they should not be talked about. The subjects which remain available for discussion are not numerous. In addition, the parties borrow one another's policies periodically, displaying a coolness in this process that would disconcert us Europeans. It happens frequently too that on the necessity of some great economic measure—the second transcontinental railway, for example—everyone is agreed. The question is not whether it shall be carried out but who shall carry it out. In such circumstances what can the names Conservative and Liberal mean? They mean nothing but government and opposition. We shall attempt later to give the characters of the Liberal and the Conservative. Let us acknowledge that we shall succeed only with difficulty; for their differences are minimal and their common points very numerous.

It might be supposed that this being so, the frontiers between the two great groups would be as elastic and indeterminate as their policies, and that politicians would pass easily from one to the other. But this is not so at all. In Canada the party is almost a sacred institution, to be forsaken only at the cost of one's reputation and career. It is held in esteem almost like one's religion, and its praises are sung in dithyrambs that are often a trifle absurd. Its members owe it absolute loyalty even in the smallest matters, and individual vagaries of opinion are sternly condemned. Oppose your party in defence of some doctrine which it formerly maintained itself but which the necessities of the moment have led it to abandon, and you will lose your reputation by your independence. Thus M. Bourassa, who separated himself from Sir Wilfrid Laurier over the question of participating in the South African War, was violently taken to task by many of his political friends. In theory you may be right, they said to him, but don't you see you are compromising the unity of the Liberal party? In the eyes of politicians the reproach was overwhelming: "Party first, Principles afterwards!" might almost have been their cry.

And you should see how the party organs treat the disloyal member who goes over to the enemy! No sarcasm, no insult, is spared him. The words, "Traitor," "Turncoat," "Knave," seem inadequate to describe the turpitude of his crime. This is somewhat ridiculous, considering that a man may change his party without changing his policies; but one has to remember that the party is a sort of a club, a brotherhood, an association of men, advancing shoulder to shoulder on the way to power, and sharing good and evil fortune alike.

The reasons for which men cling to their party are indeed both intricate and numerous—sometimes they are moved by interest, sometimes by sentiment. Family feeling, tradition, good fellowship, have much to do with it. A family has been Liberal or Conservative for generations past—its members grow up in the parental faith. Later, after marching in line with their companions under the same leaders, there would be a feeling of shame at quitting the ranks; electoral campaigns gone through together, and all the memories clustering around them, serve to create an *esprit de corps* which has not much to do with programmes and doctrines, but which constitutes an extraordinarily strong connecting link. Finally, we must not forget that, in following the fortunes of one party, a man has every chance of seeing it, sooner or later, in office. It can then shove you into employment, provide you with profitable subventions, give you some advantage which you have long coveted. There is a tacit contract which the voter on his part makes it a point of honour not to break.

In ordinary times a political machine thus perfected is almost bound to work all right, but it is not possible to keep the burning questions of race and religion always in the background.

The most consummate diplomacy could not, for instance, have prevented the religious question from being raised in 1896 over the schools of Manitoba, or the race question from coming to the front in 1900 on the occasion of the South African War.

When, in spite of their efforts, the parties find themselves face to face with these disquieting realities, they can no longer turn away from them. They must declare their stand, or at least they must speak.

Several results may then follow. Under irresistible pressure the habitual structure of groups may break up, and a new distribution of men according to their views may come into operation. Or opinion may try to canalize itself into the cadres of the existing parties. Ordinarily, however, the solution is much less simple. By reason of their heterogeneous composition Canadian parties can never take a clear position on a fundamental question. In order to satisfy nearly all their members they are almost necessarily reduced to distinctions and compromises. It follows that, because the voters do not know what to do in order to make a clear choice, since the question is not clearly posed, the meaning of the vote is generally falsified in the following manner: some, not very many, vote according to their convictions against their party; others, very numerous, vote for their party against certain of their convictions. In this latter case the need to hold on to or to win power is more pressing than the need to affirm a particular policy.

Never was this complexity made manifest in a more flagrant manner than in the general election of 1900. On this occasion French Canadians, strong pro-Boers and proven anti-imperialists, were to be seen voting in large numbers for a ministry which had established the preferential tariff of 1897 in favour of England, despatched the Canadian volunteers to the Transvaal, and declared boldly its adhesion to the imperialistic movement. On the other hand, English voters in Ontario whose imperialism was beyond suspicion were to be seen voting against Sir Wilfrid Laurier, though in sympathy with his policy. The first disapproved of the tendencies of the ministry but wished at all costs to keep at the head of the state a man of their own race; the second could not forgive him for being a Frenchman and a Catholic. As this example shows, no voter in this great consultation of the electorate was able to express his whole opinion. Such is the generally misunderstood story of Canadian politics.

However, if the question at stake were held to be really crucial and more important in its issues than the existence of parties, the Canadian public would find itself rent in two clear divisions, just as though these makeshift parties had never existed. For example, if the right to use the French language were called in question, all French Canadians, Liberal or Conservative, would unite together as one man in defence of what they regard as the inalienable patrimony of the race; while if the Catholic Church were attacked in regard to any of its essential instruments, all the faithful independently of their race or party would rally on her side.

Fortunately for Canada, there would seem to be little danger of such conflicts. In a new country of wide extent and great prosperity material questions are apt to take precedence of all others. The immediate need is to people the newly opened territories and turn them to account, to construct railroads and waterways. The country has to be made to pay. To this end the methods to be adopted are not much in dispute. The only thing disputable is by which party these enterprises shall be brought to a successful issue. For a nation divided in so many other respects it is a guarantee of quiet that on this one point everyone is agreed!

The Elections—The Party Organizations

There can be few countries in the world in which elections—whatever the questions at issue—arouse more fury and enthusiasm than in Canada; there can be none in which political contests are entered on with greater gusto. At election-time the public life of the Dominion is to be studied in one of its most curious and characteristic manifestations.

The life of a parliament is in principle five years, but ordinarily a dissolution takes place soon after the conclusion of the fourth.[1] The voting is in single-chamber constituencies, and takes place everywhere on the same day;[2] there is no second poll, and the first is always decisive, even if there has been no absolute majority. In accordance with the English system, candidates who have no declared opponents seven days before the election become members "by acclamation," as it is styled. The suffrage varies in the different provinces, and is not universal in all. One person can vote in more than one constituency. These rules, for the most part, have their source in England. We shall see, however, that in practice the United States' influence is to be seen.

It is the strong two-party organization which characterizes and dominates Canadian elections. These are principally—uniquely, one might say—a duel between Liberals and Conservatives, and there is hardly a place for any independents. Everything contributes to discourage them. In effect the law favours concentrations of votes. A provision that is hardly democratic obliges candidates to deposit a sum of $200, which is confiscated if they do not win half the number of votes cast for the elected candidate. There is not only no second ballot, but it is not well thought of by those who know its real character. Does it not tend to facilitate the birth of new parties, by encouraging differences of opinion on the first ballot? That is enough to make the party leaders, guardians of discipline, declare that they fear it greatly. What they would prefer is precisely the disappearance of dissidents, whoever they may be. "Our parliamentary régime," said one of them to me, "is fitted for two parties, no more. In the name of principle, then, we oppose the formation of secondary groups, and consequently the second ballot which might provoke them."

It is not difficult, then, to understand the weight of authority appertaining to each party. To a far greater extent than its members taken individually, it is the party that fights, talks, and promises. The programme imposes itself morally and almost materially as well upon those whom it takes under its wing. The semi-anarchy which marks our political contests in France, in which everyone is left to himself, makes it hard for us to form any idea of the rigour with which the Canadians enforce obedience in electoral matters.

It is the party, a veritable moral person, that treats with the great forces whose support it requires—railway companies, the Catholic clergy, industrial and commercial companies, etc. Large followings depend on these powerful organizations. The elections are expensive affairs, and money must be got for them somehow. These essentials are generally already dealt with over the heads of the candidates by the time the campaign begins.

The central organization of each party is reduced to a minimum. It may be said to consist in the one case of the prime minister, in the other of the leader of the opposition, each of whom indicates the general lines to be taken. There is, properly speaking, no organizing body dealing with the whole of the Dominion. Matters are seen to in each province on the spot, under the direction of some influential politician, who with a large and elaborately constituted staff conducts all the operations like a regular chief-of-staff. Canada being very much decentralized by reason of its immense extent, the freedom left to each of its provinces is considerable. They all take their cue, however, from the leader of the party, and each party hangs together well.

The provincial leaders have a tremendous task to get through, having to superintend sometimes as many as fifty or sixty elections. First of all they have to make sure that there shall not be more than one of their party candidates for each seat, for a splitting of the vote would be fatal. They have to keep an eye upon every phase of the canvassing, to be in constant communication with the newspapers, distributing all the election literature, despatching speakers to all the public meetings. A hundred other details require their attention, whilst they must contrive all the time to keep the whole field of battle in sight.

Let us glance now at the actual proceedings in a single constituency. These differ, of course, in different provinces, especially according to whether the constituency be in a town or in the country, but there are certain traditions and customs that prevail throughout and that justify certain generalizations.

Five or six weeks before the voting-day the candidates are nominated by a local convention held in each constituency. The siege of the masses has already taken place. What has still to be done—and it is no small matter—is to hold on to friends and to make sure of doubtful voters. In this work Canadian politicians are dangerously expert, with their combination of Norman shrewdness and Yankee realism.

In each local centre the candidate chooses four or five influential men, who are known in the French districts as chiefs; according to the amount of money at his disposal, he hands them sums of $20, $40, or $60, which it is understood that they are to expend in the interest of the cause. Naturally a portion of this money stops en route. The candidate is aware of this, but he shuts his eyes, having need of the co-operation of people of importance whose opinions are listened to. Besides, when these have their pockets well lined with dollars, they carry themselves with more assurance and have more go in them. Having more confidence in themselves, they inspire more confidence in others. Their bearing indicates that the party's coffers are full, and their suggestion of opulence wins many adherents.

The first action of these chiefs is to hire a place which shall serve as the headquarters of the party organization, where they stock all the pamphlets, posters, announcements, etc., as well as portraits of the candidate, and the provincial or federal leaders. Here they establish their offices, and welcome all comers with the utmost cordiality and amiability. It would seem as though they were haunted by the fear of not being sufficiently gracious. Nothing is more curious, especially in the English districts, than the difference between the reception that one receives in a business office and in a political committee-room. In addition to the expenses involved in all this, there are other items, more or less justifiable, of which the candidate is not supposed to take cognizance. Canadian public opinion is very tolerant in regard to these.

These first preparations having been seen to, the candidate takes a carriage, a sledge, or a train, and begins a round of visits and meetings. In the country districts—especially in the French ones—he goes from locality to locality, following certain traditional methods, visiting the smaller villages during the week, and keeping the Sunday for the more populous centres. It is in these, in the open space in front of the church, that he delivers his most important addresses. In most of these open spaces in the province of Quebec there are small wooden tribunes for use on such occasions. In fine weather everything goes off perfectly, but even if it rains or snows the meeting is not abandoned. Umbrellas go up, and those who are cold stamp their feet, while the orator's voice gives out the flowing periods, prefaced always with the words, "Messieurs les Electeurs!"

In the cities there is a different order of procedure. The mass of voters assemble together at monster meetings for a general exposition of the party programme, a public debate, and a visit by some personage of distinction; while smaller meetings are held in different quarters of the town, or for each separate profession.

But public meetings are not enough in themselves. House-to-house canvassing, as the English call it, is also essential. In the French districts the canvassers begin usually with the priest, unless his displeasure has been incurred, which is a grave matter, though not necessarily fatal. Then one proceeds to make the rounds of adherents and opponents, evading dangerous discussions with the latter, and talking rather of the weather, unless some one particular topic should appeal to them. All these ceremonies are carried out most politely, for the country-bred French Canadian is a lover of forms.

Visits of this kind are more difficult in the urban centres. In some of the Western cities, for instance, there are entire quarters inhabited by foreigners who only know a little English, and who are not to be reached by ordinary posters or addresses. Special posters are made out for their benefit in their own languages, but they are scarcely to be won over otherwise than by personal visits, backed up by promises and presents. These foreigners constitute very important bands of voters, whose presence sometimes dangerously warps the meaning of appeals to the voters.

Meanwhile the great forces whose interests have been solicited and secured are not being inactive. Their co-operation is the result of the negotiations made before the party programme was completed. In return for the promise of a tariff or the withdrawal of some threatened parliamentary bill, the business men make money contributions, the Church puts into play the power of its propaganda.

The Canadian government, not having the Napoleonic bureaucracy at its back, is not able to exercise its influence after the fashion of ours. Its influence is called into action rather by its office-holders, who hold out promises in its name. "Vote for the government, and you shall have such and such a subvention, new railway, or appointment." These are the words you will hear uttered by the ministerialists—no attempt to disguise the nature of the market transaction (as with us). The Opposition, instead of protesting, retaliate with promises of what they will do for their supporters should they come into office. Thus both sides call into play the powers of the state in order to catch votes.

In a country in which the entire population belongs to one or other of two religions, it is inevitable that the voice of the clergy should count for much. It must be said, however, that the Protestant parsons and ministers do not as a rule take an active part in the elections. If they intervene, it is to plead for new laws in defence of morality or to combat existing laws which violate their Protestant idea of morals. They rarely take up a position as a body on the side of either party. As we have seen already, it is quite otherwise with the Catholic clergy.

But the predominant influence, which if a party is bent on victory must be either secured or rendered neutral, is that of the great commercial, industrial, and financial concerns. The resources of the government are to be assessed in money, whether they take the form of office, subventions, or public works. Now, the great concerns are well equipped for a contest with it upon this ground, having great armies of voters dependent upon them, besides having certain public bodies under their control. You hear of gas, water, and electric companies forcing a municipality to carry out their demands; of some huge industrial company, employing thousands of hands, dictating its wishes to a provincial ministry, to whom its support is necessary; of some director of a railway through some region with no other line of communication treating on equal terms with members of the federal government, and sometimes as master of some of its ministers.

It is only natural in these circumstances that there should be bargaining. The railway companies especially require to come to terms with the government, for a session never passes in which some new bills affecting their welfare have not to be passed. It is essential to them to have a majority on their side, and if possible a minister to bring the bills forward in their interest.

The entire history of Canada is full of these bargains between financial powers and the political parties. In 1872, for instance, Sir Hugh Allan, promoter of the Canadian Pacific, gave more than $300,000 to the Conservative party for their campaign. In 1887 a sum of more than $100,000 came out of the funds of several great companies eager for concessions and subventions for distribution in twenty-two constituencies of the province of Quebec. In 1891 the promoters of a huge dock enterprise supplied nearly $120,000 for campaign funds.[3] In 1904 it is notorious—without it being possible to know the exact figures—that the Canadian Pacific Railway and the Grand Trunk Railway scattered money about lavishly—the former among the Conservatives, the latter among the Liberals, both with a view to controlling the second transcontinental line that was being sanctioned. No doubt cynicism goes too far sometimes, as in 1872 and 1891, and there is a scandal, and ministers themselves are injured. But normally it is considered quite the thing that contributions should be made to the party funds in this spirit, and without them both parties would be at a loss how to conduct their campaigns.

We come now to the voting-day. The chiefs have studied the register carefully and made an estimate of the probable number of votes. In the towns, naturally, the unforeseen has a wide margin.

In the country, where everyone is known individually, it is a case merely of bringing one's adherents up to the ballot box and keeping them out of reach of the foe.

On the morning of the great day all available conveyances have been hired, often at exorbitant prices, a practice which reveals a characteristic form of corruption. The chief organizers, taking up a central position, keep in constant touch with the progress of the voting: in such a village, things go well; in such another, electors resident some distance off have failed to record their vote—a carriage is despatched to the scene at once to bring them in. Sometimes just the opposite manœuvre is resorted to with equal success: by some ingenious stratagem the adversary's electors are kept away from the polling booth. A Conservative railway company, for example, despatches the Liberal workers miles away to execute some quite unnecessary piece of work!

At the end of the day the excitement has reached its utmost limit. Old men, invalids, cripples, are roped in. Sometimes these just turn the scales, the election being won by 40 or 50 votes out of 3,000 or 4,000. The victory can only go to a party which is perfectly organized. But it can be seen from our remarks that organization is capable of being carried to excess.

The Elections—Their General Character and Tone

The electoral campaigns in Canada, with their curious mixture of old British forms and new American free-and-easy practices, may be characterized as distinctively colonial. By the use of this word, so full of meaning to English ears. I mean to class Canada as belonging to that group of Anglo-Saxon peoples which out-do England herself, if not also the United States, in the extraordinary realism of their political life.

The charge of vulgarity is one of those brought most frequently by the English against their colonial fellow-subjects. The Canadians are not proof against this accusation in their public life. It is not that they are particularly violent: during the elections of 1904, which I followed closely, I did not hear many downright insults, and the vocabulary of the candidates struck me as containing comparatively few outrageous expressions. Without having recourse to unseemly language, however, they have a way in the Dominion of making terrible accusations in the simplest, most direct fashion, that go beyond our most violent outbursts of low abuse. The thickness of the Anglo-Saxon skin renders possible the use of certain forms of words that with us would call forth hot protests and duels. In the calmest, most unimpassioned way you hear politicians regularly accused of putting money in their pockets, without anyone, even the man against whom the charge is brought, seeming in the least shocked. The thing is of too common occurrence. This cold-blooded attitude baffles one's understanding, and one would almost prefer to witness a little violence. In the same way in parliament quite important personages may be heard to talk of the "stupidity" and "ignorance" of their "honourable friends." In France such remarks would lead to angry outbursts. In Canada the members thus alluded to hardly frown.

We must keep in mind this marked difference in temperament in order to understand the way in which the Canadians deplore our violence, while we in turn look on astonished at their brutal frankness of speech. Charges of corruption and peculation are bandied about from start to finish in their elections, and are really too prevalent altogether. Such charges are not unknown with us, but what marks them in Canada is the fact that they are not made in the heat of the moment—they owe their introduction to a plan of campaign prepared in advance, quite deliberately. By whom? Irresponsible journalists, you will surmise, calumniators by profession. Not at all. By the official agents of the great parties, who place quite circumstantial accusations against some of their opponents, with names and details, in the forefront of their campaign literature....

If physical violence is absent from Canadian elections, corruption, as I have shown already, is to be met with in diverse forms. There has been a great improvement during the last twenty years, but alcohol, money, and fraudulent elections are still far from having lost their harmful influence.

To begin with, there are the inevitable drinks which are offered by the election agents or by the candidate himself, and which have for purpose and effect merely the putting of the electors into good humour. But the actual purchasing of votes is the really serious thing. Naturally, this is carried out on a large scale only in certain districts, but there are many in which the margin between the two parties is so fine that it is all important to get hold of the doubtful voters by hook or by crook. In some constituencies in Quebec, Ontario, and Manitoba, votes are to be bought not merely from the poor people but from well-to-do farmers. Sometimes appearances are saved by the device of letting out a conveyance for the polling-day at an exorbitant price, but often the transaction is put through quite simply and shamelessly. A public man in Manitoba told me how at the close of one of his meetings a number of electors approached him to barter with him there and then for their votes.

Then there are yet other constituencies, traditionally corrupt, where the cynicism of electoral agents knows no bounds, the lists of voters and voting papers being tampered with. At an election in October 1903 at Sault Ste. Marie (Ontario) the results of the poll were thus falsified. Bogus electors were imported from the neighbouring part of the United States and given their board and lodging and generous payment in return for handing in illegal voting papers to certain venal individuals similarly remunerated who had been installed as officials in the polling booths. An appeal was made against the election with 213 charges of specific corruption. At the sixteenth case investigated the court declared themselves satisfied with the evidence already produced, and invalidated the election.[4]

Such flagrant cases as this one are of course rare, but the influence of the American "machine" has permeated the whole colony, and there are Canadian experts who have carried the science of handling votes to a dangerous perfection. Both parties warn their followers against the wiles of these people. As an illustration of what is done, let us study the pages of a pamphlet officially published by the Liberal party à propos of the general election of 1904, in which are set forth certain methods of falsifying the voting papers—methods naturally attributed in this case to the Conservatives. It contains a wealth of new and suggestive expressions: slipping, for instance, is involved in the ascribing to Conservatives votes given for Liberals: switching means the mixing up of voting papers in such a way as to profit by the confusion; stuffing is the fraudulent recording of votes by impersonation of the dead or absent; spoiling is the invalidating of the voting papers of the other side by surreptitiously marking it on the outside.[5]

The author of this brochure would have us believe that the Conservatives enjoy a monopoly of these fraudulent tactics, but the Conservative leaders address precisely the same warnings[6] to their followers, and it is scarcely credible that all the virtue is on one side and all the vice on the other. Both parties wind up by crying, "Vote for our candidates if you would put an end to these abuses." And it remains a matter for astonishment that they do not disappear!

From all that we have said, it will be gathered that election expenses in Canada are very high. The normal and legitimate outlay is considerable to start with, and when we come to the more dubious items we have to reckon up in thousands of dollars. In a very interesting article in *La Patrie*, M. Tarte, who knows both parties through having belonged to each in turn, estimates as follows the cost of the campaign in Montreal in 1904. He writes:

> *A general election is a cause of legitimate expenditure on the part of the leaders of political parties and of those members who are prepared to buy the honours they solicit. Let us pass in quick review the electoral divisions of our city.*
>
> Saint-Antoine. *Both candidates are men of means, large means. How much will they disburse through the medium of their election agents? Will it be less than $20,000 or $25,000 apiece? There have been previous elections in which the happy (!) candidate had to hand out more.*
>
> Sainte-Anne. *This division is less expensive than that of Saint-Antoine. Oh! things are not done by prayer. We believe that each candidate will keep within $10,000 or $12,000 just at first.*
>
> Saint-Louis *and* Saint-Laurent. *Ask the treasurers of both organizations, if you know them, what was the legitimate expenditure of the candidates.* La Patrie *does not pretend to exact information. We suspect, however, that without an available sum of $15,000 ready money no candidature would stand much chance.*
>
> *Before we come to the centre of the city—that is to say,* Saint-Jacques *and* Sainte-Marie—*let us glance discreetly at* Maisonneuve. *Here we have a minister as candidate. A minister is a man who is supposed to have power and plenty of money. If Monsieur P. meets with an opponent of weight, can he expect to get off at less than $25,000 to $30,000? You are either a minister or you are not! His adversary, who pleads poverty because he is of the opposition, must provide himself with at least $10,000. The opposition spends less, but it must spend. All these figures are approximate. They represent $160,000 in round numbers. In electoral expenses the numbers are always round!*[7]

Even if these figures be patently an exaggeration, even if we reduce them by a half or a fourth, they serve to indicate the really deplorable *power exercised by money*. Such expenditure is not only dangerous in its demoralizing influence upon the electorate, but also in the crippling effect it may have upon the resources of the elected member, who runs a risk of debt on his entering parliament.

We must not, however, conclude that these financial misdemeanours form the basis of the Canadian elections. That would be a great mistake. We must remember the saying of Rousseau: "The people are never corrupted, but often they are deceived." When the margin between the parties is very narrow in a constituency, bribery and corruption may serve to turn the scale. But, generally speaking, great currents of public opinion are not to be turned aside by the force of the dollar. In the chapter which follows we shall see what are the arguments that really weigh with the Canadian electorate.

The Elections—The Arguments that Tell

In all electioneering programmes there are certain points upon which the politicians lay stress, instinctively as it were, because they know them to be calculated to impress public opinion; and nothing throws more light upon the real spirit of a constituency than the kind of language addressed to it by the candidates, its licensed flatterers. In this chapter we shall study the arguments of a general character which the Canadian election organizers are most given to invoking, and which ensure victory to their party when they can make out their claim with sufficient plausibility. They are four in number: the defence of one of the two races or of one of the two religions against the other; the prosperity of the country; the promise of public works or material local advantages; and the personal prestige of the party leader.

The appeal to racial exclusiveness combined with religious bigotry is the first and last cartridge of the politicians of the Dominion. Before thinking of any other reason, or after all other reasons have been exhausted, they come to or return to this, feeling themselves here upon solid ground from which they can at will stir up the passions of the populace. I have already explained that Canadian statesmen worthy to be so called in contradistinction to the ordinary politicians hesitate in their generous solicitude for the peace of the country to let loose the currents of mistrust and hatred which they would be unable later to control. They are, however, sometimes forced to remember that there are in Canada two jealous peoples, having in many respects interests apart, and they also cannot always refrain at certain opportune moments from playing a little racial politics. Sir Wilfrid Laurier, habitually an apostle of union, has not hesitated, on various occasions, to remind his fellow-citizens of Quebec of all the advantages to be derived by them from having one of their own number as federal prime minister. "Do not forget," he said to them at Montreal in 1896, "that if there is a Liberal ministry at Ottawa, it is a Frenchman who will be at its head."[8] This was an appeal, discreet but quite undisguised, to the sentiment which has ever since accorded him the faithful and enthusiastic support of almost all the French Canadians.

If the leaders cannot avoid these racial appeals altogether, it may be guessed that the smaller fry make use of them recklessly. In the region of the Lower St. Lawrence the affirmation of the rights and claims of the French race forms the *leitmotif* of every campaign. Purely racial arguments never fail here of their effect, and the number of politicians who do not have recourse to them, openly or otherwise, is small indeed.

The English of Ontario are still more sensitive to racial and religious prejudices. The presence of our race in Canada is a perpetual subject of irritation to them, and at bottom they resign themselves to it only with difficulty. You should hear the tone in which they speak of "French domination," "the French-speaking prime minister," "these French papists" who are "rebels at the bottom of their hearts." In the elections of 1900 they selected as their scapegoat M. Tarte, Minister of Public Works, guilty (among a hundred other misdeeds) of having delivered francophil speeches in Paris at the Universal Exhibition. Their diatribes against him, repeated *ad nauseam*, soon became the stock refrain, and the great newspapers let themselves go on the subject with truly deplorable violence. "If we wish to remain faithful to the Queen and the flag in the hour of peril, how can we safely allow a Tarte to control our destinies? If Tarte were free to act as he liked, the English flag would not be floating over Toronto to-day.... Are we going to have Tarte to rule over us? Vote for British liberty, for a stronger Empire, for industrial stability and progress. Vote against absolutism, robbery, race prejudice, against treason and Tarte."[9]

The effect of this agitation was so strong in Ontario that the Conservatives won 11 seats; the number of their successful candidates went up from 44 to 55, while that of the Liberals, the followers of Laurier and Tarte, went down from 48 to 37. In Quebec, for analogous reasons, the opposite result was brought about, and the Liberal ministry carried 58 constituencies out of 65. Manifestly the French province had voted for Laurier because he was French; the predominantly English province had voted against him because he was not English.

Fortunately, though the opposition between the two races is always latent, it does not always manifest itself in these outbreaks of anger. In the intervals, material interests resume the preponderant place natural to them in all countries, but above all in new countries. The national prosperity, indeed, seems to affect people much more closely in Canada than in France. In France so many people are in receipt of fixed incomes, which are scarcely touched by the ebb and flow of economic life. In America, on the contrary, the great majority of the population are directly or indirectly engaged in commerce, industry, or agriculture, so that no one, so to speak, escapes the fluctuations of the general fortune. The result is that, in Canada as in the United States, when business goes well everything goes well. People have money, high spirits, good humour. They spend, they build, they amuse themselves; they hope to spend, build, and amuse themselves still further. No one is indifferent to the general situation, which profits everyone and the cessation of which would be a public misfortune.

In these circumstances the party which can invoke in its favour the argument of prosperity has in its hands a weapon of the first importance. If it is able with any show of truth to say to the electors, "Renew our lease of power and the existing prosperity will continue," it is sure to touch a responsive chord. If, on the contrary, it is a time of commercial crisis, it is the cue of the opposition to put all the responsibility for it upon the government, and to cry from the housetops, performance, "Put us in, and all this shall be changed!" With a few variations, this is the tune taken up regularly by either side at each federal election: the singers change but the song remains the same.

The elections of 1904 were fought out very largely, almost entirely, upon this basis. The Liberals took to themselves all the credit for the prosperity of the country, and compared it with the financial "slump" which had marked the closing years of the Conservative term of office before 1896. Here are the words, lacking assuredly in impartiality, in which one of their pamphlets set forth the question:

A DEPLORABLE SITUATION! BEFORE 1896

What was the situation during the last years of the Conservative Administration? As almost all Canadians know, business was stagnant, little or no progress was being made, the country was moribund, people were emigrating in thousands.... Confidence in the government was destroyed. These were some of the results of the last years of Tory rule. Truly the country needed a doctor to attend to it. Those were dark days; fortunately the clouds have passed.

HAPPIER DAYS! FROM 1896 TO 1904

Let us now turn over the page and look at the present state of things and at the situation during the last few years. It is undeniable that since 1896 the country has been completely prosperous, that all kinds of businesses are in progress and flourishing, that work is abundant, that every honest and active man is able to find suitable employment.... The tide of prosperity seems to have turned our way just at the moment when the Liberals assumed office. It has risen still higher regularly year by year ever since!... The vexation and despair of 1896 have given place to enthusiasm, energy, and pride. Canadians show that they are conscious of belonging henceforward to a great nation. National pride is their dominating sentiment.... The only class of people really dissatisfied is that of the Conservative politicians.[10]

It is not hard indeed to understand that the latter would not be wholly delighted over a state of prosperity so invaluable to the cause of their opponents. They endeavour by a complicated system of reasoning to show that in reality this prosperity is their doing, but their attitude lacks elegance. "If a man puts money into a business," they say, somewhat ill-humouredly, "if he adopts a wise plan in his management of it, provides for it the most up-to-date machines, and establishes agencies to ensure its commercial success, then if he goes away leaving his successors a fortune in process of formation, should the credit be given to the inheritors or to the real founder?... A great wave of prosperity passes over the world. Canada equipped by the Conservatives is qualified to profit by it. The Liberals, taking on our policy ready-made, install themselves in power, and have nothing to do except record the inevitable prosperity brought about by the Conservatives. They proclaim to all the world that Canada (equipped by the Conservatives) is prosperous. To whom belongs the credit? To the man who made the plans or to the man who inherited them? Intelligent people will reply that it belongs to the man who made the plans—to the inventor, organizer, and constructor."[11]

Although there is not lacking some truth in this plausible reasoning, one finds it easy to guess that bitter recriminations of the kind produce no good effect, but the reverse. The elector loves success and simple statements, and finds more to his taste the illustrated pamphlets in which the Liberal party demonstrates to him by means of suggestive and convincing illustrations the satisfactory way in which things are going. Let us take, for instance, some typical pictures from a series of pamphlets entitled, "Laurier Does Things." A big farmer, freshly shaved and looking very pleased with himself, meets Mr. Borden, Leader of the Opposition, who seeks to convert him to sane Conservative ideas. But the elector, shrewd and skeptical, replies, "Give me one good reason, Mr. Borden, just one, why I should put an end to such excellent management!" Mr. Borden, perplexed, has no reply to make. On another page, two groups of persons are represented. In the first, Mr. Fielding, Minister of Finance, holds out an enormous bag representing his surplus to Jack Canuck (the Canadian John Bull), who dances with delight at receiving it. In the second, Mr. Borden, in mourning, is sobbing out, "Alas! alas!" while by his side a decrepit old man, the Tory party, raises his arms to heaven and exclaims, "The country is going to the dogs!" On yet another page, we see a chorus of four personages, a farmer, a manufacturer, a workman, and a consumer, all in new clothes and good spirits, intoning together the praises of the ministry and rejoicing in their good fortune.

By dint of repeating to the Canadian public in this way that it is rich, happy, and prosperous—all which, indeed, is in large measure true—they end by carrying conviction. From this it is an easy step to satisfy the electors that a continuation of such a state of affairs is dependent upon the maintenance of the Liberal party in power. And it ends by the majority hearkening to the appeal, "Vote for Laurier and Prosperity!"

It is not enough, of course, merely to establish the fact of success. It is necessary to guarantee its continuation by new promises. Public works are what colonials demand most of all; they know that by the construction of roads, bridges, canals, and above all railways, the natural riches of the country are made exploitable and the value of land, and hence all other values, increased. Thus provinces, municipalities, and individuals are all united in soliciting from the government as much in the way of public works as possible. The minister who has the distributing of them is a great electoral power; sometimes even this distribution becomes an essentially political question, and then it is the prime minister who takes it in hand himself. It needs very remarkable adroitness to succeed in giving satisfaction in one direction without causing dissatisfaction in another, and the whole parcelling out of public favours is a work calling for diplomatic gifts, and not to be delegated to an understudy.

In 1904, for instance, the Laurier ministry had put in hand a marvellous programme from an electoral point of view—namely, the construction of a second transcontinental railway. The projected line was to traverse all the provinces, from Nova Scotia to British Columbia, and it was possible to call up a vision to electors of tremendous advantages; millions were to be expended, there was to be work for thousands of labourers, there were to be greater transport facilities, reduced tariffs, increased immigration, rise in value of land, reclamation of immense regions as yet uncultivated—in one word, a really strong impetus given to the whole economic life of the Dominion.

As may be imagined, with so alluring a programme in their hands, the ministerial candidates did not hesitate to make something out of it officially in their election addresses: "Vote for the government, and you will have this railway"; "Vote for me, who am in with the ministry, and you will have that branch line that would be so useful for you"; "Vote for me, I have influence at Ottawa, and if you do, a lot of money will be spent in the constituency. If you don't, the constituency will suffer."

These arguments may seem like old friends. Is there a single ministerialist deputy in France who has never had recourse to them? It must be admitted, however, that at home a sort of modesty forces those who use them to cover them over a little and blur their contours. This art of understatement seems to be totally ignored in Canada. Thus at Winnipeg, on the 29th of October 1904, at a public meeting organized in Selkirk Hall in favour of the Liberal candidate, Mr. Bole, the following inscription adorned the walls:

THE WEST WANTS COMPETITION ON RAILWAYS!
LAURIER, BOLE, AND PROSPERITY!
THE GRAND TRUNK MEANS 125 MILLIONS FOR WINNIPEG!

PROSPERITY—DO YOU FEEL IT IN YOUR POCKETS?
VOTE FOR THREE YEARS MORE OF PROSPERITY!
VOTE FOR BOLE AND YOUR OWN WELFARE!
VOTE FOR THE GRAND TRUNK AND HIGH WAGES!

Mr. Bole was elected by a big majority against two opponents—one a Conservative, the other a working man. He had found the argument that told!

Now for another instance of the same kind of appeal to self-interest—half ingenuous, half cynical—in a smaller sphere. This is how a local correspondent of *Le Canada* defends the member for Saint-Jérôme (province of Quebec): "The Conservatives are doing their utmost to decry the ministerial candidate, but they can't succeed.... They reproach Dr. Desjardins with not having been a great orator in parliament. That is a very paltry charge.... Fortunately, Dr. Desjardins has something better than fine words to his credit, and his record of work done since he became a member—that is, during the last sixteen months—is the best reply to his censors. Dr. Desjardins has secured for his county in sixteen months more than the Conservatives gave it in eighteen years. That represents in all the pretty figure of $175,000, made up as follows...."

This kind of language, innocent of any kind of disguise, is held in all the constituencies without giving rise to serious protest, for it is really from this *standpoint of profit and loss* that the Canadian public regards its parliamentary system. All they ask of their representatives is to take up the same point of view. Whether it be a question of a local subsidy or of a railway through the length of the Dominion, the latter must not forget that they are elected to pursue the policy of results!

Not, of course, that the Canadian electors are absorbed exclusively by their local or individual interests. They are conscious that an attitude of unity and consistency is essential to the conduct of a great colony, almost as independent as a nation. Admirers, like the English, of strong individualities, they love to put in the place of honour a man of authority and prestige. Their commercial idea of credit, which they carry into politics, makes them feel that their reputation cannot fail to be strengthened if they have at their head a personage of distinction, calculated to impress people with a sense of his worth.

That is why it is of the first importance to the success of a party that it should be led by someone who inspires confidence and whose

mere name is a programme in itself. As long as the Conservatives
had Macdonald for their leader, they voted for him rather than for
the party. So it is with Laurier and the Liberals of to-day. If Laurier
disappeared, the Liberals would perhaps find that they had lost the
real secret of their victories. Thus, in accordance with the Anglo-
Saxon habit, the Canadians attach themselves rather to the concrete
reality than to the abstract principle. They vote as much for the
man who symbolizes the policy as for the policy itself.

So much, then, for the four principal arguments which are most
effective in rousing Canadian public opinion. According to the provinces and the circumstances, they vary in their efficacy, but they
have always to be used, and when a party is at a loss for any one
of them its cause cannot fail to suffer thereby. It is not difficult to
conclude that the parliamentary life which is the outcome of such
elections must reproduce their chief characteristics. This is what I
propose to show in the following chapter.

The Parliamentary Life of Canada

The parliamentary life of Canada is inspired at once by the influence
of British traditions from afar and by the influence of American customs close at hand. Beneath forms borrowed almost entirely from
England, a political activity goes on which belongs even more to the
New World than the Old: the "properties" are English, but the piece
is American, and those who take part in it are, as someone has well
said, American actors on an English stage. From this curious mixture
of the Capitol and Westminster we get a complicated creation which
it is almost impossible to define in precise terms, owing to the contrasts it presents.

The form, let us agree, is English.... If now we look below the
surface, we find ideas and methods which are colonial or American,
but not in the least English. In truth, it is impossible for an elective
chamber to differ much from the body of voters who have chosen
it. Is it not there for the purpose of representing it? Now the Canadian electorate is very American, as we have seen, in its aims, its
customs, and its ideas. We shall find many of its elected representatives marked with the same imprint.

We have noted the arguments which tell with the electorate;
those which tell in parliament are not fundamentally different. Perhaps the rivalries between races and religions are less fierce at
Ottawa from the fact that they are discussed by men of greater

education, knowing each other better and standing in greater fear of the consequences of violence. They produce a crisis, however, every now and again—sometimes most alarming in its character. The South African War provoked the fiercest storm of this kind that the colony has ever known since the now distant days of Papineau.

But in ordinary times economic considerations preponderate, the deputies being expected above all to think of the general prosperity. The same interest holds sway in all colonial parliaments, for nothing is more essential to a young colony than its agricultural, industrial, and commercial life. An important difference is to be noticed, however, as between Canada and Australia. In Australia the democracies have generally shown active hostility to what we in France have agreed to designate as *la féodalité financière*. The Dominion, on the contrary, following the example of the United States, has generally organized its development in accordance with, and by means of, this *fédalité*. The material results have been magnificent, but from the point of view of the character of public life this has resulted in a peril which serious-minded Canadians are the first to deplore: the legitimate policy of interests tends sometimes to become a less legitimate policy of business. In the light of the preceding chapters there is in this no cause for surprise.

It is believed, in truth, that the financial influences so powerful during the elections do not stop outside the doors of Parliament. It is not enough to have helped towards the victory of a party—it is necessary to go on and secure from it this or that new bill or concession or tariff or subsidy. In the great majority of cases the parliament only thinks of the general interests of Canada, but there are particular interests which know well how to look after themselves. In order to secure favours, the great railway companies and the great industrial and commercial establishments find it necessary as well as quite natural to employ special agents in the lobbies. In America these intermediaries, whose transactions are not necessarily incorrect, go by the name of lobbyists.

This custom, imported from the United States, indicates an undisguised and to say the least too intimate connection between business and politics. The leaders have a place apart and are above suspicion, but this could not be said of certain politicians who do not hold themselves as responsible as they should to their conscience and their constituency. Too often their election expenses are in part defrayed by a big company with some new enterprise on hand; and in consequence they do not take their seats as absolutely free men, some of them, holding perhaps important parliamentary posts, being no better really than the accredited agents of some great group of capitalists. These men are of course exceptions to the general rule, and there are also many admirable examples to be seen of party loyalty and sincere disinterestedness. But truth compels us to state that side by side with them are men who are engaged in business as well as in politics and for whom, in accordance with a conception which is too American, politics itself is a form of business.

The danger of financial influence, which is real in Ottawa, is not less real in the provinces, where the legislative bodies are smaller and a few votes are enough to turn the scales. On the other hand, it is easier to know the record of each individual member, and therefore to exercise pressure upon anyone when necessary. It is a fact known to all that certain great companies sometimes acquire enough power over the local assemblies that they can rely upon securing the decision they may want in regard to almost everything in which they are interested.

In short, Canada has suffered the power of finance to invade her politics, instead of crushing it down like New Zealand. Thus financial scandals are frequent in her political history. Doubtless this is inevitable in countries of rapid growth which are obliged to give special attention to questions of business.

Do we conclude, then, by assimilating the habitual tone of the parliament at Ottawa with that of American legislatures? By no means. The rivalries of race and religion which so profoundly divide the colony have at least this advantage, that in their way they raise the character of Canadian political struggles and from time to time inject some passion to displace the discussion of material interests, giving the orators an opportunity to fight for ideas in the European fashion, which some of them do with incomparable brilliance. Thus the celebrated crises of the Manitoba schools, of the South African War, of the schools in the Northwest, give rise to really superb debates such as the American Congress never knows, and as the British House of Commons itself seldom experiences. One understands that in these conditions the Canadians may be proud of their parliament. In spite of some weaknesses it fully deserves their pride.

The political personnel of the Dominion is as diverse in character as the varied aspects of political life at which we have been looking. At its head there are men of the highest calibre, who get their inspiration direct from the highest English traditions, and who would not be out of place in any assembly in the world; taken as a whole, it may be said to comprise a large number of mediocrities of a type similar to that in the United States. There is no one characterization that would describe it.

As there is no aristocracy in Canada and hardly any leisured class, the federal House of Commons is inevitably composed of men who follow some profession or who are closely interested in the work of the nation—especially lawyers, businessmen, doctors, journalists, and farmers. Hence payment of members was found to be an absolute necessity, involving a departure from aristocratic English traditions. Members are paid $2,500 a year, and by a recent enactment a yearly stipend of $3,500 is accorded to ministers who have been more than five years in office, while the Leader of the Opposition is paid $7,000. There is probably no other country in which such a functionary is officially remunerated. The idea is an ingenious one, and proves that the two parties are disinclined to favour new groupings, and on the contrary recognize openly their use to one another.

These conditions allow of political life becoming a career and means of livelihood. In Canada it is often a career in the best sense of the word. Many members of the best families are proud to represent their fellow-citizens in parliament. The difficulty and variety of the problems awaiting solution seem to have called forth a class of public men in the Dominion distinctly superior to that possessed by Australia or New Zealand. The names of Macdonald and Laurier belong to the general history of the world, and their country is naturally proud not only of having produced them but of having known how to appreciate them.

With such leaders, giving themselves up entirely to their country and their party, Canadian political life, despite its vulgar element, assumes at times a breadth and elevation worthy of the utmost respect. Taking it as a whole, then, and in spite of the defects I have pointed out, one may say that the Dominion has been well served by the confederation of 1867.

Notes

1   Since 1867 the general elections have taken place in 1872, 1874, 1878, 1882, 1887, 1891, 1896, 1900, 1904.

2   There are some unimportant exceptions to this rule.

3   Willison, *Sir Wilfrid Laurier and the Liberal Party,* II, 18.

4   See *Mail and Empire,* Toronto, Sept. 17, 1904.

5   *Seven Years of Liberal Administration*, 1904.

6   *Facts for Liberals and Conservatives*, 1904.

7   Article of M. Tarte in *La Patrie*, reproduced in *La Verité*, Oct. 15, 1904.

8   Cited by A. Métin in *Autour du Monde*, p. 238.

9   *Mail and Empire*, Nov. 5 and 7, 1900.

10 *Seven Years of Liberal Administration*, 1904.

11 *Conservative Policy, the Policy for Canadian Development*, 1904.

Gordon T. Stewart Political Patronage Under Macdonald and Laurier 1878-1911

It is standard knowledge that patronage was endemic to Canadian politics in the 1867-1911 period. Source-books for undergraduate students contain sections on patronage and the major historians who have written about these years refer to the ubiquitous nature of patronage, describing it as the natural currency of public life.[1] Professor W.L. Morton has pointed out that the cabinet minister of the time, "a beneficiary of patronage himself...was well disposed towards being a dispenser of patronage. Indeed it was the power to distribute patronage that in the main gave his office meaning and substance."[2] In his authoritative account of this period Professor Peter B. Waite remarks of Mackenzie Bowell, minister of customs throughout the entire span of Macdonald's administrations from 1878 to 1891, that his "principal pre-occupation was patronage."[3] As well as these reminders from respected modern scholars, the official records of the period offer testimony to the pervasiveness of patronage. Commissions to investigate the civil service were established in 1880-81, 1891-92, 1907-08, and 1911-12 and all drew attention to the "patronage evil."[4] In 1909 the Department of Marine and Fisheries had the doubtful honor of being the object of a separate investigation and it failed to disappoint its critics, revealing widespread practices not only of patronage but also of corruption.[5] Newspapers, periodicals and parliamentary debates are full of dramatic stories, charges and counter-charges concerning patronage. Major political scandals of the time, involving national figures such as Charles Rykert and Hector-Louis Langevin, revolved around issues of patronage.[6] Because of this kind of evidence it is now common knowledge that patronage was of central importance to Canadian political life. Yet there has been no study made of the workings and significance of patronage. Professor Hodgetts has noted this odd gap in Canadian historical studies. "It is somewhat curious," he writes, "that the practice of patronage has never been the subject of sustained analysis on the part of Canadian social scientists and historians."[7] This article is an attempt at such an analysis.

I

A useful and informative starting point for examining the mechanics of the patronage system is to look at John A. Macdonald's own constituency of Kingston. The picture that emerges from the Kingston patronage evidence shows that patronage was distributed by the party on a bureaucratic-like basis. Appointments and contracts were not distributed hurriedly but invariably followed discussion between local party leaders in Kingston and the Member of Parliament (in this case Macdonald) in Ottawa. Those party activists seeking posts in the public service or public contracts made application, usually in writing, to the executive committee of the local Conservative Association. The committee considered all the applications, weighed the contributions of each applicant to the party's electoral campaigns and then passed on a recommendation to Macdonald who in turn would pass on the name to the appropriate cabinet minister for formal action. In no case in the correspondence was consideration given to the applicants' qualifications—the sole criterion was service to the party.[8]

Within the executive committee there was formal discussion over each piece of patronage. The local party, through its executive committee, functioned almost as an employment agency for party workers. In 1889, for example, Edward Smythe, a barrister and president of the Liberal-Conservative Association, discussed with Macdonald various jobs in the Kingston Post Office. Smythe informed Macdonald that the committee had now filled all but one of the current vacancies. "That will leave," he noted, "a vacancy among the letter carriers that we will subsequently fill up."[9] Two months earlier Macdonald had written to the executive committee to inform the local party leaders of changes in the Kingston post office that would open up new jobs. These developments, Smythe replied, "received the hearty recommendation of our Executive Committee."[10] When the committee discussed the distribution of such posts, the merits of the candidates were discussed exclusively in terms of their work in the local party organization. Writing in January 1891 in connection with the application of William A. Newlands for a clerkship in the post office, J.A. Metcalfe explained that "his [Newlands'] father and brother are active workers in the Conservative interest and William A. is a good Conservative." Metcalfe added that Newlands had followed the proper procedure, having "applied through the Executive Committee."[11] Once Macdonald received the recommendation from the committee, he passed it on to the cabinet minister in charge of the appropriate department. In response to one such recommendation to the Customs Department, the minister, Mackenzie Bowell, sent a note to Macdonald explaining he had signed the necessary papers implementing the requested appointments. Mackenzie Bowell pointed out that neither of the two individuals recommended had "passed the 'qualifying' examinations" and therefore could not be employed as landing-waiters or clerks. But they still received posts in the customs service.[12] Local party considerations took precedence over questions of qualifications.

Because party considerations were paramount it was essential for any applicant to show a solid record of work in local electoral campaigns. An example of these values occurred over the position of second engineer at the federal dry dock facility in Kingston. Thomas McGuire, a local party notable, had been told "the Conservative Association have recommended" Joseph Levitt for the post. McGuire wrote in support of Levitt and warned Macdonald about two other aspirants for the job who should be rejected because they had made contract with the Liberal "enemy." Those other two, wrote McGuire, "are Heretics while Levitt is one of the Faithful as that term is understood by the archbishop."[13] In another case the importance of long, faithful and uncontaminated party service was emphasized. In this instance the record of the family as a whole was considered. A "claim of patronage has been brought before the Executive Committee," wrote J.H. Metcalfe to Macdonald. "I do not admire the tone of the letter yet as the old man and his sons have never gone grit I feel kindly disposed toward them."[14] During the winter of 1890-91 similar considerations dominated discussion of a vacancy for a staff officer in the militia. In December 1890 S.M. Conger, president of the Prince Edward County Liberal-Conservative Association, pressed the claims of his candidate, Colonel Graveley. Conger wrote of Graveley that he was not only "a most efficient military officer...he is more...he is a staunch Conservative and has made many sacrifices for the party."[15] Another endorsement of Graveley came from R.R. Pringle of Cobourg who reminded Macdonald that "as far as this riding is concerned he [Graveley] has always worked well and he certainly has sacrificed himself when he ran for the local [elections] when nothing but defeat stared him in the face."[16] Writing from Port Hope another correspondent addressed himself to the essential point—Graveley deserved the appointment because of "his service to the party."[17]

The fact that service to the party was the most important element in appointments did not make Macdonald's or the committee's task any easier for in many cases there were several suitable party workers seeking a post. In such cases it was difficult to make a recommendation without causing dissent and factionalism in the local organization. In other cases local party notables might either try to dominate the executive committee or try to by-pass the committee and deal directly with Macdonald on patronage issues. All these factors appeared over the appointments of a landing-waiter in the customs service in Kingston, a case that well illustrates some of the local complexities involved in distribution of patronage. In this instance John Gaskill of the Montreal Transport Company and a prominent local Conservative had ignored the work of the executive committee and had pressed his own candidate on Macdonald. On January 8, 1891 Macdonald was warned by George Fitzpatrick of the consequent trouble—"Gaskill is raising a row and I hear that the Executive Committee had a real lively time yesterday. The Kilkenny Election was nothing to it."[18] Fitzpatrick sent a telegram to Macdonald asking that the appointment be held up until a local solution to the conflict was found. The situation was more tangled because Gaskill's candidate had been "insulting" to the executive committee. The committee's viewpoint was put by John McIntyre who explained to the Prime Minister that "we are all anxious to do what we can for the party...but I know the majority of the Committee will feel greatly humiliated if Gaskill is allowed to reverse every recommendation that is made."[19]

The Kingston patronage letters also reveal that Macdonald and local party leaders did not deal simply with appointments but also were actively involved in promotions within the public service and even in the creation of new posts to satisfy the patronage demands within the party. In September 1889, for example, John Haggart, Postmaster General in Ottawa, replied to the Prime Minister concerning the promotion of a clerk within the postal service. Macdonald himself had requested the promotion after hearing from the executive committee and Haggart was willing to comply except there was no vacancy to which the clerk could be promoted. Haggart, however, went on to suggest a solution. He could do what Macdonald requested by "providing in the Estimates for the coming year a first-class clerkship in the Inspectors office at Kingston."[20] There was no discussion about the necessity of a clerkship; it was simply to be created in the interests of the local party.

From this Kingston evidence we begin to get an idea of the workings of patronage, particularly the relationship between Ottawa and the localities. The Member of Parliament, in this case Macdonald, made the formal and final decisions about appointments from the Kingston area as he passed on names to other cabinet ministers. Usually the MP received the nomination from the local executive committee. It was assumed that the local party organization, by its executive committee, was the normal channel through which patronage business flowed. When acting on patronage matters the committee did so in a formal way, receiving and reviewing applications, weighing credentials, passing resolutions and forwarding the recommendations to the MP at Ottawa. One final point to emerge is that the structure of the patronage system, as revealed in the Kingston evidence, excluded outsiders from sharing in contracts and appointments. The patronage was given only to local figures who could prove their loyalty to the local party organization.

II

The Kingston evidence while informative may not be typical because of Macdonald's position as Prime Minister. This may have led him to leave much of the daily patronage business in the hands of the local leaders. It is therefore essential to examine other evidence to assess whether this pattern was representative.

One report during the period revealed a good deal about the day-to-day workings of the patronage system. This was the investigation in 1909 by Judge Cassels into the Department of Marine and Fisheries. A basic point made in the report was that since 1867 the department had been used by both the Conservatives and Liberals, when they were in power, for partisan purposes. Positions and contracts were given to reward party activists. Regular "patronage lists" drawn up by the MP and local party leaders were kept on file so business could be directed to party faithful. "The system," noted the report,

> seems to have been handed down from one administration to another since Confederation.... It is apparently based on the old maxim of 'to the victor belong the spoils' utterly ignoring the fact that the money to be disbursed is mainly contributed by the people generally and not the money of the political followers of the party at the time being in power.[21]

During the course of the investigation the activities of the department's office in Halifax provided detailed evidence on how the system worked. In the case of Halifax the MPs were active in the regular distribution of jobs and contracts. The report explained that

> patronage in Halifax extended beyond the mere naming of the merchants and others who should comprise the patronage list. It extended to the nomination by Members of Parliament representing the constituency of individuals or an individual to whom orders were to be given.[22]

The questioning of witnesses showed the way things were managed. When work needed to be done or supplies furnished "then the members would recommend...that the orders should be given to A, B, C, or D as the case may be." Mr. Jonathan Parsons, the Department's chief agent in Halifax, explained that this was done "under the rules of patronage." He further explained that these rules applied "from year to year and from month to month every year." On every occasion a contract was to be placed the MPs "would designate...which merchant or manufacturer or dealer particular orders should be given to." The questioning concluded:

> Q: That has been the cause?
> A: Yes.
> Q: Each Time?
> A: Yes.
> Q: So it is not your independent judgment that was exercised from time to time as to where the work should be done or by whom material should be furnished; that was done upon the recommendations?
> A: By the member of parliament having the patronage.[23]

The evidence also showed that aside from this regular management of patronage the MPs authorized "taking on an employee" because they "had the patronage."[24]

The 1909 Report on the Department of Marine and Fisheries confirmed the assessment made the previous year by a civil service inquiry that the organization of the department, comprehensively influenced by patronage, had "few redeeming features." The Commission of 1908 had made a broad investigation of the public service outside the home departments in Ottawa and had concluded that these outside agencies were entirely at the disposal of the party in power. "As a rule," the commissioners explained, in the outside service...politics enter into every appointment and politicians on the spot interest themselves not only in the appointments but in the subsequent promotion of the officers...in the outside service the politics of the party is of greater importance in making appointments and promotions than the public interests of the Dominion.[25]

In each locality the MP and the party leaders regarded appointments and contracts as their exclusive right to be used to reward local party workers. "In practically no case," the commissioners discovered, "is it possible to fill a vacancy in one locality by a transfer from another."[26] In the Inland Revenue Department, for example, "political appointments as in other branches of the public service, prevail and as a rule the officers in one district are confined to that one district." In Montreal all the appointments in the customs service were made "at the insistance of the members of parliament for the district." Indeed throughout the entire customs service the commissioners concluded that each riding was "looked upon as local patronage" and that posts were awarded to local people only.[27] In his evidence Dr. Barrett, inspector of Inland Revenue at Winnipeg, explained the active role MPs took in preserving local patronage exclusively for local party use. Barrett described how when a post became available "the member of the constituency says, 'No, I will not allow anyone outside my constituency to go in there.'" In Winnipeg as in Kingston, the names for appointments were "generally given by the Liberal Association of Winnipeg." Barrett emphasized that "when the Conservatives were in power they did the same thing."[28] In their general observations on this kind of evidence, the commissioners concluded that "each locality was separately guarded."[29] Even the national party leader could not interfere with this local exclusivity. Writing to a party worker who had asked for a position outside his own constituency, Wilfred Laurier pointed out how hard this would be to arrange. "I need not tell you," wrote the Prime Minister, "that it is always difficult to bring an outsider into a locality."[30]

It is important to note that this type of patronage distribution exclusively to party activists was not confined to minor posts in the customs or postal services and other such branches of the federal bureaucracy but operated at all levels. This can be demonstrated by looking at Macdonald's policies in making appointments to the bench and the bar. County judgeships and the earning of the title of Queen's Counsel (QC) were sought-after plums in the legal profession and were at the disposal of the party in power. As with the customs service workers and post office employees the positions in the judiciary were given by the party in power primarily on the basis of the candidate's service to the party. An example of the essential relationship between party service and advancement in the legal profession is contained in correspondence from 1887 between John Small and John A. Macdonald. Small wrote a confidential memorandum to the Prime Minister with a list of barristers eligible for a QC and set out against each name the reasons for his recommendation:

> Michael Murphy: defeated candidate 1882...attended meetings in recent elections...Roman Catholic;

> Daniel Defoe: strong supporter, always took a prominent part in political movements;

> James Reeve: did good work in the last election.

> James Fullerton: takes the platform in the interests of the party;

> George Blackstock: has contested elections;

> Emerson Coalsworth: rising young barrister, pillar of the Methodist Church, a strong Temperance advocate, President of the Liberal Conservative Association for his ward, was my agent in the last election.[31]

These candidates for QC had varied characteristics—some Roman Catholic, others Methodist, some with long legal experience, others just beginning to become noted in the profession—yet each shared one necessary qualification without which any other would be useless. In one way or another all had worked for their local Conservative parties either by running as candidates, being speakers or canvassers, or drawing up and scrutinizing the voters lists. It was this kind of information on good hard party work that Macdonald looked for when creating a new batch of QC's. And these criteria were well understood throughout the party. In October 1889 Robert Birmingham, the Secretary-Treasurer of the Liberal Conservative Union of Ontario, sent Macdonald "the names of a few legal friends who rendered us special service in the recent campaign in the hope that you might be able to repay them with the much sought after QC."[32]

The next step up beyond QC were county judgeships and these too were distributed with the party's interest in mind. The context in which the awarding of judgeship was discussed can be seen from a case involving the Prime Minister, Frank Smith, the Senator who was the most important Ontario Catholic in the party, and B.I. Doyle, a party worker seeking a promotion to the bench. Doyle set forth his qualifications which rested on the premise that his "services to the Party for the last 15 years entitled me to something." He then proceeded to recount the details of this party work, emphasizing that he had "stood by the party in the darkest hours of its severest trials [and] fought for it when it was down and persevered in the desperate struggle on behalf of our principles till the victory again crowned our efforts." Doyle then went on to describe the election campaigns, particularly the one of 1878, in which he had done a great deal to get out the Catholic vote. He concluded his letter with the blunt request—"I want a County Judgeship."[33] This request was endorsed by Senator Frank Smith, who confirmed that Doyle had indeed done all the party work he claimed to have done over the years. Smith wrote of Doyle that he was "a plucky, active man whom I know to have worked hard for his party." Therefore, concluded the Senator, "he deserves to get what he asks."[34] Macdonald was unable to satisfy Doyle immediately because of some rival candidates but he did promise to do what he could and in January 1880 Doyle was appointed junior judge of Huron county.[35]

Other evidence from the Macdonald papers confirms this pattern of judicial appointments being related to partisan activity. In November 1883 Robert Smith QC was recommended for a vacant judgeship in Huron. He was considered deserving of such honor because he was "ever willing to go where duty to his party called him." In April 1885 H.C. Gwyn applied to the Prime Minister for a vacant judgeship on the grounds that he had been:

> actively identified with the party...and up to a year ago and for seven or eight years previously [was] the Secretary of the Liberal-Conservative Association of North Wentworth...[36]

In May 1884 a Conservative MP recommended J.M. Hamilton of Sault Saint Marie for a judgeship, explaining that Hamilton was "very much esteemed throughout Algoma and it is of some political importance that he should be appointed."[37] About a year later another Conservative MP, N.C. Wallace, in recommending Edward Morgan, a barrister for a junior county judgeship in York, explained that Morgan had "fought, bled and almost died for the Party and has very much stronger claims than anyone else that has been proposed for the position."[38] In the summer of 1887 A.M. Boswell, a party leader in Toronto, after reporting to Macdonald about party fund raising turned to judicial patronage and recommended N.C. Stewart for a junior judgeship in that city. Stewart, explained Boswell, was "an out and out Conservative and as steady as a rock. At one time he was not a cold water man but now he is all right."[39]

This evidence concerning the legal profession confirms that at all levels of public employment, from judgeships down to landing-waiters in the customs service, the party in power distributed patronage only to those who had worked for the party. It was not enough simply to be a contributer to party funds or an occasional canvasser but necessary to prove a long period of active, dedicated work in the ridings. The immutability of this standard was well illustrated by a case from London, Ontario that developed in that spring of 1900. It concerned the family of John A. Donegan who had volunteered to fight in the Canadian contingent in the Boer War. Donegan had been killed in South Africa, leaving a widow and two sons in London. There were some efforts to find jobs for the two boys to help support the family and James Sutherland, a Liberal MP, had written to local party leaders in London asking their views of the proposal to find posts for the Donegan boys. It might be expected that in this part of Ontario the sons of war dead in South Africa would receive sympathetic treatment but the local party balked and refused to consider them for any posts. In response to Sutherland's inquiries, George Reid, a local party leader, explained that

> as for making a position for either of the Donegans in this locality, it would be very unpopular, they have never been Friends of ours in any particular and [it] would never do to appoint any one who has not been identified with the work of the party.... To appoint him for any position purely [and] simply because his father was killed in Africa would be to my mind very absurd.[40]

Reid also pointed out that the man who was doing most to find jobs for the Donegans was not a party supporter. If he had been, that might have been a reason to give the Donegans something to reward a party worker but, warned Reid, there was no point in helping the Donegans' backer for "he is a strong supporter of the enemy and of no use to us whatsoever."[41]

A comprehensive example of the normalcy of these expectations is contained in some private correspondence between Laurier and Roy Choquette concerning the Liberal party in the district of Quebec. Following the Liberal victory in 1896 Laurier had asked Choquette to report on the patronage requirements of the local party in the Quebec area. Choquette was to sound out party notables and send Laurier "une liste des nominations...sur lesquels nos amis insistent le plus pour le moment." On September 12 Choquette sent Laurier a detailed list of demands by Quebec Liberals:

> Voici ce qui en est: L'Hon. M. Joly [controller of Inland Revenue] devrait immédiatement remplacer le Dr. Fiset de St. Sauveur par le Dr. Coté, et ce, pour faire plaisir à nos jeunes amis de Québec M. l'Orateur, devrait remercier de ses services M. Fournier, pour satisfaire M. Talbot, et en même temps le Ministre des Chemins de fer devrait faire l'échange des stations du l'Intercolonial entre Castonguay de St. Charles et M. Roy de St. Moise. M. l'Orateur devrait encore destituer un nommé Gagnon, messager sessional pour donner satisfaction à M. LaForest, notre candidat contre Costigan. M. Paterson [minister of customs] ou Joly devrait remplacer Philéas Dubé, de Fraserville, officier du Douane, part M. Amédé Gagan de St. Arseire, comte de Temiscouta....[42]

Choquette then continued, in the same matter-of-fact manner, to list further patronage requirements of other important local Liberals, each of whom, typically enough, had specific rewards in mind for himself and his fellow-workers:

> Pour faire plaisir à l'ami Lemieux, un nommé Baudin, gardien de phare de la Grande Rivière, et qui a voulu le battre à son arrivée à cet endroit, devrait être remercier de ses services et remplacé par M. William Bisson.

> L'ami Fisset attend avec impatience, ce qui lui est promis depuis longtemps, la nomination du Dr. Ross de Ste. Flavie,

à la place du Dr. Gauvreau, partisan bleu enragé, comme médecin du port à la Pointe au Père; et la nomination du Dr. Boullion, de Matane, à la place du Dr. Pelletier comme médecin du port à cet endroit.

L'ami Angers aimerait avoir la reinstallation immédiate de M. Joseph Gaudreau, comme maître de poste à Grands Fonds, Malbaie.[43]

Choquette ended this list of patronage requirements by briskly noting his own demands, "Quant à moi," he wrote, "si l'ami Fisher [minister of Agriculture] pouvait me nommer Desiré Vezina à la place de Zephiron Danceuse comme homme de police à la Grosse Ile, et l'ami Mulock [postmaster-general] me nommer M. Georges Gagné, maître de poste à Ste. Pierre, à la place de madame C. Dienne, j'en serais bien content."[44]

The working of the patronage system as revealed by these examples continued right down to the eve of World War I. The Royal Commission that investigated the civil service in 1911-1912 uncovered the same practices that their predecessors have described in the 1880's and 1890's. One particular interchange between the commissioners and a witness laid out clearly the mechanics of the patronage system. The witness was Robert G. MacPherson, post-master at Vancouver. He was asked how appointments were made to the staff and the following exchange took place:

A: Appointments are made through recommendations by the patronage committee or the members supporting the government

Q: Do they communicate directly with you when vacancies occur

A: No. I will apply for one or two men to the department at Ottawa who authorize the appointment of men who shall be recommended by the member of parliament or the patronage committee as the case may be.[45]

From the other side of Canada, on Prince Edward Island, came evidence of how the system worked there. Thomas Mann, agent at Charlottetown for the Department of Marine and Fisheries, explained that appointment and purchasing worked "by patronage." If a position fell vacant, "the members supply a list of men they want put on and if they are suitable I put them on...." In the matter of buying supplies these were purchased "from the patronage people." The questioning continued:

Q: You have a list
A: It is not a list from the government, just from the local members. They do the same as when the other government was in power. They have their friends to go and so have these
Q: You have a patronage list
A: A patronage list of friends to go to the same as before.[46]

The evidence in this section has provided an overview of the workings of the patronage system in the years between 1878 and 1911. There emerges a remarkable similarity in how the system worked under Macdonald and Laurier and a remarkable stability in a system that had the same structure in 1912 as it did in the 1880's. From Vancouver to Halifax, from London to Quebec, from Winnipeg to Prince Edward Island, Conservative and Liberal administrations of the period used their power in the same way. Federal posts and contracts were given to local party activists in a regular, time-honoured manner. Although the actual decisions on patronage were made by the cabinet ministers in Ottawa, the evidence shows that much of the work in terms of identifying applicants and proposing candidates was done by the local party organization, usually working through a committee. It is also clear that the patronage system applied to all levels of the public service from judgeships down to temporary positions in the post office. The system had become so rooted a part of Canadian political culture that it was considered legitimate and normal. It was only late in the period with the Royal Commission of 1911-1912 that serious questions were raised about the impact of so extensive a system of patronage on Canadian governments and their effectiveness in dealing with the needs of society.[47]

III

To understand all the ramifications of the patronage system it is essential to relate it to the structure of Canadian society during this period. The first and most fundamental point to make here is that Canada was a small-town, rural society which was only beginning to be changed by the consequences of industrialization and urbanization. Professor Waite has reminded us of this basic fact in his authoritative study of the period between 1873 and 1896. The rural nature of Canada, he writes, "must be kept continually in mind when considering the character and setting of Canadian life. The conservativeness of the French-Canadian countryside is well known, its resistance to social change is as strong as its political allegiances, but so much of Canada was similar...Canada was rural."[48] In 1881 the census classified 81% of the population as rural. By 1911 it was down to 56%, still over half the population. But even that figure does not tell the whole story. The census for 1911 shows that out of a total population of 7,206,643 there were 5,507,214 Canadians living in rural areas or in towns with less than 30,000. As late as 1911 about 76% of the Canadian population was living in small-town or rural conditions.[49]

One characteristic related to these conditions is that Canadian society was localistic. Professor Gibson has remarked on this quality of Canadian society, pointing out that "at Confederation and for many years afterwards, the Canadian people, a small and widely dispersed population, formed a simple and individualistic society, exhibiting strong local loyalties."[50] The evidence on patronage cited above shows again and again how social and political leaders in each locality were anxious to keep "outsiders" from moving in to their traditional sphere of influence. An insight into the isolation and localism of Canadian society in this period is provided by the memoirs of the historian A.R.M. Lower. He was born and raised in Barrie, Ontario, and recalled that in 1907 when he was eighteen years old "he had not been more than sixty or seventy miles away from home." Lower wondered whether he was "exceptional" in being thus rooted. "It is remarkable," he then added, "how local everyone was in those days."[51]

Another basically important fact to be borne in mind was that there was limited economic growth during this period and that in contrast to the United States, for example, there was no dramatic advance of industrial capitalism. Even the Laurier "boom years" after 1900 rested on the development of agriculture in the West and well into the first decade of the twentieth century contemporaries regarded Canada's economy as essentially an agricultural one.[52] In 1896 Byron Walker wrote in the *Monetary Times* that agriculture was "the substratum of our well-being."[53] Two years later D.R. Wilkie in a speech before the Canadian Bankers Association explained that Canada "was essentially an agricultural country"[54] and in 1907 this characteristic was again referred to, that "the real backbone of Canada is its agricultural and its dairy and pastoral interests."[55] A 1906 piece in *Industrial Canada* pointed out that "Canada is and always will be a great agricultural country...[the farmer] is the very foundation stone of our social economy."[56]

A natural consequence of this reality was the relative insignificance of the industrial, manufacturing sector of the Canadian economy in moulding the social structure and value system of Canada. Some caution is required in broaching this topic for there is some disagreement among scholars about the nature and performance of the Canadian economy during this period. It used to be a conventional enough statement that there was little economic development between 1867 and 1900, at which point there was a take-off based on the wheat boom in the West. The picture of unrelieved gloom for the pre-1896 years can no longer be sustained, as Professor Waite has recently explained in his assessment of the new evidence.[57] There was steady growth in some manufactures; the GNP rose from $710,000,000 in 1873 to $1,800,000,000 in 1896. Clearly the economy did grow and the transportation and banking structures developed before 1900 proved a solid base from which the more rapid, diversified growth of the twentieth century could develop. Yet while acknowledging the reality of this economic growth its limitations must be kept in mind. The manufacturing firms in Canada were small, employed tiny work forces and had a very restricted impact on the social structure.[58] In 1870 the average number of persons employed in each manufacturing establishment was 4.6; in 1890 it had risen to only 5.5.[59] Manufacturing was still small-scale, decentralized and geographically dispersed.

These economic circumstances were important for sustaining such a flourishing patronage system. The key point is that there were limited job opportunities available in the private manufacturing sector and that as a consequence federal contracts and positions within the federal public service were important areas of career opportunities.[60] In a system in which there was dynamic capitalist growth as in the United States, employment opportunities at the disposal of the federal government assumed a minor place but in the case of Canada such opportunities were a foremost feature in the job market. The way in which the Donegan family immediately turned to political patronage for jobs is a good example of the role federal posts played in this respect. When it is further remembered that the major capitalist activity of the period—the Canadian Pacific Railroad—was also controlled by the state, it is clear that federal patronage played a dominant role in job distribution in post-Confederation Canada. It is revealing to note that patronage started to decline once the economy began to develop and diversify. There were several reasons for the decline of patronage after the 1914-18 war but one of the basic ones was that the advance of manufacturing reduced the heavy dependence on the federal government (and therefore the federal political parties) for jobs and contracts.[61]

The slow development of industry in Canada had another social consequence that intensified the central significance of the patronage system. Again in contrast to contemporary United States, where capitalists and businessmen formed the dominant social class, these groups were numerically small and socially insignificant in Canada. In a society where industrial development was in its infancy and where manufacturing was small-scale, the professional middle classes flourished.[62] The prestige occupations in Canada lay in this area— barristers, solicitors, clergy, civil servants. In the case of Quebec the pre-eminence of these groups is accepted readily enough. Jean-Charles Falardeau has provided a good summary of the situation in Quebec, pointing out that by the mid-nineteenth century the professional middle-classes had succeeded the traditional elites. "La noblesse professionelle," Falardeau notes, "constituent effectivement, jusqu'à l'époque contemporaine, l'élite Canadienne-Française—c'est cette élite que l'on est tenté d'appeler et que l'on appelle souvent notre bourgeoisie."[63] But while this social phenomenon of a "bourgeois" class composed mostly of professionals rather than businessmen is normally associated with Quebec, it was equally a hallmark of English-Canadian society before the industrialization of the twentieth-century. Because there was no rapid capitalist and industrial development in Canada, there failed to develop a large and powerful middle class whose members could earn a living in ways that were open to trained and educated men in the United States and Britain. Opportunities for upward mobility through business corporations or by selling technical skills were very limited in Canada. This weakened "the development within Canadian society of capitalist, urban middle-class social values and forms of social structure."[64] In these circumstances there was little choice for each generation between 1867 and 1911 but to earn a living and gain social status by entering the legal profession or gaining a position in the public service.

A nice example of the social prestige a professional man could achieve in this small-town society was given by the Civil Service Commission in their 1908 report. Looking back to the 1880's for an overview of the reasons why public service was so attractive to Canadians the commissioners pointed out the advantages:

> Owing to the small mileage of railways and to the lack of communications most of the necessities of life raised in the different localities were consumed locally. Butter, eggs, meats, foodstuffs and articles entering into daily consumption were produced in the locality in which they were consumed. The same characteristic feature was applicable to domestic servants employed in the households of officials in the public service. A generation ago there was no means by which the farmers' daughters could remove easily from the locality in which they were born, and as the supply of domestic servants was greater than the demand the wages were comparatively small.... The civil servant in these days, although not in receipt of a large income, had his wants satisfied cheaply and without stint.[65]

Not all public employees could afford servants. Nevertheless it is a valid proposition that for most of the 1867-1911 period, bearing in mind prevailing economic conditions, the public service was the biggest single area of attractive, secure and prestigious employment. Even as late as 1911 employees in the public service still talked in terms of the "dignity" and "respectability" of their position in society.[66] The only way to get one of these jobs was to have some claim on one of the two political parties. It was these basic social and economic realities that enabled the political parties to make the patronage system such a powerful organizing force in Canadian society and politics.

IV

These final two sections will put forward some general conclusions about the significance of the patronage system and its long-term consequences in Canadian political development. The first point to make is that the pervasive patronage system that lasted throughout these years confirmed the power and prestige of professional middle classes who ran the two federal parties. In Canada these middle class groups—barristers, solicitors, doctors, notaries—which controlled the political parties did not, as in Europe, face serious social or economic competition. There was no aristocratic or traditional landed class that still had an influence in public affairs; there was no lingering peasant presence upon which a political movement could be based; there was no rapidly expanding capitalist class deriving wealth and power from industrialization; there was no mass labor movement seeking to form its own party. In these conditions the federal political parties, representing the dominant middle class and particularly the professionals, were extraordinarily influential in Canadian society. To understand the ramifications of these circumstances it is useful to consider the observations made by Hans Daalder in his analysis of political development in western Europe.[67] Daalder, in tackling the question of how political elites relate to other elite groups in society, has suggested that one method of assessing the relative power of elites is to gauge the extent to which important positions within society could be obtained without reference to the political elite, without going through party channels.[68] In Canada nearly every important position in society was available only through the two political parties. Judges were appointed on the basis of partisan loyalty; QC's were distributed to lawyers who had been active in party work; senators were purely political appointments; posts throughout the public service, from the most senior down to the temporary and from Halifax to Vancouver, were disposed of by the parties to those who had worked for them. Even men with technical qualifications, such as civil engineers seeking work on the railroads, thought it wise to let their party credentials be known.[69] And in filling these positions the party leaders were approached in a supplicating manner by archbishops, bishops, deacons, priests, ministers, university principals, manufacturers and individuals from their prominent social groups. In Daalder's terms the political elite in Canada was the top power elite, no other group approaching it in terms of power and influence.[70]

The course of Canada's economy during these years helped sustain the dominant role of the parties and their patronage system. Again it is helpful to compare Canada with Europe and the United States. Jacques Ellul has written that "the nation-state is the most important reality of our days.... Nowadays it is the state that directs the economy.... The state is not just a superstructure. Marxist analysis is only valid in the nineteenth century when the emergence of uncontrolled, explosive economic power relegated a weak, liberal and unclearly delineated state to the shadows and subjugated it."[71] In Canada things did not happen this way. There was no explosive economic growth and the state was not relegated to a position of insignificance by the powerful forces of industrial capitalism. On the contrary, the state in Canada, the federal government, was the single most important energizing agency as it took the lead in stimulating economic growth, protecting infant industries, building a national transportation network as well as constructing its own physical presence in hundreds of public work projects across the country in the form of harbours, bridges, railways, post offices, customs houses and other buildings to house its bureaucracy. Upon entering office, each political party fell heir to this extensive sphere of government activity. In the United States the party in power had similar room for maneuver but in that country the party's scope for activity was circumscribed by other powerful interests in the expanding capitalist economy whereas in Canada the parties faced no rivals. Quite simply in Canada the parties were dominant and pervasive. A contemporary observer in the 1880's caught this development in the new Confederation. There was in Canada, he wrote, "an overgrowth of party-ism."[72] In these circumstances the patronage system was like water finding its own level as it permeated post-Confederation Canadian society.

Another important point to emerge from the ramifications of the patronage system is that in the 1867 to 1911 period English- and French-Canadians were more alike in their social and political behavior than has commonly been accepted. Scholars have drawn attention to the fact that a major reason for the French-Canadian attachment to the Union (1840-1867) was that the Québécois professional middle class received, through patronage, opportunities for social advancement. Jacques Monet has well described this phenomenon in the twenty years before Confederation. "For two generations since 1800," explains Monet,

> The Canadian professional class had been struggling to secure an outlet for its ambitions: so now with a kind of bacterial thoroughness it began to invade every vital organ of government, and divide up among its members hundreds of posts as Judges, Queen's Counsels, Justices of the Peace, Medical Examiners, school inspectors, militia captains, postal clerks, mail conductors, census commissioners. And the flatteries and salaries of office percolated down to other classes of society—from merchants who wanted seats on the Legislative Council down to impoverished habitants on the

crowded seigneuries—the Canadians came to realize how parliamentary democracy could be more than a lovely ideal. It was also a profitable fact. And henceforth...there could be guaranteed for all French-Canadians the possibility of room at the top.[73]

This process continued after 1867. Jean-Charles Bonenfant has described a typical pattern of upward mobility through politics—"l'homme politique était bourgeois d'une certaine aisance, ayant de préférence une formation juridique, se faisant élire à la chambre basse pour mourir plus tard conseiller legislatif, senateur ou juge."[74] Jean Falardeau in his analysis of nineteenth century Quebec society also draws attention to the relationships among politics, patronage and social status. Falardeau makes distinctions between professionals and politicians, suggesting that the political bourgeoisie represented by such leaders as La Fontaine and Laurier and the members elected to Ottawa were more susceptible to English values, while within the localities of Quebec the "pure" professionals such as doctors, advocates, notaries, derived office and rewards from political patronage but remained rooted in Quebec language and culture. By the middle of the nineteenth century these professional and political elements, flourishing off the patronage system and all its ramifications, had replaced the ailing seigneurs as "la classe dirigeante" in Quebec. Falardeau describes them in that perceptive phrase already noted as "la noblesse professionelle."[75]

All this may be familiar enough but such historical social analysis should not stop short at the Ottawa River. Most of the preceding observations about the mobility patterns, values and social aspirations of the Quebec middle classes apply almost as well to English Canada between 1867 and 1911. Of course conditions were not identical in English Canada and Quebec. In the English provinces there were more varied responses to business, finance and commerce; there were more opportunities in these fields and more social credit attached to them. Also in English-Canada there was no one dominant church to which all successful men had to defer or relate in some manner. Yet recent research has downplayed some of these conventional distinctions and shown that Quebec's response to economic change was not as reactionary as was once supposed.[76] Whatever the final verdict of scholars on these distinctions it is essential to point out the similarities that did exist. Before industrialization developed in a dynamic manner in the decade after 1900,

English-Canada was a rural, small-town and churched society with limited contacts with the secular and transforming world of industrial capitalism. The opportunities for posts and social advancement through businesses and companies were restricted. It was a society in which the most prestigious and important groups were the professional middle classes; a society in which patronage was normal, legitimate and pervasive; a society in which patronage was the single most important route of upward mobility to sought-after positions that gave security and status. English-speaking Canadians like their counterparts in Quebec turned to the patronage of the parties to become judges, senators, QC's, post office officials, customs service officials, collectors of inland revenue, medical examiners and a multitude of other positions in the public service. The operation of these social processes in English-Canada may have been less intense than in Quebec, more directly linked to business and commercial goals, but the profound similarities between French- and English-Canadians remain. There was then a fundamental convergence in how English- and French-Canadians regarded politics and political parties and the social ramifications of politics. In particular both major ethnic groups in Canada shared the same expectations and derived the same kind of rewards from the system of political patronage. On patronage English- and French-Canadians spoke the same language.

V

In the turning to the long-term consequences of the patronage system a paradox appears. On the one hand patronage helped to create and maintain a political stability, an essential condition if Confederation were to succeed, but on the other hand it helped to entrench a political culture which because of its nature pushed problems concerning the nature of Confederation to the background. On the positive side the ability of the parties to utilize patronage on so grand a scale over so long a period helped them to attract and retain supporters and thereby establish a solid base in the population. The process of establishing political stability has been analyzed by many scholars studying new nations in the modern world and one conclusion they have come to is that political stability usually requires political parties to have an extensive and influential reach in society. The political parties must be able to show that they can effectively reward supporters and so encourage loyalty to the party. Often some form of patronage or corruption is the means by which a party establishes its position. As Joseph Palombara puts it, "corruption or its functional equivalent may be critically important to a developing nation."[77] For example, in such a new nation if merit alone were the criterion for appointment to the public service then there would be a growth of bureaucratic power which would push the parties to the sidelines and thus lead to political instability as the parties became unable to attract and reward supporters. In the Canadian case patronage functioned in this manner. Patronage cemented the support of both federal parties, enabled them to exert extensive influence throughout society, and thus helped create a stable party system.

Such an achievement should not be underestimated in a country as fragmented ethnically and regionally as Canada. But for the achievement of political stability there was a price to pay. One of the adverse consequences of the patronage system was that it encouraged the persistence of localism in Canadian politics. The way in which patronage was dispersed made every local party organization across Canada jealous of its own territory and suspicious of outsiders. Local exclusivity was sanctioned by the national party leaders. Indeed, this was a deliberate object of policy in order to create strong local organizations to fight election campaigns. This tendency must be kept in perspective. Localism, given the social, economic and geographic setting of Canada at the time, was bound to be a natural characteristic of Canadian politics.[78] The parties were moulded by the type of society in which they functioned. It is therefore a question of degree. Localism was bound to exist and the parties could either simply live with this reality or try to lessen its impact or encourage its persistence. They did the last. The patronage system of the two parties encouraged Canadian political culture to remain localized. From a party viewpoint this was a good thing since it created strong, loyal, hard-working local associations that could be managed by skilled leadership in Ottawa from the center of the patronage web. But it also restricted the vision of those in politics: MPs and local party notables were not encouraged by the system to interest themselves in affairs outside their own areas. The system worked in the direction of local inwardness. Because of this the Canadian House of Commons was in a metaphorical sense "la maison sans fenêtres."[79] The MP's vision was narrowly focussed back into his locality and the windows on national issues were closed or obscured. The long reign of the patronage system contributed to a persistent parochialism in Canadian politics.

The great paradox lying at the center of Canadian political culture in this period was that this emphasis on localism and avoidance of debate on the relationships between the two racial groups were the very reasons for the success of the party system in maintaining stability prior to 1911. To explain this paradox it is useful to relate the case advanced in this article to recent work done by Arend Lijphart on elite accommodation and consociational democracy.[80] Lijphart's model seems a fruitful one to apply to Canada. He argues that European countries which have an ethnically segmented population have developed a peculiar form of democracy. In these systems each major ethnic group supports its own political party and the leaders of these parties, the representative elites, negotiate and mediate to form governments and maintain stability without sacrificing the interests of one particular group. Thus while there may be little communication and even great tension between the various linguistic blocs the elites of each group compromise in an attempt to reach solutions to national problems. The system then is characterized by elite accommodation. In a stimulating and thoughtful study Kenneth McCrea has applied the consociational democracy model to the Canadian case.[81] McCrea points out that the model can be useful for Canada only if it is modified to account for the fact that the two major ethnic blocs have never been represented by separate political parties at the national level. If accommodation does take place between the elites of each society, it must take place within the parties rather than between ethnically based parties. Having made this adjustment to the model McCrea analyzed how the system has worked in Canada and concluded that "even by the most charitable interpretation, the political system's capacity to learn and adapt to linguistic-cultural diversity has not been high."[82] The federal parties have not been able to work out solutions to national problems but have instead created a situation of "immobilism and stalemate" in which the federal government seems weak and ineffective. Accommodation within the parties which should have been going on since 1867 has not taken place. On the contrary the gulf between English- and French-Canadians has widened to the point where the continued survival of the nation is in doubt. McCrea concludes that the Canadian political system has a low learning capacity.[83]

This is a complex topic which requires multi-factor analysis. Yet one of the principal reasons for the apparent ineffectiveness of the federal party system lies in the structure of parties as they developed between 1878 and 1911. The cardinal point here is that both parties relied on patronage so heavily that they reduced the need for any genuine accommodation on such issues, for example, as language in the public service. As Brown and Cook have recently pointed out, communication between the two races hardly existed except in the realm of politics. In 1902 Lord Minto remarked that he found "the leaders of society of both races unacquainted with each other."[84] In these conditions much depended on the intercourse among the politicians of each race within the two federal parties and they found it easier and more congenial to deal with patronage and localized politics rather than "questions of race."[85]

The impact of patronage limited accommodation in the whole system of appointments and promotions in the public service. As far back as 1877 William LeSueur drew attention to the fact that in the Canadian public service no heed was paid to whether or not an employee or candidate was bilingual and no recognition or reward was given to those who happened to be bilingual. LeSueur pointed out that:

> in a service where two languages are used it is obviously unfair that a man who brings to the Service a knowledge of both, and whose knowledge of both is made use of by the Department in which he serves, should derive no advantage whatever from the fact. Such, however, is the fact. In the Department in which I serve a man who knows both French and English is made to do work requiring a knowledge of both those languages and to do it for his seniors. A senior clerk may send to a junior clerk that portion of his work which requires knowledge of a second language and the junior gets nothing at all in the way of promotion for this special qualification.[86]

It is important to emphasize that both English- and French-speaking politicians were responsible for this non-recognition of the value of two-language people in the public service—it was not a policy concocted by bigoted Anglo-Canadian politicians. The fact that a contemporary like LeSueur could put his finger on a fundamental issue like this shows that it is not anachronistic to suggest that more could have been done by the parties to incorporate linguistic duality more securely and formally into the structure of the federal administration. The parties did not do so because it did not occur to them to do so.

Whether they came from the Gaspé or western Ontario or Halifax or Vancouver the politicians of the day were interested in the public service from the viewpoint, above all, of patronage. Their interest lay in placing party workers in the service, not trying to make the civil service a setting for reasonable accommodation of French- and English-Canadian interests.[87] In such ways the patronage system, while satisfying the immediate needs of local party associations in Quebec and the rest of Canada, constricted any incipient structural accommodation between the two racial blocs.

Canadians of the twentieth century are reaping the harvest of patronage politics during the 1867 to 1911 period. Parties relied heavily on patronage to satisfy ethnic groups within each party and so avoided the need to think about genuine accommodation in terms of the relationship of English- and French-Canadians in Confederation. Patronage was a great strength yet also a great weakness in the Canadian party system. It enabled the parties to flourish and maintain political stability as long as social and economic conditions were fertile ground for patronage and as long as society placed no major demands upon the parties. But once conditions changed, as Canada became an industrialized, urbanized society, as the provinces became more powerful and, above all, as Quebec modernized and began demanding that attention be paid to the basic meaning and structure of Confederation, then the parties which had been successful before 1911 began to become less effective. Their historical development had not prepared them for finding solutions to national problems.[88]

Notes

1   W.L. Morton, "The Cabinet of 1867," in F.W. Gibson, ed., *Cabinet Formation and Bicultural Relations* (Ottawa, 1970), p. 3; an example of a source book treatment of the topic is J.H. Stewart Reid, Kenneth McNaught, Harry S. Crowe, *A Source Book of Canadian History* (Toronto, 1964), pp. 331-346.

2   Morton, "The Cabinet of 1867," p. 2. Political reminiscences of the period are full of references, charges, and counter-charges to patronage and corruption. Richard Cartwright, *Reminiscences* (Toronto, 1912), is particularly rich in this regard. So too is W.T.R. Preston, *My Generation of Politics and Politicians* (Toronto, 1927).

3   Peter B. Waite, *Canada 1874-1896* (Toronto, 1971), p. 96.

4   Commission to Inquire into the Present State and Probable Requirements of the Civil Service (1868-1870), 1st and 2nd Reports in Sessional Papers, #19 (1869), 3rd Report in Sessional Papers, #64 (1870);

Royal Commission to Inquire into the Organization of the Civil Service Commission (1880-81), 1st Report in Sessional Papers, #113 (1880-81), 2nd Report in Sessional Papers #32 (1882); Royal Commission to Inquire into the Present State of the Civil Service at Ottawa (1891-92), Report in Sessional Papers, #16C (1892); Report of the Civil Service Commission (1907-08), Sessional Papers, #29A (1907-08); Commission to Inquire into the Public Service (1911-12), Sessional Papers, #57 (1913).

5   Report of Investigation into the Department of Marine and Fisheries, Sessional Papers, #38 (1909).

6   Waite, *Canada 1874-1896*, pp. 218-221, 230.

7   J.E. Hodgetts, William McClockey, Reginald Whitaker, V. Seymour Wilson, *The Biography of an Institution, The Civil Service Commission of Canada 1908-1967* (Montreal, 1972), p. 8.

8   The evidence is taken from the John A. Macdonald Papers, Public Archives of Canada [hereafter P.A.C.], Vol. 14, Kingston Patronage. On the formalities of the process see John McIntyre to John A. Macdonald, October 11, 1891.

9   Edward Smythe to John A. Macdonald, Kingston, November 13, 1889, Private, Macdonald Papers, Vol. 14, P.A.C.

10   Smythe to Macdonald, Kingston, September 17, 1889, Private, Macdonald Papers, P.A.C.

11   J.A. Metcalfe to John A. Macdonald, Kingston, January 18, 1890, Macdonald Papers, Volume 14, P.A.C.

12   Mackenzie Bowell to John A. Macdonald, Ottawa, January 8, 1891, Macdonald Papers, Vol. 14, P.A.C.

13   Thomas H. McGuire to John A. Macdonald, Kingston, January 9, 1891, Macdonald Papers, Vol. 14, P.A.C.

14   J.A. Metcalfe to John A. Macdonald, Kingston, November 29, 1890, Private, Macdonald Papers, Vol. 14, P.A.C.

15   S.M. Conger to John A. Macdonald, Picton, December 26, 1890, Macdonald Papers, Vol. 14, P.A.C. The militia appointment involved the interests of several ridings in south-east Ontario.

16   R.R. Pringle to John A. Macdonald, Cobourg, December 28, 1890, Macdonald Papers, Vol. 14, P.A.C.

17   H. Ward to John A. Macdonald, Port Hope, December 23, 1890, Private. On the relationship of this piece of patronage to local party "strength" see also Sam Hughes to Charles Tupper, Jr., Lindsay, Ontario, December 25, 1890, Macdonald Papers, Vol. 14, P.A.C.

18   George Fitzpatrick to John A. Macdonald, Kingston, January 8, 1891, Private, Macdonald Papers, Vol. 14, P.A.C.

19   John McIntyre to John A. Macdonald, January 10, 1891, Private.

20 John Haggart to John A. Macdonald, Ottawa, September 19, 1889. In another case Edward Smythe discussed with the Prime Minister the plight
of "our old friend B. McConville," a party activist who had been given
a contract for carrying the mail and now wished the amount to be increased. See Smythe to Macdonald, Kingston, September 17, 1889, Private, Macdonald Papers, Vol. 14, P.A.C.

21 Report of Investigation into Department of Marine and Fisheries (1909),
p. 10.

22 *Ibid.*, p. 41.

23 *Ibid.*, p. 44.

24 *Ibid.*, pp. 42-43.

25 Report of the Civil Service Commission (1907-08), pps. 37, 27.

26 *Ibid.*, p. 28.

27 *Ibid.*, pp. 89-90.

28 *Ibid.*, pps. 7, 28, 440-443.

29 *Ibid.*, p. 28.

30 Hugh Falconer to Wilfred Laurier, Shelbourne, Ontario, January 13,
1908; Laurier to Falconer, Ottawa, January 15, 1908, Private Laurier
Papers, P.A.C. Vol. 950.

31 John Small to John A. Macdonald, Toronto, April 5, 1887, Confidential,
Macdonald Papers, P.A.C., Vol. 24.

32 Robert Birmingham to John A. Macdonald, Toronto, October 10, 1889,
Macdonald Papers, P.A.C., Vol. 24. Macdonald kept a list of all the barristers in Toronto and noted opposite each name the party affiliation.
He also estimated the composition of the Ontario bar as a whole according to party membership. The Toronto bar had 150 barristers eligible for the QC—95 were Conservatives, 55 were "Reformers." See List
of in Toronto, Macdonald Papers, P.A.C., Vol. 24.

33 B.L. Doyle to Frank Smith, Goderich, November 28, 1879, Private, Macdonald Papers, P.A.C., Vol. 25, II.

34 Frank Smith to John A. Macdonald, [?], December 1, 1879, Macdonald
Papers, P.A.C., Vol. 25, II.

35 N.O. Cote, *Political Appointments, Parliaments and the Judicial Bench in
Canada 1890-1903* (Ottawa, 1903), pp. 571-572.

36 H.C. Gwyn to John A. Macdonald, Dundas, April 22, 1885, Macdonald
Papers, P.A.C., Vol. 26.

37 S. Dawson to John A. Macdonald, Ottawa, May 13, 1884, Macdonald Papers, P.A.C., Vol. 26.

38 N. Wallace to John A. Macdonald, Ottawa, July 15, 1885, Private, Macdonald Papers, P.A.C., Vol. 26.

39 A.M. Boswell to John A. Macdonald, Toronto, July 7, 1887, Macdonald

Papers, P.A.C., Vol. 27 II.

40 George Reid to James Sutherland, London, May 4, 1900, Laurier Papers, P.A.C., Vol. 873.

41 *Ibid.*

42 Roy Choquette to Wilfred Laurier, Ottawa, September 12, 1896, Personnelle, Laurier Papers, P.A.C., Vol. 833.

43 *Ibid.*

44 *Ibid.* Laurier himself would act on these patronage requests, even down to the most minor, by notifying (as Macdonald had done) the appropriate minister of the necessary appointments. For example, in response to one request for Liberal appointees to the International railroad Laurier made out a recommendation naming those employees to be dismissed and indicating their replacements. See H.G. Carroll to Wilfred Laurier, Quebec, December 29, 1896; Memorandum by Laurier in Reply, n.d., Laurier Papers, P.A.C., Vol. 833.

45 Royal Commission on the Public Service (1911-12), p. 1292. Macpherson's evidence was given on July 30 and 31, 1912.

46 *Ibid.*, pp. 1416-1417.

47 With the changes wrought by industrialization and urbanization the Canadian government was forced to acknowledge that the patronage-ridden public service system was inefficient and ineffective in the new conditions. This was a basic factor pushing for change. Public opinion was also increasingly critical of patronage after 1900, and an increasing sense of professionalism within the service were additional factors. Public employees in the western provinces were particularly critical in their appearance and representation to the Royal Commission of 1911-12. See R.C. Brown and R. Cook, *Canada 1896-1921, A Nation Transformed* (Toronto, 1974), pp. 192-194, 321; Norman Ward, *The Canadian House of Commons* (Toronto, 1950), pp. 275-281; Royal Commission on the Public Service (1911-1912), pp. 16-20, 337-338; Civil Service Commission (1908-09), p. 13. The latter report noted that "it was the universal feeling amongst the officials who gave evidence...that this patronage evil was the curse of the public service."

48 P.B. White, *Canada 1873-1896* (Toronto, 1971), pp. 8-9.

49 M.C. Urquhart and K.A.H. Buckley, eds., *Historical Statistics of Canada* (Toronto, 1965), pp. 5, 14-15, Series A 15-19 and A 20-24. On pp. 5-7 Urquhart and Buckley discuss the problems of "urban" and "rural" classification in this period.

50 F. Gibson, ed., *Cabinet Formation and Bicultural Relations* (Ottawa, 1970), p. 171.

51 A.R.M. Lower, *My First Seventy-five Years* (Toronto 1967), p. 33. Some examples of suspicion of "outsiders" appear in this article. The patronage papers of both Macdonald and Laurier are full of other instances. For

example a lawyer looking for work in London, Ontario was regarded with deep antipathy because he had no roots in the area. Another individual who was not known locally was described as an "unscrupulous professional man"—i.e., with no base in the local church or community, simply interested in pursuing a career wherever he could get a job. See John Barwick to John A. Macdonald, Woodstock, February 10, 1879, Macdonald Papers, P.A.C., Vol. 251; A. McKean to John A. Macdonald, Bothwell, Ontario, September 19, 1887, Macdonald Papers, P.A.C., Vol. 271. Also see note 30 above for an example in the Laurier Papers.

52   Michael Bliss, "A Living Profit: Studies in the Social History of Canadian Business 1883-1911," Ph.D. Thesis, University of Toronto, p. 331.

53   *Monetary Times*, June 21, 1896, quoted in Bliss, "A Living Profit," p. 331.

54   *Journal of Commerce*, November 4, 1898, pp. 634-635; Byron Walker to G.F. Little, October 10, 1907, both quoted in Bliss, "A Living Profit," p. 331.

55   Byron Walker to G.F. Little, October 10, 1907, quoted in Bliss, "A Living Profit," p. 331.

56   *Industrial Canada*, March 1906, p. 484, quoted in Bliss, "A Living Profit," p. 332.

57   Waite, *Canada 1893-1896*, pp. 74-78.

58   S.D. Clark, "The Canadian Manufacturers Association," *Canadian Journal of Economics and Political Science* , Vol. IV (1938), pp. 506-508. R.T. Naylor, *The History of Canadian Business 1867-1914*, 2 Vols., (Toronto, 1975), Vol. 2, pp. 276-284 argues Canadian industrial development was stultified during these decades.

59   Urquhart and Buckley, eds., *Canadian Historical Statistics*, p. 463, Series Q 1-11.

60   Naylor, *History of Canadian Business 1867-1914*, Vol. 2, pp. 276-284. Contemporaries talked of the very recent growth of industrial capitalism in Canada and referred to the fact that there was not as yet a class of entrepreneurs who could sit back and enjoy their profits. W.T.R. Preston in *My Generation of Politics* (Toronto, 1927), pp. 204, 487 described the 1880's and 1890's as "the twenty years [which witnessed] the creation and establishment of a capitalist system." Robert Laird Borden in his *Memoirs* (Toronto, 1938), p. 151, pointed out that "we have no men of leisure or of means." Goldwin Smith in his *Reminiscences* (New York, 1910), pp. 456-457, 487 remarked that "Toronto wealth is not munificent. It certainly is not compared with the United States." All these points reflect the fact that Canadian industry was as yet only a struggling part of the social and economic structure.

61   The Report of the Civil Service Commission (1907-08), pp. 14, 17, pointed out that public service positions while still sought after were becoming less attractive as opportunities expanded in the economy. They pointed to the significance of the fact that the lower levels of the

public service were being increasingly filled by women. Norman Ward in his study of Canadian MPs emphasizes that many of them went on to important patronage positions. "The evidence is fairly strong," he writes, "that politics in Canada is by no means the precarious occupation it is often assumed to be. Until very recently, only a small number of private businesses were in a position to provide positions for 30% of their employees." See Ward, *House of Commons*, pp. 98-101, 103, 146.

62 Bliss, "A Living Profit," pp. 1, 321, 341; S.D. Clark, *The Developing Canadian Community* (Toronto, 1968), pp. 227, 234. Clark argues that "in a way scarcely true of any other Western nation, the middle class in Canada has been the Establishment."

63 J.C. Falardeau, "Evolution des structures sociales et des élites au Canada français" (Québec, 1960), pp. 10-11.

64 Clark, *The Developing Canadian Community*, pp. 243-252.

65 Report of the Civil Service Commission (1907-08), pp. 14-17.

66 Royal Commission on the Public Service (1911-12), p. 1213.

67 Hans Daalder, "Parties, Elites and Political Development in Western Europe," in Joseph Palombara and Myron Weiner, eds., *Political Parties and Political Revolution* (Princeton, 1966).

68 *Ibid.*, p. 75. Daalder talks of the "reach" or "permeation" in society of political parties.

69 For example, George Grant to John A. Macdonald, Kingston, November 26, 1883, Macdonald Papers, P.A.C., Vol. 26, Bishop of Hamilton to Macdonald, Hamilton, October 15, 1880, Macdonald Papers, P.A.C., Vol. 25 II; Bishop of Peterborough to Macdonald, Peterborough, November 23, 1887, Macdonald Papers, P.A.C., Vol. 27 I; Reverend A. McKean to Macdonald, Bothwell, September 19, 1887, Macdonald Papers, P.A.C., Vol. 27 I; Byron Nicholson to William Gibson, Quebec, November 28, 1908 (Nicholson was a newspaper editor and "literateur"), Laurier Papers, P.A.C., Vol. 950; Thomas Swan to John A. Macdonald, Mount Forest, Ontario, March 17, 1883, Macdonald Papers, P.A.C., Vol. 5 (Swan owned a carriage works business); R. McKechnie to Macdonald, Dundas, March 11, 1891, Macdonald Papers, P.A.C., Vol. 22 (McKechnie was head of a manufacturing company and former President of the Canadian Manufacturers Association). On railroad patronage see N.A. Belcourt to Laurier, Ottawa, August 31, 1904, Laurier Papers, P.A.C., Vol. 950. Also, Waite, *Canada 1873-96*, pp. 136-137, Brown and Cook, *Canada 1896-1921*, pp. 147-153.

70 Alexander Tillock Galt caught the essence of this condition in the new confederation when he wrote that "politics form the only short cut from the middle to the upper ranks." See O.D. Skelton, *The Life and Times of Alexander Tillock Galt* (Toronto, 1920), pp. 377-379. In 1880 an observer noted the dominance of fashionable society in Ottawa by politicians, civil servants and associated professionals. See J.E. Collins, *Can-*

ada Under Lord Lorne, p. 309. See also Lady Aberdeen's comments in Saywell, ed., *The Canadian Journal of Lady Aberdeen* (Toronto, 1960), p. 42. J.W. Dafoe, "Canadian Problems of Government," *CJEPS*, Vol. V (1939), p. 288, pointed out that a career in politics in pre-1914 Canada carried more "personal distinction" than since that time and that to be an MP "meant a good deal more than it does now; and to be a member was a very general, if not all but universal desire among ambitious men."

71 Jacques Ellul, *The Political Illusion* (New York, 1967), p. 9.

72 Hans Muller, *Canada. Past, Present, and Future* (Montreal, 1880), p. 7. J.D. McClockie back in 1948 described a new state form, "the party state" in which the political party was the most dominant power. See McClockie, "The Modern Party State," *CJEPS*, vol. XIV (1948), p. 143.

73 Jacques Monet, "Les Idées politiques de Baldwin et LaFontaine," in Hamelin, ed., *The Political Ideas of the Prime Ministers of Canada* (Ottawa, 1969), pp. 16-17. See also l'Hon. Charles Langelier, *Souvenirs Politiques* (Quebec, 1912), pp. 25-26.

74 Jean-Charles Bonenfant, "L'evolution du statut de l'homme politique Canadien-Français," in Fernand Dumont et Jean-Paul Montmigny, eds., *Le Pouvoir dans la société Canadienne-Française* (Quebec, 1966), pp. 117-118.

75 Falardeau, "Evolution des structures," op. cit., p. 11. The phrase "La noblesse professionelle" comes from P.J.O. Chauveau, *Charles Guerin. Roman de moeurs canadiennes* (Montreal, 1853), pp. 55-56.

76 For example, William F. Ryan, *The Clergy and Economic Growth in Quebec 1896-1914* (Quebec, 1966). Two other studies put Quebec economic development in a much clearer light than traditional works. See Albert Faucher, *Québec en Amérique au XIX siècle* (Montreal, 1973) and Jean Hamelin and Yves Roby, *Histoire Economique du Québec 1851-1896* (Montreal, 1971). Faucher, for example, deals with the economic divergence between Quebec and Ontario in terms of technical development, regional pulls and so on rather than in terms of differences in value systems. See too the assessment in Brown and Cook, *Canada 1896-1921*, pp. 127-143.

77 Joseph Palombara, ed., *Bureaucracy and Political Development* (Princeton, 1963), p. 11; Hodgetts, et al., *Biography of an Institution*, pp. 14-16.

78 Gibson, ed., *Cabinet Formation*, p. 171. See note 51.

79 Daalder, "Parties, Elites and Political Development," op. cit., pp. 64-65.

80 Arend Lijphart, *The Politics of Accommodation, Pluralism and Democracy in the Netherlands* (Berkeley, 1968). "Typologies of Democratic Systems, *Comparative Political Studies*, Vol. I (1968), pp. 17-35. "Consociational Democracy," *World Politics*, Vol. 21 (1969), pp. 207-225.

81 Kenneth D. McRae, *Consociational Democracy. Political Accommodation in Segmented Societies* (Toronto, 1974).

82   *Ibid.*, pp. 250, 259-260.

83   *Ibid.*, pp. 254, 261.

84   Brown and Cook, *Canada 1896-1921*, pp. 164-165.

85   In a letter written shortly before his death Macdonald complained, almost in a tone of surprise, that such issues should arise in Canada, that it was "a great pity that these questions of race should arise so frequently." John A. Macdonald to Alphonse Desjardins, Ottawa, January 6, 1891, Alphonse Desjardins Papers, P.A.C., MG 27I, E22.

86   Notes on Civil Service Reform by William D. LeSueur Select Committee on Present Conditions of the Civil Service (1877), p. 106.

87   McRae's comments are pertinent here. "In retrospect," he writes, "the quest to accommodate linguistic diversity in Canada may be viewed as a series of lost opportunities...and it seems likely that this low capacity of the system to devise effective solutions has helped to increase the intensity of linguistic and cultural cleavage in recent decades." McRae, *Consociational Democracy*, p. 259.

88   It is necessary not to press this case too far lest the tone become anachronistic. Professor Creighton has warned against placing politicians of post-Confederation Canada in an alien context. They were not eighteenth century politicians interested in ethnic and cultural issues. They were Victorian politicians who were successful in building a viable Canada in arduous circumstances. D.G. Creighton, *Canada's First Century 1867-1967* (Toronto, 1970), p. 8. These are weighty reminders of the dangers of anachronistic analysis. Yet, as the 1877 evidence of LeSueur shows, there were alternatives even in the context of the times. Macdonald and Laurier than can be characterized as limited in their responses to the basic problem of Confederation—and these limitations took root and flourished because the patronage system enabled the political leaders to close their minds to structural responses to the "questions of race."

P.B. Waite Politics at the Grassroots: Lessons from Post-Confederation Nova Scotia

Not the least part of the process of political accommodation was patronage, in all its many variations. From the Macdonald and the Thompson Papers there emerges the picture of an extensive network of patronage, well defined and highly developed. So much so that one has the impression that Antigonish County, for example, lived by its wharves, breakwaters, and railways. Dominion wharfmasters, Intercolonial railway employees, customs collectors, lighthouse keepers, and postmasters formed part of a well-ramified system of dominion patronage, organization, and administration....

The sequence of events in Maritime patronage went like this. A Conservative worthy in, let us say, Pictou County, thought X should have the job of collector of customs in Pugwash. He would recommend X to C.H. Tupper, the Conservative MP, who would in turn mention it to the responsible minister, Mackenzie Bowell. It could go the other way around, that Bowell would ask the Conservative MP in whose riding the vacancy occurred, whom he would recommend. If there were no Conservative MP for the constituency, then the recently defeated Conservative candidate would be approached. As a rule, the minister did not need to make too many enquiries, for a cloud of applications would descend upon him the moment the post was known to be open. Indeed, the body of the newly deceased incumbent of the office would be still warm when the letters would be off to Ottawa. With judges, the letters would often arrive before the judge was dead. If Judge Y was very ill, a candidate would write to Sir John Thompson: "Judge Y's illness is almost certainly mortal," the candidate would add cheerfully, "and please consider me as a candidate."

Thompson's own constituents in Antigonish County ate and drank patronage. The long winters and the halcyon summers seemed only to nourish that delightful preoccupation. Thompson himself was not proud of this unpleasant and important side of his work as MP for Antigonish. His constituency seemed to him greedy, rapacious, impatient, unforgiving, with alarmingly tenacious Scotch memories that kept past rights (and wrongs) clearly in the world of present reality. "I revolt against Antigonish the more I think of it," Thompson grumbled to his wife Annie in 1887.[1]

One day in October 1886, Archie A. McGillivray, an Antigonish constituent, vain, brash and greedy, heard that the Intercolonial Railway stationmaster at Antigonish town had died. "May his soul rest in peace," said Archie piously, "I hereby apply for the situation...and finding that this situation would suit me, I demand it. All I want from you is a decided answer." Thompson said no, in a letter written, Archie claimed, "in that cool faraway tone." It made Archie furious. He railed against Thompson's rank ingratitude for all that Archie had done for him over the years in Antigonish County; Thompson's "dark, ungrateful heart" would rue the day that he refused the modest exigencies of Archie A. McGillivray.[2]

B.F. Power, another constituent with more brains and more clout than Archie, preferred telegrams. The Antigonish stationmaster died on 11 October 1886; B.F. Power reminded Thompson that very day that the stationmaster was, happily or unhappily, very dead and that B.F. Power's brother Henry was quite available. When the new stationmaster was appointed, it was neither Archie McGillivray nor Power's brother, but D.H. McDonald, promoted from being stationmaster at Tracadie, eighteen miles eastward along the line. B.F. Power kept a watchful eye on D.H. McDonald, however, and two months later came the following telegram:

> If stationmaster here be dismissed for drunkenness you have a right to confer that office on me. I pay all telegrams answer before sixteenth as I will be away state salary.

That was certainly brash enough. Thompson did not ignore it, however; he telegraphed his cousin, David Pottinger, chief superintendent of the Intercolonial Railway at Moncton (1879-92) for information. The pay, said Pottinger, was forty dollars a month; but he added that D.H. McDonald was not in any trouble so far as Pottinger knew.[3] But McDonald was in trouble, and the chief superintendent soon found out.

The Intercolonial Railway rules about drinking by employees were strict and specific. In the rule book of 22 November 1886, Rule No. 59 was that only men of known careful and sober habits were to be employed in the movement of trains. Rule No. 60 was even more specific: any employee drunk on *or* off duty would not be kept on the Intercolonial Railway service.[4] What had actually happened to D.H. McDonald is not altogether clear—it seldom is on such occasions. On the nights of 6 and 7 December he and some friends had something of a party, which included McDonald getting pitched out of a sleigh into an adjacent snowbank, followed by some good-natured but very drunken wrestling in the snowdrifts in front of Antigonish's main hotel. This was not drunkenness, McDonald told Thompson, but only animal energy; all he had had to drink was whisky and milk, taken for strictly medicinal purposes. Whatever McDonald's explanations, he was dismissed for drunkenness. B.F. Power was given the position, even though he could not yet use the telegraph key and would have to learn. It was a clear patronage appointment, and David Pottinger did not altogether relish it. "The usual and proper course," he wrote to his cousin, "would be to promote some experienced person to a station like this, but I suppose we can't."[5]

It can be added that it was also virtually impossible to appoint a man from outside the county to such a position. A Pictou County man, however competent, might even be, *horrible dictu*, a Protestant; in any case being from outside the county, he could not be given an important patronage preferment in Antigonish. The reverse would also be true in Pictou County.

Thompson was less susceptible to patronage pressures outside his own constituency. In his own department, Justice, he preferred to encourage the *esprit de corps* of the civil service. The warden of Dorchester Penitentiary, New Brunswick, as indeed other wardens, had been a patronage appointment when Thompson became minister of justice in 1885. The incumbent in Dorchester, Warden Botsford, was the brother of Senator Amos Botford (1804-94). Warden Botsford died in April 1887. Within twenty-four hours Thompson had fifteen telegrams about four possible candidates, plus a letter from Sir Charles Tupper. Senator Botsford had his own ideas who should replace his dead brother. The director of penitentiaries, J.G. Moylan, also had a candidate in mind.

Thompson cut all that off. He promoted the deputy-warden, J.B. Forster. Politely, firmly, he told an irate Conservative in Dorchester that promotion of good men to the highest positions in the service was the stuff of which a good service was made. "If these officers find the higher positions disposed of according to political claims, some political advantage may result but the Service will soon be in a useless condition."[6]

Thompson was also concerned to redress the imbalance he observed in Nova Scotian appointments in the inside service. Across the whole inside service, he told Macdonald, Nova Scotia's share of the five hundred or so appointments should have been seventy; she had in 1887 only twenty-six. No Nova Scotian was deputy-minister, none was chief clerk. This argued the more cogently why Thompson should have a free hand in the choice of his deputy-minister, consequent upon the appointment of his former deputy, J.W. Burbidge, to the Exchequer Court of Canada.

> My choice would however be very limited as I could not afford to take a man about whose fitness I could entertain a doubt and I am not at all sanguine that any of the best men would accept. If not I should want to look to Ontario. New Brunswick has far more than her share now.[7]

Tilley and Costigan had clearly been doing their work! Thompson, after inviting Robert Borden of Halifax (who was tempted but said no), appointed Robert Sedgwick of Halifax.

Many of the little Maritime towns, and doubtless others in Quebec, Ontario, and elsewhere, presented curious mixtures of dominion-provincial relations, some seldom explored, or not even known. It was a process of accommodation at its most basic. In Antigonish town, by 1887, there was a small dominion public building, housing the customs office and the post office, but it had room for more than these. It so happened that the postmaster of Antigonish was also the caretaker of the building; besides these offices, he was also sheriff of Antigonish County. The county found the space convenient; it was also cheap since it cost nothing. Thus were accommodated county officials, the registrar of deeds, registrar of probate, and others. The registrar of probate was also a magistrate and did his magistrate's business there, rather to the discomfiture of the other occupants of the building. Since the Municipality of Antigonish County contributed nothing to the building, neither to cost nor upkeep, should not the situation be regularized in some way? It seemed so to Thompson. There was surely no objection, he suggested to Sir Hector Langevin, the minister of public works, to housing municipal officers in dominion public buildings, but they ought to have some regular system of tenure. Otherwise, there would be all kinds of similar demands on dominion public buildings elsewhere.

There was an odd consequence to this. The town of Antigonish discovered that much the best place to hang the town's fire bell was on that dominion building, on the northeast corner. Thompson thought that would do no harm. But the postmaster-general-sheriff thought differently. He objected; he said that the process of hanging that fire bell there on that northeast corner would ruin, positively ruin, his flower garden! It took the bishop and a peremptory telegram from Thompson to get the fire bell placed where the town wanted it.[8]

Such was the infinitude of questions, little and big, that filled so much of the life of Thompson, the conscientious administrator.

At election time the story is more familiar, noticeable from the beginning: the importing of campaign funds from central Canada. Both Nova Scotia and New Brunswick raised roughly half of their own campaign funds, but they seemed to expect, and to get, assistance from outside. This seems to have been especially the case in 1891, where it was known that American money had been imported into both provinces by the Liberals. Both Thompson and young C.H. Tupper found Nova Scotians very canny with their own money; the Halifax merchants and manufacturers never seemed enthusiastic when the time came to dig into their pockets. Senators, who did not have to fight any elections at all, were not very responsive in shelling out money for MP's who did.

In 1891 Maritime money seems to have been channelled, some of it at least, through John Haggart, the postmaster general from Ontario. There were some frank pleas. L.deV. Chipman in Kentville, trying to help W.C. Bill defeat Frederick Borden in Kings County, wrote anxiously that they had raised $1,500 in the Annapolis valley, had got $1,000 more (presumably from Ottawa), but needed a further $2,000. Chipman promised to raise this extra $2,000 himself, provided he were promised the vacant Nova Scotia seat in the senate. Thompson's response was not helpful. F.W. Borden won by 161 votes; Chipman claimed afterward that had Thompson come through with the promise of the senate seat, W.C. Bill would have won by fifty to one hundred votes. Chipman never did get a seat in the Senate.[9] Joseph Pope telegraphed Thompson from Kingston that if more ammunition were needed in Nova Scotia, Thompson could draw up to $2,500 from W.A. Allan of Ottawa. Sir John Macdonald suggested leaving Cumberland to its own devices (where Dickey, Sir Charles Tupper's successor, seemed a certainty) and sending $500 to John McDonald in Victoria, Cape Breton (who won), and $500 to J.N. Freeman in Queens (who did not).[10]

The result of the federal election in 1891 in Nova Scotia surprised everyone, Liberals and Conservatives alike. Thompson won

Antigonish by 227 votes, a much bigger majority than either 1885 or 1887. In the province as a whole, the Conservatives took sixteen of twenty-one seats compared to fourteen seats in 1887. In New Brunswick, they took thirteen of sixteen seats. In both provinces it was the best Sir John A. Macdonald's Conservative government had ever done. Even Prince Edward Island, which had given its six seats to the Liberals in 1874 and in 1887, had elected two Conservatives. Indeed, twenty-one seats of the Macdonald government's twenty-seven-seat majority, coming into the new session of 1891, were created by New Brunswick and Nova Scotia. No wonder Sir Richard Cartwright was cross; the Macdonald government, he said, was nothing but a patchwork "made up of the ragged remnants from half a dozen minor provinces, the great majority of whom do not even pretend to be actuated by any principle save...a good slice of booty."[11] There was some truth in that. The ragged remnants were New Brunswick and Nova Scotia, joined with Manitoba, British Columbia, and the Northwest Territories. The five together had presented a thirty-four-seat majority to help the Conservative government. There was not a little irony in the fact that by 1891 the shreds and patches of Confederation had won their own victory over the central Canadians who had run things so much their own way only twenty years before....

Notes

1   Thompson to Annie, 22 September 1887, J.S.D. Thompson Papers [hereafter JSDT], vol. 290.

2   McGillivray to Thompson, 18 October 1886, *ibid.*, vol. 45; 13 November 1886, *ibid.*, vol. 46.

3   Power to Thompson, 9 December 1886, telegram, *ibid.*, vol. 47; Pottinger to Thompson, 11 December 1886, telegram.

4   D.H. McDonald to Thompson, 17 January 1887, *ibid.*, vol. 48. A condensed version of the Antigonish story is in P.B. Waite, *The Man from Halifax: Sir John Thompson, Prime Minister* (Toronto, 1985), pp. 176-177.

5   Pottinger to Thompson, n.d., endorsed on Thompson to Pottinger, 29 May 1887, private, *ibid.*, vol. 52.

6   Thompson to Michaud, 15 April 1887, *ibid.*, vol. 229; vol. 52 contains the incoming correspondence on this question.

7   Thompson to Macdonald, 21 September 1887, Macdonald Papers, vol. 273.

8   Thompson to Langevin, 23 August 1888, private; JSDT, vol. 235; vol. 76, Whidden to Thompson, 24 October 1888, telegram; same, 25 October 1888, telegram.

9   L.deV. Chipman to Thompson, n.d., private and confidential, *ibid.*, vol. 124; 19 March 1891, private, *ibid.*, vol. 125.

10   Pope to Thompson, 1 March 1891, telegram, *ibid.*, vol. 124.

11   Toronto *Globe*, 9 March 1891.

H.B. Ames, M.P. Electoral Management

In these days, when charges of electoral corruption are so frequently made, when the retort generally deemed sufficient is the *tu quoque* argument, it is little wonder that the average citizen—who votes on occasion and at other times is immersed in his own affairs—should be strongly tempted to conclude that illegal election methods are a necessary evil attendant upon free institutions; indeed, that they are an inseparable adjunct of popular government. Of such vital importance is it, especially at the outset of this era of great national promise, that so dangerous a heresy be not allowed to go unchallenged nor be permitted to find permanent lodgment in the minds of our people, that it is incumbent upon every one, willing and able to defend the contrary proposition, to let himself be heard, lest we lose faith in ourselves and in the value of the constitutional liberty which we enjoy.

In this spirit the writer accepted the invitation of the Editor of *The Canadian Magazine* to contribute an article upon the topic of organisation in city elections. It will be his contention that business-like preparations and thorough organisation are, not only from a moral point of view, unquestionably preferable, but are also, from a practical standpoint as a means of vote-winning, decidedly more effective than the less scrupulous methods so often for this end substituted.

The municipal experiences of the City of Montreal, during the past twelve years, may be cited in proof of the assertion that it is possible to carry through *successfully* a series of hard-fought election contests with dependence only upon honest and honourable means. Of this "Seven Years' War" the writer can speak with a knowledge born of actual participation. The years from 1894 to 1900 witnessed a bitter struggle between two elements for the control of the Montreal City Council. An extravagant administration, long condemned by good citizens, yet strongly entrenched in the exercise of power, did not hesitate to defend itself by every means at its command, no matter how unscrupulous. Opposed to this a citizens' organisation through careful and effective work, by a sort of electoral sapping and mining, so to speak, secured with each successive election during this period, the return of a greater number of reform councilmen, until, at last, in 1900 a majority of such were elected and a new administration inaugurated.

The Montreal system of election organisation has received high praise even from those who were worsted by it. It was admittedly a triumph of clean methods. Those who took part in this work are, therefore, glad of an opportunity for describing even the details of the system, in the hope that there may be found ideas which, *mutatis mutandis*, can be developed in other cities, and may aid in securing similar triumphs for the cause of electoral purity.

How then may elections be honestly and honourably won in large city constituencies? This is the subject under review, and in the development of our theme we naturally take up its consideration under four heads:—

1. The character of the preparations which must needs be made between contests;

2. The methods which may be rightfully employed to reach the ear of the electorate;

3. The activities to be set in motion in order to bring out the maximum favourable vote;

4. The precautionary measures necessary for the protection of an honourable candidate against corrupt practices on the part of an opposition less scrupulous.

Preparatory Work

Foresight is nowhere more necessary than in preparation for an election. No sooner are the returns of to-day's battle announced than it is time to commence the preliminary arrangements for the next contest. To this end should be established in every city constituency a political club. In Great Britain such clubs are permanent institutions, with central headquarters and a paid clerical staff. In this country, however, we depend almost entirely upon volunteer service. Young men believing in the tenets of a particular party and genuinely desirous that its principles should triumph, are suitable material out of which such associations may be formed.

Of the duties naturally devolving upon a political club, one of the most important is the surveillance of the electoral lists. Although no two Canadian cities follow precisely the same procedure in the preparation and revision of a parliamentary voters' list, nevertheless, the general method is the same. It is customary for the municipal assessors to prepare the preliminary list, entering upon it the names of all ratepayers. An opportunity is then afforded for such as are entitled to qualify in respect of revenue (manhood suffrage). Here is work for the young men of an active political club. By careful canvass the names of all the "eligibles" residing within the limits of the division under the club's charge can be secured. Such a list prepared, it is not difficult with a knowledge of family history and surroundings, to determine the probable political leanings of most of those who have yet to cast their first vote. All regarded as open to subsequent conviction are urged, by notification, by appeal and by persistent personal effort, to take the necessary steps to register and thus have their names placed upon the new list. It is left to the opposing party to look after their own supporters. Conservatives can hardly be expected to register Liberals, nor the reverse. With the party which excels in this activity lies, from the outset of the campaign, a decided advantage. Many a contest has thus been won or lost at time of registration.

When the names have all been entered on the preliminary list a revision follows. There again is opportunity for valuable service. The lists may have been "stuffed," that is to say, names having no legal justification may have been intentionally added; or they may contain names incorrectly entered which require amendment; or there may yet remain upon them names of persons who have died or moved away since the assessors performed their work. The collection of the necessary evidence on these points and its submission before the Revisors is therefore imperative. Every name, that cannot be legally voted upon and yet remains upon the list, is a temptation and a danger. The party of honesty cannot use such names, while for their unscrupulous opponents opportunity for personation is offered. The more accurate and recent are the lists upon which an election is held, the better the chances of those who employ only fair means. In attending to the revision of the list the club can render most valuable service.

But, even after the lists are completed and signed the work connected with their surveillance is not ended. In Montreal, for instance, it is possible for two years to elapse between the preparation of the lists and their use in a parliamentary election. Each succeeding day brings some alteration which should be taken note of. Every change of residence or employment, every death, every permanent removal, should be recorded at club headquarters, in order that when election day arrives, it may be possible, even in a great city of several hundred thousand inhabitants, to find quickly, surely and easily each voter entitled to poll. A militant political club possessed of full, up-to-date information regarding its' voters' list, ready whenever the call comes to take the field on behalf of the chosen candidate, is the first requisite if a political party would win a close city constituency. With such preparation their candidate will be able at all times to give a good account of himself. With such an organisation in the field the battle is already well-nigh won.

Influencing Public Opinion

Let us next consider the methods employed in reaching the public ear, more especially those resorted to when an election is imminent. The fact is too often lost sight of that an election is won by the party which captures the non-partisan vote. In every constituency it is safe to assume that a considerable proportion of the voters have permanently made up their minds: so it is usually not difficult to ascertain, with a fair degree of accuracy, who are the "stalwarts" on both sides. As far as a campaign of persuasion is concerned, these only need to be discovered, properly labelled and eliminated from the problem. The remainder, however, whose sentiments are undisclosed or who declare themselves to be as yet undecided, are the electors for whose capture the most careful siege operations, the most powerful batteries are necessary.

It is customary for railway companies, for the owners of proprietary medicines, for large retail storekeepers and others to employ specialists, whose life-work it is to attract public attention to the virtue and value of the offers they make and to reach those who may become patrons. So, too, in an election campaign, there is ample scope for the highest ingenuity and organising ability in the effort to reach and convert the doubtful voter. Tons of literature are at every election uselessly printed and circulated. Much of this finds its way to the waste basket and to the ash-heap. And why? Because of lack of appreciation of the fact that men cannot be influenced *in masses*. Every individual has his personal characteristic, and it is "hand-picked fruit" that constitutes, in most instances, the successful candidate's majority. It is, therefore, necessary to carefully classify the "doubtfuls." This list must be divided and sub-divided and then it must be ascertained from what point each group can best be approached. For example, if an editorial of special aptness, say to importers,—setting forth the annoying incidents attendant upon the operation of the Dumping Clause and holding the government responsible,—appears in the daily paper, it is good tactics for the opposition candidate to see to it that this article, in attractive, readable shape, reaches every importer on his "doubtful" list. If a public meeting has been arranged for, at which a speaker particularly successful in convincing workingmen is to deliver an address, every artisan and industrial labourer on the doubtful list should have a card of special invitation and a reserved seat, that he may hear the questions at issue discussed by one who views them from the same standing as himself. The strong partisans will, in any event, come to the meeting; the man who is wanted most is he who, had he remained at home, might have voted the other way. If a series of pamphlets is being prepared for distribution, let them each view the issues from a different plane. Send to French electors literature not only French in language but French in spirit; to property owners, that which will cause a man who has a stake in the community to think of imminent taxation; to the Trades Unionist that which will coincide with his mode of thought; to the cotton mill worker and the woollen mill employee the argument for adequate protection;—one might particularise *ad infinitum*—in fine, send to each that which he will read.

In the St. Antoine division contest, one of the most successful features of the Conservative organisation was a Central Bureau of Distribution. Here was installed a competent staff of stenographers, in whose hands were placed the address books for the division. The names of the electors were numbered consecutively from 1 to 8,500 and there were specified the residential and business addresses, the language and class. A complete set of envelopes was always on hand in anticipation and were of four colours, in conformity with distinctions above referred to. From this room was first issued, and delivered to every elector, a card asking support for the Conservative candidate. Next followed a notification of the location of his committee rooms with a polite invitation to call if needing information. As the content grew warmer, editorials, pamphlets, circulars, letters—some 20,000 in all—were distributed from this centre. These were never scattered broadcast; they were always personally addressed and delivered by hand, and reached those who, it was believed, would read them. Just prior to election day there was sent to every elector, at his residence, a notification of the location of his polling booth, and if he succeeded on the day of election in reaching his office without having voted, on his desk with the morning mail he found a final reminder with the words, "Remember that this is election day." Of great service, too, was this bureau in counteracting false reports. No story could gain headway before a contradiction or an explanation went to every house in a district where the rumour unchallenged might have altered votes.

But after all, the most powerful vote-winning influence is personal solicitation. Happy the candidate who has a band of friends ready to undertake for him this service with the list of "doubtfuls." After you have reduced your undeclared vote to its minimum, these names, divided among a score of friends, each taking those known to him, may be subjected to a final interview. Misapprehensions can be explained away, prejudices removed, and few there are who, in a quarter of an hour's conversation with a man whom he knows and respects, will not make his final preference manifest. When this last resource has been exhausted, your campaign is at an end. You know whether your candidate has the majority with him or the reverse; it remains but to crystallise into actual votes the favourable sentiment.

Getting Out the Vote

The supreme test of electoral organisation is its success in bringing out the vote. The recent Montreal election in St. Antoine division is noteworthy in this respect. In 1900 there were 9,291 names on the list, of which 5,706 voted, or slightly more than 61%; while in 1904, with only 8,527 names on the lists, a total vote of 6,046 was cast, or almost 71%. The Liberal vote of 1904 was only 105 less than in 1900, but the Conservative vote of 1904 exceeded that of 1900 by 452. So smoothly did the Conservative machinery of the election run, that many during polling day, mistaking lack of confusion for absence of activity, prophesied defeat. Quite the contrary was the case, for the Conservatives who in 1900 had carried the constituency by a narrow majority of 57, had the satisfaction of seeing their candidate elected in 1904 by 614 more votes than his opponent.

As an example then of successful organisation the *modus operandi* of this election may be described. The electoral district had been divided into eleven parts. For each division there was a committee room with its chairman, its secretary, its telephone and corps of workers, a committee room having charge of from six to eight polls. To every polling booth on election day was assigned a corps of volunteer workers. They numbered from four to ten, according to the anticipated favourable vote. Within the poll sat the scrutineer. Thoroughly trained as to his duties and quite competent if need be to direct the returning officer, he was provided with a list of those entitled to vote at his poll and also with a packet of identification cards. It was the scrutineer's duty to see to it that none but those so entitled should vote at that poll. Should he require to order an arrest, he had with him information and warrant forms, while at the door stood a special constable. The identification card used in this election was invented to prevent personation. The information it bore had been twice checked in the previous canvass, and consisted of an accurate description, giving particulars as to height, build, complexion, colour of eyes and hair, colour and style of beard, nationality and certain noticeable peculiarities of the voter. As there was one such descriptive card for every elector, no man, who did not accurately correspond with its description, could vote in that poll. Near the poll at the house of a friendly neighbour was stationed the "telephone man." It is remarkable how many city electors can be reached during business hours by telephone. The necessary 'phone numbers of all presumably favourable electors had been ascertained prior to the day of election, and entered alphabetically upon a convenient card for the use of the "telephone man." From 9 a.m. till 4 p.m. his telephone was never idle. "Have you voted, sir?" "When will you come up to vote, sir?" "Shall we send someone to fetch you?" Such were the invariable questions. And these constant reminders had their effect. Business men, realising that work would be rendered impossible until they had performed their duty as citizens, came early to vote. In many instances by three o'clock the telephone man had exhausted his list.

At the door of each polling booth stood the "poll captain." Upon him rested the responsibility for getting in the entire favourable vote. In his hand he held his poll pad, containing detachable slips of paper with business addresses and polling place, one for each presumably favourable voter. As one by one the electors presented themselves at the door of the poll, a courteous question from the poll captain elicited the name, and the captain detached and destroyed the corresponding slip, inasmuch as that name no longer required his attention. At the captain's elbow were his "hustlers," each with a carriage, loaned for the occasion, ready when given a slip to go in search of a dilatory or indifferent voter and invite, indeed almost compel him, to come and vote. Thus the poll was guarded, the dilatory elector reminded and the forgetful sent for, and St. Antoine division, which bears the reputation of being a sluggish district at election times, polled the largest percentage of votes in its history.

Protection Against Corrupt Practices

When a candidate sincerely determines to carry through an election contest in an honest and honourable manner, to play the game, both in letter and spirit, according to the rules, should his opponent be not like-minded, the fair-play candidate is certainly entitled to take what precautions may be necessary to prevent and to punish corrupt practices. It is not to be expected that he will allow himself to be beaten by illegal means and then simply content himself by crying "foul." He is bound to defend his own cause and at the same time protect his constituents against fraud.

Different methods will need to be employed in different constituencies to combat corruption. If bribery is likely to be attempted, the fair-play candidate must needs make such arrangements, even to the employment of detectives, as will enable him to secure conclusive evidence to unseat and disqualify his opponent and to punish his corrupt agents.

In large cities, where there is a considerable floating population, personation is the most deadly method of stealing an election. When 25% of the names upon a voters' list are those of persons whose whereabouts is at election time no longer known even to the local residents, the difficulty of preventing personation becomes apparent. There is so little likelihood of detection, the attendant risk is so insignificant, the price paid for passing false votes is so tempting, that unless severe measures are employed, there will always be many persons ready to undertake this business. But the practice has been effectually put an end to in Montreal, at least in so far as the western portion of the city is concerned, by the method already alluded to, of descriptive cards.

When the electoral list comes into force, a competent man is employed to call upon every elector whose name appears thereon. At that time nearly all can be readily found. The canvasser during his visit asks some unimportant question, but, before leaving, takes an accurate written description of his man. The descriptive cards become, henceforth, part of the archives of the political organisation which sent him forth. Every time it becomes necessary to canvass this man, the person detailed for this work is required to fill out and bring back a new descriptive card. Thus the accurateness of every canvasser's work is carefully tested. Thus also the original description is verified and improved upon. After this description has been established by several visits it is copied upon the card which upon election day is (as has been previously shown) placed in the hands of the scrutineer.

Anyone who has had experience in city elections knows how difficult it is to get good men to act as scrutineers in certain city districts. The old practice has been to employ local men, but these are often susceptible to corrupt influences. By employing the Montreal system of cards it is not necessary that the scrutineer be a resident of the district. He needs only to be intelligent and trustworthy. With the descriptions in his hands he can effectively prevent personation, even in a poll where he is not personally acquainted with a single elector. This system will put an end to personation in any city. It enables a candidate, who will not permit fraud to be practised on his own behalf, to render it impossible for an opponent to take mean advantage of him.

In order to stamp out political corruption it is necessary in all cases that election crime, when detected, should be severely punished. It so often happens that a candidate who has been successful, who may have secured the arrest of bribers or personators of the other side, in the hour of victory is appealed to for the exercise of mercy and consents not to prosecute the prisoners. It is the expectation of this clemency which is mainly responsible for the continuance of these acts. Was it understood that electoral crime would be unflinchingly punished, cost what it may, we would soon have little or none of it.

In the recent St. Antoine election what purported to be an attempt at wholesale personation was discovered and frustrated. Six men were arrested in this connection. As their case is yet to come before the Court of the King's Bench for adjudication, it is not pertinent to discuss the incident in this article. Suffice it to say that the return of the successful candidate (it is believed, because he would not secure the abandonment of this criminal prosecution) is now being contested, but the case will be pushed to a finish.

In conclusion the writer once again reaffirms his belief that it is not only possible to win elections by honest means, but that, from a practical point of view, careful preparatory work, good judgment in influencing public opinion, thorough organisation in bringing out the vote and effective protective measures against corrupt practices, are more effective in winning votes than the lavish expenditure of money so often resorted to, and so frequently resulting in general corruption. The political party that resolutely sets its face against every form of electoral corruption, that absolutely refuses to consent to compromise, that prosecutes without flinching those guilty of fraud and that, keeping from guilt itself, forces its opponent to do likewise, that party—if there ever be such a one—will sooner or later come to power. A party thus elected, untrammelled by promises and obligations which it cannot with honour fulfil, free from the necessity of providing at the public expense for men whose claim for consideration lies in the immorality of the services they have rendered, will be in a position to claim the services of the noblest men, will have and will hold the confidence of our people and will be able to give to Canada that pure and honest administration of which this nation, now entering upon the grandest period of its political existence, stands most in need.

'A Candidate in the Late Elections'   Electoral Management: A Reply to Mr. Ames

Can elections be run without corruption? Can the great political evil of our day be eradicated? Is it possible for clean men to engage in politics and win elections by the same honourable means that they win success in business? Many clean men answer "No" and will have nothing to do with politics. Many practical politicians answer "Yes," but with a hypocrisy the brazenness of which only those on the inside can appreciate.

In the May [1905] number of *The Canadian Magazine* a man who has proven his ability to win answers "Yes," and outlines the methods by which it can be done.

There is a great deal of strength and force in his points. I have shared in the management of more than one campaign that has been won by the same kind of thorough organisation without resort to corrupt methods and a few months ago I warmly agreed with just such contentions as are made by Mr. Ames. But there is one radical omission in Mr. Ames' argument. I want to make that omission clear and ask if there is any other solution to the problem it raises than the one I point out.

An organisation such as was used in Montreal and, in a less thorough manner, in many cities and by both political parties, requires a large corps of workers. How many of these men are paid for their services? I do not mean that they are bribed. The men whose votes or support have to be bought, are not the men wanted for such work. They must be men whose honest support can be depended upon, but they must also be men in the same grade of life as the men they canvass, and not one in ten of such men can afford to take the time from daily work unless they are paid what they otherwise would be earning and perhaps a little more. It is easy to stretch such payments to the point where they become bribes to the men themselves, or provide funds for bribing others, but it is also obvious that up to a certain point there is nothing in the nature of a bribe about them. Where does the money to pay all these men and the other legitimate expenses of a campaign come from? Does it come out of the pockets of the candidate or are there others whose public spirit is so great as to lead them to contribute large sums to what they have no private interest in?

Let us see what it means to run an election in the manner outlined. I will take the St. Antoine election, where Mr. Ames was the successful candidate, as an example of one conducted with the most thorough organisation, yet without any resort to bribery or worse methods. I will agree that no election could be run in a cleaner manner. Let us see where that lands us.

There were in that constituency eleven divisions, each with a chairman, secretary, telephone man, clerks, caretakers of rooms, messengers, etc., say at least ten. In each division there were six to eight polls, and at each was a captain, scrutineer, special constable, telephone man and from four to ten "hustlers." Striking an average that means seventy-seven men employed in each division, or 847 in the constituency. How much would it cost to pay those men a reasonable wage for a day's work? The usual tariff on both sides in Toronto is $4.00 a day, and I doubt if Montreal is any cheaper, which means $3,388 for part of the work on election day. But that is not all. The four to ten hustlers did not go after their men on "shanks' mare." They had at least six carriages, single or double, at each division and these cost at the lowest average $5.00 each, which in the eleven divisions, each with six to eight polls, means a cost for livery alone of $2,310. I pass over Mr. Ames' implication that the rigs were "loaned." It is the one false note in his article. Nobody believes that liverymen are filled with such generous public spirit that they will empty their stables for a killing day for love or glory. They are not in business for their health. In every city and town in Canada where there is a real contest every rig that can be had is engaged long before election day, and there are few of them not paid for. Thus the one final day of the election must with incidentals added have cost at least $6,000.

But that is only a fraction of the work or expense. Firstly, there is the maintenance of a political club, with rent, fuel, caretaking and a dozen other expenses to be provided for. Then there is a thorough, systematic canvass for "eligible" manhood suffrage voters in which volunteers can give substantial assistance, but only paid workers will do thoroughly. Then there is another canvass for the revision of these lists, with detailed evidence to be collected and sifted. Then the keeping of the lists up to date, with every change of residence or employment or death for 8,000 voters kept track of. Then comes the preparation of hundreds of letters, pamphlets, circulars, editorials, identification cards, notices of meeting; and the addressing, sorting and delivery of thousands of letters. Mr. Ames says 20,000, but I sent out nearly that many with an organisation not to be compared in thoroughness to his. Double that number or five to each elector on the average would not be overdoing the work. Then comes the heaviest work of all—the personal canvassing of a score of "friends" who could not begin to do the work without devoting their whole time to it. Keep that pace up for two months and he will be a clever financier indeed who keeps within $10,000.

I am not guessing when I state these figures. I know what it costs to do this work for I have had to pay for it. In the late Provincial elections I determined that while I would put up the hardest fight I was capable of, have the most complete organisation, permit the paying of men who worked for me their fair pay for the work done, as for any other work, I would not, on the other hand, allow any paying for votes directly or by any subterfuge, and of course, no resort to personation or any other such means. I did everything that lay in the power of a candidate to do to stop every form of bribery, and I am quite certain that not $100 went in paying for doubtful votes. Yet in spite of that policy, honestly and effectively carried out, it cost over $4,000 to run my election. Comparing the organisation which I had with that which elected Mr. Ames, I have not the shadow of a doubt that his cost at least $15,000. Who paid for it?

But some will say, "Yours is a very corrupt constituency." It unquestionably is. In the last Dominion election the successful candidate simply bought his way into the House. His opponent's failure was due to his unwillingness or inability to spend as much money, not to any scruples of conscience. I have learned from reliable sources of so many individual instances of bribery and payment for services, that I have no hesitation in saying that that election cost the present member and his party from $15,000 to $20,000. I know that in a previous election the cost to one candidate outside of any party funds exceeded $6,000. I know that in another election the successful candidate spent $9,000, according to his own statement to me. In still another election two wealthy men contested the riding and their agents openly bid for votes in front of the polls. With a single exception, when the candidate was poor and his chance hopeless, there has not been a contest in this riding in the last twenty years in which the cost on each side did not exceed the amount mentioned for my own election. Nor is the riding an abnormal one. I remarked to a man of Cabinet rank, a member of either the present or the late Government of this Province—I will not say which—

that my riding was an exceptionally corrupt one. He looked at me with a funny smile and replied:—"There are just about seventy such ridings in this Province."

But that is somewhat aside from my point. Briefly, I say that in no close city constituency, accustomed to hard-fought contests can an organisation at all complete be run through an election at a cost of less than $3,000 to $4,000; and that the man who attempts to follow Mr. Ames' advice will find himself $10,000 poorer when he has squared up accounts a month after the polling, or rather after the time for filing protests has expired.

But there are more serious features than the money cost. Payments made for work done in an election are, in most instances, illegal though not morally corrupt. The consequence is that every candidate is forced to have an organisation to run his election which is unofficial, which makes these illegal expenditures in such a way that they cannot be fastened on him, while he shuts his eyes until such time as they are opened by the necessity of redeeming the promises made by his too zealous workers. That organisation is primarily for legitimate, though illegal, expenditures; but being thus formed in secret to evade the letter of the law, it is not to be wondered at, that it usually develops into wholesale evasion of the spirit as well. The law in its present form forces every live candidate to be a hypocrite on pain of having his election voided and himself held up to opprobrium, when in reality he is no worse than most of his fellows. I say every "live" candidate. I have known some who were as innocent as a babe of the manner in which their election was won.

Yet another and the most important of the results of these facts. If elections must under the present system cost several thousand dollars, where does the money come from? It may come in two ways—from the candidate, or from party funds which are largely from headquarters. If from the first, the necessary consequence is that the privilege of sitting in Parliament or even the Legislature is the prerogative of the rich only. We will be but a degree different from the state of decaying Rome when the wealthy distribute their money to buy the suffrages of a free people. Will the men who thus buy their way into Parliament be scrupulous guardians of the public monies, or will they be on the lookout for a chance to reimburse themselves out of the public funds? But, it will be said, most of our representatives are not wealthy men. Quite true, but what is the alternative? Omitting safe seats in which there is no real contest, the only other alternative is that the necessary funds are supplied from party headquarters. And that is, in fact, where most of the money comes from. The calculations of the headquarters' managers are based on a scale that the ordinary close constituency will require about $2,000 assistance; but varying from $1,000 in good country constituencies where the people have not been educated to the use of money, up to $5,000 in hard fought, important city constituencies, and occasionally that amount is greatly exceeded. An average of $2,000 in each constituency on each side may be an over statement as to the late Provincial elections, but it certainly is not as to the late Dominion elections. That would mean a total in the Province of Ontario alone of $400,000 in each election, and I do not believe I am at all overstating the figures. It is, of course, impossible for any one to get such figures accurately, but I have been sufficiently interested to get all the information possible from many and varied sources.

From what sources do such enormous funds come? For what purposes do the men who contribute to these amounts spend their money? Does a man, for example, who contributes $15,000 to one party do it for love of the cause, or does he expect to get it back in a railway subsidy, or a Government contract, or a more favourable tariff? It must be obvious to any man that the men who do contribute large sums to the election funds are the very men who are looking to get it back in some form with generous interest. And in the end, who pays the piper? *There is one possible, ultimate source, and one only. The people of the country foot the bills of both parties—the honest and thrifty provide the funds that are scattered among the dishonest.*

I am not a pessimist but neither do I believe in shirking the task of following unpleasant facts to their logical conclusion. I agree that there is a vital difference between the wholesale bribery which so often prevails, and the payment of the necessary expenses of a thorough organisation. But yet both lead to the same end—the alternative of making the Houses which represent the people the preserve of the rich or of providing enormous party campaign funds. So long as it is necessary to conduct a system of canvassing, and to organise the getting out of the vote, so long will the necessity for such campaign funds continue, and with the necessity the fact. Nor will legal prohibitions of these acts have any other effect than the organisation of secret forces without either legal or moral responsibility.

Is there any possible remedy? I can, for my part, see but one—

compulsory voting. The citizen who will not take the trouble to go to the polls, cannot complain if he forfeits the privilege on the next occasion. If no candidate is satisfactory, he may put in a blank ballot; if he cannot for good cause be present, he may have the penalty removed at the time. But if he must wait to be dragged or bribed to the polls, the country will be the better without his assistance till he has learned better. With such a rule no organisation to get the vote out is needed or excusable. If there is any other way in which the curse of corruption can be rooted out I shall be glad to learn of it, but for my own part I fail to see any remedy less drastic than that of the compulsory vote.

J.C. Courtney Party Leadership Selection in the New Dominion

Early post-Confederation history of the selection of party leaders in the new Dominion clearly indicated the degree to which British-modelled attitudes and practices had a firm grip on Canadian politics.... The parties in parliament admittedly deferred to the wishes of the Governor General when the Crown was involved in selecting a new prime minister. But in turn such deference was clearly based upon an implicit understanding that informal processes of contacting various party notables and weighing their expressed opinions would be undertaken by the Governor General. In this respect the Sovereign's representative, like the monarch herself, performed an essential governmental act, with some latitude of discretion (the degree of which related specifically to the occasion), and with profound implications both for the country and for the party. The retiring leader and other key individuals in the parliamentary party, therefore, were in positions to play a substantial part in choosing the new leader and, by and large, they did. Their influence was commensurate with their place in the party hierarchy. By the same token the parliamentary parties' less prominent members enjoyed relatively little influence in the selection of the leader although this was a feature much more characteristic of the party in power than in opposition, for in opposition the caucus vote on the party leadership was a vehicle that allowed an element of formal participation for backbench MPs. It would be impossible to equate that vote, however, with any measurable degree of influence over the outcome, given the likelihood of a "leadership-followership" connection between the relatively few, but important, party notables on the one hand, and the many, but nonetheless comparatively unimportant, backbench MPs and senators, on the other hand.

Parties in Office

The choice of Macdonald in 1867 as Canada's first prime minister was to be expected. His substantial ministerial experience, his role in the negotiations of the 1860s on Canadian confederation, as well as his leadership of the Canadian delegation in London during the winter of 1866-67 marked him for the prime ministership. Macdonald was so informed during the London meetings. "Lord Monck," Macdonald wrote to his sister, "is to return to Canada as Governor General, and has, but this is *entre nous*, charged me with the formation of the first Government as Premier."[1]...

The election of 1867 gave more than enough parliamentary supporters to the government side for Macdonald to be assured of the leadership of a loosely defined but nonetheless discernible group. A national political party was in its early stages of development and its first leader was to retain his position in the party for a quarter of a century and through six more elections.

In a period of little more than five years, from June 1891 to July 1896, Canada had six different prime ministers: Macdonald, Abbott, Thompson, Bowell, Tupper, and Laurier. It was an extraordinary period in Canadian party history.[2] Macdonald's death had come at a time (June 1891), when the Conservative party's many factions were becoming increasingly quarrelsome (even though the Macdonald government had just been returned to office in the recent election) and when, incredibly, there was no readily apparent successor to the party leadership. The man who might well have succeeded Macdonald, could not. It had been recognized for some time before Macdonald's death that the Old Chieftain's faithful French-Canadian colleague, Sir Hector Langevin, would succeed him. An arrangement to that effect, which had been agreed upon some years earlier, had to be abandoned because of the scandal charges which just prior to Macdonald's death had been launched against Langevin's department (Public Works). The subsequent inquiry disclosed such a state of affairs in the department that Langevin, although acquitted of personal wrong-doing, was obliged to step down from the cabinet. In retrospect, this seems the closest the Conservative party has ever come to choosing a French Canadian as its leader.

For different reasons, neither of the next two most logical potential successors to Macdonald was available. Sir Charles Tupper, then Canadian High Commissioner to London, claimed he would not accept the leadership of the party if it were offered him (although the sincerity of the disclaimer itself has been questioned by one of Tupper's biographers[3]). Tupper was so distantly removed from the Canadian capital that nothing short of a unanimous appeal by Conservative MPs could conceivably have led to his return, and such an appeal was an impossibility given the range of opinions of Conservatives over Tupper. The other possible leader, indeed the most obvious successor to Macdonald, was Sir John Thompson. An experienced politician, Thompson was highly regarded by many of his colleagues. Yet he was unacceptable to some influential Conservatives, the Ontario Orangemen in particular, not so much because of his Roman Catholicism but because he had been a Catholic convert from Methodism. Although offered the prime ministership by the Governor General, Thompson declined to accept, "bowing instead to the 'sectarian climate' of the time."[4] At the same time, Thompson was in a powerful position, for the Governor General requested his recommendation for the next prime minister. Thompson recommended J.J.C. Abbott, who in turn accepted the premiership when it was offered to him by the Governor General.[5]

Abbott, if nothing else, was frank. In his speech to the Senate about acceptance of the call to form a new government he made it clear, almost apologetically so, that the reason for his selection was the lack of agreement on other possible leaders:

> But the position which I to-night have the honour to occupy, which is far beyond any hopes or aspirations I ever had, and I am free to confess beyond any merits I have (cries of no, no), has come to me very much probably in the nature of compromise. I am here very much because I am not particularly obnoxious to anybody.[6]

Abbott was right. He was held to be an acceptable compromise leader, although less so by his own province of Quebec than Ontario, and his age (70) made it all too clear that his leadership would be short-lived. He was regarded, in other words, as a stopgap leader. His was to be a holding operation during which time the way would be prepared for Thompson to succeed him. It was agreed that Thompson would lead the party in the Commons with Abbott, the first of two prime ministers in the Senate, leading the government party in the upper house.

Abbott remained as prime minister for a year and a half. During that time Thompson emerged according to one contemporary observer as "the practical chief of the Administration [and]...the real leader of the Conservative party."[7] He was clearly expected to be the next prime minister and party leader, and it was felt that the religious difficulties would be minimized if he were able to bring into his cabinet some acceptable Ontario Protestant. To Abbott, there was no doubt about the leadership succession. "I am convinced," he wrote Thompson, "...that the feeling of the party points directly and unmistakeably [sic] to yourself."[8] On medical advice, Abbott submitted his resignation to the Governor General in November 1892, and Thompson accepted the request to form a new government. The retiring leader's role had been one of allowing the party sufficient time to sort out its affairs and to reach agreement on the leadership under a Roman Catholic. He had also paved the way for the leadership transition by acquainting the Governor General with his own views and those of the party on the succession.[9]

Unfortunately for the Conservatives, Thompson died at the age of fifty, only just over two years after he had become prime minister. The situation in the Conservative party was a repeat of that following Macdonald's death, for no acceptable successor was readily available in Canada. But to some, at least, the choice once again "pointed unmistakably to Sir Charles Tupper, the High Commissioner to London."[10] They argued that Tupper was the one man who could restore harmony in the crumbling Conservative party. Yet their views were anything but shared by the Governor General and his wife (Lord and Lady Aberdeen) who were determined not to see Tupper as the first minister. In her diary, Lady Aberdeen made His Excellency's intentions perfectly clear: "Never if he [Aberdeen] could help it should Sir Charles be again in Canadian politics. He is another of those who are able mysteriously to provide largely for his sons & daughters."[11] Lord Aberdeen cabled the Colonial Secretary of the British government for advice, and consulted with Sir Frank Smith, a Conservative senator for nearly a quarter of a century. Both agreed that the senior cabinet minister and acting prime minister in Thompson's absence, Mackenzie Bowell (who himself felt he was in line for the premiership), should be given the opportunity of forming a government. The Governor General agreed and called on Bowell.

"The history of the Conservative party for the next eighteen months," according to Saywell, "is a study in the degeneration, moral and physical, of a political party."[12] To begin with, Bowell was regarded, like Abbott before him, as a temporary compromise leader. But Bowell was suspicious, and this did not augur well for the party. According to Bowell's Minister of Finance, George Foster: "The general opinion expressed that this is a temporary arrangement naturally worries him [Bowell], and he sees a cabal in every two who converse together."[13] Additionally, as had been the case with Abbott, Bowell had no dedicated following in the party, his parliamentary seat was in the Senate, and he was seventy years of age. He was liked by his colleagues, but he was clearly not leadership material. Lady Aberdeen found him "rather fussy, and decidedly commonplace, also an Orangeman,"[14] and Foster allowed that "B. is old, vain and suspicious to a degree. What freak he may take no one knows, and this is really the most to be feared in the development of the thing."[15] All in all, it was a situation tailormade for the opposition, and the Liberals' confidence grew accordingly.

Bowell's leadership of the party and of the government proved to be so inept that by early 1896, less than a few months before the expiry of the five-year life of that parliament, seven prominent cabinet ministers resigned from his administration. The action has been unequalled in Canadian political history. Those who submitted their resignation clearly lacked confidence in Bowell's leadership of the party and the government....

There was no question that the party was weak and divided under Bowell. There was also no question that the seven bolters (or "nest of traitors" as Bowell called them) wanted Sir Charles Tupper as their leader. Tupper had just arrived in Ottawa from England and had been well briefed about developments within the party. He was also willing to accept the prime ministership. Bowell judged the situation accurately and offered his resignation to the Governor General. Aberdeen, however, was determined not to call upon Sir Charles, nor was he prepared to accept the resignation of a prime minister whose government had just presented a throne speech to parliament and on which there had as yet been no vote. The following day Bowell again attempted to resign, but for a second time the Governor General would not yield. A stalemate had developed. The party could not continue without a change in its leadership, but the prime minister could not step down. Finally an understanding was reached which permitted both sides to save some face. Bowell was to stay on as prime minister, but Tupper was to enter the House of Commons through a by-election and assume effective leadership of the party. Bowell would step down as prime minister at the end of the parliamentary session (less than four months away) and Tupper would be named his successor, although on this last point the Governor General had his own views. He "refused to pledge himself in advance regarding any future change of Prime Minister."[16] Thus 1896 was, for good reason, a key year in Canadian party politics, in so far as the governing party asserted with some success a claim to choose its own leader (even though he may not, in fact, become prime minister) independent of vice-regal wishes....

The remaining leader to be chosen whilst his party was in office prior to the introduction of leadership conventions in his party was Arthur Meighen. On July 1, 1920, Sir Robert Borden informed the caucus of the Unionist party (the name of which was changed by the caucus that day to the National Liberal and Conservative Party) that because of failing health he was forced to step down as prime minister and party leader. His wish to relinquish the party leadership was respected when caucus unanimously adopted a "resolution of regret for [his] resignation and appreciation of [his] public service,"[17] but it was ten days before Borden formally stepped down as prime minister. During that period there was rather faithful adherence to the British example of "soundings" and "consultations" within the parliamentary party—certainly more fully than had previously been the case within a governing party in Canada. Such an activity revealed a substantial difference between the opinions of the backbench supporters of the government on the one hand and those of the ministers on the other.

The depth of the party's differences of opinion was made more obvious to the retiring leader than to others by virtue of the method adopted to canvass the opinions of the Government's parliamentary supporters. A unique plan to choose the new leader was devised by Sir George Foster and approved by caucus. According to Foster:

> The selection [is] ultimately to be made by Sir Robert. Each member of Parliament supporting the late government is to indicate by letter his first and other choices, and his reasons therefor. Sir Robert is to sift these out—ascertain the possibilities of each carrying the confidence and support of his colleagues, and using his long experience and knowledge of conditions, evolve the best from the number suggested.[18]

Although Borden referred to the members' letters as "ballots" he clearly understood that the role he was expected to play was something more than that of a returning officer. As the Montreal *Gazette* pointed out, "the selection of the new leader is...in Sir Robert Borden's hands, though he will be guided largely by the suggestions of his followers and colleagues."[19]

Borden's task was complicated by the division within the party over the succession. He and virtually the whole cabinet favoured as the new leader Sir Thomas White, the former Finance Minister. Others were mentioned as possibilities, but White was the clear favourite. The majority of the government backbenchers, on the other hand, supported the Minister of the Interior, Arthur Meighen.[20] Borden reported to Meighen that 90 per cent of the backbenchers preferred Meighen as their first choice. However this simply was not the case, for an examination of the "ballots" indicates that although Meighen received more than twice as much first-ballot support as White, he was the choice of slightly less than 65 per cent of the backbenchers (see Table 1). Nonetheless, as over two-thirds of those preferring someone other than Meighen as their first choice gave him as their second choice, and as Meighen had a solid majority of the first-choice ballots, his support for the leadership was clearly of such a substantial nature that it could not be ignored.

Because of the uncertainty over the matter of the new leadership, there was considerable public speculation. This, in turn, led the prime minister to issue a statement outlining his interpretation of the correct procedures to be followed in such a situation. A more exact phrasing of British constitutional practices could scarcely be

Table 1: 'Ballot' Totals Indicating to Borden Preferences for his Successor, July 1920.

	First choice	Second choice	Third choice	Fourth choice
Arthur Meighen	65	28	4	
Sir Thomas White	27	27	4	
Sir George Foster	6	6	2	1
Sir Henry Drayton	2	5	4	
J.A.Calder	1	7	6	4
Sir James Lougheed	1	1	5	1
N.W.Rowell	1	1	4	
Hugh Guthrie		1	5	
C.C.Ballantyne			1	
Sir Arthur Currie			1	

Source: *Borden papers,* private, in possession of Mr. Henry Borden, Q.C., as provided by Professor R.C. Brown.

imagined:

> Much confusion and misunderstanding seem to prevail in the press regarding the power and responsibility of a retiring Prime Minister in respect to the selection of his successor.

> The selection of a new Prime Minister is one of the few personal acts which, under the British constitution, a sovereign (in Canada, the representative of the sovereign) is required to perform. A retiring Prime Minister has no right whatever to name his successor, nor has he any responsibility with respect to the selection of his successor, except as follows:

> The sovereign or his representative may not see fit to ask the view of the retiring Prime Minister with respect to the selection of his successor. For example, the Queen, on the final retirement of Mr. Gladstone, did not ask his advice or his views on that question. In such a case, the retiring Prime Minister has no right whatever to express his views or tender any advice on the subject. If, however, the sovereign or his representative asks the views of the retiring Prime Minister, he has a right to express them, but they need not necessarily be followed. In expressing such views, he does not tender advice as a Prime Minister, because he has already retired from office. His advice is to be regarded simply as that of a person holding the position of Privy Councillor, who has acquired a wide experience in public affairs which would give a certain value to his opinion on the subject.[21]

As the weight of the cabinet ministers' opinions could not be ignored, the Governor General was informed of them by Borden, and White was issued an invitation to form a government. His refusal, on health and business grounds, left Borden free to recommend Meighen if he could persuade "the anti-Meighen faction in the Cabinet to accept Meighen's leadership and remain in the Government."[22] This was accomplished after much consultation. Meighen agreed to undertake the formation of a new government and he was sworn in as prime minister on July 10. The retiring leader's role had been a substantial one. He had determined satisfactorily the location and intensity of support for his various potential successors and his exhaustive consultations over a period of several days prepared the way for the acceptance of the new leader within the parliamentary party.

Parties in Opposition

Those members of the Commons sitting in opposition to Macdonald's government following the 1867 election scarcely constituted a loosely knit coalition, much less a political party. There were Nova Scotia anti-confederationists, Quebec *Rouges*, and Ontario Reformers: each group anti-ministerialist, but with little else in common with the others that would seemingly enable rapid development of a parliamentary party. The most logical and, at the same time, the most acceptable, first leader for such a disparate group, George Brown, had been defeated in his attempt to get into the Commons in 1867. There was no better evidence of the apparent hopelessness of the opposition's plight than the fact that when parliament met after the 1867 election the opposition did not choose a leader, and it was the government, not the opposition, who assigned the leader of the opposition's seat to the Reform MP, Sandfield Macdonald. Yet within six years Sir John A. Macdonald's government had been replaced by the Liberals led by Alexander Mackenzie. By 1873-74, the party system had developed to the stage in Canada of fostering active anti-party competition as well as establishing within parliament a credible alternative to the party in power.

Alexander Mackenzie had clearly emerged as the chief opposition spokesman during the early post-Confederation years. Less than two years after the 1867 election he acknowledged this when he wrote:

> The newspapers call me the leader of the Opposition. I am nothing of the kind. I would not allow the party to pass a vote naming me such when they proposed to do it last session. But at the same time, I am doing the work which devolves on the leader, until some one fit to be a political prophet shall arise to be a judge over them. Still, I feel a kind of obligation not to leave, without it is [sic] so agreed.[23]

The election of 1872 gave the opposition forces good reason to be encouraged for, although they had failed to defeat Macdonald's party, they had nonetheless narrowed the gap considerably between the numbers on the two sides of the House. The results convinced Mackenzie that the Liberals had to choose a leader as soon as parliament met, and he recorded in a letter to his brother the party's deliberations on this matter. The letter of March 1, 1873, describes fully the process utilized to choose the first leader of the Liberal party.

We had a meeting of the Ontario members on Tuesday afternoon. I gave them my reasons for calling them together, and told them that Dorion had also called a meeting of the Quebec members, both meetings being with a view of forming a complete organization under one leader; that I had hitherto acted as leader, although not elected to that office; that I was now resolved to retire from the position; that we should have a friendly, open discussion on the subject, advising them to come to no decision until we could all meet together. I urged them to consider whether it would most advance the general interests of the party to make the choice from Quebec rather than from Ontario. I then said that my own impression was that the preponderating power Ontario held, would probably induce members from all sections to select one of the members from that Province, and in that case I thought Mr. [Edward] Blake should be chosen, as his splendid abilities and his standing in the country gave him many advantages, while his legal knowledge gave him additional power, placing him ahead of all others in the House. Blake then spoke, agreeing in the general plans I suggested, but protesting against my conclusions.

He spoke of my success during the last five years, and said the local Government was defeated through my efforts, and the late elections were carried by my influence and exertions, and consequently if an Ontario man were chosen, it must be me; and at any rate he could not listen to any proposal. One or two expressed themselves in favor of Blake in preference to me, all the others avoided any comparison, but discussed the matter fully. Finally it was delegated to a committee to consider. This committee was previously appointed to confer with a committee from Quebec, respecting the speakership and other matters. Our committee were Rymal, Young, Blake, Richards and myself, the others [from Quebec], Dorion, Holton, Letellier, Huntington and John Young. We had three long meetings, during which we arrived first at the conclusion that it was advisable to have the leader from Ontario, Blake and I agreeing that all Ontario would take Dorion freely if they considered that step advisable. They were unanimous against it. I then proposed to agree on Blake, each of us promising our utmost effort to support him. He would not listen to it. I also declined. The general meeting was adjourned till 4 o'clock this afternoon. The committee met again at 10, and I was pressed to yield which I reluctantly did. Dorion reported the result of the general meeting [to caucus]. Holton moved and Geoffrion seconded the motion to adopt the committee's report and declare me leader of the whole party. This was at once put by the chairman (John Young) and carried unanimously, seventy members being present.[24]

By early November the following year, Macdonald's government was so discredited by the Pacific scandal that its defeat appeared imminent. Macdonald resigned and Mackenzie accepted the Governor General's request to form a government. The changeover had been simplified by the opposition party's action of formally selecting a leader earlier in the life of the parliament.

Mackenzie's Liberals easily won the election of 1874 but they were defeated at the polls four years later. Mackenzie had failed to provide the leadership necessary to see the government successfully through a difficult economic period and he proved to be no match for Macdonald. Yet, following his government's defeat, Mackenzie chose not to offer his resignation to his party's caucus as might realistically have been expected. Macdonald had done this five years earlier when his government had resigned and his party was forced into opposition[25] and, although his resignation was not accepted, the gesture had established a precedent that would be followed by other leaders in both parties in the years ahead. Mackenzie's increasingly stubborn attitude toward the parliamentary group (he eventually stopped attending caucus meetings completely), as well as his unwillingness to bend on certain matters of policy, led to growing dissatisfaction with his leadership.

Although the details are unclear (there are two differing interpretations of the events immediately prior to his decision to retire), it is a fact that Mackenzie announced his resignation to a surprised House at 2:00 a.m. on April 28, 1880. The statement was as brief as it was to the point.

Mr. MACKENZIE: I desire to say a word, or two with regard to my personal relations to the House. I, yesterday, determined to withdraw from the position as leader of the Opposition, and for [sic] this time forth I will speak and act for no person but myself.[26]

The background to Mackenzie's decision is clouded by contradictory accounts, but clearly Mackenzie had determined that in preference to forwarding his resignation to caucus he would make a simple announcement in the House of Commons. Laurier's biographer, O.D. Skelton, claims that a resolution was passed by the Liberal caucus "asking Mackenzie to consider the question of the leadership," and when this was put to him by a committee of five from caucus, Mackenzie reacted by stating he would shortly step down as Liberal leader. Mackenzie's version of his resignation was to the effect that a party conspiracy led by Edward Blake was determined to so undermine his position as leader that Mackenzie would resign and Blake would succeed him. Mackenzie stepped down even though, he maintained, a majority of his former cabinet colleagues assured him that they could "break down the compact" and "restore order" in caucus if he remained as leader.[27] In spite of the apparent contradictions, "it is not impossible," according to one of Mackenzie's biographers, "that both versions contain a large degree of truth."[28]

With Mackenzie out of the way, the Liberal caucus was free to choose a new leader, and there was no question who he would be. The man who had refused Mackenzie's offer of the leadership eight years earlier, Edward Blake, was the indisputable favourite. The Liberal caucus met (with Mackenzie not in attendance) the day following Mackenzie's resignation, and a brief account in the *Globe* summarized its activities.

> The Liberals of both Houses of Parliament met in caucus for the purpose of selecting a successor to Mr. Mackenzie in the leadership of the party. Scarcely a member was absent.... The utmost unanimity prevailed. The genial member for South Wentworth, Mr. Joseph Rymal, occupied the chair, a position to which he was entitled both by seniority and merit. After the object of the meeting had been explained it was moved by an Ontario Liberal, and seconded by a New Brunswick Liberal, "That the Hon. Edward Blake be elected leader of the Liberal party of Canada." Before the motion

could be put every member present rose to his feet as if to emphasize his endorsation of the nomination, and amidst cheers the motion was declared carried. Mr. Blake, on being called upon, acknowledged in grateful terms the honour conferred upon him.... At the conclusion of Mr. Blake's speech a committee was appointed to convey to the Hon. Mr. Mackenzie the warm thanks of the Liberal party for his past valuable and untiring services during his long and useful parliamentary career, and their cordial appreciation of his integrity and usefulness to his party and country.[29]

Blake led the Liberals in two general elections, but both times the party was unsuccessful in its attempt to replace Macdonald's Conservatives. Following the 1887 election Blake, in poor health and dispirited by his party's electoral loss, determined to resign. Within two weeks of the election he sent a letter to all Liberals elected to the new House of Commons informing them of his intention to resign and reminding them that at the time of the opening of parliament "it will devolve on the liberals at once to choose their leader for the new Parliament."[30] In point of fact, Blake yielded to considerable pressure and agreed to stay on as leader but for the first parliamentary session only. Meeting in mid-April for the first time since the election, the caucus unanimously re-elected Blake to the party's leadership and at the same time set up an advisory committee of eight MPs to assist the leader in an attempt to ease his workload.[31] Blake's health did not permit him to continue much longer, however, and on June 2, 1887, he forwarded his resignation to caucus and it was accepted five days later.

During the period from June 2-7 several prominent Liberals were mentioned as potential successors to Blake. They included Sir Richard Cartwright and David Mills, both Ontario members of the House of Commons, and Oliver Mowat, the premier of Ontario. Little serious attention appears to have been paid to Wilfrid Laurier as a likely successor, but Blake was determined to see him as the next leader. Blake's opinion was that "there is only one possible choice—Laurier."[32] During their years together in the House, Blake had seen in Laurier a potentially great leader, and he argued that the party would be strengthened by choosing as its new leader a French-speaking Roman Catholic from Quebec. "To many members of the party the suggestion came as a surprise," Skelton records,[33] but it was equally true that "the knowledge of Mr. Blake's preference probably determined the action of the caucus."[34] When caucus met on June 7, Cartwright moved and Mills seconded Laurier's nomination, an action which effectively committed Laurier's major opposition to his support at the same time as it left him free to accept the leadership if he so wished with no substantial opposition. Laurier, however, took some time to deliberate the matter; it required much persuasion by Blake and others to bring him to the point of agreeing to accept the leadership. This was finally done on June 23, 1887, when Laurier announced his acceptance of the request contained in the Cartwright-Mills motion. Even then, Laurier was convinced that Blake would return to the leadership shortly, once his health had improved, in which case he would all too willingly step down. Others claimed that the selection of Laurier was understood to have been on a temporary basis only, making it possible for the selection of someone like Cartwright once Blake retired from politics.[35] If that were the case, then there is an element of irony in Laurier's service as Liberal leader, for he remained in that position until his death in 1919—a term unequalled by that of any other party leader in Canadian history.

Prior to the introduction of leadership conventions, the only Conservative leader to have been chosen while the party was on the opposition side of the House was Robert Borden. Borden's selection as Conservative leader followed the party's poor showing in the November general election of 1900. In that election Sir Charles Tupper suffered personal defeat, a circumstance he seized upon to tender his resignation to the party as its leader.[36] The most likely successor to Tupper would have been George Foster ("beyond question...the most outstanding figure in the party," according to Borden),[37] but Foster too had been defeated in the 1900 election. The absence of a parliamentary seat was not an impossible handicap, but it "had no doubt an influence in determining the choice of the Conservative caucus," observes Foster's biographer.[38] Sir Charles Hibbert Tupper was ruled out as a possible successor to his father because of "strong opposition to a dynastic succession" within the party.[39] With the opening of parliament in early February 1901, caucus met twice to choose a new leader. To Borden's surprise his name was proposed by Sir Charles Hibbert Tupper. Although he initially declined, Borden agreed under great pressure at the second meeting to accept.... Borden, in fact, remained at the head of his party for the next twenty years, and was the last leader to be chosen by a party in opposition prior to the introduction of national leadership conventions.

General Principles of Leadership Selection

Prior to any comparative analysis of the differences between leadership selection by parties in office and those out of office, what of the fact that without exception the leaders chosen in office were leaders of the Conservative party and, with one exception only, those chosen in opposition were leaders of the Liberal party? Can the differences, in other words, be explained as differences in leadership selection techniques between parties in power and parties in opposition? It is, after all, one of the facts of Canadian political history that Liberal leaders right up to St. Laurent's selection in 1948 were chosen whilst the party was in opposition and that, with Borden's exception in 1901, it was sixty years after Confederation before the Conservatives had to choose a leader when they were out of office. Yet it seems highly improbable that the differences could be accounted for as a function of the specific parties rather than as a function of the party's position in parliament. The obvious point about Borden's selection in 1901 was that it was made in basically the same tradition as the preceding three opposition party selections: following considerable intra-party discussion a caucus motion on the party leadership was adopted by the members of that body (both Conservative MPs and senators) and accepted by the nominee (see Table 2). In office the Conservatives relied, when possible, on intra-party negotiations and agreements (1892 and 1896); but in the absence of such agreements or lacking an obvious successor the party relied, to an extent that varied with the particular situation, upon vice-regal consultations with party notables (1891, 1894 and 1920). There is no reason to believe that from the 1870s through to the early twentieth century the Liberal party would have acted differently had a leadership vacancy occurred when it was in power. Had the Liberals in 1873 been without a leader when the Macdonald government resigned (they in fact had chosen Mackenzie nine months earlier), the parliamentary party notables might well have participated in a consultative operation of some kind with the Governor General to select from their midst an acceptable leader to head a new government. Laurier once remarked that it had been a mystery to him that on Macdonald's death Tupper had not been sent for immediately by the Governor General,[40] an interesting comment in that it questions only the decision arrived at in 1891, not the process used to make the decision. In short, the attitudes of personnel of both parties were not noticeably different on the matter of techniques used to select new leaders. The fact that neither the Liberals in opposition nor

Table 2: Leaders Selected Prior to the Introduction of Leadership Conventions in Their Party

	Year of selection	Name	Methods by which selections were made
In government	1867	John A. Macdonald	The exercise of the prerogative power of the Crown by the Governor General in naming the Prime Minister.[a]
	1891	J.J.C. Abbott	The exercise of the...Prime Minister.
	1892	John S.D. Thompson	The exercise of the...Prime Minister.
	1894	Mackenzie Bowell	The exercise of the...Prime Minister.
	1896	Charles Tupper	Agreement reached by, various party notables in the cabinet.
	1920	Arthur Meighen	Retiring leader was instructed by caucus to play an influential role in discussions, negotiations and, finally, advice to the Governor General. Caucus members advised the leader individually by ballot of their first, second and third choices for their leader and their reasons therefor.
In opposition	1873	Alexander Mackenzie	Formal selection by unanimous vote of caucus acting on a recommendation of a ten-man caucus committee.
	1880	Edward Blake	Caucus vote on a motion from the floor.
	1887	Wilfrid Laurier	Caucus vote following the strong recommendation of the retiring leader.
	1901	Robert L. Borden	Caucus vote on a motion from the floor.

[a] The first four party leaders on the Government side were selected as a result of the use of the royal prerogative of the Crown by the Governor General. Depending upon the time and the circumstances of the appointment to be made, the Governor General usually sought the advice of and held consultations with various party notables.

the Conservatives in office were critical of the techniques utilized by their opposites to choose their leaders would seem to indicate substantial acceptance of the processes used, even if the party itself had no occasion to use them.

For the party in power the Governor General did play an important role in many of the leadership discussions. The discretionary powers of the Crown were clearly exercised in the selection of Macdonald, Abbott, and Bowell. A more formal consultative process, with the Governor General acting exclusively on the advice of the retiring leaders, was followed when Thompson and Meighen were chosen. The contest between the governing party and the Governor General early in 1896 over the normally fused but potentially separate positions of party leader and prime minister made a rather special case of Tupper's selection, but it by no means challenged the continued existence of the Crown's discretionary power.... What had been established by 1920, and what did represent a break with earlier post-Confederation Canadian politics, was the decreasing involvement of the Governor General as one of the major participants in the search for new political leaders.

The caucus assumed greater importance when the party was out of power than when it was in power. In fact, in the Conservative party the parliamentary caucus' only opportunity to participate formally in the selection of its leader came when the party was in opposition. Yet what did such participation really mean? In all four instances of leadership selection in the opposition party the matter was handled by way of presentation of a motion to the caucus either on behalf of a caucus committee or by one or two party notables. Unanimity was a dominant feature of such meetings. As no motions proposing other members of the party for leader were presented, this would seem to suggest that much in the way of private discussions, of "soundings" within the party, had preceded the caucus meetings. In two cases (Borden, and more particularly, Laurier), a considerable amount of extra-caucus persuasion was needed to bring about acceptance by the nominee following the introduction of the motion in caucus. With such evidence it would be unfair to judge the caucuses' role as being anything more than a purely formal one, their powers more apparent than real.

The key to the leadership of a party obviously lay with the opinions and decisions of its more prominent and influential figures, regardless of whether or not the party was in power. The retiring leader might have been sufficiently able to judge the mood of his party to avoid protracted struggles and infighting and to ensure a relatively smooth leadership transition by timing his exit carefully. Such was the case with Abbott when he stepped down in Thompson's favour. A successful or a popular leader wishing to retire could virtually guarantee the succession to the man of his choice. Blake's support for Laurier (over Cartwright, Mills and Mowat) was sufficient to tip the scales in Laurier's favour, and Macdonald was not exaggerating his own power within the Conservative party when he told Tupper in 1888 that he could designate Tupper as his successor if Tupper were agreeable.[41] In other cases of clearcut succession, the leader, having lost his credibility in the party, was virtually powerless, and as a consequence was forced out when an attractive alternative supported by several prominent members of the party became available. Most certainly Bowell, and quite possibly Mackenzie, was removed in this way. On those occasions when no clearly acceptable individual stood out as the obvious successor, yet when a new leader had to be chosen (1887, 1891, 1894, 1901 and 1920), the party elite had no choice but to determine the amount of weight to be attached to the opinions expressed by various individuals within the party. The Borden-Meighen changeover best illustrates that point, for in 1920, if Borden and virtually the whole of the cabinet had had their way, the much more numerous backbenchers would have had to accept as leader a person other than the one a clear majority of them favoured.

The future of the party under various potential leaders was also a major consideration when leadership changeovers took place. *Party* was foremost in the minds of the participants as they attempted to judge its likely electoral success with different individuals at its head. The party whose future they were concerned with, of course, was the parliamentary party, for national organizations, party headquarters, staffs, elected executive officers, annual meetings and the other accoutrements of modern political parties were yet to come. Theirs, the parliamentary party, was in every sense of the word *the* party.

They were concerned, like any politicians, about timing. Entrances and exits to and from the leadership had to be so timed as best to preserve party unity. Had Thompson succeeded Macdonald directly, had the way not been prepared by Abbott, there would have been, in Lady Aberdeen's words, "a stampede of Ontario supporters."[42] Had Mackenzie not resigned in 1880 when there was much displeasure with his leadership, he himself recognized that "any other course would have broken up the party more or less."[43]

Had an arrangement not been made in January 1896, whereby Tupper could assume effective leadership of the party, the Conservatives knew all too well that they would be in a hopeless condition to fight the election of that year.

Political notables were interested as well in broadening the party's appeal when they searched for a leader whose qualities would quite possibly make the party more attractive in areas of electoral weakness. Blake was convinced in 1887 that by choosing Laurier as its leader the Liberal party would reap substantial benefits in future elections in Quebec and would not, at the same time, run the risk of losing its traditional support in Ontario. Blake's argument in favour of Laurier, therefore, was based on the likelihood of a net political gain for the party in forthcoming elections with such a man as leader. Macdonald's offer to Tupper in 1888 to name him as his successor was refused by Tupper in part because he knew Macdonald had previously promised it to Sir Hector Langevin and would not hear of Macdonald going back on his word, and in part because he felt the party would benefit more politically by having a French Canadian succeed Macdonald. Blake and Tupper acted in those circumstances with a primary interest in vote maximization for the party. They wanted not to reinforce areas of party strength so much as to effect an arrangement that would assist in improving the party's fortunes in areas of relative weakness. Mackenzie, on the other hand, argued in 1873 when he was chosen Liberal leader that the "preponderating power Ontario held" in the party left little choice but to select the leader from that province. As the Liberal party was in a somewhat earlier stage of development at the time than the Conservatives, and dominated as it was by its Ontario wing, Mackenzie's views were understandable. Eventually, however, at the end of Blake's leadership, the party was ready to be convinced that something other than an Ontario Protestant leader was needed if the party were to stand a reasonable chance of regaining power.

Finally, there was no doubt but that experience in national politics and service in parliament as a private member, then as a cabinet minister, counted for a great deal when new leaders were to be chosen. Each of the leaders included in Table 2 had participated to some extent (most, quite fully), in parliamentary politics, and as a result it was not difficult to predict his likely success or failure as a leader. There were certainly genuine misgivings about Bowell when he was chosen as leader, and for good reason. Borden feared that his own period in parliament (less than five years) had not been sufficient time to prepare him for the leadership when he accepted it in 1901, and his first few years as Conservative leader seemed to confirm those fears. But it is also worth noting that George Foster, one of Borden's potential rivals for the leadership and a man with some eighteen years in the House, was effectively removed from the competition by virtue of his defeat in the 1900 election and his subsequent absence from parliament at the time Tupper's successor was chosen. How this feature of leadership selection would be altered in years to come with party conventions!

Notes

1   Joseph Pope, *Memoirs of the Right Honourable Sir John Alexander Macdonald*, 2 vols. (Ottawa: J. Durie and Son, 1894), I, 319.

2   The political history of the period is covered in Lovell C. Clark, "The Conservative Party in the 1890's," *Report of the Canadian Historical Association* (1961), pp. 58-74; Lovell C. Clark, "Macdonald's Conservative Successors, 1891-1896," in John S. Moir (ed.), *Character and Circumstance: Essays in Honour of Donald Grant Creighton* (Toronto: Macmillan Company of Canada, 1970), pp. 143-162; and John T. Saywell, "The Crown and the Politicians: The Canadian Succession Question: 1891-1896," *CHR*, XXXVII (December 1956), 309-337.

3   J.W. Longley, *Sir Charles Tupper* (Toronto: Makers of Canada [Morang], Ltd., 1916), pp. 211-215.

4   Clark, "The Conservative Party," p. 62.

5   In so doing, Thompson effectively blocked D'Alton McCarthy from the party leadership, McCarthy's claim was not a strong one. He was one of the most outspoken of the Ontario Orangemen in parliament and had made the effort during the search for a new leader to press his own claim for the leadership on Thompson, no doubt pointing out at the same time that Thompson's Roman Catholicism made him unacceptable to the Protestantism wing of the party. See J. Castell Hopkins, *Life and Work of the Rt. Hon. Sir John Thompson* (Toronto: United Publishing Houses, 1895), p. 190, and Steven Miller, "The Canadian Prime Ministers, 1867-1948: An Essay on Democratic Leadership" (unpublished Ph.D. dissertation, Department of Political Science, Cornell University, 1958), pp. 256-257.

6   Canada, *Debates of the Senate* (June 17, 1891), p. 98

7   Hopkins, p. 239.

8   Public Archives of Canada (hereinafter cited as PAC), *Thompson Papers*, vol. 166, 20780, letter from Abbott to Thompson of November 10, 1892.

9   See Saywell, "The Crown and the Politicians," p. 314. At least some of the Ontario Conservative Orangemen who had previously reacted un-

favourably to the suggestion that Thompson become party leader had, during the course of Abbott's premiership, changed their minds. Writing to Thompson to assure him of the support of the "boys," one Ontario MP and Orangeman, Sam Hughes, stated: "What! the pervert? the ultramontane? the roman catholic? the defender of Mercier's Jesuit Estates Act? *Yes*, all say yes." Hughes to Thompson, August 20, 1892, as quoted in Clark, "Macdonald's Conservative Successors," p. 146. "Pervert" was the expression current at the time to refer to a Roman Catholic convert.

10   Clark, "The Conservative Party," p. 62.

11   John T. Saywell (ed.), *The Canadian Journal of Lady Aberdeen, 1893-1898* (Toronto: The Champlain Society, 1960), p. 166.

12   Saywell, "The Crown and the Politicians," p. 319.

13   As quoted in S. Morley Scott, "Foster on the Thompson-Bowell Succession," *CHR*, XLVIII (September 1967), 275.

14   Saywell (ed.), *Journal of Lady Aberdeen*, p. 161.

15   Scott, "Foster on the Thompson-Bowell Succession," 275.

16   Saywell, "The Crown and the Politicians," p. 329. See also Longley, pp. 225-226.

17   Henry Borden, *Robert Laird Borden: His Memoirs*, 2 vols. (Toronto: Macmillan Company of Canada, 1938), II, 1031.

18   W. Stewart Wallace, *The Memoirs of the Rt. Hon. Sir George Foster* (Toronto: Macmillan Company of Canada, 1933), p. 205. Both Foster and Borden acknowledged the proposal as being Foster's, but years later H.H. Stevens claimed responsibility for it. See Ruth M. Bell, "Conservative Party National Conventions, 1927-1956: Organization and Procedure," (unpublished M.A. thesis, Department of Political Science, Carleton University, 1965), p. 18.

19   R. MacGregor Dawson (ed.), *Constitutional Issues in Canada, 1900-1931* (London: Oxford University Press, 1933), p. 382.

20   See Roger Graham, *Arthur Meighen*, 3 vols. (Toronto, Clarke Irwin and Co. Ltd., 1960), I, 287-301, and Borden, II, 1030-1040.

21   Dawson (ed.), p. 386.

22   Graham, I, 292.

23   William Buckingham and Hon. George W. Ross, *The Hon. Alexander Mackenzie: His Life and Times* (Toronto: Rose Publishing Company, 1892), p. 612. See Thomson, *Alexander Mackenzie: Clear Grit*, p. 119.

24   Buckingham and Ross, pp. 329-330. On the selection of Mackenzie in 1872 see also Thomson, pp. 146-148, and O.D. Skelton, *Life and Letters of Sir Wilfrid Laurier*, 2 vols. (Toronto: Oxford University Press, 1921), I, 172-174.

25   In November 1873, Macdonald begged caucus to accept his resignation

and choose a younger man, but his request was refused. See Donald Creighton, *John A. Macdonald: The Old Chieftain* (Toronto: Macmillan Company of Canada, 1955), pp. 180-181.

26 Canada, *Debates of the House of Commons* (April 27-28, 1880), p. 815.

27 Skelton, I, 220-221; also PAC, *Mackenzie Papers*, Reel M-199, Mackenzie to Charles Black, May 20, 1882, 2356-2357, and *Mackenzie Letterbook*, vol. II, Mackenzie to L.H. Davies, May 20, 1880, 673-678.

28 Thomson, p. 362.

29 *Globe*, April 30, 1880, p. 2.

30 A copy of Blake's letter is to be found in Queen's University, *Douglas Library Notes*, vol. IV, no. 3 (August 1955), n.p.

31 See Margaret A. Banks, "The Change in Liberal Party Leadership, 1887," *CHR*, XXXVIII (June 1957), 115.

32 Skelton, I, 341.

33 *Ibid.*

34 Sir John S. Willison, *Sir Wilfrid Laurier and the Liberal Party: A Political History*, 2 vols. (Toronto: George N. Morang, 1903), I, 34.

35 See Banks, 122-125.

36 A copy of Tupper's letter of resignation addressed to the "members of the Conservative party in the Senate and House of Commons" and dated January 17, 1901, is to be found in *The Times* (London), February 11, 1901, p. 6. The resignation was accepted by caucus at its first meeting of the new parliament, February 5, 1901.

37 Borden, I, 73.

38 Wallace, p. 114.

39 Muller, "The Canadian Prime Ministers," p. 411.

40 Canada, *Debates of the House of Commons* (February 7, 1916), p. 586.

41 Macdonald's offer to Tupper was recalled some years later by Tupper. See W.A. Harkin (ed.), *Political Reminiscences of the Rt. Hon. Sir Charles Tupper* (London: Constable and Co., 1914), p. 147.

42 Clark, "The Conservative Party," p. 62.

43 *Mackenzie Papers*, Mackenzie to Black, May 20, 1882.

K.Z. Paltiel Party Finance Before World War I

Disciplined parties did not emerge until some time after 1867. Party lines had been blurred by the coalition ministry which had brought about Confederation[1] and their delineation was further impeded by the continued survival of "loose fish" or "ministerialists" who would back whichever group held office but whose support at the hustings could not be relied upon. The fundamental problem facing a parliamentary leader at that time was the creation of a stable working majority. One essential instrument was the allocation of funds raised by the party leaders themselves amongst their followers.[2] Such monies came from their personal resources and contacts in the business world, particularly those who had benefited or expected to benefit from government favour. The personal burden on Sir John A. Macdonald, for instance, was not inconsiderable. As one contemporary put it:

> He was pretty deeply in debt for a good many years, but I think his indebtedness was due to political exigencies and not to speculations or personal extravagance. I have heard him speak with much bitterness, and I do not doubt with much truth, of the scandalous way in which he was often pillaged by his political supporters and of the niggardly contributions he received from wealthy members of the party. But this is a very common experience with public men.[3]

Thus Macdonald and Sir Georges Etienne Cartier became involved in soliciting and collecting funds from government contractors, such as Sir Hugh Allan and the group bidding for the construction of the Pacific Railway. When the Pacific Scandal was revealed, the leaders' personal connection could not be repudiated and the Conservatives went down to defeat in 1874. But the last word in the matter should be left to Macdonald whose explanation to the Governor General best describes the financial structure of the parties in those days:

> It has been stated in the English press that I should not have mixed myself up in these money matters, but should have left it to our Carleton and Reform Clubs. This may be true, indeed is true, if such clubs existed; but, as a matter of fact,

the leaders of political parties have always hitherto acted in such matters, and there can be no special blame attached to a leader for continuing the invariable practice on this occasion.[4]

The Liberals in this period found themselves in a similar position. The 1872 and 1874 campaigns were financed "with a very trifling expenditure of money"[5] according to party sympathizers but Macdonald estimated that the Liberals in 1872 spent more than a quarter-of-a-million dollars in the effort to oust the Conservatives.[6] According to George Brown the party depended almost entirely on a few members who "could come down handsomely";[7] amongst whom was the president of a bank which allegedly benefited from government deposits when the Liberals won. However, it was not until ten years after its defeat in 1878 that the Liberal Party was able to regularize its income and financial structure, the years of Mackenzie and Blake having been marked by a hand-to-mouth existence on a modicum of funds.[8]

In devising the National Policy of tariff protection and railway building in 1878 Macdonald found a program which appealed to the manufacturing interest and was designed to attract funds to the party coffers.[9] In the years that followed, fund-raising emerged as a specialized task of the party organization as disclosed in 1891 in the McGreevy Scandal, the second major Canadian railway scandal.[10] The charges involved members of the federal cabinet who were alleged to have diverted government funds allotted for railway subsidies to the support of government candidates in the Province of Quebec. From 1882 to 1887, Thomas McGreevy, M.P., had fulfilled the functions of principal collector and treasurer of the Conservative Party for federal campaigns in Quebec. Together with the federal Minister of Public Works and the Postmaster General (both posts traditionally having had vast sources of patronage at their disposal), McGreevy was a member of a three-man team acting on oral and written orders from his ministerial colleagues regarding the distribution of funds in the elections of 1882 and 1887.[11]

This nascent specialization removed the leadership from direct contact with the fund-raising process, an essential step in the evolution toward the contemporary structure.

With Wilfrid Laurier's accession to the leadership in 1887, the fund-raising pattern of the Liberal Party took a similar turn. The unofficial group of party collectors typical of the period of Mackenzie and Blake gave way to organizers like Edgar and Preston in

Ontario and Pacaud and Tarte in Quebec who were intimately concerned with provincial as well as federal campaigns and who devoted a major portion of their time to party political affairs.[12] When the party won power in 1896 these activities became centralized within the Cabinet; a pattern which was to be repeated in the latter years of the King régime. Like their Conservative rivals the Laurier Liberals learned to make their policies acceptable to manufacturing and railway interests. The incumbent Ontario Liberals under Mowat were, according to Cartwright, "all more or less mixed-up with the manufacturing element in one way or another."[13] The election of 1891 demonstrated that the program of commercial union with the United States alienated business. In 1891,

> They [the Liberals] faced an organized and aggressive campaign by the business interests which considered themselves in peril. Manufacturers...wholesalers...bankers...worked quietly and effectively in town and city. Most effective of all the anti-reciprocity forces was the Canadian Pacific....[14]

> In every constituency but one—that of Marquette, where Robert Wilson won a six-vote victory, wholly through oversight, Van Horne declared—through which the main line of the Canadian Pacific ran, a Conservative was elected.[15]

The Liberals turned to rival railway interests as illustrated by the Baie des Chaleurs Railway scandal in which Ernest Pacaud, one of Laurier's organizers, obtained $100,000 for the provincial party ($10,000 of which reached Laurier) from a railway concession.[16] Laurier's Cabinet included, amongst others linked with the business world, Sir William Mulock and the Hon. William Paterson who were well connected with Toronto banking and Ontario manufacturing interests.[17] Once it was in office, the Liberal Party did not hesitate to exploit all the sources of patronage afforded a party in power. In the words of a sympathetic observer, Laurier himself had "a large toleration for patronage."[18] Elsewhere the same commentator states:

> There was...a system of purchase of public supplies and distribution of public contracts which effectually excluded political opponents from any profitable access to the treasury.... From the privileged dealers in supplies subscriptions were taken, and from many contracts there was a generous

return to the party fund.[19]

It should occasion no surprise that members of Laurier's Cabinet were denounced as "corruptionists."[20]

Under Laurier efforts were also made to systematize the organizational and fund-raising apparatus of the party. Around 1891, Joseph Israel Tarte began to switch his allegiance to the Liberals, joining the party at its first convention in 1893.[21] For four years prior to the victory of 1896, he worked as Laurier's full-time chief organizer in Quebec, raising funds, setting up a permanent office in Montreal and organizing Liberal clubs in the constituencies.[22] Although Tarte received only $1,200 of the $4,000 annual salary suggested on his behalf by Laurier, "his travelling expenses were high and his postal bill [from 1894 to 1896] alone was about $1,000."[23] After 1896, Tarte continued these activities from within the Cabinet as the salaried Minister of Public Works, organizing election campaigns and liquor plebiscites for the party in Quebec and New Brunswick.[24] His close involvement with these activities made it difficult to escape charges of corruption and he was forced to leave the Government in 1902.[25]

Once in power, the Liberals tended to divide organizational responsibilities on a regional basis among Ministers from the areas concerned. Thus Clifford Sifton took charge of fund-raising and organization in Western Canada with an occasional foray into Ontario.[26] Similar roles were played by Charles Hyman, W.S. Fielding, Andrew Blair, William Pugsley and Raymond Préfontaine.[27] In contrast to Sir John A. Macdonald's active role, however, the Liberal Party's fund-raising structure in the Laurier era was not concentrated under the party leader. Laurier was clearly aware of and occasionally assisted the activities of the fund-raisers.[28] But centralization occurred only at the regional level. Fund-raising remained in the control of the regional leaders with dire results for Laurier when he was abandoned by Sifton in the Reciprocity Campaign of 1911[29] and other leaders in the Unionist crisis of 1917. As a contemporary observer put it: "The former Liberal leaders of Ontario, New Brunswick, Manitoba, Saskatchewan and Alberta were members of the Union cabinet. The party organizations, the party rolls, and the party war chests had gone with them."[30]

The dependence of the two parties on the business community was re-emphasized in the election of 1911, which returned the Conservatives to office under Borden. Aroused by Laurier's espousal of reciprocity, the financial community supported his opponents. The Canadian Pacific Railway headed by Sir William Van Horne threw its considerable weight against the Liberals,[31] and Sir Hugh Graham, publisher of the Montreal *Star*, employed the talents of his staff and about a quarter-of-a-million dollars on behalf of the Conservatives.[32] About $200,000 was channeled to the Quebec Nationalist leaders, Armand Lavergne and Henri Bourassa, in order to defeat the Liberals by splitting the French-Canadian vote.[33] Protectionism and big business had successfully asserted their power.

Notes

1 Hon. Sir George Ross, *Getting into Parliament and After*, William Briggs (now The Ryerson Press), Toronto, 1913, pp. 17-18.

2 Donald Creighton, *John A. Macdonald, The Old Chieftain*, The Macmillan Co. of Canada Ltd., Toronto, 1955, pp. 47ff.

3 Rt. Hon. Sir Richard J.G. Cartwright, C.M.G., P.C., *Reminiscences*, William Briggs (now The Ryerson Press), Toronto, 1912, p. 49.

4 Cited in Joseph Pope, *Memoirs of the Right Honourable Sir John Alexander Macdonald, G.C.B.*, The Musson Book Co., Toronto, 1894, p. 553.

5 Cartwright, *op. cit.*, p. 192.

6 Creighton, *op. cit.*, pp. 140-141.

7 *Regina v. Wilkinson* (H.T. 40 Vict. 1877) Quoted in *Upper Canada Queen's Bench Reports*, Vol. 41, 1878, p. 11.

8 Khayyam Z. Paltiel and Jean B. Van Loon, "Financing the Liberal Party," in Paltiel et al., *Studies in Canadian Party Finance*, Committee on Election Expenses, The Queen's Printer, Ottawa, 1966, pp. 152-154.

9 W.T.R. Preston, *My Generation of Politics and Politicians*, Rose Publishing Co., Toronto, 1927, p. 126.

10 *Report of the Royal Commission in reference to certain charges against Sir A.P. Caron*, Queen's Printer, Ottawa, February 6, 1893, Sessional Papers, No. 27.

11 *Ibid.*, pp. 161-164.

12 Paltiel and Van Loon, *op. cit.*, pp. 176-182.

13 *Laurier Papers* , Letter from Cartwright to Laurier, October 15, 1887, quoted in W.R. Graham, "Sir Richard Cartwright, Wilfrid Laurier, and Liberal Party Trade Policy, 1887," *Canadian Historical Review*, XXXIII, No. 1, p. 12.

14 O.D. Skelton, *Life and Letters of Sir Wilfrid Laurier*, Vol. I, Oxford University Press, Toronto, 1921, p. 416.

15 *Ibid.*, p. 418.

16 *Royal Commission of Inquiry into the Baie des Chaleurs Railway Matter, 1891,*

Reports, Proceedings and Depositions, Quebec, 1892, pp. 51-65; see also Joseph Schull, *Laurier, The First Canadian*, The MacMillan Co. of Canada Ltd., Toronto, 1965, pp. 254, 257.

17 Paltiel and Van Loon, *op. cit.*, pp. 156-157.

18 Sir John S. Willison, *Sir Wilfrid Laurier*, Makers of Canada series, Oxford University Press, London and Toronto, 1926, p. 468.

19 Sir John S. Willison, *Reminiscences, Political and Personal*, McClelland and Stewart Ltd., Toronto, 1919, pp. 280-281.

20 *Ibid.*, p. 277.

21 Laurier Joseph Lucien Lapierre, "Politics, Race and Religion in French Canada; Joseph Israel Tarte," unpublished Ph.D. dissertation, University of Toronto, Toronto, 1962, pp. 242-250.

22 *Ibid.*, pp. 303-304, p. 311.

23 *Ibid.*

24 *Ibid.*, p. 366, p. 398.

25 *Ibid.*, p. 526. Tarte is responsible for the deathless phrase "Les élections ne se font pas avec des prières—Prayers do not win elections."

26 John W. Dafoe, *Clifford Sifton in Relation to His Times*, The Macmillan Co. of Canada Ltd., Toronto, 1931, p. xiv.

27 Willison, *Reminiscences, Political and Personal, op. cit.*, p. 277; Schull, *op. cit.*, pp. 458-459.

28 Paltiel and Van Loon, *op. cit.*, pp. 181-182.

29 Skelton, *op. cit.*, Vol. II, p. 372.

30 Schull, *op. cit.*, pp. 591-592.

31 *Ibid.*, p. 523; see also Dafoe, *op. cit.*, p. 364.

32 Mason Wade, *The French Canadians*, 1760-1945, The Macmillan Co. of Canada Ltd., Toronto, 1955, p. 602.

33 *Ibid.*, p. 598. See also Robert Rumilly, *Histoire de la province de Québec*, Éditions Bernard Valiquette, Montréal, 1948, v. XVI, p. 75.

Paul Rutherford The Politician's Dominion:
Party Media Relationships in
Early Canada

Neither the cleric nor the businessman could lay claim to the type of
influence over the press enjoyed by the politician. Journalism and
party seemed inextricably linked—by tradition and necessity.[1] True,
that once prominent hybrid, the newspaperman-cum-politician, had
become a much less common breed after Confederation because both
party politics and daily journalism, at the top anyway, required full-
timers. But the typical publisher or editor remained addicted to playing politics, for him a grand sport that added spice to life and gave
significance to his calling. ('The game of politics is a great game,'
mused Willison; 'it is played with men as the standing figures on the
board, and it is full of joy to the journalist who loves his work, his
country and his kind.')[2] Besides, the results of the game often gave
him, or at least his newspaper, sustenance in the form of readers, subsidies, and patronage. The typical politician saw newspapers as essential vehicles of publicity, indeed a surrogate for organization, which
could confound foes, strengthen party discipline and morale, and educate electors. (So Laurier claimed, 'the publication of a newspaper is
a very great advantage always for the prosperity and well-doing of a
political party.')[3] He was, then, quite prepared to reward friendly journalists and to punish the disloyal or hostile.

The resulting marriage, however, was at times a stormy one.
That old question of dominance could easily cause trouble: politicians naturally assumed they were the masters, journalists their servants, a presumption that not every editor or publisher would stomach. The party chieftains had difficulty realizing that their reputed
organs must curry favour with a wide range of readers, and this
meant these dailies had to be more than just the mouthpieces of a
party. Put another way, the publisher and editor was forced by the
logic of mass communication to carry news or advocate views, perhaps highlight stories, that might be harmful to the best interests
of the party. More important, the politician and the journalist had
differing views of politics. The bias of the politician made him see
politics as a contest between two teams intent on winning office;
the bias of the journalist made him see politics as a war of ideas
in which right must triumph. Is it any wonder the politician's hold
over the press was challenged, even by faithful journalists? Some-

Figure 1: Newspaper Circulations and Political Loyalties

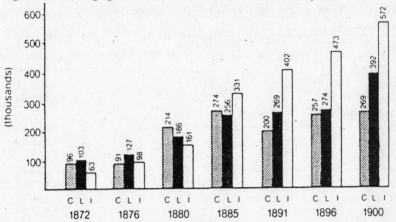

C = Conservative, L = Liberal, I = Indipendent.
The circulations listed are a combination of the totals of the daily and weekly editions of the daily newspapers. The figures and political lables (except where evidence suggests otherwise) are taken from assorted newspaper directories. Some newspapers where not included because their political loyalties could not be ascertained.

times, events seemed to promise a renewal of the struggle for a free press, this time against the mastery of party instead of government.

The cause of freedom, however, got sidetracked because of the outbreak of a civil war of sorts between party newspapers, albeit Conservative and Liberal rivals, and a motley crew of self-styled independents and mavericks. The economics of journalism underlay the conflict. One route to commercial success, at first it seemed the only route, required a party label to attract a loyal readership. (Hector Charlesworth noted of his grandmother, 'She was a staunch Tory, and every day read the *Mail*...from the first column to the last.')[4] This maxim made each city, eventually from Halifax to Victoria, the site of at least one Conservative and one Liberal daily. The balance of forces between the two camps remained roughly equal, sometimes the Liberals ahead, sometimes the Conservatives, winning more readers, until the late 1890s when the defection or death of old Conservative warriors (especially in Quebec) plus the political dominance of the Liberal party in Ottawa and the provinces gave the Liberal press a definite edge. Still the Liberal achievement

Table 1:
Selected Newspapers and Federal Patronage 1891-1901 (in dollars)

	Conservative years (July 1891-June 1896)	Liberal years (July 1896-June 1901)
HALIFAX		
Herald	33,951.75	1,152.73*
Chronicle	38.00	27,811.31
SAINT JOHN		
Sun	54,853.28	1,215.56*
Telegraph	–	45,548.65
QUEBEC		
Chronicle	14,672.49	555.83*
Telegraph	45.20	10,478.29
L'Événement	2,016.03	120.10*
L'Électeur/Soleil	17.70	11,297.25
MONTREAL		
Gazette	12,149.50	698.09*
Star	2,020.79	754.63*
Herald	105.83	97,796.57
Witness	41.13	6,196.36
Minerve	2,869.16	203.30*
Le Monde	1,599.18	203.52
La Presse	2,166.81	50.74
La Patrie	4.20	10,177.70
OTTAWA		
Citizen	4,648.29	336.79
Journal	1,331.16	2,040.24
Free Press	269.25	5,505.76
TORONTO		
Mail	418.10	
Empire	9,707.31	
Mail and Empire	2,989.29	983.41*
World	4,546.04	83.30
Telegram	67.84	5.80
News	132.30	21.45
Star	504.40	5,367.73
Globe	80.40	12,276.35
HAMILTON		
Spectator	4,742.66	565.30*
Herald	847.10	2,173.45
Times	–	5,037.95
LONDON		
Free Press	2,885.74	364.60*
News		392.40

Table 1 Continued

	Conservative years (July 1891-June 1896)	Liberal years (July 1896-June 1901)
WINNIPEG		
Manitoba Free Press	1,329.55	2,503.52
Nor'Wester/Telegram	1,118.82	13.50*
Tribune	54.45	1,038.47
VANCOUVER		
News-Advertiser	580.55	189.60
World	42.05	1,685.05
VICTORIA		
Colonist	1,407.90	109.70
Times	37.25	786.05

* All or a large part of this patronage was received in 1896-97.

was eclipsed by the triumph of the 'Independents.' After the mid-1860s the sectarian papers, even more the people's journals, pioneered a new strategy of non-partisan politicians to win a mass readership irrespective of people's political preferences. The circulation of the so-called independent press zoomed upwards in the 1880s, due not only to the appeal of popular journalism but also to a few converts from the ranks of the party press as well. Although the most prominent independents were located in the big cities of central Canada, notably Toronto, before long maverick dailies and non-partisan newcomers had appeared across the land, even in some small towns. Yet the challengers did not sweep aside their party rivals: in 1900 the party press claimed 77 dailies, boasting a combined circulation of 660,699 (or 53 per cent of the total daily and weekly circulations of the daily press), while the independent press had a mere 37 champions, though with a combined circulation of 572,461 (or 46 per cent of the total).

The civil war, of course, was waged on the editorial pages. Controversy revolved around the prosperity of any link between party and press, given the common assumption that the newspaper moulded public opinion. The self-styled independents argued that the fettered journalism of a party organ could never benefit the public. 'The primary object of such a journal is not to serve the interests of the public at large,' asserted the Toronto *Telegram* (15 May 1876), 'but to promote the policy of a particular faction.' Indeed, 'the party organs...do nothing but defend their own and abuse the other,' agreed the Toronto *World* (7 April 1884). That made the party paper, in the words of a newly intransigent *Monde* (15 October

1892), 'l'ennui du bon gouvernement et l'ennemi des gouvernés.' Its apologies for the misdeeds of friends and assaults on the virtue of rivals could not but threaten the new democracy: 'Thus the public mind has been debauched, the properties of life outraged, the self-respect of voters ruined, and the parliaments of Canada made the stamping ground of monied adventurers and political sharks' (Toronto *News*, 29 September 1883). The party organ betrayed the newspaper's mission to voice the popular will and to uplift public opinion.

Contrast this invective with the self-praise of the independent press. 'An independent press desires above all things the good of the country for which it denies itself the temporary benefits which partisanship gives,' claimed a smug Montreal *Star* (5 July 1882), 'and it desires to do full justice to men and measures of all parties.' This gave the independent press a special role in political life: not just to tell 'the truth about the affairs of the country and about political doings' (Montreal *Star*, 16 April 1886), but to protect 'popular rights' (Toronto *News*, 14 May 1885) against any infringement. Early on, when it was hardly independent in any real sense, *La Presse* (3 September 1886) maintained that such papers were 'les intermédiaries utiles entre la certitude aveugle du ministériel et la scepticisme de l'oppositioniste.' An independent press acted as 'la soupape de sûreté, ouverte à tous les doutes, à toutes les répugnances, à tous les mécontentements, à tous les courants souterrains' which might otherwise never find a voice until the political fabric was shattered by public anger. Likewise, *Le Monde* (15 October 1892) claimed that the 'liberté de pensée, de parole et d'action' of the independent dailies made them great 'reformateurs,' in the words of Charles Dana 'daily humanitarians and utilitarians.' In short, the independent press was nothing less than the true voice of the Canadian democracy.

The party press, if thrown on the defensive, responded in kind. Much was made of the need for a 'strong and forceful' public opinion, the result of views 'arrived at by conviction,' not 'simply parrot-like repetition of the opinions of the predominant mob.'[5] That was the task of the newspaper—not just any newspaper but one which, announced Edmond Larrau in *La Patrie* (25 February 1882), 'représente une idée; une idée qui est le partage d'un group, d'une dénomination politique, d'une classe dans la société.' So when *La Minerve* enjoyed a brief renaissance in 1898, there came the proud proclamation that it was 'un journal conservateur, fidèle à son passé et respectueux des grandes traditions politiques du parti de Lafontaine, de Morin et de Cartier.'[6]

The trouble with the independent press, it seemed, was that these papers represented nothing. 'The so-called independent journalist is a man who has a whole wardrobe of nearly made convictions,' asserted the Hamilton *Spectator* (10 January 1887), 'which he changes to suit the weather, the fashion, or, mayhap, the condition of his purse.' He could exercise no lasting influence over public or party. Indeed, the London *Advocate* (26 October 1874) once claimed 'the demands of our institutions require that the great newspapers shall take side with one party or the other,' so entrenched was party in the Canadian constitution. That was why the revitalized *La Minerve* (1 September 1898) could think its rebirth meant a return to 'sa place au conseil de la nation.'

The demands of party journalism by no means required servility. 'It is his highest duty to elevate the ideas and the tone of his party and to guide it in the ways of progress and purity,' the Montreal *Herald* (8 May 1879) said of the party journalist. 'The plain duty of the journal, in giving its opinion on political matters,' the Toronto *Globe* (3 February 1888) charged in its own defence, 'is simply to express what it believes would conduce most to the public interest.' Apologists had squared the circle, arguing the organ could serve the public as well as the party. Their reasoning assumed that any devotion to party, 'la cause commune,'[7] grew out of principle not payment. Such fealty, held the true believer, merely gave substance to the journalist's mission to lead the public in the ways of righteousness.

A good deal of the rhetoric in support of party journalism was specious. Apologists failed to admit the extent of the connections between party and press. All kinds of money was funnelled into the upkeep of needy papers. An unhappy Maurice Laframboise, who may have lost $30,000 trying to sustain Montreal's *Le National* (1872-79), admitted that in French Canada it was impossible to assure newspapers 'une existence exempte de profonder perturbations sans l'aide généreuse et persistante d'amis dévoués, sans de puissantes contributions de la part du parti dont ils partagent les vues et défendent les intérêts.'[8] The Ottawa *Times* in the early 1870s was something of a ministerial organ, changing hands when the government at Ottawa changed. Conservative monies started, and for a time sustained, the Toronto *Mail* and later the Toronto *Empire*. L.-A.

Sénécal apparently funded the short-lived Quebec *Times* (November 1881-January 1882) to reach the English-speaking electorate on behalf of Chapleau's election campaign.[9] He performed a similar function, though the results were more lasting, in the founding of *La Presse*. Rumour had it that when the CPR set out to buy control of the Toronto *Globe* in 1882, Ontario Liberals moved swiftly to organize a purchase by wealthy friends, among them Robert Jaffray and George Cox, of Mrs George Brown's holdings.[10] Clifford Sifton, in his own right, invested in the Brandon *Sun* and the *Manitoba Free Press*, though he tried in vain to hide his ownership. In September 1895 the *Printer and Publisher* reported that *La Minerve* was 'controlled financially' by J.-P. Caron, a leading Conservative, and that 'a controlling interest' in *Le Monde* had been acquired by another Conservative, J.-A. Ouimet. In 1899 George Cox, now a senator, arranged a consortium of wealthy friends to buy and revitalize the Toronto *Star* in the Liberal interest. Quebec's Conservatives were able to go to J.D.R. Forget, a grand financier, to fund the waning *Le Journal* of Montreal (1899-1905).

Victory at the polls signalled to loyal publishers that they would receive a share of government patronage, mainly advertising or printing contracts. The origins of the practice went back to the early days of journalism, though only after mid-century did newspaper subsidies consume large sums of public money.[11] Party chieftains took great care to reward the faithful with government contracts; at least as early as 1876, the Ottawa government had an official list for departments which designated the newspapers deserving business, a list periodically updated and always revised when office changed hands. Equally, party journalists assumed that compensation for past services, and future exertions, was their due; in the 1870s James Moylan, admittedly the proprietor of an Irish-Canadian weekly, regularly published official announcements without approval but submitted bills to departments anyway, a practice to which Macdonald gave his blessing.[12]

The actual amounts of money involved could sometimes be sizeable. According to *La Patrie* (30 March 1897), the Quebec government bestowed around $10,000 on *L'Événement* and another $19,000 on *La Minerve* in the single year 1895-96. But it was the federal government which had the most funds to disburse. The auditor general's reports during the 1890s can be used to compare the practices of Conservatives and Liberal office-holders, each over a five-year period (Table 1). There was not too much difference in purpose or habit, whatever the claims otherwise. Ottawa gave the press contracts worth roughly $125,000 in 1890-91, rising to $172,500 ten years later. Although the monies were shared among a wide range of journals, the largest sums usually went to big-city dailies. In 1895-96, for instance, the Belleville *Intelligencer*, a daily closely associated with Prime Minister Mackenzie Bowell, received $159.85 in advertising, whereas the Montreal *Gazette* got $1,057.27. The most lavish contracts came from printing, not advertising. So the Moncton *Times* earned $81,650.18 from job printing in the Conservative years, much of this probably for the purposes of the government-owned Intercolonial Railway. Of the $97,796.57 the Laurier government gave the troubled Montreal *Herald*, $86,590.31 arose out of printing jobs—indeed in 1900-01 the lucky company won almost $50,000 in such contracts alone. Party favouritism was obvious. Why else would the Conservative *Sun* of Saint John receive $54,853.28 in the early 1890s and the rival *Telegraph* $45,548.65 during the Liberal years? The major organs were handsomely rewarded: the $12,696.60 the *Empire* (and later the *Mail and Empire*) garnered from government advertising in the Conservative years was matched by the $12,276.35 the *Globe* acquired in the Liberal years. The Conservative régimes seemed a bit niggardly in their treatment of francophone organs, by comparison with anglophone dailies (perhaps Quebec's Conservative governments looked after the former?), but the Laurier government remedied that (witness the $10,177.10 for *La Patrie* and the $11,297.25 for *L'Électeur/Le Soleil*). Maritime dailies did especially well out of printing contracts, the central Canadian faithful earned their subsidies mostly in advertising contracts (the Montreal *Herald* was an outrageous exception), and the prairie and Pacific organs had to make do with modest sums from both sources. Largely left off the lists were the independent or maverick papers—as long as they remained such. The Toronto *News* and especially the *Telegram* received negligible contracts over the course of the decade. Even the Montreal *Star* and *La Presse* got very little, given their huge circulations. But a switch in loyalties earned decent subsidies for two 'independents,' the Toronto *Star* and the Hamilton *Herald*, in the Liberal years.

Did any of this matter? Observed the Hamilton *Spectator* (9 January 1882): 'The fact is no journal of standing of either party looks upon its government patronage as being of importance to it. Every such journal has scores of private patrons whose account is vastly greater with it than that of the Gouvernment[sic].... If there is any want of independence in the Canadian press it is not because of the money it receives from the Canadian Government.' True enough, the annual sums bestowed upon a newspaper usually constituted only a small portion (less than 5 per cent?) of total revenues. And yet opposition or independent papers loved to disclose the subsidies paid to ministerial organs to prove their venality. An irate La Patrie (20 August 1879) carried a list of supposed Liberal papers—'Les Vendus' it called them—which had apparently been bought off by Chapleau and Sénécal. Likewise, a self-righteous Toronto Globe (19 May 1885), though the recipient of monies from the Ontario government, published a list of Conservative dailies and their earnings under the suggestive title 'They Don't Count.'[13] The publication in 1899 of the news that the Montreal Witness had received a paltry $694 from the Laurier government, while much larger sums went to more reliable organs, so frightened the Dougalls they planned an editorial explaining the money meant no loss of independence.[14] In 1901 Willison estimated that 'within the last five years between three and four hundred thousand dollars of party money,' by which he meant mostly patronage money, 'has been put into Liberal papers in Canada.'[15] In short government 'pap' did matter. The money was welcome: it could make a difference in the profit-and-loss statements of lucky publishers, even if it was rarely the means of economic salvation it had been for the feeble papers of the 1850s and 1860s. Acceptance did indicate some sort of bond. Politicians did not give patronage out of the goodness of their hearts.

Finally, politicians could bestow upon journalists all sorts of favours. In 1872 Isaac Buchanan, a leading Hamilton Conservative, urged upon Thomas Patterson the wisdom of hiring a stalwart protectionist, such as John McLean, to aid the forthcoming Mail.[16] Party organizers were sometimes set to work as circulation boosters, a practice which apparently helped the weekly Mail reach quickly a fair-sized readership in rural Ontario. Quebec's government railway in the 1870s, the Quebec, Montreal, Ottawa and Occidental Railway, offered printing and advertising contracts to La Minerve, Le Canadien, the Montreal Gazette, and Le Nouveau Monde—in fact the railway commission's Montreal office was owned by Alphonse Desjardins of Le Nouveau Monde.[17] When Martin Griffin, the Mail's editor, accepted the post of parliamentary librarian at Ottawa in 1885, he was merely following in the footsteps of many a loyal journalist who found peace and comfort in the provincial or federal civil service. Government departments typically preferred to release news first to representatives of friendly journals, a habit which caused J.E.B. McCready (the *Globe*'s correspondent in the 1880s) a lot of trouble.[18] The *Monetary Times* (21 August 1891) reported a peculiar arrangement whereby half the profits resulting from a paper contract between the New England Paper Co. and the Ottawa government 'should be applied towards the extinction of a debt due by *La Presse* newspaper, though the agreement does not appear to have been carried into effect.' In 1897 William Templeman of the Victoria *Times* was called to the Senate, like many a publisher before and after. In 1901 Laurier helped to persuade Toronto money-men to lend Berthiaume some $300,000 to consolidate his paper's debts.[19] Sufficient evidence has come to light, then, to show that the happiness of a journalist, be he reporter or publisher, could depend upon the assistance of friendly politicians.

What services did the journalist offer in return? First, the party organ acted as a newsletter, publishing news about friends or foes—necessary to keep partisans abreast of what was happening within the party, what conspiracies the other side had concocted, where politics was going. During any election campaign that information was vital to victory, the news because it enabled a quick response to, say, an enemy gambit and the views because they could be used by local candidates on the hustings to win over voters.

Second, the organ was a devout booster of the party leader, the rank and file, and their cause. Always, the journalist should strive to bolster morale: 'Say something to encourage our people and inspire them to work,' A.S. Hardy (premier of Ontario) urged Willison in the midst of the provincial election campaign of 1898.[20] In victory the organ gloated, telling all readers right had triumphed[21]; in defeat the organ counselled courage and perseverance, sure evil would fail in the end.[22] The party leader, whoever he might be, was the recipient of constant adulation, his ego often stroked with detailed reports of his comings and goings plus effusive editorials praising his works. The virtues of the party's policies were repeated ad nauseam and its traditions reinterpreted to suit circumstances, which gave both parties an important intellectual gloss. Best of all, the boosterism of the party journalist meant that the party could always count on powerful champions, no matter how gross the actions of leaders or followers, an attribute of political life especially striking when the Pacific Scandal and other such news of corruption surfaced. (Defending the party might produce some extraordinary editorials—a classic instance was *La Minerve*'s efforts to calm French-Canadian anger over the Riel execution late in November 1885—as editors scrambled to explain away what seemed patently unacceptable to the public.)

Third, the organ served as a censurer—of the enemy mostly. 'Bite someone or something occasionally just to show that you want to hurt somebody now and then,' was another of Hardy's maxims.[23] Sometimes the enemy was within, as in the case of D'Alton McCarthy (the renegade Conservative) whose support for Tariff Reform led the Toronto *Empire* to read him out of the party late in 1892. Much more often, though, abuse and ridicule were showered on the opposing leader (Macdonald was stereotyped a corruptionist, Blake a moral coward)[24] and his policies or views, always dangerous to the public interest. Indeed, the chief editorial focus of the major organs was normally on the manifold sins of the enemy. All in all, a network of newspapers seemed essential to give the party substance, to make it a community of ideas and interests as well as a formidable foe able to compete in the game of politics.

No wonder politicians occasionally cracked the whip. A misbehaving journalist could not be allowed to get off scot-free. In 1892 leading Liberals, primarily Oliver Mowat (premier of Ontario), engineered the removal of Edward Farrer, of annexationist fame, from his editorial chair at the *Globe*. An erring newspaper soon found its patronage cut off. Chapleau withdrew provincial patronage from Tarte's *Le Canadien* early in 1882 because of the paper's ultramontane leanings; the dispute ended amicably a year later when Tarte returned to the party fold.[25] The Toronto *Mail*, while Conservative the beneficiary of hefty advertising contracts, lost these in the late 1880s and early 1890s during its years of mugwumpery. In 1891 Mercier's men threatened disaster for Quebec City's *La Justice*: unless it submitted to the *parti national*, the paper would lose its right to publish on *L'Électeur*'s printing presses.[26]

Sometimes a politician actually sponsored a newcomer to challenge or replace an erstwhile friend. Macdonald did this three times in Toronto: the *Atlas* (1858), the *Mail* (1872), and the *Empire* (1888). In 1883 Mercier and his cohorts launched Montreal's *Le Temps* because *La Patrie* refused to accept Mercier's leadership—Beaugrand's surrender was soon followed by the death of *Le Temps*.[27] Late in 1895, Laurier and other Liberal chieftains appear to have inspired the birth of Montreal's *La Bataille*, again to argue properly the Liberal case, moderate to the core, when *La Patrie* would not.[28]

The actual management of the views and news of the press required close attention. Now and then, the politicians themselves acted as directors to censor the opinions of an organ: Laurier served for a brief time at *L'Électeur* in the early 1880s and G.W. Ross (eventually a Liberal premier of Ontario) did the same at the *Globe* during the next decade. Mostly, though, the politician stayed away from direct involvement but devoted much time to guiding his favourite organs. Macdonald was a master of this art. His correspondence is full of letters pertinent to the problems of press management. Once, while in Washington to assist in the negotiation of an Anglo-American accord, he sent off a letter to a crony urging him to arrange with 'the friendly newspapers' a trap for Brown and the Liberals in the forthcoming debate over the agreement.[29] In 1872 he was in constant communication with T.C. Paterson over matters large and small, both the handling of the National Policy and the hiring of assorted journalists. Throughout the mid-1870s, he and Thomas White exchanged letters on the *Gazette* and the Montreal scene. In 1886 Macdonald tried in vain to curtail the anti-Catholic 'incendiarism' of the *Mail* under the management of C.W. Bunting and Edward Farrer.[30] So it went. Even a devoted tactician such as Macdonald must have found the task of guiding his newspapers, at times, a tedious chore.

Willison's correspondence of the 1890s sheds light on the problem from the journalist's point of view. Because Willison was editor of the country's premier Liberal organ, he received guidance from everywhere. Sometimes the matter was important: during 1895 and 1896 J.D. Cameron, Manitoba's provincial secretary, pressured Willison to ensure the *Globe* did not compromise Manitoba's stand on public schools. Often the matter was very minor: late in 1897 Richard Cartwright (a federal minister) asked for an editorial which would sooth Lord Strathcona (Donald Smith, the CPR magnate) who was angry at some reflections on himself in an earlier *Globe*. Willison, of course, had many more dealings with the party leaders. Laurier's letters, as befitted a man who had taken up Macdonald's mantle, were a judicious blend of praise and understanding but always loaded with suggestions and sometimes mild complaint when the *Globe* seemed at odds with the party good. Only rarely were his missives full of iron when Willison proved too presumptuous. The issues discussed could be weighty, pertaining to the tariff, racial discord, party unity, and the like. There was, at times, a real exchange of views between the two men. By contrast, the letters of A.S. Hardy were full of niggling advice and much criticism, clearly reflecting the belief that the *Globe* was not fulfilling its tasks as a party organ. Hardy even took it upon himself to question the *Globe*'s style of reporting![31] In both cases, of course, the party leader was the master and Willison the servant. Willison might disagree, and a compromise might be arranged, but he clearly was not his own man. The duty of the party journalist was, at bottom, to obey.

This duty could become very irksome. Even the long-suffering Patteson once exploded. In May 1875 he received a remonstrance from Cobourg's Conservatives, who felt slighted because a full report of a local banquet had not appeared in the *Mail*. That was too much. Patteson had printed for private development a long letter explaining the difficulties of running an effective party organ. He specifically repudiated 'the right of any section of the Liberal-Conservative party to interfere with the management of this newspaper, or to dictate what should receive preference among the many things *all* of which it is impossible to publish.' He satirized the presumption that 'it is a very easy task to run a paper, to please everybody bent on self-glorification and to do justice alike to all Conservatives,' an especially quarrelsome bunch it seemed. Sadly, he concluded that it was his lot in life to 'offend a larger or smaller number of persons every day, and bear the brunt of it in addition to the other labours devolving on him.' All this he did for 'an inadequate salary.'[32]

The more sensitive Willison eventually, if briefly, broke free from party fetters. The *Globe*'s success had made him a person of some influence in party councils. But throughout the 1890s he had tried to turn the *Globe* into a more impartial, and complete, record of politics, though still very Liberal in its views. That course might win him kudos from other journalists, but not from politicians however (and notably Premier Hardy). What seemed a crescendo of party criticism, a persistent desire to reincarnate Brown's *Globe*, exasperated Willison and offended his sense of amour propre. 'Personally I resent the assumption of every Liberal politician that I am his hired man, that he has the right to dictate or shape my course as a journalist,' he wrote angrily to Clifford Sifton in 1901. 'I claim as much freedom as any other Liberal.'[33] Partly, the outburst grew out of Willison's conviction that he deserved gratitude, not criticism: Willison was addicted to adulation. Partly, too, it reflected a disdain for the abilities of the little men who always carped: Willison was something of an intellectual snob. Most of all, though, it was the cry of a man who loved his profession and found he could not realize his ideal journalism in a party context. Little wonder that late in 1902 he resigned from the *Globe* to seize the opportunity offered by Joseph Flavelle to edit an avowedly independent Toronto *News*. Willison swiftly became the scourge of what he called 'the theory of hereditary partisanship, and the remarkable notion that loyalty to a party leader is as sacred an obligation as loyalty to king and country.'[34] The ultimate irony, of course, was that the *News* experiment proved an expensive flop, the paper soon falling into Conservative hands and Willison returning to the ranks of party journalists but now on the other side of the fence.

Willison's experiences were not altogether unique. There were some journalists loyal to a fault. Witness Ernest Pacaud, publisher of *L'Élec-teur*, which aptly lived up to its boast as the 'Organe des Libéraux du district de Québec,' or David Creighton, manager of the Toronto *Em-pire*, which came to represent to contemporaries the acme of party journalism. Yet no matter how extensive the connections between party and press, politicians were never able to turn journalists as a group into their docile tools. Journalists did dissent and occasionally 'kick over the traces,' whether moved by principle, profit, or plain cro-chetyness.

Take first the example of the independent dailies. Their support for any politician or party was always qualified by the notion that the press must be a tribune of the public and so an adversary of the powerful. The intransigent Protestant moralism of the Montreal *Witness* ensured it would remain an ally of dubious merit, often full of bile, for the Liberal party in Catholic Quebec. After 1878 Gra-ham's *Star* combined strong support of the Conservative cause at election time with sometimes harsh criticism of Conservative prac-tices between elections. Robertson's *Telegram* may have moved into the Conservative camp by the late 1880s, but the paper's jingoism and nativism made it a constant nag, no doubt something of a thorn in the side of Macdonald and his successors. Maclean's *World* flirted first with Blake's Liberals, later with Macdonald's Conservatives (where the money was), yet never gave up its freedom to argue eccentric causes. The Toronto *Mail*'s effort to voice the revolt of the 'classes' turned it into a critic of nearly every politician. Likewise, *L'Étendard*'s ultramontane fervour, at least during most of the 1880s, meant it would never wholly trust any political figure or anything as secular as a party. In 1893 and 1894, *Le Monde*'s devotion to the ideas of democracy and nationality brought it into sympathy with Mercier, a by then discredited politician whose corrupt practices were condemned by both parties (though the paper continued to receive federal advertising contracts throughout). The declared independence of these dailies, then, did have some substance, if not always as much as they might boast.

Equally important was a persistent factionalism in the ranks of the rest of the press, outside of the thoroughly disciplined organs that is. Factionalism was an ever-present reality of party journalism in French Quebec, really a reflection of that penchant for feuding common among French-Canadian politicians. Around 1880 Tarte's ultramontanism, for instance, made *Le Canadien* a critic of the opportunist views of the dominant Chapleau faction in the provincial Conservative party. In 1886 *La Presse*, though supposedly in Conservative hands, flirted for a time with Mercier's *parti national*, perhaps to ensure a refuge for Chapleau should he decide that events warranted leaving the Macdonald cabinet over the Riel execution. During the late 1880s, Quebec's *La Justice* voiced the aims of the so-called Conservative-Nationalists who were sometimes uneasy members of Mercier's Liberal-dominated coalition government. In 1896 *La Presse*, on the verge of independence, became a severe critic of 'la faction ultra-tory' of Ontario's Conservative party, since its nativism imperilled Confederation. Off and on, Beaugrand's *La Patrie* was at loggerheads with Liberal chieftains at home and in Ottawa because of the newspaper's yearning for the old *rouge* causes of separation of church and state or annexation to the United States.

But there were also many mavericks in the less heated politics of English Canada. A disgruntled Toronto *Leader*, feeling abandoned by its tory friends in the mid-1870s, challenged the alliance of Catholic Quebec and Orange Ontario on which the Conservative party still counted for success. During the early 1880s, the Conservative Quebec *Chronicle* strenuously objected to the pro-Montreal bias of the province's Conservative governments. At the end of the decade, the Ottawa *Citizen* (influenced by the fact that Catholics were a significant local force) rejected the nativist views of the provincial Conservatives, under William Meredith, who were trying to ride into office on the Protestant horse. The Winnipeg press was especially prone to breakaways: the *Times*, a Conservative organ, was much upset with the Macdonald government in 1883 because of its new tariff on agricultural implements; the *Manitoba Free Press* split with the Liberal Greenway government in the late 1880s over its railway policies; the *Tribune*, very Liberal in provincial politics, never quite trusted a federal party led by the French-Canadian Laurier and controlled by Ontario men. And in British Columbia, where party politics was not properly introduced into the local scene until the late 1890s, newspapers could shift, apparently at leisure, from one group of politicians to another.

Far more threatening to the party's rule, though, were the new conventions of journalism fostered by the maturing of the daily press. The purblind partisanship of days gone by no longer fitted the dignity of so vigorous a fourth estate, a point reiterated by the *Printer and Publisher*. 'Many a bright man has had his patriotism crushed to powder by the stern onslaughts of a press dominated by party feelings and prejudices,' it told journalists. That was a disgrace to 'modern newspaperdom.'[35] Besides, 'the tendency of politicians (both sides) was to make use of the press without adequate return,' the journal warned.[36] Better to deal with politicians in the same fashion as any other supplicants for press publicity. Usually, Willison is credited with leading the daily press toward a more impartial style of political reporting, though in fact other publishers and editors were also moving in the 1890s to free their news columns of blatant bias. Indeed, even on the editorial pages, the public men of the 1890s were more likely than their predecessors have been to receive fair treatment. The failure of outright organs such as the Toronto *Empire* and *La Minerve* was taken as proof that the party-dominated daily had gone for good (which, by the way, was not correct). The public and the advertiser expected the newspaper to espouse the ideal of community service, not just party service. A few dailies actually experimented with political neutrality: during the federal election campaign of 1900, for example, the Ottawa *Journal* opened a column to Conservatives and Liberals, reserving the editorial page for criticism of instances of excessive partisanship and eventually (on 6 November 1900) admitted its liability to make a clear choice between the combatants. The business imperative balanced the dictates of party fealty, a change which Walter Nichol of the Vancouver *Province* praised as a laudable feature of the modern age.[37] That was the key. The politician, whatever his influence over individual journalists, could not fully control what was now an industry.

Not surprisingly, the very institution of party did come under attack in the press. During the late 1870s and early 1880s, the anti-party cause was a prominent aspect of the Radicalism sponsored by the people's journals of English Canada. Less often, the occasional *nationaliste* paper in French Canada, say *L'Union Nationale* in the late 1860s or *Le Monde* in the mid-1890s, would provide a reasoned critique of the party system. Any newspaper declaration of independence, of course, produced an obligatory denunciation of the evils of partyism. Critics charged that parties lacked any firm grounding in principle and were held together only by a lust for the spoils of office: the result was the dominance of 'machine' politicians, corruption in high places, needless appeals to racial and sectarian animosities, and on and on. The litany of sins placed at the door of party conveyed the impression that it was, in fact, the enemy of all things good. Remedies varied: an organization of independent voters (Montreal *Star*), electing every official in sight (Toronto *News*), a political realignment (Winnipeg *Sun*), a new party (Farrer's *Mail*). The common hope was to destroy partyism, 'the madness of the many for the gain of the few' (Toronto *Telegram*, 29 January 1887). None of the remedies proved especially practical, though. Indeed, the experience of third parties such as the Equal Rights Association or the Patrons of Industry suggested that things were better left as they were. That accounted for the declining vigour of the anti-party cause during the 1890s, even among the self-declared independents. The rhetoric of anti-partyism remained useful as a means of expressing indignation, not fostering change.

Besides, the stream of abuse had elicited an even more convincing defence of the party system from Liberal and Conservative apologists. Whatever the ills of partyism, parties were vital instruments of political organization, necessary else government would become the plaything of transient factions. (A party 'includes a leader who must be a superior man; a following of trained intelligences which in turn lead the people; defined principles; a well understood plan of progress; and all combined for the good of the country according to the principles accepted as the best.')[38] Besides, the two-party system had history and nature behind its existence. The Liberal-Conservative dichotomy was entrenched in the British constitution and its Canadian offshoot. That opposition was 'an expression of human character,' a conflict rooted in 'human nature' between those who yearned for change and those who wished to preserve.[39] The editorial pages of party dailies, sometimes independent papers as well, often reflected on the special attributes of the two parties. So the Conservative apologist made much of the claim that his was a party tradition and progress and patriotism locked in combat with an enemy which was dangerously radical, too parochial, pro-American but anti-national, even irreligious. His Liberal foe replied that his was the party of liberty, always on the side of reform, menaced by a tory enemy imbued with the spirit of reaction and bent on creating privileges. The variations in this imagery were legion. But, always, the apologist linked his celebration of his party with a dark picture of the enemy. That publicity gave the two-party system a solid foundation in myth essential to its survival in the new democracy. Here again the daily press had played a central role in legitimizing the patterns of authority.

Notes

1   See Colin Seymour-Ure's *The Political Impact of Mass Media* (London 1974), especially 156-201, for an excellent discussion of this symbiosis.

2   J.S. Willison, 'Journalism and Public Life in Canada,' *Canadian Magazine* (October 1905) 554.

3   Laurier to M. Jerome, 12 August 1901, cited in H. Blair Neatby, *Laurier and a Liberal Quebec: A Study in Political Management* (Toronto, 1973), 158.

4   Charlesworth, *Candid Chronicles* (Toronto 1925), 19.

5   Montreal *Herald*, 23 March 1896.

6   1 September 1898.

7   *L'Électeur*, 10 April 1885.

8   Cited in Beaulieu and Hamelin, *La Presse québécoise*, vol. 2, 189.

9   *Ibid.*, vol. 3, 45.

10 Hammond, 'Ninety Years of the Globe,' Ontario Archives, 214.

11 See R.A. Hill, 'A Note on Newspaper Patronage in Canada during the Late 1850s and Early 1860s,' *CHR*, 49 (March 1968) 44-59.

12 Norman Ward, 'The Press and the Patronage: An Exploratory Operation,' in J.H. Atchison, editor, *The Political Process in Canada. Essays in Honour of R. McGregor Dawson* (Toronto, 1963), 8.

13 I am indebted to Brian Beaven for this example.

14 Undated clipping (from the Montreal *Gazette*) and note, Dougall Papers (vol. 5).

15 Willison to Clifford Sifton, 29 January 1901, cited in A.H.U. Colquhon, *Press, Politics and People: The Life and Letters of Sir John Willison, Journalist and Correspondent of The Times* (Toronto, 1935), 98.

16 Buchanan to Patteson, 19 February 1872, Patteson Papers.

17 Young, *Promoters and Politicians*, 91.

18 McCready, 'The Special Correspondent,' *Canadian Magazine* (October 1907) 548-552.

19 Heintzman, 'The Struggle for Life,' 52.

20 'Memo for Mr. Willison,' included with Hardy to Willison, 8 February 1898, Willison Papers.

21 For instance this comment from *Le Nouveau Monde*, 17 February 1880: 'Chaque élection nouvelle est l'occasion d'un nouveau triomphe pour les conservateurs. Quand les libéraux dégringolent du pouvoir, ils tombent à plat, l'opinion publique les déserte comme des péstiférés et ils se trouvent bientôt reduits à leur plus simple expression.'

22 For instance this comment from *La Patrie*, 3 December 1881: 'En attendant, libéraux, chacun a son porte. Dans ces jours de crise et d'affollement populaire, restons eximer et attendons avec confiance l'heure de la rétribution.'

23 'Memo for Mr. Willison.'

24 Note this little bit of abuse from *La Minerve*, 25 June 1896: 'Laurier est, par ses études et ses préférences bien connues, anglo-saxon de langue, d'idées, de tendances et d'esthétique; il est canadien-français par un pur et regrettable accident.'

25 LaPierre 'Joseph Israel Tarte,' 121-125.

26 Rumilly, *Histoire de la province de Québec*, vol. 6, 214-215.

27 Beaulieu and Hamelin, *La presse québécoise*, vol. 3, 80.

28 *Ibid.*, 355. *La Bataille* disappeared in March 1896.

29 Macdonald to Alexander Morris, 21 April 1871, reproduced in Joseph Pope, *Correspondence of Sir John A. Macdonald* (Oxford, 1921), 145.

30 Macdonald to Bunting, 25 May 1886, reproduced in *ibid.*, 380.

31 Hardy to Willison, 16 August 1898, Willison Papers.

32 11 May 1875, Patteson Papers.

33 Willison to Sifton, 29 January 1901, cited in Colquhon, *Press, Politics and People* (Toronto, 1935), 99.

34 Willison, 'Journalism and Public Life in Canada,' 555.

35 January 1894, 2.

36 January 1897, 1.

37 Bruce, *News and the Southams* (Toronto 1968), 165-166.

38 Toronto, *Mail*, 26 July 1880. The *Mail* did admit this ideal was never quite realized in practice.

39 Respectively in the Halifax *Citizen*, 14 September 1872, and the Halifax *Chronicle*, 6 December 1894.

John English The End of the Great Party Era

> We cannot return to the days when the people and even the
> parliaments knew nothing of what was going on behind
> their backs until they were asked to give their lives to vindi-
> cate the bargains of the diplomats. All that is past....
>
> Craig Forrester in Douglas Durkin, *The Magpie*

J.W. Dafoe and Craig Forrester took their places on opposite sides of
Winnipeg's barricades; nevertheless, both agreed in one respect: the
Unionist experiment, however brief, had been a decisive moment in
Canadian political and party history. The events of 1917, Dafoe later
wrote, marked 'both an end and a beginning to what might be called
the era of the Great Parties.' The 'efforts at the realignment of parties,
the attempt to newly appraise political values, and to redefine political
relationships...[were] testimony to the dissolving, penetrating power of
the impulses of 1917.'[1]

Dafoe recognized that Unionism was a much wider stream than
merely a conduit for Canadian pre-war sentiment. Even in the absence of war one might have expected a movement similar in tone
if not in intensity. The rapid economic growth, the flood of immigrants, urbanization and the consequent depopulation of rural Canada, broke down traditional allegiances, disrupted local communities, and promoted social disturbance. The turmoil of 1914-18 accelerated these tendencies; it did not give birth to them. Writing
on German unification in the nineteenth century, Robert M. Berdahl has argued: 'The process of economic modernization involves
a radical transformation of the traditional structure of an agrarian
society. It involves the destruction of an older social order in which
the bonds of individual loyalty and dependency are based on personal and local obligation; it requires the creation of a new society
in which individuals become highly dependent on many others from
whom they are far removed personally and geographically.' In the
face of the resulting disintegration, nationalism 'acts as a force for
the reintegration of society.'[2] Berdahl further claimed that nationalism as an ideology as distinct from an idea is functional: 'It serves
a definite purpose of elites, as, for example, furthering economic
development or binding a community together during a period of
social upheaval.' In David Apter's words, it forms 'the link between

action and fundamental belief.'[3]

Union government reflected the aims of what Apter would term a 'nationalizing elite,' English Canadian in origin and deeply concerned with the need to bind together a fragmented Canadian community.[4] To attribute 'the clash' between French and English Canada solely to cultural differences is unsatisfactory. This cultural differential has been a factor since the beginning of the nineteenth century but the degree of antagonism has varied immensely. Moreover, modern studies of nationalism show that there is no intrinsic reason why regional loyalty must necessarily conflict with national loyalty.[5] Cultural reasons alone are therefore insufficient explanation for the variation in the degree of hostility between English and French Canada. The analysis of the preceding chapters suggests that prior to the First World War the community of interests, which in the absence of a common culture binds a nation together, no longer obtained in Canada.[6] Ontario had become an urbanized province with a new industrial élite which possessed close economic, cultural, and social ties with the 'new west.' French Canada, however, continued to exalt the values of a traditional society and, in response to the aggressive character of Anglo-Canadian nationalism, had developed its own kind of nationalist expression. As a result, the equilibrium which had permitted French Canadians to accept the existence of a community of interest with English Canada gradually disappeared. Yet not only French Canada shunned the new nationalism: the Maritimes, the oldest English provinces which the new immigrants avoided and where economic stagnancy seemed permanent, also baffled the Unionists.[7] So, too, did rural Ontario where only a blatant political bribe purchased the loyalty of the Ontario farmer in December 1917. These ineffable political realities punctured the integrative vision of Unionism's 'nationalizing élite,' but not before the Canadian party system was changed fundamentally.

The traditional party system, based upon, in Berdahl's terms, 'the bonds of individual loyalty and dependency,' could not survive the nationalizing influence of the 1917 campaign; no longer did constituency boundaries and interests define the party contest. National politics did matter: individuals, again in Berdahl's terms, became 'highly dependent on many others from whom they are far removed personally and geographically.' The venerable patterns of constituency politics, which industrialization, urbanization, and immigration already threatened, crumbled as new pressure groups and leaders replaced traditional party structures in the organization of the campaign. About this, Borden had few regrets, and, with the help of others, he moved to assure the endurance of this fresh political landscape. In accomplishing this, nothing was so important as the reform of the federal civil service. The fulfilment of this campaign pledge exceeded even its proponents' hopes: '...The sense of the uniqueness of the opportunity this [coalition government] provided gave strength to the reformer's broom which swept in a wide and ruthless arc, to leave the newly constituted [Civil Service Commission] in full legal command of personnel administration throughout the entire civil service.'[8] In a stroke, the reformer's broom swept away what observers from Siegfried through Skelton had regarded as the life-blood of the Canadian party system.

Local Conservatives and many members of Parliament regarded the sudden removal of patronage—the most potent lever at the constituency level—as sheer robbery, and Robert Rogers led them in a futile but persistent resistance to the theft. An illustration of what happened and what they objected to can be seen in the correspondence between Arthur Meighen and his Portage la Prairie 'bagman,' Jack Garland. On 25 May 1918 Garland wrote to Meighen requesting a small favour of the type so readily granted by Canadian politicians since Confederation: 'I am told that Harry Johns has sent in his resignation as caretaker of the Post Office. If such is the case do you think there would be any chance for Chas. Gordon. Gordon, as you know, after he was dismissed by the [Liberal] local government, went out farming and met with an accident which has left him for all time unable to do hard work, was in Jacket for nearly a year and he is the very sort of man to look after a position such as this in his condition.' Here was a rich opportunity to reward a party man and to win goodwill, an important political commodity in a small town like Portage la Prairie. Meighen's private secretary therefore forwarded Garland's letter to Public Works Minister Carvell with a note asking him to do all that was possible to meet the request from 'a very close friend of Mr. Meighen.' On 29 May B.K. Dibbee, Carvell's secretary, replied: 'In the absence of Mr. Carvell, I beg to acknowledge receipt of your favour of the 28th instant regarding the position of Caretaker at the Post Office at Portage la Prairie. These positions are now filled through the Civil Service Commission, and Mr. Gordon should be advised to apply to them and take the necessary examinations.' Meighen's irritated secretary wrote at once to the chairman of the Civil Service Commission, W.J. Roche, a former Conservative minister and a fellow Manitoban. Roche's reply was friendlier than Dibbee's but the substance was the same: commission regulations could not be breached whatever Meighen's fate in Portage la Prairie might be. Charles Gordon did not become the caretaker of the Portage la Prairie post office.[9]

While Meighen did not join Rogers in the latter's implacable resistance to the new political order, he, like many other Conservatives, quietly lamented many of the changes, not least because of their impact upon his political future. To a friend he voiced his frustration with the constraints which Union government imposed upon its members: 'I am down here pretty much alone, so far as the west from our old standpoint is concerned. I cannot take the course that a Minister could take under old conditions, and consequently I cannot engage the party support which it has all along been possible to engage.'[10] Political men could not behave in what they thought was proper political fashion; the government of men seemed to have become mainly the administration of things.

Without the tie of patronage, limited by the nature of coalition government, and with the party press almost mute, Unionist members found themselves isolated from their constituencies. But many Canadian politicians escaped these afflictions, and this fact more than any other fuelled Rogers' assault on Union government. On a very practical level, Liberalism in its various guises was the prime beneficiary of the Unionist reforms. Federally, Union government meant that the Liberals, for the first time since 1911, had a share of federal advertising, judicial work, and appointments, from the judiciary to the poll clerks. When they did not get their share, they complained vigorously.[11] What exasperated Conservatives was not so much the sharing of federal patronage but rather the Liberal control of patronage in the provinces where the dent of reform was almost invisible.

After the fall of the Hearst Conservatives in Ontario in 1919 the Tories held not a single province, and the importance of this in the collapse of the Conservative-dominated Union government should not be underestimated. In Nova Scotia, for example, most federal patronage passed through the hands of the Unionist minister, A.K. Maclean, into the control of the powerful Liberal machine of Premier George Murray. But although Murray received a fair share of the federal patronage, the provincial patronage was reserved exclusively for Liberals. Not surprisingly, the provincial Tories were outraged. Thus, when a Nova Scotia Tory was asked for his explanation for the Conservative débâcle in the 1921 federal election, he pointed out that his friends had been 'sullen and resentful because they felt the old Conservatives had been sacrificed.' This, 'even more than hard times and war discontent, was responsible for the horrible showing we made here.'[12] Another Nova Scotian, F.B. McCurdy, the public works minister in the Meighen ministry, echoed these complaints. Federal civil service reform, he gently chided Borden, 'is certainly unsuited to Nova Scotia where the local provincial government continues to care for its supporters.' McCurdy added, not as criticism but as analysis, that as much as 10 per cent of the electorate drew 'emoluments' or received 'recognition' in some way or another from the province.[13] It was, very simply, a way of life that Nova Scotians of both parties expected to continue. And, in a few years, McCurdy and his friends did reap their rewards.

What had changed, however, was both the rewards and the manner of their disposition, and it is in this respect that the Unionist experience left enduring results. There are, Peter Clark and James Q. Wilson have argued,[14] three kinds of rewards which political parties can use to attract support and party workers: material, solidary, and purposive. The first describes patronage in the popular sense: jobs, contracts, career incentives, and the like, whether legally permissible or otherwise. The second refers to the 'sense of fellowship' one derives from association with like-minded individuals. The third is ideological reward: the party is seen to further or represent ideals to which an individual strongly adheres. In the case of material rewards, the provincial governments and, therefore, the provincial parties controlled most after 1917. This was in part the result of Union government and its reforms and in part a reflection of the character of Canadian social and economic development. Prior to the war, Clifford Sifton's 'army'—the immigration agents and officers—swarmed about the west performing public and party service. The railways, so dependent on the politicians' aid, threw themselves into the political fray, often on both sides. But during the war and after, immigrants no longer found much welcome on Canada's shores and plains, and the railways which had brought them here had, in many cases, been nationalized and 'politically purified' by the Union government. Inevitably, with the end of the war, the federal government ceased its dominant role in Canadian economic life. In the provinces, however, new tasks abounded. The proud owners of Buicks, Reos, and, of course, Fords demanded new and better roads; the millions who made their homes in Canada's cities sought the amenities of modern life; and these were generally the responsibilities of the provinces. So too were the natural resources whose rapid exploitation continued in peace as in war.

As a result of these broadened functions, the provincial governments became, in Christopher Armstrong's words, 'semi-independent principalities treating with one another and the federal government.'[15] Provincial parties established a similar and related independence and, indeed, paramountcy. With the reduction of federal patronage, the breakdown of federal party lines, and the wider ambit of provincial governments, the opportunity for Ottawa to interfere with, much less control, provincial parties diminished. In comparison with pre-war days, one might say that the party's heart was cut off from the arteries and other vital organs. In this sense, one can appreciate Meighen's complaints that he felt 'all alone' at Ottawa, and McCurdy's yearning to return to the old system of political appointment, 'a non-rigid system with a human touch...in which all affected had a voice.'[16] Without adequate material rewards, Unionism depended upon 'purposive' incentives, and these, quite simply, were not enough.

Union government also broke down the 'solidary' fellowship of the Conservative party. The popularity of Bob Rogers' 'smokers,' at which, during wartime prohibition, one could find good whisky as well as good tobacco, is also explained by the opportunity which these occasions gave to Conservatives to feel comfortable and to have their prejudices confirmed while meeting with old friends. This was not the atmosphere of Unionist gatherings where suspicion mingled uneasily with solemnity. Many went elsewhere, some to the new political groupings where purposive incentives did apply. The most notable of these groupings was the Progressive party which harnessed western Canadian feelings of resentment and made a specific sectional appeal in contrast to the characteristically general appeal of the traditional parties. But the most significant and lasting example of party commitment born of a spirit of resentment, perhaps even of vengeance, occurred not in the west but in Quebec. Not long after Meighen replaced Borden, the former Tory organizer Sir William Price gave a melancholy summary of Quebec politics to his new leader: 'It must be understood that today in this Province the Liberal Party is looked upon by its adherents as the Party of French Canadians—in other words as a National Party.'[17] The emotion lingered, accompanied by a lasting distrust of 'centralization' and of Union government's heir, the Conservative party. Against a party commitment of this nature, material incentives could make no headway. This was, perhaps, Unionism's most fateful legacy.

In those earlier days when Borden was fashioning the Unionist coalition, he believed he was fathering a party which would transcend the variety of Canadian political cultures, a party which would define and indeed represent a definable national interest. Harking back to a tradition as old as the English Civil War which declared party and public interest to be antithetical, Unionism proposed to abolish party by declaring itself the embodiment of the public interest.[18] But between this idea and the reality fell far too many shadows—the bitterness of the disenfranchised, the outrage of the French Canadian, the promises unfulfilled—and these shadows fell darkly along the path that future Conservative politicians would have to tread.

It was, however, not only the Conservative party but also Canadian federalism and the Canadian party system which bore the consequences. Rather than strengthening the nation state, the attempt to end partyism instead reduced the possibility for national action. 'National government' became, to too many Canadians, a symbol not of innovation and creativity but of domination by an arrogant majority. Thereafter they would prefer the muddle, the contradictions, and the ambiguities of brokerage and consensus politics. In this Mackenzie King had no equal. Thus the Union government which divided us most was succeeded by that prime minister who would divide us least.

Notes

1 J.W. Dafoe, *Laurier: A Study in Canadian Politics* (Toronto, 1922), 176, 180.

2 'New Thoughts on German Nationalism,' *American Historical Review*, LXXVII (Feb. 1972), 75, 76.

3 *The Politics of Modernization* (Chicago, 1965), 314.

4 *Ibid.*, and Karl Deutsch, *Nationalism and Social Communication* (New York, 1953), 18-20.

5 The following is much influenced by David Potter, 'The Historian's Use of Nationalism and Vice Versa,' *American Historical Review*, LXVII (July 1962), 924-950.

6 Potter writes, 'There is certainly at least one other important factor besides common culture which may bind an aggregate of individuals together, and this is community of interest, not in the narrow sense of economic advantage only, but in the broad sense of welfare and security through membership in society.' *Ibid.*, 935.

7   Census figures indicate this most dramatically (percentage of total Canadian population for the three Maritime provinces at 1871, 1881, 1911 and 1921 respectively): Prince Edward Island: 2.55, 2.25, 1.30, and 1.01; Nova Scotia: 10.51, 9.32, 6.83, 5.96; New Brunswick: 7.74, 6.65, 4.88, 4.41. *Sixth Census of Canada, 1921* (Ottawa, 1924), 1, 3.

8   J.E. Hodgetts, *et al.*, *The Biography of an Institution* (Montreal and London, 1972), 50.

9   Garland to Meighen, 25 May, Mitchell to Carvell, 28 May, Dibbee to Mitchell, 29 May, Mitchell to Roche, 30 May, Roche to Mitchell, 31 May 1918, PAC, Meighen Papers, v. 42.

10   Meighen to Staples, 21 Nov. 1918, *ibid.*, v. 2.

11   See, for example, PAC , Borden Papers (BP), Borden Diary, 15 Sept. 1918.

12   William Hall to Meighen, 10 Feb. 1922, Meighen Papers, v. 67.

13   McCurdy to Borden, 21 Dec. 1921, BP v. 277.

14   'Incentive Systems,' *Administrative Science Quarterly*, VI (1961), 129-166.

15   christopher Armsrong, 'The Politics of Federalism: Ontario's Relations with the Federal Government, 1896-1941,' unpublished Ph.D. thesis, University of Toronto, 1972, 2. See also H.V. Nelles, *The Politics of Development* (Toronto, 1974). Nelles argues in a similar vein and concludes that the provincial government became a 'client' of business interests.

16   McCurdy to Borden, 21 Dec. 1921, BP, v. 277.

17   Price to Meighen, 29 Dec. 1920, Meighen Papers, v. 44.

18   On the anti-party tradition, see Richard Hofstadter, *The Idea of a Party System* (Berkeley and Los Angeles, 1969), chap. 1; and Austin Ranney, *Curing the Mischiefs of Faction* (Berkeley and Los Angeles, 1975), 22-57.

PART 2   The Second Party System

The period from the end of the First World War to the Diefenbaker revolution was the era of classic regional brokerage in Canadian politics. The parties that emerged and crystallized were quite different from those of the first half of the century and they differed from one another. The Liberals became what Reg Whitaker called *The Government Party*; the Conservatives suffered from *The Tory Syndrome* (as George Perlin named it) in permanent opposition; and a variety of third parties broke the hold of the two old parties which had monopolized the first party system.

The first reading presents in summary form Whitaker's brilliant analysis of the role of the Liberal party as the preeminent vehicle for accommodating the demands and needs of what had become, in electoral terms, a four region country. In fact only the Liberals were equipped to play this brokerage role for only they commanded sufficient strength all across the country. The Conservatives (with the help of the electoral system) had been shut out of Quebec and had been pushed out of the prairies. It was in this context that protest parties of one sort or another disrupted the two-party system. It all meant that national elections were no longer genuinely nation-wide contests.

Joseph Wearing, John R. Williams, and Walter Young all reveal something of the politics of the second party system as well as the parties they are describing. In Wearing's piece on the Liberal party we see the development of new, national extra-parliamentary party organization, though the old caucus-based party was clearly uncertain of what role it might play or how new lines of intraparty authority would fit with responsible government. As Williams reveals, much of the formal apparatus of the national organization, at least in the Conservative case, bore "little resemblance to the actual operation of the party." In his sketch we see how the national party really worked. Finally, Young describes the essence of the Co-operative Commonwealth Federation(CCF), a party and a movement that rejected brokerage politics and dedicated itself "to more fundamental or value-oriented change." That sort of party could have only limited success in a party system whose primary latent function was accommodation and national consensus building.

It was the Liberals' 1919 national convention that called the new parties of the second system into being. That convention defined a policy agenda, established the new extra-parliamentary organizations, and selected a leader. This transformation of party—leader relations was especially critical given the important place leadership has always played in Canadian parties. The short excerpt by R.K. Carty speaks to this change. It is followed by Chubby Power's reminiscences of just what the Liberals' conventions were like. Few knew better than he. For many years Power was one of the party's premier political organizers, and he was a leadership candidate in 1948. Even this brief account of that contest is enough to reveal just how different the leadership politics and conventions of the second system parties were from those of our era.

Civil service reform during the First World War had marked the end of patronage, and inevitably the pattern of party and electoral finance changed too. The two readings that deal with this issue are both taken from contemporary accounts. In the first, written at the end of the second system, a political scientist named E.E. Harrill describes what the parties needed money for, and where and how they got it. Chubby Power provides a contemporary working politician's view of the problem of election spending and reiterates a number of suggestions he first made in the late 1930s for needed reforms. In fact it wouldn't be until the mid-1970s, after the report of the Barbeau *Committee on Election Expenses*, that some of these changes would finally be made.

One of the biggest challenges parties faced in the second system was that of communicating with supporters and voters. Gone were the days of the partisan press, and in its place parties faced a relatively nonpartisan multimedia society. Soderlund et al. describe this, but it is Whitaker's study that perhaps provides the best portrait of how the new world of mass advertising quickly embroiled the parties. Whitaker believes that this forced the parties to think harder about what and how and to whom they wanted to communicate. In doing so Canadian electoral competition began to shift, and prepare itself for the television politics of the third party system.

Ironically, the end of the second party system was signalled in much the same way as that of the first: by a massive Conservative landslide. At the time John Meisel used the metaphor of the "stalled omnibus" to describe what had happened. In a later essay he came to argue that there had been a decline in the role of parties and that they no longer played such a central part in the public life of the nation. In that essay he offered a number of explanations for what had happened without really trying to assign relative weight to them. In retrospect, the emergence of Federal-Provincial diplomacy stands out as probably the most important. It absorbed the tasks of regional accommodation which had been the primary latent function required of parties in the second party system. The third party system would make new demands of parties and so inevitably call new political parties into being.

R. Whitaker The Government Party

Environmental Constraints

The environmental constraints on the Liberal party would appear to have been dominated by three factors. The Canadian political system is liberal-democratic, which, as C.B. Macpherson has ably argued,[1] is a system characterized by a fundamental, or structural, ambiguity: the coexistence of the democratic and egalitarian values of the political institutions based on universal adult suffrage and the inegalitarian nature of the liberal capitalist economic structures upon which the political structures arose historically. The Liberal party was operating in an environment in which two sometimes contradictory forces were at work in shaping the party's role. On the one hand, the party had to finance its operations as a party as well as to manage a capitalist economy as a government, both of which left it vulnerable to the demands of the corporate capitalist world. On the other hand, the party had to get votes, which left it vulnerable to the demands of public opinion. Contradictions were not always in evidence between these two forces, but when they were the party was in a state of crisis. Crisis can mean not only danger but opportunity. The Liberal party demonstrated superior skill at calling in one of these forces to redress the balance when the other became too dominating. In the King period this often meant calling in the force of the voters to compensate for the opposition of private economic interests, but in the St. Laurent period it more often meant calling in the force of corporate capitalism to restrain and manage public opinion. In either event, both the political power of the voters and the economic power of corporate capitalism were in effect resources with which the party, as an intermediate force, could bargain. The ambiguity of this role was heightened, and even cultivated, by the ambiguous ideological role of the party fashioned by Mackenzie King. That the party never rejected the support of the vested capitalist interests, while at the same time never entirely losing its credibility with the voters as a party of democratic reform, left it precisely the flexibility and freedom of action to 'wheel and deal' in the centre of the political spectrum and to make the kind of practical accommodations necessary to maintain its hold on power.

The third environmental factor, this somewhat more specific to Canada, was the regional diversity and political fragmentation inherent in a federal society as decentralized as Canada. This factor is at the same time so obvious as to be almost taken for granted, and yet so important that it can scarcely be overestimated. The relatively weak impact of the dominant *class* cleavages of modern industrial society on Canadian party politics in the face of economic regionalization and cultural divisions not only simplified the role of the Liberals as the centre party exploiting the ambiguities and contradictions of liberal-democracy—rather than becoming a victim of them, as in the case of the British Liberal party—but also gave a very particular cast to the structure of the party. It is no exaggeration to say that the structure of the Liberal party in this era can *only* be understood in the light of the impact of federalism on the inherited political structures of the British parliamentary system.

Party Finance

The relationship between the party and its financial supporters was a complex one, to a degree which rather forbids easy generalizations. The celebrated Beauharnois affair of 1930 was a highly misleading guide to the financial state of the party. The penury into which the party fell following the defeat of that year illustrates two points: first, whatever the motives of corporate donors to political parties, a party which sustained a major defeat was quickly abandoned. This was particularly crucial for the Liberal party whose traditional links had been more to government contractors than to significant sections of big business whose interests closely related to party policy or ideology. A party which depends heavily on government contractors is in obvious difficulties when faced with a period out of office. The second point to emerge from this period is that the party was clearly unwilling to compromise its policies in return for financial support. In the case of the banks and the mining companies, as well as the railway unification issue and the wheat marketing board, there is evidence that the party— and here the decisive role of the party leader must be emphasized— would not alter policy at the behest of businessmen armed with financial inducements. On the other hand, the party's own ideological bent, while it might distance itself from some capitalist interests, drew it close to certain sectors of the corporate world. Capitalism is not a monolithic set of interests, except in those comparatively rare moments when it is challenged by other classes from below or external enemies from without. There were always some sectors of the corporate world, even if not the greater part, which were willing to work with the Liberals, particularly where their interests coincided closely with Liberal policy. Even while still in opposition there were those who found such an identity of outlook—particularly the retail chain stores and the meat packing industry. Later, the Liberal party in office was able to greatly widen the scope of its friendly relations with the corporate world, as the identity of interests broadened and deepened with the years of power.

With the victory of 1935 a major structural problem in financing the party—its separation from office—was ended. Another problem soon manifested itself, however, in the form of [Ontario Liberal Premier] Mitch Hepburn's financial blockade of the federal party. The capacity of a strategically well-situated provincial party to dominate certain crucial sectors of private financial support for the party, in this case the resource industries, and to use this financial power to attempt to force its own policy goals on the federal party, was a salutary lesson to the national party both as to the growing decentralization of the structure of Canadian federalism as a result of the growing peripheralization, or Balkanization, of the economy, as well as to the continuing vulnerability of the party, even in office, to the withdrawal of financial support for the campaign fund. Any government in a liberal-democracy is aware of the crucial significance of 'business confidence.' This general dependence of governments on the private sector was matched by the dependence of the Government party on the continued support of the same interests for the party treasury. In both cases, on the other hand, the party was not without resources of its own with which to bargain—although in neither case was it in a position to ignore these interests altogether. The party's principal resource was its continued hold on office. Hepburn's blockade could only work in the long run if he were able to dislodge the Liberals from power at Ottawa. Failing that, the Liberals would have to be dealt with as the Government party, and business could not afford to ignore the implications of this for its continued relations with government.

The contract levy system which Norman Lambert enforced in the late 1930s was predicated upon the desire of business to maintain good public relations with government as a major purchaser of goods and services from the private sector. This system not only was maintained after Lambert's departure from active party work, but was extended and deepened. Two developments made this consolidation possible. The enormous growth of government intervention in the private sector, arising out of the demands of the wartime economy and commitment to interventionist Keynesian fiscal policies following the war, along with the maintenance of relatively high levels of defence expenditure in the Cold War period, had a specific meaning for the financing of the Government party. A greatly expanded state sector which involved government in continuous interaction with private corporations as sellers of goods and services to this sector, enhanced the scope for party finance—on a contract levy system where tenders were in force, or on a straight patronage basis where public bidding was not the practice. That this growth of state activity was expressed initially through the federal government, and that this centralization was closely associated with the policies of the Liberal party, also meant that the position of the federal party was reinforced in relation to its provincial counterparts. Of course, business generally wishes to retain good relations with government parties, especially when government intervention in the private sector becomes less predictable than in the past. There is also the motive of wishing to purchase access to decision-makers in case of difficulty. Thus, with or without the specific connection of government contracts, the federal Liberal party was able to increase its capacity for financing its activities as a partisan organization through the 1940s and 1950s. Another sign of this improved financial position was the growing regularization of funding over the inter-election period, reflected in the growing ability of the party in the 1950s to finance its day-to-day operations on a normal business basis—a condition which had certainly not existed in the 1930s.

Party finance was not an isolated factor; party organization was intimately, even inextricably, bound up with the problem of party finance. Adequate financing was the necessary, although not the sufficient, condition for the vitality of the party as an organization. The genesis of the National Liberal Federation in the early 1930s was as much, if not more, a matter of fund-raising as it was a matter of creating an extra-parliamentary organization for electoral purposes. Vincent Massey was selected by the party leader most of all because of his presumed access to sources of party funds, and his desire for post-election assignment to the London High Commission was used by Mackenzie King as a club to force Massey unwillingly to abandon a policy-making role to concentrate on fund-raising. Norman Lambert, as Massey's successor, was above all a finance chairman and 'fixer' for linking financial supporters with government business. Following the war the close connection between the NLF officials and fund-raising continued, from Gordon Fogo through Duncan MacTavish through Alan Woodrow to Bruce Matthews.

This concentration of the extra-parliamentary party on fund-raising may indicate an endemic condition of cadre parties, with their aversion to mass membership participation in policy-making or leadership selection, and their extreme vulnerability to a small number of corporate donors, but it also illustrates two specific factors of the Canadian political experience in this era. First, the Liberal party, especially under King's leadership, was haunted by the spectre of the Beauharnois affair, and found considerable political utility in a formal separation of the fund-raising apparatus from the parliamentary leadership of the party. Duverger's notion of 'contagion from the left' impelling cadre parties into extra-parliamentary organization proves to be of limited significance here. There is very little evidence of demands for participation by the rank-and-file membership in policy-making or even leadership selection in this era of the Liberal party's history. Nor is there much, if any, evidence of a perception of electoral threat from mass party techniques of campaigning. The move of the Liberal party toward extra-parliamentary organization had much more to do with the demands of party finance.

The second major factor forcing the national party's attention on party finance was the divergence between the concentration of economic power in the private sector—both in the corporate and in the regional sense—in a small handful of influential corporations in Toronto and Montreal and the decentralized nature of the former political system. As a political organization, the Liberal party was based on the constitutional distribution of elective offices into more than two hundred local constituencies and nine provinces (ten after Newfoundland's entry into Confederation). However, much as the central regions might dominate the party as a whole, such centralization could in no way match the centralization of private economic power. Indeed, the autonomy of the local units of the party in a political and electoral sense was one of the characteristics of the Liberal party as an organization, and the very structure of the formal institutional arrangements of election under the parliamentary system of single-member constituency voting ensured that this would be so. Consequently, the scope of such political activities as electoral organization and policy-making on the part of an extra-parliamentary national office was necessarily limited; on the other hand, the importance of the small number of party donors in two concentrated geographical locations meant that local units of the party at the provincial and constituency level were generally incapable of generating the necessary contacts for fund-raising purposes—but for the crucial exception of the provincial units in these areas. With this exception and its consequent problems aside, it is clear that party finance would necessarily be one area of party activity best left to an extra-parliamentary wing of the national party. Hence the high degree of concentration on this one activity most relevant to the extra-parliamentary national party.

Party Organization

There is no doubt that the Liberal party was a cadre party in many of the senses that Duverger uses the term: parliamentary in origin, small in membership, deriving support from local notables, etc. Yet I have already suggested that there is little evidence of Duverger's 'contagion from the left' as a factor shaping the party's structure. The growth of an extra-parliamentary party alongside the parliamentary party did not come about as the emulation of a successful mass socialist party organization on the left—since such never did develop fully at the national level in Canada—but rather as the consequence of electoral defeat, in 1930, or the fear of defeat during the Second World War. Even when, as in the latter case, it was fear of a leftward trend in public opinion and the possible capitalization of the CCF on this trend which moved the party to change its approach, the specific *organizational* changes introduced in the party were not very significant; changes rather took place on the level of policy and party programme. There was no democratization of the party organization or any shift of influence from the parliamentary to the extra-parliamentary party; rather the parliamentary leadership skilfully manipulated the extra-parliamentary structure to help initiate desired policy changes. Once the next election was won, the organization reverted to its former state.

The point is that a cadre party operating in a federal system is particularly vulnerable in an organizational sense to the loss of office, not only because the fruits of power are useful resources for party organization but also because the party lacks a firm and loyal *class* basis of support in the electorate. Moreover, the fact that the party's provincial bases are not really bases at all, but rather problematic elements in the overall structure of the national party, with different electorates, different concerns, and even different sources of party funding, means that a national cadre party out of office cannot rely on the provincial parties as a second, fall-back position for the national party in its hour of organizational need. Conversely, if it does (as in the case of Ontario in the 1930s), it may be creating organizational and political problems for itself in the long run.

The alternative in this situation is for the defeated cadre party to create an extra-parliamentary structure to undertake some of the functions normally carried out by the cabinet ministers while in office...

The basic outlines of the structure of the party began in the local community where the MP or the defeated candidate held the key to local patronage. The crucial organizational problem for the party at the local or constituency level was how to interest enough people in the party to put together the hundreds-strong organization needed for election day, ranging from returning officers to poll clerks to scrutineers, inside and outside, to drivers, and to the other odd jobs required. Direct cash payments were by no means un-known, but indirect promises of patronage or influence following success at the polls were also featured as commodities of exchange. Regional or provincial clusters of MPs and candidates would then in turn become clients to the regional or provincial cabinet minister who was the leading figure in the political organization of the area, and who controlled higher levels of government patronage as a re-wards system for maintaining the allegiance of his Mps. Finally the cabinet ministers were themselves clients to the prime minister, who held such powers as that of appointment and firing over them, not to speak of the power of dissolution of Parliament. It must be re-membered that the reciprocal nature of the exchange relationship in clientist systems meant that it was not a one-way street of influ-ence. Secondly, at the national level, it always remained true that the relationship between the cabinet ministers, and thus between the leaders of the various regions within the party, were as much relations of mutual accommodation as hierarchical, involving hori-zontal rather than vertical patterns of interaction.

This in turn reflects the particular cast which federalism gives to cadre parties in office, which can be called a *ministerialist* system of party organization. This system places a premium on the regional representativeness of the executive, and encourages the emergence of regional power-brokers as key cabinet ministers, who thus play a double role as administrators and as political leaders of regions. When the administrative powers of patronage are severed from the political role of regional power-broking, ministerialist organization becomes a liability rather than an asset to the party. Hence the attempt to create an extra-parliamentary wing of the party as an electoral alternative, particularly when the party leader, as in the case of King from 1930 to 1935, is unwilling to personally assume the organizational burden.

On the other hand, when the party returns to power the extra-parliamentary party diminishes drastically in importance in the face of the return to ministerialism. In the case of the Liberal party after 1935, however, one can see a new factor entering into the parliamentary versus extra-parliamentary equation. In the absence of strong class bases to national politics, cadre-ministerialist party organization rests most comfortably on what can be loosely called a patron-client model. The regional discontinuities of the country lend themselves to a clientist type of politics in which one sees vertical integration of subcultures and horizontal accommodation among the élites generated by these subcultures. So long as politics revolves mainly around questions of patronage and regional bargaining, ministerialism fits in well with the needs of the party as an organization. Even out of office, as with the creation of the NLF in the early 1930s, the promise of future patronage considerations is a powerful weapon to line up political support. Yet to the extent that the forces of industrialism and urbanism and events such as depressions and world wars intrude on this somewhat petty little political stage (the provincialism and sordidness of which was noted by earlier outside observers such as Lord Bryce and André Siegfried),[2] the attention of governments is drawn inevitably toward wider problems, which demand universalist, bureaucratic solutions rather than the old-fashioned particularist solutions of patronage political cultures. Under the pressure of these external forces, ministerialist government becomes administrative government, politics turns into bureaucracy, and the Liberal party becomes the Government party. Paradoxically, ministerialist organization thus becomes an impediment to the political health of the party as a patronage organization, as well as the source of the necessary instruments of that type of politics. In these conditions there is a continued need for some sort of extra-parliamentary wing of the party to maintain the necessary contacts between the party's external supporters and the largesse of the government, to co-ordinate the patronage side of the party's operations, and to remind it constantly of its role as an electoral as well as an administrative organization. Thus the NLF did not disappear entirely after the return to office in 1935, as had happened in 1921. The partisan ceasefire in the war years coupled with the intense and accelerated bureaucratization and centralization of the wartime government led to such a political crisis for the Liberal party that it found it necessary to call the extra-parliamentary party back into existence to help get the electoral machine functioning once again. Ministerialism thus generated its own limitations.

The electoral victory of 1945, in which the party's ability to respond to *class* politics as well as regional politics was tested, and the return of prosperity in the aftermath of war, laid the foundations for an apparent reversal of the relationships just indicated. After the war the extra-parliamentary party was relegated to the status of a mere paper 'democratic' legitimatization of ministerialist organization. Even party publicity was in effect 'farmed out' to a private advertising agency in return for government business, thus directly linking party publicity with state publicity. The Liberal party's transformation into the Government party had reached its logical culmination, with the virtual fusion of party and state. The Liberals won two general elections under this arrangement, and convinced most observers that they could continue indefinitely. But they lost the third election, and then suffered a devastating collapse when faced with the necessity of running while out of office, suddenly bereft of ministerialist organization, yet lacking any real extra-parliamentary party organization.

Ministerialist organization thus appears as a curiously ambiguous factor in party organization. Partly as a result of this ambiguity, the role of the national leader in the Liberal party was of paramount importance. When the party was out of office in the early 1930s the leader was in a very real sense the sole representative of the national party. In the aftermath of defeat, it is no exaggeration to assert that Mackenzie King had become the sole personal embodiment of the party in any significant way. The parliamentary party remained, but without clear responsibilities, and often without either the inclination or the ability to function as a continuing party organization. Hence King's frantic efforts to set up an extra-parliamentary organization for purposes of election planning and especially fund-raising, since the responsibility for these activities was forcing an intolerable burden on his own shoulders. It should also be noted that when out of office the potential patronage powers of the leader of the opposition in a future government are almost the only inducements available to the party for organizational purposes.

This places the leader squarely at the centre of the political stage, to a degree which would appear to almost match the domination of the party by an incumbent prime minister. There is no doubt that Mackenzie King returned to office in 1935 in a stronger and more commanding position over his parliamentary party and his ministers than that which he had enjoyed before defeat. The circumstances of that period of opposition may have been exceptional, and no attempt should be made to generalize on the role of the leader of a party on the strength of this example. What is clear, however, is that the crucial role of the leader in the party organization was enhanced by this experience, and that the creation of an extra-parliamentary party was not a detraction from the role of the leader but rather an instrument of the leader's continued influence over all aspects of the party's operations.

The well-known patronage powers of an incumbent prime minister, his direct relationship with the voters, his prerogative of dissolution, and his financial control over the fortunes of individual candidates, all demonstrate that the role of the party leader while in power is of enormous importance. Yet ministerialist organization, as well as the concentration of the prime minister on policy and administrative matters, tended to push the Liberal party in power toward a somewhat more diffuse distribution of responsibilities for party organization than had been the case while out of office. This tendency became quite striking when a new leader, Louis St Laurent, who showed not the slightest interest in matters of party organization, allowed a still greater degree of devolution of responsibility in these matters to his ministers. Paradoxically perhaps, the greater strength of ministerialism in the St Laurent years is in itself an indication of the discretionary role of the leader in shaping the party organization; Liberal leaders had the capacity to leave their personal stamp on the party structure, even if, as in St Laurent's case, this stamp was delegation of authority to his cabinet colleagues. Under King's direction the party organization, as well as the cabinet, was under tighter control. Yet it must also be pointed out that this greater control was only a matter of degree. It is clear from the historical record that King's ability to dominate his colleagues was limited, the limits being well recognized by King himself. Ministerialism was more than a tactic of a certain kind of prime minister; it was a structural feature of cabinet government in a regionally divided society. The historical circumstances and the accident of personality might allow greater or lesser scope for ministerialism, but the *fact* of ministerialism was not subject to these vicissitudes. National party organization when the Liberal party was in office derived its basic structure from the interplay of the leadership of the prime minister and the ministerialist distribution of responsibilities.

The domination of the extra-parliamentary by the parliamentary leadership was an inevitable feature of a cadre-ministerialist party in a federal political system. This did not make the administrative task of the extra-parliamentary officials an easy one, in the sense of a division of responsibilities and recognition for their work. In the case of both Vincent Massey and Norman Lambert, the problems of status and position were acute. Massey was obviously over-qualified in the sense of social prestige and self-evaluation for the instrumental task which King had set him. The severe personal problems which beset the relationship between the NLF president and the party leader during Massey's short tenure indicated that in future less 'weighty' persons would have to be selected for the NLF. Norman Lambert was much less prestigious a figure than Massey—as well as being more appropriate for the position in terms of skills and interests—but Lambert's difficulties in dealing with the party leader arose from another, although related, source. In order to do the job of national organizer, fund-raiser, party 'fixer,' and director of the party publicity office, Lambert believed that as NLF president he must be given official recognition by the party leadership, in order that the requisite authority be vested in the position. The reluctance of the party leader to grant this recognition, and the consequent inability of Lambert to deal on a level of equal footing with the cabinet ministers, meant that his capacity to carry out his duties was constantly hemmed in by frustration and sometimes by direct opposition of elements of the parliamentary party.

In this situation there would appear to be more than the structural constraints of ministerialism and federalism at work: to King, party organization work was 'dirty work,' slightly tainted, not quite respectable, and above all to be kept at arm's length to avoid any possibility of his own office being infected with scandal. To St Laurent, party politics was rather boring and unworthy of much attention, best left to those with a taste for that sort of thing. In either event, the result was the same: the extra-parliamentary party lacked prestige and authority. Lambert, as well as some of his financial collectors, found this invidious position intolerable, and eventually parted ways with the Liberal parliamentary leadership. While direct historical evidence of dissatisfaction on the part of later incumbents in the NLF presidency is lacking, it is clear that none of Lambert's successors held positions of any greater prestige than Lambert. If they were satisfied with their role it could only be because their expectations were lower than Lambert's had been. Finally, when one reaches the level of the secretariat of the national office, there is no question of the strictly instrumental role expected of these officers. People like H.E. Kidd and Paul Lafond displayed the utmost modesty and self-effacement in their dealings with the parliamentary leadership, as well as in their relationship to the NLF president and executive. They were the closest thing in the Canadian context to party bureaucrats. It is a mark of the domination of the parliamentary leadership as well as the weak level of extra-parliamentary organization in this country that these party bureaucrats never became, as sometimes happened in the European context, 'apparatchiks,' men of indirect but powerful influence on the party. Since they were not holding the levels of power they could not manipulate them. More to the point, there is no evidence that they harboured such ambitions; if they had, they would not have assumed such positions.

The weakest aspects of the extra-parliamentary party in this era were the policy-making function and the question of leadership selection. Mackenzie King derived his ultimate legitimacy as party leader from the 1919 convention, but it was a legitimacy which he never allowed to be put to the test of renewal by the assembled party membership. Since there was no provision in the party constitution and no overwhelming party demand for national conventions during King's tenure, a generation passed without a single assembly embodying the membership base of the party in any significant sense. The advisory council meetings held infrequently over the years were the closest approximation to conventions but in terms of numbers and of authority they were far from substitutes. Advisory councils were effectively dominated by the parliamentary party and rarely fulfilled other than honorific and formal duties. The one apparent exception was the 1943 meeting which adopted the welfarist programme which the party carried into the 1945 election campaign. This was not the result of autonomous action, however, but of superbly executed manipulation by a parliamentary leadership which wished to legitimize new directions in policy which had been planned by the civil service and advisers to the prime minister.

Massey's attempts at policy-making in the early 1930s met the active hostility of the party leader and the indifference of the parliamentary caucus as a whole. That the party leadership expended considerable anxiety and energy at the various advisory council meetings over the question of preventing anything remotely critical of the parliamentary party's policies from being aired is a striking indication of how far parliamentary control over policy went; the extra-parliamentary membership was not only to be powerless in deciding policy, but it had to be *seen* to be powerless as well. The smallest hint of disagreement over policy among Liberals—which is to say, the hint of any dissension from the policies adopted by the parliamentary leadership—was to be avoided at all costs. Democratic legitimation of the internal processes of decision-making in the party was accepted, but only at the most rarefied and abstract level, that of the mandate of the party leader derived from the majority vote of a party convention at one point in time. The autonomy of the parliamentary party in policy-making was justified in rhetorical terms by the invocation of the constitutional supremacy of Parliament. Whatever the merits of that argument, it was rendered somewhat problematic by the increasing bureaucratic influence on the policies of the parliamentary leadership, to the extent that by the last years of the St Laurent period virtually all Liberal policy was formulated by the permanent civil service. Policy-making was delegated to an institution which was, in the formal sense at least, non-political as well as non-partisan. The exclusion of the extra-parliamentary party membership from policy-making may thus be viewed as a matter of practical expediency rather than as one of constitutional principle. The party membership was not judged competent to formulate policy.

The 1948 national convention which chose Louis St Laurent as King's successor best illustrates these relationships within the Liberal party. The extraordinary lengths to which the party leadership went, in this unique example of a national party meeting throughout the period of this study, to prevent any public manifestation of criticism or disagreement within the membership extended not only to policy questions but to the matter of leadership itself. The evidence clearly indicates that the convention format was manipulated throughout to ensure that King's chosen successor should receive as little opposition as possible. On the other hand, the necessary democratic legitimation seemed to demand that St Laurent receive some token opposition. Both imperatives were carried out in a remarkable example of stage-managed conflict, in which the two genuine opponents of St Laurent were effectively utilized for maximum public effect and minimum internal impact. Even in the case of the selection of the party leader, then, the 'democratic' mandate becomes highly questionable, and the domination of the party by the parliamentary leadership is seen to be decisive.

Conventions at the constituency level during this era would appear to have served equivalent legitimation purposes for the parliamentary élite. Nomination votes by the constituency association membership were often, although not always, called before elections. Rarely were these exercises more than empty formalities. Sitting members were virtually assured of renomination; defeated candidates from the previous election had the inside track; and if neither of these conditions obtained, the local cabinet minister and his organizers would normally anoint the man they wanted for the nomination. The association would then ratify the choice. It did not happen like this in every instance, but it was the general rule. Observers of contemporary Canadian political culture who have noted the 'quasi-participative' nature of Canadian democracy[3] might examine the role of the Liberal party, the dominant party in Canadian politics for well over a generation, in the political socialization of its members and supporters. The Liberal party was certainly no training ground for participatory democracy, however loosely that phrase might be defined. If anything, the dominant values which it propagated as a mediating institution between the state and the mass of the citizens were those of deference and unreflective loyalty.

Deference and loyalty are political values appropriate to the clientist web of relationships which formed the basic structure of the party. Clientist relationships, moreover, flourished in the era of one-party dominance, when the Liberals as the Government party monopolized the basic medium of exchange in patron-client politics: patronage. But the general condition referred to earlier, the transformation of politics into bureaucracy in the period of one-party dominance, had a double effect on the party as an organization. The use of the state as a reward system for party loyalty effectively drained away the human resources of the party as a partisan organization into levels of bureaucracy and judiciary where they could no longer be of political use to the party. Second, as an inevitable consequence of the first problem, the party had to rely heavily on direct co-operation from the bureaucracy or the private sector to replenish its parliamentary leadership. Thus it merged more and more intimately with the senior civil service, both in terms of policies and personnel, and with the corporate élite outside the state system itself but in regular contact with the government. For these organizational reasons, as well as for the more general ones mentioned earlier, the party became less and less distinct as an entity, its separation from the state system and the private sector more and more blurred. The Government party was becoming in a curious sense a non-partisan party, so long as its hold on office was not challenged. Some might prefer to argue that it was a case of the bureaucrats being made into Liberals. Yet however one approaches the question, it seems reasonable to conclude that the Liberal party, as a political party, was growing less distinct, that the party was more a vehicle for élite accommodation, involving not only the élites of the two linguistic and cultural groups in Canada but the bureaucratic and corporate élites as well, than a partisan organization. When partisanship got in the way of élite accommodation it was partisanship which was usually discarded. No better example of this can be found than in the examination of federal-provincial relations within the Liberal party in this era.

Federal-Provincial Party Relations

The relations between the federal and provincial wings of the Liberal party...may be most usefully divided into two parts: the central provinces of Ontario and Quebec and the hinterland or peripheral areas of the West and the East.

Quebec, as the homeland of French Canada, held a special status within the national Liberal party, based on tradition and a mild form of consociational tolerance. Yet it was Ontario, with its strong and semi-autonomous economic base, which mounted the toughest challenge to the dominance of the national party in this era. In both cases the federal party ran into difficulties with its provincial counterpart, to a moderate degree in Quebec and to an extreme degree in Ontario. In Quebec, electoral defeat for the provincial party in the mid-1930s gave the federal party, which remained ascendant in its own electoral sphere, the opportunity to control the provincial party, even to the extent of guiding it back into office briefly. Eventually, the federal party settled into a pattern of constituency collaboration with its provincial party's enemy, and more or less accommodative intergovernmental relationships with the Union Nationale in terms of federal-provincial affairs, including accommodations which sometimes drastically undercut the political position of its provincial counterpart. In Ontario, a politically (and even financially) stronger provincial party in the mid-1930s waged open war on the federal party, even extending its campaign to Quebec, both on the intergovernmental and political fronts. This vigorous challenge was finally defeated by intelligent mobilization of the federal party's resources, and the intervention of an external event, the coming of the Second World War. Following the provincial defeat, the federal Liberals managed very well in Ontario by allowing a much weakened and discredited provincial party to flounder unaided in the further reaches of opposition, while dealing with the Conservative provincial government in federal-provincial relations with little regard to partisan considerations. Thus, in both cases, the long-run result was the same: the federal party prospered in the two largest provinces without a strong provincial wing. Little was done to aid the provincial parties, and, in the Quebec case, much was done to damage the provincials. This distant relationship was matched by an emphasis on intergovernmental relations with the provincial administrations of the opposite political colour. In other words, executive federalism overrode federal-provincial party solidarity. The Government party at Ottawa preferred to deal with other governments.

Intra-party relationships with the hinterland regions of Canada were not normally troubled by financial competition between the federal and provincial wings. The financial superiority of the federal party was almost always evident. In the Atlantic provinces this financial strength in conjunction with competitive two-party systems and patronage political cultures resulted in highly integrated party organizations and low levels of intra-party strains. Newfoundland was a somewhat exceptional case, representing one-man provincial rule in close co-operation with the federal Liberal party and the federal state, but even here there was a close meshing of the two parties, albeit with rather more provincial direction than in the Maritime provinces. Basically the Atlantic provinces represent a case study of the Liberal party as an integrative device within Confederation drawing the provincial units into the federal sphere of influence and control, a political reflection of economic and administrative domination of poor and underdeveloped provinces by the federal government.

The West presents a striking contrast with the Atlantic region. Although very much in a state of economic inferiority to central

Canada, the western provinces resisted a status of political inferiority to the Government party at Ottawa, first by giving relatively weak electoral support to the party in federal elections and second by tending to strike out on experimental routes with the party system in provincial politics. Thus the Liberal parties in Manitoba and British Columbia entered coalitions at the provincial level while maintaining their full partisan identities in federal politics. Even in Alberta unsuccessful moves were attempted in this direction. In all cases severe intra-party strains became apparent. Only in Saskatchewan was a consistently high level of federal-provincial party integration maintained, due to tradition, strong partisan leadership, and relative provincial political strength. Yet even in Saskatchewan prolonged relegation to provincial opposition bred growing internal party disunity. The Liberal party at Ottawa during its long period of domination grew further apart from its provincial counterparts in the West which were either co-operating with its federal party competitors or floundering in opposition. Eventually, a pattern of intergovernmental relations with provincial administrations ranging in partisan colouration from quasi-Liberal to social democracies to Social Credit began to predominate over the kind of intra-party integrations which the Saskatchewan Liberal machine had once represented. The Liberal party's experiences in the West were very different from those in central Canada. Yet the same basic result was reached from different routes: executive federalism proved stronger than federal-provincial party solidarity.

The underlying reasons for the prevalence of executive federalism over political federalism in Canada have been explored at length by other writers. Attention has also been given to the general question of federal-provincial intra-party relations.[4] This study in effect constitutes a documentation of the growing 'confederalization' of the Liberal party over a period of almost thirty years. It should be emphasized that this process does not necessarily imply the attenuation of federal dominance over provincial wings of the party. Indeed, in most cases examined, the federal party emerged as the most successful. That this took place in the two central provinces, those best situated in economic, political, and even cultural (in the case of Quebec) terms to mount effective challenges to federal domination of the Liberal party, is a striking indication of the ability of the senior level of the party to maintain its superior position. But confederalization did mean the separation of the two wings in terms of senior personnel, career patterns, party finance, and even ideology. This means that by the 1950s the Government party in Ottawa was loosely linked with unsuccessful opposition parties in Quebec City, Toronto, and three western provinces—parties whose weakness was more or less enforced by the very success of the federal party. Nor was this distinctly asymmetrical relationship simply an accident: rather it reflected a crucial problem in federal-provincial relations.

The problem revolves around the inevitable conflict in which two wings of the same party in the same province must engage for the available human resources. An increasing separation and insulation of the two wings at the level of parliamentary leadership was never matched by an equivalent separation of the membership at the constituency level. The critical problem faced by all parties of the mobilization of the party rank and file at election time to perform the multiple organizational tasks necessary for successful electioneering, could become itself a cause of contention and competition between two wings of the party in the same area. Only in the extreme—and in the Canadian context, unlikely—eventuality of complete jurisdictional accord between the province and the national government might political conflict at the governmental level not cause conflict at the party level. Another factor capable of overriding intra-party divisions might be a cross-provincial ideological cohesiveness within the party: in the case of a brokerage party like the Liberals, this was never true in practice, and doubtful in theory. Nor could pure patronage politics serve to override divisions... A preoccupation with patronage politics was itself a disturbing factor in federal-provincial intra-party relations.

E.R. Black has suggested that 'just as the virtual independence of a provincial government's policy-making depends to a considerable extent on its provincial resources, so the effective control of provincial organization by the local officers depends upon the local unit's political resources in comparison with those of the central party: such resources are considered to be size and commitment of membership, financial capabilities, quality and appeal of leadership, and, of course, electoral success.' Black then goes on to note that while the policy objectives and organizational requirements in the federal and provincial arenas are often quite different, nevertheless 'both sets of leaders must rely in large measure on the relatively small group of people and on the same resources in their field work.'[5]

In the case of Hepburn's challenge to federal domination, it was precisely this lack of organizational differentiation at the local level which proved to be his undoing. To blockade successfully the federal party Hepburn had to mobilize the local Liberal activists to withdraw their allegiance and support from the federal Liberals. This he attempted to do by discrediting the federal party in the eyes of Ontario voters and by forming alliances with federal Conservatives. Yet so long as the Liberals remained in office in Ottawa, this campaign achieved little success. Thus Hepburn was driven by the logic of his position to more and more extreme opposition to his own national party. Since he was ultimately unable to extend his efforts beyond his own province, the much wider base of the national party was not sufficiently undercut to give tangible evidence of success. Hence his struggle developed in a manner which seemed irrational and self-defeating to the local Liberal activists. The financial resources of the provincial party were not enough to counteract the political resources of the federal party, especially after the outbreak of the Second World War. In the end it was the provincial party which was driven into opposition; the provincial Liberals have never, since Hepburn's failure, attracted the kind of local organizational strength characteristic of the federal Liberals in that province.

In Quebec a superficially different, but essentially similar, pattern developed. Provincial disputes spilled over into federal constituency politics; the federal party reasserted stability by the subordination of the provincial wing, first by directly placing it in office, later by abandoning it to successive terms of opposition while collaborating with its opponent. The capacity of the federal wing to enforce a permanent opposition status on its provincial counterpart derived from its superior political and financial resources accruing from the national office, and its evident unwillingness—except in the very special circumstances of 1939—to utilize these resources on behalf of the provincial party. Superior political and financial resources combined to ensure superiority in the attraction of human resources. Yet, in the long run, the provincial Liberals were able to rebuild their strength, not through prior solution of their financial problem but by generating new and separate organizational structures which could serve as alternative sources for the mobilization of human resources. In other words, political resources were developed independently of the federal party.

To a degree in Manitoba and much more so in British Columbia, coalition arrangements in provincial politics put severe strains on constituency organization and the loyalties of local party activists. There is definite evidence for British Columbia that the federal Liberals were in a much stronger position when the provincial party went into opposition in the 1950s than when it had been the dominant provincial coalition partner earlier. Saskatchewan, in the period of joint Liberal rule in both capitals from 1935 to 1944, appears to offer a contrast, inasmuch as party integration was smoother than it was later when the provincial party was out of office. In this case, Saskatchewan is closer to the example of the Atlantic provinces where intra-party unity was bought at the price of clear federal domination—exercised in the Saskatchewan case, however, with some autonomy at the level of the federal cabinet by Jimmy Gardiner as the regional prairie power-broker at Ottawa. In other words, federal Liberal domination within Saskatchewan did not preclude regional representation of some significance within the cabinet, a regional power which was backed precisely by the high level of intra-party integration and the bargaining leverage this placed in Gardiner's hands. Saskatchewan thus represented a model of party politics as a vehicle of regional representation quite different from those adopted elsewhere in the West. The Liberal parties of the Atlantic provinces, on the other hand, did not appear to utilize party integration as a bargaining lever within the federal cabinet to the same extent. Here party loyalty overrode regional discontent and the same local activists could be mobilized equally for either level of electoral politics with the same well-integrated set of rewards backed by the political financing of Montreal and the co-ordinated patronage inducements of the federal and provincial states. Only in Newfoundland is there real evidence of this Liberal loyalty being translated into any real provincial influence on the federal party, but here the small size of the province and its state of underdevelopment and poverty severely limited its power. The Maritimes aside, it is clear that in the case of Saskatchewan federal-provincial integration as a vehicle of provincial political representation is not without strain when one party loses office. In the late 1940s and 1950s it became apparent that a certain tension between the two wings at the leadership level was being reflected in problems at the local level.

There is a sense, then, in which federal and provincial wings of a party are often locked into a rather self-destructive relationship. If, as many observers have argued, political parties act mainly as recruitment agencies for the staffing of elective office—and the weakness of the Liberal party as a channel of demands on the political system through extra-parliamentary policy formation appears to give added weight to this emphasis—then federal and provincial wings of the same party are necessarily locked into competition for the same pool of human resources. Provincial weakness matched by federal strength guarantees the latter wing against too much competition. Dealing with governments of another political colour at the provincial level, on the other hand, avoids this problem. The claims of other governments can be treated as a matter of intergovernmental negotiation. The claims of party become a complicating factor, adding new levels of conflict which can be avoided when the problem is simply intergovernmental. The intra-party dimension of federal-provincial relations is thus a matter of *additional* complexity. It is difficult to generalize beyond this from the limited time period that has been examined, but it does seem safe to conclude that a Government party will prudently seek to avoid such complications. They may opt, as the federal Liberals did in Ontario and Quebec, for underwriting the position of their provincial wings as permanent opposition parties, thus keeping the party name before the provincial voters while at the same time minimizing their impact on the federal level. Thus the dominant strategy of the federal Liberals in confronting this organizational problem in Ontario and Quebec was to downplay partisanship between levels of government.

In a country as diverse and as decentralized as Canada, and especially in the case of provinces as crucially influential in relationship to the federal government as Ontario and Quebec, a party in power in Ottawa could not afford the intra-party strains involved in attempting to use the party as an integrative device in federal-provincial relations. Instead, the Liberal party reverted to intergovernmental, even interbureaucratic, relations as the major channels of accommodation. This not only helped account for the weak and underdeveloped nature of extra-parliamentary national party organization in this era, but also strongly reinforced the tendency already present in the Government party to transform politics into bureaucracy and party into state.

Perhaps this may be the final, paradoxical, conclusion to be drawn from this study. The curious lack of definition of Canadian parties, which has troubled so many observers of our politics, is only reinforced as the evidence concerning their structure is marshalled. The Liberal party was an organization seeking not so much to consolidate its distinct partisan identity as to embed itself within the institutional structures of government. Its fulfilment was not so much organizational survival as it was institutionalization as an aspect of government: control over recruitment channels to senior levels of office. The deadening of political controversy, the silence, the greyness which clothed political life at the national level in the 1950s, were reflections of a Liberal ideal of an apolitical public life. In place of politics there was bureaucracy and technology. This in no sense meant that Canada stood still. Profound changes were taking place in the nation's political economy. But these changes tended to take place outside the realm of traditional public debate. Instead, it was between the great bureaucracies, whether public (federal and provincial) or private (Canadian and American), that debate and policy refinement took place. The Liberal party had truly become the Government party—an instrument for the depoliticization and bureaucratization of Canadian public life. The vision of Mackenzie King in his almost forgotten *Industry and Humanity* had begun to take shape: 'whether political and industrial government will merge into one, or tend to remain separate and distinct' was King's question for the future in 1918. He concluded that 'the probabilities are that for years to come they will exist side by side, mostly distinguishable, but, in much, so merged that separateness will be possible in theory only.'[6]

Notes

1   C.B.Macpherson, *The Real World of Democracy* (Toronto, 1965), and *Democratic Theory: Essays in Retrieval* (London, 1973).

2   A. Siegfried, *The Race Question in Canada* (1906; new ed., Toronto, 1966); James Bryce, *Canada: An Actual Democracy* (Toronto, 1921).

3   R.J. Van Loon, "Political Participation in Canada: The 1965 Election." *Canadian Journal of Political Science*, III, 3 (Sept. 1970), pp. 376-399; Robert Presthus, *Elite Accommodation in Canadian Politics* (Toronto, 1973).

4   D.V. Smiley, *Canada in Question: Federalism in the Seventies* (2nd ed., Toronto, 1976).

5   E.R.Black, "Federal Strains Within a Canadian Party," in H.G. Thorburn, ed., *Party Politics in Canada* (3rd ed., Scarborough, 1972), pp. 129-130.

6   Mackenzie King, *Industry and Humanity* (1918; new ed., Toronto, 1973), p. 246.

J. Wearing The Liberal Party

The Philosophical and Historical Traditions

The ideological origins of the Liberal party of Canada lie within the corpus of nineteenth-century British liberalism, but the party's principles have also been very much shaped by Canadian circumstances and its own response to the problems that have arisen throughout the last hundred and fifty years of Canadian history.[1] Its philosophical ideals are largely drawn from the heterogeneous collection of principles that make up the British liberal tradition, as one can readily see in perusing the political views of Canadian Liberal party leaders. In early nineteenth-century Canada, Robert Baldwin, arguing for the rights of an elected legislature against the presumptions of the Crown's representative and his Canadian advisers, found inspiration in the Whigs' belief in the supremacy of Parliament. George Brown's vigilance over Tory plans to aid the churches and to grant special school rights to Roman Catholics was likewise a typically whiggish response. Edward Blake, excoriating John A. Macdonald's government for its extravagance in building the Canadian Pacific Railway (let alone the whole question of state intervention in the domain of private enterprise) was in the best tradition of Gladstonian public frugality. The anticlericalism of the early nineteenth-century French Canadian *Rouges* came from continental European liberalism, though the ideas of British liberalism became more prominent in French Canada at the time of Wilfrid Laurier, who sought to avoid having religious difference as the basis of party politics. His liberalism was in the manner of John Stuart Mill and Gladstone: combining a belief in reform, progress, individual rights, parliamentary democracy and the perfectibility of human nature. The two election platforms in which he proposed free trade with the United States were quintessential nineteenth-century liberalism.

Mackenzie King's views reflected the new positive liberalism of T.H. Greene and L.T. Hobhouse in seeing the necessity for state intervention as a means of enhancing the individual liberty of society's weaker members. But King was not one to let his political ideals lead him into precipitate action. Apart from old-age pensions, his commitment to social security did not produce much legislation for over fifteen years until his wartime government accepted the Marsh Report—a Canadian equivalent of the social welfare plan devised by a British liberal, Lord Beveridge, for postwar Britain. More recently, Pearson, with his extension of social welfare and his commitment to international as well as national conciliation, and Trudeau, with his return to an emphasis on individual rights (both legal and linguistic), have kept the Canadian Liberal party well within the mainstream of British liberalism—even when the latter has been reduced to little more than a rivulet.[2]

That is not to say that Canadian liberalism has always been faithful to these principles nor has it been free of the opportunism and moral flaccidity to which parties in power are especially prone. As two writers on Canadian ideologies have said, "practical politics tend to be not un-ideological, but ideologically fuzzy." Indeed, according to one study of the party, the conflicting strands of Mackenzie King's liberalism verged on hypocrisy as his government played its "by now familiar role as the defender of the people against the big interests and the defender of the big interests against the people."[3]

It would perhaps be more generous to say that the foremost Canadian Liberal leaders, whatever their philosophical underpinnings, have been pragmatists above all. Furthermore, the experience of practical politics has added some distinctively Canadian themes to Canadian liberalism, themes which—though distinctive—have not always been mutually consistent. In the pre-Confederation legislatures of the Canadas, Nova Scotia and New Brunswick, responsible government was the first big local issue to divide Tories and Reformers. After the cause was won, however, there was a party realignment, largely based on the religious controversies of the day, which put the Reform or Clear Grit opposition on the side of giving no state aid to religious denominations. Following Confederation, the Liberals in Ottawa were at best a loose amalgam of pro-Confederate Scotch Presbyterians (farmers from southwestern Ontario and businessmen from Toronto), anti-Confederate, anti-clerical Quebeckers, and other anti-Confederates of varying hues from Nova Scotia and New Brunswick. As the years passed, other strands were added to the Liberal party. From Ontario, came Oliver Mowat, the durable nineteenth-century premier and the first defender of provincial rights against centralizing Conservative governments in Ottawa. He allied himself with another Liberal premier, the nationalist Honoré Mercier from Quebec. When the Liberals, finally under Laurier, ended the long period of Conservative rule in Ottawa, they had become staunch defenders of French Canadian interests and provincial autonomy, although these two goals came into conflict when provincial governments in Manitoba and Ontario severely curtailed the use of French as a language of instruction in the schools.

The Ontario farmers who settled in southwestern Manitoba took their Scotch Presbyterian brand of liberalism with them and, in the other three western provinces, the lure of federal patronage permitted Liberal loyalties to take hold, at least to begin with. The Progressive revolt after the First World War was much influenced by American agrarian populism. It ended permanently the two-party system in Canada, even though the Progressives did not set out to create just another political party like the two older ones. Many of them took independent political action simply as a means of giving farmers a voice in Ottawa and of putting pressure on the Liberal party to recommit itself to the principles of free trade and the reform of government institutions. Others, like the United Farmers of Alberta, had more radical goals which the Liberal party could not be expected to endorse. And while most moderate Progressives gradually returned to the Liberal fold, the radicals became a nucleus of the socialist CCF party.

Electoral success (or the lack of it) also had its effect on what the Canadian Liberal party stood for. In the nineteenth century, the Liberal party, mostly in opposition in Ottawa and mostly in government in the provinces, was a staunch defender of provincial rights. In the twentieth century, the situation has been reversed; the Liberal party has almost monopolized power in Ottawa and provincial Liberal governments have increasingly become a rarity. During the latter period, when the federal Liberal party held power in Ottawa, it was not reluctant—at least until recently—to exercise federal powers vigorously. It won recognition of Canadian autonomy within the British Empire, mobilized the nation during the Second World War, introduced the social welfare legislation of the postwar period, and took responsibility for managing the Canadian economy on the Keynesian formula. When Newfoundland joined Confederation in 1949, the Liberal party had become the spokesman for the federal power and the wheel had turned full circle. Unlike the Maritime anti-Confederates of eighty years before who became Liberals, Newfoundland anti-Confederates became Progressive Conservatives and the Confederates, led by Joey Smallwood, became Liberals. (There was one notable exception: Donald Jamieson, who opposed Newfoundland's entry into Confederation, later became a federal

Liberal cabinet minister and, later still, leader of the Newfoundland Liberal party.)[4]

The Organizational Beginnings

The organizational beginnings of the Liberal party go well back into the nineteenth century, when riding organizations were created to elect Reformers to the pre-Confederation legislatures. Eventually modest provincial offices were established and, by the First World War, provincial policy conventions were held. Attended by hundreds of constituency delegates, they were held annually (or almost annually) in every province except Quebec and P.E.I. Thus, even though the party was soon dominated by its elected members, its origins nevertheless conform to Duverger's model of the mass-membership party—though membership was never large enough anywhere, with the possible exception of Saskatchewan, to really qualify for the adjective "mass."[5]

Before 1932, sporadic attempts were made to amalgamate these provincial associations into some kind of national organization: the policy convention of 1893, the creation in 1912 of a Central Information Office (with a young director by the name of Mackenzie King), and a National Liberal Advisory Committee three years later.[6] Typically, interest in party organization arose when the party was out of power and flagged when it got back into office.

The bitter party split over the conscription issue in the First World War gave the matter particularly pressing urgency. A convention was called in 1919, not only to elect a new leader, Mackenzie King, but also to deal with the party's organization. It approved the creation of the National Liberal Organization Committee with an executive (the leader and nine vice-presidents named by their respective provincial associations) and a national council (six from each province, including the provincial leader). A head office was set up in Ottawa with an organization branch and an information branch, incorporating the existing information office.[7]

As soon as the party regained power in 1921, everyone lost interest in the new organization. The provincial parties were slow to appoint representatives to the executive, as were the constituencies in meeting the $250 levy that was intended to finance the office.[8] Mackenzie King was wary lest it hobble him in his wheeling and dealing with both the Progressives and the factions within his own party. Gradually its functions were taken over by his ministers who, reverting to earlier practice, took it upon themselves to deal with the organizations in their respective provinces. The Central Office was kept active producing campaign literature in the 1921 and 1925 elections, but it was always short of funds.[9]

It was not until 1930 that, prompted by defeat and scandal, King was forced to reconsider seriously the establishment of a national organization. The scandal arose after it became known that the Beauharnois Power Corporation, which wanted a hydro-electric power concession on the St. Lawrence River, had given a large political donation to the party's chief organizer, Andrew Haydon. King got himself off a potentially dangerous hook by denying that he had any knowledge of the party's fund-raising activities. But the affair confirmed King's intention to institutionalize the distance between himself and those discredited individuals, the party's fund raisers.[10]

The National Liberal Federation

In 1931, King revived the National Liberal Organization Committee which, a year later, gave birth to the National Liberal Federation. It was to be a true federation in which federal and provincial interests would have an equal voice and, in recognition of the federal principle, each provincial association would have an equal representation on the 69-member General Committee. (The name was later changed to Advisory Council and membership eventually increased to 236 in 1955). The smaller Executive Committee likewise recognized the principle of equal provincial representation.[11]

The Federation, unlike the earlier National Liberal Organization Committee, was to become a permanent fixture; however, there was an uncertainty as to what its functions should be—a situation that has a familiar ring today. Should it be the vehicle for gathering expert opinion on policy for the enlightenment of the parliamentary leadership or should it serve as a forum for the party rank-and-file to voice their policy concerns? Should it be responsible for keeping the party organization in good shape between elections? Would that in turn necessitate getting involved in patronage and fund raising? Should it run federal election campaigns or merely co-ordinate the campaigns of the provincial organizations? Should it confine itself simply to producing a newsletter or should it also get into the increasingly sophisticated business of advertising, marketing surveys, and public relations?

Vincent Massey—the patrician, first president of the Federation—gave his priority to policy and organized the first Liberal "thinkers" conference in Port Hope during the summer of 1933. Mackenzie King was, however, suspicious of Massey's attempts to shift the party to the Left and also saw the conference as interfering with the leader's prerogative to set party policy. Massey was allowed to hold the conference only if it had nothing directly to do with the Federation and King used the lure of an appointment to the Canadian High Commission in London to make Massey promise that the Federation would restrict itself to organizational concerns in future.[12]

The Advisory Council of the NLF did provide a regular forum for policy debates and resolutions by party members, but it was not large enough to be considered a genuine gathering of the rank-and-file. With its deliberations held under the watchful eye of cabinet ministers, meetings generally praised the government; in fact, the absence of controversy prompted a later president, Senator Fogo, to tease delegates that they were not true Liberals in allowing so many resolutions to be presented and passed in such cursory fashion. Too much of the discussion went on in the smoking room outside the meeting hall and in the bedrooms of the hotel, he added. On the other hand, Brooke Claxton, a cabinet minister who described himself as "a kind of messenger boy" between the prime minister and the cabinet and the Council, warned the Advisory Council that, because the party was in power, they must be careful lest their resolutions put the government on the spot. On another occasion, recognizing that many of the delegates would like to have seen "resolutions put in sharper terms," he reminded them that the proper procedure was for the Council to pass general resolutions, which were put before the government confidentially—who then drafted the election platform. One wonders why he was so concerned, since the ministers kept careful control of the proceedings in any case.[13] Finally, meetings of the Advisory Council grew less frequent and, in the mid-fifties, took place at three-year intervals instead of annually as called for in the constitution. A suggestion made at the 1948 convention to hold a full-scale policy convention of rank-and-file delegates every four years was also ignored.

Political Organization and the Federation

While Massey's interest lay in the lofty concerns of policy, Norman Lambert, the first general secretary of the Federation (and later party president, when Massey got his high commissionership), was a master of political organization. But these concerns, like those of policy, encroached upon an area where the parliamentary party traditionally held sway.

From the days of Laurier, a system had evolved whereby key cabinet ministers from the various provinces took responsibility for party matters in their own bailiwicks. The minister kept in touch with the MPs and defeated candidates in his province or region, looked for promising candidates, held nomination meetings, and was consulted by other ministers over the distribution of federal patronage in his area. Particularly in the later King ministries, these political lieutenants exercised formidable political power in their own right: such men as Fielding, Ralston, and Ilsley from the Maritimes; Lapointe, Claxton and Power from Quebec; Murphy, Howe and Martin from Ontario; Dunning, Crerar and Gardiner from the Prairies. However, not every minister in King's cabinets had the appropriate talents. One who did, Chubby Power, commiserated with King: "Unfortunately, it is not always possible to make a good organizer out of a good Minister, and some of your best colleagues in the Cabinet were utterly incapable of understanding anything whatsoever about practical organization."[14]

A very different aspect of political organization under King was the completely informal network of personal contacts that he maintained throughout the country. The network was said to have consisted of several hundred names of people whom King had met in one way or another—a high school teacher, a farmer, a lawyer. Though not necessarily prominent people, they provided King with useful information about public opinion across the country on a level with which he, as a politician, had to deal. Although much of this was also done through his personal correspondence, every morning an official from the Federation presented King with a short list of those of his contacts who happened to be in Ottawa on that day. Depending on what was the current political problem, he might ask to have one of these people pay him a short visit. In a similar way, he kept in touch with his network whenever he travelled throughout the country. This had very little to do with the Federation; in fact, it was a function that a more active extra-parliamentary organization would have performed. In any case, it gave King a source of information that was very different from what came to him from the civil service, cabinet, or even the caucus.[15]

Because the party had been out of power when the Federation was established in 1932, Lambert had become very active in organizational matters. When the party returned to office in 1935, he hoped that the Federation would retain some responsibility in this area. He realized that it would have to have some influence over patronage, if it were going to exercise any real power. As long as Lambert was active, the party office did get involved in such matters, though more because of Lambert's undoubted talents than because of any formal recognition that this was an appropriate sphere for the Federation. Though it was described as "the gateway to departmental favours," the national office was not nearly as involved as Lambert would have liked. Ministers tended to know either too little or too much about what Lambert called the "business side" of party organization. Those who knew too little naïvely eschewed such partisanship; those who knew too much refused to share their patronage prerogative with anyone apart from cabinet colleagues.[16]

For his part, King regarded the whole patronage business as distasteful. Lambert was chafed by his leader's disdain, especially when it meant that King procrastinated over his appointment to the Senate. Years later, Lambert (by then a senator) was still bothered that the "business side" of political organization had "to be concealed from the public as something unclean and untouchable."[17]

Senator Fogo, who succeeded Lambert as general party factotum during the war and was formally elected president in 1945, was primarily a fund raiser and not active in party organization as Lambert had been. He believed that the party office should operate between elections only as a service branch with educational and promotional responsibilities and that it should not do very much even during elections. Allan McLean was styled National Director rather than General Secretary when he was appointed in 1945; but in spite of the grander title he seems to have been less of a force in the party than either Lambert or Fogo had been. In 1949, McLean was replaced by H.E. 'Bob' Kidd who, reverting to the earlier nomenclature, assumed the title of General Secretary. Kidd had formerly been an advertising executive with Cockfield Brown Inc., which handled the major share of the Liberal party's advertising business. His appointment has been interpreted as indicating a shift away from the traditional organizational practices of Lambert to the new emphasis on advertising, public opinion analysis and public relations. This, in fact, was where Kidd's responsibilities lay when he took up his position in the party office. Activity between elections was directed at maintaining a large mailing list (100,000 or more addresses) of people who "are potential points of strength throughout the country." But this concentration on so-called opinion leaders was difficult to sustain. Publishing was very expensive, the provincial associations could not be counted on for distribution and it was difficult to get subscribers for the party's quarterly magazine, *The Canadian Liberal*, even at the modest subscription price of $1.00.[18]

King may not have had much taste for party organization, but he saw the necessity for having people who did—and did not hesitate to blame them when things went wrong. With his successor, Louis St. Laurent, party organization got progressively less attention from everyone. Ministers became ever more preoccupied with the challenge of administering huge departments and could find neither time nor energy to undertake the inevitable travelling and speechmaking required of those who became heavily involved in party affairs. In the immediate postwar period, Brooke Claxton, a cabinet minister from Montreal, had been the minister most active in such party matters as organization, advertising, publicity and general liaison with the Federation. When he retired in 1954, he left a gap which could not be filled by the remaining political ministers: an aging Jimmy Gardiner, a politically insensitive C.D. Howe and an ex-bureaucrat, Jack Pickersgill, for example.

The ministers may have become less politically-minded and less representative of their respective regions, but they refused to share their responsibilities. In 1945, the cabinet felt no compunction about summarily relieving the Federation of any campaign responsibilities without even consulting the party president, Senator Wishart Robertson. In the other postwar elections up to 1957, the Federation was usually represented on the campaign committee by its president, general secretary and associate general secretary; but campaign strategy, such as it was, remained firmly in the hands of the few politically-minded ministers. The result was that, according to John Meisel in his book on the 1957 election, there was really "no high command" in the campaign. The Federation had the more mundane task of acting as a "news exchange" and "clearing house." It produced a speaker's handbook, pamphlets, leaflets, free-time political broadcasts and helped with the leader's tour and national advertising. But even the important job of publicity was taken over by the party's advertising agency, Cockfield Brown, and the provincial party offices jealously guarded their own prerogatives in the campaign.[19]

By 1957 the Liberal party had become an extension of the cabinet and, when ministers went down like ninepins before the Conservative onslaughts of 1957 and 1958, not much of the party was left.

Notes

1   The Liberal party has not had attention lavished on it by scholarly writers such as one might have expected. In the last few years, a start has been made on filling the lacuna. The most notable is Reginald Whitaker, *The Government Party: Organizing and Financing the Liberal Party of Canada 1930-58*. David E. Smith's *Prairie Liberalism: The Liberal Party in Saskatchewan 1905-71* is an excellent study of the party in one province. J.W. Pickersgill has very much a Liberal perspective in *The Liberal Party*.
There are several theses: P.H. Heppe, "The Liberal Party of Canada." Ph.D., Wisconsin, 1957; P. Regenstreif, "The Liberal Party of Canada: An Analysis." Ph.D., Cornell, 1963; J.W. Lederle, "The National Organization of the Liberal and Conservative Parties in Canada." Ph.D., Michigan, 1942; E.E. Harrill, "The Structure of Organization and Power in Canadian Political Parties: A Study in Party Financing." Ph.D., North Carolina, 1958; Brian M. McFadzen, "The Liberal Party and MacLaren Advertising Co., Ltd., 1957-65." M.A., Queen's, 1971.
A number of biographies provide valuable insights into the organization of the party, especially R. MacG. Dawson, *William Lyon Mackenzie King, 1874-1923*; H.B. Neatby, *William Lyon Mackenzie King: The Lonely Heights, 1924-1932* and *William Lyon Mackenzie King: The Prism of Unity, 1932-1939*; J.W. Pickersgill & D.F. Forster, *The Mackenzie King Record*, 4 vols.; J.L. Granatstein, *Canada's War: The Politics of the Mackenzie King Government, 1939-1945*; John English & J.O. Stubbs, eds., *Mackenzie King: Widening the Debate*; Denis Smith, *Gentle Patriot: A Political Biography of Walter Gordon*; Robert Bothwell, *Pearson: His Life and World*; George Radwanski, *Trudeau*; Walter Stewart, *Shrug: Trudeau in Power*; Anthony Westell, *Paradox: Trudeau as Prime Minister*. There are three notable autobiographies: Lester B. Pearson, *Mike: The Memoirs of the Right Honourable Lester B. Pearson*, 3 vols.; Judy LaMarsh, *Memoirs of a Bird in a Gilded Cage*; Walter L. Gordon, *A Political Memoir*.

2   W. Christian & C. Campbell, *Political Parties and Ideologies in Canada: liberals, conservatives, socialists, nationalists*. Frank H. Underhill, *In Search of Canadian Liberalism*. M. Hamelin, ed., *The Political Ideas of the Prime Ministers of Canada*.

3   Christian & Campbell, p. 41. Whitaker, p. 141.

4   In addition to the material mentioned in footnote 1, useful material on the early history of the Liberal party in the various provinces is contained in the following works: Martin Robin, ed., *Canadian Provincial Politics*; Hugh G. Thorburn, ed., *Party Politics in Canada*; H. Blair Neatby, *Laurier and a Liberal Quebec*; Norman Ward, ed., *A Party Politician: The Memoirs of Chubby Power*; Peter Neary, "Party Politics in Newfoundland, 1949-71: a survey and analysis", *Journal of Canadian Studies*, (November 1971); S.J.R. Noel, *Politics in Newfoundland*; L.G. Thomas, *The Liberal Party in Alberta: A History of Politics in the Province of Alberta, 1905-1921*; F.C. Engelmann & M.A. Schwartz, *Canadian Political Parties: Origin, Character, Impact*; W.L. Morton, *The Progressive Party in Canada*. See also my article, "Pressure Group Politics in Canada West before Confederation", *Canadian Historical Association Annual Meeting*, 1967. Wayne E. MacKinnon, *The Life of the Party: A History of the Liberal Party in Prince Edward Island*.

5   Maurice Duverger, *Political Parties*, 2nd ed., Introduction and Book I. See also my article, "Ontario Political Parties: Fish or Fowl?" in Donald C. MacDonald, ed., *Government and Politics of Ontario*.

6   Murphy Papers, vol. 34, folder 156, Party Organization, a memorandum printed for the 1919 convention; vol. 17, Laurier to Murphy, 17.11.15. Regenstreif, pp. 125-129.

7   *The Story of the Convention and The Report of Its Proceedings*, pp. 203-204. Murphy Papers, vol. 17, folder 79, Murphy to Lemieux, 4.12.19; vol. 13, folder 59, Meeting of the Executive Council of the National Liberal Organization Committee, 24.2.20.

8   Murphy Papers, vol. 17, folder 79, Murphy to Lemieux, 4.12.19; vol. 13, folder 59, Meeting of the Executive Council of the National Liberal Organization Committee, 24.2.20; vol. 15, folder 72, Murphy to Kyte, 24.1.21.

9   Neatby, pp. 327-328. Regenstreif, p. 134. Whitaker, p. 9.

10   Murphy Papers, vol. 11, folder 50, Murphy to Fraser, 18.8.26; vol. 28, folder 98, Murphy to Moore, 19.4.26. Regenstreif, p. 136. Neatby, *The Lonely Heights* , p. 385. K.Z. Paltiel, *Political Party Financing in Canada*, pp. 25-26.

11   Regenstreif, pp. 166-180. Interview with H.L. Kidd, 14.1.72.

12   Whitaker, pp. 37-43. H.B. Neatby, *The Prism of Unity* , pp. 38-39.

13   LPC, vol. 861, file: 1943 Advisory Council Proceeding of Meeting; vol. 862, file: 1948 Advisory Council, Meeting of; vol. 863, file: 1952 Advisory Council. Regenstreif, pp. 181-186.

14   See my article, "President or Prime Minister" in Thomas A. Hockin, ed., *The Prime Minister and Political Leadership in Canada*. N. Ward, ed., *A Party Politician*, pp. 273-274.

15   Interviews with J.R. Scott, 2.9.72; Gordon Dryden, 18.9.79.

16 Whitaker, pp. 86-95.

17 LPC, vol. 861, file: 1943 Advisory Council Proceeding of Meeting. Whitaker, pp. 91, 95-96, 103-104.

18 LPC, vol. 647, file: British Columbia Liberal Association, 1956-1957, 1958-1959. Memo by Kidd, 24.9.57: Ontario Liberal Association, 1950-52, Kidd to Hale, 30.3.51; file: British Columbia Liberal Assoc. 1953-55, Kidd to Deachman, 29.9.55. Interviews with Kidd, 14.1.72; Paul Lafond, 26.8.77. Whitaker, pp. 166, 185-194. Regenstreif, pp. 191-202.

19 LPC, vol. 631, file: Office of the Prime Minister 1954-55, J.L. McDougall to St. Laurent, 14.10.55; vol. 660, file: Ontario Liberal Association 1949, W.G. Hale to Kidd, 21.2.49; H.S. Hamilton to Kidd, 13.5.49; vol. 661, file: GE-1957 Ontario Liberal Association: Bulletins, "Organizational Responsibility—Electoral Districts, 1952"; vol. 678, file: Correspondence & Memoranda October to December 1961, Liberal Organization in the 1957 Campaign [written by Kidd]; vol. 647, file: B.C. Liberal Assoc., 1953-55; Memo by Kidd, "Record of Conversational with John L. Gibson, former Independent Liberal for Comox-Alberni, B.C.", 17.2.54; vol. 644, file: Working Group on Constitution (1), Report of the Committee Appointed to Study the Functions and Constitution of the National Liberal Federation [December 1959]; General Considerations, July 1959, Interviews with Pickersgill, 13.1.72; Kidd, 14.1.72; Lafond, 26.8.77. Whitaker, pp. 165-170, 179-194, 206-215; Meisel, pp. 63-72, 179.

John R. Williams The Conservatives' National Organization

In theory the national organization of the Progressive Conservative party is represented by the clear cut diagram shown in Figure 1. In reality this diagram bears little resemblance to the actual operation of the party, and for the most part this symmetrical sketch represents what the party would like the public to believe is the organization. Apparently the Conservatives have never thoroughly analyzed the function and role of many parts of their organization, which like Topsy have just "growed." Such organizations as the young Progressive Conservative association and the women's association have been created mainly to counteract similar activities in the Liberal and CCF parties rather than because Conservatives felt a real need for them. Consequently, much of the organization exists almost entirely as "window dressing" to impress the public.

The leader is by far the most important figure in the whole organization. It is he who carries the party banners in elections, decides upon party strategy and tactics, is ultimately responsible for obtaining funds to support the party, and even to a large extent enunciates party policy. However, the leader alone cannot carry on all the functions of a political party, although at times Conservative leaders, as in the case of R.J. Manion, have practically been compelled to do so. Since the end of World War I, there has been a growing demand for a functioning party organization headed by a national association which could exert influence upon the leader and the parliamentary group. This movement has been spearheaded by men anxious to give the rank-and-file members of the party more of a voice in party affairs, but little in the way of a genuine organization has developed. The leaders and the parliamentary group, with the exception of John Bracken, have been cool toward the development of an association which might eventually place them in a subordinate position.

Development of a Dominion Association

As early as May, 1920, a conference of twenty-one Conservatives from all parts of Canada met in Toronto to urge the reorganization of the party. Little came of this meeting. Since the national association of Sir John Macdonald's day had long ago disappeared, there was no group

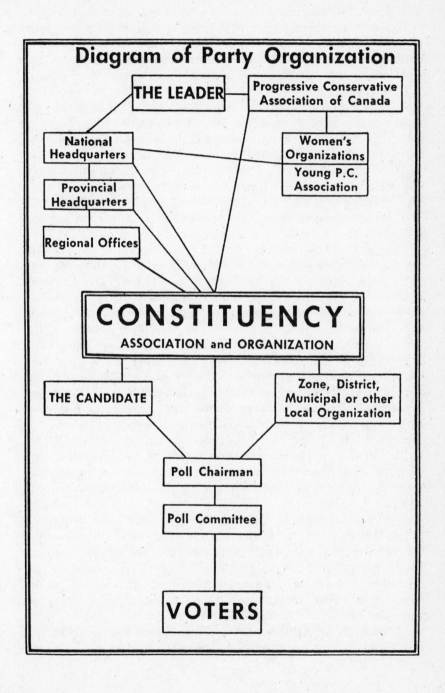

Diagram of Party Organization

THE LEADER

Progressive Conservative Association of Canada

National Headquarters

Women's Organizations
Young P.C. Association

Provincial Headquarters

Regional Offices

CONSTITUENCY
ASSOCIATION and ORGANIZATION

THE CANDIDATE

Zone, District, Municipal or other Local Organization

Poll Chairman

Poll Committee

VOTERS

in the party which could represent itself as the spokesman for the rank-and-file members. Finally, in large measure due to the insistence of John R. MacNicol, a party conference was held in Toronto on November 17, 1924, to establish a permanent organization called the Liberal-Conservative Association of Canada.[1]

This association exercised no real power in the party and did little more than exist in name. In fact, it was kept alive by the almost single-handed efforts of the late John R. MacNicol.[2] By 1941 there were only two thousand sustaining members in this Dominion Association.[3] Occasional "annual" meetings were held in Ottawa. Since the meetings were attended almost entirely by Conservatives from Quebec and Ontario, party members in such outlying areas as British Columbia and Nova Scotia complained that the association was dominated by a small clique.[4] Consequently, the association was not influential except in the central provinces.

There was apparently no formal written constitution for this association, although a so-called Dominion executive did exist and there were officers at the head of the association.[5] The only real contribution made to the operation of the party by the association was through the Dominion executive, which played a role in calling the conventions of 1927 and 1938. The only other occasion upon which the Dominion executive actually exercised any major influence in the course of Conservative party history was when it met (reinforced by ex officio members of the Senate and House of Commons) in Ottawa, November 7, 1941, ostensibly to consider the problem of rebuilding the organization and to decide the means by which a permanent party leader should be selected.[6] This meeting is most noted for the fact that it elected Arthur Meighen leader, but it was also this meeting which marked the first real attempt to organize a vigorous national association. Many of the suggestions made at this time were later realized during the years when John Bracken was leader.[7]

Previous attempts to reorganize the party had been attempted, but all had failed. At the 1938 convention the organization committee had presented a resolution, which was overwhelmingly approved by the delegates, to create a national Conservative council similar in membership to that of the executive of the Dominion Association. This council never met, although the resolution provided that it be convened not later than September 15, 1938.[8]

Manion thought that as leader he was obligated to establish this council on a functioning basis, and he attempted to persuade the provincial associations to name delegates to form the Dominion executive council. Only two or three provincial associations complied, and Manion quickly realized that he could not accomplish anything without more co-operation from the party members.[9]

The plan evolved at the 1938 convention was not put into effect because of the laxness of the provincial associations and the feeling current among Conservatives that a Dominion council was unnecessary. However, by the time of the 1942 convention, Conservatives had been jarred awake to the fact that they might not be able to survive as a party unless they built up an association to integrate the work of party members and to improve public relations. Consequently, a resolution similar to that of 1938 was passed at the 1942 convention authorizing the establishment of a Dominion Progressive Conservative Association. A constitution was outlined and provision was made that the association be set in operation not later than March 15, 1943, with the understanding that six members of the new association would bear the responsibility and authority for enforcing this resolution so that it could not be ignored as had earlier plans for a revitalized organization.[10] This Dominion Progressive Conservative Association was officially brought into existence at the first annual meeting held in Ottawa, March 13 and 14, 1943.[11]

Nature and Functions of the Progressive Conservative Association

The constitution of the Dominion Progressive Conservative Association provides for two types of membership: executive and general. General members pay the annual membership fee, attend meetings, participate in discussions at such meetings, and receive information, but they do not have the privilege of voting.[12] The executive membership consists of 113 persons, including ex officio officials and additional persons elected as executive officers of the association.

The Dominion Association is empowered to set up a committee on policy and resolutions to study party policies and report on them to the association at each annual meeting. The constitution clearly vests in the association authority to call national conventions, although for all practical purposes it is the executive officers who exercise this power. Establishment of a permanent party headquarters in each province is required by the constitution, and it lays down the rule that each federal riding shall form a Progressive Conservative association.

Beginning in 1943 annual meetings of the Dominion Progressive Conservative Association have been held regularly in Ottawa except in 1949. These annual meetings have been a fine device for enabling officers of the association to survey major problems in organization and public relations. Most of the meetings have considered reports by committees on the constitution, publicity, and organization. Association officers are elected by the executive members at these annual meetings. Resolutions are also passed at a great rate, but they apparently have little significance for policy or strategy. While the association concerns itself with the entire range of party affairs, including policy, at these meetings, in reality the party leader makes many decisions without consulting the association or the executive officers.[13]

Close co-operation between the parliamentary group and the association has been obtained by appointing to the committee on resolutions members of the House of Commons representing caucus committees. In this way it is possible to integrate the legislative program of the parliamentary group with the general principles of the party as approved by the annual meetings. However, because of the fear among members of the parliamentary group that the association would encroach upon their prerogatives, the resolutions committee at the 1947 meeting asserted that its report was not binding upon the party since an annual meeting is not a policy-making convention, and the report would be of value only because of the suggestions which were to be considered by the leader and caucus.[14]

Although annual meetings may promote a certain amount of party enthusiasm and unity, it is difficult to see that they are the "democratic" institution which they are hailed as being by party officials. For the most part the voting personnel at the annual meetings is composed of the same people who control the party in the House of Commons and in the provincial legislatures. Consequently, the party rank and file have no voice in the decisions reached, although they can make suggestions, and they are treated to a good show once a year. However, these meetings are valuable in providing a sounding board for the leader and publicizing the party program.

Below the Dominion level of organization exists a federal organization which reaches into the provinces. In most provinces there is a federal organizer directed by the national headquarters; in some cases he may also be the provincial organizer representing the provincial association. It is the task of the federal organizer in the province to organize Dominion riding associations, prepare lists of supporters, speak before influential groups, and raise party morale in that province.[15] The organizer and headquarters office in each province are the only evidence of the federal organization at the provincial level, and there are no meetings of federal association units at this level. The Conservative party has practically disappeared from provincial politics in the provinces of Quebec, Alberta, and Saskatchewan, but since the party still contests many of the federal ridings in these provinces, organizations and associations are still maintained. For the most part these organizations are artificial affairs kept alive by a few persons because of a family attachment to the Conservative party or because of an opportunistic desire to win a federal judgeship, postmastership, or Senate seat, should the Conservatives succeed in forming a Dominion Government. There is some inducement to a few people to maintain these shadow organizations because of the slight prestige which accrues to them from being officers in practically defunct organizations. At annual meetings of the Dominion Association they are likely to be lionized simply because they are the only Conservative standard bearers from a particular province and because of the wishful thinking in the national organization that such individuals represent the nucleus for rejuvenating local organizations. Since these shadow associations have no real "grass roots," but do have the privilege of participating in all national events such as conventions, they are quite useful to the national officials for influencing conventions and annual meetings.[16] Playing a major role in such pseudopolitical organizations does not appeal to the more capable and aggressive politicians in these provinces, even though some of them may inherit strong Conservative family traditions. Maurice Duplessis and Camillien Houde, both quondam Conservative provincial leaders in Quebec, soon realized the futility of spending their time and energy in a shadow organization, and they have both succeeded quite well on their own independent efforts after leaving the Conservative party.

Below the provincial level in the more populated areas there may be found intermediate organizations called regional offices. The regional office attempts to co-ordinate party activities in that area and gives general assistance to the riding associations. For the most part these intermediate offices have little significance.

Organization in the Ridings

It is at the level of the federal riding that elections are won and lost in Canada. Unfortunately for the Conservatives, the riding is the weakest link in their organization. In 1941 when there were 243 federal constituencies a Conservative survey indicated that the party was insufficiently organized in 204 of them. Today with 263 constituencies there is little evidence to indicate that the Conservatives are any better equipped in the ridings of Canada to contest general elections. Like the organization at the provincial level, many of these ridings are organized in token fashion by people who have a vested interest in the party machine. The national office, anxious to make as good a showing as possible in each election campaign, shortsightedly encourages them to run candidates so that the national officials may claim to be contesting as many federal seats as possible. Thus the appearance of party decadence is postponed until after the campaign, but there is no improvement in riding organization.

Some measures of the inadequacies of party organization at the riding level is indicated by the results in such provinces as Alberta and Saskatchewan in the 1949 general election. In Alberta the Progressive Conservatives contested fourteen out of seventeen ridings, and ten of these candidates lost their deposits. Much the same situation repeated itself in Saskatchewan, where all twenty ridings were contested by the Progressive Conservatives, but their candidates lost deposits in eighteen of the twenty ridings and carried only one constituency. The one successful Conservative in Saskatchewan was John Diefenbaker. Many Conservative candidates in Saskatchewan failed to carry even 10 per cent of the vote cast in a riding. In Quebec many candidates received less than 3 per cent of the vote in some constituencies.[17]

Part of the decline in party organization at the riding level may be explained by the preference of Conservative leaders to concern themselves with the broad sweep of national politics rather than to become involved in the intricacies of local politics. Under R.B. Bennett all local organization almost entirely disappeared except where it was kept alive by the individual members in the House of Commons.[18] Part of the decline in organizing work is also due to the lack of enthusiasm among young people, who feel that the Conservative party does not provide a future for them. Consequently, they are not likely to devote their efforts to building a local riding organization for what they feel is a lost cause, as well as a cause which has no appeal to them or genuine interest in them.[19] In addition, because of the long record of Conservative defeat, few aggressive young men interested in politics wish to become identified with the party. To improve the organization at the riding level the national party has done everything that could be done with large sums of money and high-powered publicity, but there has been practically no attempt to improve the personnel of party workers at this level. Fine pamphlets have been published on how to organize a local riding association, but, beyond describing what the ideal riding association should do, the national party has not ventured.

In theory the Progressive Conservative riding association is intended to "form a centre of political activity and strategy, and to stimulate and co-ordinate the work in the various districts, municipalities and polls within the constituency."[20] A few constituency associations actually succeed in realizing this ideal, but the great majority fall far short. In the successful riding association, this ideal is attained through an active executive composed of the officers, representatives from each poll area in the riding, and representatives of the women's and young people's organizations. It is this executive which is responsible for organization and maintaining party morale in the riding. The executive usually meets several times a year, depending upon the effectiveness of the officers and the urgency of the political situation. Annual meetings are held by most riding associations to elect officers, receive reports of committees, and discuss local politics and tactics. The most important meetings of the associations are to nominate candidates. Between meetings an efficient executive will see that there exists a poll committee in each voting subdivision to check on the political propensities of the voters, arrange occasional meetings to be addressed by party notables (including the constituency representative in the House of Commons or legislative assembly if he is a Conservative), distribute party literature, secure publicity in the local newspaper, and enroll new members in the riding association.[21]

While many riding associations are not as active as they should be, a few are very well organized and carry their responsibilities easily and well. In a few constituencies the Conservative riding association keeps a complete file of all voters. When a newcomer arrives in the constituency he is immediately visited by a member of the executive, his political affiliation is noted, and if he is likely to vote Conservative he will be urged to attend party meetings. For the active riding association the national party is willing and anxious to provide all possible help in organizing a constituency.

Auxiliary Associations

In addition to organizations directly in the line of the federal hierarchy there are affiliated organizations for women and young people. Unfortunately for the party, none of these groups have heretofore been used for much more than "window dressing." The leader and members of the parliamentary group have referred to young Conservative associations as proof that the Progressive Conservative party appeals to the young men and women of Canada. Actually the party as it is now constituted has little appeal to young people. However, party officials have seized upon the cliché that the party is composed of youth and repeated it so often that even they seem to believe it although there is small justification for such a contention.[22]

There seem to be several reasons for the existence of a young Progressive Conservative organization: (1) to keep abreast of the Liberal Party and the CCF, both of which have such associations; (2) to appeal to young voters; and (3) to segregate the more aggressive young men who might threaten the vested interests of the older members if they were to participate in the regular party organization.[23] Of the various functions of the young Progressive Conservative association probably the least successful is that of attracting young voters. The association is headed by a president elected at the annual meeting of the young Progressive Conservatives, and generally supervised by an executive secretary. This organization keeps busy issuing pamphlets assuring Canadians that the future belongs to the young people, who should take advantage of this fact by joining the party with a future.[24] By the spring of 1950 there were 130 Young Progressive Conservative clubs throughout Canada. Apparently few people take the organization seriously. In 1933 at a conference of young Conservatives, party officials revealed their real attitude toward the young members of the party much more effectively than does the sugar-coated literature distributed by national headquarters. J. Earl Lawson, MP and later national director, made it clear to the young Conservatives attending this meeting that their organization was purely educational and not intended to give their members a voice in party affairs. In outlining the party policy toward young Conservatives, Mr. Lawson asserted:

No party can afford to have two organizations striving for authority within a riding. There have been tried and experienced and capable riding organizations throughout the country long before you young fellows were ever thought of—or thinking of joining junior Conservative clubs. I don't intend to mince words with you. We can't disrupt the work and views of these organizations simply because some of us within the party thought it a good idea to form the Federation of Young Canada Conservative Clubs. I want to be perfectly frank with you. I cannot see for the life of me why you should try to force your view upon long-constituted capable authority.[25]

In addition to the young Progressive Conservative association, which does little more than publicize its existence, there is also a Progressive Conservative student federation which is also primarily "window-dressing." However, the members of this organization are somewhat more iconoclastic than the young Progressive Conservatives. Conservatives are careful to point out that the student federation "is an independent organization, not connected officially with the Party."[26] Local branches of the federation at such universities as Queens and Toronto are quite active and have succeeded in carrying out worthwhile programs in which the students themselves discussed political or economic problems and issues with outside speakers. Although the individual member may find it a valuable experience to belong to the federation, there is little indication that the federation exerts much influence upon the regular party organization.

As with youth, the Conservatives have been extremely loath to grant women much influence in the party, and for the most part few women have been anxious to play an active role. As in the case of young people, the more aggressive and active women are not likely to be Conservatives unless there is a strong family tradition.[27] Apparently the Conservatives have never decided upon the part which women are to play in the Conservative party. Consequently there prevails a split in party policy, with some party officials urging that women help to organize their constituencies for elections and with others holding that women's groups should confine themselves to purely social activities and not interfere in the serious business of politics.[28]

There is a Dominion Women's Progressive Conservative Association which was organized in 1946 from the Women's Committee of National Association established in 1942. This organization meets at the time of the annual Dominion Association meeting. At the 1950 annual meeting Sybil Bennett, niece of R.B. Bennett, was elected president. The delegates to this annual meeting of the women's group are appointed by the women's provincial associations. By 1949 there were slightly over two hundred local associations which were expected to hold monthly meetings for the purpose of hearing speakers, discussing papers, and publicizing the activities of the party.[29] On the national level, the women's association publishes a monthly "News Letter to Progressive Conservative Women" which is a chatty little publication describing the organizing work of the national chairman and the progress made by the women in their provincial and local meetings. Beginning with a circulation list of 250 subscribers, the popularity of this publication has steadily grown. By the summer of 1949 there were over eight thousand paid-up members receiving this news letter.[30]

Women are represented on the executive of the Dominion Progressive Conservative Association by the president and secretary of the national women's organization and the president of each provincial women's association; in addition, there must be one woman in the representation of each province. The major influence of women in the party is exerted through these representatives on the Dominion executive and through those few hardy souls who have persevered against many obstacles both inside and outside the party. Most evidence seems to indicate that women in the Conservative party play a slightly less active role than do their sisters in the Liberal party of Canada or the Republican and Democratic parties in the United States, and they are not nearly so important to the party as are women in the CCF in Canada or in the British Labour Party.

The National Direction

Supervising the entire operation of the Dominion organization is the party's national director. In the party machinery outside Parliament, he is second in importance only to the leader. Upon him falls the responsibility of providing for all the details of conventions, elections, and annual meetings as well as directing the national headquarters staff and keeping in touch with all constituency associations. He also serves in a twofold fashion as a liaison officer: (1) between the parliamentary group and the organization outside Parliament, and (2) between the provincial and national organizations. His job is perhaps more strenuous and demanding than that of any other party official, including the leader, and it should be filled by a competent organizer who can devote all his time to problems of organization and publicity. Above all else he must be thoroughly acquainted with political factors in all parts of the country and be willing to work long hours attempting to adjust the party machinery to these diverse factors while at the same time integrating the various sections and interests within the party into a smoothly running organization.[32] Unfortunately, prior to the time that R.A. Bell became national director this post was filled by men who gave only part-time attention to it, and, in fact, some of them did not function at all between general elections.

The inadequacies of the national organizers during the 1920's and 1930's and their failure to devote themselves wholeheartedly to the organization are important reasons for the decline of the party. In startling contrast to the Liberals, the Conservatives have lacked continuity of organizers. For each general election from 1921 to 1945 there was a different national organizer, and as a result not one of them had the opportunity to develop the experience necessary for successfully fulfilling the requirements of the job. This continual change of organizers was partly a reflection of the chaotic conditions within the party; as one leader replaced another, each appointed an organizer who would be personally loyal to him.[33]

Until recently little thought has been given to the qualifications and functions of the national organizer. Appointments seem to have fluctuated about equally between millionaires and party hacks. The Hon. Robert Rogers was the major organizational figure during a large part of the Borden Government. He was a wizard on political tactics in the provincial field, but his techniques were a little too crude to succeed in the infinitely more complicated Dominion field.[34] The organizer at the end of the Borden regime, James Calder, was successful when aided by the wartime pressures of 1917, but he failed lamentably as organizer in the election of 1921.[35] After Calder, Arthur Meighen in quick succession appointed J.W. Black, who encountered nothing but reverses, and S.F. Tolmie, who achieved little.[36]

With the appointment of General A.D. McRae as party organizer in 1926, there were indications that the Conservatives had at last found an organizer who would hold the office for many years and devote himself willingly to the task of building up a favorable public opinion. A millionaire, he spent large sums of his own in organizing the 1927 convention and in fostering the candidacy of R.B. Bennett for the leadership.[37] His great wealth and his close relationship with many businessmen facilitated the important task of collecting funds for the party coffers. Noted for his affability, McRae mingled much with newspaper correspondents and other publicists, and by 1930 he had developed a smoothly operating publicity bureau which was a potent and successful weapon in the election of 1930.[38] Following the victorious election of 1930 McRae was rewarded with appointment to the Senate in 1931.[39] He continued to exert some influence upon Conservative policy and strategy, although he made no effort to maintain the organization following a breach with R.B. Bennett. In fact, the elaborate party headquarters were closed immediately after the election.[40]

By the end of 1934 the party began to prepare for a general election in 1935. Typical of the tardiness with which the Conservatives prepared to meet the onslaught of the Liberals was the way in which Bennett postponed appointing J. Earl Lawson as federal organizer until the campaign was practically at hand. Lawson, who had been first elected to the House of Commons at a by-election in 1928, was serving his second term in the Commons when appointed organizer. Apparently his chief qualification for the post was his parliamentary experience. Several of Lawson's pronouncements on party affairs indicate it would have been difficult for the party to have selected a more inept organizer.[41] In addition, Lawson was further handicapped by Bennett's appointing him Minister of National Revenue and thereby placing him in an impossible dual role. A large measure of responsibility for the party defeat in 1935 must rest upon Lawson, as well as upon the short-sighted leader who did not appoint him organizer until a few months before the election.

In accepted Conservative fashion, the national organizer ceased to exert much influence after the 1935 election, and the formal machinery, already severely atrophied by Bennett's neglect, practically disappeared. Bennett's successor, R.J. Manion, however, was acutely aware of the need for organization, and he set about the task by appointing Dr. J.M. Robb national organizer. This appointment was particularly unfortunate.[42] Robb was a general practitioner in the small backwoods town of Blind River in northern Ontario. Dabbling a bit in Ontario politics, he had been elected twice and defeated four times in six provincial general elections. Although he had served as Ontario Minister of Health, he evinced no great ability in provincial politics, and he had never ventured into the federal field before his appointment as organizer. Thus he had practically no contacts among members of Parliament or other party notables. Removed from his normal environment, he had little idea of how to conduct a national campaign. Lacking any kind of journalistic experience, he had few conceptions of the role of publicity except of the most rudimentary sort. In addition, to complicate further Manion's problems with finance, Robb had no wide acquaintanceship among business interests that might have been willing to help finance the 1940 campaign. After learning something of how to conduct a political campaign in the hard school of experience, Dr. Robb retired to his medical practice following the defeat of 1940, and the party was again left without a national director.[43]

Finally, in April, 1943, after Gordon Graydon had made an extensive survey of party organization and pointed out the need for a regular national director, John Bracken appointed R.A. Bell to the post. Without doubt Bell was the most competent of the many persons to hold this position. Well acquainted with party history, tradition, and politics, Bell spared neither himself nor his staff in working to improve the organization. Bell was the best available man for the post, and it was in large part through his efforts that the party has been held together in the period of 1943-1949. Consequently it was a severe blow to the party when Bell announced in August, 1949, his decision to resign as national director in order that he might resume the practice of law.[44] Bell's resignation after the party's defeat in the general election of 1949 follows the familiar pattern for retiring organizers. Although Bell had long expressed the desire to resume his law practice, it is doubtful if he would have resigned in case of a party victory. This resignation may indicate a general deterioration in party organization and the desire of George Drew to surround himself with men who had been closely associated with him in Ontario provincial politics. On August 3, 1950, W.H. Kidd was appointed national director to succeed Bell.

The national director is appointed by the party leader and is responsible only to the leader. An informal relationship exists between the national director and the executive of the Dominion Association, but in the case of conflict between the leader and the executive, the director's first loyalty is to the leader and only to the leader.[45] A close relationship exists between national headquarters and the parliamentary group, and it is maintained by the director, who performs a liaison function between the two. He regularly sits in meetings of the caucus, where he is available for questioning, and in caucus he can speak freely in describing organization plans to members of the parliamentary group. Very often he is consulted before the caucus reaches a major decision. Should he not be present in caucus, the leader or chief whip will acquaint him afterward with the opinions of the caucus relating to organization. However, Dominion headquarters is not under the control of the parliamentary group, and the relationship between the two "must be characterized by a measure of give and take."[46]

During election campaigns the national director supervises campaign publicity, co-ordinates activities in all ridings as much as possible, plans speaking tours for the leader and other party officials, and is kept occupied marshalling party forces in all parts of the Dominion. Like a military chief-of-staff, he plans, co-ordinates, and can act only in the name of the leader. Before the general election of 1945, R.A. Bell was responsible for the establishment of a school for candidates in Ottawa. Of only several days' duration, it was a splendid example of what can be done by a national organizer to acquaint candidates with problems of campaigning, to instruct them in party history and policies, and to give them an elementary conception of the nature of Canadian government. In addition, Bell toured all ridings giving talks on organization and pointing out to candidates and campaign managers how they might best improve the effectiveness of their appeal to the voters.

In preparing for a national convention or annual meeting, it is the national director who investigates the facilities of the meeting place, arranges for amplifiers and radio broadcasts, acts as liaison agent with the press, plans decorations, carries on research to determine procedure at previous conventions, and with the help of his staff sets up the complicated machinery for certifying and registering delegates.[47] In addition, he must be a diplomat in settling disputes between groups at meetings, and very often he has the responsibility for smoothing over differences within the party so as to give the public the impression of party amity.

Between elections and conventions the director supervises the staff at national headquarters, answers inquiries on party policy and organization, tours the country to encourage local party organizations, speaks at party rallies, and directs all aspects of public relations.[48] In case of a by-election, he usually visits the constituency, helps the local officials organize their campaign, and may accompany the leader on a speaking tour of the riding.

National Party Headquarters

The Dominion headquarters over which the director presides is the point of origin for most party publicity and organization work. Like the Liberal party and the CCF, the Conservatives maintain their central office in Ottawa, where the party leader and the parliamentary group can make full use of their services. Until 1943 the Conservatives rented a suite of rooms in an office building on Wellington Street. Rent for the suite with a mailing room in the basement amounted to $200 a month.[49] Between elections little use was made of this suite. In 1943 the party purchased a large, old brick residence on Laurier Avenue for $8,700. Cost of renovating this building for use as a national headquarters amounted to $3,000.[50] Officially named "Bracken House" while John Bracken was leader, and now referred to as Dominion headquarters, the building is owned by a corporation, Bracken House, Ltd., established under Ontario law. Maintenance and repairs have been financed out of rent from garages in the back of the building and from the sale of waste paper.[51] The advantages which accrue from the party's ownership of its own headquarters are many. In addition to saving $200 a month in rental, the building provides far more working space than did the office suite. Even more important, however, is the greater degree of permanency for the headquarters of the organization than was previously the case, and it is no longer possible for the headquarters to be closed between elections, as was customary before 1943. The permanent building also provides a satisfactory meeting place for the women's organization and the young people's association.

The size of the staff in the national headquarters up to 1943 followed the vagaries of election campaigns. After the successful election of 1930 until March, 1935, there was no activity in national headquarters. For the 1935 campaign a staff was hastily improvised and then allowed to disintegrate almost as soon as the election was over. From 1936 until planning began for the 1938 convention there were only two people on the staff, the executive secretary and a mailing-room boy. In preparation for the convention of 1938 the staff was expanded to twelve people, and it remained at about that size in preparation for the 1940 campaign. After the 1940 fiasco, the staff quickly melted away. At the time of the 1942 convention there were only two regular employees on the staff, and most of the convention plans were made by party workers in House Leader Hanson's office. With the election of Bracken to the leadership, the appointment of R.A. Bell as national director, and the purchase of Bracken House, a regular staff of about fourteen persons was established. In the summer of 1948 the headquarters staff was increased to twenty-four and remained at that number after the convention. During the election campaign there were thirty full-time employees, but after the 1949 election the staff was cut down to twelve.

During the periods between elections and conventions, the national headquarters settles into a routine for handling day-to-day business. There are letters of inquiry on party policy or requests for literature which must be answered. Lists of officers in the constituency and provincial associations are kept up-to-date. Major newspapers from all parts of the Dominion are read, and items of political significance are clipped and filed for future use.[52] The staff collects advertisements issued by Canadian political parties and pastes them in large scrapbooks for later reference. Pamphlets and broadsides distributed by Canadian and British parties are saved and analyzed for suggestions to improve Progressive Conservative publicity material. When Parliament is in session, the *House of Commons Debates* are received and studied by the staff. While Parliament sits the staff is prepared to answer questions which a member of the parliamentary group may ask in connection with preparing a speech. Other services provided members of the parliamentary group include obtaining railway tickets and reservations, helping to arrange rallies in the constituencies, and providing extra secretarial aid when needed.

Part of the task of the national office is to maintain a record of party activities and party finances. One of the greatest advantages of a permanent headquarters is that it provides a place where records can be kept over a long period of time. In the past this advantage did not exist, and party workers today are often handicapped by the absence of party records from the 1920's and 1930's which were largely destroyed in 1940 and 1941. A permanent party headquarters lessens the possibility of such wholesale destruction of files.

Perhaps the most important function of the national office lies in the area of public relations. Members of the headquarters staff are available for speeches on party policy and organization. They are often called upon to represent the party at formal occasions such as the Governor-General's Dominion Day lawn party, at the funeral of a prominent public personage, or at a public ceremony when Parliament is not in session. In the field of public relations, the headquarters staff concentrates upon the preparation and dissemination of publicity. This publicity takes many forms. Pamphlets and one-sheet broadsides are issued by the national office during and between elections. The nature of the arguments in these publications has altered little since World War I, but they are a good deal more colorful. Cartoons ridiculing the Liberal Government, depicting the menace of communism, or bewailing the large government surplus are favorite features of the one-sheet broadside. On the reverse side of these sheets is an exhortation to support the Progressive Conservative party.

In most instances the appeal to the voter is on an abstract plane bearing little relation to the realities of Canadian political life. Instead of outlining the party policy on family allowances or housing in specific terms, party publicity has relied on vague and high-sounding generalities of "sound government," "enactment of a Canadian Bill of Rights," and "justice for veterans."[53] Conservative publicity shows an almost psychopathic concern over "the communist menace," "the Canadian Way of Life," and "Free Enterprise," but it does little to tie these phrases down to material problems in Canada. Consequently, hundreds of thousands of Canadian voters are relatively untouched by Conservative publicity because it has little or no meaning for them.

A bimonthly newspaper, *Public Opinion*, is published by national headquarters. Started in 1942, its circulation has risen to about 30,000.[54] However, this figure should not be taken to indicate that there are 30,000 Canadians paying the subscription of a dollar a year for *Public Opinion*. In the first place, *Public Opinion* is the "premium" included with membership in the Dominion Association, and all dues-paying members (approximately 4,500) receive the party newspaper. Secondly, each riding association is allowed one hundred free copies to distribute among party supporters. Of course, not all associations take advantage of the offer, but if all 260 of them did, 26,000 copies would be circulated free on this basis.[55]

During 1943 *Public Opinion* was devoted to publicizing John Bracken, fostering the idea that the Progressive Conservatives were a brave new party, and building up interest in the young Progressive Conservative organization and the women's associations. *Public Opinion* combines some valuable and readable features with a great deal that is nonsensical or downright wishful thinking.[56] One of the more valuable contributions of *Public Opinion* has been an attempt to acquaint the Conservative subscribers with the members of the parliamentary group through a series of articles on "The Men around John Bracken." This series ran from October, 1946, to October, 1947. Another series, not quite so extensive but helpful, was entitled "Know Your Members" and under this heading there appeared in each issue a brief sketch of several members, with their photographs.[57] Other articles on organization and party policies have been valuable as an attempt to make the Conservative rank and file aware of the possibilities for improving the party. Unfortunately, however, many of the more recent issues have been devoted to sensational charges against the Liberals and the CCF, criticisms of the "bureaucracy," and exorbitant praise for all Conservative pronouncements.[58] *Public Opinion* compares favourably with such party publications in the United States as the *Democratic Digest* or the *Republican News*, and it handles the same type of material with the traditional deprecation of the opposition and inordinate praise for the party's own accomplishments. However, without doubt it is far inferior to the Liberal party's magazine, *The Canadian Liberal*, on almost all counts.

Another area of publicity covered by the national headquarters is radio. The staff prepares fifteen-minute radio broadcasts describing party policies for use in general elections and by-elections. In several by-elections one-minute radio announcements have been prepared by the national office on behalf of the local candidate.[59]

After Bell became national director motion pictures were used fairly extensively for publicity. Under direction of the headquarters staff, professional photographers have made motion pictures on John Bracken and his life, the 1948 convention, and George Drew. The movie on the 1948 convention is well done and particularly valuable because it gives a general impression of the procedure and atmosphere at a Canadian national convention.

Besides the material intended for the consumption of the general public, the national office produces many publications of a more or less esoteric character. A series of pamphlets on organization have recently been published to instruct party members on the purpose, nature, and techniques of organization.[60] Each contains a suggested constitution for every type of local association as well as a specific outline for organizing constituency associations.

Another useful publication is the *Scrutineers' Manual* published to serve as a guide for Conservative scrutineers and workers at Dominion elections. This little manual is full of information on precautions for scrutineers, duties before the polls open, procedure for checking ballot boxes at the close of polling, and methods of counting ballots.

Notes

1 See *Canadian Annual Review, 1924-25*, p. 205. The leader, Arthur Meighen, was named honorary president; in recognition of their services in the creation of this association John R. MacNicol was elected president and Robert Rogers was made treasurer. There were to be two vice-presidents, a man and a woman, from each province (*ibid.*, p. 205).

2 John R. MacNicol was a staunch and well-to-do Conservative who devoted a great deal of time and money to the problem of building Conservative associations in South York, in the province of Ontario, and in the Dominion. He served continuously in the House of Commons from 1930 until defeated in 1949.

3 John W. Lederle, "The National Organization of the Liberal and Conservative Parties in Canada" (unpublished doctoral dissertation in the University of Michigan Library, Ann Arbor, 1942), p. 155.

4 "Memorandum" from R.A. Bell, Dec. 6, 1947, p. 1.

5 The officers consisted of a president, nine ex officio vice-presidents who were also presidents of the provincial Conservative associations, a treasurer, and an executive secretary. Until 1941 the Dominion executive consisted of (*a*) officers of the association, (*b*) the national party leader, (*c*) provincial leaders, (*d*) the national Conservative organizer, (*e*) two representatives from the Dominion Young Conservative association, (*f*) the chairman of the press committee, and (*g*) representatives from the provincial Conservative associations distributed as follows: Ontario—7, Quebec—7, the seven remaining provinces—4 each, and the Yukon—1. See the Dominion Conservative Association, *The Conservative Party of Canada* (Ottawa 1941) inside back cover. At the meeting of the Dominion executive held in Ottawa in Nov., 1941, Mr. MacNicol announced that at the request of the Conservative association of Ontario and of the Quebec association, the number of representatives from the provincial Conservative associations (*g* above) had been doubled, and that later the two representatives from the young Conservative association had been increased to four (*Minutes of the Conservative Representatives in Ottawa, November 7th and 8th, 1941* [hereinafter referred to as *Minutes, 1941*], p. 6.)

6 Following the electoral debacle of 1940, the parliamentary group, thoroughly frightened by the catastrophe, turned to MacNicol and his much ridiculed association for help in strengthening the relationship between the voters and the parliamentary group. An organization committee under the chairmanship of Gordon Graydon had been sent out

to survey the national situation. The caucus had been asked for a joint meeting with the Dominion executive on the first Saturday following the reassembling of Parliament in order that the report of this committee on organization could be fully considered. See *Minutes, 1941*, p. 5.

7   For the first time since 1920 a complete survey of party organization was made. The effect of inadequate attention to organization was soon discovered through this survey, and Gordon Graydon reported "that a decade of non-continuous nation-wide organization and publicity...has left heavy damage in its trail" (*Minutes, 1941*, p. 29).

8   For a detailed description of the plan for a Conservative council, see *Proceedings of the Convention of the National Conservative Party of Canada, Held in the Coliseum, Landsdowne Park, Ottawa, on July 5, 6 and 7, 1938* (hereinafter referred to as *Proceedings, 1938*), pp. 294-295. The resolution also suggested the appointment of a national organizer with headquarters in Ottawa, a permanent party headquarters in every province, common associations in each province for both the federal and provincial fields, and regular annual meetings of each provincial association (*ibid.*, p. 294). Also see the *Globe and Mail* (Toronto), July 6, 1938, p. 1.

9   See *Minutes, 1941*, pp. 4-5.

10   *Official Report, 1942*, p. 312.

11   See the *Gazette* (Montreal), March 15, 1943, pp. 1, 18, for account of the first annual meeting, including debate on the constitution and the election of Gordon Graydon as the first president of the association.

12   See the constitution of the Dominion Progressive Conservative Association, clause III, section B. R.A. Bell pointed out that the general members are not allowed to vote because of earlier experience with the Dominion Conservative Association of the 1920's. In the earlier association all members enjoyed the right to vote, and as a consequence members living close to Ottawa dominated the association to the disadvantage of people in outlying areas. Under the present arrangement, most of the general members who attend annual meetings are from the vicinity of Ottawa, but since they cannot vote they have no more influence than general members in British Columbia, who are represented by the same proportion of executive members as are Ontario Conservatives (interview with R.A. Bell, July 7, 1949). Actually, of course, this arrangement provides the means for secure control of the association by an inner circle of party officials.

13   "Memorandum" from R.A. Bell, p. 2. Bell writes: "Generally speaking, the necessity for changes arises on short notice and decisions must be taken by the Leader after consultation with such advisers as he chooses without reference to the Association or its Executive" (*ibid.*, p. 2).

14 "Minutes of the Progressive Conservative Association of Canada, Appendix d" (1947). Also see R. MacG. Dawson, *The Government of Canada* (Toronto, 1947), pp. 550-551.

15 "Memorandum" from R.A. Bell, received Dec. 6, 1947, p. 2.

16 Party officials are also anxious to give some appearance of party activity in these provinces so that at national conventions the Progressive Conservatives will not reveal their national weaknesses by being unable to obtain delegations from these provinces. Actually, the associations in these provinces are of little real value, and, as in the case of Quebec, may cause great disunity at party conventions and also play a role in selecting the party leader which is entirely out of proportion to their real importance. These "shadow" organizations, like the Republican party organizations in some Southern states, exert little real influence outside the party but are possessed of real power within the party.

17 See the *Evening Citizen* (Ottawa), June 28, 1949, p. 20. The statistics on which the above comments are based were derived from a summary of the results of the 1949 general election compiled by the Canadian Press.

18 Interview with the late Sir Henry Drayton, June 16, 1948.

19 In an interview on June 30, 1948, M. Grattan O'Leary said that when addressing local meetings in Ontario he was appalled at the number of old men and women in the audience. Seldom were these meetings attended by young people, and most of the audiences were composed almost entirely of middle-aged or older people. The frequent repetition of this spectacle has made him wonder about the value of such meetings. Instead of talking to older men and women who will fast die out as party supporters, O'Leary thought the speakers should have been appealing to young people who have many years of voting before them.

20 The Progressive Conservative Party, *Constituency Organization* (Ottawa, 1948), p. 6.

21 For a thorough discussion of what is expected of the riding association and its executive committee, see the Progressive Conservative Party, *Constituency Organization* (Ottawa, 1948). This pamphlet of forty-two pages outlines the methods for establishing and maintaining riding associations. Also valuable is the Progressive Conservative Party, *Meetings and Procedures* (Ottawa, 1949). These two pamphlets in a series of five are the product of a growing awareness in the party of the value of organization. They were written by the national headquarters staff, and their publication was one of R.A. Bell's contributions to the party; he was the prime mover in this series of pamphlets on organization.

22 An amusing incident occurred at the nominating meeting in Carleton county, June 13, 1949, when the various candidates and their seconders spoke to the Carleton voters in Richmond. George Drew, the Pro-

gressive Conservative candidate, began his speech with the assertion that the Progressive Conservatives were a party of young people who were rising all over Canada in righteous indignation to throw out of office the "old" Liberal Government. His Liberal opponent, John H. Macdonald, a young man of thirty-six, was completely ignored by Drew. M. Grattan O'Leary, Drew's seconder, proceeded to disparage Macdonald as an untried, inexperienced youngster who did not have a chance against a veteran campaigner twenty years his senior. The Minister of Reconstruction and Supply, R.H. Winters, who seconded Macdonald, aptly pointed out the disparity between Drew's claims and O'Leary's comments.

23   R. MacG. Dawson observes: "Segregation probably makes both sections of the party somewhat happier: the younger members are given a sense of importance and responsibility and are freed from the dampening influences of their seniors; the older members may then go their own gait undisturbed by the nagging impatience and ebullience of youth. In short, segregation, while conducive to internal peace, is probably bad for both groups." (*op. cit.*, p. 533).

24   See the Progressive Conservative Party, *Young Progressive Conservative Organization* (Ottawa, 1949), p. 5. Also indicative of the manner in which the party has attempted to organize the young people are the Young Progressive Conservatives of Canada, *Organizers' Handbook* (Ottawa, n.d.) and *How to Organize a Discussion Group* (Ottawa, n.d.).

25   *Mail and Empire* (Toronto), Sept. 9, 1933, p. 4.

26   *Young Progressive Conservative Organization* , p. 10.

27   A case in point is that of Miss Jeanne Travers, president of the Ottawa Progressive Conservative Business Women's Club. A Conservative because of family ties, she has persisted in trying to organize women in the party despite almost constant opposition from the regular organization (interview with Jeanne Travers, Sept. 29, 1948).

28   In talking with several members of the Conservative parliamentary group, the writer asked why women were not more active in party affairs. They all agreed that politics is no place for women. The rank and file probably agree in large measure with this opinion. At the Carleton nomination meeting in Richmond, June 13, 1949, Eugene Forsey, the CCF candidate, was seconded by a Mrs. MacCordick, and the audience, predominantly Conservative, snickered, made lewd remarks among themselves, and shuffled their feet. They refused to give her the attention they had allowed the other non-Conservative speakers—to say nothing of the rapt attention they had accorded Mr. Drew and his seconder. One farmer who applauded Drew at great length observed: "That CCF feller oughta know a woman wouldn't do him no good."

29   Letter from Miss Hilda Hesson, former chairman of the women's association, July 18, 1949.

30 *Idem.*

31 See Dean E. McHenry, *His Majesty's Opposition* (Berkeley, 1940), pp. 102-105.

32 See statement of task of party organizer made by General A.D. McRae, quondam federal Conservative director, at 1938 national convention (*Proceedings, 1938*, p. 72).

33 The Liberals had only two different national organizers during the same period that the Conservatives had six. This stability in the Liberal organization is no doubt in large part due to the long and astute leadership of W.L. Mackenzie King. See J.W. Lederle, *op. cit.*, p. 166.

34 See M. Grattan O'Leary, "The Rival Chiefs of Staff," *Maclean's Magazine*, XLIII, No. 13 (July 1, 1930), 8. For an illuminating account of the methods employed by Robert Rogers in the province of Manitoba, see "Report of the Royal Commission Constituted to Inquire into All Matters Pertaining to the Manitoba Agricultural College," especially p. 46; "Report of the Royal Commission Constituted to Inquire into and Report on All Expenditures for Road Work during the Year 1914"; and "Report of the Royal Commission Appointed to Investigate the Charges Made in the Statement of C.P. Fullerton, K.C."

35 O'Leary, "The Rival Chiefs of Staff," *loc. cit.*, p. 8.

36 *Ibid.*, p. 8, and *Canadian Annual Review, 1923*, p. 163.

37 O'Leary, "The Rival Chiefs of Staff," *loc. cit.*, p. 8.

38 Because of the wealth of such men as McRae and Bennett, the Conservatives could afford a large staff of journalists, secretaries, and publicity men who used the most modern equipment, so that party headquarters resembled a propaganda bureau found in "connection with vast research foundations in the United States" (*ibid.*, p. 8).

39 In Canada it is customary for the leader of a successful party to appoint the national organizer to the Senate in recognition of his services. A seat in the Senate provides the organizer with a stable income and a position of recognized social and political prestige without burdening him with onerous duties. For a discussion of McRae's role as an adviser to Bennett, see Lederle, *op. cit.*, p. 143.

40 Usual procedure at this time was to open a national office for the general election campaign, and then to lock the headquarters as soon as the campaign was over, and to forget it until the next election (interview with R.A. Bell, July 7, 1949).

41 It was Lawson who had implied to the young Conservatives that there was no room for them in party councils. When informed that in two ridings membership on the executive had been granted to young Conservatives, Mr. Lawson retorted: "Well, that's holding out the olive branch farther than I ever would have done" (*Mail and Empire*, Toronto, Sept. 9, 1933, p. 4).

42　One observer commented that Robb was appointed by Manion solely because of the "imaginary necessity to 'do something' for a party regular, bankrupt in executive experience and sales ability" (H.L. Marshall, "Sunshine or Shadow for Conservative Party?" *Saturday Night*, LVIII, No. 8, Oct. 31, 1942, 17a). Selection of Robb indicates how little thought leaders have given to the qualifications necessary for a successful organizer.

43　Lederle, *op. cit.*, p. 167.

44　See the *Evening Journal* (Ottawa), Aug. 26, 1949, p. 16. His resignation was effective in September (*ibid.*, Sept. 23, 1949, p. 16).

45　"Memorandum" received from R.A. Bell, Dec. 6, 1947, p. 2, and interview with R.A. Bell, Aug. 6, 1948.

46　*Ibid.*, p. 3.

47　See "Minutes of Meeting of the Executive Officers of the Progressive Conservative Association of Canada, held in the Progressive Conservative Caucus Room, House of Commons, July 26, 1948," pp. 2-3. In the summer of 1948 R.A. Bell attended the Liberal national convention in order to get ideas for organizing the forthcoming Progressive Conservative convention.

48　In summing up his functions as national organizer, R.A. Bell described them as sixfold: (1) co-ordination and direction of organization—including receiving reports from local ridings and suggesting organization techniques to them; (2) co-ordination of women's organization with general organization; (3) co-ordination of young people's activities with general organization; (4) supervision of public relations; (5) supervision of research and information; and (6) administration—including direction of national headquarters and finance (from interview with R.A. Bell, July 7, 1949).

49　Lederle, *op. cit.*, p. 172.

50　Interview with R.A. Bell, July 7, 1949.

51　Total garage rent is $20 a month. All information on purchase, ownership, and maintenance of Dominion headquarters was obtained from R.A. Bell in interview of July 7, 1945.

52　Besides the daily newspapers, the Dominion headquarters subscribes to publications such as the CCF *News* (Toronto), the *Commonwealth* (Regina), and the *Canadian Liberal*.

53　See "The Progressive Conservative Party's Practical Proposals for a Better Canada" (Ottawa, 1948). In the Introduction to this thirteen-page pamphlet there are repeated the same clichés which are used over and over again in all party publicity. Also see "12 Reasons for Joining the Progressive Conservative Party Now" (Ottawa, 1947), "4 Questions for Canadian Women" (Ottawa, 1948), "Why Protection Is Necessary?"

(Ottawa, 1921), and "Do You Realize the Extent of the Employment Given by Manufacturing?" (Ottawa, 1921).

54 Interview with C.V. Charters, July 7, 1949. Charters was director of public relations from early in 1947 until July, 1949.

55 See "Report of the Publicity Committee," in "Minutes of the Progressive Conservative Association of Canada, March 28th and 29th, 1947, Appendix c." Apparently not even the lure of "something for nothing" could persuade all riding associations to accept this offer. In addition, each riding association could put another hundred names on the subscription list at an annual charge of $40.00 (*ibid.*).

56 Among its better features in 1945 and 1946 was a series of pictures of government buildings in Ottawa with a brief statement of the history or function of the building. For instance, see *Public Opinion*, IV, No. 2 (Aug., 1945), 1. Later there appeared a series of pictures and articles entitled "Salute to Canada and Great Canadians," paying tribute to prominent men in major Canadian occupations: Tom Moore, former president of the Trades and Labour Congress of Canada; E.S. Archibald, director of the Dominion experimental farms; and P.D. Ross, publisher of the *Journal* (Ottawa). For an example, see *ibid.*, V, No. 8 (Aug., 1946), 1.

57 For example, see *ibid.*, VI (March, 1948), 5, or VI (April, 1948), 5.

58 Headlines from a few of these issues give some conception of the subject matter favored in *Public Opinion*: "Govt. Farm Policies Cause Food Scarcities—Raise Prices," VI (April, 1948), 8; "Finagling in Civil Service Appointments," VI (March, 1948), 8; "Red Tape Makes Waste," VI (Feb., 1948), 8. Headlines on the front page usually blazon some ridiculous assertion that indicates the lengths to which Conservatives must go to raise their morale. For example, under the headline "A Dying Government" a lengthy article was devoted to the contention that the King Cabinet was composed of tired men supported by "uneasy" private members (VI, March, 1948, 1, 7). In the summer of 1948 *Public Opinion* claimed "Parliament Session Ends on Despondent Note for Liberals," and an article alleged that Louis St. Laurent would not contest the Liberal leadership since he had not proved his mettle as a vote-getter in the Quebec provincial election of 1948 (VI, July-Aug., 1948, 3).

59 For the York-Sunbury by-election, Oct. 17, 1947, one of these one-minute scripts announced: "YOUNG PEOPLE OF YORK-SUNBURY: YOU are the ones most vitally concerned in making your voices heard. Let YOUR ballot be a protest against a Government who NEEDED and USED You in War; but neglected to provide shelter where you could live and bring up a family when you got home. Against a Government whose remedy for unemployment is a wholesale exodus of trained young men and women to other Provinces and to the United States, instead of wise policies for Maritime development. You, married student veterans, hit

HARD by increased costs of living—PROTEST. Vote SANSOM who fought WITH and FOR you" (from collection of radio scripts in national Progressive Conservative headquarters).

60   This series includes five pamphlets: (1) *Constituency Organization*; (2) *Women's Organizations*; (3) *Young Progressive Conservative Organization*; (4) *Meetings and Procedures*; and (5) *Party Handbook*. All of these pamphlets have been issued in French as well as in English. This valuable series is the creation of R.A. Bell, who relied heavily upon his personal experience in organization when he prepared this material. The pamphlet on women's organization, however, was written by Miss Hilda Hesson, national director of the women's Progressive Conservative association.

W. Young A Party-Movement: The CCF and the Rejection of Brokerage Politics

> For most of its history the role of the CCF has been that of a voice crying in the wilderness, a conscience informing, animating, goading old parties into some overdue reforms.
>
> Andrew Brewin (1943)

The CCF began in the West because it was there that the roots of protest had grown strong in the soil of discontent, that the isolation of the frontier, the malevolence of nature and eastern business were most keenly felt, driving the people to build their own organic society expressing values foreign to industrial capitalism. Chief among these values were co-operation and fellowship. It began in the West because many workers, isolated and alienated like the farmers, created their own societies either through their trade unions or through the simpler fellowship of learning and discussion.[1] And it was in the West that many immigrants settled, bringing to the plains the philosophy of the British Labour party and from the United States, the populist and semi-socialist movements such as the Non-Partisan League. There was both cause and contact. A common link among these elements was their belief in fellowship; in some it was represented by the social gospel, in some by the brotherhood of trade unions, and in others by the necessary unity of the working class.

The CCF was created by the bringing together of the politically active farm groups, the labour and the socialist parties that had united in the Western Conference of Labour Political Parties, and Fabian intellectuals from eastern Canada, and the Ginger and Labour group from the House of Commons. If there was a catalyst it was James Shaver Woodsworth. The socialism the CCF espoused was the product of its Fabian element and meant different things to each of the groups that formed the party. Those who supported the CCF did so for various reasons, but reasons which, at that time, precluded support for the Liberal or Conservative parties.

The farmer supported the CCF because it offered him a means of overcoming the deficiencies of his situation. For the farmer's benefit the socialism of the CCF excluded public ownership of farms and, later, small businesses, was not too vehemently against profit or property if there was enough for all, and supported the idea that the farmer should be his own boss—free enterprise as opposed to private enterprise. In addition, the anti-establishment attitude of the CCF fitted well with the resentment and envy felt by the farmer toward the "fifty big-shots" and the eastern bosses.[2] The CCF offered to realize the frustrated ambitions of the farmer in a manner not inconsistent with either the Protestant ethic or free enterprise (on a small scale).[3] The Regina Manifesto was one step further from the doctrines of the Progressives, a step for which the failure of the Progressives had prepared the farmers. The ideology and structure of the CCF were consistent with the society they had built on the prairie.

The differences in the strength of the party in the three prairie provinces was the result of a number of factors. In Manitoba its strength was in the urban ridings; the rural population stayed within the Liberal-Progressive tradition. The Manitoba Farmers Union was never more than a lukewarm supporter of the CCF. Winnipeg was a major urban centre, the home of the Grain Exchange, the major rail and stock yards. Manitoba was closer to the rural Ontario tradition than Saskatchewan.

In Saskatchewan the farmers' organizations were actively involved in the formation of the CCF. There, more than in Alberta and, certainly, more than in Manitoba, the one-crop economy prevailed. There was, as well, a stronger infusion in Saskatchewan of immigrants with some European experience of socialism, particularly the socialism of the British Labour party. Alberta had been pre-empted by the United Farmers of Alberta before the founding of the CCF, and when that party fell from power in 1935 and dwindled, it took the CCF down with it. Social Credit answered the same needs there that the CCF answered in Saskatchewan, although with a more simplistic ideology. It nevertheless offered an explanation for the farmer's plight and proposed what seemed to be an adequate solution, that is, one consistent with the aims of the agrarian producer.

Outside the wheat belt the CCF could not count on the same support because nowhere else was there as large or as homogeneous a group which shared similar economic and social conditions, attitudes, and geography. It had to rely for its membership on alienated groups in urban centres such as the immigrant community in North Winnipeg and the working classes in Toronto and Vancouver. In Quebec and in the maritime provinces the party failed to win a foothold because it was not indigenous and consequently was seen as an alien force. It was opposed by the Catholic church because it was seen as godless and as a threat to private property, and by the liberals in Quebec because it was Anglo-Saxon and centralist. In the maritime provinces, although it had some success in Cape Breton in Nova Scotia, it conflicted with a rigid traditionalism in politics and an isolationism that prevented any real progress despite the generally depressed state of the economy.

The CCF lacked the pragmatism of approach and outlook needed to cope with the variety of attitudes that existed in Canada. The image of the party was forged on the anvil of prairie radicalism from iron supplied by Fabian intellectuals. Its approach was that of a movement, predicated on the assumption that there is universal agreement on the cause and cure of sin and that if such agreement is lacking it is the result of ignorance which education will remedy. The intellectual attitude prevalent in the CCF was, naturally enough, that socialism was the answer and that socialists knew the real truth. It followed from this that one answer was as valid in Quebec as it was in Nova Scotia or Saskatchewan. Intellectually this was probably true, but politically it was false, and as a guide for the party, almost suicidal.

Most Canadians were unwilling to see business, profits, and competition as evils, and were unmoved by the educational activities of the CCF. Those who were victims of capitalism often viewed their misfortune as simply the luck of the game. The CCF assumed the existence of a Canadian working class. Objectively such a class existed, but the members of that class did not, for the most part, accept their position as such. Their aspirations and attitudes were middle class. They were not prepared to support a party that was not identified with the status to which they aspired. Democracy and the rags-to-riches philosophy were a part of the Canadian ethic. Those who accepted the major premise of unlimited upward mobility for those with energy and initiative could not support the CCF.

The kind of class consciousness that leads to concerted action to overthrow or radically alter existing institutions is often generated by confrontation with the blank wall of despair such as that faced by the single unemployed in 1935, which led to the Ottawa trek. Because of past experience and because of the dominant attitudes expressed by established political leaders and by the press, most Canadians were persuaded that things would get better. The CCF began by proposing ways of making things better, and as prosperity returned, argued that things would get worse and, finally, accepted implicitly the liberal assumption by basing its electoral appeal on equality of opportunity rather than on equality of condition. It was never able to arouse the unity of sentiment that true class consciousness implies because the working class did not see its position as static and hopeless.

Those who found themselves alienated from society could and did accept the socialist argument. Trade union leaders and activists were attracted to the CCF because they were outsiders like the farmers. Many were committed socialists and their support for the CCF was natural for this reason. But, unlike a large proportion of their followers, they felt most keenly the antipathy of society toward trade union activity. Despite their pre-eminence in their own union or in the Congress, society did not accord them any status higher than that of their rank and file; indeed, in some cases it was lower because they were seen as the co-ordinators of disruption in a capitalist society. John Porter has pointed out that such rights as trade unions have were granted as concessions.[4] It is not surprising that the men who represented trade unionism would gravitate toward the CCF, nor is it surprising that many of their union members, whose lack of interest in the trade union *movement* is a notorious fact, would show little if any interest in Canada's socialist party. For them the union was merely one aspect of the acquisitive and competitive processes of a capitalist society.

Throughout its history the CCF shared the general socialist assumptions about the utility of education and about the purity and altruism of the awakened proletariat. As a party it accepted the liberal notions about the essential rationality of the citizen; it was not until 1957 and 1958 that there was any indication in the party's campaign literature that it recognized that lengthy argument and documented prophecy of impending depression had little impact on the electorate. The function of the party as an educational movement between elections meant that the election campaigns themselves were fought on the same basis. Because of these beliefs and because of the immense amount of energy devoted to spreading the CCF gospel, its leaders were prepared to wait, secure in the knowledge that the truth would win.

To hasten the process the advantages of socialism and the deficiencies of capitalism were displayed through a constant barrage of criticism and analysis. Yet the voters the CCF had to woo to win were part of the system, accepted it, and worked in it. Socialism was seen by the press and much of the public as destructive and the CCF as an engine of chaos. Significantly, during the war it was treated as fascist by its critics, and afterward as communist;[5] it was always anti-capitalist, and to non-socialists that meant anti-democratic. Only a modification of its ideology and a muffling of radical members would have helped offset the negative public image, but the requirements of the movement prevented such action.

The CCF was not unacceptable to all Canadians at all times. As the Gallup Poll figures showed, it "enjoyed" a remarkable surge of support during the latter stages of the Second World War when the social change and dislocation of the times and the peace-time orientation of the party made it attractive. But it was the movement that triumphed as Mackenzie King read the signs and moved leftward. In any case it was not the socialism of the CCF that appealed to that part of the electorate, roughly one-quarter, that supported it, it was the image of the party as an instrument of change.

Because it was a movement of protest the CCF attracted to its ranks liberals, committed socialists, dedicated anti-capitalists of various sorts, and those who were simply opposed to authority in all its forms; anarchists, malcontents, and rebels. These elements made the CCF a fighting party, but by virtue of the strength of their commitment, the more doctrinaire socialist and anarchist elements were more dominant than their numbers warranted. Unlike those who were solidly behind the party but not part of the sub-movement of socialist ideologues, the doctrinaires were prepared to give boundless time and energy to debate and criticism. They tended to be the activists in constituency organizations and delegates to conventions. Their presence helped preserve the movement and contributed to its critique of society. For some of these elements the CCF provided an outlet for genuine social protest founded on philosophical grounds; for a few it merely institutionalized bitterness and provided a legitimate channel for the expression of anti-authority neuroses. Most political parties can tolerate a maverick or two, but the CCF seemed to attract more than its share.

For the rest of the community the CCF came to be represented by those who spoke the loudest and most often; and these tended to be, at conventions at any rate, the rebels, those who deviated most vehemently from middle-class mores, who were dedicated to the destruction of the foundation of Canadian society—the free market economy. Coldwell's calm, rational approach was overlooked by people anxious to find a justification for their fears about the CCF, and for the press, the behaviour of the activists on the party's left wing provided much better copy than anything the party leaders might say.

The presence of militants in the ranks was also an asset. Because it was a movement the CCF attracted only those who were dedicated, and who gave freely of their time and money and stayed with the party through defeat after defeat. Limited in funds, the CCF depended on volunteer help in election campaigns, and was able to command and receive prodigious effort from its members, whose tireless canvassing succeeded in getting out the socialist vote and, in more than one instance, winning the seat.

The militants opposed the development of the CCF as a political party and made a fetish of their opposition to making ideological sacrifices in order to win office. Success, they feared, would transform the CCF from a vehicle of protest into a disciplined party in which there would be little room for the rebel. They preferred to see the CCF remain as a perpetual gad-fly that bit the hide of the establishment and goaded the "old line" parties into reform while providing the outsiders of Canadian society with a platform and a haven. By 1956 this attitude had become prevalent throughout the party, even among those who, in many respects, were the most anxious to make the CCF more a party. In his address to the national convention in 1956 Lewis, then national chairman, said:

> One of our major roles in Canada has always been and should always be to be the conscience of the Canadian people in the political and social struggles of this country. And to be that conscience we need not necessarily be in power. We can—if we are true to our principles and our objectives, consistent in our determination to fight the big interests in this country, determined to represent at all times the interests of the Canadian people and of common people everywhere—we can continue to be as we have always been, the political and social conscience of Canada, plaguing the unjust people, needling the people who destroy democracy, demanding with untiring effort a greater share of the goods of this life and the comforts of modern existence for ever increasing numbers of our people.[6]

The CCF's structure was, in some ways, a hindrance to its success as a party. Paradoxically it accepted the premises of democracy within the party itself but rejected them within the context of the Canadian political system. Within the party there was debate, divergence, and compromise. There was room for positive leadership, or "directed democracy" as it was described, yet the necessity for compromise or for pragmatism within the larger sphere of Canadian politics was never fully accepted. In theory the party members set policy at the national conventions, but in practice the leaders performed a function similar to that of Rousseau's legislator. Although there is much evidence to demonstrate the relevance to the CCF of Robert Michels' Iron Law of Oligarchy, it is also true that the activities of the leaders were limited by membership participation—enough at least to make participation in the party battle more awkward than if their control was absolute.

The position of the party's leaders was further limited by the conditions of the times. When Woodsworth was leader, the CCF was small, growing, and achieving many of its aims. The charismatic nature of his leadership provided great impetus whereas his own inclinations kept the CCF from developing that side of it that was party. Under Coldwell and Lewis, the party experienced both its greatest successes and greatest strains, first during the early stages of the Second World War and then as the support generated by the dislocation of war evaporated in the prosperity of peace. The long decline after 1945 denied Coldwell the electoral successes a party leader needs to strengthen his hand. A succession of failures encourages independence and irresponsibility among the militants in a party. Perpetual failure tends to produce a membership dominated by the zealot who, in a democratic party, finds ample scope for his individuality. Coldwell's task became less that of leader and more one of grand arbiter in a house of all-sorts.

Despite these disabilities, which were largely the product of the conjunction of the roles of the movement and the party, the CCF altered the shape of the Canadian party system and provided an impetus for reform that was lacking in the Liberal government. It achieved this measure of success partly because its Members of Parliament learned to use that institution to great effect and, in so doing, demonstrated a competence to the leaders of the "old line" parties that was impressive; and partly because the CCF represented an alien force that stood for values seen as anathema by those same leaders. In some ways the Communist party was less feared because it was so obviously "outside." The CCF, on the other hand, was clearly working within the system, and working surprisingly well for its numbers, while steadfastly opposing some of the fundamental values of the system. It was a distinctly different political phenomenon.

Neither at the beginning nor at the end was the CCF like the other parties in Canadian national politics. It retained its unique character throughout the twenty-eight years of its existence. Starting as a confederation of radical parties and protest movements, it attracted and held as members and active politicians men and women of exceptional dedication and, in many cases, exceptional ability. When it became part of the New Democratic Party, it was no longer a confederation of movements and much less a movement than it had been in the forties. Most of those who had helped form the CCF in 1932 stayed with the party; some had been active in its councils throughout and helped to reshape it into a party and, finally, into the New Democratic Party.

What made the CCF unique was, first of all, that it was a socialist party which survived and remained a potential threat to the other parties on a continent in which socialist parties have a gloomy history of schism and failure. Some of the reasons for its success relative to similar parties in the United States have been debated elsewhere,[7] and there may be something in the composition of the Canadian "fragment" that is more conducive to the continued life of socialism—if at times by the merest thread—than in the United States. And, no doubt, the marriage of a federal state to a parliamentary system has played a part in generating the regional pressures that provide fertile ground for such parties as the CCF.[8] The "brokerage" thesis is also useful for the light it sheds on the success of the CCF—if staying alive can be so counted—because if this was the view held by such prime ministers as Mackenzie King, then clearly its impossibility contributed much to the strains which helped generate and nurture the CCF.[9]

These theories, all of which have an intellectual fascination, offer possible general explanations for the fact of the CCF. It began because, for various reasons, enough people were sufficiently dissatisfied with the *status quo* that they first created their own movements and parties and subsequently joined forces in the CCF. It came into being because the existing system was unable to satisfy these people or could not cope with them. In this respect, the system referred to was more than the party system; it was the sum total of the political, economic, and social systems that had failed in various ways to satisfy the expectations of these people or cope with their demands. Their dissatisfaction came from the failure and remained to compel them to take action to remedy their own situation. The economic and social plight of the wheat farmer led him to protest; the inability of the existing political system to satisfy his demands compelled him to create his own party in order to express these demands and, ultimately, to bring about the changes he sought.

If the function of the party system is to "organize public opinion and link it to expert opinion for the purpose of finding a sound and acceptable definition of the national interest,"[10] then in the thirties, for a significant public opinion, it had failed to function. Its failure in this context could be traced to the rigidities of the parliamentary system that are inconsistent with federalism and that demand a kind of superficial brokerage function of the major parties which they are ill-equipped to provide and Parliament ill-equipped to enact. Its failure could equally well be attributed to the fact that the parties in the system were controlled by, or were fragments of, the "charter group" elite described by John Porter. Congealed by their origins, frozen in an attitude of obeisance to the elite and the value system espoused by that elite, the parties could not, of their own volition, make the adjustments required by the demands of the "protestant minority." It was assumed by the elite and its parties, that its position not only reflected the best interests of the country at large, but encompassed the views of all its citizens as well. In the absence of evidence to the contrary, it inevitably thought of itself as the embodiment of the Canadian consensus.

When the adjustments were made, they were only made under the threat of socialism as represented by the CCF. In the absence of a third party with a strident voice advocating values contradictory to those of the ruling elite, the parties of that elite could not justify, even within the context of the brokerage function, any legislative activity that interfered with the interests of the ruling group. With such a party on the scene, however, operating within the political system and therefore legitimate, the major parties had to respond to stave off the threat which this party constituted. Actions taken to meet this threat were justified by the nature of the challenge. When Mackenzie King wheeled his party to the left, he justified his action by pointing to the danger of the CCF. The old parties, in such circumstances, actually performed the brokerage function which they did not, in fact, perform before.[11]

In other words, before the twenties the two major parties mediated between the conflicting elements *within* the ruling group.

There was no clash of values; there was only conflict of interest. But with a vocal minority threatening to destroy the system which the ruling elite had created for itself and which nurtured it, the major parties had to become brokers and seek to create a broader and more genuine national consensus in order to forestall the CCF. This was not a particularly difficult transition to effect, since, as already mentioned, a majority of Canadians shared the values of the elite. The extension of the powers of the federal government and the widening of its authority during the war provided a demonstration of the inclusiveness of the government and gave the impression that it had a wider interest and was responding to the needs of all Canadians. This impression was accomplished, for the most part, with no major change in either the values or the structure of the party in power.

The extent to which the CCF was considered a threat can be seen by the lengths the press and business went to denigrate it and label it subversive. The degree of panic felt by the establishment can be measured by the extent to which it saw the CCF as constituting a root and branch attack on the institutions of capitalism, requiring a massive counter-attack in the form of elaborate and extensive propaganda campaigns. The CCF was not as revolutionary as it was seen to be, but the point is that it did appear as a threat and accommodations were made to avoid the danger of losing all in the maw of "state socialism." Business feared loss of property and power; the Liberal government feared loss of office as well.

Undoubtedly the existence of the CCF strengthened the hand of the Liberal party by enabling it to exact firmer and richer support from the business community. The lengths to which the Liberals were prepared to go in meeting the CCF challenge is indicated by their actions enabling the intervention of the Communist party (LPP) in the 1945 general election. Having defended the Communists' right to exist and resisted their poisonous advances, the CCF had the grim satisfaction of seeing the Communists used by Liberals as a weapon in the defence of the capitalist establishment. There was as well some satisfaction to be derived from the fact that such movement to the left as occurred in Liberal policy was facilitated by the CCF threat, which was offered by King as an excuse and a reason to his party's right wing.[12]

The ignorance that is the foundation of faith in free enterprise extended to the nature of those agencies which, like the CCF, sought major reform but not revolution. Had the CCF formed the government there would have been significant changes because its leaders held different values and had a different perspective, but the extent of change was over-estimated. What the establishment feared was not the CCF party so much as the CCF movement and the image of that movement that their own propaganda had created.

The CCF [was] more successful than the Progressive party in influencing the system because it was a movement dedicated to more fundamental or value-oriented change than were the Progressives. The fact that the CCF was a movement meant that its participation in the party battle did not contaminate its goals so much that its influence in politics was lost. Its operation within the political system and its gradual acceptance of the rules of the game did bring about a dilution of its ideology in the programmatic sense, but did not significantly alter the party's goals. In a curious, paradoxical way, its strict adherence to the parliamentary rules of the game, its earnest profession of liberal values in defence of civil liberties, and its obvious honesty made it more acceptable to more people and, therefore, more of a threat. At times it seemed as though many commentators thought—if they did not say—"if only the CCF was not socialist." If it had not been socialist, it would not have been the CCF. It would not have remained a movement and, consequently, would have disappeared because it would have had no more reason for continuing to exist than had the Progressives.

There is a sense in which it may be said that all parties are ideological. Those which reflect the dominant values of the particular society have no need to express their ideology as a manifesto or declaration of principles. Political scientists who despair of finding a single coherent statement in the Liberal or Progressive Conservative "philosophy" have ignored the haystack in their search for a single needle. Liberalism and Progressive Conservativism are, in effect, what Liberals and Progressive Conservatives do when in office. Their behaviour reflects, by and large, the dominant values of Canadian society. The "ideological" party—that is, the one with a manifesto—is usually an agency for expressing dissatisfaction with the *status quo*. It is directed toward change, not maintenance.

It is almost invariably a movement as well as a party and can only attract people to its ranks by convincing them of the validity of its particular *weltanschauung*, something the "old line parties" do not need to do because they express the prevailing *weltanschauung*. To achieve its ends the "ideological" party must not only campaign, it must educate through whatever means are available to it. It must secure a reasonably permanent body of support among the electorate since its nature is to have a program of long-run goals that cannot be adequately achieved in one term of office. When it wins supporters, they tend to stay with it, as CCF/NDP voting history shows, because in so opting to oppose the *status quo* they have made a definite and identifiable commitment that is difficult to cast off. For one thing, the internal pressures of the party-movement they have espoused help them resist any return; for another, a return to the *status quo* would constitute an admission of error. To switch from Liberal to Conservative requires no great struggle with one's conscience since both parties reflect, with few real variations, the dominant values. One can switch allegiance from the Roughriders to the Argonauts without demonstrating any lack of faith in football. When the ideology is one that is as inconsistent with the *status quo* as was that of the CCF, then the need for education, for propaganda, is that much greater.[13] The party with an ideology is also a movement; its goals are more than the mere acquisition of power. The parties without such an ideology in this sense are mechanisms for achieving power; the party-movement is a mechanism for propagating and enacting beliefs through power.

A functional analysis would demonstrate that both kinds of parties perform functions which, in some respects, have little influence on the primary goals of each. Both provide focus and coherence for the electorate, offering a point of contact with the processes of government. They fulfil constitutional roles in the processes of electing leaders and nominating candidates. The list is long. There is one respect, however, in which the party-movement is functional to the democratic system and the "normal" party is not or, indeed, may even be dysfunctional. That is in the respect already discussed: the party-movement compels the traditional parties to perform functions which, in the absence of the threat the party-movement constitutes, would not be performed. Put succinctly, its presence demands the performance of leadership.[14] As with streams which meet no obstacles, which have no rapids, political parties grow placid, stagnant, and putrid in the absence of fundamental opposition. The two-party system predicated on the "ins and outs" thesis stagnates from the lack of the aerating qualities of robust ideological debate and vigorous local party activity.

The Canadian party system is unlike both the American and British party systems with which it is often compared. Many in the CCF chose to see it as a two-party system and hoped that the CCF would eventually replace the Liberal party as the party of the left.[15] Frank Underhill has described it as a multi-party system in disguise, more like the American than the British system.[16] Certainly since 1922 third and fourth parties have been a part of this system and a necessary part of the calculations of political leaders, and in this sense alone it must be admitted that the party system is "more multi than two." But it is not possible to say that the Canadian party system is "more like" either one or the other of the older systems. It suffers from the worst features of both, compounded by the peculiarities of the Canadian constitution.

The parliamentary system exerts pressure toward the maintenance of a two-party system which in a federal state produces strains that help create third and fourth parties. The parliamentary system also emphasizes strong central control of parties, an emphasis heightened in Canada by the wholly natural centralist attitude of federal politicians. Federalism exerts opposite pressures, its nature demanding vigorous regional or provincial party branches. The result of this network of tensions has been central control of national parties with very weak provincial branches and weak linkages between them, and strong provincial parties which are either indigenous, as in the case of Social Credit in Alberta, or independent of the national party, as was Hepburn's Ontario Liberal machine. There is no guarantee of easy relations between a national prime minister and provincial premiers of nominally the same party. They are more characteristically rivals than collaborators.

The local branches of national parties have no autonomy because they have no viable control over their Members of Parliament. They lack control because of the nature of the parliamentary system which requires cabinet or front-bench domination of the parliamentary party. In the national context, local politicians are beholden to Ottawa and not, as is the case in the United States, the centre more beholden to the branches. There is nothing to tie the national party—branches and centre—together, so what articulation there is in the structure is very weak. Between federal elections, the provincial branches of the national parties are dormant, dependent almost entirely on the centre for stimulus and direction.

The provincial parties, by comparison, are both more active and more independent. They represent provincial interests and tend to act in competition with the centralist tendencies of the national parties. The fact that the national Liberal party had to establish a separate organization to fight the 1965 federal election in Saskatchewan, campaign support having been effectively denied it by Ross Thatcher's provincial Liberal party, offers a recent and perhaps extreme example of this phenomenon. Although they share personnel, the national and provincial parties tend to maintain a separate and often divergent existence.

Given the existence of weak and dormant local units and consequently of relatively little local input through the national party machinery, the direction of the national party is handled entirely by and from the centre with little feedback. The fact that the formal headquarters apparatus of the major national parties is traditionally small is indicative of the tight "in-group" control of these parties and of the irrelevance of feedback from the provincial branches. The growing reliance on professional advertising men for high campaign strategy has offset whatever trend there has been toward the broadening of the base of these parties. Major party decisions are traditionally taken by a small caucus or inner circle, and are based on its assessment of the national political scene and the advice of professional public relations firms.

Consequently there is a built-in propensity toward stagnation in the absence of viable or seemingly viable third and fourth parties. These minor parties, struggling to achieve major status, have provided the inputs which the major parties lack. Starting from a regional or class base, they have represented and consequently brought to the attention of the major parties the particular attitudes or grievances of sections of the country that the major parties have ignored or failed to deal with. By providing as well the kind of ideological confrontation which is typically absent in contests between the two major parties, they have served to stimulate the older parties and reactivate their previously dormant philosophies. The multi-party system in the setting of parliamentary federalism functions to prevent the stagnation which a pure two-party system necessarily produces. Two parties alone cannot successfully represent all the interests or act as a broker—honest or otherwise. Attempts to represent a national consensus have been usually based on the assessment of a few with limited access to the attitudes of the whole. The result has been that the national consensus has in fact been the view of the most dominant voices in the old parties. And these are the voices at the centre; historically, the voices of the elite or the establishment.

The CCF's ideology and structure, which was a product of the ideology, helped to offset the fissiparous effects of parliamentary federalism. Unlike the two major parties, which had no specific ideology as a reference point, the CCF had democratic socialism as elucidated in the Regina Manifesto. It provided a single body of doctrine federally and provincially. It was the tie that bound the party together into a national unit. The CCF was not immune to the pressures that divide parties; there was... a high degree of independence within provincial CCF parties. But the separation was not as great as in the two old parties. National CCF leaders played a more active part in provincial politics on behalf of their provincial sections than was ever the case with the Liberal or Conservative parties.

Pure autonomy was not possible because all sections of the CCF were part of a single movement. Agreement on basic goals superseded differences over policy. Because the movement sought to elucidate, it relied on the central office for information, material, and direction. Because it was surrounded not so much by an opposition as by enemies, it bound itself together with biennial conventions, newsletters, and the adulation of a leader. Its structure was highly articulated; democracy and socialism made it so.

A clearly defined ideology also strengthens the central control since the goals of the ideology transcend the goal of power for its own sake. The preservation and elaboration of the ideology enhances the centre and increases the dependence of the branches on the central leadership. The ideology and the structure which follows from it integrate the party, increase its strength, and act as a powerful preservative. There is always the danger of internal division on ideological questions—the history of the British Labour party bears this out—but finally the splits heal because in one way the dissidents have nowhere else to go, and in another the basic consensus with respect to the long-range goals of the movement usually remains.

The success of the CCF as a movement was the extent to which the CCF as a party performed an input function, as measured by legislation enacted by the Liberal government, which reflected the ideas, if not the ideology, of the CCF. The relationship between the CCF *qua* movement and the CCF *qua* party was close and interdependent. The movement succeeded to the extent it did because the party was able, at one point at least, to pose a threat to the established order through legitimate channels—it could not be suppressed as was the Communist party because the CCF accepted the rules of the game, although there were those in the CCF who felt this was an act of treachery. Thanks to the British Labour party which, like the eldest child in the family, broke a trail for those that followed, democratic socialism was accepted within the parliamentary tradition. The movement and party aspects intermeshed, one aiding the development and aims of the other while at the same time hindering its development and distorting its aims.

As the argument is pursued it is increasingly difficult to disentangle one from the other because, of course, the CCF was a *party-movement*. Speculation about what would have happened had the CCF cast off its ideological raiment and met the other parties on their own ground, or if it had hewn to a more consistently doctrinaire position than it did, is idle. To understand the CCF and the role it played, it is necessary to see it as both a party and a movement, and to see the crucial interaction of these two aspects of the single organism that was the Co-operative Commonwealth Federation in Canada.

Notes

1 See text of which this excerpt is ch. 10, W. Young, *The Anatomy of a Party*, ch. 7; University of Toronto Press, 1969.

2 See Daniel Bell, "Interpretations of American Politics," in D. Bell, ed., *The Radical Right* (New York 1963); and Peter Viereck, "The Revolt against the Elite," in the same volume.

3 See Richard Hofstadter, "The Pseudo-Conservative Revolt," in Bell, *The Radical Right*, 70, 86.

4 Porter, *Vertical Mosaic*, 311.

5 The Communist party gave credence to this criticism by its public exclamations of support. In 1960 Tim Buck claimed that the Communists had successfully infiltrated the New Party (NDP). Vancouver *Sun*, Aug. 31, 1960.

6 Report of the Fourteenth National Convention (1956).

7 See G. Horowitz, "Conservatism, Liberalism and Socialism in Canada: An Interpretation," *CJEPS*, XXXII (May 1986).

8 See S.M. Lipset, "Democracy in Alberta," *Canadian Forum* (Nov., Dec., 1954).

9 See J.T. McLeod, "Party Structure and Party Reform," in A. Rotstein, ed., *The Prospect of Change* (Toronto 1965); and John Meisel, "The Stalled Omnibus: Canadian Parties in the Fifties," *Social Research*, XXX (1963). For a brilliant analysis of the relationship of the electoral system to the party system, with particular reference to the CCF, see Alan C. Cairns, "The Electoral System and the Party System in Canada: 1921-1965," *Canadian Journal of Political Science*, March 1968.

10 Meisel, "Omnibus," 367.

11 Frank Underhill has argued the reverse, that "the old parties were too much under the control of one class group to function as honest brokers any more." (*In Search of Canadian Liberalism*, 198). In fact, the old parties were always under the control of one class group and what brokerage they performed was within the context of the class group's interests.

12 At a cabinet meeting June 22, 1944, Mackenzie King justified his opposition to J.L. Ilsley's budget proposals, claiming they "would be just fatal to the Government and play into the hands of the CCF..." J.W. Pickersgill and D.F. Forster, *The Mackenzie King Record*, VII (Toronto 1968), 29. The extent to which the CCF loomed large in King's consideration during this period can be seen in this volume, e.g. pp. 30-32, 127, 137, 146.

13 Addressing the British Columbia NDP Convention in April 1968, T.C. Douglas said that the NDP was not interested in minor changes such as tariff reform and its like. "Our movement," he stated, "is fundamentally concerned with the basic structure of society itself." He characterised Canadian society as "a society of shabby values."

14 The effect of the CCF on the Conservative party is described in J.L. Granatstein, *The Politics of Survival* (Toronto 1967), 69, 149-150, 166-167. Granatstein points out that "The CCF had...forced the old parties to adjust their platforms and policies," 189.

15 See for example, Donald MacDonald, "The Three P's and Political Trends," *Canadian Forum*, XXVI (Dec. 1946).

16 "The Party System in Canada," "The Canadian Party System in Transition," and "Concerning Mr. King," in *In Search of Canadian Liberalism*.

R.K. Carty The Coming of Leadership Conventions

The conscription crisis and subsequent general election in 1917 tore the Liberal party apart, with many (English-speakers) deserting to enter the Conservative-led Unionist government. In the aftermath of the war Sir Wilfrid Laurier faced the task of finding a way to bring mutually disaffected Liberals back together. He settled on a plan for a large national convention charged with defining Liberal policy for the future. But Laurier died between the calling of the convention and its meeting in August 1919 which, willy-nilly, was transformed into a gathering to choose a new leader. The caucus itself chose a house leader in the customary way but no one assumed that this made him the party's national leader.[1]

The convention of 1919 marked a significant shift in the life of the party, for the politicians were handing over to partisan activists the power to choose their leader. This was all the more unusual because there really was no formal, mass extraparliamentary national party organization, or even regular party conventions—this was only the second such meeting in Canada since 1867! The 1917 election had reduced the Liberal caucus to little more than a Quebec rump, visibly unrepresentative of the country's diverse regions. The appeal of a convention was that it could overcome this deficiency and provide the party with a mechanism for incorporating all the regional interests in the selection of its leader. That similar conventions had already been used in many provinces, some influenced by neighbouring Americans, no doubt helped to make the Liberals' 1919 national convention seem a natural development.

But however expedient, the Liberals' use of a convention to choose Mackenzie King as their leader was still seen as an exceptional device for coping with a special situation. Thus, the very next year, when the Conservatives came to replace Robert Borden they resorted to traditional practices in choosing Arthur Meighen. His electoral defeats at the hands of King made the Conservatives reconsider, and in 1927 they copied the Liberals by using a convention to select R.B. Bennett as their new leader. Bennett won the next election. His victory, like King's, legitimated the use of leadership conventions, which were soon being portrayed as the democratic face of Canadian parties.

Table 1: Major Party Conventions 1919-58

Convention	Winner	No. of delegates	No. of candidates	No. of ballots
1919 Liberal	King	947	4	3
1927 Conservative	Bennett	1,564	6	2
1938 Conservative	Manion	1,565	5	2
1942 Conservative	Bracken	870	5	2
1948 Liberal	St. Laurent	1,227	3	1
1948 Conservative	Drew	1,242	3	1
1956 Conservative	Diefenbaker	1,284	3	1
1958 Liberal	Pearson	1,380	3	1

Source: R. Krause and L. LeDuc, "Voting Behaviour and Electoral Strategies."

In fact, the three Liberal and five Conservative conventions held prior to the 1960s were hardly models of party democracy. On the whole they were smallish (up to 1,500 delegates), not very competitive events. Between 40 and 50 percent of the delegates came in some ex officio capacity, while many of the constituency representatives owed their places to an MP and voted as he wanted. As Chubby Power (himself a candidate for the Liberal leadership in 1948) acknowledged, this "indirectly perpetuate[d] the old custom" of caucus selection.[2]

For all that, conventions did make a difference. Three times they chose men who were not members of the parliamentary party. (One of them, John Bracken, the Progressive premier of Manitoba, made the Conservatives change their name to the Progressive Conservatives, to the subsequent delight of all who relish the idiosyncracies of political language.) And on several occasions conventions downplayed parliamentary experience and opted for the more junior candidate. In both of these ways conventions opened up the party leadership to individuals who would not have been selected under the traditional rules.[3]

In both parties, national conventions stimulated the development of extraparliamentary organizations to direct their affairs between conventions. Eventually these organizations grew to compete with the caucuses as the decision-making heart of the party, with the issue of leadership at the centre of the struggle. The problem was that while it was clear that the party-in-convention chose the leader, there was no agreement on who might depose him. Mackenzie King is alleged to have told his parliamentary colleagues that he was finally responsible only to the wider party that had chosen him. But it was in the Conservative party that the tension between extraparliamentary organization and caucus was to be fully fought out.

After defeats in the 1963 and 1965 general elections, many prominent Conservatives, led by the party's national president, decided that Mr. Diefenbaker had to be replaced as leader. Diefenbaker disagreed and, commanding the support of a majority of the Conservative caucus, refused to budge. Despite the position of the parliamentary party, after some prolonged maneuvering the party organization managed to call a leadership convention for 1967. Caucus members were forced to recognize it, and some, including Diefenbaker himself, became contestants... By then, the second party system was over.

Notes

1   D.D. McKenzie of Nova Scotia (who went on to run a poor fourth at the 1919 convention) has been lost to history, largely ignored by academic and party literature alike. At the 1984 Liberal leadership convention the party propaganda circulated to the delegates to remind them of previous leaders didn't even include McKenzie in a footnote.

2   C.G. Power, *A Party Politician: The Memoirs of Chubby Power* (Toronto: Macmillan, 1966), p. 371.

3   For a stimulating paper see Ian Stewart, "The Ins and Outs: Status Cleavages at Canadian Leadership Conventions," in George C. Perlin, ed., *Party Democracy in Canada* (Scarborough, ON: Prentice-Hall, 1987).

C.G. Power Two Liberal Leadership Conventions

1919

Political organizing is not confined to federal and provincial election campaigns. There have been four national conventions of the Liberal Party, in 1893, 1919, 1948, and 1958. I attended three of these, and had an opportunity of closely examining the activities of the last two; that of 1948 as a candidate for the party leadership, and that of 1958 as a member of the organization committee and as chairman of the committee on political organization. These national conventions, broadly speaking, are held for the purpose of consulting the rank-and-file members of the party, and of giving them an opportunity to discuss and formulate party policy. In the last three, the choice of a party leader by direct vote of the delegates was the most important work accomplished.

There has been a great deal of controversy about leadership conventions, centring on the contention of some shrewd political observers that when the leadership is to be decided it becomes so important in the minds not only of the delegates but of the people of Canada that all other questions are subordinated to it. Thus it is difficult, if not impossible, to direct the attention of delegates to matters of equal importance, such as party policy and organization, with the result that the delegates usually return home with little or no idea of the issues to be put before the people of the country for discussion and decision. Prior to the 1958 convention, indeed, Norman Lambert, a former secretary and chairman of the National Liberal Federation and the chief organizer of the Liberal campaigns of the period 1930-5 and 1940, held strongly to the belief that only one item should be submitted to the convention, the choice of a leader. Lambert's view received some support, but not sufficient to be generally acceptable.

Before 1918 the Liberal Party leader had always been selected by a caucus of the sitting Liberal members of the federal Parliament. Sir Wilfrid Laurier was selected in this way, and the 1893 convention was held merely for the purposes of strengthening the party organization and formulating policy. Similarly in the Conservative Party, Arthur Meighen was selected in 1920 as leader and prime minister by the Conservative-Unionist party caucus. The selection of Mr.

Meighen by what was termed a privileged few made him a target for the attacks of both Liberals and Progressives during the election campaign of 1921, and since that time Conservative leaders have also been selected at conventions. A similar procedure has been followed by the Social Credit Party, and by the CCF and the New Democratic Party.

The obsession of conventions with the choice of leaders has resulted in the adoption of platforms that as a rule contain items that, through want of full discussion by delegates who often have fundamental differences of opinion, are a conglomeration of verbose language and ponderous phrases with little substance or meaning, calculated only to meet the divergent and often uninformed views of those who participated in the discussion. As far back as the general election of 1921 Mr. Mackenzie King, as the new leader, found himself embarrassed by some of the policies in the 1919 convention resolutions, and was impelled to say that he considered that the platform need not be explicitly followed by the leader. It would, he said, be considered as a chart and compass indicating the direction the party would follow. The Conservative Party, which formulated a platform in its 1956 convention and chose as leader Mr. John Diefenbaker, prudently decided not to publish the details of the party resolutions or the platform adopted at the convention. As late as 1958 the Liberal Party sought a substitute for the party platform, and endeavoured to draw public attention to what was called the 'Pearson Plan.'

Notwithstanding these apparent deviations, I would say that it is a good thing to have meetings of this kind at which party policy can be strenuously debated. It leaves the impression with the rank and file that they have had their say in the formulation of party views and the advancement of party ideals and ideology. There is never, as any experienced politician can testify, a dearth of resolutions. They come from private individuals and from associations of all sorts—youth, women, ridings, provincial federations, labour groups—and they deal with all manner of questions, including matters outside federal jurisdiction. The resolutions are dealt with by a committee that sits almost continuously for several days prior to the meeting of the convention. The committee screens the resolutions, not with the idea of altering the sense, but merely in an endeavour to make them more comprehensible, and to consolidate resolutions relating to the same subject and having the same end in mind. In this process a great many are eliminated, but all the authors are usually present or represented at the convention itself, and when the subject matter comes to be discussed in the committee on resolutions set up by the convention itself (usually composed of persons who were not members of the preliminary committee) there is opportunity for debate. This opportunity is somewhat lessened by the tendency to gallop through the items to enable the delegates to be present in the main hall of the convention to listen to formal speeches delivered by provincial leaders or others prominent in the party. As a rule the debate is altogether too hurried and too confused, and the end result is always unsatisfactory. But the members of the party have at least the satisfaction of being able to say that they did have some influence, and that they have a stake in the party's fortunes. This enables them to return home with the feeling that they have a personal interest in the success of the party, and to dissipate the idea that decisions are handed down from the hierarchy. They have had an opportunity of expressing their views in a democratic way.

Also subject to criticism is the constitution of the delegations which attend the conventions, though I can think of no other means to obtain the fullest possible representation of party views. The Liberal Party conventions have arranged for representation mainly by stipulating that three delegates from each federal constituency be elected at a local convention. The weakness in this is that very often the constituency delegates are the choice of the federal member of Parliament and reflect his views and vote as he directs. There is also representation *ex officio* of federal members of Parliament, Senators, and defeated candidates at the last election; of youth and women's organizations; of university Liberal groups; of provincial Liberal parties, and of members of provincial legislatures. But the majority of the delegates are those selected by the constituencies. This in a sense indirectly perpetuates the old custom of selecting the party leader by members of the parliamentary caucus. It must be admitted, of course, that the member of Parliament ordinarily selects persons who have been most active in his local organization; these are the persons delegated to carry on the work of ward or county organization, whose function it is to persuade the electors to support the party. It is difficult to argue that they should not have something to say in the selection of the leader, and the determination of party policy.

The greatest aid to party organization that comes from conventions arises from the opportunities for personal contacts. The meeting of a large number of persons actively engaged in the same kind of work, the acquaintances formed, and, above all, the exchange of information and experience, are of great value. Leaders of the party have to pick out the persons on whom they can most rely for the essential function of organizing the constituencies for electoral purposes, and if little or no attention is paid to the resolutions or even to the directives of the convention in organizational matters, it is largely because the workers have their own methods of proceeding. At any rate, a sentiment of cohesion is engendered between the leaders and the persons who will, through their local efforts, have a large influence on the fortunes of the party.

The national Liberal convention of 1919 provided an excellent example of what I mean. The timing was a gamble, since it was barely two years away from the election of 1917, when the Liberal Party in eight provinces had been split asunder. On the other hand, other circumstances rendered it opportune. The death of Laurier in February 1919, and the disappointing record of the Unionist government, made a resurgence of Liberal sentiment across the country almost inevitable. Had Laurier been alive at the time of the convention, it might have been embarrassing for many of those who had abandoned him in 1917 to give him the same meed of praise and loyalty which they could easily proclaim after he had passed into the ranks of Canadian statesmen. Furthermore, though coalitions bring men of great prestige and high standing into the government, they do not as a rule attract the allegiance and activities of the rank and file; by 1919, within the ranks of those who had supported the Union government in the constituencies, a tendency had developed to return to former allegiances. The welding together of organizations during the 1917 campaign had been purely temporary.

Liberal leaders of provincial governments who had given their support to Unionists (George Murray in Nova Scotia, W.E. Foster in New Brunswick, W.M. Martin in Saskatchewan, T.C. Norris in Manitoba, and Charles Stewart in Alberta) had all placed their provincial Liberal organizations at the disposal of the conscriptionist Unionists for the purposes of the 1917 election. In addition to these premiers there were thousands of Liberals who for patriotic or conscientious motives had abandoned Laurier and thrown their support to his opponents. The division between the conscriptionists and the anti-conscriptionists had been wide and deep-seated. Outside Quebec men had been torn between what they considered to be their conscientious duty to keep Canada in the war and their undoubted devotion to Laurier's personality; when they decided to set aside this sentiment of affection, they looked askance at those who remained loyal in the face of the strong and well-publicized rush of patriotic fervour toward Unionist candidates. Those who remained solid in their Liberal convictions risked social ostracism. This did not make for the best of feeling between wings of the party so divergent in their outlook, and the 1919 gamble consisted of an attempt to bring together these persons so recently at daggers drawn, and to mould them into a harmonious and militant political party.

This objective was not immediately realized, and the vote for the leadership gave some indication that various factions were still very much alive. However, the fact that so many Liberals of different convictions came together at all, and formulated a political platform, gave the new leader an opportunity to bring into play his remarkable talent for conciliation and compromise.

The credit for making this convention representative of Liberalism in all its diversified facets belongs almost entirely to two men: Andrew Haydon, a barrister of Ottawa, who was secretary-treasurer of the convention, and Charles Murphy, a former minister in the Laurier cabinet, who was chairman of the national convention committee and of the committee on arrangements. Murphy was the real organizer of the convention, and was responsible for its successes. There was, and had been much to criticize in Murphy's complex character, but he was devoted to the cause of Liberalism and intensely loyal to Laurier and to his memory. He had a flair, almost a genius, for organization and worked tirelessly to bring together the various sections of the party so that the convention would be harmonious.

It must have been extremely difficult for him to arrange matters so that honours and prestige would be placed on the shoulders of men for whom he had the most intense dislike. To Murphy, anyone who had abandoned Laurier and gone over to the enemy during the conscription crisis was nothing less than a traitor. Nevertheless, he so arranged matters that many whom he had most bitterly denounced, and whom he continued to denounce after the convention, were placed in positions of honour during the proceedings. He must be given great credit for overcoming his personal feelings in his desire to make the convention a party triumph. It must be added that in after years his loyalty to the party gave place to a bitter and well-publicized hatred for Mackenzie King. His letters against King, bitter, sardonic, and spiteful, pointing out all King's defects of character, were addressed to dozens of people across the country. Some of them made lively reading.

Apart from the main division arising out of the events of 1917, there existed in 1919, within the ranks of Liberalism, diverse tendencies that have not yet wholly been resolved. Liberalism then as now contained many persons whom, for want of a better name, I shall call 'Whigs'; and a possibly larger number holding far more radical views about (for instance) the tariff and social welfare. These divisions sometimes coincided with sectional interests, and at other times revealed an occupational or administrative stratification. In Quebec the ruling provincial group under Sir Lomer Gouin, Alexandre Taschereau, and others was inclined to express the ideas of the business interests of the province. Others, largely to be found among the members of Parliament, favoured a low tariff and a wide expansion of social benefits. Most of these men looked up to Ernest Lapointe and Jacques Bureau as their leaders. This group, elected to the federal Parliament almost entirely on the one issue of anti-conscription, also felt that it was in their electoral interest to persist in their stand in the selection of a new leader for the party.

The final test came in the balloting for the leadership. Gouin and his friends, allied to Rodolphe Lemieux and some of his adherents in federal politics, strongly supported W.S. Fielding for the leadership. Fielding had been premier of Nova Scotia; for years an efficient and well-thought-of Minister of Finance in the Laurier cabinet, he was renowned from coast to coast as a wise and prudent administrator. Though he had not joined the Unionist government in 1917, he had given it his support. More recently, in the House of Commons, he had cut himself adrift from the followers of Sir Robert Borden. Fielding's support was to be found largely among the older men and in the ranks of the business community. Prior to the convention, other possible candidates included William Martin, premier of Saskatchewan, who refused to allow his name to be put in for nomination; and George P. Graham, who had been at one time leader of the Liberal Party in Ontario, a great favourite of Laurier, and a minister in his cabinet. Graham was extremely popular in all ranks of the party, but though he had refused to accept a post in Unionist government he was considered by the more radical anti-conscriptionists as a waverer in the conscription crisis. He had voted for the Military Service Act but had refused to be a candidate on behalf of the Unionist party. In the election of 1917 he was defeated in his own riding. The persons who rallied to his support did so largely on the grounds of personal friendship. Another candidate was D.D. McKenzie of Cape Breton, who, after Laurier's death, had been appointed temporary House leader of the Liberal group. He had remained solid in his allegiance to Laurier, and was elected in 1917 as a Laurier Liberal candidate; but he had no great strength or support outside Nova Scotia since he was little known and his type of oratory, though at times quite humorous, was not appreciated.

In the discussion of resolutions at the convention, and in the speeches, few references were made to the differences of view about the primary issue of the 1917 election. Indeed, a successful endeavour was made to avoid anything that might arouse the latent antagonism between sections of the party, although there was a strong conflict of opinion on tariff matters.

It must be emphasized that during the convention attention was almost entirely centred on the choice of the leader. It appeared early in the convention that the two men who could be most influential, at least among the younger members of Parliament from Quebec, were Jacques Bureau and Ernest Lapointe, who were strongly supporting the candidature of Mackenzie King. King had no prestige and no great reputation among us. He was considered a bit radical, which did not hurt him in our view, though I think it was one of the reasons why the provincial Liberal group from Quebec were a bit afraid of him. But the word had gone around that he, of all Laurier's colleagues, had been most faithful to him. Some doubt may be thrown upon this theory by what has appeared subsequently in the relation of the story of the formation of the Union government, with which King seems to have at least flirted; but it was firmly implanted in the minds of the Quebec members that King had been solidly and faithfully a supporter of Laurier. As such he could be held up before the electorate of Quebec as anticonscriptionist, and we members who would support him would be absolved of all suspicion of having compromised with the conscriptionist enemy.

That, I think, was the principal (and perhaps the only) reason why King received so much support from the Quebec delegation. That he was proposed by Sir Allen Aylesworth and seconded by Sydney Fisher also helped, because these two ex-members of Laurier's cabinet were known to have been faithful supporters of his throughout the crisis. Dozens of estimates have been made of the proportion of Quebec delegate votes going to King as against that going to Fielding. I think it is possible that Fielding received a greater number of votes from Quebec than is generally believed, because the provincial ministers and all those over whom they had any authority must have voted for him; that is indicated by the very large number of votes he actually received—only a few less than King when the other candidates were eliminated and the two came down to the wire.

What I would like to make clear is that it seems to me that there was never any strong sentiment in favour of King personally. He simply represented the protest against conscription, and the protest of those who wished to avenge Laurier....

1948

No national Liberal convention was held between 1919 and 1948, the full period of Mr. King's leadership. I was a conspicuously unsuccessful candidate for the leadership in 1948, but before commenting on that I should like to recount some of the salient episodes in my relationship with the party in the period immediately preceding the convention.

Certainly, after my resignation from the cabinet in 1944, my relations with the party became confused. In the election of 1945 I refused to be sponsored as a candidate by Mr. King; much to his annoyance I declared that in my view the policy should be: 'King if necessary, but not necessarily King.' I was elected without direct sponsorship by any party, and without calling myself an Independent. I felt that if I called myself an Independent I would give the impression that I was closely allied with nationalist Tories, who were probably the most vigorous opponents of Liberalism. Though I was never able to convey the idea to many other people and certainly not to the Liberal leaders, I considered myself not a follower of the party but an ally; and this made my position a difficult one. On a number of occasions between 1945 and 1948 I was obliged to make myself rather obnoxious to the leadership by criticizing the party's policies, actions, and tendencies....

On January 20, 1948, at a dinner held under the auspices of the National Liberal Federation, King requested the federation to arrange for a convention; and on March 19 Gordon Fogo, chairman of the National Liberal Federation, in the name of the federation issued a call for a national convention of the Liberal Party. The purposes of the convention were to be (1) to consider the platform of the Liberal Party of Canada, (2) to consider the question of party organization, and (3) to consider the question of party leadership. The convention was called to meet in Ottawa on August 5, 6, and 7....

During the whole of the [1948 Quebec] provincial election campaign, when anyone mentioned the possibility of my being a candidate for the federal leadership, I strenuously denied it. But towards the end of the campaign my notes show that I had a telephone message from Sir James Dunn, who arranged to fly from his home at St. Andrews, New Brunswick, to Quebec City to have lunch with me. At this luncheon he stated that he had been asked to ask me to be a candidate at the convention; that a great many of the leading businessmen were afraid of Gardiner, and many more thought that St. Laurent could not win an election. He added that Howe was now running the government to suit himself, to which he, Dunn, took some exception. I noticed that Sir James was not an altogether disinterested observer, since apparently some ruling of Howe's had caused difficulty for Algoma Steel, Dunn's own company. I did not commit myself on whether I would be a candidate, and stated that in any event I could make no announcement at that time as it might prejudice Godbout's chances of victory. I assured him that not all federal members supported St. Laurent. I stated further that the only thing that might induce me to accept the nomination would be if Howe were to be the directing force behind St. Laurent. In that event there would be no change for the better in party politics, as Howe had consistently disregarded parliamentary procedure, and apparently did not believe in a government responsible to the people through their representatives. Actually he favoured government by boards, committees, crown companies, and commissions, all headed or controlled by the same person: Howe.

I discussed the matter with some of my friends, who strongly urged me to run. The newspapers got hold of the rumour but I refused to comment, and asked all the newsmen as a favour that there should be no hint of any movement of that kind, at least until the Quebec provincial campaign was over. My notes show that there was great disappointment after the election, and much disgruntlement and talk against St. Laurent, particularly in his own constituency of Quebec East, where his candidate had been defeated. The Liberals had held only one seat in Quebec City. The organizers said

St. Laurent could not make a good impression on the electors, and would not be able to hold Quebec for them in the coming federal elections. Many of the delegates said they would not attend the convention. We also heard St. Laurent felt very discouraged, and stated that he would not be a candidate for the leadership. Finally King telephoned to urge him to continue in the fight, and many cabinet ministers and other leading Liberals did the same. St. Laurent announced that he would remain a candidate.

About this same time, Colin Campbell of Ontario, who had been handling Mr. Gardiner's campaign for the leadership, came down to Quebec to see me. He was enthusiastic over the number of votes he hoped to get, particularly in western Canada and in Ontario. He was also hoping to attract support in Quebec. I told him I thought there was not the slightest chance of Gardiner's getting many votes out of the Quebec delegation. Campbell seemed disappointed about this, and returned to Toronto.

During the next few days I kept receiving telephone calls (some, I think out of curiosity) asking whether I would be a candidate—some offering support if I would. Finally, on August 1 or 2, I informed some of the newspapermen that I would be a candidate at the convention. It is difficult for me to analyse what my sentiments were at that particular time. I was clearly of the opinion that St. Laurent had been such a failure in the provincial campaign that he would make no headway federally even in Quebec. I also feared that as a French-Canadian Catholic, he would get little support in English-speaking Canada.

I did a little checking concerning my own prospects of making even a reasonable showing at the convention, and I came to the conclusion that unless there were several candidates, and unless I was able to have enough votes on the first ballot to keep from being eliminated, my chances were extremely poor. If, on the other hand, I could remain in the running after the first ballot, there was some chance that I might accumulate votes from those who were eliminated, and finally get into the running against Gardiner and St. Laurent. I never had anything like a glimmer of hope that I would be successful; but I was coming more and more to the conclusion that since I had in the past three or four years, in the House of Commons, in speeches, and in magazine articles, protested against the government's method of procedure and continued wartime controls, I could not at this time whitewash the past and give a blank cheque for the future. This was the time, when Liberals of all shades and degrees were assembled, to set forth my views, and if anyone wanted to vote for them, and for what I considered to be the true precepts of Liberalism, then I would give him an opportunity.

When I arrived in Ottawa on the Monday night preceding the convention, it was soon made clear to me that I had no chance whatsoever. Many of the delegates who spoke to me (I canvassed no one and asked no one to vote for me) said they believed in the same kind of Liberalism as I did, but were committed to support St. Laurent. This was largely based on their conviction that to carry the country they must have someone who could carry Quebec, and that St. Laurent was the only one who could make any showing in that province. In any case, all the ministers including the Prime Minister were putting forth every effort to get St. Laurent elected on the first ballot.

I had secured a proposer of my name at the convention in St. Pierre Gagnon, a former member of the legislature from the County of Kamouraska. Gagnon lived not far from my country place at St. Pacôme, and he readily signed my nomination paper. When I reached Ottawa I still had no one to second my nomination, and it was some days before anyone offered to perform that necessary chore for me. Then Senator T.E. Crerar said he would be glad either to propose or to second my name. A day or so afterwards I suggested to him that, since the chances of my election were so poor, I would have no objection if he wished to withdraw his offer. Crerar stated most emphatically that he would do nothing of the kind, that my views on Liberalism were the same as his own, and that he had nothing to lose. He suggested, however, that as I had rather a lot at stake perhaps I had better think it over. I had several chats with Angus Macdonald, who stated that he himself had seriously considered entering the field, and that the delegates from his province of Nova Scotia were all in favour of it; but he did not think he could win enough support from the other provinces. He assured me that if he did not run he would vote for me, but would not, in view of the divergent views of the Nova Scotia delegates, openly support anyone. I thought that Angus could not get many votes outside his own province and that it would hurt his prestige if he did not make a good showing. Angus told me that his wife was rather keen for him to run.

On the opening day of the convention Sir James Dunn came to see me and said that Howe and he had settled their difficulties, and that he would be able to export steel to Europe, as he desired.

He suggested that in my best interests, and since I knew I had no chance of winning, I could now in honour retire. I had expressed my views, he said, and there was no use in my antagonizing the party and hurting my future chances. If I persisted, he suggested, I could not expect to receive anything, but if I retired now I could pretty well write my own ticket. He also stated that he would see that I was appointed a director of Algoma, and retained as legal counsel. I told him that I was in the fight to the finish, and that before I consented to run I had carefully considered all the factors, and that it had become a matter of principle with me. Nevertheless, the rumours of my retirement continued to persist until I was tired of denying them.

I attended the Quebec caucuses and meetings of the committee on resolutions, and some of the meetings of delegates, including one held for the purpose of advancing St. Laurent's candidature. I felt like a lonely man during that period, because I did not wish to approach anyone for fear he might be immediately looked upon as a supporter of mine; a great many who normally were friends, I think did their best to look the other way. It was most uncomfortable for the three days the convention lasted. I decided that since I was going to lose anyway, the best thing I could do was to give the most forceful and frank expression of my own views on the Liberal Party, the policies it had followed in the past, and what should be done in the future. I was handicapped in this since the supporters of St. Laurent, fearing that Jimmy Gardiner might make a first-class fighting speech if he were given sufficient time, endeavoured to cut down the time that would be permitted to the candidates. It was first fixed at twenty minutes, during which the candidate could speak in both languages if he desired; later there was a determined effort made to cut it down still further. There was even a suggestion that five minutes would be enough, and I rather imagine that had the matter come to a vote, and not been pushed very rapidly by the chairman, there would have been a great deal of support for five or ten minutes rather than twenty.

Twenty minutes to explain a program and a theory for the guidance of a great political party like the Liberal Party is not a very long time. However, I did rather carefully prepare my speech, and when the lots were chosen for the order in which the speeches would be given it was found that Power was to be first, with Gardiner second, and St. Laurent last. My speech, I think, was well received by the delegates, who cheered not too often but with a reasonable degree of apparent approval. Gardiner's speech seemed to me quite long and involved, and certainly gained no votes for him. St. Laurent's speech was a matter-of-fact statement, and while it did not inspire, I think it gave confidence to those who listened to him. Here was a man they could trust, a man of equable temperament and solid capacities. St. Laurent won hands down, Gardiner getting some three hundred votes, and my own vote amounted to an insignificant fifty-six as against over eight hundred for Mr. St. Laurent. Gardiner and I at once moved that the vote be made unanimous.

When it was all over, I was not too depressed. Many people, and the newspapers generally, had said that I had succeeded in expressing the views and the thinking of those who considered themselves Liberals across the country. The fact that I obtained such a small number of votes would have made me the laughing-stock of a great many people, I think, had there not been a general idea throughout the party that I had said what somebody had to say at the time, and that in the long run it would be for the greater benefit of the party.

I have never regretted my experience in going before the convention. My campaign was a short one, and I gave myself no trouble in the way of canvassing. I really thought at the time, too, that I would have made a poor prime minister; but I had in mind the thought that the Liberal Party was due for a defeat shortly and that I would be a more successful and efficient leader of the opposition than either of the other candidates. I have often wished for a chance to prove to myself what I have always had in mind, that I would be a first-class leader of an active opposition in the House. However, that opportunity has been denied me, and I have had to be satisfied with being an opposition leader within my own party.

E.E. Harrill Party Finance in the Second Party System

There are four purposes for which the national party funds are expended:

1. tour of the party leader and associates;
2. headquarters organization—rent, salaries for a greatly expanded organization, and supplies;
3. national advertising—radio [and television], pamphlets, newspapers, and magazines; and
4. contributions to individual candidates through the national organizer in each province.

A breakdown of expenditures shows that tours and other travel expenses require approximately ten per cent of the national fund; the headquarters organization uses about ten per cent and national advertising about forty per cent. The remaining forty per cent goes to the individual candidates. In 1935 a national tour by the leader could be managed for about $1,200; in 1949, however, one leader's tour cost nearly $20,000. The headquarters organization requires only small clerical and managerial staff to operate between elections, but during a campaign the staff and costs are greatly expanded.

The parties depend largely on advertising agencies to make arrangements for their paid broadcasts as well as for their printed publicity. Broadcasting stations have been accused of charging political parties the rate they normally quote for the best listening time, regardless of what time the political broadcast or spot advertisement goes on the air. "National advertising, however, is placed and guaranteed by agencies of impeccable standing, yet the top rates are charged just the same."[1]

Printed advertising can run into substantial sums for the national party organization. Each party prints a number of pamphlets for wide distribution—apparently to all party candidates.

On the constituency level the expenses of the candidate, in descending order of their cost, are: payment of workers, local advertising (newspaper, radio, pamphlets, fliers, and gimmicks of various sorts), rent and office expenses, cars, travel, and refreshments (alcoholic and nonalcoholic) for various occasions. In some constituencies the emphasis may vary. Most party workers on the local level are paid for their services.

A Quebec Liberal organizer listed workers as the big item of expense in that province. He reported that it was surprising to discover the kind of people who demanded money for working in a campaign. Wealthy men wanted thirty or forty dollars per day for their sons who, he claimed, were "not worth a damn." He said he had to pay them "because the old man thought it was good for John to earn some of his vacation money and, anyway, the old man thought the party had plenty." There were, he said, in the rural areas in French Quebec, men who were called "chiefs." These men could carry an election in their districts because of the position they held in the area. They might, however, be working for nothing, although some people seemed to feel that they were getting money and keeping it.

Political parties frequently complain that newspapers charge higher rates for political advertising than for anything else. In 1938 in a meeting of the Special Committee on Electoral Matters, one member of Parliament asserted:

> I have found that even reputable newspapers...increase the cost of a column if it is given to a candidate over the cost of giving it to an advertising concern for ordinary advertising. Hotels also increase their cost. That is true. There is no question about that.[2]

Committee rooms, though simply local centres for distribution of literature and information, require, as do offices, considerable rental expenditure.

Rents for halls and school auditoriums used for speeches vary greatly. Some candidates have reported charges of ten dollars or less, but others have recalled figures of fifty dollars and up.[3] In the rural areas where halls are cheapest the candidate, because of widely scattered population, has to hold more meetings than are required in urban locations.

In some ridings travel may in itself be expensive. A member of Parliament testified to this: "...but there are districts...which are twelve hundred miles in extent with widely separated places, where you have to travel one hundred miles to get to a district with no settlement intervening."[4] Hiring of cars to carry voters to the polling places on election day appears to be an almost universal practice for both the major parties, though it is forbidden in the elections act. Blair Fraser states:

There may be local exceptions, but I do not know of any constituency in which cars are not hired by the Liberal and Conservative candidates. All kinds of excuses and devices are used, such as deferring payment until the day after election or having it made by somebody else.[5]

Parties cannot win victories by buying votes directly. All agree that the outright corruption of the old days is a thing of the past. It is admitted that in certain areas it may still be the thing to do to pass around a little gin, whisky, or beer. The Maritimes have the reputation of clinging to this practice. In Ontario and Quebec some candidates admitted that in small home meetings they might hand beer around. They said, however, that such refreshments no longer are considered an expensive campaign item.

The CCF and Social Credit generally run much more economical campaigns than the two older parties. One CCF official claimed that ninety per cent of the political work of the CCF was done by volunteer workers. The Liberals and Conservatives generally admitted this, as illustrated by one MP.

> As to Mr. Heaps and the CCF, I know that their followers still have the apostolic zeal. They would do anything for nothing; but we have not got that in the old parties. The apostolic spirit has faded away, unfortunately, and I do not imagine that it will ever come back.[6]

It is acknowledged with little or no disagreement that most of the money for the Liberal and Conservative Parties comes from business sources. They depend primarily on corporations, businessmen, and trade associations for their financing. There is no restriction on political contributions from corporations; therefore these donations, however large, are perfectly legal. Practically all the national fund comes from these business sources. (Men who should know agree that the two old parties each spent about seven million dollars on the 1962 election. About half of this sum was paid out of central funds and the other half out of funds raised and spent by the constituency organizations.) The size of contributions from individuals and individual companies apparently has traditionally and fairly consistently been large. Of course, information about specific amounts has generally been available only when some scandal was uncovered. In the early 1930's the Beauharnois scandal revealed that one power company was contributing more than $800,000 to both major parties in one year. This sum is perhaps extraordinary. It would appear that a donation of a thousand dollars is expected today from local firms and that for larger businesses the scale rises considerably.

Senator Power remarked that manufacturers who used to give to the Conservatives for tariff protection now give to both parties. It was his opinion, though he disclaimed actual knowledge, that the big contributors were transportation interests, banks, insurance companies, paper companies, and contractors.

Mr. Richard Bell, the Conservative national organizer in 1953, explained that the biggest share of campaign funds came from business contributions. He gave no names but mentioned at various times an aluminum company, textile firms, and shipping companies. These big contributors were primarily national companies, and national collectors did not ordinarily go below the "third level" of business. He explained that the two top levels of business would be the national firms, while the third level would be, for example, a wholesale drug house in a fairly small town. Such an establishment would give a thousand dollars to the national fund; the same company might also give two hundred and fifty dollars to the local party fund.

It is difficult to get anything like specific names and specific amounts, but occasionally they do come out. The greatest publicity given to campaign funds in modern times was focused on a 1930 investigation of the Beauharnois Power project by a Special Committee of the House of Commons. In its fourth report to the House on July 28, 1931, the Committee stated:

1. Mr. R.O. Sweezey has admitted in his evidence that he was responsible for the following contributions:—

2. For contributions for political purposes aggregating $864,000 and which includes the sum of $125,000 paid to John Aird Jr., of which mention will be made hereafter. Of this total, approximately $300,000 were Company funds and the balance was raised by Mr. Sweezey personally and probably at least in part came out of the large profit made on the sale of the Syndicate assets to the Beauharnois Power Corporation and, therefore, indirectly out of the moneys borrowed on the sale of the Company's bonds. Mr. Sweezey

states (Evidence page 821) that he contributed personally to the Liberal Party "somewhere around $600,000 to $700,000." This large sum was paid to Senators Haydon and Raymond. On page 822, Mr. Sweezey says that the total contributions to the Liberal party would run up well over $700,000 and in this there was included a sum stated by Mr. Sweezey to be in the neighbourhood of $100,000 and by Mr. Griffith to be around $120,000 which were Company funds.

3. Mr. Sweezey is unable to state how much was paid to them but he and Mr. Griffith agree that out of the sums paid to Senator Raymond, the Liberal party of the Province of Quebec was to be taken care of. Mr. Sweezey says that he has no knowledge of how much went to the Province of Quebec nor does he tell how much of the total amount was paid each of the two Senators. He, however, ventures the statement that the amount received by Senator Raymond might have been in the neighbourhood of $200,000.

4. On page 822, Mr. Sweezey is asked the question, "Then you spoke of contributions to the Conservative party. What amounts were they and to whom were they paid?" Answer— "They were small amounts. Some of them were to help personal friends whom I had been helping, as a matter of fact, for a number of years in their campaign work." Mr. Sweezey spoke of contributing $6,000 to the campaign of Mr. Leslie Bell, and Mr. Bell in his return under the Dominion Elections Act is said to have published this contribution, as required by Section 80 of such Act. Contributions were also made, according to the testimony of Mr. Sweezey and Mr. Griffith, to General McCuaig, understood to be a collector for the Conservative Campaign fund in Montreal, of $10,000. Mr. Sweezey is not clear as to whether there were any further contributions to the campaign fund of this party. Mr. Griffith, however, states that there was a contribution to Mr. Cartier and that the total contributions to Conservative candidates or party organizers were $25,000. Mr. Sweezey, on the other hand, thinks the amount was $30,000 but refers to Mr. Griffith for the correct amount.

5. Contributions were also made to Mr. W.R.P. Parker, President of the Ontario Liberal Association, amounting to about $3,000. There was also a suggestion with reference to a proposed contribution to the Conservative Federal Campaign Fund through its organizer, General McRae. This, however, was not made. Asked if the reason for its not having been made was that Mr. Bennett would not accept it, Mr. Sweezey in his reply said, "I do not know what it was but I presume that may be so."[7]

In the individual constituency the candidates collect some of the money necessary for their campaign. Here they draw on small local businesses, soliciting individual contributions of relatively small sums. Miss Aitken reported that money in her constituency was collected by a financial committee and by her official agent. The latter wrote a letter of solicitation to every member of the Conservative Party in her riding and to hundreds of small merchants, tradesmen, service station owners, and businessmen. She acknowledged that although this resulted in donations of two, five and fifteen dollars, she had to find larger donations.

"We went to rich people who believed in our cause, and many gave generous donations—two hundred, five hundred, even one thousand dollars from individuals. We went to friends of the candidate who had already expressed their faith in her and had promised financial support."[8]

Sometimes a candidate can afford to finance his own campaign or at least a substantial portion of it. Miss Aitken refers to one candidate who spent about four thousand dollars out of his own pocket.[9] Professor Williams observes that the party often prefers "fat cats" who can finance their own campaigns and perhaps contribute additional sums to the central party fund.[10]

In lieu of money, services are sometimes rendered. A party worker in one constituency boasted that she was not paid by the party or candidate for her services. She was a member of an engineering firm and several years before had decided that political work was good public relations. In 1953 she was giving two months full-time service in the constituency organization. This practice paid off, she said, though there was nothing illegal about it. Her firm knew what government jobs were to be offered and was in a position to get them. She also referred to a man high up in the constituency organization—as head of a business machine company he expected something in return for his nonpaid services—and to a taxicab company owner who furnished a fleet of automobiles on election day free of charge.[11]

Naturally this sort of help comes more freely to the party in power. Some companies apparently give to both the Liberals and the Conservatives—a practice noted by Mr. Edward W. Bickle, a collector for the Conservative Party in Ontario. Bickle further remarked that in the federal field the companies gave larger sums to the Liberals, then (1954) in power.[12] This practice of giving to both major parties is pretty well substantiated by leaders of both parties. There is no agreement on the moral judgment to be passed on this practice. Any such judgment may depend on the purpose of business in making these substantial donations to political parties. The scandal in the Beauharnois affair of the 1930's lay in the effort of the power company making political contributions to secure specific favours from the government. This company gave largely to the Liberals (who were in power) from whom the company had obtained initial concessions for developing power on the St. Lawrence River. Prime Minister King admitted that the Liberal Party was in the valley of humiliation as a result of this exposure but denied that there was any connection between the governmental concessions and the political contributions of the company.[13]

A fair estimate would be that at least fifty per cent of the general funds of the two parties comes from industrial and commercial concerns, and probably at least forty per cent from businessmen who are so closely identified with particular companies that it is difficult to distinguish between them. The remaining ten per cent of the general fund then would come from individuals as such. The individual contributions would be much smaller.

The CCF money comes from sources very different from those of the Liberals and Conservatives. The national fund depends largely on the CCF provincial organizations for its supply of money. Business interests have made some offers of contributions to the national CCF organization. C.J. Woodsworth, son of the former national leader of the CCF recalled that his father had refused to accept at least one contribution from a large company.[14] In the provincial organizations, the CCF gets more help from the Political Action Committee of the Canadian Congress of Labour than from any other one source. The Ontario provincial secretary guessed that in the 1953 national campaign in Ontario the Political Action Committee had spent about eighteen or nineteen thousand dollars for the CCF in advertising and in other kinds of campaign work.

On the constituency level a CCF official in Montreal stated flatly that they had to raise all their money locally and that in many cases it was all they could do to raise the deposit required to run a candidate. The local units of the CCF party contribute to the provincial organization, and it in turn contributes to the national organization for national expenses. There is very little of the flow of money down from a central fund to candidates because the national fund has very little income other than that from the provincial organizations. Sometimes supporters and friends conduct a special drive for a particular candidate. The CCF does not accept funds from business organizations or associations. It does accept aid from labour union locals and the labour PAC. This financial aid comes on the constituency and provincial levels.

The Social Crediters have conducted relatively inexpensive campaigns, but where their money comes from cannot be known exactly. A national campaign fund may very well be the "On to Ottawa" fund, or the educational fund may also be used for campaign purposes. Several political leaders of other parties believe that companies, especially oil companies, contribute to Social Credit in Alberta. The Social Crediters themselves are vague about their income, its size, and sources. They assert that the local candidates raise their own money. Dr. Hansell said that local organizations conducted sales, held dinners and devised other similar ways of raising money on the local level. Mr. Paynter, the national organizer, admitted soliciting from companies for funds on a local level but denied it is done on a national level. He referred frequently to the practice of taking up collections at Social Credit meetings.[15]

The Social Credit people have a great deal of zeal. In the Alberta and national organization—not so much in British Columbia—the leaders have been men who were active fundamentalist evangelists. On the provincial and on the constituency levels the methods used for raising funds have been those commonly associated with religious activities of that sort in this country.

The money-raising practices of the Liberals and Conservatives are very much the same. Collectors are chosen by the party leaders and their close advisors to solicit funds—largely in Toronto and Montreal, the sources of the big money. The same men may do this collecting over a long period of time. In the Conservative Party the national leader names a man financial chairman to take charge of collecting money for the national party organization—usually a businessman, a lawyer, or an accountant. This man has to be completely reliable because there is no accounting for the funds. The national financial chairman may have as much as one-half million dollars come to him in a matter of days.[16] In 1953 it was a Toronto lawyer, a former president of the Toronto Board of Trade. This chairman selected a committee to help him—a subcommittee in Toronto and another in Montreal.

The collectors for the Liberals and Conservatives appear to be from the same social and economic group. A former Conservative collector, a prominent Toronto businessman, said that at the time he was collecting for national Conservative organization his partner was collecting for the Liberals, and a common secretary kept up with both funds.

The Conservative practice is for the national organizer to make up his budget, dividing the sum agreed to by the national collector into the four categories of expenses discussed earlier. The national organizer then consults with each provincial organizer for the national organization, who decides (subject to review by the national organizer) on allotments to individual candidates in his province. The amount going to individual candidates varies according to needs. The collector of funds, the national organizer, and the provincial organizer for national purposes are all responsible to the national leader and not to the party association or any provincial organizations.

In some instances, contributions—or parts of contributions—are earmarked by the donor for particular candidates. In these cases the collector informs the national organizer, who sees that the provincial organizer turns over the designated amount to the particular candidates. This may be against the better judgment of the organizer, but he does it anyway.

In these two major parties the leader appears to remain as aloof as possible from the financial end. Professor Lederle, writing in 1942, reported that at least letters of appreciation for contributions were written by Mr. King. Mr. Bickle, with experience as collector for both the provincial and national organizations of the Conservatives, said that neither Mr. Frost, the Ontario premier at that time, nor Mr. Drew, then the national leader (1954), ever asked the identity of donors. Out of hundreds, or possibly thousands of contributions that came across his desk, Mr. Bickle reported, perhaps one out of a hundred donors asked him to tell the leader about the contribution—which he would then do. Generally speaking, he felt, the leader did not know about funds and would refer to him people who wanted to contribute.

The national leader may be aloof from the details and technicalities of collection and disbursement of party funds, but it is he, and not the party association or any other party organization, who bears the responsibility and who ultimately wields the power. Arthur Meighen, former national leader of the Conservative Party, stated that the party leader's responsibility was personal and could not be evaded.[17]

The Liberals who discuss it at all deny that governmental contracts are awarded on the basis of political contributions. Blair Fraser reported that ninety-eight per cent of defence production contracts were given on the basis of open bids. The other two per cent were special secret jobs. But, he added, "not all departments are as sensitive about patronage as defence production."[18] John Lederle, not feeling at liberty to disclose his evidence, stated categorically that in the central office and in various provincial headquarters of the party, the lists of recipients of government contracts are carefully checked over and that at the proper time, a request for financial assistance is made. "At the time of awarding of public contracts the organization officials will ordinarily be consulted with respect to the party patriotism of the contract seekers."[18]

Political parties in Canada receive the overwhelming share of their funds from sources whose interests are reflected in the policies of the respective parties. Opinions on the motivation behind this political giving to the two old parties are not difficult to gather from the collectors of these contributions and from the officials of the parties. These reasons have included, in the relative frequency with which they were expressed:

1. Preservation of private enterprise.
2. Preservation of the two-party system.
3. Preservation of a climate of opinion that is favourable to business.
4. Civic duty.
5. Habit.
6. Gaining of access to the ear of persons in high places.
7. Gratitude for specific policies or privileges.
8. Hope for specific policies or privileges.
9. Hope for direct aid.

10. Keeping up with competitive companies seeking government business.

11. Prestige.

At the end of World War II when the CCF was thought to be a real threat, the Conservatives received a much larger campaign fund, largely from business interests, than they had previously enjoyed. When the CCF failed to materialize as a strong major party the contributions to the Conservatives fell in subsequent elections. Perhaps this may be attributed partially to the poor showing of the Conservatives in 1945, but the Liberals apparently had as much as ever to spend—at least their type of campaign was not noticeably affected.

The CCF disclaims receiving funds from business interests, except on rare occasions, and attributes this not only to an aversion to the source but also to the dislike of the capitalist business managers to the socialistic policies of the CCF

The Social Credit Party, on the local levels at least, solicits funds from business, presenting the specific argument that it is opposed to socialization and will preserve private enterprise.

Evidences of contributions given to political parties in support of a specific policy that affects a specific company can rarely be found. From the stated policies of the Canadian parties, from the type of men in the positions of authority in the parties, from the general atmosphere in which the parties exist, businessmen can expect a continuation of governmental policies favourable to private enterprise (or which they think to be favourable at any rate), whether the Liberals or Conservatives win a general election. This may account for the generally accepted notion that most individual business firms of any size contribute to both these parties.

The type of solicitor chosen by the two parties is indicative of this appeal to business self-interest. The Conservatives assert that they choose a man or men of unimpeachable business or professional standing—one who has achieved success in business or in the professional world associated with business. The Liberals, although less frank in discussing persons and sums, obviously use the same tactics.

Contributing by the same companies to both the older parties bolsters the general theory that the motivation behind the giving is for preserving private enterprise, or the two-party system, or to preserve that indefinable thing called "climate of opinion favourable to business." It indicates to some observers a form of insurance—the company protects itself whatever the outcome of the election. The policies of the Conservatives and the Liberals are harmonious with the desires of the business community, so it supports the party system in which these two parties dominate. It is possible that many businessmen who contribute are not only concerned with preserving the *status quo* but may also share with the spokesman for the Beauharnois power company the belief that "gratefulness was always regarded as important in dealing with democratic governments."[20] The feeling of civic duty or patriotism cannot be overlooked as contributing to the motivation of business in giving to the Liberals and Conservatives.

It remains for the psychologist to study the pull exerted by social and class ambition on businessmen when they are approached by their social and financial peers or superiors for political contributions. Along with self-interest, apparently habit and desire for prestige may contribute to the success of the two old parties in securing financial support from business.

Notes

1   Blair Fraser, "Our Illegal Federal Elections," *Maclean's Magazine*, LXVI (April 15, 1953), 85.

2   Canada, House of Commons, Special Committee on Electoral Matters, *Minutes of Evidence*, June 23, 1938, C-4.

3   Canada, House of Commons, Special Committee on Electoral Matters, *Minutes of Evidence*, March 30, 1939, A-13, A-14, A-15.

4   Canada, House of Commons, Special Committee on Electoral Matters, *Minutes of Evidence*, June 23, 1938, A-6.

5   Fraser, *op. cit.*, 84.

6   Canada, House of Commons, Special Committee on Electoral Matters, *Minutes of Evidence*, March 30, 1939, A-31.

7   Canada, House of Commons, Special Committee on Beauharnois Power Project, *Report*, Session 1931 (Ottawa: King's Printer, 1931), p. xxi.

8   M. Aitken, *Hey Ma, I Did It!* (Toronto: Clarke, Irwin & Company, Ltd., 1953), p. 141.

9   *Ibid.*, p. 140.

10   J.R. Williams, *The Conservative Party of Canada* (Durham: Duke University Press, 1956), p. 265. Politicians have been known to complain that once a millionaire had run in a riding, it was spoiled for subsequent candidates with less money.

11   Interview with ward chairman, August 3, 1953.

12   Interview with Edward W. Bickle, July 7, 1954.

13 Canada, *House of Commons Debates*, July 30, 1931, pp. 4379-4380.

14 Interview with J.S. Woodsworth, August 13, 1953.

15 Interview with Peer V. Paynter, July 9, 1954.

16 On the lack of any accountability for funds see "Ottawa Spotlight," *Montreal Star*, July 4, 1953, p. 6, and Canada, House of Commons, Special Committee on Beauharnois Power Project, Session 1931, *op. cit.*, pp. xxii-xxv.

17 Letter from Arthur Meighen, July 8, 1954.

18 Fraser, *op. cit.*, 83.

19 John W. Lederle, *The National Organization of the Liberal and Conservative Parties of Canada*, Ph.D. Dissertation, University of Michigan, 1942.

20 Canada, House of Commons, Special Committee on Beauharnois Power Project, Session 1931, *op. cit.*, p. 823.

C.G. Power The Problem of Election Spending

...I would like to enter a plea for major and, I believe, urgent reforms in the raising and spending of campaign funds by Canadian political parties. I believe that their size, real or reputed, brings pressure for stupid, senseless and futile expenditures; that they can and should be limited by law; that the hypocritical concealment of their extent and sources gives rise to unhealthy rumours and suspicions which undermine faith and confidence in democratic institutions; and that in the interests of Canadian democracy, the sources of campaign contributions and the size of funds should be indicated to the public.

No group of people would be happier to see restriction of election expenditures than those who come under the head of political organizers. They would like to see spending cut to the point where, for example, just because one side plasters every pole in the county with its candidate's picture, the other need not follow suit. They would like to be rid of all the little chisellers who come around with schemes which, because they have already sold them to the other side—advertisements in often valueless publications, for instance—they literally blackmail you into buying for your own man, usually at rates the vendor dare not charge for ordinary commercial purposes. Restrictions of campaign spending would certainly be a cure for an organizer's headaches.

Apart from the official costs of an election, defrayed by the state itself, supporters of parties and individuals are spending...an average of considerably more than $40,000 to elect a member to the House of Commons. When you pause to consider that the C.C.F., the Social Crediters and splinter-groupers are going along largely on a shoestring, the cost of getting a representative of either of the two major parties into the House of Commons begins to be apparent.

This theoretical average of $40,000, of course, includes a proportion of overhead—four years of it—in the central organization's publicity, radio, advertising, and what not, and that for all parties.

Moreover, the amounts vary in different constituencies. For instance, in an election held nearly 30 years ago in a Montreal Island constituency the amount legally expended and publicly reported by one candidate was $105,000. The loser in the same constituency on the same occasion spent $44,000. These sums, needless to say, constitute a record at least for known legal disbursements. In other constituencies as little as $400 or $500 has been sufficient to carry the day.

Yet the war chest is always empty. Even in the heat of an election campaign, central party funds are usually in the red and the faithful are out scrounging for dollars. As the race goes down to the wire the demands from individual candidates become more and more urgent, more and more insistent. Candidates themselves have a tendency to minimize or conceal information as to the money they have received from supporters in their own ridings and constantly, persistently and tearfully call on headquarters for more and more money.

This adds enormously to the cost of an election. With a ceiling on slush it would disappear. It would also enable the candidate's organizer to ward off exaggerated local demands. The racketeer would look for other means of turning a penny. Hence the corrupt practices in which he engages would, I believe, largely disappear, for it is on the constituency level that corrupt practices mainly occur.

What are these practices? In the main they are the direct bribery of electors, treating, impersonation of voters and the transportation of citizens to and from the polls, the last of which may surprise many an honest citizen who regards himself as entitled to a free ride to the ballot box in a car provided by his own party's candidate.

Take bribery, or the buying of votes by one device or another.... There was a time, of course, when votes were literally bought for money in the market place. I well remember an incident, more than 40 years ago, when the Liberal buyers set up shop on one side of an actual market and their Tory competitors for votes on the other, while the vendors, the voters, moved from one side to the other, offering their franchises to the highest bidder. It was a tight election and toward the end of the day single votes were going for as high as $75 and $80 and one transaction was even recorded for an even $100. When the exchange, or rather the polling places, closed, the winner's majority was two votes. Thirty-five thousand dollars had been spent by one side, $30,000 by the other. Another $300 in the loser's kitty in the last five minutes would have turned the tide.

Such things could not happen in these enlightened times. We have become smoother operators. Nowadays staunch friends of candidates become distributors of largesse for the limited period of the campaign and surreptitious deliveries of coal, large orders of groceries, or even electric washing machines are made at the right moment.

Treating, for election purposes, is defined as the giving, or providing, of any meat, drink, provision or refreshment for the purpose of corruptly influencing voters.... As in most things concerned with elections, the activities of one party cancel out those of the other, with the result that if both abstain from undercover goings-on—as they would be forced to do if expenditures were restricted—the result of the polling would be the same.

Personation (usually called impersonation by the public) is defined as applying for a ballot paper in the name of some other person, alive or dead.... It does not appear to have penetrated into our election practices to any great extent west of the Ottawa River, but by all accounts it flourishes in Montreal, where it goes by the name of "telegraphing" and its exponents as "telegraphers."

...Of all our corrupt electoral practices on the constituency level this is undoubtedly the most heinous and the most difficult with which to cope, since its operators are professionals, thugs and gangsters who stop at nothing. The practice has increased considerably since women secured the vote, not because the ladies are more politically immoral than their men-folks, but because women are not generally as widely known as men. Many businesswomen reside in boardinghouses and are seldom known even to their immediate neighbours. A similar statement applies to female domestic help. Then to challenge the identification of a woman come to vote is extremely difficult. The result is that the feminine telegrapher has become an important part of the machinery of electoral corruption in those areas where impersonation is widely practiced.

In all these despicable practices money is the motive power. It is my argument, therefore, that if we severely curtail its use on the constituency level we shall make rapid strides toward removal of these crimes against democracy, by taking away the incentives which attract the chisellers and the gangsters. I do not suggest that we shall be able to achieve the millennium overnight. But we can move a long way toward it.

No doubt exists...that if we were to restrict the amounts of money which central organizations are permitted to spend, we would be doing a good day's work for democracy. For again, in this field, the scales are often weighted in favour of the party which, for one reason or another, is able to raise the preponderantly large campaign fund....

Granted an even-money status as between major parties in any election, restriction of their expenditures would be helpful to all and would also assure a much better opportunity for fighting our elections on issues, rather than with money. As things are now, if one party engages to carry advertisements in each of the 100 daily newspapers in the country, then the other must do so—and one half-page advertisement will cost the central organization $9,475 for a single appearance. If neither party were to advertise due to restrictions on spending, I venture to assert that the outcome of the election would not be affected in the slightest degree.

Free radio time for discussion of the issues of the day, particularly over the CBC, has relieved the parties of some part of the financial burden, for a half hour's talk by a national leader over the coast-to-coast network costs $5,500. It would do no harm, either, if the parties were forced, by lack of money, to eschew the use of the mails, excepting, perhaps, one mailing during a campaign, which costs close to $20,000 for postage alone.

There remains the question of publicizing the names of donors, and I do not think I am giving away any secrets of state when I say that those charged with the raising of campaign funds seriously fear that many present donors would no longer come across if the size of their donations were to be set down opposite their names, or the names of their corporations in a public report. I could also venture to believe that the publication of such names might in some cases be a source of embarrassment to the recipient party. But, actually, that is precisely what those who believe that reform is urgent are getting at. To publicize the names of those who contribute to central campaign funds would be an extremely healthy cathartic, both for donor and recipient. It is precisely the kind of medicine our democratic political process requires if it is to remain—or, perhaps I should say become—honestly democratic.

We may restrict and publicize as much as we like, but if we do not equip ourselves with the teeth of penalty, and give them a sharp biting edge, we may just as well not bother. The obvious point at which to lay on the penalty is the candidate. It becomes, therefore, a question of forcing the men and women who contest seats for the House of Commons to police their own elections. This admittedly is no easy task, but the results would be well worth the inconvenience, for they would give back to the Canadian people the confidence in democratic election practices which I believe they have lost. And if our people lack confidence in their own free institutions, believing them to be no longer free of external pressures, how long do you think those institutions will last?

When this subject was debated in 1938 I said in the House: "Our present democratic system is built on confidence. Destroy that confidence and the value of our institutions is almost entirely impaired. A greater threat by far to democracy than the 'isms' that now infest our body politic is the belief that electoral manipulation, electoral manoeuvring, electoralism as it is called in our province, is undermining the very basis of democracy."

W.C. Soderlund,
W.I.Romanao,
E.D.Briggs and
Ronald H.
Wagenberg

From a Single Medium to a Multimedia Society

Canada's first mass medium, the newspaper, was virtually without competition until the early 1930s, by which time it was mature in the sense that it was regarded as an important and serious-minded institution.[1] As with all adulthood one could applaud the arrival of sobriety and restraint while harboring a twinge of nostalgia for the youthful vitality and passion they replaced. For those who found relinquishing the latter qualities altogether too painful to bear, there was an alternative: abandon print communication altogether and embrace instead a rapidly growing infant, radio, which had begun to intrude into Canadian life. The progression was from a relatively simple communications system, politically relevant to a small attentive public, to a complex, technologically sophisticated series of systems with the potential for much wider influence.

Radio broadcasting as we know it began on the North American continent in the 1920s. In Canada, a Marconi station was first licensed as a commercial operation in Montreal with the call letters of XWA (later CFCF).[2] Radio, while started in Montreal, developed almost simultaneously in the 1920s across the country. From its inception radio was a cultural, and hence a political, football. Politicians did not immediately recognize radio's potential; indeed, the fact that licensing of would-be broadcasters was initially entrusted to the Department of Marine and Fisheries, under the assumption that it should be viewed as an extension of marine services, is an indication of how little it was at first understood.

But mere toy though it might have been, it was fantastically popular, and it ran into two immediate problems that necessitated government interference in its operations. First, Canadian stations had great difficulty competing with stronger American stations broadcasting on the same wavelengths, in the absence of agreements on the allocation of exclusive spectrum usage. Second, there was already concern before the twenties had ended that fledgling Canadian radio was becoming the instrument for the transmission of American culture. In arguments that were to be repeated by later generations of Canadians, it was maintained that most Canadian stations carried popular American programs because it was easier and less expensive to do that than it was to produce domestic content.[3]

The Aird Commission, which submitted its report in 1929, indicated that Canadians preferred Canadian broadcasting. While the statement was ambiguous, in that Canadians have always shown a preference for broadcasting content originating in the United States, the Commission's conviction was clear: "the destiny of Canada depends upon our ability and willingness to control and utilize our own internal communications for Canadian purposes."[4] One of the recommendations of the report resulted in the creation of the Canadian Radio Broadcasting Commission and later, in 1936, in the creation of the Canadian Broadcasting Corporation.

This is not the place to review in detail the operations of the CBC or to recount the transformations through which it has been put in more than 50 years by the various committees, commissions, and ministries that have pried into its workings. What should be noted here is that radio brought a new dimension to the traditional relationship between politicians and the media. Politicians' interest in the press had always been narrow and selfish. Newspapers were useful as personal and party mouthpieces, as tools in the perpetual propaganda contests that constituted politics, but publishing in the collective sense was not thought of as essential to the national interest. Radio, on the contrary, from the time of the Aird Commission Report, was considered a sort of national resource to be managed in such a way as to provide a protective shield against foreign (i.e., American) cultural intrusion. The strength of this resolve was certainly not constant over the years. At times, in fact, it was almost nonexistent. The resolve did survive and by the time television appeared in the early 1950s, it found expression in any discussion about the role of the media, including the printed press.

One-third of all Canadian homes had some sort of radio receiving device by 1930. In urban centres it was more like half. The unending gloom of the Great Depression served to reinforce the attractiveness of technology's magic to such an extent that neither bread lines nor dust storms could prevent 75 percent of households acquiring radios by the time economic recovery was in sight. Politicians could hardly avoid concluding that radio presented an ideal means of reaching more people faster than ever before.

Yet there was no stampede to politicize the microphones and there were no attempts to develop a party radio. One reason for the latter was the fact that many of the private radio stations were owned by press barons who were disinclined to resurrect a practice that print journalism had only recently escaped. Another and more practical reason was that partisanship might discourage advertisers even more quickly in radio than in newspapers. In any case, radio remained unsullied by party labels. It was used for electoral campaigning, on a local and regional basis, during the late 1920s, and, with some initial trepidation, for federal campaigns. Both Prime Minister Mackenzie King and Opposition Leader R.B. Bennett utilized it to attempt to reach nation-wide audiences, though with undetermined effect as far as impact on the voters was concerned.

It was President Franklin Roosevelt who was to demonstrate how effective radio could be for political communication. His famous fire-side chats over coast-to-coast radio in the United States came to characterize the Depression as surely as unemployment, but with the opposite effect. The talks were a soothing ointment applied by a kindly parent to the hurts of millions and, as time would tell, they paid handsome dividends in the form of electoral success.

In Canada, those dark days also served to heighten realizations of radio's potential. In Alberta, William (Bible Bill) Aberhart had already discovered that the air waves were ideal carriers for the evangelical messages of the Calgary Prophetic Bible Institute. When, in 1932, he decided that the spiritual salvation offered by Christianity had to be supplemented by the material salvation promised by Social Credit, it was naturally radio that transmitted the Good News. Aberhart was a master performer before a microphone. His voice ranging up and down the octaves, he thundered and cajoled and pleaded with his listeners to have faith in Christ and Major Douglas (the Social Credit theorist) in about equal proportions. He found his way into almost every Alberta home on a regular basis and he was accepted in the vast majority of them for the same reason that Roosevelt's chats were welcomed by Americans—and many Canadians. Here was a voice of hope, of understanding, of deliverance when none seemed to be likely from any other quarter. Social Credit swept to power in the Alberta election of 1935 and maintained a stranglehold on that province until 1971. Much of the thanks (or blame) could be laid at radio's door. At least, as John H. Irving has put it, "It may be doubted if there could have been a Social Credit movement without Aberhart's use of the radio."[5]

Aberhart was not the only Canadian politician who found radio an effective propaganda instrument. While the successes were not of the same magnitude as experienced in Alberta, the political broadcasting experience in neighboring Saskatchewan was very similar. There, a young Socialist Baptist minister, T.C. Douglas, found similar success for the fledgling Co-operative Commonwealth Federation (CCF) through his radio broadcasting orations in the early 1940s. In Quebec the newly organized Union Nationale under Maurice Duplessis used radio as the principal avenue for attacking the entrenched Liberal regime of Louis Taschereau in 1935 and 1936. Again the offensive succeeded and forty years of Liberal rule came to an end. On the other hand, when R.B. Bennett's desperate Conservative Government tried to recover from the threat of defeat in the federal election of 1935 by resorting to a series of broadcasts in the form of dramatized political discussions critical of the Liberals and Mackenzie King, they were nevertheless swept from power.

By itself radio certainly did not ensure electoral victory, but it conferred an advantage on those who took the trouble to master the techniques of using it. The political careers of those who possessed such skills were considerably enhanced. To ensure that party radio did not arise and some equity in broadcasting opportunities was guaranteed to all political parties, a 1939 White Paper on political broadcasting recommended that all parties represented in Parliament should have free broadcast time during elections. This first occurred in the 1940 campaign and was made a permanent feature of Canadian broadcasting in 1944. The free time, which was proportional to each party's numerical strength in the House of Commons, could be supplemented by as much paid advertising as a party could afford.

The traditional press did not fold its type and slink into the underbrush with the appearance of radio. Publishers were understandably nervous for a time, mainly about radio's impact on advertising revenues. They sermonized frequently on the desirability of a pure, commercial-free CBC system on the British model, and when that battle was lost in 1938, "they ranted and raved, throwing a tantrum inspired by a sense of betrayal and some fear."[6] But the tantrum was mitigated by the fact that many publishers were by that time deeply involved in radio ownership themselves, and, in any case, newspaper operations did not seem to have been significantly affected. Profits were scarcely high during the Depression, and the number of dailies declined to a low of 87 by 1945. But radio listening did not seem to be a substitute for newspaper reading. There were several reasons for this. Radio was perceived to be an entertainment medium and the most popular listening periods were early afternoon and evening hours. Moreover, the new medium generated new advertisers rather than enticing the old ones to shift from print to voice. Traditional publishing thus was little altered by the coming of radio. It appears, however, that publishers gradually adopted a more serious demeanor, as befitted the senior communication medium now that the frivolities could safely be left to the newcomer to provide. Both newspapers and radio faithfully recorded events, including political comings and goings, on a day-to-day basis, but more as observers from afar than as partisan participants.

Communication systems became more complex and all-encompassing. With the beginning of television broadcasting in 1952 the multimedia era had truly arrived. From the point of view of those already in the marketplace, however, the danger was that television would be the ultimate medium all by itself. It did, after all, combine the best features of radio and the movies; it had a public acceptance that made the earlier reception of radio seem lukewarm; and, as time proved, it appeared capable of unending improvement and expansion.

By 1960 most of the older media were in desperate straits. Movie attendance had fallen by 50 percent; radio was almost totally eclipsed; and advertising had fled from even the giants of the consumer magazine industry that the only choice seemed to be between immediate and lingering death. Newspapers, however, again demonstrated their basic resilience. They were not totally unaffected by television's savage rampage. They too lost advertising dollars, as older people were found to prefer to receive news via television rather than expend the greater effort that newspaper reading required. Newspaper circulation, which had climbed more or less continuously for more than two hundred years, continued to increase, although the rate of growth slowed perceptibly. Newspaper publishers had less cause for alarm than most of their media cousins.[7]

Television was not very innovative in its early days. Televised newscasts, for example, consisted mainly of on-camera readers, supplemented by still photographs of events, and occasionally by filmed footage. But this was a classic case of the whole that was greater

than the sum of its parts. Television had impact. It had the imme-
diacy movie newsreels lacked; it could briefly convey a good deal
more information than a newspaper headline; and, of course, its
visual dimension brought events into everyone's living room with a
reality that not even the most dramatic radio reader could match.
Television could convey messages that affected viewers on both the
cognitive and affective levels. These need not be wholly consistent
with one another. Verbal accounts of an event might, for instance,
be objectively phrased and dispassionately rendered, but the pictorial accompaniment might well make a far stronger statement, or,
in the extreme case, serve to make quite a different impression than
the carefully modulated words. Pictures indeed tended to speak
louder than words, and the possibility of conscious or unconscious
pictorial bias, present in the media to some extent since newspapers
began publishing photos in the late nineteenth century, was now
far greater.

It has not been incidents of visual distortion that have troubled
the relationship between politicians and television or other media
personnel. Political events continue to be a major focus of attention
for all media, and politicians have learned to play to the television
cameras before all else. Strangely, political leaders unanimously declined the offer of free-time telecasts during the 1953 federal election, but since then practically everything has come to be framed
with an eye to the 30-second television newsclip. Great efforts are
devoted to staging "media (i.e., TV) events" that will display the
party leader or other prominent figure in what is hoped will be a
favorable light. A premium is put on good television image and on
the ability to package and market that image.

Since the coming of television (the federal campaigns of 1957
and 1958 were the first in which television was extensively used)
politicians have courted the media more assiduously than ever before, but have rarely been able to establish an easy relationship with
them. Federal and provincial leaders have complained that their
treatment by the media has been unfair. Prime Minister Trudeau
has probably given voice to such complaints more frequently than
most of his predecessors or contemporaries, though John Diefenbaker in the last years of his prime ministership could also scathe
journalists bitterly, and even Lester Pearson was known to grumble
at the attitudes of the gentlemen of the press. The most general
complaint has been that the media are too critical, that they con-

centrate on trying to embarrass and emphasize the negative aspects of practically everything.[8]

Some evidence suggests that the media have at last become what journalists have long aspired to be: a genuinely independent Fourth Estate. The media that were hard hit by the television tidal wave in the fifties have managed to reclaim a sufficient portion of the public's attention to remain viable and profitable. Each now appears to occupy a more or less comfortable niche. A live-and-let-live philosophy and a degree of mutual support have come about and it is now not unusual to see radio advertise on television, and in turn promote television programming.

Notes

1   For an excellent overview see W.H. Kesterton, *A History of Journalism in Canada* (Ottawa: Carleton University Press, 1984) and Paul Rutherford, *The Making of the Canadian Media* (Toronto: McGraw-Hill Ryerson, 1978).

2   A concise history of Canada's early broadcasting system is contained in *The Canadian Broadcasting Corporation: A Brief History* (Ottawa: Canadian Broadcasting Corporation, 1976), pp. 1-2. See also Frank W. Peers, *The Politics of Canadian Broadcasting: 1920-1951* (Toronto: University of Toronto Press, 1969).

3   See Canada, Department of Communications, *Report of the Task Force on Broadcasting Policy* (Ottawa: Supply and Services, 1986), pp. 381-472.

4   *Report of the Royal Commission on Radio Broadcasting 1929* (Ottawa: The King's Printer, 1929), pp. 12, 13.

5   "Interpretations of the Social Credit Movement," in Hugh Thorburn, ed., *Party Politics in Canada* (Toronto: Prentice-Hall, 1963), p. 92.

6   Rutherford, *The Making of Canadian Media*, p. 83.

7   For a discussion of newspaper circulation development in Canada, see *Royal Commission on Newspapers* (Ottawa: Minister of Supply and Services Canada, 1981), pp. 63-66.

8   For up-to-date treatments of media influence on politics see Daniel Tavas, *The Newsmakers: The Media's Influence on Politics* (Toronto: Nelson, 1990) and Walter I. Romanao and Walter C. Soderlund, *Media Canada: An Introductory Analysis* (Toronto: Copp Clark Pitman, 1992), pp. 310-332.

R. Whitaker Advertising, Parties and Elections: The Case of the Liberals

> *...we stripped away all the mysticism of political campaigns and "sold" Liberalism as we would sell any other product or service–by modern merchandising methods...Walsh has always approached its political assignments with the same techniques that it employs successfully to sell automobiles, fountain pens, hosiery, etc. for other clients...Given a free hand, Walsh proceeded to formulate a plan that would sell a Government to a people, just as we would sell any other product or service to people...[I]nferior products can annihilate superior ones, if shrewdly, consistently and heavily impressed upon the public.*
>
> Walsh Advertising Agency, *A Formula for Liberal Victory* (1948)

> *Jello isn't very solid either, but they sell a hell of a lot of it.*
> American political public relations man

The rise of the advertising and public relations industries in the twentieth-century capitalist economy has been one of its more noteworthy structural changes....It would seem that the rise of mass advertising techniques in politics tended to coincide with the decline of traditional, localized, patronage-oriented, machine politics. As patron-client politics has been slowly transformed into the more universalist categories of bureaucratic politics, techniques of communication with the *mass* of voters has obviously become a more pressing concern. This does seem to involve, in a curious way, a greater emphasis on issues.[1] Although ad men are commonly denounced for debasing politics with personalized images, they are in another sense technicians advising their political clients in the best way to present their electoral promises and programmes to the widest possible mass audience. Just how far one can blame the ad men themselves for a state of affairs which may be more a symptom than a cause of the lowest-common denominator standard of mass society, is a matter of some considerable conjecture, which I could not hope to answer here. Nor will I attempt to answer the question of the empirical effect of advertising on partisan voting behaviour.[2] Instead, in keeping with the overall focus of this study, I will examine the *organizational* aspects of political advertising: the links between the ad agencies and the party, and the effects of advertising on the party organization. And here, it must be said at the outset, the effect of the ad men was indeed to focus the attention of the party on its ideas and programmes. However much the packaging and selling of these programmes might displease the high-minded and the fastidious, the ad agencies were in another sense clearly in the balance against the older, localized patronage politics. As agents of mass socialization for the newer bureaucratic politics, their influence ought not to be underestimated...

Advertising agencies and politics in Canada

It is thus to the advertising agency that one must turn in Canada to study the link between politics and the techniques of modern mass persuasion. K.Z. Paltiel has noted the decline in the influence within parties of the press barons of earlier eras, like the Siftons, the Atkinsons, and the Lord Atholstans, and their replacement by the ad men—in conjunction with the rise of radio and television: 'The advertising agency and the public relations consultant have taken the editor's place in the counsels of the parties. The rise to party prominence of such advertising men as Senator Keith Davey, the former national Liberal organizer, Senator Allister Grosart who performed a similar function for the Conservatives during Mr. Diefenbaker's rise to power, and Mr. Dalton Camp who precipitated the latter's undoing, bear witness to this process.'[3] And it was the Liberal party which from the 1930s through the 1950s led the way into the new era of political advertising—whether as a cause or an effect of its superior political and financial status among federal parties at this time being difficult to determine...

The First World War gave a major impetus to the development of advertising and most particularly to the involvement of advertising agencies in the preparation of government propaganda appeals to citizens on such issues as voluntary enlistment and the sale of government bonds. The many businessmen who took up leading positions in the government war effort naturally turned to the publicity methods with which they were already familiar, and to the agencies with which they were familiar. Following the introduction of conscription, advertising agencies found their way into politics as well. H.E. Stephenson and C. McNaught note that 'the same advertising agency which had explained the terms of the Military Service Act to the public was allotted the task of preparing the publicity campaign for the Union Government' in the election of 1917.[4]

There is only scattered evidence on the extent to which advertising agencies were utilized by parties in political campaigns of the 1920s and 1930s. Paltiel has stated that it was in the 1940s that 'both the Liberals and the Conservatives began to employ advertising agencies to help plan their campaign activities.'[5] Although the use of agencies and their services did become more pronounced in the 1940s, and while it does seem to be true that more formal bargains were struck between the party and its agencies in this decade, the relationship in fact appears to have more venerable roots reaching into the 1930s at least. In the 1935 federal campaign, for example, slightly over $50,000 was spent nationally on radio publicity through the agency of Cockfield, Brown and a further $17,000 was spent on billboards and weekly newspaper advertisements through the agency of R.C. Smith. The publicity end of a special dinner commemorating the twentieth anniversary of Mackenzie King's leadership of the party held in Toronto in 1939 was handled by Harry Cockfield, a principal partner in Cockfield, Brown.[6] Moreover, as will be shown later, the distribution of advertising dollars from the government among the various friends of the Liberal Party in the advertising world was already a major patronage problem for Norman Lambert in the late 1930s.

The Second World War gave an even greater impetus to the advertising industry than its predecessor. By 1944 almost $37 million was being spent nationally on advertising through agencies (about half the total amount spent on advertising) and the agencies were earning almost $6 million in fees. Significantly, two-thirds of the total billings were going to eleven agencies each making more than $1 million per year in gross revenues.[7] Giants were already emerging within the industry.

The federal government was leading the way in the use of advertising, particularly through its gigantic Victory Bond campaigns, the greatest promotion campaigns ever to take place in Canada up until that time. Throughout the war the federal government spent at least $30,444,537 on advertising, of which more than two-thirds went through ad agencies.[8] In fact, by war's end, the federal government headed the list of the largest advertisers in the land.[9] This meant that there was a very substantial 'pork barrel' for advertising patronage in the making; it also meant that the attention of politicians would inevitably be drawn to the potential of ad agencies for political as well as governmental work. Everything was in the cards for a happy and lasting *ménage à trois* between the government, the party, and the ad agency.

To the Liberals a more specific spur came with the realization of the sagging popularity of the wartime government and the sudden perception of a strong electoral threat from the left. The now famous Gallup poll of 1943 which showed the CCF leading both the Liberals and the Conservatives in national popularity was a salutary shock to a party which had carried the country in a landslide vote only three years earlier. The awareness that not only did the government need to better its image but that public opinion on a wide spectrum of issues had shifted clearly to the left, presented the Liberals with a decisive challenge which called for the services of experts, not amateurs or old-fashioned machine politicians.... One facet of the strategy devised to renew the party's electoral hold on the country was to turn to the services of the advertising agencies which were at that moment shaping Canadian public opinion on behalf of the war effort. If experts could package and sell a war, presumably they could package and sell the Liberal party.

Not that the Liberals were lacking in ideas for substantive approaches, although the ideas came largely from the senior levels of the civil service. The new Keynesian economics being channelled into Canada by W.C. Clark and his bright young men in the Department of Finance did offer a strategy which could not only avoid a return to depression at war's end (which was the chief fear of the public) but could do it through the wide extension of public welfare and social security programmes: a winning combination of policies with which to face a strong social democratic challenge. The advertising agencies were to have a viable product to market, but the Liberal party clearly realized that a good product alone would not necessarily be accepted on its own merits. Hence the need to develop an appropriate sales pitch. The civil service and the cabinet would produce the product and the ad men would undertake the job of selling it. Just what this meant in specific terms may be seen in an almost embarrassingly frank presentation made in the form of a large, glossy brochure by Walsh Advertising to the National Liberal Federation detailing Walsh's contribution to the New Brunswick provincial Liberal victory in 1948 (Walsh was the official Liberal agency in both the 1944 and 1948 McNair campaigns).[10] Although Walsh was not chosen as the Liberals' national agency, it did represent the party in Ontario and New Brunswick: its thinking as exemplified in this brochure does perhaps represent an insight into how ad agencies saw their role in political assignments in the 1940s. Certainly Walsh seems to have thought so highly of it that they specifically deposited a copy in the Public Archives of Canada, presumably for the edification of future generations.

Whether edifying or not, the gist of the Walsh 'formula for Liberal victory' was as follows. After being retained by Premier McNair as 'advertising and public relations counsel' to the New Brunswick Liberal Association, Walsh was given the full co-operation of the civil service and free access to all government records; thus saturated with information, Walsh ad men were able to put together a *Speaker's Handbook*, the 'foundation' of the campaign. Then the actual campaign work was begun: province-wide newspaper advertisements on every theme, and with a local 'dealer tie-in'—the name of the local candidate included; radio bulletins so short that by the time the low attention span of the listener led him to turn the dial, the message was already over; and so on.

Rather more interesting than Walsh's specific techniques, however, was their philosophical rationale, a vision of political man as standing somewhere between a Hobbesian consumer and a Benthamite behaviourist:

> Walsh has always approached its political assignments with the same techniques that it employs successfully to sell automobiles, fountain pens, hosiery, etc. for other clients. Perhaps that is the secret of the agency's success in the political field. After all, voters are human beings. And all human beings are motivated, in all their actions, by a comparatively few well-known and measurable impulses. These may be broadly defined as Fear, Hunger, Sex, and Rage. To reach and incite these impulses, there are five portals of entry—sight, sound, touch, taste, and smell—with the first two being of paramount importance.

> Given a free hand, Walsh proceeded to formulate a plan that would sell a Government to a people, just as we would sell any other product or service to people....

Walsh researchers, having probed deeply into the 'subconscious or inner feelings of the people,' had concluded that Canadians were, 'in their secret hearts,' *satisfied* with what they had, but *afraid* of losing it.

Liberalism was the political product which could best answer this consumer dilemma, by a positive exploitation of this fear: if the idea of *progress* could be distinguished in the voters' perceptions from that of *change*, and the former identified in the public mind with the familiar and habitual act of voting Liberal, then the future of Liberalism would be assured: '...Liberalism was presented not as a political party, nor as a vague, ideological theory, but as a *mass* expression of each individual's inherent human desire for progress and security. The objective was to make each individual discover within himself the exciting realization that Liberalism and his own personal hopes and aspirations are synonymous.... In other words, we gave people the opportunity to gratify the inherent desire for change and to mitigate an equally inherent fear of the unknown in a single action—voting Liberal.' Walsh was also at pains to point out that while the Liberal party was doubtless a worthwhile product, there was no guarantee that a good product can sell itself. Indeed, inferior products can annihilate superior ones, 'if shrewdly, consistently, and heavily impressed upon the public.' In case the Liberals missed the significance of this point, Walsh was careful to add that 'only professional advertising people of long experience can do this.... We at Walsh are not politicians. But we are professional students of human behaviour and human reaction to stimuli.'...

Cockfield, Brown and the National Party

The agency the Liberals chose to advertise their wares nationally was not the fast-talking Walsh group, but an agency that, being Number One, did not have to try harder: Cockfield, Brown and Company, of Montreal, Toronto, Vancouver, Winnipeg, and anywhere else where there was money to be made from salesmanship. Cockfield, Brown was not only the biggest advertising concern in the country; its president claimed in the late 1950s that *per capita* it was the largest agency in the world. Beginning with a merger of a Toronto and a Montreal firm in 1928, Cockfield, Brown began its existence with over $2 million in billings and never looked back. One of Cockfield, Brown's special assets was its research department, apparently the first such department in a Canadian agency: its research capacity was certainly one of its attractions to clients such as the Liberal party.[11] But Cockfield, Brown was politically attractive to the Liberals as well. In the 1935 federal election, the Toronto office contributed $2,000 to the Liberal bagman on Bay Street.[12] In the 1940 election, the Montreal office of Cockfield, Brown was the chief Liberal agency, assisted by Walsh and

Canadian Advertising of Montreal. And Cockfield, Brown was already gaining a lion's share of the lucrative government advertising pot. It was only natural when the government decided in 1940 to set up a special group of large agencies to push the War Savings Campaign, that one of the agency's two principal partners, Harry Cockfield, should have been chosen as chairman of the campaign.[13] The most successful ad agency in the country and the most successful political party seemed to be made for each other.

Two key figures in speeding this marriage were Brooke Claxton for the party and H.E. 'Bob' Kidd for the agency.... Claxton was the organizational genius of the national Liberal party in the 1940s and early 1950s. Along with Jack Pickersgill, he probably had more to do with the organization of national campaigns than any other cabinet minister. That this involvement coincided with the period of some of the Liberals' greatest electoral triumphs is unlikely to have been entirely accidental. A man with an academic background, Claxton was much more than an old-fashioned organizer. Although he had a quick eye, not to speak of a strong stomach, for some distinctly traditional patronage practices—such as collecting campaign contributions from a carefully tended list of corporations receiving contracts from his own mammoth Defence Department 'pork barrel,'[14] he was still something of the intellectual in politics who always kept watch on issues as well as on organization. And part of his concern with issues was an interest in their efficient packaging and selling. Claxton seems to have been one of the first federal politicians to take real advantage of the services of the ad agencies to advance his own career as well as the fortunes of his party.[15]

Kidd was an ad man who had 'worked with and in the Liberal organizations since 1925,' first in Vancouver where he arrived after immigrating to Canada after the First World War, and later in Montreal where he moved within the Cockfield, Brown organization.[16] Kidd seems to have had a predilection for putting his advertising and PR skills into the service of Liberal politics, and by 1949 was to become the secretary of the National Liberal Federation. Unlike some of his more recent professional colleagues in similar positions, his self-effacing manner prevented him from rising above a service capacity in the party; indeed, there is no evidence that he ever harboured ambitions to do any more than that. As a servant of the party, however, his role was not at all unimportant, even if less glamorous than that of the Keith Daveys of a later era.

In Claxton's first entry into politics, his successful capture in 1940 of the Montreal seat of St Lawrence–St George from the Conservatives to whom it had been entrusted since 1925, he personally retained the services of Cockfield, Brown. Following the election, a small debit balance in Claxton's account with the agency was written off, and his agent thanked Cockfield, Brown for a 'further contribution to his cause.' Kidd, who was a close personal friend of Claxton, undertook to advance the latter's political career with some PR work between elections. A year after Claxton's first appearance in Ottawa as an MP, Kidd was working on some press publicity for him. 'In my opinion,' he suggested to Claxton, 'it would do no harm to begin and to maintain a carefully directed publicity drive, the purpose of which would be, primarily, to acquaint the Canadian people with your career and to make people who don't know you as enthusiastic and devoted as those who have had the good fortune to work with you during the last campaign.' Claxton, professing himself to be 'just a little embarrassed,' nevertheless admitted that he 'like[d] this very much'.[17] Kidd then began a systematic effort to send out copies of Claxton speeches and personal information to editors around the country. As he explained: 'A tremendous effort is necessary to sustain...the increasing rate of public attention which an individual like yourself is gradually attracting. It is easier to start it than to sustain it, but I would say that in sustaining it alone, can you look for reasons for ultimate success and power, and once you are firmly established as a national figure (it may well happen this year or next) I believe you will agree that you have acquired political capital of considerable value.'[18]

Kidd was right: within two months Claxton was appointed parliamentary secretary to the prime minister, was given major responsibility for steering the revived National Liberal Federation along the desired lines, and within a year and a half was appointed minister of national health and welfare. His political capital proved to be of considerable value indeed. In this rise to prominence Claxton's own abilities can hardly be discounted. Yet he himself put considerable value on the publicity skills of Kidd and Cockfield, Brown. Sometimes, however, the frothy effusiveness of the PR practitioner made even its beneficiary wince. When Kidd described a Claxton speech on foreign policy as 'masterly...a document of historic significance,' Claxton was somewhat taken aback. 'I must say,' he replied with disarming candour, 'that when I delivered it I thought it a very poor speech and just another set of platitudes..."governor generalities.'"[19] At least it can be said for Claxton that he was too intelligent to believe his own publicity.

The other side of the agency-party relationship even at the local level is demonstrated by an inquiry from Kidd in late 1942 concerning an advertising account with the Montreal Tourist and Convention Bureau which Cockfield, Brown wanted. Claxton, who seems to have had some influence with the bureau, promised to push for making money available for such an account.[20] But compared to the advertising dollar of the city of Montreal, Ottawa was the big time; here, Claxton would no doubt be a friend in court. Such a friend was worth cultivating.

In the spring of 1944 Cockfield, Brown's research department conducted an opinion poll in St Lawrence–St George on Claxton's behalf—in itself a somewhat innovative practice at that time—and from March of that year to the beginning of the 1945 election campaign the agency did $2585 worth of paid work for Claxton in his constituency. In the 1945 campaign itself, Claxton spent $5109 on advertising (almost 40 per cent of his total budget) of which $2750 went to Cockfield, Brown. By this point, numerous other ad agencies were clamouring to get on the bandwagon as well: trying to find a place for them all in the campaign was something of a problem. That these services were by no means all over-the-table agency-client contracts can be seen by notations in Claxton's campaign records of 'donations, etc.' from the agencies or their personnel. And a massive, ninety-page, typewritten analysis of the campaign in detail, with recommendations for improved efficiency in the future emanated from the Cockfield, Brown offices after the election. Claxton wrote a warm letter of appreciation to the agency for their assistance that 'took so many forms that it is hard to single any out, but perhaps the most gratifying was the way in which your executive were always willing to help me personally.' None of his political attachments, Claxton averred, were more valuable than those with the Cockfield, Brown people, 'as friendly as they are able.' '*Everyone*,' he concluded, 'thinks my own publicity in St Lawrence–St George was the best any candidate had in any election.' Years later, in reply to the receipt of a Christmas present from Cockfield, Brown, Claxton gracefully stated that 'my connection with Cockfield, Brown and Co. has been one of the happiest results of my being in public service. Nothing has contributed more, both to such success as I have had, and to the enjoyment (such as it is) of this life.'[21]

Such a mutually beneficial arrangement could not be confined to a single Montreal constituency, or to a single Liberal member, however important. In 1943, the watershed year for the organizational revival of the Liberal party nationally, a formal arrangement was made between the National Liberal Federation and Cockfield, Brown. The latter would become the party's single national agency on a continuing basis. Other agencies might work on the provincial campaigns, responsible to provincial committees, but only Cockfield, Brown would have responsibility for the national advertising. What the precise terms of the agreement were is unfortunately not clear from the documentary evidence now available. Nor is this altogether surprising, considering the circumstances: as the author of an internal Cockfield, Brown memorandum two years later rather delicately put it, 'the agreement we entered into with the party was a confidential one. I hope that neither its terms or conditions are known to anyone outside our office.'[22]

The reasons for this reticence are obvious: the relationship was to be a patronage one, party work in return for government contracts. This has indeed been the classic arrangement with ad agencies in Canadian politics, one now so well known as to have been officially noticed in a public government report in 1969.[23] The use of political advertising as a 'loss leader' by agencies is thus no longer a very startling piece of news. What is still murky, however, is the exact nature of the bargain struck. At one pole one might imagine the entire range of advertising services offered at cost, with the agency's commissions from the media being rebated to the party. And, to be sure, at one point the president of the NLF, Gordon Fogo, did inform the secretary of the NLF that the arrangement with Cockfield, Brown was 'not intended to show them any ultimate profit.'[24] A few years later the same secretary, in dealing with another ad agency involved in a by-election, suggested that 'in all the advertising we have done the 15% commission has been paid by the newspapers to the advertising agency. In most cases the advertising agencies have rebated this to us.'[25] If such were in fact the practice in all cases, the donation to the party would be very considerable indeed. But this appears to be highly overstated.

One problem with the model of political advertising at cost in exchange for government advertising is the sheer diseconomy of such a bargain from the agencies' perspective. Not only is there uncertainty over the outcome of an election and thus of the ultimate pay-off, but the volume of government business necessary to recoup the loss involved in the political advertising would seem to be quite enormous. As one expert in the advertising field told the Task Force on Government Information in 1969:

> If an agency spends, in time, talent and out-of-pocket, $15,000 on a political campaign (and this is not a large amount, if one considers men assigned to travel with a candidate plus the back-up staff), then taking into account the 15 per cent commission agencies get from the media on billings, it will take $100,000 in government billings to replace this amount. And on the basis of current agency net profit, it may take a million dollars before the agency breaks even. That is one of the reasons that some very good agencies will not touch government business. They cannot afford to get embroiled.[26]

Granted that the net profit of the industry may have been different in earlier decades, the point remains: the *quid pro quo* cannot, in the nature of things, be a simple question. As the task force concluded, ad agencies 'do indeed get paid for much of the work they perform during elections. They get a 15 per cent commission from the media on billings; that is their normal commission on any kind of advertising assignment. What they do not normally get paid for are such extras as special television effects, art work, and men assigned to travel with candidates.' As O.J. Firestone suggests, agency earnings on political accounts may, in a narrow sense, be greater than on commercial accounts, since 'as a rule, advertising agencies do little media, product or consumer research, and a minimum of artwork, in political advertising.' However, the *net* position of the agencies may normally be worse on political accounts, because they are also required to provide other services 'such as public relations services for a minister or other help for individual politicians trying to get elected.' The final result is well summarized by Firestone: 'Agencies continue to mix commissionable advertising efforts with unpaid political work. Then they rely on getting government advertising to make up for any losses or non-earnings they have had during an election campaign.'[27] The specifics of any agency-party relationship will thus have to be discovered, not inferred.

It is difficult to establish the precise dollars and cents bargain struck between the Liberals and Cockfield, Brown. One problem is the rather loose terminology that often went back and forth in communication between agency and party. Echoing Fogo's statement quoted earlier, Kidd informed Fogo's successor, Duncan McTavish, that 'I believe Cockfield, Brown has taken the position that they do not wish to consider service to the National Liberal Federation from a profit standpoint. They are more than pleased to be able to make the resources of the organization available to the Party whenever they are required....' This self-sacrificing statement was, however, to back up an agency invoice including a $650 commission. If the party were to 'raise our eyebrows at this charge,' Kidd went on, the agency would withdraw it. In the event, the commission and similar charges were paid.[28] Indeed, it is clear from the documents that the Liberals did normally pay the commission on their regular media advertising.[29]

If commissions were normally charged, which is hardly surprising, the question remains as to what Cockfield, Brown's actual contribution to the Liberal cause constituted, apart from the services they could offer any commercial client. Claxton informed Mackenzie King after the 1945 election of the status of Cockfield, Brown's contribution: 'It is often thought that the commissions earned through handling political advertising would leave a firm doing political business with money in pocket. This was not the case with Cockfield, Brown. In direct expenditures and contributions of money, Cockfield, Brown and Company spent $9,000.00 more than they received from all sources, and, in addition, made contributions in the services of the experienced senior executives for which no charge was made.[30] A straight financial contribution to Liberal campaigns might be part of this bargain. This could take the form of a write-off of a portion of the agency's fees. In 1953 this write-off totalled $5000. Contributions might also be given on special occasions, such as the 1948 national convention, when $3650 was billed without commission.[31]

Above and beyond this type of clear-cut contribution there were other services provided free as well. For example, certain cabinet ministers were given special consideration. In the 1949 and 1953 elections, 'as a gesture of good will.' Cockfield, Brown provided free posters for Robert Winters' campaign in his own constituency. In a by-election organized under the general supervision of Walter Harris, a Cockfield, Brown man was loaned free, expenses included, for the direction of the advertising campaign. Paul Martin had a special relationship to Cockfield, Brown (as did Martin's ministry) which even superseded the normal devolution of advertising at the Ontario constituency level to the Walsh agency. C.D. Howe was also the beneficiary of some Cockfield, Brown largesse on occasion. Often such matters seem to have been played by ear: if the agency thought it could collect, it would: if unsure, it would write off an outstanding amount.[32] The situation was not always obvious, to either side....

After the initial arrangement was made, the Liberals, mindful of the spectre of the CCF hovering menacingly on their left, wished to begin a public relations campaign well in advance of an election which could by law come no later than 1945. Cockfield, Brown prepared a pre-election plan in December, 1943 which was submitted to Senator Wishart Robertson, president of the NLF, in January. In the same month, H.E. Kidd of the agency appeared before Jimmy Gardiner, Chubby Power, and Ian Mackenzie for the job of directing the campaign from the Ottawa end. His services were to be 'loaned' from the agency for the duration.[33] Kidd arrived in Ottawa to work with Claxton and Jack Pickersgill from the prime minister's office, and later with Gordon Fogo as party chairman, on plans for the coming campaign. An extensive survey of a sample of forty-three ridings was undertaken to test the party's standing as well as to try out some possible election slogans for consumer reaction.[34] But problems arose almost at once. The party decided against immediate commencement of the campaign. A second pre-election campaign plan, with an estimated budget of $150,000 for all media was approved by the cabinet's publicity committee in April, with special reference to the coming Saskatchewan provincial election, which was seen as the major test of the CCF. Although the programme was authorized by Jimmy Gardiner, and the first ads set in type, 'financial arrangements were not completed' and the campaign largely remained in the Cockfield, Brown files. In any event, the Liberals spent two and a half times as much on election advertising in Saskatchewan in 1944 as they had in the previous provincial election, but only about one-fifth of the total, a mere $5505, was channeled through Cockfield, Brown as the national agency.[35] The nub of the problem was the puzzling difficulty the Liberals were experiencing in raising money nationally. Traditionally, inter-election periods have been the most difficult time for Canadian parties to collect money, but as the election period in 1945 was to demonstrate, the Liberals were, for reasons which remain quite unclear, in some trouble concerning fund-raising in the late stages of the war-years.[36]

It is not possible to reconstruct a coherent picture of just how much money was being spent by the Liberals on advertising in the first year of their arrangement with Cockfield, Brown. The secretary of the NLF reported that $14,537 had been paid to the agency from March 1944 to January 1945, but invoices totalling some $23,000 were sent from the agency during the same period. How much was paid for, how much written off, and how much represents duplication of other charges is impossible to sort out. The point is clear, however, that whatever funds were forthcoming fell far short of the first hopeful estimates of the agency. For example, one item alone in the original December 1943 plan had included a series of twenty-six quarter-hour radio broadcasts for which production and time charges would have totalled $73,000. The Liberal party simply did not command the financial resources to pay for the publicity campaigns familiar in the world of private enterprise.[37]

Nor could the party count on the kind of continuous and steady financing that private corporations relied on. And Cockfield, Brown was evidently unprepared for dealing with such a client. The Liberals were in a difficult situation: they knew that a massive advertising campaign would be required to ensure the defeat of the CCF, but they were not at all sure how to pay for it. Early in 1945 Kidd and Fogo worked out a tentative campaign estimate that 'would come to a pretty substantial figure'—around $200,000. Since the total cost of the national advertising campaign to the NLF in 1940 had been only $68,222.30 (Quebec included), this would indeed indicate a major increase. But as *Marketing*, the advertising journal, correctly prophesized at the beginning of the election campaign: 'The power of advertising will be a strong factor in the forthcoming federal and Ontario provincial elections but there will not be nearly as much advertising as the various parties and candidates wish to employ.' After the election was called, a scaled-down budget was agreed upon for $143,000. Ultimately, all that and possibly a little more was in fact expended.[38] But the process was painful, to say the least.

Trouble began almost as soon as the campaign got underway. Cockfield, Brown demanded payments in advance of expenditures. The party could not find the dollars: Fogo, 'at the end of his tether,' told the prime minister that $35,000 was desperately needed for publicity expenditures. With Norman Lambert's quick intervention, the money was advanced by Senator Armand Daigle, one of the party's Montreal bagmen, but the agency was indignant.[39] Kidd, already beginning to see things somewhat more from the party's point of view, tried to mollify his employers by pointing out that the Liberals were now (after the advance) $8,000 ahead:

I would like to take this opportunity to point out that Mr. Fogo has at no time protested against payments in advance of expenditures—these payments are an indication of his integrity and intention to abide by our agreement. What he did hope to receive was a few days breathing space when his maximum outgo hit at a time when funds were just coming in.

It would be extremely unfortunate, and I think bad faith on our part, if we broadcast the impression that the Liberal party were hard up for funds. This is not so—and we have no reason for saying so.

In a memo a few days earlier Kidd pronounced his intention to comment on the behaviour of the agency 'at some future date when there is time to view these events in their proper perspective.'[40]

The money did come through; *Marketing* complimented Cockfield, Brown on the quality of its Liberal advertisements,[41] and 'Unity-Security-Freedom...Vote for a New Social Order' proved to be a more compelling selling point than the CCF programme of nationalization. The marriage between the Liberal party and Cockfield, Brown had proved itself, but not before some rough ground had been passed over.

One significant result of the 1945 campaign was the Liberals' realization of the invaluable service of H.E. Kidd as the institutionalized link between the party and the agency. Kidd had worked 'day and night for the Federation for eighteen months,' Brooke Claxton testified to his Cabinet colleagues. And to Mackenzie King, Claxton confided that Kidd's work had 'extended far beyond the preparation of advertising material...he was in Ottawa assisting in the whole work of organization....'[42] In effect the Liberals had gained the services of a full-time national organizer for the duration, as well as a direct link to their ad agency. Properly grateful, the party helped secure him a vacation in the West Indies, when the pace of his activities in the party's service led to health problems after the election.

Following the election Kidd returned to Cockfield, Brown's Montreal office. But his heart does not seem to have been in it. Complaining to his friend Claxton about the boring detail of normal commercial work, he sounded a plaintive note: 'Please remember me to Jack Pickersgill and other friends. Needless to say, I find it difficult to adjust myself to commercial activities. I miss keenly the broader horizon and the more interesting tasks which occupy the minds of the men at Ottawa (in my opinion!).'[43] It seems that this sense of 'broader horizons' drew Kidd strongly toward party work: perhaps there is a hint here of the psychological considerations that can on occasion attract men from the private sphere to the insecurities of politics. After directing the advertising for the 1949 election, Kidd tried to convey to the surviving principal of the agency, G. Warren Brown, the peculiar flavour of an election campaign:

> It has been very interesting to get a glimpse of a political party in battle. You hear strange voices on the telephone from all parts of the country.... Men and women never heard of before—all confident, demanding and determined. I hardly realized the large number of people who are engaged in a political campaign. In our case it is absolutely true to say that the strength of the Liberal Party's power lies not in the Cabinet so much as in the roots of the organization which extend deep into the electorates of every province.[44]

Kidd was to provide perhaps the most significant contribution the agency was to make to the Liberal party. After taking charge of the publicity side of the national Liberal convention to choose King's successor in 1948, Kidd was appointed secretary of the National Liberal Federation, a post he was to hold for over a decade. Regenstreif reported that upon assuming this new office, Kidd 'severed his formal connections with his old firm.'[45] This was not in fact the case. Kidd continued to be a member of Cockfield, Brown and was even, in 1956, promoted to the office of vice-president 'in charge of the Ottawa office of Cockfield, Brown.'[46] In fact, there was no real Ottawa office, other than the NLF offices, but Kidd did double duty as both party secretary and agency representative, using two separate letterheads for his correspondence. While working for the Liberals he continued to do agency business, such as handling the account of the Canadian Bankers' Association. This was not necessarily to the detriment of the party; the latter association carried on anti-socialist propaganda in elections which the Liberals felt to be to their benefit.[47] But the point is that the NLF for over a decade was under the permanent direction of a member of the party's ad agency. The most striking evidence of all of the intimacy of the agency-party relationship is that Cockfield, Brown paid Kidd's salary throughout the period of his work with the NLF.[48] Considering Kidd's position in the agency this must have constituted a very considerable contribution to the party, and must certainly figure as a major part of the *quid pro quo* of the patronage relationship. Even if the party had paid for his service, the fact yet remains that the permanent call on the services of someone of Kidd's talents, not to speak of contacts in the media throughout the country, would have just as surely been of invaluable assistance. Some of the implications of this cosy arrangement were not lost on the opposition in Ottawa. In 1951 the CCF leader, M.J. Coldwell, frustrated by rather devious attempts of the government to cover up the extent of Cockfield, Brown's government advertising business, cast some less than oblique references in Kidd's direction: 'It seems to me that Cockfield, Brown and Company are receiving very large advertising fees from this government, very large commissions therefore for the magazines and periodicals. And when we know who is the representative of Cockfield, Brown in this city—the national secretary, I believe, of the Liberal association—it seems to me that they are getting a very large amount of advertising, and that the commission is very considerable.'[49]

The relationship was not without its critics from within the party as well, although they did not normally dwell on questions of patronage. Many of the complaints came from the more old-fashioned politicians and organizers who had an instinctive mistrust of the slick new operators from the world of Madison Avenue. Norman Lambert was suspicious of the agencies, believing that the increasing tendency to turn over campaigns to their direction 'was one reason for the great increase in the amount of money spent by the parties because the advertising company finds ways of spending money.' Chubby Power felt that the ad men were one of the biggest problems in political campaigning, due to their lack of political principles, and that in any event they were not worth their cost.[50] After the liberal defeats of 1957-8 C.D. Howe suggested privately that 'in my opinion, Cockfield, Brown have not done much for us over the year, except advocate spending money uselessly.'[51] One Liberal MP, in answer to a request from the NLF for ideas on improving party organization, was more direct yet: 'I may be old fashioned,' he admitted, '[but] I would steer clear of the average professional advertising agency, the only thing they can convince *me* of—is a desire to be sick.'[52]

...Of course there were many tasks to which an advertising agency could be put, other than the planning and execution of a national advertising campaign during elections. One was the continual cultivation of the media for the enhancement of the Liberal image day to day. Kidd was tireless in the NLF offices in monitoring the press, planting stories, admonishing hostile reporters, and generally watching for opportunities to put the best Liberal face forward. In these endeavours the Montreal office of his agency was always willing to help. The Cockfield, Brown research department, a pride of the agency, was sometimes called upon to supplement the inputs into the party's fact files from the civil service, helping to provide favourable data for party speakers.[53] Opinion surveys in the constituencies were another item, although in this era it seems that primary reliance was placed on the Gallup polls. The agency handled the distribution and advertising of the CBC 'Nation's Business' broadcasts by cabinet ministers. And special occasions, such as the rather infrequent national conventions, national summer conferences, or special testimonial dinners for prime ministers, which required press liaison and public relations services, invariably found Cockfield, Brown men in charge of such arrangements.[54] In other words, in an era of growing media emphasis, ad men were beginning to displace the old style political organizers who had traditionally looked after these matters.

There were other purposes to which the agency could also be put which were rather less obvious—and less legitimate as well. There is definite evidence that in the 1945 campaign at least $15,948 was collected in campaign funds from four companies, Massey-Harris, Dominion Woollens and Worsteds, Firestone Tire and Rubber, and G.H. Wood and Company, in the form of cheques made out to Cockfield, Brown and not to the Liberal party.[55] The attraction of this arrangement from the contributors' point of view was that the donations could be written off for tax purposes as advertising expenditures. There was a certain hesitation on the part of the agency concerning the problem of receipting these donations, as well there might be, since the procedure was quite certainly illegal. But illegal or not, it did continue, and while no documentary proof of the practice could be found beyond the 1945 election, there is evidence that contributions to parties through advertising agencies have been a continuing feature of the political scene in Canada.[56]

As the years went by, the agency-party relationship became closer and closer. After the 1953 election a cabinet subcommittee on publicity began fairly regular meetings as an institutionalized link between the cabinet and the NLF. In 1956-7, with another election of the regional power brokers of the cabinet, a representative of the prime minister, the NLF, and Cockfield, Brown was a summation of all the important organizational forces in a national campaign. The intimacy of the party-agency relationship meant advance knowledge of election dates was entrusted to the agency—with concomitant problems of security when the agency was eager to get started. Only the Cockfield, Brown officials were allowed to see the advance plans for the 1953 election, as the NLF reminded the agency of the party's 'dependence on you to protect its position....'[58] In other words, the ad agency was privy to the kind of arcana normally reserved to the inner circle of the cabinet.

Federal-Provincial Organization of Advertising

The generally decentralized nature of Liberal campaign organization was paralleled by decentralization of campaign publicity. The 1945 campaign proved that an arrangement with a national agency need not preclude the use of other agencies at lower levels. As one party document noted: 'In the 1945 election publicity was decentralized. Each provincial committee and in many instances the constituency committees, had their own publicity people. The duties of publicity people in the provincial and constituency levels being to insure the greatest possible presentation in newspapers of the activities of their candidates.' The practice continued in later elections. There was certainly no shortage of agencies ready and willing to offer their services to a party which gave every indication of continuing its control over the Ottawa government advertising dollar into the indefinite future. As Kidd reported in 1953, one ad man met with Liberal officials, offering on behalf of his agency 'to accept any assignment we care to give him, in the hope that he may get some reward after the Liberal Government has been given a new mandate.'[59]

Walsh Advertising, the Ontario provincial Liberal party agency, regularly took charge of that province's publicity in campaigns. Walsh's president, W. George Akins, chaired a provincial standing committee on publicity, which also included individuals from other agencies with special tasks: for example, G.A. Phare of R.C. Smith and Son, a pioneer in radio advertising, took charge of Ontario radio spot ads in 1949.[60] One agency which was assiduous in cultivating the Liberal party was MacLaren's of Toronto, one of the largest and fastest growing agencies in the country. Already involved in 1949, MacLaren's was making cash contributions to the Liberal cause in the early 1950s. In 1953 MacLaren's offered various forms of help to the campaign.[61] MacLaren's was later to be the agency that picked up the pieces after the Liberal disaster of 1958.

Putting all these agencies into harness simultaneously was not always an easy task. In 1945 the NLF treasurer recommended that Vickers and Benson of Montreal be given a 'substantial' amount of Liberal advertising. The secretary of the NLF wondered if his impression was correct that the arrangement with Cockfield, Brown included the understanding that 'they were going to divide some advertising among certain Liberal companies.' Gordon Fogo was clear in his mind: 'As I understand our arrangement...it will not readily lend itself to distribution of the advertising amongst several concerns.'[62]

Fogo was speaking of the national campaign, of course, but what he seemed to have forgotten was that in Liberal campaigns there were always two 'national' organizations—one in English Canada and another in Quebec. The publicity organization was parallel in this regard as well. Although it was the Montreal office of Cockfield, Brown which was involved in national party work, Quebec always remained a special case, out of reach of the agency's control. Vickers and Benson did gain a portion of the business in that province, which was not altogether surprising in light of the fact that a Liberal MP from Montreal was an executive of the firm.[63]

A persistent problem was that of French-language ads. Outside Quebec, these sometimes rested with the NLF and Cockfield, Brown.[64] But the 'special situation' of Quebec was recognized in the original agreement between the party and Cockfield, Brown. The agency agreed to work with the Quebec organization and to 'bring in as our associates for the French advertising the Canadian Advertising Agency.'[65] By 1949 Vickers and Benson was involved in some of the French advertising as well. In the same year Claxton concluded an understanding with the Quebec party organization that English and French ads would be handled separately, without regard to province.[66] In this election, a committee of six Quebec ministers and senators with organizational responsibility made final decisions on copy and distribution. Nor was this seen as mechanical translation of English into French: instead 'des changements radicaux' were necessary. 'Il s'agit,' as one committee member put it, 'non pas de traduire, mais d'adapter les idées de base des brochures à notre milieu particulier le Canada-français.' And the NLF's French secretary agreed wholeheartedly. A key figure in linking this Quebec committee and its publicity to the national campaign in 1949 and 1953 was Brooke Claxton; the maintenance of continuity and co-operation was 'very largely on a personal basis.'[67]...

Quebec advertising may have been a special case, but even the distribution of responsibility to other agencies at the provincial level was not without its inter-agency rivalries and complexities. In effect, the strains which often accompanied federal-provincial relations within the party organization were reflected in strains between federal and provincial ad agencies. This point should not be overemphasized: in general the decentralized publicity organization worked as well for the Liberals in these years as did their decentralized campaign organization. Efficiency and co-operation stand out far more than division and conflict. But this success was not without at least some attendant strains. Ontario was one example, and its problems were directly related to the failures and disasters of the provincial Liberals. Ottawa Liberals won elections with tireless regularity; Toronto Liberals lost with equal reliability. Ad agencies associated with the Toronto Liberals found correspondingly greater difficulties in successfully practising their trade. Hence, at federal election time the serene functioning of the Cockfield, Brown–NLF machine would sometimes sputter and cough at the provincial intakes. One Ontario agency prominent in the mid-1940s–R.C. Smith Advertising–was eased out of the picture altogether by the end of the decade.[68]

Walsh Advertising was the pre-eminent provincial agency in Ontario in the 1940s and 1950s, and was always attempting to move in on the national account as well, with little response from national party figures who tended to be deeply suspicious about both the competence and the expansiveness of Walsh's services.... Walsh was always ready to formulate self-assertive and sometimes eccentrically grandiose plans. The standing committee on publicity of the Ontario Liberal Association, chaired by Walsh's president and staffed with other Walsh men, issued a report in late 1952 suggesting a vast scheme of provincial, regional, and constituency meetings of publicity officers under the 'expert guidance' of 'advertising specialists,' and the creation of a regular party press as a 'ready medium of official party communication.'[69] Since the NLF had been providing such a press to a generally unappreciative and uninterested party audience for years, since an Ontario Liberal paper had gone under for lack of sales, and since there was no possibility of raising the funds necessary for the Walsh vision, Kidd in Ottawa might have been grinding his teeth in frustration. The air of unreality in Toronto was heightened when set against four successive election routs, in two of which the Liberals had been reduced to a third party in the legislature. Such foolishness scarcely enhanced the confidence of the federal party in either its Ontario party or its Ontario ad agency.[70] ...

Another province where the publicity situation presented a face of some complexity was 'that great and uncertain political country' of British Columbia.[71] Of course the political situation in British Columbia was confused enough from the federal perspective during the days of the coalition government. But following the Social Credit victory in 1952, political advertising was even more confused, owing to Premier W.A.C. Bennett's blithe disregard of national partisan allegiances in dispensing advertising contracts. Whether Bennett actually believed in non-partisan allocation of the government ad dollar, or whether, as may be more likely, he preferred to make his own alliances without reference to what was done east of the Rockies, the result was the same: a situation unique to that province. For example, James Lovick and Company was the agency for the Alberta Liberal party and also ran government tourist campaigns in British Columbia, campaigns so partisan as to rouse BC Liberal leader Arthur Laing to denounce 'purely political propaganda to advertise Premier Bennett.'[72] British Columbia was, as so many easterners before and since have discovered, a world of its own. This could cut both ways. In 1957-8 Cockfield, Brown was able to pick up the lucrative contract from the BC Travel Bureau to advertise centennial celebrations; it was quite unthinkable that such a contract would have come their way from, say, Tory Ontario.

In 1945 the Stewart, Bowman, and Macpherson agency ran the provincial side of the federal campaign, with promises to Cockfield, Brown of 'all kinds of co-operation.' 'I need hardly tell you,' Kidd reminded his agency's Vancouver office with barely repressed bitterness, 'that this proved an illusion in as much as he [Stewart] persuaded the newspapers to give him the space he required, and squeezed out national advertising on the party's important subjects such as family allowances, full employment, etc.'[73] Relations with the BC Liberals had reached such a low level by 1949 that the secretary of the NLF could not even get a reply from the secretary of the BC Liberal Association even after a stream of letters to Vancouver. Understandably, in such circumstances the federal party decided to try to put its own people in charge of federal publicity. A tour by St Laurent in April of 1949 was publicized by the Vancouver office of Cockfield, Brown, which reported to Kidd that they had 'arranged publicity, news reels, window displays, radio broadcasts, eclipse of the moon, and earthquake.' Modestly, they added: 'Hope our efforts will reflect the glory of Cockfield, Brown and H.E. Kidd.' After the provincial electoral disaster of 1952, in which the coalition's account was handled ineptly by Stewart, Bowman, Macpherson, the time had come for a clean break with the past. Cockfield, Brown was asked to handle publicity in British Columbia for the federal election the next year. Yet such was the peculiar nature of the province that not even this could put Ottawa's fears to rest. Kidd put his foot down firmly on the idea that the agency's Vancouver office should handle not only the provincial campaign but the placing of national ads as well, and admonished Montreal not to give Vancouver authority to do anything 'on our account.' 'Not that I don't trust them,' he hastened to add, 'but the people of BC are known to be enthusiastic. Sometimes their enthusiasm takes them the wrong way, but we have hopes that the faithful will respond...to the clarion call of the Great White Father.' The Great White Father's call seems to have had disappointing results. Or at least one might infer this from the fact that the next election in 1957 saw BC publicity handled by McCann, Erickson, a Canadian subsidiary of one of the largest American agencies.[74] Somehow neither the Liberals nor Cockfield, Brown ever quite solved the problem of acclimatization to the west coast.

Advertising Expenditures

Throughout the period 1944 to 1958 it is not possible to reconstruct the total amount of money spent by the Liberals through ad agencies at all levels. It *is* possible to estimate how much was spent on national advertising through Cockfield, Brown in general elections. Table 1 gives the overall picture. Although these figures are only estimates, they are probably reasonably accurate. One of the striking features is the steady decline in total expenditures from 1949 to 1958. There seems to be a combination of factors at work. Neither in 1953 nor (mistakenly) in 1957 was there much fear of losing, and expenditures were held down. Then in 1958 the situation was so hopeless that money was scarce anyway. Another observation must be one of surprise at the generally low level of national expenditure, compared to amounts at least doubled in the late 1960s and early 1970s.[75] The big

Table 1: Estimated Amounts spent on national advertising for the Liberal party through Cockfield, Brown in general elections 1945-58.

1945	$161,361
1949	188,890
1953	178,867
1957	164,119
1958	146,620

Sources: invoices, statements, etc., NLF, v. 602, 809, 815, 836 and 843.

difference, aside from inflation, is that television had not yet come into its own in this era. Moreover, then as now, considerable amounts were spent at the provincial level. For example, in 1953 it was estimated by one source that $82,000 was spent separately in Ontario; about 46 per cent of the national total.[76] Finally, as already explained, French-language advertising was also excluded from the national totals.

Naturally enough, Cockfield, Brown wished to encourage greater spending. Their first hopeful estimate in 1957 was for a budget of $548,666. By the end of that disheartening campaign they had to settle for little more than one-quarter of that figure. In 1953, after a final, reduced estimate had been accepted, Claxton called a meeting of the NLF and Cockfield, Brown representatives in his office three weeks before the polls and announced a 'radical scaling down' of advertising spending. As one participant in the meeting later recalled, 'Mr. Claxton announced that the election was in the bag and the purpose of the meeting was to save every possible expenditure.' The change was fundamental: in 1949 advertising had been a 'major vehicle' for the party campaign. Now it was felt that the Liberal image could live off its own fat; 'getting out the vote' would be the major thrust. The howls from Cockfield, Brown and from some provincial quarters were loud, but Claxton was, as usual, right.[77] All of which seems to indicate that the Liberal party was selling itself as much as it was being sold by its ad men.

How the money was spent can be seen in Table 2 based on the 1953 campaign. Most of the Liberal radio time was under the direction of the provincial committees, although Cockfield, Brown did provide a man to co-ordinate the distribution of transcribed radio speeches throughout the country.[78] Production costs, especially for 'spot' bulletins on private stations, normally rested with the prov-

Table 2: Breakdown of space and time charges for Liberal advertising, by media and by province, general election 1953.

	$	%		$	%
Print media:					
Dailies	19,562	20.0	Ontario	43,100	44.1
Weeklies	30,960	31.7	Quebec	16,850	17.2
Weekend	19,168	19.6	BC	9,188	9.4
Farm	7,861	8.0	Manitoba	8,511	8.7
Financial	831	0.9	Saskatchewan	7,932	8.1
Labour	1,628	1.7	Alberta	6,128	6.3
Foreign-language	3,948	4.0	Nova Scotia	2,425	2.5
Veterans	315	0.3	New Brunswick	1,888	1.9
			Newfoundland	1,213	1.2
Radio	13,518	13.8	PEI	431	0.4
			Yukon and NWT	126	0.1
Total	97,791	100.0		97,792	100.0

Source: NLF, v. 815, Cockfield, Brown account, 28 Oct. 1953, media breakdown, Nov. 1953.

inces and their agencies. Similarly, the special status of Quebec in advertising, as outlined above, accounts for the relatively low figure for that province in the table.

One factor inflating these rather modest figures was the practice of charging 'political rates' by the media. Even hiring such a prestigious agency as Cockfield, Brown to purchase space did not prevent newspapers, especially weeklies, from taking the opportunity to gouge the political parties for a little extra. This practice—now illegal under the Elections Expenses Act of 1974[79]—was a major problem in the 1940s and 1950s. The worst of it was that neither the party nor its agency could budget accurately for this factor, since the papers in question often quoted a commercial rate and then invoiced the agency at a higher, 'political' rate. Despite a general feeling that the practice was 'scandalous' and 'virtually dishonest,' there was little the party could do in the face of a threatened publicity shut-out in rural areas served by weekly papers.[80] And the drain on the publicity budget could be considerable. In 1949, 218 out of 656 weeklies upped their rates *after* accepting lineage, representing a 41 per cent increase in charges over the original quotations. Some Saskatchewan papers went from two to ten cents a line. An advertisement in 1953 was placed in eighty papers—twenty-nine of which had 'known' political rates, others of whom might charge such rates without quoting them. Even some major dailies, such as *Le Devoir*, charged political rates.[81] And this despite the fact that many papers, particularly small weeklies, were dependent to a considerable degree on the placing of federal government advertisements for much of their operating revenue. This ingratitude was irritating to the Ottawa Liberals, to put it mildly.

Cockfield, Brown's activities for the party were not confined to election campaigns. A regular year-to-year advertising and publicity arrangement was also in force, which might vary in extent according to the political circumstances and the party's financial position. In 1954, $5879 in publicity expenditure was billed through Cockfield, Brown by the NLF; this dropped to a mere $644 the following year, but rose to $7281 in the pre-election year of 1956.[82] These figures, it might be noted, represent actual amounts paid out by the NLF to the agency; in the nature of the *ad hoc* party-agency relationship, this may be an underestimate of the actual volume of business.

The Television Medium and Liberal Advertising

The role of the advertising agency in national Liberal campaigns in this era may seem, when all is said, to have been modest and conservative by present-day standards. Certainly there is little or no evidence of the ad men controlling or directing the party's policies. The 'boys in the back room' were obviously *advisers* in certain technical aspects of media use: ultimate power lay squarely in the cabinet and the office of the prime minister. Not a single instance can be found in the available records of the ad men persuading the party to adopt a particular issue, or not adopt another. Kidd tried to serve both his masters, the party and the agency, with equal fidelity—and with equal sense of his own subordinate position. If anything, when relations became strained, Kidd tended to take the party's interests as primary, and to plead its case with the agency. So far as the nature of the product being sold, the relations between the Liberal party and Cockfield, Brown were along the classic lines of the agency-client type. Cockfield, Brown packaged and sold what the party produced. The ad men may have worn grey flannel suits, but *éminences grises* they were not. Others have suggested that in the 1960s and 1970s the ad men have taken on a more direct policy-making role in the party councils.[83] But it was not so in this earlier era.

Cockfield, Brown's political advertising was not as aggressive or as ostentatious as the kind of political puffery already evident in the United States in this era. Indeed, in striking contrast to the tinsel and plastic garishness of American presidential campaigns, the national campaigns orchestrated for the Liberals seemed restrained, dignified, deferential—perhaps even a trifle *bureaucratic*. The quiet, competent style had the same solid stamp as that of an official government poster; authority without overstatement. Indeed, those schooled in the Cockfield, Brown style could be quite put off by signs of 'Americanization' of Canadian politics. One agency man accompanying the prime minister on a 1953 election tour of Windsor reported with evident distaste to Duncan MacTavish that Paul Martin's local organization had been influenced by the techniques of American ad men from across the river—a master of ceremonies telling the rally crowd how to respond, the use of cue cards, etc. 'The worst aspect of the Windsor show resulted from a resort to American electioneering methods which shook me almost through the cement floor of the arena.... It must be remembered that Windsor is at all times influenced by methods employed across the line and, while the above tactics shocked us, they probably went quite unnoticed by the Windsorites.' But reporters from the Parliamentary Press Gallery, he added, 'were not impressed.'[84]

The decisive watershed separating this older era of publicity from that of today was, of course, television. Television was just making a first appearance in Canada in 1953 and was of no significance in the national election of that year. But 1957 and 1958 witnessed the first extensive use of television in a general election. That this coincided with the end of the twenty-two year Liberal era may be merely accidental, but it is much more likely that there is some connection between the two events. The entire publicity programme built up by the Liberals and their ad agency, and the resulting image of the party in the minds of voters, was in many respects a pre-television, print-media phenomenon. The restrictive rules established by the CBC against 'dramatization' meant that *any* use of television in this era would be limited and primitive, but even at this level the Liberals were quite lost in the new medium. While some solid empirical evidence would be needed to show that Diefenbaker rose to power on the strength of his television image—evidence that is simply not available—it *is* certain that television was an unmitigated disaster for the Liberals, a disaster so frightful that the party leadership itself was appalled and shaken. It is worth looking at this story, for in retrospect one can almost mark the end of an entire era in Canadian political campaigns.

Some preliminary investigation of the use of television in the United States was undertaken by Cockfield, Brown in 1953 with the NLF footing the bill, but little or no use was made of the medium in that election, except for some CBC free time, with the latter providing technical assistance. Considerable preparatory work was undertaken prior to the 1957 election, with Kidd suggesting to Cockfield, Brown that an 'all out effort on television for the party' should be mounted. Television, he predicted with considerable accuracy, will be 'the biggest headache of all,' and suggested the need for a lot of expert help. A man from CBC Montreal was installed in a special studio in Ottawa to prepare Liberals for the new medium. Later a Quebec broadcaster by the name of Réne Lévesque was added for French-language work. Closed circuit lectures and demonstrations were provided, but despite having 'at our disposal the best of equipment, knowledge, and enthusiasm to have done a first class job...it was never given a full rein of appreciation.' This latter statement was merely diplomatic. In fact, 'the principals in the contest'—the cabinet ministers—took no notice of the services being provided them. Only one minister, Ralph Campney, bothered attending a single session. The trouble was, as Kidd confided to his agency, that 'the attitude of most politicians...is one of caution and fear.' Some had appeared in free time shows in 1956 with consequences 'disastrous for the personalities involved....' St Laurent refused to appear on such programmes: 'He recognizes that ultimately he will make his appearance on television, but he prefers to see what his colleagues will do on the television screen.' The example was not encouraging, and by late 1956 signs of panic were beginning to appear in the party.[85]

Early in the 1957 campaign the extent of the disaster became apparent when the long-awaited appearance of the prime minister on the television screen called forth an anguished plea from the arch-Liberal *Winnipeg Free Press*. Under the headline, 'LIBERALS, BE HUMAN' the *Free Press* noted sorrowfully that St Laurent, reading from a manuscript on his desk, 'refused to make any concessions to the television camera.' Liberals, the editor concluded, were 'just not at home in [this] merciless medium': 'If you cannot loosen up and act like ordinary people,' he advised earnestly, 'it would be decidedly to the advantage of the Liberal party to give up the television time that has been allotted to you.'[86] This Hobson's choice was indeed all that was left to the party by this stage. From $30,000 to $35,000 had been spent on production. Close to $15,000 more had been invested in buying time for 'spots' and ten-minute programmes in Ontario. But the party had 'convincing evidence that our TV programmes were doing us more harm than good...' All further television was cancelled in mid-May, despite the fact that cancellations would in many cases be billed anyway by the stations. This painful, and costly, decision was necessary, Kidd told Mac-Tavish, not because of the technical backing, which was 'marvellous,' but 'because our masters have not seen fit to make use of the facilities which we established for them here....'[87]

To make matters worse yet, the Liberals were also the victims of what appears to be either a misunderstanding or worse with regard to television production. A Toronto film and television producer, S.W. 'Spence' Caldwell, offered his services for the 1957 Liberal television effort. The NLF understood that he would charge only costs and out-of-pocket expenses, for as Caldwell told Kidd 'several times,' he did 'very substantial business in Ottawa and there were other reasons why he was anxious to do everything he could to facilitate the Liberal case on TV.' Or, more succinctly, he was quoted as saying: 'we want to earn as many gold stars as we can.' Kidd became suspicious of Caldwell, however, sensing 'that he had set a trap for us,' a sort of 'Trojan Horse operation.' When the election results were known, MacTavish recalled, Caldwell 'changed [his] tune' and began charging large amounts. Some money, $10,000 at least, was paid, but Caldwell billed the party for an additional $43,852.72 in 1958, and continued to try to collect this amount, along with threats of legal action, into the 1960s. The Liberals successfully stood fast against this claim, but well might Kidd conclude, from all points of view, that the party needed some basic discussions on television and its use, for 'future ways of handling this difficult and cruel medium.'[88] C.D. Howe summed up the situation most admirably with reference to his own defeat in Port Arthur by Douglas Fisher of the CCF: 'My opponent,' he informed another defeated Liberal MP, 'was a polished television artist, and his gains all took place in the area covered by television. I may tell you that television is no good for us 'old boys.'[89]

Electoral Defeat and the Agency-Party Relationship

The 1957 electoral disaster marked the end of an era in more ways that one, for it also signalled the beginning of the breakup of the relationship between the Liberals and Cockfield, Brown. Despite the fulsome praise traditionally lavished by both partners to the agreement on each other, there was one key consideration which kept the marriage happy: the electoral success of the breadwinner, the Liberal party. When the party was no longer in a position to follow through on its contribution—the government advertising post—the romance turned sour. Cracks began to appear immediately after the election with a somewhat cool exchange of letters between Kidd in Ottawa and Cockfield, Brown in Montreal on the agency's billing. An executive committee made an accounting of its overall contribution. 'It was the feeling of the meeting that the amount of our work and efforts should be made known in the right places, and that in this connection Duncan MacTavish was particularly mentioned.' But 'recognition' was not enough. Some $17,000 was assigned to such items as travel, staff time (195 man days), and research, and the agency wished to explore the possibility of collecting as much as possible of this amount from the party. Kidd, clearly angry, stated that research was a service that the agency would normally render a client, that there was no prior agreement on such a billing, that the party was being charged for the time it took the agency to answer inquiries, that in sum 'this is a new development in the relation between Cockfield, Brown and the Federation.' So far as staff time went, Kidd asserted that 'this is an attempt to assess the value of the company's services to the Party and probably should not be placed opposite the total revenue secured [for] the company, not only in the various election campaign expenditures, but on other matters as well.'[90]

It was the last part of Kidd's argument which was the weakest, in light of the fact that the Liberals no longer held the government's purse strings. Hence the agency was changing its perspective on the whole matter. The first victim of this change was Kidd himself. He was given a choice of staying with the party or returning to the agency. Kidd's heart by now seemed to be much more with the party than the agency and he formally resigned his position with the latter about the end of 1957 and accepted a full-time appointment as secretary of the NLF, a post he had in fact held for the past nine years. His old friend Brooke Claxton was troubled by this development, justly warning him that his future in the NLF might not be secure inasmuch as Duncan MacTavish would not be around forever as president. It was 'quite possible and even probable, that the incoming President and Executive may have quite different ideas about the Federation's work and the manner of carrying it out....' After the 1958 Conservative landslide, the Liberal party began to look to revamping its party organization, and the 'old guard'—of which Kidd was seen, rightly or wrongly, as a representative—was under fire. By the close of 1959 it had been decided to replace Kidd as secretary. In vain Claxton appealed to A.B. Matthews, Bay Street bagman and now NLF president, to remember Kidd's contributions to Liberal election publicity since 1945: 'With all the emphasis I can use I say Bob had more to do with this than any other single person, that it was superbly well done and that no one could have worked more effectively over longer hours or with greater success. Beyond question he has sacrificed his business career and his health in the interest of the Liberal cause.' Jack Pickersgill still recalls with some bitterness the 'rather brutal' firing of Kidd.[91] Sentiment, however, has little place in either politics or business, when losing numbers start appearing on the board.

Early in 1958 a changeover also occurred in the top ranks of Cockfield, Brown, but the agency decided to stick with the Liberals in the election of that year. Yet the writing was on the wall. And other agencies were more than willing to move in and pick up the pieces, foremost among them MacLaren's of Toronto which 'contributed' the services of Richard O'Hagan full time to the NLF during the 1958 campaign, services described by Senator J.J. Connolly, the campaign co-ordinator in Ottawa, as 'invaluable.' Walsh also tried to move in on the national scene, as did the Ronalds agency. But MacLaren's was by 1958 the largest agency in Canada, topping Cockfield, Brown for the first time in total billings. A cynic might suggest that only the best would do for the Liberal party, and in early 1959 the Ontario party dropped Walsh and appointed MacLaren's, presaging a changeover on the national level in the same direction. As if in confirmation of MacLaren's growing partisan role, the Diefenbaker government dropped its last official government account with the agency, the Fisheries Department, and hired a Tory firm.[92]

Thus Maclaren's took over where Cockfield, Brown left off, and the agency that in the days of the pipeline debate had represented the Liberal party, the government of Canada, and Trans-Canada Pipe Lines, all at the same time, relapsed into a position of political neutrality, to which they have steadfastly adhered ever since....

Government Advertising Patronage

Having examined the agency-party relationship from the electoral viewpoint, it remains to examine the reverse side of the coin: the partisan nature of government advertising distribution among the agencies.

After helping elect the Conservatives in New Brunswick in 1952 while on leave from his ad agency, Locke, Johnson & Company, Dalton Camp recalls that he had never considered gaining government advertising accounts. The readers of Mr Camp's memoirs may permit themselves a slight incredulity on this point, while taking more seriously his memory of what transpired in a meeting between himself and the new premier, Hugh John Flemming. The latter showed Camp a letter from the president of Walsh Advertising, suggesting a renewal of Walsh's account with the New Brunswick Tourist Bureau:

> 'Seems like a nice fellow,' Flemming said, placing yet another call.
> 'Two months ago they were down here telling people you weren't good enough to be Premier of New Brunswick,' I said, somewhat more heatedly than intended.
> Flemming looked puzzled. 'What's that?' he asked.
> 'They're the Liberal agency,' I said, my irritability barely contained.
> 'Well,' he said softly, reflectively, almost to himself, 'We can't have that, can we?'
> And so it came to pass that Locke, Johnson & Company Ltd. became the agency for the New Brunswick Travel Bureau....[93]

Camp adds that the return of this trophy to his agency gained him a promotion and, more importantly, experience in the travel industry. The mixture of politics and travel advertising has turned out well for Mr Camp. Today the firm of Camp Associates rests its business almost entirely upon two pillars: the accounts of the Ontario and New Brunswick governments, especially their tourism budgets.[94]

Camp Associates are by no means the only agency to have relied heavily on political connections for their clientele. One of the few wholly French-language agencies in Quebec history was Huot Advertising, which at its peak grossed $2 million in billings. Huot was,

Table 3: Federal government advertising contracts by agency, 1940-56 (Crown corporations excluded), in dollars

	1940-6	1945-7	1949-50	1952	1953	1954	1955	1956
Cockfield,Brown	1,121,212	861,020	933,469	852,912	880,890	927,468	913,677	1,008,775
MacLaren's	444,421	301,906	803,329	1,043,291	773,825	1,109,460	949,105	1,115,781
Walsh	689,197	688,388	510,327	1,015,678	884,230	1,090,054	731,910	789,196
Ronalds	12,654	96,418	380,058	804,827	794,324	775,595	687,907	845,949
Canadian	478,770	195,133	121,253	97,157	63,572	104,459	83,072	86,427
R.C. Smith	1,613,402	955,450	110,128	10	6,237	11,720	7,798	
'Advertising Agencies of Canada'[a]	17,748,464	5,350,578						
'Associated Advertising Agencies'[b]	568,592	837,510						
Others	1,295,589	635,932	96,308	64,735	83,557	55,165	56,327	55,731
Total	23,972,301	9,922,335	2,945,872	3,878,610	3,486,635	4,073,921	3,429,796	3,941,859

[a] A special non-partisan grouping of ad agencies during the war, chaired by Cockfield, Brown, but including Conservative agencies as well. *Marketing*, 8 Sept. 1945
[b] A consortium of Liberal agencies

however, fatally dependent on the patronage of the Union Nationale Party, and when the Quebec Liberals won in 1960 the agency 'began a downfall from which it never recovered.' In 1963 it was merged into a new agency.[95]

The federal Liberals have always been shrewd enough to avoid too heavy involvement with agencies whose overall dependency on the party might prove unhealthy. Certainly neither Cockfield, Brown in the 1940s and 1950s nor MacLaren's in the 1960s and 1970s could be considered *dependent* on the party's fortunes, given the wide range of lucrative commercial accounts both agencies boasted. Nevertheless, the electoral success of the party could bring a very welcome and profitable dollop of government business on top of their commercial accounts: the icing, as it were, on the largest advertising cake in the country.

Given the patronage nature of the party-agency relationship, and given the number of agencies which offered their services at election time, it was inevitable that conflict and jealousies should arise over the distribution of the government advertising dollar. Norman Lambert's role as the patronage 'fixer' behind the scenes from 1935 to 1940 was nowhere more evident than in the settling of the various claims from the advertising agencies which had helped the party in the 1935 election. One of the chief problems was that C.D. Howe did not particularly like Cockfield, Brown and preferred to give his business to MacLaren's. Lambert continued to argue Cockfield, Brown's case until Howe finally agreed that he would leave the advertising contracts to Lambert, with his own advice to be taken into consideration. Other ministers were not always so co-operative, and were apt to give contracts to their own favourites despite the impact on the overall distribution, and ministerial prerogatives were such that Lambert sometimes had to throw up his hands in resignation. One such incident occurred in 1939 when P.-J.-A. Cardin, minister of public works, switched his ministry's advertising from MacLaren's to a Quebec agency; Lambert simply told MacLaren's that he could give them introductions, but could not look after their business for them. It appears that in this era at least, part of the bargain struck between the agency and the party included a straight kick-back on the contracts awarded. For example, when the Agriculture Department was considering Cockfield, Brown, Lambert told the agency that a 5 per cent return to the party was expected; the agency representative seemed to be in agreement with this arrangement. When the Department of Trade and Commerce gave their advertising to

Table 4: Federal government advertising contracts by agency, 1940-56 (Crown corporations excluded), in percentages

	1940-6	1945-7	1949-50	1952	1953	1954	1955	1956
Cockfield,Brown	4.7	8.7	31.6	22.0	25.3	22.8	26.6	25.6
MacLaren's	1.9	3.0	27.2	26.9	22.2	27.2	27.7	29.3
Walsh	2.9	6.9	17.3	26.2	25.4	26.8	21.3	20.0
Ronalds	0.1	0.1	12.9	20.8	22.8	19.0	20.1	21.5
Canadian	2.0	2.0	4.1	2.5	1.8	2.6	2.4	2.2
R.C. Smith	6.7	9.6	3.7		0.2	0.3	0.2	
'Advertising Agencies of Canada'[a]	74.0	53.9						
'Associated Advertising Agencies'[b]	2.4	8.4						
Others	5.3	6.4	3.2	1.7	2.4	1.3	1.6	1.4
Total	100.0	100.0	100.0	100.0	100.0	100.0	100.0	100.0

Note: percentages may not total exactly due to rounding

MacLaren's in 1938, Lambert spoke to an agency representative who confirmed that $2000 would go each year to the NLF in gratitude. Other variations on the *quid pro quo* can also be found in the Lambert diaries. For example, in 1941 Harry Cockfield informed Lambert that Howe was supporting his agency for the tourist publicity budget; in return for this support, Cockfield, Brown was putting on a 'big publicity campaign' in Howe's Department of Munitions and Supply 'at cost.'[96] There were many possible forms which the patronage relationship might take: generalizations appear difficult. One theme common to the twenty-two years of Liberal rule after 1935, however, was that Cockfield, Brown got too much business in relation to the party's other agencies. This cry, originating from the competition and sometimes picked up by certain cabinet ministers, was no doubt an inevitable result of Cockfield, Brown's pride of place as the national agency for the party.

Following the 1945 election Kidd's first assignment upon his return to Cockfield, Brown was to 'provide immediately a breakdown of advertising expenditures made by the Government since 1940 through the various advertising agencies.' Claxton invited Kidd to come to Ottawa and offered the assistance of an official to go through the departmental records.[97] The problem was the age-old political problem of successful parties—the just distribution of patronage. All the agencies which had done their bit during the election had to be rewarded, but Cockfield, Brown kept a watchful and proprietorial eye over the proceedings to ensure that its senior position in the agency hierarchy was respected. When Kidd moved over to the NLF as secretary he sometimes had to placate rival agencies with data showing their share of the pie.[98] Indeed, there even seem to have been conscious efforts to downplay the amount of billings received by Cockfield, Brown, for the benefit of the opposition, and even perhaps for that of the other agencies. This becomes more obvious in the light of Tables 3 and 4, which summarize what little information was made public about government advertising accounts in this period.[99]

A number of aspects of these figures require explanations. First of all, there is no breakdown available by specific agency for the 'Advertising Agencies in Canada,' the non-partisan group set up to promote the war effort, even though three-quarters of the total advertising spending during the war went through this group. Harry Cockfield of Cockfield, Brown was the chairman of the consortium and it is not unreasonable to suppose that this agency received a good proportion of the total business; on the other hand, known Tory agencies were also cut in on this deal as well.[100] 'Associated Advertising Agencies,' which appeared briefly around the war's end, was a consortium of Liberal agencies only, but the specific break-down of account allocation among agencies is unknown. By the 1950s the picture becomes clearer, with Cockfield, Brown; MacLaren's; Walsh; and Ronalds each taking between one-fifth and one-quarter of the total business on the average. Canadian retained a smaller share. R.C. Smith, once closely connected to the party,[101] seems to have fallen into disfavour and to have dropped altogether from the picture by the last couple of years of the St Laurent gov-ernment. The 'other' category includes a shifting miscellany of agen-cies with very small bits of business with different departments, in-cluding small amounts going to foreign agencies for promotions abroad. Here and there, Conservative agencies (McKim; McConnell, Eastman; J.J. Gibbons, etc.) do appear with small contracts but never as major advertisers.

Long-term agency-client relationships were built up with particu-lar government departments: MacLaren's was largely centred on fi-nance, defence and the RCMP. Walsh specialized in defence, labour, post office, trade and commerce, and veterans' affairs; Ronalds in defence and finance. Cockfield, Brown's departmental specialization was even more concentrated, being centred almost exclusively on the single biggest advertising account in Ottawa, the Canadian Gov-ernment Travel Bureau. Table 5 shows the total billings by the Travel Bureau through Cockfield, Brown from 1942-3 to 1957-8. In the twelve-year period from the end of the war to the defeat of the Liberals in 1957-8, Cockfield, Brown did $9,607,791 worth of busi-ness with the bureau.

Yet even with this steady source of earnings, Cockfield, Brown does not *seem* to have been 'top dog' among the agencies, with either Walsh or MacLaren's or both apparently out-billing them in any given year; in fact, this appearance is quite misleading, but it was one which both the government and the agency were at pains to cultivate, even to the extent of deliberately covering their trail in replies to parliamentary questions. On more than one occasion, written returns to questions evaded stating the amount spent by the Travel Bureau on the entirely disingenuous pretext that the media, not the bureau, paid the agency commission. But the greater prob-lem was that the bulk of Cockfield, Brown business lay with the Crown corporations which did not report the disposition of its ad-

Table 5: Total publicity billings by Canadian Government Travel Bureau through Cockfield, Brown, fiscal years 1942-58

1942-3	$ 15,670
1943-4	
1944-5	27,362
1945-6	
1946-7	604,785
1947-8	500,726
1948-9	737,750
1949-50	910,568
1950-1	608,377
1951-2	857,733
1952-3	930,568
1953-4	896,184
1954-5	952,825
1955-6	948,025
1956-7	929,353
1957-8[a]	730,897
Total	9,650,823

[a]In 1957-8 the bureau also spent $521,654 through three new Conservative agencies: Locke, Johnson ($455,982), Hayhurst ($53,363), and Harold F. Stanfield ($12,309)

Source: *Public Accounts*, 1942-58

vertising dollars: TCA, CNR, and the Canadian Steamship Lines (accounts which dovetailed neatly with the Travel Bureau account). The total advertising budgets of TCA and CNR are only available from 1950 and after (see Table 6). Unfortunately we cannot be sure what proportion of these figures was billed through agencies, and how much of that through Cockfield, Brown. In the case of CNR, however, Donald Gordon testified before a parliamentary committee in 1956 that Cockfield, Brown and Canadian Advertising had together done $454,408 worth of business in Canada for CNR (in what proportion was not clear), and that Cockfield, Brown had indirectly handled an additional $500,404 in billings in the United States through an American 'correspondent' agency, presumably taking a small cut in the process.[102] A similar agreement was in force for TCA's American advertising, but on the Canadian side Cockfield, Brown was the sole agency. Whatever the exact amounts earned by these accounts, it is obvious that they were quite sufficient to establish Cockfield, Brown's pre-eminence in the government feeding trough. That it was impossible to precisely quantify this pre-eminence no doubt well suited both the agency and the party.

Crown corporations did have a certain autonomy from political influence, and Cockfield, Brown began to suffer from the restiveness of both the CNR and TCA in the late years of the St Laurent government. In 1956 the CNR decided to rationalize the somewhat curious arrangements for its American advertising, by eliminating the middle man and dealing directly with an American agency—in this case the giant McCann-Erickson agency, just then moving into Canada. TCA moved in the same direction with its American accounts. Worse for Cockfield, Brown was CNR's decision to phase the agency out of its Canadian account as well, and to shift over fully to Canadian Advertising. When TCA put out for bids from other agencies as well, questions were inevitably raised about Cockfield, Brown's reputation, questions which seemed to embarrass Donald Gordon. In the end, TCA stuck with the agency which had served them since their inception,[103] but the loss of the CNR must have been a major blow.

If all were not well with Cockfield, Brown's government business by the mid-1950s, the election defeats of 1957 and 1958 gave the *coup de grâce* to the agency's presence in Ottawa—and to that of the other Liberal agencies as well. Within a month or two of Diefenbaker's accession to office in 1957, *Marketing* was reporting wholesale shifts in departmental advertising from Liberal to Conservative agencies, such as McKim's (the agency of Tory president Allister Grosart); Foster; Locke, Johnson (Dalton Camp); and newcomers such as O'Brien of Vancouver (headed by a personal friend of John Diefenbaker). Walsh, Ronalds, and Canadian were quickly pulled out of a massive campaign for the Bank of Canada already underway, and Walsh, always the brashest of agencies, decided to contest the matter in court, filing suit in Exchequer Court for $160,580 and costs. The suit was counterpetitioned by the government, and the matter seems to have disappeared from further view. Considering Walsh's own *modus operandi* in the nether world of party advertising and government patronage during the Liberal years, it is not altogether obvious what legal or moral claim it had in mind—in any event the partisan changeover in 1957 only confirmed (as the Liberal return in 1963 reconfirmed) the patronage nature of government advertising. Ironically enough, the only bit of government business retained by Cockfield, Brown during the Diefenbaker years came from the same source which had given the agency trouble in the Liberal era because of its relative political independence, TCA. In 1960 the public airline undertook once again a prolonged search for a new advertiser, interviewing no less than twenty-seven agencies, but decided to divide its business between Cockfield, Brown and the Conservative agency of Stanfield, Johnston and Hill.[104] By this point, of course, Cockfield, Brown was already easing its way out of partisan identification.

In conclusion one is led to the observation that from the point of view of the agency, the patronage business was ambiguous. When it was good—as it was during the 1940s and 1950s—it was very good. It would certainly appear, in the absence of contrary evidence, that for Cockfield, Brown, MacLaren's, Walsh, Ronalds, and perhaps Canadian, the many fat years of government earnings must have very handsomely compensated them for whatever sacrifices they made to the benefit of the Liberal party. Certainly Cockfield, Brown must have been averaging somewhere between $1.5 and $2 million worth of billings per year in the 1950s, which would seem to indicate an adequate return on their rather modest political investment. But when things went wrong, they went very, very wrong—as they did from 1957 to 1963. It is obviously a chancy business, and for any agency it must be something of a calculated gamble.

From the party's point of view, the risks would seem to be less. After all, the rewards will come not from the party's own resources but from the public treasury—with the added bonus that official government advertising in recent decades, the thin line between 'state' publicity and publicity for the *party* in office, especially near election time, becomes more and more difficult to distinguish. It is scarcely possible to say, for instance, if an official advertisement announcing the extension of a welfare programme, replete with highly visible references to the minister and the prime minister, is more of a governmental or political advertisement; the connection is obviously so close that there is little point in even attempting to make distinctions. It is simply the media-era version of the local wharf construction announcement. The major difference from the past is the key intervening role of the advertising agency between the party and the electorate. There seems every reason to believe that this role is becoming more, rather than less, important.

One example of the deepening relationship between the agencies and the political process is the recent extension of advertising services to party leadership campaigns and even to constituency nominations—a paradoxical result of the so-called 'democratization' of the Liberal and Conservative parties in the 1960s. Another factor supporting the party-agency relationship is the massive growth of provincial budgets in the 1960s and 1970s. The concomitant rise in provincial expenditures on advertising has apparently lessened the risks incurred by political agencies, who may now fall back on friendly provincial treasuries when the wrong party is in office federally. Camp Associates, for instance, can presumably wait out the eventual return of the Tories to Ottawa in relative affluence so long as Ontario and a Maritime province or two retain Conservative administrations. Another example of the same phenomenon is the career of the NDP agency, Dunsky Advertising of Montreal, which offers publicity assistance to a federal party with little or no hope of achieving office in the foreseeable future. That something more than faith in the social democratic cause may be involved in this otherwise charitable activity can be seen in the fact that Dunsky not only holds the accounts of the major trade unions affiliated with the party, but became the chief agency for the provincial NDP governments of Manitoba, Saskatchewan, and British Columbia. The latter account included the billings of the largest automobile agency in North America, the nationalized Insurance Corporation of British Columbia, but was entirely lost to Dunsky with the defeat of the Barrett government in 1975.

With these types of intricate interconnections established between advertising agencies and all three major political parties in the country, it is unlikely that the agency-party relationship will change drastically in the near future. If anything, with rising levels of expenditures on both party and government advertising, the agency-party relationship is undoubtedly even stronger today than at any time in the past. Thus the examination of the relationship between the Liberal party and its advertising agencies from the 1930s to the 1950s is of much more than antiquarian interest; it is an examination of a present situation in embryo and early development.

Notes

1   The difference between the patronage style of political campaign and the newer communications orientation which comes with advertising is well illustrated by the reaction of Angus L. Macdonald to observing a media-centred provincial campaign in Manitoba in 1932. Macdonald wrote to J.L. Ralston about the implications for Nova Scotia: 'Can it be

that we could conduct a campaign in this Province with radio hire and other publicity as our major items of expense? Speed the day!' JLR, v. 12, Macdonald to Ralston, 12 Dec. 1932.

2   For a recent empirical investigation of the effects of advertising on voting behaviour in Quebec, see Kristian S. Palda, 'Does Advertising Influence Votes? An Analysis of the 1966 and 1970 Quebec Elections,' *Canadian Journal of Political Science*, VI, 4 (December 1973), pp. 638-653. Palda concludes that there is indeed a relationship between advertising and voting. A recent American study of the effects of television advertising in the 1972 presidential election came to similar conclusions regarding that medium. See Thomas E. Patterson and Robert D. McClure, 'Television News and Televised Political Advertising: Their Impact on the Voter,' paper delivered at the National Conference on Money and Politics, Washington, DC, 27-28 Feb. 1974.

3   *Political Party Financing in Canada* (Toronto, 1970), p. 77.

4   H.E. Stephenson and Carlton McNaught, *The Story of Advertising in Canada: A Chronicle of Fifty Years* (Toronto, 1940), pp. 159-185, quotation from p. 174.

5   *Political Party Financing*, p. 77.

6   NPL, Diary, 1935, list of expenditures; 14 July 1939. WLMK, v. 270, Norman P. Lambert to King, 1 July (228963-4), A.D.P. Heeney to Lambert, 19 Jul 1939 (228965). Cockfield was again brought in for high-level consultations with Lambert on billboard, newspaper, and radio advertising for the wartime election of 1940. NPL, Diary, 25 Jan. 1940.

7   *Marketing*, 3 Nov. 1945. Statistics from 1941 to the present can be found in Dominion Bureau of Statistics, *Advertising Agencies in Canada* (Ottawa, 1968).

8   The amount of government spending is calculated from figures in an unpublished Sessional Paper, no. 257 (12 Aug. 1946), Public Archives of Canada, v. 505. The proportion spent through ad agencies is estimated from figures in another unpublished Sessional Paper, no. 14B (19 May 1947), PAC, v. 515. The proportion is only a rough estimate, since the time periods are not exactly comparable in the two sets of figures, but it is no doubt generally accurate.

9   *Marketing*, 12 Dec. 1958.

10   PAC, Walsh Advertising Agency, *A Formula for Liberal Victory* (1948).

11   *Marketing*, 12 Dec. 1958; see also 21 Nov.

12   *NPL*, Diary, 1935, list of contributions. There were personal connections as well. The head of a newly formed Toronto Liberal Businessman's Club in 1933 was a member of the Cockfield, Brown staff. WLMK, v. 198, H.R.L. Henry to W.R.P. Parker, 3 Jan. (168203); Parker to Henry, 4 Jan. 1933 (168212). Duncan Marshall, a minister in the Hepburn government and later a Liberal senator, was an executive of the firm from 1923 to 1934.

13   *Marketing*, 3 Feb. 1940, 12 Dec. 1958.

14   BC, v. 155. Claxton to A.R. Renaud, 18 May 1949, includes list of contributors, either actual or potential, for the 1949 campaign. Another list in file 26 ('Broadcasts, Elections, 1949') contains a list of defence supplies 1 April to 30 Dec. 1948 with exact amounts of contracts. At least three-quarters of the names on the first list also appear on the second.

15   As Kidd remarked to Pickersgill a decade later, 'It was largely you and Brooke, I believe, who brought into being the programmes of reform which, having Mr. King's acceptance, we were able successfully to develop as our principal appeal in the '45 election.... Brooke was a tower of strength in the party councils,' NLF, v. 633, Kidd to Pickersgill, 13 Aug. 1954. Pickersgill has described Claxton as 'the link between Mackenzie King and the political organization of the Liberal party.' MKR, II, pp. 5-6. He also wrote his own advertising copy for the Department of National Defence when he was minister. James Eayrs, *In Defence of Canada: Peacemaking and Deterrence* (Toronto, 1972), III, pp. 67, 121, 127.

16   BC, v. 44, Kidd to Claxton, 16 March, 24 June 1943. Although born in Sweden, Kidd was of English parents.

17   BC, v. 28, Campbell Smart to A.M. Mitchell, 22 April, Mitchell to Smart, 23 April 1940; v. 44, Kidd to Claxton, 3 June, Claxton to Kidd, 4 June 1941.

18   BC, v. 44, Kidd to Claxton, 16 March 1943. Kidd did not leave his client's own constituency unattended. A 'Hansard Club' was set up in 1940, with Kidd as secretary, to function for the 'greatest benefit of members as well as our party representative for St. Lawrence–St. George,' Kidd, notice, n.d., BC, v. 44.

19   BC, v. 44, Kidd to Claxton, 15 July, Claxton to Kidd, 21 July 1943.

20   BC, v. 44, Kidd to Claxton, 27 Nov. 1942, 1 Feb. 1943; Claxton to Kidd, 23 Dec. 1942, 28 Jan., 9 and 23 Feb. 1943.

21   BC, v. 44, Cockfield, Brown memorandum, 25 April 1944, with attachments; report, 2 May 1944, BC, v. 28, 'Breakdown, Election Expenses,' 5 July 1945; v. 29 and 30 also include material on the various agencies involved, seven in all. *Ibid.*, Claxton to Anderson; BC, v. 44, Claxton to Kidd, 26 Dec. 1951.

22   NLF, v. 602. Kidd to G.C. Hammond, 11 May, 1945. Almost all the information available on the Liberal-Cockfield, Brown relationship comes from the National Liberal Federation files. It might be noted that a written inquiry from the author to the Montreal office of Cockfield, Brown and Company concerning access to any remaining records of the Liberal party account, elicited no response, not even an acknowledgement. Apparently, the sensitive nature of the subject has not lessened appreciably in thirty years.

23 Task Force on Government Information, *To Know and Be Known: The Report of the Task Force on Government Information* (Ottawa, 1969), pp. 324-338. See also Firestone, *Public Persuader*, pp. 67-77, 182-186; interview with Hon. J.W. Pickersgill, 15 July 1974.

24 NLF, v. 596, Fogo to A.G. McLean, 7 Feb. 1945. J.L. Granatstein, 'Financing the Liberal Party, 1935-1945,' in M. Cross and R. Bothwell, eds *Policy by Other Means: Essays in Honour of C.P.Stacey* (Toronto: 1970), p. 194. Granatstein's article is far and away the best piece on Liberal party organization in print—and the first to utilize the archival goldmine in the Norman Lambert diaries at Queen's University, except for Neil McKenty's biography of *Mitch Hepburn* (Toronto, 1967).

25 NLF, v. 599, McLean to Annis, 13 July 1948. The agency in question was R.C. Smith of Toronto.

26 Submission of J.S. Crosbie, president, the Magazine Advertising Bureau of Canada, to the Task Force on Government Information, 30 Jan. 1969; quoted in Task Force, *Report*, p. 335, and in O.J.Firestone, *Public Persuader: Government Advertising* (Toronto: 1970), p. 69.

27 Firestone, *ibid.*, pp. 68-69.

28 NLF, v. 629, Kidd to MacTavish, 8 Oct., Kidd to Archibald, 14 Oct. 1954.

29 See, *inter alia*, NLF, v. 826, Cockfield, Brown memorandum, R.G. Bartlett to S.D. Denman, 23 Oct. 1952 ('I understand that our commission is added to the net price when we bill the National Liberal Federation'), and Kidd to Bartlett, 1 April 1953; v. 809, Bartlett to Paul Lafond, 3 Aug., and Lafond to Fogo, 5 Aug. 1949. ('All Cockfield, Brown invoices include full agency commission, and thus prices on individual invoices as well as on the total are boosted by some 17%').

30 NLF, v. 603, Kidd to Archibald, 8 June 1945. Granatstein, 'Financing the Liberal Party,' p. 194, writes that 'how this fact squared with Fogo's belief that Cockfield, Brown was working without profit is unclear.' Unclear indeed!

31 NLF, v. 621, G.C. Hammond to Alan Woodrow, 23 Dec. 1952; v. 868, Hammond to A.W. Cooper, 30 July 1948. A vice-president of the agency suggested to Kidd that 'you might like to draw this to the attention of Gordon [Fogo] at some convenient time.' Hammond to Kidd, 2 Aug. 1948.

32 NLF, v. 815, Denman to Hammond, 2 April 1953; v. 617, Kidd to Walter Harris, 23 July 1952; v. 603, Kidd to H.R. Conway, 18 April, 1945; v. 806, Conway to Kidd, 25 May 1949; v. 632, Kidd to MacTavish, 21 Nov. 1955. In 1954 a Claxton radio speech was advertised and the agency pondered the cheque. If the party 'has any political funds,' the agency suggested, 'we should collect...if not, then I think we should absorb the charge.' NLF, v. 629, Hammond to Kidd, 27 Aug. 1954. The federation paid, commission included. Kidd to Archibald, 29 Oct. 1954.

33 NLF, v. 863, 1955 advisory council, proceedings, p. 69; BC, v. 44, Robertson to Claxton, 29 March 1944.

34 J.L. Granatstein, *Canada's War: The Politics of the Mackenzie King Government, 1939-1945* (Toronto, 1975), pp. 385-387.

35 NLF, v. 602, Kidd to MacLean, 1 Sept. 1944; v. 602, note in file on 'CCF Saskatchewan Election, 1944'; Hammond to Kidd, 25 July 1944. According to the note, the following amounts were spent by the various parties on advertising: 1938, Liberals $10,462; CCF $140; Conservatives $1070. 1944, Liberals $25,613; CCF $16,530; Conservatives $5027; Social Credit $56.

36 See Granatstein, 'Financing the Liberal Party,' pp. 194-195.

37 NLF, v. 602, Cockfield, Brown account files; Kidd to Fogo, 2 Nov. 1944; v. 603, Cockfield, Brown estimate, 18 Dec. 1943. After its 1943 revival the NLF was budgeting for $100,000 per year and about $8000 a month—for all purposes. Yet by Aug. of 1944 the demands of Cockfield, Brown and of that traditional sinkhole of Liberal money, the Quebec organization, had pushed the federation 'beyond what was originally contemplated in our budget,' and the NLF president was fearful that the 'matter will get out of hand.' NLF, v. 620, Robertson to J.-A. Blanchette, MP, 1 Aug. 1944.

38 NLF, v. 603, Kidd to T.L. Anderson, 26 Jan. 1945; v. 602, 1940 advertising budget, Cockfield, Brown, 'National Liberal Committee, Estimate of Advertising,' 24 April 1945, files on Cockfield, Brown account, invoices, statements, etc. *Marketing*, 21 April 1945.

39 NPL, Diary, 2, 12, and 15 May 1945. Granatstein, 'Financing the Liberal Party,' p. 194.

40 NLF, v. 602, Kidd to Hammond, 11 May, Kidd memorandum, 1 May 1945. This was a recurrent problem in the party-agency relationship as is well illustrated by a memorandum in the NLF files concerning the Ontario provincial election of 1945 detailing the shortfall of funds for projected publicity: '...because of the way in which campaign funds are raised and distributed, no long range advertising plans can be made.... If the entire amount that was eventually spent was on hand early in the campaign, a working plan could be put into effect. But, when moneys are made available for advertising in scattered amounts over a five week period, it is not possible to work out a plan, and there has to be a considerable degree of makeshift.' NLF, v. 632, memorandum, n.d., n.a.

41 19 May 1945.

42 BC, v. 44, Claxton to C.D. Howe, 30 Nov. 1945; Claxton to King, 2 Dec., 1947.

43 *Ibid.*, Kidd to Claxton, 3 Aug. 1945.

44 NLF, v. 806, Kidd to Brown, 25 May 1949.

45 'The Liberal Party,' p. 197.

46 *Marketing,* 24 Feb. 1956. It is not clear what this promotion actually sig-
nified. Dalton Camp was also promoted to a vice-presidency of his
agency in the same year, but comments drily that 'advertising agencies
proliferate executive titles; I looked upon my elevation...much as I did
on becoming a lance-corporal in the army—an assumption of greater
responsibility without any apparent corresponding benefit.' *Gentlemen,
Players and Politicians* (Toronto: 1970), p. 256.

47 NLF, v. 806, Kidd to J. McNab, 8 Feb., Kidd to Archibald, 9 March; v. 614,
Kidd to Vernon Knowles, 25 July 1949.

48 Interview with Hon. J.W. Pickersgill, 15 July 1974.

49 *Can. H. of C. Debates,* 7 March 1951, p. 999.

50 Both quoted in E.E. Harrill, 'The Structure of Organization and Power
in Canadian Political Parties: A Study in Party Financing,' unpublished
PHD thesis, University of North Carolina, 1958, pp. 209-210.

51 CDH, v. 109, file 75(7), Howe to W.A. Fraser, 30 Jan. 1959.

52 NLF, v. 826. E.T. Applewhaite to Kidd, 25 Aug. 1952. Sometimes the ad
men caused hostility among others in Ottawa as well. In 1956 Kidd
complained to his agency about expense account charges by Cockfield,
Brown men working on a Liberal television series. He explained that
'sometimes the way advertising men spend money in Ottawa excites
the envy and dislike of civil servants who don't have expense accounts.... That is the tradition of business, I know, but it doesn't go
down with people here....' NLF, v. 837, Kidd to D.R. McRobie, 16 Oct.,
Kidd to Archibald, 1 Nov. 1956.

53 As one example, in 1953 Brooke Claxton wanted data on comparative
GNP growth figures. Cockfield, Brown undertook 'rather extensive research,' and a tentative allocation of $3000 was set aside in the budget
for such purposes. NLF, v. 826, Kidd to S.D. Denman, 16 March 1953;
BC, v. 61, Kidd to Claxton, 27 March 1953. Civil servants often contributed their expertise to this process as well. NLF, v. 606, Mitchell Sharp
to Kidd, 30 Oct. 1944.

54 BC, v. 44, Kidd to Claxton, 13 July 1947, NLF, v. 614, Kidd to Fogo, 26
Feb. 1949, notes a summer conference billing from Cockfield, Brown
of $1165. A twenty-fifth-anniversary dinner for Mackenzie King was
held in 1944, with a PR campaign orchestrated around it. NLF, v. 597,
Kidd to MacLean, 30 June 1944. A dinner for St Laurent in Quebec
City excited some sarcastic press about the ubiquitous ad men in attendance.

55 NLF, v. 602, amounts were as follows: Massey-Harris, $7500; Dominion
Woollens, $5000; Firestone Tire and Rubber $2750; G.H. Wood and
Company $689.42; Total $15,948.42.

56   *Ibid.*, Kidd to Hammond, 4 Jan., Hammond to Kidd, 13 Jan. 1945. The practice was publicly alluded to during the 1972 federal campaign.

57   NLF, v. 631, contains minutes of committee meetings from 1954 to 1956; v. 838 has similar records for 1957. See also Regenstreif, 'The Liberal Party,' pp. 196-197.

58   NLF, v. 815, Kidd to Denman, 16 March 1953; see also Kidd to Denman, 10 April. Fears about security were hardly groundless. Dalton Camp recalls that early in the 1956 Nova Scotia provincial election, an anonymous informant handed him a thick roll of Cockfield, Brown pamphlets 'in first-proof stage, uncut, the ink still damp.' *Gentlemen, Players and Politicians*, p. 214.

59   NLF, v. 806, 'Notes re Organization,' n.d. (1949), n.a.; v. 621. The agency, Tandy Advertising, was pulled into the Ontario campaign. NLF, v. 828, MacTavish to Kidd, 21 June 1953.

60   NLF, v. 807, Phare to L.L. Leprohon, 18 May 1949. Phare was the inventor of the standard rate card in 1932. *Marketing*, 1 Dec. 1958. R.C. Smith and Son were campaign contributors ($1000 in 1940). NPL, Diary, 1940 list of contributors.

61   BC, v. 29, Claxton to J.A. MacLaren, 28 June 1949. $1000 was contributed in late 1957, NLF, v. 620, Fogo to Kidd, 19 Nov. 1957. NLF, v. 826, W.G. Abel to Kidd, 13 Aug. 1953; BC, v. 61, Kidd to W.F. Harrison, 16 April 1953.

62   NLF, v. 596, McLean to Fogo, 1 Feb., Fogo to McLean, 7 Feb. 1945.

63   NLF, v. 808; BC, v. 30, Alan MacNaughton to Claxton, 4 June 1953.

64   NLF, v. 831, Denman to P. Lafond, 14 March 1957: 'Historically, the reason has been that the local influences prevalent in Quebec do not obtain in other provinces and therefore the specific appeal to the Quebec voter would not in most cases apply to French speaking people outside the province.' But this was not always the case, in fact.

65   NLF, v. 802, G. Warren Brown to Robertson, 16 March 1944.

66   BC, v. 155, notes on interviews with Senators Beauregard and Gouin, 13 May 1949.

67   NLF, v. 818, Lafond to Kidd, 16 April, L.M. Gouin to Lafond, 3 April, Lafond to Gouin, 7 April 1953; v. 635, Kidd to MacTavish, 11 Dec. 1956.

68   As late as 1948 R.C. Smith was put in charge of an unsuccessful federal by-election campaign in Oshawa. NLF, v. 601, G.F. Stiritt to MacLean, 18 Aug. 1948. But by the turn of the decade the agency had lost all its federal government patronage.

69   BC, v. 50, 'Report of the Standing Committee on Publicity of the Ontario Liberal Association,' Dec. 1952.

70   As Dalton Camp remembers the 1948 national convention, the Ontario Liberals were 'leaderless, poor-mouthing, and gauche...so crudely in-

ept, so preposterously vulgar.' *Gentlemen, Players and Politicians*, p. 2. Camp's disdainful words were no doubt echoed on more than one occasion by Ottawa.

71   The phrase is that of H.E. Kidd. NLF, v. 827, Kidd to Conway, 6 July 1953.

72   *Marketing*, 6 July 1956. The authoritative *National List of Advertisers* lists Lovick as the Alberta Liberal agency in the mid-1950s.

73   NLF, v. 806, Kidd to A.D. Black, 25 March, 1949. Kidd plaintively asked his agency's Vancouver office to phone the official in question and 'let me know what the score is in the Provincial office....'

74   NLF, v. 807, Kidd to Black, 4 March (see also Chapter 9 of *The Government Party*); v. 806, Black to Kidd, 14 April, 1949; v. 827, Kidd to H.R. Conway, 6 July 1953; v. 631, F.W. Ellis to Kidd, 30 May 1957.

75   Paltiel, *Political Party Financing*, p. 38, and Paltiel, 'Party and Candidate Expenditures in the Canadian General Election of 1972,' *Canadian Journal of Political Science*, VII, 2 (June 1974), pp. 341-357.

76   *Marketing*, 15 March, 1957.

77   NLF, v. 836, Denman to Kidd, 21 Jan. 1957. Kidd protested to Claxton the day after the meeting. NLF, v. 616, Kidd to Claxton, 6 July 1953. The secretary of the Nova Scotia Liberal Association complained about undue emphasis on 'organization and bringing in a vote on election day' and wanted more advertising. NLF, v. 621, Kidd to MacTavish, 3 July 1953.

78   In 1949, the Cockfield, Brown radio man was employed 'full time' in Ottawa during the campaign, and the agency believed that the 'operation was most successful.' NLF, v. 826, Denman to Kidd *et al.*, 26 March 1953.

79   21-22 Eliz. II, 1973, Bill C-203, s.99.3.

80   NLF, v. 611, Kidd to R. Conway, 26 May 1952. The worst of it was that the weeklies, which were most prone to change 'political rates,' were highly thought of by the Liberals in terms of voter impact. As Kidd informed a member of the prime minister's staff, 'The weekly press...is a much more important force than is commonly realized.... The weekly editors, of whom there are eight or nine hundred, have a good deal of influence in their communities and they are certainly in a position to promote a line of thought or to influence opinion if they want to.' NLF, v. 623, Kidd to W.R. Martin, 1 Oct. 1952.

81   NLF, v. 826, Cockfield, Brown invoices; v. 601, J.W. Stebenne to I.B. Gardner, 16 Nov., *Le Devoir* to Gardner, 10 Nov. 1948. For the general practice, see Blair Fraser, 'Our Illegal Federal Elections,' *Maclean's*, LXVI (17 April 1948), pp. 24-25; Harrill, 'The Structure of Organization and Power in Canadian Political Parties,' p. 209; Committee on Election Expenses, *Report* (Ottawa, 1966), p. 52.

82   NLF, v. 800, cheques issued for years 1954, 1955, and 1956.

83   Brian M. McFadzen, 'The Liberal Party and MacLaren,' (Queen's University, unpublished M.A. Thesis, 1977), pp. 125-131, argues that MacLaren's was reluctantly, but inevitably, drawn into policy-making as well as image-making in the Pearson era.

84   NLF, v. 824, W.A. Munro to MacTavish, 23 June 1953; see also J.W. Pickersgill, *My Years with Louis St Laurent: A Political Memoir* (Toronto, 1975), p. 194.

85   NLF, v. 826, files on television, Denman to Kidd, 6 April 1953; v. 836, Kidd to McRobie, 16 Nov. 1956; v. 837, Kidd to R.W. Harwood, 24 Feb. 1956, memo, Gordon Atkinson, 2 July 1957, Kidd to McRobie, 13 Feb., Kidd to Harwood, 1 March, Kidd to M. Wood, 25 Oct. 1956.

86   NLF, v. 838, *Free Press*, 3 May 1957.

87   NLF, v. 836, Kidd to Archibald, 25 May, Kidd to MacTavish, 15 May, 8 Aug. 1957. 'From a public relations standpoint,' Kidd suggested, 'it would be a mistake' for the Liberal Party to contest the billed cancellations. In the event, some Liberal broadcasters cancelled their charges as a campaign contribution. See NLF, v. 839, M.T. Brown to Kidd, 17 June 1958. Pressure was brought to bear on others to drop the charges. *Ibid.*, Kidd to Walter Harris, 23 Nov. 1957.

88   NLF, v. 837, Kidd to MacTavish, 23 May 1957, Kidd to Miss Thurber, 25 Sept. 1958; v. 838, Kidd to MacTavish, 11 July, Caldwell to MacTavish, 27 Aug., MacTavish to Caldwell, 16 May, Kidd to MacTavish, 11 July 1957; MacTavish to Lafond, 25 March 1963.

89   CDH, v. 108, file 75(5), Howe to H.A. Mackenzie, 27 Aug. 1957.

90   NLF, v. 836, McRobie to Kidd, 9 Sept., Kidd to McRobie, 23 Oct. 1957. John Meisel reports that no less than 40 Cockfield, Brown employees worked on the election. *The Canadian General Election of 1957* (Toronto, 1962), p. 65.

91   NLF, v. 843, P.C. Logan to Kidd, 11 Feb. 1958; BC, v. 79, Claxton to Kidd, 27 Nov. 1957; Claxton to Matthews, 30 Nov. 1959; Pickersgill interview. Background to the changeover is given inDenis Smith, *Gentle Patriot: A Political Biography of Walter Gordon* (Edmonton, 1973), pp. 57-59.

92   *Marketing*, 7 March, 2 May, 1958, 27 Feb., 20 March, 17 July 1959; NLF, v. 876, McRobie to Kidd, 7 Jan. 1958; v. 846, 'Newspaper Advertising Copy Plan (for discussion),' n.d.; v. 850, advertising estimates, 6 Feb. 1958; v. 847, Connolly to W.A. Ellis, 31 March, Connolly to E.V. Rechnitzer, 31 March 1958; v. 875, G. Marler to MacTavish, 14 Dec., MacTavish to Marler, 20 Dec. 1957. McFadzen, 'The Liberal Party and MacLaren,' p. 57, suggests that Cockfield, Brown 'fell from favour,' resulting from the defeat of 1957-8 and the 'controversy created by apparent conflicts of interest involving the Trans-Canada Pipelines, the agency, and its government employer.'

93   *Gentlemen, Players and Politicians*, p. 93.

94   Camp Associates has recently gained a certain notoriety in the press for their close relationship with the government of Premier William Davis. See 'Ontario Ads Net $525,000 for Camp Agency,' *Globe and Mail*, 30 Nov. 1974.

95   Frederick Elkin, *Rebels and Colleagues: Advertising and Social Change in French Canada* (Montreal: 1973), pp. 31, 121. Ironically, the Quebec Liberals 'had some trouble' finding an agency in 1960, finally settling on Collyer, of which former Liberal MP Roland Beaudry was vice-president and financial director. *Marketing*, 1 July 1960. It seems that ad agencies have been little better than either journalists or political scientists in predicting electoral transformations.

96   NPL, Diary, 31 Dec. 1936, 9 Jan. 1939, 7 Feb. 1937, 7 March 1938, 10 Nov. 1940.

97   BC , v. 44, Kidd to Claxton, 2 Aug., Claxton to Kidd, 3 Aug. 1945.

98   In 1951, MacLaren's indicated some discontent with their state. NLF, v. 613, H.S. Hamilton to Kidd, 22 Sept., Kidd to Hamilton, 22 Oct. 1951.

99   'Public' is a somewhat ambiguous term in this context, in which data has been consolidated and compiled from very disparate sources. It should be emphasized that the raw data has actually been put together here for the first time. Sources from which the columns have been compiled in detail are as follows: 1940-6: PAC, *Sessional Papers*, v. 505, no. 257 (12 Aug. 1946); 1945-7: *ibid.*, v. 528, no. 149A (18 Feb. 1948); 1949-50: *ibid.*, v. 570, no. 175B (22 June 1951); 1952: *ibid.*, v. 601, no. 172 (26 Jan. 1953); 1953: *ibid.*, v. 612, no. 172 (12 Jan. 1954); 1954: *ibid.*, v. 625, no. 169A (8 Feb. 1955); 1955: *ibid.*, v. 641, no. 199 (1 March 1956)—see also NLF, v. 632, Kidd to Stuart Garson, 8 Nov. 1956; 1956: *Sessional Papers*, v. 650, no. 188 (27 Feb. 1957)—see also *Marketing*, 19 July 1957. All these figures have been cross-checked with the relevant sections of the *Public Accounts*, 1944-57, and in places supplemented by figures from the latter source. The years indicated in the columns sometimes overlap and for this reason have not been totalled for the entire period. Moreover, some indicate fiscal years and others calendar years, depending upon the nature of the information asked in Parliament. The data do not, therefore, give us a chronologically very coherent picture, but they do indicate the relative share of dollars earned by the various agencies at specific points in time.

100   *Marketing*, 8 Sept. 1945.

101   R.C. Smith was a financial contributor to the party in 1940, donating $1000 to the bagman in Toronto, NPL, Diary, 1 March 1940.

102   Canada, House of Commons, 1956, Sessional Committee on Railways and Shipping, *Minutes of Proceedings and Evidence*, 20 March 1956, pp. 198-199.

103 *Marketing*, 16 and 23 March, 7 Sept. 1956. In answer to a question from Tory ad man William Hamilton in a committee hearing, Gordon replied: 'If you asked me how we chose between Cockfield, Brown, and the Canadian Advertising Agency, I do not think you should press that point.... I do not want to have this conversation create the idea, or let it get abroad, that we are critical of Cockfield, Brown or that we regard their services as inferior to some other agency. I do not want that to go out of this room.' Committee on Railways and Shipping, p. 200. It did, of course. See *Marketing*, 30 March 1956.

104 *Marketing*, 19 July, 16 Aug., 1957, 18 April, 17 Oct. 1958, 28 Oct. 1960.

John Meisel The Stalled Omnibus and the Decline of Party

I The Stalled Omnibus

"Traditionally, Canadian politics have been governed by the two-party system, and the two historic parties, Conservative on the one hand and Liberal on the other, have shown many of the traits which have marked the two historic parties in the United States.... Both are great, nation-wide, easy going, omnibus vehicles, whose occupants often have difficulty in recognizing their fellow passengers or in understanding why the driver of the bus let them in."–G.V. Ferguson (1927).

Background

The similarities between American and Canadian parties are, indeed, so striking that their differences are often overlooked. The most far reaching and fundamental of these differences concerns them not individually, but taken together. The two-party *systems* differ in some important respects and notably in the degree to, and manner in, which each contains the various interests and groupings that constitute their respective countries' political community. It is, of course, true, as Austin Ranney and Willmore Kendall have insisted, that the United States does not have a one-party system but many, and that generalizations about *the* American party system tend to overlook the enormous variation from state to state in the relative strength of the parties and also in the relations among them.[1] But no one seriously questions that, insofar as Congress and the Presidency are concerned, the United States supports a two-party system that contains the pressures and interests of all the major groups seeking expression through political means. The same cannot be said of Canada where, for over four decades, the major two parties have repeatedly failed to satisfy the aspirations of important minorities. These have consequently organized themselves into minor parties that have won office in several of the provinces and which have also played an effective role in national politics. We are here concerned with the latter, and the following figures therefore show only the percentages of votes polled by the minor parties (and independents) in national general elections since 1921.

Table 1: Percentage of votes polled by minor parties: 1921-63

Year	Percentage of vote polled by minor parties	Year	Percentage of vote polled by minor parties
1921	29	1945	32
1925	14	1949	21
1926	9	1953	20
1930	6	1957	20
1935	25	1958	13
1940	18	1962	26
		1963	26

There is, of course, nothing sacred about a two-party system, but in the Parliamentary setting it has some clear advantages. The chief of these are that the responsibility for the government's performance can be unmistakably identified with one party and that it makes it easier than any other democratic system for the government's policies and program to be reasonably coherent. But its most immediate and, in the short run, most practical advantages, so far as Canada is concerned, are 1) the majority of politicians and the politically active people seem to consider the absence of it as a sort of political fall from grace; and 2) the machinery of government, and particularly of Parliament, is closely geared to it. The reaction in Canada to the failure in three out of the four most recent elections of any party to win a Parliamentary majority is, therefore, considered in the country as something akin to a national disaster.

We are not concerned with the difficult task of assessing the importance or gravity of the present situation. Our purpose is to probe into the reasons for the current impasse and to make a guess about the future. Let us begin our analysis by examining the functions performed by the party system in Canadian society.

Function of Party System

The Canadian party system, like those in all liberal democratic states, must organize public opinion and link it to expert opinion for the purpose of finding a sound and acceptable definition of the national interest. To do this, it must perform other tasks: it must, for instance, "sublimate private interests by finding principles that merge them with general interests,"[2] and it acts as a broker of ideas, or of class and regional interests. It must, in short, create a national consensus on the broad purposes of government and on the general means most suited to achieve them. It is precisely in this function of maximizing consensus that American parties have been so successful and that their Canadian counterparts have lately experienced considerable difficulty. One of the chief reasons for the difference is that the ease with which consensus can be achieved depends on the degree of underlying group cohesion. And this, in turn, depends on the extent to which there has developed a secular political culture.[3] "The United States," as Seymour Martin Lipset has rightly argued, "has developed a common homogeneous culture in the veneration accorded the Founding Fathers, Abraham Lincoln, Theodore Roosevelt and their principles. These common elements, to which all American politicians appeal, are not present in all democratic societies" (note 3, p. 80).

Canada is one of these. It has no distinct national flag, no nationally and universally accepted national anthem, no nationally meaningful "political" holidays. And while it would be unrealistic to assert that there are *no* secular symbols representing common experiences and common values of English and French Canadians and of the various regions and sections, it nevertheless remains true that by comparison with the United States, Canadians are hardly a nation. In these circumstances, one of the chief and most important latent functions of the political parties and of the party system is to foster and develop a sense of national unity and of national being. Parties are still among the relatively few genuinely national forces in Canada and the degree to which they succeed in developing a consensus in the short run depends to a great extent on the way in which they and other agencies have succeeded in fostering a sense of Canadian nationalism.

It is of course possible to argue that the differences between the American and Canadian party systems should be ascribed to contrasts between the Presidential and Parliamentary forms of government or to differences in the electoral laws and practices in the two countries. But I accept L. Lipson's conclusion that "parties appear primarily to be the product of their society and are only secondarily the offshoot of advertising governmental institutions."[4] This view is strengthened by Canadian experience:[5] the traditional two-party system functioned satisfactorily for the first half century after Confederation and no change in the system of government preceded the failure of the old parties to contain expressions of regional and sectional discontent.

If the electoral system cannot be held responsible for the stresses that have recently interfered with the smooth working of the traditional two-party system in Canada, what other causes can be found to explain it? Before exploring this question it will be instructive to sketch briefly the changes Canadian parties have recently undergone.

Party Differences and Changes

The main features of, and the differences between, the major Canadian parties, as they had developed from the time of Confederation to the eve of World War II can briefly be sketched as follows: both parties, trying to appeal to a sprawling and diverse electorate, became pragmatic, opportunistic and flexible. And since they shared the object of their affection—the Canadian public—they came to exhibit a certain family resemblance. They were, in short, the classic omnibus-type party described by G.V. Ferguson in the quotation at the beginning of this article. Some contrasting tendencies could nevertheless be detected. On the whole, the Conservatives showed a greater attachment than the Liberals to the United Kingdom and the Empire; but they were also more nationalistic and more suspicious of the United States. In their attitude to the nature of Canadian federalism, the Conservatives tended to be more centralist. After 1891 they appealed primarily to the Protestant and British elements in the population and have been slightly more prone to reflect the interests of business and wealth.

The Liberals have been less concerned with defending the imperial tie and generally have been more pro-American. They have been more jealous of provincial rights, as was to be expected of a party which by 1896 had become the favourite of French Canada. They were identified less than the Conservatives with the English elements in the population; they had a greater appeal to the farmer, to lower income groups, to Roman Catholics.

The standard textbook on Canadian government summarized the situation as follows: "...certain broad tendencies and attitudes can be traced as fairly indicative of each party's general position. It may, for example, be asserted with some confidence, that the Liberals desire a lower tariff than the Conservatives; that they are more inclined to favour the primary producers, especially in Western Canada; that they are more nationalistic and less Imperialistic; that they are generally more tolerant of sectional and racial differences. In short, Liberals and Conservatives approach a new or old problem not with a predetermined philosophy behind them, but with a certain leaning or bias which, however, each is prepared to modify—and sometimes to modify substantially—should the circumstances warrant it."[6]

While Dawson's characterization sums up fairly the parties' general tendencies prior to World War II, it is doubtful whether it was accurate in 1947 when the book was first published. By 1957 it was clearly wrong. The Liberal party that went down to defeat in 1957 was no more "inclined to favour the primary producers, especially in Western Canada" than were the Conservatives and, if anything, it was considerably less tolerant of sectional interests, as was evidenced by the opposition to it of a growing number of provincial premiers. For, among its other gerontic symptoms after twenty-two years in office (of which six were years of a world war), the most serious was the decline of the influence on its leaders of the party as compared with that of the senior civil servants. This gave the Liberals a centralist bias which made them insensitive to regional and sectional pressure. "A party long in power...comes more and more to think in national terms, particularly if most of the speculation and planning is done not by the party as such, but by Ottawa-based and Ottawa-minded civil servants. When the regional interests ultimately come to find the national emphasis no longer tolerable, when they find the national government too intransigent, they turn to a party seemingly more receptive to provincial and regional pressure."[7]

By 1957, the Conservatives had become the champions of the provinces and they consequently benefited from the Liberals' centralism. But the party that had adopted Mr. Diefenbaker as its leader late in 1956 underwent other and equally important modifications. Influenced greatly by eastern business interests and generally representing what is considered the old British, Tory element in the past, the new leader—something of a prairie radical—proceeded to make it the party of the underdog. He appealed to all the groups who felt themselves neglected by the Liberal government: old age pensioners, newly naturalized Canadians, people living in the less prosperous regions, and also to all those who had reacted unfavourably to the arrogant complacency which had come to mark the Liberal government in the mid-1950s.[8]

Once in power, these tendencies found reflection in many of the Conservative government's policies. All sorts of welfare payments were increased or new ones instituted, some legislation dis-criminating against so-called "new Canadians" was abolished, and public works projects in underdeveloped areas of the country were approved. At the same time, however, the government acquired a reputation of indecision, of incompetence, and of failure to cope with Canada's growing economic difficulties. The Conservative party had never attracted appreciable numbers of intellectuals; nothing that the party did while in office remedied this failing. But it was not only the eggheads, it was also the business community and the urban population generally—particularly the people living in the larg-est cities—that slowly turned against the government. And, as has been noted already, the Diefenbaker party failed utterly to establish a permanent foothold in Quebec, even after it had polled half the vote there in 1958.

The Liberals have, of course, benefited from Conservative weak-ness. Under the leadership of Lester Pearson, who has surrounded himself with able lieutenants, the party also changed its physiog-nomy becoming, to all intents and purposes, the party of business, wealth, and the upper middle class.[9] But it kept many of its old sources of support, with two critical exceptions: the prairies and Quebec. Hence its failure to dislodge the Diefenbaker government in 1962 and hence the inability of the Pearson government to com-mand a clear majority in the House of Commons after the 1963 election.

II   The Decline of Party

In seeking to identify the main manifestations of, and reasons for, the decline of party, relative to other political factors, I distinguish be-tween long-run factors, most of which are universal in liberal democ-racies and appear to a greater or lesser extent in most highly indus-trialized and post-industrial societies, and those which are of more re-cent origin and uniquely Canadian.

Long-run Reasons for Party Decline

Rise of the Bureaucratic State

Modern political parties evolved from small cliques of power-wielders when the extension of the franchise necessitated the organization of mass electorates. The greater participation of the public in political life led, in conjunction with other factors, to the emergence of the positive state—one which increasingly participated in virtually every aspect of the human experience. But the "ancestors" of our political institutions and the political parties serving them evolved at a time when governments were dealing with a limited range of problems, and when only a small minority of the population was politically active. Under these conditions parties were able to act as suitable links between the small electorate and the even smaller number of political decision-makers.

The continuous expansion of governmental activities has created mounting problems for the legislative and representative system. Up until the First World War, the Canadian parliament dealt with only a small number of issues, met seldom and required little specialized and technical knowledge to operate. Now the number and complexity of the areas in which the federal government operates are so vast that it is quite impossible for MPs to be abreast of what is going on. At best, each can become reasonably well-informed about one or two areas.

The expansion of government activities and the increasingly complicated nature of government decisions have reduced the capacity of elected officials to deal with many important public issues and necessitated the restructuring of many governmental institutions. Thus MPs and even cabinet ministers are often incapable of fully understanding the problems and options confronting them, and the normal structures of ministries is being supplemented by a large number of quasi-independent administrative, regulatory and judicial boards and commissions not directly responsible to the elected representatives of the public or to party politicians. In short, an important shift has occurred in the locus of power of liberal democracies, from elected politicians to appointed civil servants, whose links to political parties are indirect and increasingly tenuous. This means that parties, supposedly in control of the political process and responsible to the public for its performance, are often little more than impotent observers of processes they cannot control and the results of which they can only rubber stamp.

A good illustration is the case of irregularities in the sale of reactors by Atomic Energy of Canada Ltd., a crown corporation, to Argentina and Korea. There were strong suspicions that bribes had been paid and that the foreign exchange regulations of some countries had been violated. Enormous commissions were also allegedly paid to shadowy foreign agents. One of the reactors was sold at a loss of over 100 million dollars. The Public Accounts Committee of the House of Commons held extensive hearings and questioned closely Mr. J.L. Gray, president of Atomic Energy of Canada at the time of the sales. His stonewalling of the issue, and that by everyone else connected with the matter, was so effective that the House of Commons committee failed to shed light on the sales and finally had to let the case rest.

Pluralism and the Rise of Interest Group Politics

Before the expansion of governmental activities and the increase in their complexity, the usual pattern of lawmaking was relatively simple. Ministers or the whole cabinet, with or without prompting by their civil servants, decided on the broad outlines of what needed to be done. Civil servants, drawing on expert knowledge and advice, prepared the necessary background papers and draft proposals. These were discussed by the ministers, in the absence of their civil servant advisors, and ultimately presented to parliament for enactment. The basic decisions were essentially those of politicians and their officials. More recently, a more involved process of legislation has evolved, partly because of the need to deal with problems having enormous ramifications, partly in an effort to make government more participatory, and partly in response to the claims of a market-oriented, pluralist society in which political parties depend on the financial support of powerful economic interests or of unions. Before any law or important administrative decision is decided upon, an intense consultation between officials and representatives of various vested interests takes place. There has been a striking increase in lobbying by interest groups who have the resources and capacity to do so. Many important decisions are arrived at through private consultations between civil servants and spokesmen for various vested interests, during which politicians play no role. By the time ministers enter the decision-making process, the die is cast and only minor changes, if any, can be made. The *general* interest, therefore, as aggregated by political parties, tends to receive scant attention and parties are left with little choice but to approve what has already been decided by others. The process of consultation is for the most part totally non-partisan and most ministers engaged in it act as governmental decision-makers, far removed from their party personas. For the government party caucus to disown government policies already decided on after considerable negotiations would be politically harmful and is hardly ever heard of. Convincing testimony to the relative impotence of parties is found in Robert Presthus's study of Canadian interest groups, which shows that the latter spend considerably more time and effort lobbying bureaucrats than members of parliament. Furthermore, it is clear that having recourse to pressure group participation in policy-making is not a feared or temporary phenomenon. The Canadian government, like many others, has institutionalized the practice by appointing large numbers of advisory committees and other bodies designed to ensure the pressure of interested parties in the policy process.

Incipient Corporatism

A related phenomenon received wide attention during the ill-fated, mid-1970s anti-inflation program of the federal government. Although the case is derived from Canadian experience, the phenomenon is not unique to this country. Efforts to control prices and wages required the cooperation of both management and labor. The idea was that economic policy would emurge from regular consultations between the federal government and representatives of labor, industry and business and that a group comprised of these interests would become institutionalized as a permanent consultative body. In the end, this structure was never established. It is difficult to see how this kind of change in the governmental process could have been made without undermining the power of parliament and hence of political parties. Compromises delicately wrought by a tripartite council would not likely be upset by the House of Commons even if members of the majority party wished to repudiate the deals made by their leadership.

Recourse to the tripartite consultative process reflects a tendency toward a new form of corporatism—a process of arriving at collective decisions through the efforts of representatives of the main "functional" interests in the country rather than of its territorial delegates. Because corporatism is usually associated with fascism, it is viewed with suspicion; but there is nothing inevitably authoritarian in it. There are corporatist elements in the usually highly regarded Swedish politico-economic system. But whatever its general merits, corporatist institutions supplement legislature and reduce the importance of political parties.

A more recent example of a variant of the corporatist approach concerns the Trudeau government's so-called "Six and Five World." This policy designed to reduce inflation was conceived and launched entirely without any involvement of the Liberal party and its success depended very heavily on the government's ability, in private conversations and negotiations with industry, to ensure voluntary compliance by the private sector with the guidelines. While decidedly non-partisan, it diverged from the corporatist model by not resting on the collaboration of government, business and industry, as well as labour. The latter was bitterly hostile to the program and vigorously repudiated it. It should, however, be noted that in the execution of the scheme, Senator Keith Davey, the quintessential Liberal party activist, played a key role on the committee guiding the implementation of the "Six and Five" program. But he was asked to perform this task because of his personal qualities and not because of his party connections.

Federal-Provincial Diplomacy

Another and increasingly threatening cause of the decline in the importance of parties lies in the changing nature of Canadian federalism. Accommodation between the various regions of the country (and to some extent, between special interests which happen to be in part regionally based) is taking place more and more through two mechanisms which are largely unrelated to party politics. The first of these is the federal-provincial prime ministerial conference, where Ottawa and the provinces hammer out compromises touching virtually every aspect of human experience. Most of these are the result of delicate bargaining on the part of eleven governments which sometimes cannot help but take positions imposed by other negotiators and which therefore cannot be anticipated by legislative caucuses, let alone by party supporters.

The second procedure through which policies are agreed upon by the federal and provincial governments is the regular meeting and consultation among federal and provincial officials. There are now thousands of such encounters annually and hundreds of formally established committees, task forces and work groups in which decisions are made which bind the participating governments. As with prime ministerial meetings, these encounters reach decisions which can be reversed or altered only at great cost—one not likely to be risked by rank-and-file members of political parties.

It can be argued that governments, at the ministerial level, are composed of leading party politicians and that their actions are in a sense those of political parties. This is technically correct, but the infrequently and unfocused expression of party opinion and the almost nonexistent party activity between elections deprive elected officials of any viable contact with their party organisms. There is, in contrast, a striking frequency and intensity of contacts between office-holding politicians and civil servants and spokesmen for vested interests. It is no exaggeration to argue that although ministers, and through them, the officials who serve under them, formally reflect party interests, they do not do so in any meaningful way. Between elections, except for occasional and exceedingly rare party gatherings, the cabinet *is* the party, insofar as the government side of the equation is concerned. Thus, such major policy changes as the introduction of wage control in the 'seventies and Trudeau's 1983 resolve to play a mediating role between the superpowers were introduced without any party involvement of any sort.

The Rise of Electronic Media

Until the advent of radio and particularly of television, politicians were the most effective means through which the public learnt about political events. In many communities across the country the political meeting was not only an important means of communication but also prime entertainment. Political issues were personalized by politicians who, in addition to adding colour to the consideration of matters of public policy, lent the political process a gladiatorial dimension that heightened its public appeal.

Television has, to a great extent, changed all that. The average Canadian spends several hours a day watching all manner of programs among which political material plays a relatively minor role. The entertainment value of face-to-face politics has declined since there are so many other exciting things to watch. And the public perception of the political process and of political issues that remains is derived from television treatment of the news and of political personalities. Public taste and public opinion on almost everything is being shaped by television programs and television advertising. Politics and politicians are filtered by a medium in which the primary concern is often not enlightenment, knowledge or consciousness-raising but maximal audiences and profits. This has meant that even major political events like the choosing of national party leaders are dominated by the requirements of television. The organization and scheduling of meetings are arranged so that the most appealing events occur during prime time, when they are broadcast, and all other aspects, even the quality of discussion and the time spent on critical issues, are made subservient to the demands of the electronic media.

Television has to some extent wrested the limelight from party politicians; but, on the other hand, it provides a matchless opportunity for the public to witness the party game. Its coverage of the most colourful political events—leadership conventions, elections, and so-called debates between party leaders—furnishes unprecedented opportunities for parties to be seen in action. The problem is, of course, that the exposure is chosen by the media largely for entertainment value, rather than as a continuous in-depth exploration of the dominant political issues and partisan strategies. The focus tends to be on the people who report and comment on political news rather than on the political actors themselves. One result of this tendency is that public opinion on political matters is shaped as much by media intermediaries as it is by the protagonists representing the various parties. Furthermore, the key role of television is changing the character of political leadership. It is now virtually impossible for anyone who is not "telegenic" to be chosen as party chief. His or her presence and style on television can make or break a politician; yet, these are only some (and not the most important) attributes of an effective political and governmental figure.

Investigative Journalism

Although television has come to occupy a key position in the manner in which the public perceives political and party life, it has not eclipsed the more traditional ways of reporting and analyzing news and of entertaining the public. Newspapers and periodicals still receive considerable attention, particularly among the politically most active members of the public. Partly, no doubt, in response to the competition provided by TV and partly because of the intense rivalry among some of the major printed media, newspapers and magazines have recently resorted to numerous ploys designed to attract attention and a wider audience. Among these, investigative journalism—a return of sorts to the old muckraking days—has been particularly important. Many of the major papers and some of the periodicals have sought to discover governmental lapses and to reveal wrongdoing on the part of local, provincial and federal authorities. These efforts at exposing flaws and shortcomings, errors, dishonesty and inefficiency perpetrated by governments have often led to the establishment of judicial and quasi-judicial inquiries and to the corroboration of the sins unearthed by sleuthing journalists. The watch-dog function of the print and electronic media is important to the present argument because it can be seen as an encroachment upon, or at least a complement to, the role of opposition parties. They, of course, are the agents par excellence, according to conventional theory, for keeping governments on their toes and for publicizing their misdeeds.

Although opposition politicians and investigative journalists no doubt derive mutual benefit from one another's activities, the recent increase in the role of the media as agents unearthing governmental malfeasance, regardless of how beneficial it may be, detracts from one of the most essential roles of opposition parties—that of criticizing the government. This is not to say the activities of the journalists inhibit or hamper opposition politicians; on the contrary, the latter exploit them; but the relative importance of government debate is reduced when much of the combat occurs outside the party arena—on the printed page or the television screen. One of the questions presented by the new or perhaps revived emphasis in the media on tracking down governmental errors of commission or omission is in fact whether the often vigorous and reportorial initiative of the media does not reflect a decline in the energy and resourcefulness of opposition parties. Like many of the arguments presented above, this is a question requiring systematic research.

Whatever the reasons, a considerable challenge of, and check on, governments today originate outside the realm of political parties and tend to reduce the effectiveness of the party system. The media may be able to report governmental failings, but they cannot provide alternative governments—one of the functions of opposition parties. By sharing with others the task of exposing and criticizing official actions (and by often being outdone by them), opposition parties lose some of their credibility as alternatives to the current power-holders.

Opinion Polling

Increasingly widespread use of opinion polls by the small groups of officials and cronies working with the party leader has diminished the need to rely on the knowledge of public attitudes by local militants and elected politicians. The vast, sensitive network of contacts, reciprocal favours, and exchanges of information which characterized the relationship between party leaders and their followers has to some extent been attenuated by the use of scientific sampling, sophisticated interviewing techniques and subtle statistical analyses. While the results are in some respects more reliable, there is also a decided loss: the interplay between public opinion and the leadership exercised by politically informed and concerned activists is substantially reduced. There is likely less debate and argument, since local party people are no longer encouraged to take the pulse of their "parishioners" and to mediate between the grass roots and the leadership. Public opinion, as defined by pollsters, guides political decisions more and political decision-makers are less involved in forming public opinion. Two consequences, at least, are relevant for our purposes: the character of political leadership and of political styles has changed and the party organization is no longer needed as an essential information network.

The Domination of Economic Interests

There is little agreement among scholars about the exact role of economic factors in the sociopolitical realm. Are the forces and relations of production basic causes of all other aspects of social organization or can social organization be manipulated through political means? Whatever one's judgment, one does not need to be an economic determinist to acknowledge that governments have frequently found it difficult to resist certain kinds of economic pressures or to work against certain economic realities. This vulnerability is enhanced by the greatly increased number and power of multinational corporations. These vast, global-girdling enterprises are rarely dependent on their operations in any one political jurisdiction and are adept at playing one interest against another. The behaviour of the oil companies before, during and after the oil crisis of the seventies is a case in point. Even those who doubt that Canadian industry and business can withstand governmental pressure cannot ignore the fact that the multinationals, recognizing no loyalties other than to their balance sheets, can obviate, ignore, influence and even dominate Canadian governments. A striking example came to light in the autumn of 1977 when Inco, a Canadian-based multinational, which has benefited from lavish tax and other concessions, announced that it would lay off 3,000 employees in Canada. Against arguments to the effect that the company was at the same time using funds provided by Canadian taxpayers to expand productive capacity overseas, a senior vice-president indicated that "fears of government takeover and other economic recriminations in Indonesia and Guatemala forced Inco...to cut back production in Canada where massive layoffs could be made with little prospect of serious political interference." This episode provides an illuminating vignette illustrating the impotence of the Canadian government and of Canadian political parties, in the face of economic pressure from industry. This subservience of the political realm to the economic is related to the prevailing value system and dominant ideologies: when parties and governments buckle under economic pressure, they do so because they do not believe in interfering with private enterprise.

One-Party Dominance

Finally, among the long-run, general factors leading in the decline of party in Canada is the very nature of the Canadian party system. Its chief feature during this century has been that it is a one-party dominant system, in which the important alternation is not between different parties but between majority and minority Liberal governments. Increasingly, the line between the government and the Liberal party has become tenuous, leading Liberals have become ministerial politicians and the opposition parties have been out of office for so long that they are seldom perceived as being capable of governing, sometimes (according to one scholar) even by themselves.

Canada has long been in a situation in which there has been a serious loss of confidence in the government and in the government party and at the same time no corresponding or compensating sense that the opposition might do better. The latter was perceived as inexperienced, fragmented and disposed to attack on principle everything and everyone who had anything to do with the government. Public opinion polls taken after the 1975 Conservative leadership convention showed a major decline in Liberal support and a corresponding upsurge in Conservative fortunes, but the election of a Parti Québécois government in November 1976 reminded Canadians of the woefully weak position of the Conservatives in Québec and of the fact that, in the past, only the Liberals (among the major parties) have tried to find a satisfactory accommodation between French and English Canada. The fear of national disintegration drove many voters back towards the Liberals, albeit with very little enthusiasm. Despite extensive doubt about the Liberals' capacity to provide adequate government (particularly west of the Ottawa River), the Conservatives were able, after the 1979 election, to form only a minority government which was toppled a few months after coming to power by the combined vote of the Liberals and the NDP.

This reinforced the already strong sense, among most leading Liberals, that they are indispensable and (since the Canadian public seems to recurrently favour them), nearly infallible in dealing with Canadian problems. The sense of self-assurance—an increasingly important element in the party's physiognomy—has itself contributed a great deal to the decline of party in Canada.

Among the many other consequences of one-party dominance, one requires special notice in the present context. The less favoured parties (unless they are essentially doctrinaire organizations which attract ideologues regardless of electoral opportunities) experience great difficulty in attracting candidates of top quality. Highly successful and ambitious individuals do not, for the most part, wish to foresake promising careers in exchange for a difficult electoral campaign and, at best, an almost permanent seat on the opposition benches. In a system in which parties in power alternate, able deputies know that part of their career is likely to be spent in the cabinet and they may therefore be attracted to a political career even if their preferred party does not, in the short run, seem to stand a good chance of election.

Short-run Causes: The Liberal Style

Disdain of Parliament

Prime Minister Trudeau is not, as has often been noted, a House of Commons man. He seems to hold parliament in low esteem and is on record as questioning the intelligence of his opponents. He seldom uses parliament as the platform for important pronouncements, preferring to deliver policy statements or general reflections on the state of the country in public speeches, television interviews or press conferences. Having entered politics relatively late in life, and having been strongly critical of the Liberals, Pierre Trudeau's personal circle appears to be outside the ranks of the party he now leads, and outside of parliament. The two intimate colleagues who entered politics with him, Jean Marchand and Gérard Pelletier, were also not at home in the House of Commons milieu and have retired from it.

A significant decision of Mr. Trudeau, in the present context, was his move in 1968 to establish regional desks within the privy council office, which were designed to keep abreast of developments and ideas in the regions. A more party-oriented prime minister would have relied on his party contacts and on colleagues in the

House of Commons rather than on civil servants, and there was much criticism of the prime minister's move in the House of Commons and privately, among Liberal back-benchers. The desks as such have been abandoned but the government continues to bypass the House of Commons on some critical issues.

Examples abound of the Trudeau government wishing to bypass parliament, presumably so as to escape unfavourable or contentious publicity. After the first election of the Parti Québécois, for instance, opposition spokesmen sought an extensive House debate and the establishment of a parliamentary committee which would engage in a searching and continuous consideration of Canada's crisis of unity. The government provided for a three-day parliamentary debate and refused to establish the requested committee. Instead, the prime minister created special national unity groups of officials in the privy council office and established a task force on national unity under Jean-Luc Pépin, a former cabinet minister, and ex-Premier John Robarts of Ontario. Important government decisions, like those dealing with the testing in Canada of the Cruise missile or with the abandonment of Via railway lines, are announced when the House is recessed, and frequently news which is likely to embarrass the government is released late on Friday, thereby precluding its receiving the immediate attention of the House. These moves bespeak a lack of enthusiasm for using parliament as an instrument for fashioning—as distinct from merely legitimizing—national policy. And to play down parliament is to play down political parties, since their chief national arena is the House of Commons.

Confusing the Public

A certain amount of sophistry is indigenous to politics when it comes to governments justifying their failure or unanticipated changes in their policies or strategy. But the public is not likely to maintain respect for either its government or the whole political system when it is confronted by an administration which, after an election, completely repudiates a major policy stand or when it welcomes into its ranks a former opposition member who has been a vociferous leader against one of its most important pieces of legislation. The Liberal party has done both, thereby weakening confidence in the integrity of our political parties and of their practitioners.

One of the principal differences in the platforms of the Liberal and Conservative parties in the 1974 election was the question of how to combat inflation. The Conservatives advocated a temporary price and wage freeze (pending the development of a permanent policy), for which the Liberals excoriated them, arguing that the public would never accept such controls. Having done much to undermine confidence in officially sanctioned constraints, and having given the impression that Canadians could not be trusted to cooperate in such a program, the government in 1975 introduced its own anti-inflation program, which froze wages and tried (unsuccessfully) to control prices. Not surprisingly, the government that campaigned on a vigorous anti-controls platform encountered considerable opposition when it tried to apply them.

The general language policy of the Official Languages Act of 1969 is one of the most important Liberal government attempts to promote national unity. Robert Stanfield, then Conservative leader, succeeded in persuading his party to follow him in supporting the language bill, but he was challenged and about twenty of his followers broke party ranks. None of them was more implacably opposed to efforts designed to assure that both French and English speaking Canadians could deal with the federal government in their own language than Jack Horner, the member for the Crowfoot constituency in Alberta. Mr. Horner had consistently been one of the most savage opponents of efforts to protect the French language and to create in Canada an ambience agreeable to francophones. However, after unsuccessfully contesting the Tory leadership, Mr. Horner became disillusioned with the leadership of his successful rival, crossed the floor of the House, and ultimately became a Liberal cabinet minister.

It is not always easy to distinguish between our two old parties but some basic diverging orientations do in fact divide them. One is the attitude they adopt towards French Canada. Although the official leadership of the Conservative party has, under Robert Stanfield, Joe Clark and Brian Mulroney, been sympathetic to the aspirations of French Canada, the party has always been plagued by a bigoted wing of members who lacked comprehension of and sympathy for Quebec. Mr. Horner, as a leading member of this group, was a strange bedfellow for the Liberal MPs, the former targets of his venom. While this move gave the Liberals a much needed prairie seat and Mr. Horner a cabinet post long before he might otherwise have received one (if ever), it made a mockery of what our political parties allegedly stand for.

Decline in Ministerial Responsibility

It has been a cardinal principle of the cabinet system of government that individual ministers are responsible for anything that is done by the ministries and departments for which they are responsible. The civil service is supposed to be an anonymous body without political views, obediently carrying out the commands of its masters, the politicians. This has always been something of a fiction, of course, since senior civil servants must provide useful advice and so there is no point in their totally ignoring the partisan and political constraints impinging on the ministers. The tendency for ministers and deputy ministers to see the world in like fashion is particularly pronounced in a one-party dominant system in which the collaboration between a minister and his or her deputy may continue for many years. All this notwithstanding, the principle of ministerial responsibility has had a long and respected tradition in Canada, at least in the sense that ministers, as politicians, have assumed complete responsibility for the actions of their civil servants and their departments. The political party in office has thus been the beneficiary of all the popular things done by the public service and the victims of its failings.

Recent developments have altered the once well-established principle of ministerial responsibility. First, there is a rapid turnover in the various ministries. The result is that few ministers have a chance to master the complex business of their ministry before they are assigned a new portfolio. While an alert and hard-working minister can be briefed fairly quickly by his new subordinates, it takes a prodigious amount of work and insight, and a great deal of time, to be able to become the effective head of a department and to lead it. Until this happens—and many ministers of course never gain the upper hand—the politicians are in a sense the captives of their officials. Ministers may, under these conditions, take formal responsibility for what is done in their name but the real power lies elsewhere.

The Trudeau government has gone further than any of its predecessors in accepting ministerial *lack* of responsibility for the actions of officials and in so doing has brought about an important revision in our constitutional practice. Trudeau's ministers have steadfastly refused to resign when consistently harassed by opposition members, sometimes for the excellent reason that the bloodthirsty cries of their opponents were unjustified and irresponsible. But there have been several instances when, under previous custom, ministers would have backed down, whereas members of the Trudeau cabinet, supported by their leader, refused to assume responsibility for the actions of people working under them. The most notorious, and on other grounds, exceedingly troubling, case of this concerns revelations, made in 1977, about RCMP break-ins and other illegal acts in 1972 and 1973. The government's cavalier manner of responding to this situation need not detain us here, although it is another instance of the government undermining public trust in the political process. The relevant point is that the government defence was simply that the then solicitor-general (the "responsible" minister) had not been informed of the RCMP's actions and since the particular minister had been moved to another department, the principle of ministerial responsibility was no longer applicable. The former solicitor-general at first failed even to make a statement to the House about the whole affair, although he later did deliver one. Members of the RCMP repeatedly broke the law and no minister took responsibility for these extremely serious transgressions. If a party holding office is no longer accountable for what is being done by officials under one of its ministers, the party system cannot ensure that governments are responsible to the electors. This state of affairs makes a mockery of democratic procedures and further diminishes the credibility of political parties.

Plebiscitary Tendencies

All of the short-run causes for the decline of party mentioned so far were laid at the doorstep of the Liberals. While that party has been an important cause of the process of party attenuation, it should not, of course, be assumed that it is the sole culprit. The opposition parties have been unable to present an acceptable alternative and have failed to convince the public that they could remove some of the ills currently afflicting the country. Nor can party politicians of any stripe be held responsible for the fact that much of the political decision-making has shifted from the conventional sites to federal-provincial negotiations, where parties do not fit neatly.

A recent factor that might possibly further impair the viability of parties is also not the Liberals' making, although Mr. Trudeau's reaction to it might exacerbate its effect on the place of parties in our system. The Parti Québécois' insertion of the referendum into our political process takes away from the monopoly enjoyed by parties in deciding certain issues. The PQ is of course not the first to introduce direct consultation of the public to Canadians. W.L. Mackenzie King had recourse to this device during the conscription crisis in the Second World War, and two referenda were held before Newfoundland became part of Canada. But the commitment of the PQ government to conduct a referendum to decide whether Quebecers wish to break or redefine their relationship with the rest of the country has brought forth an indication that Ottawa might itself conduct a similar vote.

Referenda normally ignore political parties and emphasize policy options, thereby diminishing the importance of parties in the political process. If they are held very infrequently, and only with respect to such fundamental issues as the nature of the country and its constitution, then they are unlikely to do much damage to the role of parties. But once they are used in one case, it may be impossible to prevent them from being applied to other issues—for example, the reintroduction of capital punishment, or language legislation—and they might slowly usurp some of the functions performed by parties. Any federal recourse to referenda is therefore seen by some opposition members as a potential further encroachment on the traditional role of parties.

Conclusion

The above catalogue of factors and developments reducing the relative importance of parties touches only some of the highlights; it is a partial and superficial lo k at a very complex phenomenon. This article's emphasis on federal politics has, for instance, led it to neglect the all-important provincial sphere and the interaction between federal and provincial party organizations. And our skimming of the high points has led to a neglect of some serious questions posed by these developments. We might have asked, for instance, whether the reason for the Liberal party's role in reducing the importance of parties is to be found in the fact that it is a quasi-permanent government party or in some special characteristics associated with Canadian Liberalism at the federal level. Does the Ontario Conservative party play a similar role in the decline of party in that province?

Our purpose here is not to answer these kinds of questions, important though they are, but to indicate that significant changes are occurring which alter the role played by political parties. If a series of limited advantages is allowed to reduce the overall effectiveness of a major mechanism for decision-making without producing at least an equally useful alternative, then the cost to society may be unexpectedly high. One is reminded in this connection of one of R.K. Merton's celebrated "theories of the middle range:"

> Any attempt to eliminate an existing social structure without providing adequate alternative structures for fulfilling the functions previously fulfilled by the abolished organization is doomed to failure.

Now it is true that no one is consciously trying to eliminate Canadian parties or even to reduce their importance, and that Merton was thinking of the return or rebirth of a structure whose function was needed. But the parties' sphere of influence and effectiveness is being reduced, by design or not. It may be to the country's advantage to reassign the functions of parties if they are being neglected: society might find other ways of performing these needed functions. There is a danger, however, that the alternatives may be less satisfactory and in other respects—in the field of individual freedom, for instance—potentially very harmful.

The Canadian party system is far from being perfect, but the world is full of examples showing how appalling some of the alternatives can be. That considerable reform is needed is clear. We can benefit from some of the changes occurring now and from ones which could be instituted. Students of Canadian parties need to decide which features deserve preservation and which require change. And before they are in a position to do that, they must undertake more extensive study of the issues raised here

Notes

1   "The American Party Systems," *American Political Science Review* (vol. 48) and *Democracy and the American Party System* (New York: Harcourt, Brace and Co., 1956) particularly chap. 7.

2   Neil A. McDonald has thus succinctly summarized the argument of A.N. Holcombe. See McDonald's *The Study of Political Parties* (New York: 1955).

3   See Gabriel Almond, "Comparative Political Systems," *Journal of Politics* (vol. 18), pp. 391-409 and Seymour Martin Lipset, *Political Man* (New York: Doubleday and Co., 1960).

4   "The Two-Party System in British Politics," *American Political Science Review* (vol. 47). For the view that "Canadian politics should be seen as the product of the failure of British Parliamentary institutions to work

in a complex of North American federal union" see Seymour Martin Lipset, "Democracy in Alberta," *Canadian Forum* (vol. 34). See also D.H. Wrong, "Parties and Voting in Canada," *Political Science Quarterly* (vol. 73) and F.H. Underhill, "Canadian Liberal Democracy in 1955" in G.V. Ferguson and F.H. Underhill, *Press and Party in Canada* (Toronto: Ryerson Press, 1955).

5   See also Leslie Lipson, "Party Systems in the United Kingdom and the Older Commonwealth," *Political Studies* (vol. 7).

6   R. McG. Dawson, *The Government of Canada* (Toronto: University of Toronto Press, 1957).

7   J. Meisel, "The Formulation of Liberal and Conservative Programmes in the 1957 Canadian General Election," *Canadian Journal of Economics and Political Science* (vol. 26).

8   For a full account of the party metamorphosis at this time see J. Meisel, *The Canadian General Election of 1957* (Toronto: University of Toronto Press, 1962).

9   See J. Meisel, "The June 1962 Election: Break-up of Our Party System?" *Queen's Quarterly* (vol. 59).

PART 3 The Third Party System

In the 1960s, national politics in Canada was reshaped with the development of executive federalism which drained the second system's parties of their brokerage functions. New patterns of national political competition, and with that new party structures and organizations were called into being. As Joseph Wearing recounts in his book *The L-Shaped Party*, the Liberals pioneered many of the new centralized campaign forms while attempting to give their extra-parliamentary organs a participatory cast. Later, in the 1970s, the Conservatives would lead in the development of new fund-raising techniques that allowed their organization to leap-frog the governing Liberals. The New Democrats, for their part, attempted to build a national party based on an explicit and formal partnership with the trade union movement.

John Courtney's paper demonstrates that the rules of the game for the third party system are quite distinctive. The critical role of political parties in the country's governing processes has finally been recognized and institutionalized, allowing them to play a fuller part in national politics. It has also made it possible for parties to be regulated by the state. This new environment has had an especially dramatic impact on party finances and electoral activity, which in turn has stimulated demand for further public regulation. It seems likely that the 1990s will see a second major round of legal changes governing the role and activities of Canadian parties.

A good deal of the agenda for further regulation and change is set out in *Reforming Electoral Democracy*, the four volume final report of the Royal Commission on Electoral Reform and Party Financing released in early 1992. Given that there is not a large literature about the organization and activities of national parties in the third system, the research reports prepared by the Commission will provide a rich source of material when published in 1992 and 1993. Here we have an extract from the Report that describes the basic constitutional and organizational forms of the national parties. As a marriage between the second party system's CCF and the Canadian Labour Congress, the NDP is sometimes characterized in the media as a tool of organized labour. Keith Archer's piece, taken from his book on the party, provides an assessment of just how accurate that portrayal really is.

Canadian party leadership is often precarious, not only because of the exaggerated expectations parties often have of their leaders, but also because the parties themselves are rather amorphous organizations. Leslie Pal describes ten sides of the leader-party dynamic, and while he is particularly interested in prime ministers, much of what he says is true for all party leaders. Indeed the invention of leadership reviews in the two old parties has made the position of opposition party leaders even more difficult. Joe Wearing's rules for leadership candidates reveal much about how modern party leaderships are won and, by implication, sustained. Lawrence Hanson's paper describes the delegate contests in the 1990 Liberal leadership contest. It reveals just how deeply into the party personal factionalization reaches in a contemporary leadership contest.

In two further excerpts from the Royal Commission report we have accounts of two aspects of party life: nominations and finances. The nomination process has been slow to change: it remains the private (unregulated) business of constituency party associations and provides local party activists with their greatest opportunity to make their preferences felt. As this account indicates, popular images of it as conflictual and overrun by narrowly-based ethnic and interest groups are misleading. (For a striking example of the conflict version see the National Film Board's *The Right Candidate for Rosedale*). Though it is a remarkably open process, most party nominations in fact continue to go uncontested. Party finances, on the other hand, are quite unlike those of the preceding period. The reforms of the mid-1970s, including the infusion of large sums from the public purse, have altered the ways parties have raised and spent money and in so doing changed the very character of them as organizations and as competitors.

At the beginning of the century, Siegfried observed that Canadian "parties exist apart from their programmes, or even without a programme at all" so that electoral contests were marked by "the absence of ideas or doctrines". In his essay Brian Tanguay explores the extent to which this is true in the electronic age. His analysis would not likely surprise Siegfried, though the latter would probably be interested to read Tanguay's analysis of the extent to which the imperatives of Canadian party competition have drawn the NDP into the same pattern as their two larger opponents.

Television, and later the computer, helped usher in the third party system. Jeremy Wilson's essay on horserace journalism reveals much about how contemporary journalists go about reporting politics and what implications this has for the relationship between party and media, and for modern parties' competitive behaviour. Wilson's study draws on data from the 1979 general election and by good fortune that is also the subject of an insightful National Film Board study of media-party relations called *History on the Run*. Where the media is concerned, readers should also become viewers and watch that film with Wilson's analysis in mind.

If television transformed the processes by which party politicians communicate with supporters and voters, then attitude and opinion polling transformed the ways in which the public communicates with politicians. Polls have also altered the character and substance of the conversations and the ways in which parties organize their approach to the electorate. David Walker, academic political scientist turned pollster turned campaign strategist and MP, provides a look at this side of modern parties. His judgment about their impact on modern Canadian party politics echoes that of Tanguay, but he concludes that polling is now firmly established as a central feature of party life in the third party system.

John C. Courtney Recognition of Canadian
Political Parties in Parliament
and in Law

Within many of the parliamentary systems founded on the Westminster model, part of the long-standing tradition of political parties has been based on their "nonexistence" in law and in Parliament. Such has been the case in Canada. Politicians and jurists alike have subscribed to the view that parties were neither acknowledged in the operations of Parliament nor recognized as legal entities in the courts of law. A typical expression by a politician of the view that parties were "unknown" to Parliament was delivered in the House of Commons in 1955. In the words of a CCF member of Parliament who addressed his colleagues on the subject of parliamentary rule changes:

> We have here 265 elected representatives of the people of Canada. We are not...here as representatives of either the Liberal, Conservative, CCF or Social Credit parties. I do my utmost to represent all the people in my constituency and I hope that we shall never change our rules in the House of Commons to the extent that we shall ever give official recognition to the existence of political parties.

> It is a valuable feature in the whole British parliamentary system that political parties as such are not recognized. If they are not recognized and if, in the first place, I owe my loyalty to this house as a member of the House of Commons and not as a member of the CCF, then it also is very important that we do not strengthen the hands of political organizations in Canada as such.[1]

From an examination of many such statements by parliamentarians, it appears that the unwillingness to acknowledge formally the presence of political parties within Parliament has rested on three complementary ideas: (a) a view of representation that was inherently individualistic; (b) a belief that the collective wisdom of individual members was to be preferred to the necessarily narrower and more particular points of view of political parties; and (c) a notion that a greater loyalty was owed to Parliament than to any political party. Clearly the party system was seen only as an instrument of election.[2]

Yet, as is so often the case in politics, some of the practices belie the theory. Over the years a good many changes have in fact been introduced in Parliament clearly contradicting the claims that parliamentarians have made regarding the "nonexistence" of parties. Since at least the late 1920s, separate rooms have been reserved for each of the parties for the purpose of holding regular meetings. In 1927, the Commons adopted a procedural change whereby an amendment to the amendment of a main motion would be accepted by the Speaker and voted on independently, a change that was of considerable import to the then existent third party and to all subsequent minor parties. Since the early 1950s, the Wednesday edition of *Hansard* has included a separate appendix listing the party affiliation of every member of Parliament. The House of Commons seating plan (printed primarily for distribution to visitors to the public galleries of the House) has for years not only acknowledged pictorially the old and basic fact that members of the same party sit together in the House, but, since 1968, it has also indicated the political affiliation of every member by including individual lists for each party. The numerical composition of parliamentary committees has traditionally resembled as closely as possible the relative standings of the parties in the House of Commons. Moreover, the principle has long been accepted that each party will itself select members of its own caucus to fill the positions it has been allocated on each committee.[3] In 1965, an all-party business committee was formally constituted under the standing orders for the purpose of planning the business of the House.[4] Such institutional phenomena have underscored the long-standing ascendancy of political parties in the House of Commons: since the 1870s, governments have been formed by, opposed by, and defeated by political parties. Members of Parliament might have preferred to think of themselves as representatives in some way "independent" of party (even though something as familiar to them as their recorded vote would not support such a notion), but clearly the whole operation of parliamentary government has been based on the existence of political parties. That parliamentarians have chosen to ignore one of the essentials of Canadian politics by continuing to subscribe to the view that parties were not to be acknowledged formally has served merely to widen the gap between theory and practice.

The claim that parties did not "exist" has had a good deal more truth to it in law than in parliamentary practice. Like trade unions in the early stages of their development, political parties in Canada have characteristically been looked upon as independent, private and voluntary associations beyond the jurisdiction of any law court. So rarely has a litigation involving a political party been brought before the courts that examples are difficult to locate. The most recent one, however, serves the purpose well. In 1971, an advertising agency in Montreal took legal action against the Progressive Conservative Party of Canada. According to the writ filed with the court the party was defined as "a group of persons associated for the pursuit of a common political purpose in Canada." Young and Rubicam Ltd., alleged nonpayment of a $70,000 debt outstanding from the 1968 election. The Quebec Superior Court upheld the decision of a lower court in dismissing the case. It noted that although the suit was "well founded in facts and in law" the court had no jurisdiction to hear the case for "no claim of this kind can be drawn up against a political party" as it has "no legal existence."[5]

Since the mid-1960s, a large number of changes have taken place that suggest that the traditional view of parties in Parliament and in law is no longer adequate. Canadian political parties now operate within a markedly different context than they did fifteen years ago. A variety of regulations, rules and statutory provisions affecting parties in some form or another have been introduced, making them the subjects of law and administrative regulations in such divers areas as broadcasting, taxation and election expenses. It is the purpose of this article to examine and to account for those developments in the Canadian party system that have contributed to the growing legal and parliamentary recognition of political parties, as well as to note at least some of the implications of such moves for parties now in the system and for the successful creation of new political parties. Changes prompted by the political events of 1963 ushered in the new era.

I

The federal election of 1963 confirmed what some astute observers had even then recognized as emerging and dominant features of the Canadian party system: third parties were a fact of Canadian political life, and it was increasingly apparent that no one party could count on winning a majority of the seats in the House of Commons. With the federal election of 1963, the Canadian electorate had voted for the fourth time in six years, and in only one of those contests (1958) had a majority government been elected. In 1963 the victorious Liberals wasted no time in seeking to consolidate their position as the new governing party in a "house of minorities." The government proposed and won support for an amendment to the Senate and House of Commons Act that entitled, for the first time in Canadian history, a party leader other than the prime minister and the leader of the opposition to an additional annual allowance. The definition of what was to constitute a "political party" was the critical element. According to the Act only those members who led a party with "a recognized membership of twelve or more persons in the House of Commons" would receive the additional stipend of $4,000 per annum.[6]

Two obvious questions arise from such a statutory definition. How was "recognized" membership to be determined? Why was "twelve" chosen as the cut-off number? The answers to both questions suggest an approach to parties in the Canadian Parliament fundamentally and unmistakably pragmatic.

With respect to the first question, the split in 1963 of the Social Credit party, which gave the new *Ralliement des créditistes* thirteen members and left the old Social Credit with the remaining eleven, came within weeks of the adoption of the legislation and brought the matter quickly to a head. With seventeen MPs, the New Democratic party accordingly made a claim to be seated next to the official opposition and to be granted speaking privileges in the House in keeping with its new-found status as the third largest party in the House. Social Credit, with fewer members than the *créditistes* and with parliamentary representation too small to entitle its leader to the additional allowance, nonetheless claimed speaking and seating priority over the *créditistes* on the grounds of historical precedence. The Speaker, not surprisingly, chose not to become involved. He made it clear that the "recognition" of a political party was the members' responsibility. "To my mind," he stated, "this is a question for the House to decide." The importance of the subject was obviously not lost on the Speaker given his closing remarks to his fellow MPs:

I cannot conclude this statement without some reference to the significance of these events for the future of the definition and status of parties in this house. It is not my place to evaluate the significance of these matters for the future of the ever changing structure and character of political parties; yet it is my duty, I believe, to bring to the attention of the house the novel character of the situation now before it, and more particularly the payment of allowances and the effect on the organization of parliament and parties and of the work of this house that naturally must be reflected by the emergence from time to time of new groups that invite the house to accord them the status of parties. Profound constitutional questions arise; for example, can a group of members which did not exist as a party at the time of the election of a parliament be recognized as a party before it has submitted itself to the electorate?[7]

In the event, the 1963 issue, like other less quarrelsome ones since, was resolved on a purely ad hoc basis through the adoption of a parliamentary committee's recommendations that were based on a combination of the NDP and Social Credit claims. The pressures of the moment were relieved, but beyond acknowledging the preeminence of the House in such matters and tacitly accepting the challenge to resolve each issue of "recognition" on its own merits, no long-term solution was given to the matter by members of Parliament. Nor has there been any since. The parliamentary counsel to the House of Commons acknowledged as much when he later wrote, in a background paper prepared for the Speaker, that the matter had been settled "but only for the time being."[8] Only one thing appeared reasonably clear. New legislation granting allowances to some, but not all, party leaders had become intermingled with procedural claims pertaining to speaking privileges and seating order. Technically the matters had nothing to do with one another. Yet the timing of the events was virtually certain to produce a combination that would lead to the injection of the phrase "recognized membership of twelve or more persons in the House of Commons" into future debates over regulations and statutes dealing with political parties. The term, indeed more specifically the number, would gradually assume an authenticity of its own.

Where did the number come from in the first place? It is now certain that the minority situation in which the new government found itself in Parliament provided the major motivation for the proposal to grant allowances to leaders of parties with twelve or more supporters. It is also certain that the proposal was exclusively the government's. The various opposition House leaders were informed of the government's intent, but they were not consulted about it. None objected to the proposal when it was presented to them for information, but the idea did not originate with them. According to the government House leader of the time there was little difficulty justifying the new allowances. Both Social Credit and CCF-NDP had survived for some thirty years; neither was likely to disappear at an early date; and their leaders had responsibilities above and beyond those of other MPs.[9] Stanley Knowles, NDP house leader at the time, concurred: "The extra work of those involved deserved to be covered, and we agreed that it was time to recognize a reality, namely that the House of Commons had become a multi-party institution."[10]

Much more to the point, however, was the fact that either or both of the Social Credit party (24 MPs) or the NDP (17 MPs) could ensure the government's survival on crucial votes. This was undoubtedly the primary reason for selecting in a strictly arbitrary fashion a number that would reflect, more or less, the long-term average parliamentary representation of the CCF-NDP and Social Credit. (The government House leader subsequently admitted that had he been more prescient he would have made sure that the number had been ten members rather than twelve so that both the Social Credit and the *créditiste* leaders would have received the allowance following the Social Credit split.) According to one government supporter at the time the Liberals were most anxious to ensure survival by accommodating the Social Credit group (especially their western wings) as much as possible. A Liberal cabinet minister active in presenting the government's case was even more forthright. The leader's allowance, he conceded, was dictated by a practical political consideration: "by a necessity of maintaining as much goodwill as possible in the House of Commons for a government which did not have a majority of its own supporters."[11]

Within two years of the adoption of the leaders' allowance legislation, the standing orders of the House of Commons were changed so as to recognize the right of "a spokesman for each of the parties in opposition to the government" to comment briefly in reply to a minister's statement on motions to the House.[12] Early in 1966, the argument was made by Progressive Conservative opposition members that the new standing order should be interpreted in the light of the 1963 amendment to the Senate and House of Commons Act—an argument that, if accepted, would have barred spokesmen for both the Social Credit and the *créditiste* parties given the decline in membership of those parties to five and nine members respectively in the 1965 election. Mr. Speaker rejected the Conservative argument by pointing out that, at least as far back as 1951, Speakers had accepted the principle that one spokesman for *each* opposition party would be allowed to comment on ministers' statements. He noted that the practice had been referred to in Arthur Beauchesne's authoritative work on Canadian parliamentary rules in its fourth edition (1958). Unless the House was prepared to define more precisely the standing order with respect to the right to comment on ministerial statements (something it so far has not chosen to do), the Speaker ruled that such a right should be accorded to the leader of the official opposition and, in his own words, to "spokesmen for the New Democratic Party, the Ralliement Créditistes, and the Social Credit Party" but not to "independent members."[13] The 1965 addition to the standing orders and the subsequent Speaker's ruling were important in two respects. (1) The fifteen-year custom of granting speaking privileges to a spokesman for each of the smaller parties in the House had been codified, but only after it had clearly emerged as an acceptable norm in the operations of the House. (2) The interpretation placed upon the new standing order by the Speaker (and subsequently accepted without challenge or argument in the House) was such as to distinguish that rule from the statutory definition pertaining to political parties. Significantly, the grounds for accepting separate arguments with respect to parliamentary procedures and statutes had been maintained.

II

For the past forty years Canadian broadcasting policy has clearly accepted the existence of political parties. In the Broadcasting Act of 1936 the Canadian Broadcasting Corporation was given full powers to guide and to oversee political broadcasting. According to section 22 of the Act, the CBC was empowered "to prescribe the proportion of time which may be devoted to political broadcasts by the stations of the Corporation and by private stations, and to assign such time on an equitable basis to all parties and rival candidates." In its original statement on the matter of political broadcasts (July, 1939) the board of governors of the CBC noted that:

> ...A Dominion general election is concerned with national problems.... [Our] proposals are...based on the fact that a federal campaign is essentially a contest in which opposing political parties seek to secure election of members of Parliament in order to control or influence the administration

of the country's affairs. It follows, therefore, that the network broadcasting *arrangements will be concluded exclusively with political parties*, and not with individuals as such, however important their place in public life.[14]

The governors saw their action as a "sincere attempt to establish a more rational and democratic basis for the conduct of broadcasting in general elections."[15]

The CBC devised a plan, in several respects modelled on the BBC election broadcasting policy in Great Britain, composed of five essential factors to be taken into account in allotting air time to political parties during an election campaign. The formula was based on some undisclosed mix of the following:

1. The standing of the parties in the House of Commons at dissolution.

2. The popular vote secured by each of the parties in the previous election.

3. The number of candidates nominated by each of the parties in the preceding campaign.

4. The standing of the parties in the House of Commons at the preceding dissolution.

5. The listener's right to hear an equal representation of the points of view of all existing parties.

In the event that new political parties might otherwise be debarred from sharing in broadcasting privileges because they failed to meet some or all of the foregoing provisions, a separate formula was designed to provide them with air time. Such a party was, among other things, expected to have:

1. Policies on a wide range of national issues.

2. A recognized national leader.

3. A nationwide organization established as the result of a national conference or convention.

4. Candidates nominated in at least three provinces and in at least one-quarter of the constituencies.

5. A campaign the nature of which demonstrated that the party had attained national proportions and significance.[16]

The CBC, no doubt anticipating complaints from, and quarrels with, at least some of the political parties over the allotment of time, noted cautiously that "the scheme must be considered largely as an experiment. Whether it is employed in subsequent elections will depend on how satisfactorily it works in the approaching one."[17]

There were objections following the 1940 election[18] and there have been intermittent ones since, but the key elements of the CBC formula have remained much the same. At the time of the 1972 federal election, for example, the CBC, acting under the joint requirements of the regulations of the Canadian Radio-Television Commission (CRTC) and the provisions of the Broadcasting Act (1968), provided free radio and television time

> to bona fide parties which are national in extent and which reflect a significant body of opinion throughout the country. While it is impossible to lay down an exact definition it is suggested that such parties should meet the following requirements:
>
> i. Have a recognized national leader.
>
> ii. Have a nationwide organization established as a result of a national conference or convention.
>
> iii. Have representation in the House of Commons.
>
> iv. Seek the election of candidates in at least three of the provinces and put into the field at least one candidate for every four constituencies.[19]

Regular free time political broadcasts between elections are allotted on essentially the same basis except that the provision regarding the Commons representation (iii) refers to "a group in the House of Commons under a recognized leader to whom the House had accorded privileges in the conduct of Parliamentary business."[20] Given Standing Order 15(3) adopted in 1965 and the Speaker's ruling of the following year, presumably any party whose leader has been accorded the right to comment in the House on ministerial statements would meet this particular CBC requirement.

There could be little doubt that the CBC formula for election campaign broadcasts had been designed in such a way as to favour those parties already in the system. The corporation's policy for "parties not represented in the House" was discretionary: free network time *may* have been allotted to parties with no representation in the House of Commons, if on or before nomination day, they provided "definite evidence" that they had a recognized national leader, a nationwide organization established as the result of a national conference or convention, and had candidates running in at least three provinces and one-fourth of all constituencies. The time allotted any such party, however, was not to have come at the expense of the established ones. It would have been "over and above the amount given to the federal political parties" already in existence and in no circumstances could it have exceeded "the smallest allotment received by a party" otherwise qualified.[21] As the formula was hammered out prior to each election with the appropriate radio and television authorities by some of the most experienced political-managerial talent available to the respective parties, and as the formula was dependent upon the number of seats held by all parties at dissolution as well as upon the seats and votes obtained in the preceding election, it is scarcely surprising that the broadcasting time was monopolized by the parties already institutionalized in the system. Only twice since 1953 have any parties other than the four established ones (five during the time of the Social Credit split) received free broadcasting time under the CBC formula.

Moreover, the broadcasting regulations themselves may have forced smaller parties into an unrealistic and basically futile expansion of electoral efforts at the very time that their scarce resources could have been used to greater advantage by concentrating on a relatively small number of seats. Such a suggestion has been advanced, for example, with respect to the NDP fortunes in Quebec.

The implications of the formula ought to have been obvious to any of the party personnel involved in reaching periodic agreements on the allotment of broadcast time. The CBC's commitment to some sort of "fairness doctrine" for *existing* parties meant that on the basis of a comparison of popular vote with broadcasting time the older and more national parties were bound to fare less well than the newer and more regional ones. The amount of air time allotted to the Liberals and Progressive Conservatives together never equalled (and, in a few cases, was even more than twenty percentage points below) the combined popular vote obtained by those two parties at the time of the preceding election. The CBC's 1939 reference to the listener's "right to hear an equal representation of the points of view of all existing parties" had not constituted the sole criterion for the allocation of time, but neither had it been ignored.

The free broadcast time for the 1974 election was the last to be allocated by the CBC. A new policy was contained in amendments to the Canada Elections Act adopted by Parliament prior to the

1974 election but effective only after the election. Henceforth the CRTC will be responsible for the allocation of the parties' shares of a block of time (6-1/2 hours) that all broadcasters will be required to provide during the last twenty-nine days of the election campaign. The allocation of any additional free time under the amended Act is to be determined between the parties and the television networks, with the CRTC involved only in the event no agreement could otherwise be reached.[22]

The impact of the new provisions regarding "registered" political parties and election broadcasting will likely be to reduce the amount of air time of the older and larger political parties and to benefit parties that have never had much in the way of popular support and, indeed, have never elected a member to the House of Commons. The distribution of free broadcast time in the 1974 election pointed in such a direction. Although it was not required to do so in 1974, the CBC chose to apply the provisions of the amended Act by allocating broadcast time to all registered parties that were entitled to have their party affiliation appear on the election ballots. Accordingly, the combined television time for the Marxist-Leninist and Communist parties amounted to nearly 6 per cent of the total.

III

Registration of political parties was first advocated federally by the parliamentary Committee on Election Expenses in its 1966 *Report*. Its two-year investigation of party and campaign financing led the committee to conclude that political parties ought to be recognized as legal entities so as to encourage "the development of the Canadian democratic system." Inevitably, the committee asserted without explanation that acceptance of the principle of legal recognition would mean that "political parties would not only enjoy legally recognized rights, but would equally incur legal obligations." Significantly, the committee's case for legal recognition of parties was argued on financial and political rather than on legal grounds: the electors were entitled to know "what the democratic system cost them." To ensure accurate financial reporting, agents would be named by parties and candidates. They would be held responsible for a full and exact accounting of their respective party's or candidate's financial affairs.

The committee's recommendations, which served as the basis for the widespread changes in the Canada Election Act adopted by Parliament in 1970 and in 1974, were unlike any proposed previously in Canadian party history. They were truly revolutionary by Canadian standards; as the committee itself acknowledged, they might even "necessitate changes in party structure"![23] The following were among the key committee recommendations subsequently adopted as part of the legislation governing the operation and financing of political parties: the registration of parties, the doctrine of financial agency, the acknowledgement of party affiliation on the ballots, and the consent of the regional leader for a party candidate to be accepted as such by the chief electoral officer.

With the adoption of the massive changes to the Canada Elections Act in 1970, the chief electoral officer was required to maintain a registry of political parties. In the process he was granted considerable power, both discretionary and mandatory in nature. According to the Act any party may file an application for registration so long as the application has been signed by the leader of the party and included all the necessary factual information.[24]

Registration is not automatic, however. It is up to the chief electoral officer to decide *whether to accept or to reject* the application outright. According to Act, the chief electoral officer is specifically instructed not to register a political party where he is of the *opinion* that the name or abbreviation of the party requesting registration so nearly resembles that of any party either (a) *"represented in the House of Commons immediately prior to the coming into force of this section,"* or (b) already registered with him, as to be *likely* to be confused with such a preexisting party.[25] At the time of the 1974 election the chief electoral officer utilized this power when he refused to register a party calling itself "The Communist Party of Canada (Marxist-Leninist)" because it too closely resembled the previously-registered "Communist Party of Canada." He agreed, however, to register that party under the name of "The Marxist-Leninist Party of Canada."

In addition to this discretionary power, the chief electoral officer has certain mandatory ones. He *must delete* from the registry those parties not meeting certain conditions. For example, the chief electoral officer is instructed via sections 13(8.1) and 13.3(1) of the Act (1974) to remove from the registry any party failing to appoint an auditor within thirty days of that party's organization.

Immediately prior to an election two separate sets of circumstances come into force under which a party *could* be deleted from the registry. (A) On or after the forty-eighth day before the election, the chief electoral officer *could* remove from the registry any party

(a) not represented by at least twelve members of Parliament that (b) by enumeration day had failed to file with the chief electoral officer a necessary statement of information. (B) Within thirty days of an election, the chief electoral officer could remove from the registry any party (a) not represented by at least twelve members of Parliament on the day preceding the dissolution of Parliament on the day preceding the dissolution of Parliament that (b) *had failed to nominate candidates in at least fifty* constituencies by the thirtieth day before the election. In each of the two instances (A and B) the power to delete could be exercised only if both of the two conditions (a and b) had been met. If neither of the two conditions, or if only one of them, had been met, then no deletion of the party name from the registry could take place.

The phraseology of this particular section of the Act could scarcely have been more awkward. Was it necessary to construct one long sentence of twenty-three lines containing reference to two different sets of circumstances within which *deletions* might take place by using no fewer than four negative expressions? The chief electoral officer, in a booklet entitled "Election Expenses and You" distributed to every household in Canada in 1974, simplified the language of the *Act* and he did a better job of explaining registration than parliamentarians:

A "registered political party" is defined in the Canada Elections Act as a political party which was either:

(1) represented in the House of Commons on the day before the dissolution of Parliament, immediately preceding the general election;

or

(2) thirty days before polling day at the general election had officially nominated candidates in at least 50 electoral districts in Canada.[26]

Under these conditions six parties qualified as fully registered at the time of the 1974 election: Liberal, Progressive Conservative, New Democratic, Social Credit, Marxist-Leninist, and Communist. Within a year the number had grown to ten and several more (including the Green Party and the Nude Party) had requested application forms.[27]

How many of the post-1974 group will in fact qualify at the time of the next election remains to be seen.

The intent of the registration provisions was clearer than the wording. Parties with a prescriptive claim based on twelve or more members in the House of Commons, as well as those with enough organizational ability to nominate at least fifty candidates for an election, would be assured of recognition. The discretionary powers of the chief electoral officer were designed to ensure some degree of fairness for parties failing to meet either or both of the conditions for registration; as a minimum this would almost certainly mean those parties with some historical precedence in the system. That, at least, appears to be the way in which the chief electoral officer interprets the matter. He is fully aware of the possibility of having to exercise such discretionary power in at least one instance in the near future—by leaving the Social Credit party on the registry at the next election even though it currently has fewer than twelve MPs and even if it fails to nominate fifty candidates.[28]

Registration has, in the period of a few years, emerged as a basic feature of the party system. It is now clear that certain rights and privileges will be accorded only to registered parties. Almost as a form of copyright, the names and abbreviations of existing parties are protected through registration. Candidates of registered parties are entitled to have their party name listed on the ballot alongside their own. Registered parties can benefit from particular features of the 1974 election expenses legislation—for example the tax credit scheme (advantageous to individual taxpayers) by which political parties may now collect funds. A share of 6-1/2 hours of prime-time broadcasting is guaranteed registered parties... It is clearly in a party's interest to become registered and to maintain its status as a registered group.

IV

The argument was made in the 1960s by the Committee on Election Expenses and others that if parties were to be granted certain privileges they should also be bound to assume certain obligations. To give weight to the argument required recognition of parties before courts of law. The Committee on Election Expenses argued that the principle of disclosure and limitation of a political party's income and expenditures "would be defeated if the financial agent of the candidate or party were permitted to plead that certain expenditures were made without his permission or knowledge." It was the committee's intent to guard against financial abuses by requiring each party to appoint "one or more official agents who would have the sole right to incur expenses on the party's behalf."[29] The principle of financial responsibility on behalf of the party would have to be spelled out carefully in statute. This has been done as part of the 1974 amendments to the Canada Elections Act:

> A prosecution for an offence against this Act...may be brought against a registered party and in the name of that party and, for the purposes of any such proescution only, the registered party shall be deemed to be a person and any act or thing done or omitted by an officer, chief agent, or other registered party within the scope of his authority to act on behalf of the registered party shall be deemed to be an act or thing done or omitted by that party.[30]

...Given the provisions of the Canada Elections Act regarding the doctrine of agency and a party's legal and contractual responsibilities arising therefrom,... it is virtually certain that Canadian courts in the future would accept such a case as *Young and Rubicam v. Progressive Conservative Party of Canada* that had been thrown out in the Quebec Superior Court in 1971 for lack of jurisdiction.... Canadian political parties no longer exist as purely voluntary and informal associations unknown to the law and without legal capacity. At least for the purposes of prosecution under the Canada Elections Act they now have assumed legal personality. It seems only a matter of time until the first cases involving political parties will be heard before Canadian courts.

V

Amendments to the Canada Elections Act adopted in 1970 brought to an end the practice dating back to 1874 of listing, next to a candidate's name, his address and occupation. Those two pieces of demographic information have been replaced with something new to federal ballots—the name of the candidate's political party.[31] But only candidates of registered parties are entitled to use their party name on the ballots. All others than those who wish to label themselves as "independents" are listed by name only. Party registration with the chief electoral officer, once again, has become the yardstick by which the privilege is either granted or withheld.

If candidates were to be allowed to include party labels alongside their names on the ballots, then any possibility of two or more candidates running against one another and using the same party label would have to be ruled out. A recent incident highlighted this point. In the last general election before the Canada Elections Act had been changed to allow party labels to be included on the ballots, two men contested the same Toronto seat as "Liberal" candidates. Ian Wahn had been the Liberal member of Parliament for the constituency since 1962 and had once again received the party nomination in the riding for the 1968 election. His defeated opponent for the nomination, Russell Taylor, nonetheless ran as a candidate in the election and proceeded to campaign as a "Liberal." He distributed election material and published advertisements to the effect that he was a "Liberal." Mr. Wahn, who had no objection to Mr. Taylor running as an "Independent Liberal," sought a court injunction to prevent his opponent from describing himself as a Liberal candidate. The request for an injunction was turned down in the Supreme Court of Ontario on the grounds that the dispute was a private matter and the court could not interfere in election procedures. In the event, both men continued to campaign as "Liberals" and Mr. Wahn was elected handily.

It was obvious, therefore, that under the amended Canada Elections Act someone would have to accredit or certify any candidate wishing to use a party label on the ballot. That task would clearly have to fall to party personnel and not to a public official such as the chief electoral officer.[32] Following the recommendations of the Committee on Election Expenses, the responsibility has fallen to the leaders of the recognized parties. According to the 1970 amendments to the Canada Elections Act:

> where a candidate has the endorsement of a registered party and wishes to have the name of the party shown in the election documents relating to him, an instrument in writing, signed by the leader of the party or by a representative designated by the leader...stating that the candidate is *endorsed by the party*, shall be filed with the returning officer at the time the nomination paper is filed.[33]

This section of the Act obviously enhances the position of the leaders of recognized parties in so far as they have been granted a power whereby they may accept or reject candidates nominated by the local constituency association. But as the act of choosing the party candidate is undoubtedly the most important single task that riding associations perform, and as the reference in the Act to a candidate "endorsed by the party" could be interpreted in a variety of ways, the seeds have been sown for potential intraparty disputes over the use to which that power might be put.

Such was the case at the time of the 1974 election when the Progressive Conservative leader, Robert Stanfield, refused to endorse Leonard Jones as the party's candidate in Moncton constituency. Mr. Jones had succeeded in winning the nomination at the local Progressive Conservative association meeting, but as his views on bilingualism were, according to Mr. Stanfield, contrary to "my party's established policy and my own principles,"[34] the Conservative leader deliberately bypassed him and named the former Progressive Conservative member for Moncton as the party's official candidate there. Mr. Jones apparently felt he was left no choice but to run as an "Independent." (He did, and he won.) However, as a purely speculative question, had he chosen to pursue the matter through the courts might he have been able to obtain a judgment on the meaning of the phrase "endorsed by the party?" Would the courts have held the leader's rejection of a candidate properly nominated at a local association meeting to be a sufficient (presumably it would be a necessary) condition in establishing "the party's" position on the matter? Given the arguable nature of the endorsement provisions of the Act, such might well be the sort of questions courts will be called upon to answer in the future.

The Jones case is also of interest in that the vehicle whereby the leader was able to step into an intraparty dispute was not of the party's own making. Rather, it was a statutorily-defined set of conditions enabling the leader to act authoritatively so as to alter a local association's decision with which he did not agree. In this particular instance it appears that the leader's prestige in some parts of the country may well have been enhanced, for Mr. Stanfield's move was seen as a sign of decisiveness and political courage; in other parts of the country the party may have been hurt by what many saw as interference by the leadership in a local association's business.[35] Be that as it may, there can be little doubt that the provisions of the Act, combined with the precedent established by the Jones case, provide a leader with the means to deal swiftly with a difficult political situation resulting from sharp differences over policy between the party's leadership and a particular candidate.

VI

In 1968, for probably the first time in Canadian history, the existence of political parties in the House of Commons was acknowledged in a Speech from the Throne. MPs were informed in very general terms of the government's intention so far as parliamentary parties were concerned:

> So that the Official Opposition, to which we in Canada give formal recognition as a vital part of our democratic process, as well as the other parties in opposition, may be in a position to cope more effectively with the heavy load of action each session must face, you will be asked to make new provisions for the Official Opposition, and the other parties in their Parliamentary role.[36]

The government had been urged for some time to provide a measure of financial support to the opposition parties so that they might establish reseach bureaus. The reasoning was obvious. Opposition parties found increasingly that they were unable "to compete with the expertise, inside knowledge, and extensive bureaucratic resources available to the government."[37] Their plea was for a "counter-bureaucracy," albeit a modest one by government standards.

When the plan was formally initiatied in 1969 a total of $195,000 was approved by Parliament to finance research offices for the three opposition parties. The total was allocated roughly in accordance with the number of MPs in each party, although the Social Credit party fared relatively better than either of the two other opposition parties given its small number of members. In the words of the prime minister, the government

> decided to do this by alloting a substantial amount of money to the Leader of the Opposition and a lesser amount to the leaders of the other parties which are recognized under the rules and regulations of the house, that is, those parties which have more than 12 members.[38]

As the principle behind the programme was to assist the opposition parties in their task of criticizing the government no funds were allocated to government members of Parliament. That quickly changed. Under pressure from Liberal backbenchers the original plan was modified at the beginning of the programme's second year. Not only were the government backbenchers to be included in the scheme, but as a group they were to receive the largest single allocation of any party in the House. Since then the Liberal research office has consistently received more than any other party's office.

Such a development suggests that the original aim of assisting opposition parties in their task of formulating reasonable criticisms of government policies was supplanted by a different view of how the "research" money might best be spent. Each party has been free to establish its own practices and priorities. Although some have used the money for blatantly political tasks more than others, all have most certainly welcomed the funds. Naturally it would be in a parliamentary party's self-interest to attempt to capitalize on the availability of funds and to maximize the amount of financial support it might obtain at any given time. By the same token the government must, in critical situations at least, be anxious to maximize its returns from the financial support it has agreed should be paid to its opponents at any given time.

Not surprisingly, the periodic redistribution of the funds has become a highly political act. Originally in 1969 the funding was based on lump sum grants that were to be revised annually. Following the near-defeat of the Liberal government in the election of October, 1972, and the return to a minority government situation (the first since the research assistance programme had been established), the Liberals were clearly going to be dependent upon NDP support for survival. The Social Credit representation was too small to save the government single-handedly and the Conservatives were determined to defeat the government. A formula that did away with the matching Social Credit and NDP lump support was speedily introduced and was in operation a month before the new Parliament opened. A comparison of party standings of the new House with those of the old at the time Parliament was dissolved reveals that the NDP stood to gain by far the most from the change: for each additional member elected to the new Parliament the Social Credit party received an additional $750, the Progressive Conservatives $1,265, and the NDP $3,916. For the first time in its brief history the formula, by which funds were determined, included a specific reference to "twelve" as the basic number of members needed for a party to qualify for assistance:

for parties with 12-20 members of parliament: $40,000 per party

for parties with additional members over 20 and up to 40: $2,000 per additional MP

for parties with additional members over 40: $1,500 per additional MP.

As a result of the next election in 1974, the Social Credit representation was reduced to eleven members and the majority Liberal government was no longer dependent upon the parliamentary support of another party. Under the formula Social Credit failed to qualify for a research bureau allocation. But within a month of the election the Social Credit leader, Réal Caouette, expressed no concern about the likelihood of the allocation being lost to his party. He was confident that his party would continue to be recognized in the House of Commons for the purposes of speaking privileges and research funds. History was the ground for his optimism. According to Mr. Caouette, the other parties in the House were not likely to object to Social Credit being accorded recognition as it had been a part of the Canadian political scene for some forty years. But he was certain that they would object to any group of less than twelve members in the House receiving similar privileges.[39] His confidence was not misplaced. On October 1, 1974, the formula was abandoned and lump sum payments were reintroduced. All opposition parties including the Social Credit received an increase in their research allocations even though all were returned with fewer members of Parliament.

Conclusion

The fiction that political parties do not exist in law or in Parliament need no longer be maintained. In a variety of ways the "existence" of parties has been accepted and provided for in statutes, formalized procedures, and custom, without much in the way of a complementary change in the theory of the place of parties in a parliamentary system. Of the major steps taken in the direction of acknowledging the existence of parties within the parliamentary system and recognizing them in statute, most have been taken in the last fifteen years. The ground-work had been prepared by incidental changes in parliamentary procedures in the 1920s and by some of the early broadcasting regulations of the 1930s. But the big shift started in 1963 when a new minority government proved to be most anxious to establish "goodwill" with the smaller parties in the House.

Such practical adjustments as have been made so far have been carried out within Parliament exclusively: its standing orders, speaking privileges, research allocations, and legislation. Courts have yet to confront the issue. But when they do, and that is no doubt only a matter of time, it will likely involve prosecutions under the election, broadcasting and taxation statutes. At that point, jurists will have no choice but to accept something they have so far rejected: the legal capacity of political parties.

So far as the parliamentary changes are concerned, the crassness and opportunism of the 1963 move (perhaps the abrupt change in the funding of party research allowances in 1972 ought to be included in this category) apparently tell a good part of the story. But such could by no means be considered as moves unique to the Liberal party. It would likely be difficult to find any party above currying favour with an opponent if its political survival were at stake. To judge the moves on those grounds alone misses the more important point respecting the gradual change and development of the party system over time and the unquestioned fact of 1963 (reinforced in 1972) that adjustments were required within the system so as to accommodate minor parties. The principle of equity would have been a sufficient and a proper reason, but for the timing. The unhappy dimension to such changes undoubtedly has come from the very arbitrariness of the acts themselves given the circumstances in which they were introduced.

In some of the provinces with laws relating to political parties, the experience has been much the same. In Manitoba, for example, special allowances are provided to a leader of a "recognized opposition party" defined as "the members of the assembly who belong to a political party that is represented in the assembly by four or more members."[40] This provision of the Legislative Assembly Act was added in 1970, a year following the Manitoba provincial election in which the NDP won twenty-eight seats, the Progressive Conservatives twenty-two and the Liberals four. Quebec, too, has approached the matter in much the same way. The laws governing leaders' allowances have been changed to include a provision regarding the percentage of popular vote (a minimum of 20 per cent) obtained by a party in an election as an alternative to the number of seats won by a party. This was obviously done to accommodate the *Parti québécois* whose six seats in 1970 and seven in 1973 (out of more than 100 seats in the legislature) by no means reflected its 12 per cent and 30 per cent of the popular vote in the elections of those two years. Following the 1976 Quebec election, the province's law was once again altered to accord certain privileges to the *Union Nationale*, that party having fallen short of the twelve seats and/or 20 per cent vote needed to acquire party status in the National Assembly. The arbitrariness of the most recent Quebec change was reinforced by the provision, the first of its kind in Canada, that it would last only for the duration of the present Legislature.[41] Presumably there was an unacknowledged acceptance of the premise that each new Legislature would deal with the issue on grounds appropriate to its political complexion at the time.

If the dominating theme behind the changes in the laws and regulations governing political parties continues to be one of pragmatism in keeping only with the political realities of the moment, then perhaps no major problems exist. One simply accepts the likelihood of periodic changes and leaves it at that. Yet such an explanation is unsatisfactory. It overlooks the fact that part of the arbitrariness, federally at least, is as a direct result of the continuing marginal support for the Social Credit party and the problems this obviously has created. The long-term prospects for the party are not bright, but if it manages in the next few elections to win in the order of ten to fifteen seats in the House, its presence will necessarily continue to require special solutions of an ad hoc nature if further procedural, regulatory and statutory provisions relating to political parties are to be implemented. Mr. Caouette, perhaps fearing the worst, introduced a private members' bill in 1975 to amend the Senate and House of Commons Act. It was as pointed as it was brief:

> Every political party enjoying the status of a party in the House of Commons shall continue to enjoy such status, including the rights and privileges accorded by custom, so long as the party maintains some representation in the House.[42]

The bill did not get beyond first reading.

One hesitates to dwell at length on the Social Credit party but its example highlights yet another point, that is the problem inherent in defining parties according to the number of members they happen to have in the legislature at a particular time. At the time the number is agreed upon the move may simply be seen as an act of discovering a realistic number that is mutually satisfactory to all concerned. The easy solution, one that clearly has been adopted by Canadian politicians, has been to establish a number low enough to encompass all parties represented at that time in the House. Difficulties can only result when one or more of the parties falls below that number, as the Social Credit experience indicates. Then the matter becomes one of testing the degree of commitment to the number *as a base* beyond which a party would be certain to lose its privileges. Since the 1974 election the Social Credit leader has continued to receive the additional $4,000 leader's allowance even though the number of Social Credit members of Parliament has fallen below the statutory minimum of twelve. Approval of the move, presumably following an all-party agreement to ensure parliamentary support, was given in October, 1974. At the same time, the allowance was made retroactive to the July election date earlier that year when Social Credit dropped to eleven members of Parliament. All this was done with the clear provisions of the law notwithstanding.[43]

The cynical explanation of the changes (parties look after their own interest first) may not be wide of the mark. Yet it excludes a far more important and obvious reality. By the late 1950s, the Canadian party system was, indeed it had been for some time, far removed from the two-party system idealized by nineteenth-century politicians and political commentators. Canadian third parties might never have come close to winning an election federally, but neither were they about to disappear. At least that proved to be the case with those parties created in the 1930s who could benefit from the experience of their short-lived predecessor of the 1920s. Once a serious claim had been staked by the parties over a series of elections (once, in other words, they had shown their political viability) it was only a matter of time until they were in a position to argue for and to expect fair and reasonable treatment as competitors within the system. Accordingly, adjustments were made in parliamentary procedures and privileges, statutes governing broadcasting and elections, and so forth. The rules, regulations and statutes were designed to provide *guarantees to the parties then in existence* as, for example, in the CBC denying any new party more free broadcasting time than the smallest amount granted to any party with representation in the House of Commons. The obvious hurdles need not be repeated, apart from noting that "recognition in the House" has come to serve as the definitive standard to be met for a great variety of privileges ranging from free airline passes for party leaders to regular meetings of party officials with the chief electoral officer for the purpose of suggesting improvements to the Canada Elections Act.[44] Had such rules, definitions and standards been in effect during the 1930s, it is debatable whether either the CCF or the Social Credit would have succeeded in making a breakthrough into the party system. Alternatively, once into the system with the protection it affords, a small party might so successfully carve out a niche for itself and receive more in the way of assistance and recognition than it would otherwise have any right to expect, that its existence would be prolonged. Perhaps Social Credit currently fits that description.

In other words, the obvious difficulty with stipulating at any one time the minimum criteria to be met to qualify as a "recognized" party in Parliament stems from the fact that at different times and in different circumstances the dominant and popular view of what constitutes an acceptable party system is likely to be different. On the one hand, to place restrictions or to grant privileges in such a way as to impede natural changes in the party system would be unwise for no other reason than it could generate unnecessary tensions within the society. If, shortly after World War I, the farmers' protests had not been allowed to take the form that they did (in the establishment of the Progressive party) because of statutory and regulatory barriers weighted in favour of the existing parties, what avenues would have been available to those whose moves were prompted by such profound dissatisfaction with the policies and leadership of the two older parties that no reconciliation was at that time possible within the confines of the two-party system? On the other hand, to define "political party" in such a way as to make time and assistance guaranteed by statute far too easy for any group to obtain serves no better purpose. Such a structure could, in the long run, prove to be as damaging to the political system as one in which the restrictions were too severe. That the balance between the two extremes must be sought by the practising politicians who have immediate political interests of their own to protect may not be ideal. But so far, at any rate, the brief Canadian experience has suggested that in the absence of a better alternative the pragmatic approach has a good deal to commend it. It enables historical, rational and practical arguments to be brought together in the search for policies that are both fair and realistic.

Notes

1   E. Regier in *House of Commons Debates*, July 12, 1955, 6002.

2   See *ibid.*, March 11, 1955, 1958, for the speech of W.G. Weir, MP, who stated, in part: "We are elected as individuals. The party is only used as the machinery for the election." See also remarks of J.M. Macdonnell and C.G. Power, *ibid.*, 1958 and 1959.

3   "Independent" MPs and members who have withdrawn voluntarily or who have been forced out of a party caucus often tend to lose committee assignments. See *Debates*, March 19, 1968, 7783-92.

4   See Donald Page, "Streamlining the Procedures of the Canadian House of Commons, 1963-1966," *Canadian Journal of Economics and Political Science* 33 (1967), 41-42.

5   *Young and Rubicam, Ltd.*, v. *Progressive Conservative Party of Canada*. Superior Court of Quebec, 803-933, March 22, 1971. (Translation from original).

6   *Senate and House of Commons Act*, R.S.C., 1970, c. S-8, s. 41(2).

7   *Debates*, September 30, 1963, 3007-09.

8   "A Political Party," paper prepared by Maurice Ollivier, Parliamentary Counsel, Ottawa, January 31, 1966, 6.

9   Correspondence with the author from Hon. J.W. Pickersgill, December 19, 1973.

10   Correspondence with the author from Stanley Knowles, MP, January 22, 1974.

11   Source of remarks not to be attributed. Facts for the paragraph were gathered from correspondence with, or interviews with, the author and former and present MPs.

12   Originally provisional Standing Order 15(2)(a), now S.O. 15(3).

13   *Debates*, February 18, 1966, 1435. Beauchesne's reference was to the speaking rights of "the Leader of the Opposition or the Chiefs of recognized groups." See *Rules and Forms of the House of Commons of Canada* (4th ed. rev.; Toronto: Carswell, 1958), citation 91(1). The House had moved a considerable distance from the position articulated by W.L. Mackenzie King when, as prime minister in the 1940s, he argued forcefully against according any parliamentary recognition to third parties. See *Debates*, November 15, 1940, 132-35, and February 16, 1944, 553-54.

14   "A Statement of Policy of the Canadian Broadcasting Corporation with Respect to Controversial Broadcasting," issued by authority of the Board of Governors, July 8, 1939 (mimeo), 2-3. (Emphasis added.)

15 *Ibid.*, 3.

16 *Ibid.*, 4-5, 7.

17 *Ibid.*, 3.

18 See Frank W. Peters, *The Politics of Canadian Broadcasting 1920-1951* (Toronto: University of Toronto Press, 1969), 278-80 and 322-44.

19 "Party Political Broadcasts," CBC Board of Directors, Programme Policy pamphlet (revised; March, 1972), 4.

20 *Ibid.*, 7.

21 *Ibid.*, 4.

22 Under the amended Act, registered parties are entitled to consult with the CRTC regarding the allocation of the 6-1/2 hours broadcasting time. If, through consultations, agreement can be reached by representatives of all parties, such an agreement applies during the forthcoming election. If no agreement can be reached, the time is allocated by the CRTC. *Canada Elections Act*, 1974, ss. 99 and 99.1. *Ibid.*, and interview with Mr. John Kerr, director of federal election broadcasts, CBC, Montreal, June 23, 1976.

23 *Ibid.*, 40.

24 *Canada Elections Act*, 1970 and 1974, s. 13.

25 *Ibid.*, ss. 13(4) (a) and (b). (Emphasis added.)

26 "Election Expenses and You" (published by the Chief Election Officer, 1974), 3.

27 "Contact" (published by the Chief Electoral Officer), number 12 (June, 1975), 19.

28 Interview, J.-M. Hamel, chief electoral officer, Ottawa, June 11, 1975 and subsequent correspondence, July 19, 1976.

29 Committee on Election Expenses, *Report*, 39 and 32.

30 *Canada Elections Act*, 1974, s. 13.8.

31 *Canada Elections Act*, 1974, s. 31(1).

32 The chief electoral officer has stated categorically his opposition to any move to empower him to arbitrate in any intraparty disputes regarding nominations. Interview, June 11, 1975.

33 *Canada Elections Act*, s. 23(2)(h). (Emphasis added.)

34 *Canadian Annual Review of Politics and Public Affairs, 1974*, ed. by John Saywell (Toronto: University of Toronto Press, 1975), 57.

35 See the *Globe and Mail* (Toronto), May 27-31, 1974, and *Canadian Annual Review of Politics and Public Affairs, 1974*, 57-58.

36 See *Debates*, September 12, 1968, 6.

37 Edwin R. Black, "Opposition Research: Some Theories and Practice," *Canadian Public Administration*, 15 (1972), 26.

38 *Debates*, November 15, 1968, 2791. See also *Debates*, November 15, 1968, 2790-99 for statements of party spokesmen indicating some difference of opinion over the basic principle of the scheme. In the prime minister's phrase "this measure is to enable *leaders of opposition* parties to avail themselves of some technical facilities, to resort to the services of economists, sociologists, jurists, and to alleviate their difficult duty in criticizing the government's legislative measures" (2791). (Emphasis added.)

39 *Star-Phoenix* (Saskatoon), August 7, 1974, 33.

40 *Legislative Assembly Act*, R.S.M., 1970, c. L110, S. 61 (1, 2 and 6).

41 *Legislative Act*, S.Q., 1970, c.5, s.2; S.Q., 1971, c.9, ss.10, 15; S.Q. 1974, c.7, s.9; and *An Act Respecting the Legislature Act and the Election Act*, S.Q., 1976-77.

42 Bill C-418 (1974-76), first reading, December 1, 1975.

43 Commissioners of Internal Economy, Minutes, October 22, 1974.

44 Correspondence with the author from D.W. Benson, assistant to the president, Air Canada, October 2, 1975, and interview with chief electoral officer, June 11, 1975.

Royal Commission on Electoral Reform and Party Financing

The Constitution and Organization of Parties

The structure of the large national parties reflects our parliamentary heritage and the federal nature of the country. Their structure also reflects various tensions within the parties as they try to reconcile the conflicting demands of the parliamentary party, the electoral campaign team and the party associations nationally, provincially and locally.

Party Structure and Organization

The basic organizational structure of the parties represents their efforts to manage and direct their activities toward achieving their objectives. Their structure is also affected by low levels of political participation, which limits the number of volunteers available. Parties must assign most organizational tasks to party officials and paid staff. For the larger parties, their goals are primarily electoral—winning office. For others, such as the Christian Heritage Party and the Greens, their goals lie much more in raising the consciousness of the Canadian public. In these respects, these new parties are much like the CCF in its early days.

Key structural dimensions of the largest parties encompass the distinctions between the party leadership—including party professionals responsible for the national election campaign—and the parliamentary party and the extra-parliamentary party, including local associations and rank-and-file members. These distinctions underscore a central tension in the Progressive Conservative, Liberal and New Democratic parties, namely calls for openness, mass debate and autonomy of local associations on the one hand, and pressures for legislative flexibility and executive action on the other. In keeping with the role of these parties as primarily electoral machines, the forces for executive action have come to predominate in key areas related to running national election campaigns. Furthermore, it is the party leader who has tended to dominate not only the extra-parliamentary party but also the parliamentary party. Particularly now, with the personalities of party leaders dominating election campaigns, party structures have come to revolve in large measure around the party leader in the House of Commons.

The three largest parties have roughly similar organizational formats. In all three, the biennial convention is considered the party's supreme authority. Between conventions, the party's national executive, or the federal council in the case of the NDP, renders decisions. The real power, however, tends to reside in the executive or steering committees and in the national party offices. At election time, the national campaign committees predominate, as they draw on key party personnel and prominent figures and, in the case of the governing party, cabinet ministers.

Yet for all the influence enjoyed by party leaders and a party structure operating apparently to their advantage, a central management team does not control all party activities. Party leadership has surprisingly little control over important areas of party activity, especially candidate selection.

Furthermore, the three largest parties must deal with the provincial wings of their parties, that is, the wing of the party organized to compete for power at the provincial level. The need to develop appropriate organizational structures in this respect is complicated by the nature of Canadian federalism. Party structures must take into account that both voters and members may have different party preferences at the federal and provincial levels. There is also often considerable tension between the federal government and provincial governments, even when the same party is in power at both levels.

The need to reconcile these federal-provincial considerations has important implications for the way in which party members participate in party affairs and the manner in which functions such as candidate selection are handled. Although these parties face a similiar dilemma in dealing with their provincial wings, each has found a different structural solution to the problem.

The Progressive Conservative Party operates with separate federal and provincial parties although all their provincial legislative members have automatic convention delegate status in the federal party. While it normally employs a field organizer in each province, the provincial parties have no role in the federal party. In the Atlantic provinces, the field organizer shares office space and support staff with the provincial party. In the other six provinces, the party maintains separate offices. The federal party has direct links with grassroots federal constituency associations, bypassing the provincial level.

Each province is represented by a vice president on the national executive committee, but such members are not necessarily linked with the provincial party. Although provincial party leaders, the president, women's president, youth president and vice presidents of each provincial association sit on the national executive, this body rarely meets. The more critical decisions are made in the executive committee of the national executive, which meets more frequently, and in particular, in the steering committee. The steering committee can act in the name of the executive committee between meetings of the latter, and thus holds de facto authority for most decisions affecting party operations. The relative absence of formal structural links with provincial parties gives the Progressive Conservative Party flexibility in cultivating a national orientation and at the same time maintaining informal links with the parties at the provincial level that are not Progressive Conservative.

Between 1932 and 1968, the Liberal Party of Canada was called the National Liberal Federation of Canada; and in some important respects it is still a federation of 10 provincial and two territorial units. In four provinces known as the 'split' provinces—Quebec, Ontario, Alberta and, most recently, British Columbia—the federal Liberal Party exists alongside the provincial Liberal Party. In these provinces, the Liberal Party of Canada is represented through provincial associations; for example, by the Liberal Party of Canada (Ontario) in Ontario and by the Parti libéral du Canada (Québec) in Quebec. These associations have separate or concurrent responsibilities with the national party for fund raising, for setting rules for the candidate selection process, for policy development and the adoption of resolutions for national policy conventions, and for the maintenance of membership lists. These provincial associations are governed by separate constitutions. However, if a conflict arises between the constitution of the national party and the provincial association, the national policy of the party takes precedence.

In the remaining provinces and territories the structure of the Liberal Party is integrated—they are called 'unitary' or 'joint' parties—and the provincial organization functions as a branch of the federal party. In most of the western provinces the provincial half of the joint party is weak or virtually non-existent, which means that the integrated party really has meaning only in the four Atlantic provinces. The Liberal Party of Canada, however, does keep separate offices in Quebec, Ontario and Alberta, and fund-raising offices in

Newfoundland and British Columbia. Further, there are 12 regional presidents that sit on the national executive.

Before 1990, one could become a member of the national Liberal Party in the provinces with joint parties only by joining both federal and provincial parties. After constitutional amendments passed in 1990, it became possible to take direct membership in the federal party in all provinces and territories through local constituency associations. Finally, even in the integrated provinces, few joint federal-provincial constituency associations remain. Where they exist, one association tends to be a shell for the other—in New Brunswick and Nova Scotia, for example, the provincial constituency associations are the real engines of activity.

The NDP has by far the most integrated structure of the three largest parties, having joint organizations in all provinces and territories except Quebec. Although its constitution does not use the term confederation, it does provide for an autonomous provincial party in each province. There is no provincial party representation on the federal executive, but the federal council comprises the leader, president, several Members of Parliament, representatives from various trade unions, the secretary and treasurer of each provincial party, as well as three additional representatives from each provincial section. In recent years, the size of the council has increased from approximately 110 to 175 members to accommodate expanded representation for women, Aboriginal persons and ethnocultural groups. Membership in the provincial party brings with it automatic membership in the federal party. Provincial offices, executives and conventions serve both levels. In recent years there has been concern in the NDP that provincial associations occupy most of the attention and energies of the membership. As a consequence, a Council of Federal Ridings was established recently in most provinces "to combat the dormancy of the federal party at the provincial and constituency levels between federal elections."

In a break with party tradition, constitutional amendments were passed in 1989 recognizing the NDP of Canada (Québec) as a separate entity from the Nouveau parti démocratique du Québec. In that province it then became possible to belong to a provincial party other than the NDP and still belong to the federal party, something that is not permitted in other provinces. In August 1990, when the Quebec provincial party refused to support the federal candidate in a federal by-election, the federal party severed all links with the provincial associations.

When the two parties with integrated or partially integrated federal-provincial structures collect funds under the rubric of federal income tax credits, the provincial wing can use these funds in the provincial, and possibly even the municipal, electoral arena. The law is not explicit on this issue, but those responsible for handling party finances in at least two parties expressed concern about potential abuses from the lack of clear legislation or guidelines.

In contrast with the Progressive Conservative, Liberal and New Democratic parties, the Reform Party of Canada is unencumbered by provincial wings; it has decided not to compete for power at the provincial level. Central to the party's decision-making process are the party assemblies, which meet at least every two years, and the executive council. While in theory the assemblies can decide most matters, most power resides in the party's executive council. It is composed of the party leader, the provincial or territorial directors, the chief executive officer of the party fund and provincial or territorial representatives where they have constituency associations.

The Reform Party constitution has a unique provision for referendums: party members "may initiate a formal referendum of the Party membership by submitting a petition to the Secretary of the Party requesting such a referendum and signed by not less than 5% of the Party membership." (Article 8(b)) Referendums can relate to "any important constitutional, social, economic, or political issue". (Article 8(a)) Significantly, however, the results of such referendums are merely advisory; they are not binding on the leader or the executive council. Overall, the Reform Party's constitution gives more power to the party leader than those of most other parties. "Between Assemblies, interim policies and objectives of the Party shall be those determined by the Leader in consultation with and approved by the Executive Council," provided party principles are maintained. (Article 1(d))

The constitutions of the Liberals and the NDP, because these parties have federal organizational forms, leave the local nomination process to be specified in their provincial associations' constitutions. This decentralization leads to varying practices within the same party and hampers efforts by the leadership to encourage local associations to accept changes in the nomination process. For example, the British Columbia NDP has a series of provisions governing appeals of nomination contests, while the Manitoba NDP has none; the constitution of the the Ontario Liberals has rules governing nomination finances, but there are none in the New Brunswick party.

Although the Progressive Conservative and Reform parties' constitutions tie their constituency associations directly to the national party, neither is significantly more centralized than the Liberals or the NDP for nomination practices. Essentially, the rules are left to be specified in local associations' constitutions, subject only to age provisions for party membership, a local resident qualification for constituency association membership and a minimum notice requirement for a nomination meeting. The Reform Party's national constitution requires that local party members "shall conduct a thorough search...to find the best possible candidate." (Article 4(a)) This suggests greater central control than the other parties, yet it still indicates that the traditional right to choose the local candidate remains with the constituency association. Among the other parties, the Christian Heritage Party's constitution has by far the most extensive rules governing the nomination process in constituency associations and the operation of provincial and territorial councils and the party youth caucus. For example, the constitution requires members to reside in the constituency of the local association, and it specifies the term of office of executive members of associations and councils and the frequency of meetings of the executive and membership of constituency associations.

The organization of the three largest parties also takes into account non-territorial characteristics. In 1973, the Liberal Party set up a Women's Commission and a National Youth Commission. The Progressive Conservative Party operates a PC Youth Federation and a Participation of Women Committee to promote the involvement of women throughout the party. The creation of special committees and commissions for multiculturalism and Aboriginal people in the Liberal, Progressive Conservative and New Democratic parties indicates how current issues and concerns are handled organizationally by the parties. It was not until the 1960s that these special party groupings were actively included. These organizations have become more prominent in the management of the parties' processes and activities.

These sectoral constituencies are within each party, but the NDP also has to accommodate organized labour. The party was formed as a grouping of social and economic interests. From the outset, organized labour was a special player in NDP ranks, providing financial support, volunteer labour, meeting halls and public expressions of support. The integral link between the NDP and the labour movement is recognized in the party's national constitution. Article VIII

(1)(f) of the constitution states that the membership of the council shall include "one member representing each of the fifteen affiliated organizations with the largest number of affiliated members." This clause effectively guarantees the trade unions 15 members on the council, given that they are the largest organizations affiliated with the NDP. Keith Archer observes that labour leaders typically "occupy approximately 20 to 25 per cent of the executive and officer positions" in the party. Yet overall, according to Archer, "Only a small, and declining, proportion of union members in Canada belong to locals affiliated with the NDP."

One of the most important management tools available in any large public organizations is its constitution. Typically, it provides a formal guide to the structure and the distribution of power within the organization, articulates the organization's values and goals, and specifies the rights, obligations and duties of its members and officers. A constitution is especially important for the leadership; giving it authority for its actions, for managing the activities of the organization, and in particular, for creating an organizational culture and mobilizing the membership to achieve the organization's goals.

If the constitution is to serve its purpose, there must be a reasonably good fit between the constitution's provisions and the organization's practices. Too large a contrast between formal constitutional provisions and party activities can lead to cynicism and a crisis of authority at critical moments.

To varying degrees the three largest parties suffer in that their formal constitutions only partially approximate the reality of their organizational structures. At the same time, they give party leaders only limited means to mobilize party members. There are areas where party constitutions provide no rules or guidelines about appropriate behaviour. In other areas, practices or local norms clearly contravene the constitution, yet little or no effort seems to be made to enforce party regulations. Finally, given the formal autonomy assigned to local associations, party leaders are actually constrained from intervening in most aspects of candidate selection.

Indeed, the only real authority party leaders have over candidate selection is that provided by law—the requirement that party leaders concur with the nomination of the party's candidate in each constituency. If the leader withholds approval, this action is seen as interventionist. Unfortunately, party constitutions offer little in the way of intermediary steps that could support party goals for candidate selection and the like.

The Liberals and Progressive Conservatives have both been concerned with what are seen as abuses in candidate and leadership delegate selection and with the need generally to update their constitutions in changing circumstances. The Liberal Party, for example, struck the Liberal Reform Commission in June, 1990, charging it with reviewing a variety of key party organizational matters. Yet doubts remain about whether the three largest parties have the organizational capacity to address the issues now confronting them.

The federal nature of the Canadian political system has influenced the rules and procedures of all the parties, resulting in considerable variation in the rules that exist and the way in which they are applied. Several questions are pertinent. Are these differences appropriate in national parties competing for national office? Do the party constitutions contribute to public confidence in our electoral system and in the parties when they regulate only to a very limited extent such important activities as candidate selection? Finally, do the structure and constitutional framework of the parties really serve the objective of building a broader and more active membership and of mobilizing that membership behind goals deemed important by the national party?

Keith Archer The NDP: A Trade Union Party?

The formal change from the CCF to the NDP was intended to link the party much more closely with organized labour. The change did not involve forming a new alignment, but rather using the renewed labour unity provided by the creation of the Canadian Labour Congress CLC as an opportunity to solidify the linkage which already had been developed through the CCF. It also provided the party with an opportunity to shed its image as a party responding to the economic depression of the 1930s in favour of one capable of tackling the issues facing a country in the midst of postwar prosperity and unprecedented industrial growth.

The varied and complex links that exist between the party and organized labour can be divided into three general types: personnel links, union contributions to the party's revenues, and direct union affiliation with the party. To understand the overall relationship between organized labour and the NDP, this chapter explores these aspects of that relationship.

Personnel Relations

The personnel linkage between organized labour and the NDP is amorphous and difficult to measure. Links may be formal and entrenched in the party's constitution, they may be informal and established by convention, or they may be informal, ad hoc, and subject to considerable variation over time. Additionally, the unionist involved in the NDP may participate on behalf of a central labour organization (such as the CLC or a provincial federation of labour), as a representative of a national or international union, such as the Canadian Automobile Workers (CAW), on behalf of an affiliated or unaffiliated union local, including directly chartered locals, or purely as an individual.

The party's *formal* personnel links with labour began to emerge in the years leading up to the creation of the NDP. The National Committee for the New Party (NCNP) played a large role in formalizing the nature of union participation in the new party's councils and in deciding upon the rules of union affiliation.[1]

The formal union representation on party decision-making bodies is outlined in the constitution. Article v.2 declares that the party's convention is the "supreme governing body of the Party and shall have final authority in all matters of federal policy, programme and constitution." The allocation of delegate seats at a convention thus provides an insight into the depth and breadth of the union-party linkage. There are a number of delegate categories at NDP conventions. All members of the Federal Council and the federal parliamentary caucus are entitled to delegate status. Constituency associations, through the provincial wings of the party, are accorded delegates based on their size and according to the formula set out in the constitution. In addition, delegates are awarded to the youth wing of the party and to two categories of union delegates: central labour[2] and affiliated organizations.

The party was careful to ensure that the formula for allocating convention delegates would guarantee that labour would not dominate the convention. For example, at the 1987 federal convention, 240 of the 1391 delegates (17.3 per cent) were from affiliated unions and 72 (5.2 per cent) were from central labour.[3] The 1987 data, where delegates with union credentials made up almost one-quarter of the total delegates, are consistent with the general pattern of union representation at party conventions. Union delegates as a proportion of total delegates were 19.7 per cent in 1973, 25.8 per cent in 1975, 22.5 per cent in 1977, 24.0 per cent in 1979, and 17.4 per cent in 1981. Even at the 1971 convention which elected David Lewis as leader and in which the role of organized labour in the party was being challenged directly by the Waffle candidate, James Laxer, organized labour could muster only 32.3 per cent of all delegates.[4]

However, caution should be used in interpreting the data on delegate status at party conventions. Some delegates may be very active union members, but appear under another delegate category if, for example, they also belong to caucus, council, the youth wing, or a constituency association. Thus, the number of delegates who are union members always exceeds those who have union delegate status. Conversely, it should be obvious that the role of labour in the party is strongest when unionists are unified in their outlook and orientation, a characteristic which organized labour in Canada is seldom accused of possessing. The effect of labour representation at conventions is accurately conveyed by Wiseman in his study of the Manitoba NDP: "The change in composition of delegates from CCF [to NDP] conventions was more apparent than real. The new affiliation provisions permitted many CCFers to appear as labour delegates.... It is doubtful that more than 5 per cent of the Manitoba delegation [to the NDP founding convention] would have been ineligible to attend had it been simply another CCF convention."[5] Furthermore, and along a more substantial vein, he notes that the resolutions presented by organized labour to the conventions of the Manitoba NDP "were almost always restricted to [labour's] specific legislative concerns."[6]

In the two-year period between conventions, the party is governed by the Federal Council, which meets at least twice a year at the call of the executive. As with the convention delegates, there are several categories of council member, including the federal party's 12 officers, 20 members selected from the federal caucus, 40 members from the provincial parties' table officers, 30 members selected from the provincial parties' conventions, and 12 members representing the largest affiliated organizations. In addition the council may appoint up to 5 additional members. Therefore, total membership on the Federal Council numbers between 116 and 121, of which 12 (approximately 10 per cent) are specifically allocated to affiliated unions. The Federal Council invariably has more than 12 union officials as members at any given time, but their place on council is not formally determined by their union status.

Between meetings of the Federal Council the executive has the authority to conduct and administer the affairs and business of the party. The executive consists of the 12 officers (leader, president and associate president, 8 vice-presidents, and treasurer) and 14 members elected by and from the Federal Council. Unlike council members and convention delegates, there are no specific provisions for the officers or executive of the party to have union representatives among them. A literal reading of the party's constitution would suggest that these offices could be filled without any union representation at all. But such a reading of the party's constitution would lead to a mistaken interpretation and would be analogous to a literal reading of the Constitution Act 1867. That document refers to the cabinet as the Queen's Privy Council, whose members are summoned from time to time by the crown. In fact, Canada's constitutional conventions require that the governor general make appointments to the Privy Council on the recommendation of the prime minister. There is a further constitutional convention that the prime minister will ensure adequate representation within cabinet from the various regions as well as from religious, ethnic, linguistic, and gender groups. The constitutional convention is less clear in defining what constitutes adequate representation for each group, but it does ensure that the prime minister will remain sensitive to group representation in the selection process.

For the NDP, there is likewise a strong convention making for adequate union representation within the inner councils of the party. Typically, there are prominent union representatives on the party executive and among the table officers. Although there is no definitive understanding of the number of union representatives considered to be adequate, it is typical to find that labour leaders occupy approximately 20 to 25 per cent of the executive and officer positions.[7]

The personnel links between organized labour and the NDP extend well beyond membership in the formal councils of the party. As early as the 1940s the CCF was encouraging labour unions, and especially CCL unions, to create their own political action committees, a step which the CCL itself had taken in the early 1940s.[8] The CLC has maintained a Committee on Political Education (COPE) almost since its inception, and although small in size and resources (3 full-time staff), it maintains continual contact and communication with the party. It also attempts to co-ordinate the political activities of its affiliates and encourages union locals to affiliate with the NDP.

Labour unions also have provided the party with both personnel and organizational resources to conduct party conventions and contest elections. Desmond Morton describes one of the important contributions of labour to the party's founding convention: "CCF conventions had been gatherings of only a few hundred delegates, meeting annually in hotel ballrooms and halls. For the Founding Convention, trade unionists contributed their organizing expertise. From the decorations to the labour troubadours...it looked and was professional. The new image was being fashioned."[9] In an era in which the electronic media were playing a greater role in delivering "politics" to Canadians, and "image" was becoming a more important political commodity, the organizational resources of labour became of greater importance to the party.

The campaign techniques which the NDP began to develop in the 1960s also placed a premium on personnel and organizational resources. The party's major campaign innovation was developed during a by-election in the Toronto constituency of Riverdale in 1964. In short, the technique involved massive door-to-door canvassing throughout the campaign, with a party worker visiting a voter's home three or four times before the election.[10] This technique appealed to the NDP, not only because it was relatively cost-effective, but also because organized labour could provide the army of canvassers needed for such a labour-intensive effort.

There are many other minor ways in which labour contributes to the personnel and organizational needs of the party. Many unionists serve as table officers of constituency associations, and many constituency associations hold their monthly meetings in union halls. Unions often provide personnel and vehicles on election day and other material support to assist in campaigns to get out the vote.

Given its wide range, it is not possible to measure the overall personnel contribution of labour to the party. Although labour does make a significant contribution, there are also very real limits on its contribution as an organization. On the party's decision-making bodies, labour is not able to provide more than a minority voice, albeit a significant one. Informally, the types of contributions are wide ranging, but only some of them are sponsored by the organizations themselves. Much of the overlap in personnel between the union movement and the NDP lies in individual Canadians, acting not in their capacity as union officials, but rather as individuals exercising their democratic rights. And this type of support may owe very little to the formal alliance that emerged between organized labour and the NDP.

Financial Contributions

The financial relationship between organized labour and the NDP is only somewhat more straightforward and measurable than the personnel linkage. The passage of the Canada Elections Act in 1974 has, among other things, shed light on the financing of candidates and political parties in Canada. Parties are now required to submit audited financial statements each year to the chief electoral officer, which are then made public, and to disclose in their reports the names of all persons or organizations donating $100 or more to a candidate or party. The legislation also introduced a system of public funding for political parties by providing tax credits for political contributions.[11]

Despite the mandatory public disclosure of revenues, it is not possible to determine definitively the various sources of NDP funding. The party's unique organizational structure complicates its financial arrangements considerably. The NDP is a federated party in which there is no complete separation between federal and provincial levels.[12] Membership in the NDP is available through the provincial wings of the party, and provincial membership brings with it automatic membership in the federal party. It is not possible to join the federal wing of the NDP without joining a provincial wing. And, because the party's constitution precludes membership of other political parties by its members, one cannot even belong to the federal Liberals or Progressive Conservatives while being a member of a provincial wing of the New Democrats. This provision sets the NDP apart from both the Liberal and the Conservative parties, neither of which prohibits members of other federal parties from joining and both of which maintain much clearer distinctions between their federal and provincial wings.

One of the implications of the NDP's membership policies is that the federal and provincial wings have a much closer and more intertwined financial relationship than is true of the other major parties. This fiscal overlap affects the way in which the party's revenues are reported to the chief electoral officer. The returns of registered parties report the contributions each party receives for a given fiscal period under a number of headings. Although the categories have changed somewhat over time, typically they include contributions from individuals, business or commercial organizations, governments, trade unions, other organizations, and miscellaneous. Since 1974, the NDP has been the only party to list the revenues of the provincial wings of the party. It does so even though these funds generally fall under the jurisdiction of the provincial wings. The fiscal responsibility is complicated, however, because the federal party levies a 15 per cent tax on all revenues raised by the provincial sections and, during election campaigns, it can also exact an assessment from each provincial section, thereby effectively controlling the expenditure of at least some of these funds.[13] However, and this is the issue that is most problematic in calculating the relative weight of union contributions, the provincial revenues are not broken down according to source. Consequently, this discussion of the proportion of funds which the party receives from union sources will be limited to the funds raised and controlled by the federal wing of the NDP.

The data on the NDP's revenues from 1979 to 1986 are presented in table 1.[14] Because conclusions about the size of union financial contributions will vary according to whether federal or provincial data are used, both are presented. Focusing on federal revenues first, table 1 shows that the party's revenues grew considerably, although not consistently, from $4.7 million to $7.8 million annually between 1979 and 1986. The lion's share of the funding in each year came from individuals contributing to the party... Overall, individual contributions ranged from a low of 54.4 per cent of the federal party's revenues in 1979 to a high of 83.6 per cent in 1983. As well, there has been a reasonably steady growth in contributions by individuals over time.[15]

Contributions from trade unions to the NDP are of two types: annual dues paid by unions affiliated with the party, and other donations made outside the formal affiliation mechanism. In a pattern similar to that for individual contributions, union contributions through affiliation fees have grown steadily and consistently in absolute terms and have remained remarkably stable in relative terms. The data also indicate the marginality of affiliation fees to the overall fiscal outlook of the party. At no point during this period have affiliation dues constituted as much as 10 per cent of the party's revenues; instead they have ranged from a high of 9.0 per cent in 1981 to a low of 5.0 per cent in 1983.

The major variation in financial contributions to the NDP over time is in the category of "other union contributions." The very clear pattern is for contributions from unions to increase dramatically during election years, but to fall off equally dramatically in non-election years. Union contributions to the NDP's election war chest come from many different sources. The most significant donations tend to be from the headquarters of national or international unions (contributions in 1984 included $122,500 from the Steelworkers, over $40,000 from the Food and Commercial Workers, $29,000 from the Service Employees Union, among many others) as well as from national, provincial, or regional labour councils.

It is very significant that during election years organized labour is able to contribute between $1.5 million and $2.1 million to the federal NDP as well as additional funds which are then turned over to the federal office. However, these data must be interpreted in light of two other fiscal realities; even at their high point during an election year, union contributions are outweighed by individual contributions, and they are significantly outweighed by individual donations in non-election years. In addition, although the $2.1 million contributed to the NDP in 1984 enabled the party to marshall an effective national election campaign, the amount pales in comparison to the $5.3 million and $11.0 million which corporate sponsors contributed to the Liberal and Progressive Conservative parties, respectively.

Table 1: New Democratic Party Revenue, 1979-86

Source	1979	1980	1981	1982	1983	1984	1985	1986
Individual	$2,584,536	$2,817,387	$2,868,724	$3,774,971	$4,998,350	$4,156,000	$4,611,704	$5,036,131
Business/Commercial	169,298	91,369	109,062	144,324	41,432	51,665	58,417	177,960
Government	97,752	26,828	39,619	143,358	67,155	181,010	69,890	74,585
Union								
Affiliation Dues	319,196	338,271	353,300	316,106	299,688	417,480	566,833	633,928
Other Union	1,382,420	1,364,557	161,886	157,033	336,851	1,741,575	302,568	538,856
Other Organizations	5,523*	7,678*	2,367	1,320	2,590	1,950	34,644	4,642
Interest	46,417	61,460	102,167	123,316	77,710	141,678	105,863	127,292
Miscellaneous	136,139	212,897	218,687	106,054	147,755	665,545	534,397	391,269
Provincial Election Rebates	—	—	—	—	—	—	—	810,995
FEDERAL TOTAL	4,741,281	4,920,447	3,855,812	4,766,482	5,971,531	7,356,903	6,284,316	7,795,658
Provincial Revenues	1,278,885	1,810,210	2,146,770	2,341,715	2,697,121	3,155,793	3,867,695	6,843,667
TOTAL	6,020,166	6,100,657	6,002,582	7,108,197	8,668,652	10,512,696	10,152,011	14,639,325

* Includes public corporations and unincorporated organizations.

Source: Canada, Elections Canada, *Registered Party Fiscal Period Returns*, selected years.

Union Affiliation with the NDP

We have noted that the NDP did not introduce the idea of direct union affiliation with the party. The first union had affiliated with the CCF in 1938, and there had been continuous provisions for union affiliation thereafter. However, union affiliation with the CCF had always remained low. Nelson Wiseman describes the situation in 1952: "CCF success in attracting trade unionists was not great. In 1952 there were less than 15,000 affiliated unionists in Canada and 10,000 of these were from the miners' union in Nova Scotia. There were no union affiliates at all, at that date, from Manitoba. The 2 per cent per month affiliate fee, whenever and wherever collected, provided only marginal income for the CCF; the Manitoba party collected $80 from this source in 1945 and $50 in 1950."[16] The highest level of affiliation with the CCF had occurred in 1944, at which time 100 unions with approximately 50,000 members were affiliated with the party. This number constituted approximately 6.9 per cent of the unionized work force in that year.[17] By the early 1950s growth in the affiliation movement had effectively halted and with the growth in the union movement throughout the decade, members of affiliated locals fell to between 1 and 2 per cent of the unionized work force.

Although the NDP did not introduce the idea of union affiliation, it did evince a resolve to make the affiliation movement successful. Except for the minor change which gave affiliated members the same rights at constituency meetings as individual party members,[18] the NDP adopted the affiliation formula used by the CCF. Immediately after its creation, the NDP began to work on strengthening its ties with labour in general and in rebuilding the affiliation movement in particular. For example, in the summer of 1962 an NDP-union liaison committee recommended the declaration of a political month, whose purpose was: "(a) to keep trade union membership continuously aware of their political responsibilities; (b) to increase affiliated and individual memberships; and (c) to establish an identity of interests between trade unionists and the party."[19]

Various institutional arrangements were established to increase participation in the affiliation movement. Late in 1964 the CLC executive met with administrative personnel in the party at which time the group agreed to establish regular liaison through quarterly meetings. In addition, the CLC agreed to insist in persuading delinquent unions to bring their payments to the party up to date.[20] The key officer from the CLC side of the arrangement was the director of

Table 2: Unions Affiliated with the NDP and Membership of Affiliated Unions as a Percentage of Total Union Membership, Selected Years

Year	Number of Affiliated Locals	Members of Affiliated Locals ('000s)	Total Union Membership ('000s)	Union Members Affiliated (%)
1961	278	71	1423	5.0
1962	612	186	1449	12.9
1963	689	218	1493	14.6
1964	683	216	1589	13.6
1969	764	256	2075	12.3
1974	754	283	2732	10.4
1979	745	295	3397	8.7
1984	730	267	3651	7.3

Source: NDP files, "Organizations affiliated with the NDP," selected years; Canada, Labour Canada, *Directory of Labour Organizations in Canada*, 1984.

political education. An examination of party files shows that virtually every year the CLC's director of political education would mount a drive to increase the affiliation of trade unions with the party, usually by contacting the political education directors of national or international unions, who in turn would contact the union locals.[21] More generally and symbolically, the CLC executive committee continued to pass resolutions in favour of affiliation. Typical of these efforts was a 1969 resolution recommending "to all affiliated organizations that a special all-out effort be made in the next two years to increase substantially the affiliation to the NDP, and their [the locals] participation in the Canadian COPE program."[22] On the party side, the federal secretary assumed the major responsibility for increasing affiliation. As in the CLC, much of the communication between the federal secretary and the national or international unions was through the latter's political action or political education co-ordinators.[23] The federal secretary also maintained close contact with party or union organizers and either directly or through the organizers established contact with union locals.[24]

Despite the prodigious effort on the part of the NDP and the CLC to increase affiliation, the affiliation movement did not grow appreciably. There was a change in the size of the affiliation movement after the transition from the CCF to the NDP, but the change

Table 3: Organizations Affiliated to the NDP, by Province, April 1985

Province	Number of Affiliated Locals	% of Affiliated Locals Nationwide	Number of Affiliated Members ('000s)	% of Affiliated Members Nationwide
British Columbia	56	7.7	30.5	11.4
Alberta	20	2.7	5.7	2.1
Saskatchewan	33	4.5	10.5	3.9
Manitoba	42	5.8	12.0	4.5
Ontario	552	75.6	202.3	75.7
Quebec	12	1.6	2.9	1.1
New Brunswick	5	0.7	.6	0.2
Nova Scotia	7	1.0	2.3	0.8
Prince Edward Island	2	0.3	.5	0.2
Newfoundland	1	0.1	.05	0.0
TOTAL	**730**	**100.0**	**267.35**	**99.9**

Source: NDP files.

was much more modest than originally anticipated. As table 2 illustrates, by 1962 over 600 locals with almost 200,000 members had affiliated to the party, accounting for 12.9 per cent of the unionized work force. In terms of the proportion of union members affiliated to the party, 1963 was the high water mark, when 14.6 per cent of unionized workers belonged to affiliated locals. Although this might appear to represent an encouraging increase in labour's support for the party less than three years after its founding, it should be borne in mind that only 29.8 per cent of non-agricultural paid workers were unionized in 1963.[25]

After 1963, the data indicate marginal changes in the number of union locals affiliated coupled with marginal increases in the absolute number of union members who belonged to affiliated locals. More striking is the steady decline after 1963 in the proportion of union members affiliated with the party. By 1969 it had dropped to 12.3 per cent, and it continued to fall—to 10.4 per cent in 1974, 8.7 per cent in 1979, and finally to 7.3 per cent in 1984.

It is important not to overdraw the parallels between the experiences of the CCF and the NDP with the affiliation movement. By the 1950s the affiliation movement with the CCF was collapsing both relative to the overall growth in the union movement as well as in absolute terms from over 100 locals to less than 50. For the NDP, however, there has been an overall stabilization in the affiliation movement at approximately 750 locals, a level significantly below expectations in 1961, but nonetheless stable. The relative decline of the affiliation movement with the NDP is due to two facts: few locals which did not join in the years immediately after the party's creation have joined subsequently; and very few of the unions which have emerged since 1961 have decided to affiliate.

To gain a fuller perspective on the potential political effect of union affiliation with the NDP, it is useful to examine the regional distribution of affiliated locals. The data in table 3 illustrate the significant regional strengths and weaknesses of union affiliation across the country. Of the 730 union locals affiliated in 1985, more than three-quarters (75.6 per cent) were located in Ontario. Most of the remaining affiliates were from the West (20.7 per cent). Less than 2 per cent of unions affiliated with the NDP in 1985 were Quebec-based locals, and slightly more than 2 per cent were from the Atlantic region. Nowhere in the country is union affiliation strong. East of the Ottawa River it is almost non-existent.

Conclusion

In evaluating the linkage between organized labour and the NDP it becomes obvious that the party, like its organizational predecessor, the CCF, is not a labour party or a party controlled by organized labour. Rather it is a social democratic party with links of varying strength to the union movement, some of which are purposefully weak.

The personnel links can most readily be judged a success, in large part because the party's founders intended to provide only modest personnel overlap with organized labour. Unions are an important segment of the party, but the relationship between party and labour was so designed that labour's position would be clearly and distinctly a minority one. Furthermore, even within its minority role, labour tends to under-represent itself on party decision-making bodies.[26]

The financial contributions to the party from organized labour are important and substantial, but do not overshadow other sources. Affiliation fees constitute a minor proportion of party financing, largely because so few locals are affiliated. The other financial contributions from unions are highly variable; large and significant during election years and modest during non-election years. In comparison with the corporate financing of the Liberal and Progressive Conservative parties on a year-to-year basis, irrespective of whether an election is being held, union financial contributions have not enabled the NDP to compete on an equal footing.

The most disappointing linkage in the union-party relationship is the strength of the affiliation movement. Considerable efforts to increase affiliation have yielded few dividends. The substantial growth in affiliation that was expected in 1961 simply has not materialized. This failure is an important barometer of the ability of organized labour to deliver on its commitment to the party. It is not due to a lack of effort or commitment on the part of the union leadership, particularly within the CLC. Rather, it arises largely from the way in which the affiliation movement has been institutionalized, and from the logic that flows from that structure.

Notes

1 Morley, *Secular Socialists*, 109-112.

2 Article VI.5 of the NDP's constitution states that "central labour bodies composed of affiliated organizations, and not eligible for direct affiliation to the Party...shall be entitled to representation as follows: one delegate from each such central labour body and two delegates from each such central national and provincial body."

3 Archer and Whitehorn, "Opinion Structure among NDP Activists," table 1.

4 NDP files, "Report of the Credentials Committee," selected years.

5 Wiseman, *Social Democracy in Manitoba*, 102-104.

6 *Ibid.*, 117.

7 Interview with Bill Knight, federal secretary of the NDP, 19 September 1988.

8 Lewis, *The Good Fight*, 298-303.

9 Morton, *NDP: The Dream of Power*, 22-23.

10 Morton, *The New Democrats 1961-1986*, 53-56; Morley, *Secular Socialists*, 83-100.

11 For a more detailed discussion, see Stanbury, "The Mother's Milk of Politics," 797-798.

12 Wearing, *Strained Relations* , 181-182.

13 Interview with Knight, 19 September 1988.

14 Data are presented for the period 1979-86 to illustrate the important differences in party fund-raising in election years and non-election years.

15 Data are from Elections Canada, *Federal Parties Fiscal Period Returns* , 1974-1986.

16 Wiseman, *Social Democracy in Manitoba*, 80.

17 Horowitz, *Canadian Labour in Politics*, 80; Labour Canada, *Labour Organizations in Canada*, 1977, xviii.

18 Morley, *Secular Socialists*, 111-112.

19 NDP files, minutes of Federal Executive Meeting, 22-23 August 1962.

20 NDP files, report of NDP-CLC meeting, 3 December 1964.

21 NDP files, letter by George Home, director of political education, CLC, 22 January 1971.

22 NDP files, recommendations endorsed by the Canadian Labour Congress Executive Council Meetings of 3-5 December 1968 and 17-20 February 1969.

23 NDP files, letters from Clifford Scotton to Olive Smith, co-ordinator, political action committee of the Textile Workers Union of America, 16 February 1967; to Neil Reimer, director, District 9, Oil, Chemical and Atomic Workers, 27 February 1970; and to L. Henry Lorrain, 1st vice-president, International Brotherhood of Pulp, Sulphite and Paper Mill Workers, 2 March 1970.

24 NDP files, letters from Michael Lewis (25 March 1966) and C.C. (Doc) Ames (30 March 1966) to Terry Grier.

25 Labour Canada, *Labour Organizations in Canada*, 1977, xix.

26 For example, at NDP conventions held between 1973 and 1981, less than one-quarter (24.2 per cent) of those with credentials from affiliated unions actually attended the convention: NDP files, "Reports of the Credentials Committee," selected years. The executives of locals decide whether or not to send their delegates and many do not attend for a variety of reasons.

References

Archer, Keith and Whitehorn, Alan. "Opinion Structure Among NDP Activists," Paper presented to the annual meeting of the Canadian Political Science Association, Windsor, Ontario, 9-11 June 1988.

Canada. Elections Canada. *Registered Parties Fiscal Period Returns*. Selected years.

Canada. Labour Canada. *Directory of Labour Organisations in Canada*. Selected years.

Horowitz, Gad. *Canadian Labour in Politics*. Toronto: University of Toronto Press 1968.

Lewis, David. *The Good Fight: Political Memoirs 1909-1958*. Toronto: Macmillan, 1981.

Morley, J.T. *Secular Socialists: The CCF-NDP in Ontario. A Biography*. Montreal: McGill University Press 1983.

Morton, Desmond. *NDP: The Dream of Power*. Toronto: Hakkert, 1974.

Morton, Desmond. *The New Democrats 1961-1986: The Politics of Change.* Toronto: Copp Clark Pitman 1986.

Stanbury, W.T. "The Mother's Milk of Politics: Political Contributions to Federal Parties in Canada, 1974-1984." *Canadian Journal of Political Science* 19(1986): 795-821.

Wearing, Joseph. *Strained Relations: Canada's Parties and Voters.* Toronto: McClelland and Stewart 1988.

Wiseman, Nelson. *Social Democracy in Manitoba: A History of the CCF-NDP.* Winnipeg: University of Manitoba Press 1983.

Leslie A. Pal The Cauldron of Leadership: Prime Ministers and Their Parties

The contemporary prominence of political leaders, magnified by the media's preoccupation with prime ministers and premiers, encourages the casual observer to dismiss the importance of political parties. To the vast majority of Canadians for whom casting a ballot is the full extent of their political engagement, parties are not much more than labels for different policy positions, or logos beneath a leader's beaming photograph. The party is, sometimes justifiably, reduced in the minds of many to its parliamentary rump—the handful of MPs or MLAs who carry the party banner between elections.

The three major Canadian political parties consist of much more than this, of course. They consist of thousands of volunteers scattered over every region, in every city and town. Our prime ministers, while they must ultimately present themselves before the "many-headed Caesar," or electorate, need first to be elected leaders by their parties. Parties formulate policies (often ignored), and aggregate interests (usually difficult). They meet periodically to consider the highest matters of government, but also organize picnics at the constituency level. It is true that Canadian political parties are not of the all-embracing variety one sees in Western Europe, but they do perform a bewildering array of tasks.

Our interest here is in the relation of leaders, especially prime ministers, to their party. As Weller puts it, "parties are the foundations on which prime ministers must build. There the transactional link is most obvious. Prime ministers hold their position because they lead the elected majority in the popular chamber. That majority is maintained by party discipline."[1] But surprisingly little information exists on what should, after all, be a crucial link in modern democratic politics.[2] Several reasons might explain this. First, party activity is often tedious and pedestrian. It is scattered across the nation in every constituency, large and small. Outside of leadership conventions, which have the virtues of drama and concentration, party routine is rarely exciting enough to attract the media. A second reason is that, despite their public purpose, political parties are actually private organizations. Moreover, they are engaged in a struggle for power with each other and against other parties. Accordingly, they prefer some secrecy, or at least discretion, on sensitive matters. The details of their relations with leaders are confidential in the extreme, rarely open to systematic study. Finally, parties are amorphous and shifting. Between elections they wither as volunteers drift away.

Aside from a few outstanding efforts, our knowledge of prime ministers in the party arena is almost entirely anecdotal, or else based on the perhaps atypical phenomenon of leadership conventions. Thus it is really not much more than a series of *aperçus*—of brief but unconnected illuminations which cast light on the parts without revealing the whole.

The Party Arenas: Ten Aperçus

1. Political Parties as Coalitions

There is no more venerable truth about political parties than that they aggregate interests. Their aim is to fight and win elections, but a democratic system demands organization in every capillary of the formal political system. In presenting a platform, political parties present a national agenda. They must therefore be able to muster troops at the constituency level as well as to demonstrate that they truly represent the nation and its interests. It is important to remember, however, that individual groups and interests within the party will never allow themselves to be entirely submerged in some collective party personality; they will assert themselves in a process of internal decision-making. Parties are therefore in fact loose coalitions of various interests bound either by the enjoyment of power (if they are in office) or the desire to gain it (if they are not).

In a country like Canada, the most salient divisions are regional and linguistic. The major parties have had to deal with reconciling East and West, Quebec and the rest, within their own ranks. This generates sometimes unbearable tensions. The Conservative party has traditionally had difficulty with Quebec, and only long years of patient work by Joe Clark, capped by the appeal of Brian Mulroney as a native son in 1984, succeeded in explaining the party's base there. During the 1976 Tory leadership campaign, various factions were known to support either the Western candidates (e.g., Jack Horner and Joe Clark) or the Quebec candidates (Claude Wagner and Brian Mulroney).[3] When John Turner became leader of the Liberal party, his main rival was Jean Chrétien. Pierre Trudeau was seen by some Western Liberals as preoccupied with the problems of Quebec and central Canada.[4] These internal tensions go back to the days of Macdonald and Laurier, and are a basic fact of political party life.

In recent years, other sociological groups have begun to visibly claim their rightful place in party affairs. Most notable among these are women and youth, though ethnic groups (especially among the Liberals) are emerging as well. Women's and youth caucuses were established in each major party in the 1960s and 1970s, and women's policy issues are now debated separately and at length. Women, now more active in political parties, are increasingly expressing their frustration with the so-called old boys' network which often excludes them from key leadership roles.[5] When Flora Macdonald ran for the Tory leadership in 1976, she was seen by many as "the women's candidate."[6] The 1984 general election had a separate leadership debate on women's issues.

In addition to these sociologically defined interests, each party contains clusters of politically defined constituencies. Former leaders, current premiers, senators, MPs, party executives, and an odd assortment of "backroom" types make up what is often referred to as the Establishment. Sheila Copps, for example, claims that when she ran for leader of the provincial party, the Ontario Liberal Establishment failed to back her, mobilizing instead behind David Peterson.[7] Sean O'Sullivan complained of the Tory Establishment's attempts to control the party's youth wing.[8] In normal times, between elections, this Establishment exercises substantial influence. During leadership conventions, though easily outnumbered by grassroots delegates, its members often act as synapses in the collective consciousness of party, passing critical information, processing demands and providing cues.[9] They are by no means united, and swirl in shifting coalitions, depending on issues at hand.

2. The Party and Ideology

Some sort of glue is needed to bind this rag-tag coalition. One adhesive element is ideology, or a shared vision of current problems and future prospects. It is by no means the only bonding agent, nor is it the most powerful. Yet parties are obliged by their public purpose to demonstrate a belief in some sort of coherent vision. The vision itself may be difficult to articulate, in part because it arises from the various constituencies mentioned above, but a vision there must be nonetheless.

Perhaps, however, calling a shared vision of this kind an ideology is not appropriate. It may explain the contortions political analysts suffer in pigeonholing parties by ideology.[10] Are the Liberals liberal, and the Conservatives conservative? To some degree one can find echoes of ideology in party platforms, but they are difficult to identify clearly. The two main parties are noted for this infidelity. It may be more accurate to say that political parties have *icon*ologies rather than *ide*ologies. Icons are symbols of complex and often inexpressible things, and an iconology may be defined as an eclectic collection of powerfully charged symbols. They do not make a system, nor do they necessarily compel policy conclusions, but they do define a shared, characteristic discourse which can clearly distinguish one party from another.

The Tories and Liberals each, for example, carefully nurture the icons of past leaders. Macdonald, Diefenbaker and, increasingly, Stanfield are symbols, in the Tory mind, of the traditions and practices of greatness. Laurier, Mackenzie King, St. Laurent, and Pearson, on the other hand, are icons of Liberal vision, compromise, competence, and internationalism. The Tories have a complicated visceral allegiance to the concepts of free enterprise and competition, while the Liberals vigorously embrace the idea of cultural and economic sovereignty. Internal dissension among Tories has a long history, but is mitigated by the belief that Conservatives are principled and hence prepared to do battle for what's right. Among Liberals, the long party tradition of compromise and consensus has instilled the dread of self-destruction by attacks on the leader. The extraordinary attention paid in 1986 to criticisms of John Turner's leadership betrayed the extreme Liberal sensitivity on this issue.

Senator Keith Davey has been involved in Liberal Party politics since 1949, but is apparently not able to define a Liberal in terms other than a list of icons. A Liberal likes the *Toronto Star*, bilingualism, John Turner, Pierre Trudeau, David Peterson, Canadian content, Air Canada, and multiculturalism, among other things, but hates Ronald Reagan, Margaret Thatcher, sacred trusts, foreign control, Doug Fisher, and separatism.[11]

While the lack of a clearly articulated ideology is a commonly noted fault of party leaders, it is certain that without a firm grasp of the party's iconology, no leader can hope to succeed. Brian Mulroney, despite his lack of parliamentary experience and apparent absence of ideology when he became leader, was able to skilfully tap key party icons, using their energy for his own purposes. His connections to Diefenbaker and his articulation of the party's resentment at losing power in 1980, when it had been within its grasp, were brilliant examples of how would-be leaders can invoke symbols in their own behalf.[12]

3. The Party and Elections

...The media bring leaders into our living rooms, revealing foibles with an electronic intensity completely beyond the grasp of print journalists. The media game has special rules which a prime minister must master. The phenomenon of "tagging," whereby leaders are quickly labelled as "strong and arrogant" (Trudeau), "wimpy" (Clark), or "untrustworthy" (Mulroney), makes immediate mastery a major priority for every leader. Parties now routinely employ media consultants who drill leaders on the rituals and tactics of media combat.

Despite their clear and growing influence in focussing our political attention on leaders, the media have by no means completely expunged the importance of party. It remains a fact that elections, while they are increasingly fought *in* the media, are fought *with* party machines.[13] Parties remain important as instruments of political success and as the training ground for future politicians. In Canada it is simply inconceivable that someone should aspire to political leadership without reasonably close ties to his or her party. As in most things, Prime Minister Trudeau was the exception to this rule, a man who within only four years of joining his party became its leader. But of the other leaders of the two main parties—Mulroney, Clark, Stanfield, Diefenbaker, and Drew; Turner, Pearson, St. Laurent, and Mackenzie King—all had long associations with the organizations they eventually led. Election of leaders by party conventions has eroded the connection to some degree, since almost anyone with the right organization can contest the leadership. But plausible candidates must at least be of the clan, if not necessarily in the family.

Parties are political instruments as well, indispensable to fighting and winning elections. At the federal level, there are almost 300 seats or constituencies that require candidates. Parties perform the nominating functions at the grass roots. They handle the routine of local campaigns, and are critical to "getting out the vote." No amount of clever media hype will budge voters from their sofas— indeed, *too* clever a media campaign may dispose voters to stay home, comfortable in the knowledge that their party will win. This is the moment at which ordinary party organization can make the difference—the reminders to vote, the personal phone calls, the offers to provide transportation to and from the polls—mundane as they are, these efforts may often make the difference between winning and losing. Sheila Copps, for example, recounts how she lost her first election by 15 votes out of 20,000 cast: "In almost any local or provincial election, especially in urban areas, more people stay at home than vote. And those stay-at-homes can make or break a candidate."[14]

Beyond offering these mundane election services, political parties are increasingly important as organizations in the soliciting of campaign contributions, a long-standing feature of Canadian politics, especially to parties in power. In the past, these contributions were solicited by a few notables or functionaries within the party, and usually somewhat discreetly. However, since the 1974 Election Expenses Act, party financing has become big business, and political parties have become increasingly sophisticated in encouraging donations.[15]

4. The Party and Purpose

This brings us to the reiteration of a fundamental if somewhat obvious truth about political parties. Their *raison d'être* is to win elections. All of their other activities ultimately must square with this goal and its reward, power.[16] Several simple corollaries accompany this fact.

First, parties are not policy-making or generating machines. In order to win elections, of course, one must be able to present a platform, some reasonably coherent vision of the party's public purpose. However, ... prime ministers and premiers are increasingly the focal point for the Canadian policy process. As a focal point, they must balance their activities over a wide range of arenas. The party as a machine or instrument remains indispensable in mobilizing voters at the constituency level, but policy matters have to be addressed simultaneously in all arenas. Policy conventions have grown in popularity in recent years among political parties, but leaders continue to treat any resolutions agreed to by these conventions as advice and not instruction.

Second, if winning power is the primary function of the party, it is not surprising that most leaders eventually neglect the party between elections. The machine gets rusty, volunteers drift away, meetings become infrequent. Once elected to its head, most leaders see the party, outside of its electoral role, as a nuisance. Mackenzie King, for instance, allowed the Liberal party to atrophy drastically during World War II, and then realized, to his chagrin, that the 1945 election would be unwinnable without the Liberal organization.[17] Pierre Trudeau is sometimes blamed for having won power at the expense of his party. He believed in appealing directly to the voters over the heads of the party, and quite deliberately allowed the Liberal organization (especially in the West) to decline.[18] He loathed the normal duties of the party leader among the faithful: appearances at local events and meetings with constituency executives.[19] John Turner, upon assuming the leadership, promised to revitalize the party at its roots. His efforts were a response to the drubbing the party had received in the 1984 election. Turner's atypical attention to the party between elections is clearly linked to his judgement that the party had lost its effectiveness as an electoral weapon.

Finally, the fact that parties are in business to win elections helps explain the special character of their relation to the leader. The leader, in service of the led, must be seen to further the party's electoral goal. As long as he remains successful in that quest, the party will follow. But should he falter and stumble, his followers are often quite prepared to trample him underfoot in their stampede to appoint a new champion. Party members therefore have, to use Burke's phrase, a dignified obedience, a proud submission to their leader which retains, even in servitude, a terrible potential of retribution should the leader fail. The Conservatives have been noted for exercising this punishment upon leaders who lose: Diefenbaker,[20] Stanfield,[21] and especially Joe Clark[22] all felt the sting of rejection. Indeed, the "leadership review" which eventually forced Clark out in favour of Mulroney proved so painful that the party has now limited its use. The Liberals are also cautious about formal review mechanisms, but John Turner clearly felt the intense heat of party disappointment after the 1984 electoral debacle. Two years later, with party fortunes still ambiguous, he had to defend himself against criticisms by the "old guard" of Trudeau supporters in the party.

5. The Party and Its People

In some ways, prime ministers would be better able to handle their parties if they had only to deal with paid personnel. While the paid staff of all Canadian political parties has grown substantially in the last ten years, the vast majority of party members and workers are still volunteers. They receive no direct benefit or reward other than the party's success as a whole, or perhaps the success of the individual candidate they have supported.

The demographic profile of party members is what one would expect. For both Liberals and Conservatives, they tend to be drawn disproportionately from the middle- and upper-income groups, with higher levels of education. Women play a prominent role at this level, in sharp contrast to their under-representation in candidacies and executive functions. Party members are more ideological than the average citizen, meaning that they are capable of articulating a reasonably consistent political position on a wider range of policy issues.

Why do they join and contribute their time this way? Surely it is not for the intrinsic rewards of envelope-licking and doorbell-ringing. Their motives are complex, but can roughly be organized into three categories. The first, and most benign, is a simple desire for camaraderie and social intercourse. As Jean Chrétien has put it: "Politics is a game of friends."[23] Political parties are like massive clubs, and party members often enjoy the opportunity to meet a wide range of different people and to build up social contacts, as well as the satisfaction of working with others for a common goal. The second category of motives is more clearly political. People with convictions on certain political issues are prepared to fight for the victory of those convictions through the medium of a political party. They believe, in short, in "the cause" and are prepared to advance it as best they can.

These first two categories help us understand the support that political parties may draw upon when they are out of general favour. The NDP, the Tories, and recently the Liberals need volunteers with conviction, who are prepared to give of their time and energy for little or no direct compensation. It would be foolish, however, to ignore the fact that over time, even the most selfless volunteer may begin to yearn for a more tangible recognition of his or her sacrifices. This is the third type of motive for political involvement. The most tangible rewards are appointments or perks doled out by government, so that political success becomes a sine qua non of party survival. Brian Mulroney, when he ran for the Tory leadership, made it quite clear that upon election, his government would ensure the bestowal of patronage on Conservatives.[24] For party supporters who had endured almost twenty years in the political wilderness, and who had briefly gained control and then lost the government under Joe Clark, it was an irresistible promise.

Donald Johnston has put the issue graphically:

> Separating the powermongers and the patronage-seekers from the dedicated is a chronic problem of political parties. This process is easier following defeat when hard work rather than a place at the public trough is the only reward. When the beast is dead, parasites migrate to another warm body.[25]

The motivational reality which underlies party support suggests a number of key prime ministerial strategies. A prime minister will always have to retain some degree of control over the patronage system, and will have to use that system to proffer incentives when appropriate.[26] Senatorships, Royal Commissions, obscure boards and agencies—the deliberate and judicious distribution of these and other plums will keep the spirit of self-sacrifice from flagging. As important, if not more so, is the need to provide *symbolic* rewards. Most party volunteers crave nothing more than respect and acknowledgement. These can be provided in various ways: the leader can solicit advice, compliment the work of volunteers, proclaim the importance of party democracy, and appear at local functions.

6. The Selection of Leaders

Before 1919, Canadian political parties followed British practice in electing their leaders from within the parliamentary wing. The caucus elected the leader. Since 1919 (1927 for the Tories) the parties have selected their leaders by open convention.[27] Delegates from all the ridings, members of the parliamentary party, and others specially designated arrive by the hundreds to select, by run-off ballot, the new leader. This selection process has several consequences for the relations of leader and party.

First, the leader, once elected by the party, can plausibly claim national and broad party support. This run-off system assures that the leader must be elected by a majority, however slim, and since no provincial breakdowns of the votes are given, there is no chance of discerning an imbalance in regional support. Since the leader is elected by *all* of the party, he or she may claim a moral and symbolic power of representation which would simply be unavailable under a different, more restricted, system.

Second, the dynamics of convention elections reduce the importance of parliamentary experience among leadership aspirants. The hallmark of a parliamentary career is skill in the parry and thrust of debate, but modern Canadian politics places relatively little emphasis upon it. Question Period is often a revue of theatrical accusations and denials, and media image matters as much as, if not more than, parliamentary substance. Convention delegates know this, and so a long career in formal politics is no longer regarded as crucial for leaders. Brian Mulroney, Joe Clark, and Pierre Trudeau are proof of this new reality. Some substantial connection with the party is still important, however, as the Clark and Mulroney examples show.

Finally, the convention process can create difficulties for the new leader. Defeated rivals may nurse a grudge, or protest a specious loyalty while they plot anew. In some instances, as happened with Joe Clark, the new leader is under constant threat of revolt and must use every resource just to maintain control of the party. In other cases, as with Mulroney and perhaps Turner, the wounds heal more rapidly. But the smoothness of this process will in part reflect on the leader's abilities. Possessing the prime ministership is the leader's key weapon: grudges and dissension will eventually evaporate in the face of the resources and prestige available to the prime minister.

7. The Leader's Power in the Party

...Leaders are plugged into pre-existing and ongoing political and social processes, and their leadership consists of an ability to harness these various processes in the service of a single vision. It is wrong to conceive of the leader's power as something "possessed" or imposed; it is rather the use of strategic intervention to alter and direct flows of power in other arenas that defines the leader's influence.

In these terms, a leader's power in the party which elected him may be reduced to waiting for opportunities and nurturing the resources available for intervention. In formal terms, the leader of each of the major parties has few opportunities to direct party affairs. Each party has a national executive, of which the leader is a member, to oversee party affairs. The nomination and selection of delegates is controlled by the local riding. The leader may try, of course, to influence those processes informally or use prestige to encourage certain outcomes, although not on a regular basis.[28]

In formal terms, then, the leader has in fact relatively few opportunities and resources to intervene in party processes.[29] Informally, however, the scope is much wider. A key asset in this regard is his symbolic role as leader, though if he also occupies the prime ministership he obviously has more tangible instruments at his disposal. He can work behind the scenes to encourage his supporters to outflank his foes, he can use his platform as leader to alter or amend terms of debate on key issues, he can force issues as "tests" of his leadership, he can, over time, demonstrate capacities of moral leadership which attract new support for his position, he can encourage coalitions and discourage alliances. None of these means is immediate or necessarily direct, which helps explain those awkward episodes when party leaders seem at war with their own supporters. Tories, who have been out of power much longer than the Liberals, have been afflicted by this more frequently.

8. The Prime Minister as Leader

A central fact which helps explain both the opportunities and constraints faced by prime ministers is that they are simultaneously leaders of a *party* and of a *government*. The contrasts, indeed the contradictions, are sharp: (1) the party is partisan, while the government is in the broad public interest; (2) the leader can only influence the party, whereas he may command the government; (3) party loyalty is to his person, government loyalty to his position; (4) the party is most alive during elections, the government is most alive between them; (5) the leader is elected by his party, but the government is elected by the people. There are other contrasts, but these reveal the tensions which all prime ministers face—in effect, the tensions in managing the dynamics of two related yet often conflicting arenas.

As party leader, the prime minister is expected to be concerned with partisan advantage and party affairs. The reward of the party faithful through patronage may extend from obviously partisan appointments to the awarding of contracts to loyal ridings. Partisanship means stirring up the troops occasionally with attacks on opponents. And yet, as government leader, the prime minister must preserve the fiction that he is above mere partisan concerns and is engaged in furthering the public interest. Appointments should be made on merit, contracts awarded on the basis of efficiency, and ad hominem attacks should be avoided in favour of principled debate.

The tensions between party and government are reflected further in the loyalty which the leader may demand: in the party it is a loyalty to his person as one of them, to his qualities and abilities. To appear prime ministerial is to appear distant and aloof. Every leader must somehow balance the dignity and distance of his role as prime minister with the familiarity and openness expected by party followers. His influence over his party comes from his formal role as prime minister, but he can never forget that as party leader he heads a voluntary organization quite jealous of its autonomy; as government leader he has a much greater ability to issue formal commands and assume obedience. In part, the temptation of power is to embrace the formal role since, superficially at least, it is an arena of recognized authority. Since the party may to some degree be safely ignored between elections, the temptation can seem sweet indeed. But as stated earlier, parties are indispensable weapons in electoral struggle, and the true challenge for any leader is to play all these arenas and their demands. Pierre Trudeau appeared to embrace his formal prime ministerial role to the disadvantage of his party role; Prime Minister Mulroney is perhaps doing the reverse.

9. The Party and the Voters

In their struggle for power, political parties must of course appeal to voters. They must either play on a pre-existent loyalty, diminish a lingering doubt, or activate neutrality. Looked at from this perspective, political parties are really just the nodal point for a vast, shifting and temporary coalition of voters. The party must hammer together, by election day, a plausible coalition of socio-economic constituencies which ordinarily might be opposed to each other. This is the aggregating and integrating function of parties writ large.

In modern politics the media expect the leader to articulate the party's national profile. In doing this, the leader may initiate subtle yet far-reaching changes in the sociological base of a party. This role was not lost on the pre-television generation of party organizers. In the 1930s, for instance, a belief grew among some Tories that their party was perceived as being too right-wing; accordingly, John Bracken was recruited to the leadership in the early 1940s and brought with him a change in the party's name to *Progressive* Conservative.[30] Pierre Trudeau was an attractive leadership candidate in 1967 because, in part, he could be counted on to appeal to Quebeckers as well as to women and youth. In his second bid for the Tory leadership, Brian Mulroney had a tremendous advantage in being able to plausibly claim that he could "deliver Quebec."

In retrospect, those leaders whom we designate as great are often the ones who, whatever their reputations while in office, have managed to forge, on behalf of their parties, new and enduring coalitions. Macdonald created a coalition of Quebec and Ontario; Laurier's coalition was built of Quebec and the West. Pierre Trudeau changed the sociological profile of his party to include many more ethnic Canadians.

10. Leaders, Parties and Policy

These preceding glimpses or *aperçus* lead to some tentative conclusions on political parties, their leaders, and public policy. Perhaps most important is the realization that party and government are very different arenas which demand different skills and behaviour. The demands they make on the prime minister are often contradictory. Many observers have attempted to deal with these arenas as two stages: *first* the leader arises in the party, *then* the leader assumes the prime ministership. It is much more fruitful, however, to remember that these arenas operate simultaneously, and hence may tug the prime minister in different directions.

Political parties are not machines, however often that analogy may be used for them. They are ragged coalitions of many interests, centred around a few key ideas and, more often, icons, aiming to win power but having to rely largely on volunteers. Prime ministers are easily and understandably distracted by their governmental responsibilities, but the very fact of prime ministership gives them certain leverage over the party. The prospect of patronage is extremely effective in welding together disparate party factions. The power over cabinet appointments and some parliamentary perks helps discipline the caucus. Modern elections focus on the leader, and leaders who lose risk the wrath of the followers. By the same token, however, leaders who win power, especially those who do so regularly, attain an almost unrivalled authority over their followers.

The fact remains, however, that prime ministers are also party leaders, and the forces described above place constraints on their actions. MPs, for example, may toe the line in the Legislature but are quite prepared to vent their views in caucus. No prime minister can completely disregard these internal caucus debates, though he can try to channel them. Parties can also have a cherished commitment to certain policies that no prime minister may reject with impunity. It is not that they are unable to reject the policies or practices, only that they must be prepared to carry the party with them. In this regard, as in others, Pierre Trudeau seems to have been an exception. His solitary decision in 1978 to cut $2 billion from federal expenditures not only departed from government policy but was made without the consultation of key ministers.[31]

It is clear from the preceding review that political parties have a modest role in policy formation. The dynamics of parties demand that leaders give a respectful hearing to party policy resolutions, but the discipline of power requires that these resolutions be considered guides and nothing more. However, the party's informal policy role can be strategically important. The prime minister, as leader, needs to secure party support from among its many factions and coalitions. A process of anticipating reactions can thus occur, whereby the party does not *formally* determine policy, but informal and potential responses may affect policy design. As well, no leader can ignore the iconology of the party—it contributes a vocabulary of symbols and concepts whereby policy is shaped in a party's image.

Ultimately, a prime minister's success depends on adroitly playing these various arenas, and that often demands a politics of position rather than principle. Principles matter, of course, but they need to be translated into terms appropriate to each of the key arenas. This in turn requires a sensitivity to the dynamics and opportunities that arise independently in the political process. In the 1984 election, for example, Brian Mulroney capitalized brilliantly on the patronage issue: it echoed the resentment of his party against those who had so long enjoyed the fruits of power, it expressed a fundamental principle of good government, and it could be clearly articulated in the media. Good political issues do not simply arise; they are made. Their fabrication requires a measure of luck, but ultimately depends on the successful, and often instinctual, exercise of strategic leadership.

Notes

1   Weller, *First Among Equals: Prime Ministers in Westminster Systems* (London: George Allen & Unwin: 1985), p. 18.

2   See, for example, the skimpy treatment of this issue in the leading textbooks on Canadian politics: Van Loon and Whittington, *The Canadian Political System: Environment Structure and Process* (Toronto: McGraw-Hill Ryerson: 1981), Chap. 10; Jackson et al., *Politics in Canada: Culture, Institution, Behaviour and Public Policy* (Toronto: Prentice-Hall: 1986), pp. 465-473; Gibbins, *Conflict and Unity: An Introduction to Canadian Political Life* (Toronto: Methuen: 1985), pp. 306-309.

3   Brown, Chodos and Murphy, *Winners, Losers: The 1976 Tory Leadership Convention* (Toronto: James Lorimer: 1976).

4   For an amusing description, see Gwyn, *The Northern Magus: Pierre Trudeau and the Canadians* (Toronto: McClelland & Stewart: 1980), Chap. 16.

5   On women in politics, see Bashevkin,S., *Toeing the Line: Women and Party Politics in English Canada* (Toronto: University of Toronto Press: 1985).

6   Brown, Chodos and Murphy, *Winners, Losers*, p. 72.

7   Copps,S. *Nobody's Baby* (Toronto: Deneau: 1986), p. 41.

8   O'Sullivan,S. *Both My Houses* (Toronto: Key Porter: 1986), pp. 34-35.

9   Senator Keith Davey is the backroom politician extraordinaire. See his autobiography, *The Rainmaker: A Passion for Party Politics* (Toronto: Stoddard: 1986).

10   See for example Christian,W. and Campbell,C. *Political Parties and Ideologies in Canada* (Toronto: McGraw-Hill Ryerson: 1986)

11   Davey, *The Rainmaker*, p. 327.

12   Martin,P., Gregg, A. and Perlin G., *Contenders: The Tory Quest for Power* (Toronto: Prentice Hall: 1983).

13   For instance, televised leadership debates have relatively little impact on election outcomes; Leduc and Price, "Great Debates: The Televised Leadership Debates of 1979." (*Canadian Journal of Political Science*; March 1985).

14   Copps, *Nobody's Baby*, p. 18.

15   Stanbury, W., "The Mother's Milk of Politics: Political Contributions to Federal Political Parties in Canada, 1974-1984." (*Canadian Journal of Political Science*; December 1986)

16   See Winn, "Elections" in *Political Parties in Canada* edited by C. Winn and McMenemy (Toronto: McGraw-Hill Ryerson: 1976)

17   Whitaker,R., *The Government Party* (Toronto: University of Toronto Press: 1977), Chap. 4.

18   Johnston,D., *Up the Hill* (Montreal and Toronto: Optimum Publishing: 1986), p. 57.

19   As described in McCall-Newman, C., *Grits: An Intimate Portrait of the Liberal Party* (Toronto: Macmilan: 1982), p. 340.

20 Newman, *Renegade in Power: The Diefenbaker Years* (Toronto: McClelland & Stewart: 1973), Chaps. 24-25.

21 Stevens, *Stanfield* (Toronto: McClelland & Stewart: 1973), Chaps. 12-13.

22 Simpson, *Discipline of Power: The Conservative Interlude and the Liberal Restoration* (Toronto: Collins: 1986).

23 Chrétien, *Straight from the Heart* (Toronto: Key Porter Books: 1985), p. 23.

24 Martin, Gregg and Perlin, *Contenders*.

25 Johnston, *Up the Hill*, p. 135.

26 Prime Minister Trudeau ended his time in office with a barrage of appointments. Having held them vacant for so long may have enhanced party discipline.

27 For background, see Courtney, *The Selection of National Party Leaders in Canada* (Toronto: Macmilan: 1973) Chaps. 1-2.

28 When Don Johnston mentioned to Pierre Trudeau that he was interested in running for office, Trudeau was encouraging. "[There] was little he could do to help, however, since it would have violated Party convention for him too give the nod to any particular person in a Liberal nomination race." Johnston, *Up the Hill*, p. 31.

29 See McMenemy, Redekop and Winn, "Party Structures and Decision-Making." in *Political Parties in Canada*, Winn and McMenemy, eds.

30 Morton, *The Progressive Party in Canada* (Toronto: University of Toronto Press: 1950).

31 As described in Chrétien, *Straight From the Heart*, pp. 117-118.

Joseph Wearing Joe Wearing's 12 Rules for
Winning a PC or Liberal
Leadership Contest

Joe Wearing is both a political scientist, who has written about Canadian parties, and a longtime Liberal party activist who has participated
in many leadership contests. These rules summarize his observations
and experience of party leadership contests. He says "they are intui-
tively derived without any specific pretension and are provided with
examples taken mostly from the 1983 Conservative and 1984 Liberal
conventions."

Rule #1

You have to have a secure and sizable home base. Otherwise, if you
cannot demonstrate drawing power where the cards are stacked in
your favour, how can you convince people of your growth potential
anywhere else? One of the clearest examples was Crosbie's base in
Newfoundland. Chrétien secured a base in his home province of Quebec with some difficulty and Mulroney's base in that province was, to
some extent, an illusion. Though he actually split the Quebec delegation with Clark, he had to claim massive support at home to have
credibility elsewhere. A base need not be strictly geographical. Clark's
base consisted of paid party organizers, but he perhaps relied too
heavily on them to the exclusion of others in the party; certainly David
Crombie thought so. Turner's base lay with the ex-officio delegates.
None of the other candidates had any base within their respective parties, or if they did—John Munro, Eugene Whelan, Mark MacGuigan,
for example—it was much too small.

Rule #2

You must also demonstrate broad national appeal. In the recent conventions, Mulroney, Turner, and Chrétien were able to show this.
Johnston began to show it too late. The most notable candidate to
flout this rule was Crosbie, who campaigned as if Quebec did not exist
and thus damaged his credibility as a candidate of national stature.

Rule #3

You have to be regarded as a serious candidate by the media. This rule is obviously related to the previous rule, because the media play such a vital role in moulding delegates' perceptions of how the various candidates are doing in other parts of the country. The real breakthrough in Crosbie's campaign came when journalists saw him not just as a colourful, intelligent candidate, but as one with real winning potential (even though he failed Rule #2).

Of all the candidates, Mulroney, both in 1976 and 1983, was eminently skilful in generating media interest. For example, in 1982, when he decided to put himself in readiness for another crack at the leadership, it was six years since the previous leadership convention. Many media people had never met him and were sceptical. So he used a series of fund-raising dinners to conquer (or reconquer) them.

A related skill is getting the media to follow *your* agenda rather than someone else's—Mulroney's experiences in the 1976 campaign showed him the importance of this. In 1983, his organization leaked Gallup poll results to *The Globe and Mail* in the week before the convention to give his campaign (especially his fund-raising) a final boost. According to the poll, delegates believed Mulroney had the best chance of beating either Trudeau or Turner, even though he was behind Clark on the first ballot. The Mulroney people did *not* show *The Globe and Mail* the scenario of a final ballot between Mulroney and Crosbie that Crosbie won.

The media's refusal to see either John Roberts or David Crombie as major candidates had a debilitating effect on their campaigns. Similarly, even though the media saw Jean Chrétien as Turner's principal challenger, they refused to see him as a winner or a potential prime minister. Media interest in Johnston did not come until well after the halfway point, by which time it was too late.

Rule #4

Before the convention is called, you must line up people with good networks in the party, including good fund-raisers and a respectable number of caucus supporters. Put all of these people into key positions when the campaign begins. The Mulroney candidacy of 1983 is the pre-eminent manifestation of this rule. He learned this lesson in 1976, when he had only three MPs and his campaign was managed by a group of his old friends, mostly Quebecers from St. Francis Xavier University and Laval law school. In 1983, he secured much more caucus support and set up a decentralized organization with key organizers in each province. Crosbie, who started to put together his campaign team in 1981, also had some good network people. Michael Wilson, being from Ontario, had close links with the provincial Conservative Party and counted on getting the networking skills of the fabled Big Blue Machine. But Ontario Tories were hoping for Davis himself as a candidate and so Wilson's campaign never got the backing it needed. An outstanding example from an earlier convention is the network presented to Robert Stanfield by Dalton Camp. Duff Roblin might have got it had he not procrastinated so long about becoming a candidate.

On the Liberal side, Turner had no paucity of network people, but he had considerable difficulty in getting them all to mesh. Jean Chrétien was at a disadvantage in Quebec for having earlier declined the Quebec leadership with its control of the party machine. John Roberts had virtually no support in cabinet or caucus and this was a serious impediment.

Rule #5

You can no longer take a passive approach to the selection of delegates, as you could at earlier conventions. The organizing of candidate slates is now a part of the leadership selection process in Canada, even if, as we said above, half the delegates were uncommitted when elected in 1983 and 1984. Obviously, delegate-selection strategies have to vary according to party rules in each province and the strength of local organizations.

In general, (a) try to get early delegate-selection meetings in the ridings where you expect to do well (John A. Macdonald used this tactic in general elections in the days before all ridings voted simultaneously); (b) if the local organization is weak, use outside, paid organizers to pack the delegate-selection meeting; (c) if the local organization is well established, recruit from among the local party notables who are already in place; (d) run a slate in order to capture all the delegate positions in ridings where you are strong. However, slates can be risky in well-organized, non-metropolitan ridings, where they are liable to cause resentment and the risk of a backlash; (e) a *joint* slate with another candidate may be a clever move in order to prevent a sweep by a strong opponent.

Rule #6

When wooing delegates, try to meet as many as you can in small, private gatherings close to their own home turf. This takes a lot of time, money, and incredible stamina. If you have been accepting invitations to speak at fund-raising dinners and annual meetings across the country for the last several years, then you already have a big advantage. Attempt to ingratiate yourself with every delegate, not just the nominally undecided. Remember, every delegate is a potential *second-ballot* supporter.

Every major candidate attempts to do this sort of thing now. Those who did it to particularly good effect were Joe Clark before the 1976 convention, Brian Mulroney before the 1983 convention, and Jean Chrétien, who hardly ever turned down an invitation to speak at a Liberal riding association's annual meeting. By contrast, Claude Wagner passed up the opportunity to become known by the Conservative rank and file after he was elected to Parliament in 1972. He is said to have been the most sought-after guest speaker among Conservative MPs, yet he declined most invitations.

Rule #7

Delegate tracking is important. Every candidate's organization attempts to track delegates' leanings through a hierarchical structure: a contact in each riding reports to an area chairman who reports to a provincial chairman, who, in turn, reports to a national chairman. The problem is that delegates lie, often from the kindest of motives. So your organization has also to do independent tracking. Use phone-banks and pretend to be an "independent" survey research firm. (This is why delegates tend to get about fifteen calls a day asking them how they intend to vote.)

Rule #8

For convention week, find a co-ordinator who can keep everything, including you, the candidate, from falling apart. During the final week, appearance is everything. (When is it not in politics?) Your organization has to appear in control, even when it is not. Your people have to spread much good will and confidence (though not too much). Remember Keith Davey's maxim, "Lead to your weakness in conventions," because the delegates will know all the candidates' foibles by this time and will be primarily concerned about having their fears alleviated.

Rule #9

Have the courage to give a short, unscripted, impromptu (or memorized) speech. The two notable examples of candidates who broke this rule and got a lower first-ballot vote than expected were Paul Hellyer in 1968 and Jean Chrétien in 1984. Do not worry if your demonstration eats into your allotted speaking time. Remember, your "big speech" will be delivered in 40^0 C heat when the delegates have already suffered from a surfeit of speechmaking. If you are forced to cut your speech short, the delegates will be thankful.

Rule #10

You have to demonstrate *some* momentum as balloting progresses, both to prove you can win and to have the necessary numbers. Momentum comes from having made links with other candidates' camps through existing personal friendships. As Peter White of Mulroney's 1983 campaign said, "The key strategy has got to be coalition building." Close ties of friendship between the Mulroney team and the Wilson team were crucial in bringing many of Wilson's supporters "on side" when Wilson withdrew after the first ballot. There were similar ties between the supporters of Davie Fulton and those of Robert Stanfield at the 1967 PC convention. Three candidates who singularly failed this test were Clark in 1983, Mulroney in 1976, and Davie Fulton in 1967. The candidate with the *greatest* momentum is not necessarily the final victor—for example, the vote totals for Crosbie in 1983 and Robert Winters in 1968 grew faster from ballot to ballot than did those of Mulroney and Trudeau.

Rule #11

Pick your opponents carefully. Jean Chrétien thought his chances would have been better if Donald Macdonald had entered the race. Macdonald and Turner had been keen rivals and, if a contest between them had become bitter, "the only compromise acceptable to both camps might be good old Jean Chrétien." A year earlier, Mulroney was very relieved when the two premiers, Davis and Lougheed, decided not to run for the Conservative leadership.

Once all the candidates are in and out, there is still the consideration of whom you want to meet on the final ballot. Mulroney wanted a runoff with Clark; Crosbie wanted a runoff with Mulroney; and Clark wanted a runoff with Crosbie. This is admittedly the most difficult rule to implement. One thing you might attempt is to bolster the strength of your preferred final-ballot opponent by discouraging your second-ballot supporters in his camp from switching to you. A more drastic and dangerous course is secretly to direct some of your supporters to vote for your preferred final-round opponent on the penultimate ballot. Rumours abound that some of Frank Miller's supporters did this at the Ontario PC convention in 1985 in order to get Larry Grossman rather than Dennis Timbrell onto the final ballot against Miller. Whether by coincidence or not, Grossman *did* move from third place to second—eliminating Timbrell by just six votes—only to be beaten by Miller on the last ballot.

Rule #12

You apparently do *not* have to have a happy, smoothly functioning organization. The two most recent examples are Mulroney's 1983 and Turner's in 1984.

Lawrence Hanson Contesting the Leadership at the Grassroots: the Liberals in 1990

Canadian political parties are entering a transitional phase in terms of the manner in which they choose their leaders. Recently, a number of provincial parties have used either a direct vote of all party members or a system which combines the direct vote approach with the existing convention system. This latter procedure has now been adopted by the Liberal Party of Canada which will first use it when they meet to choose Jean Chrétien's successor.

Although these changes are important, it should be remembered that the leadership process has evolved continually throughout this century. Between 1919, when the Liberals became the first to hold a national leadership convention, and the conventions of the early 1980s, the process has been altered in a number of significant ways. Over this period, conventions in both the Liberal and Conservative parties were characterized by an increasing percentage of delegates chosen at the constituency level, while the proportions of ex-officio delegates such as Members of Parliament declined. This trend was again apparent in 1990 when the Liberal party's constituency representation increased from seven to twelve locally elected delegates per riding. In addition, both parties also created new categories to attract more individuals from particular groups, such as women and youth, into the party.

Beyond numbers, the processes by which constituency (and other) delegates have been chosen has also been transformed. As recently as the late 1960s, the selection process was an affair dominated by the party elite, with delegates often being chosen and then instructed by local Members of Parliament to cast their ballots for a particular candidate. However, based on data from the 1983 and 1984 Conservative and Liberal leadership conventions, Carty argued that delegate selection at the constituency level has become a more competitive, open and organized process, and that constituency politics in general are undergoing an important transformation.[1] By comparing the selection processes of delegates to the 1984 Liberal convention to those who attended the 1990 Liberal convention we will be able to reach some conclusions about the extent to which the trend toward openness, competitiveness and factional organization has continued and even accelerated.

What costs do these developments pose for the parties? To answer, it is necessary to estimate the extent to which they leave them vulnerable to manipulative tactics such as leadership campaign organizations packing selection meetings with people recruited solely for the purpose of voting for identified would-be delegates. By comparing the selection experiences of delegates who voted for Tom Wappel, a candidate whose campaign was identified strongly with the issue of abortion, it will be possible to assess whether or not the leadership selection process is overly susceptible to manipulation by single issue and special interest groups.

The 1990 Delegate Selection Process

Although there were fourteen different types of delegates present at the 1990 Liberal leadership convention we are concerned only with those chosen in the constituencies.[2] At the 1984 convention, such delegates made up 57 per cent of the entire body. However, as a result of the 1986 rule change which increased the number of constituency delegates, this figure rose to 69 per cent at the 1990 convention, making locally elected delegates an even more important target of leadership candidates' campaign efforts.

In his analysis of the 1984 leadership campaign, Carty develops a four-part model of delegate selection contests at the constituency level: (1) delegate positions are contested; (2) those seeking them ask others to come to the selection meeting to vote for them; (3) would-be delegates identify themselves with particular leadership candidates; and finally, (4) they run on slates with other delegate hopefuls. Table 1 compares the experience of constituency delegates to the 1984 and 1990 conventions in terms of this framework.

The differences between constituency delegate selection in 1984 and 1990 are startling. Although the rate of contested delegate selections remained roughly constant, the nature of these contests changed considerably. In 1990, three-quarters of all delegates asked others to come to selection meetings to support them, up from the roughly 60 per cent who sought such support in the previous campaign. In 1984, only two-fifths of the delegates identified themselves with a particular candidate prior to the vote at the selection meeting, while in 1990 more than 80 percent of the delegates had identified themselves in this fashion.

In 1990, 85 percent of the delegates ran as members of a slate, as opposed to the 38 percent who sought election in this manner

Table 1: Constituency Delegate Selections

	Percent 1984	Percent 1990	Percentage Change
1. Selection contested	75	76	1
2. Asked others to come and support	59	74	25
3. Prior identification as supporter of a particular candidate	41	83	102
4. Ran as part of a slate	38	85	124
5. Ran on an identified slate	24	76	216
6. Trench warfare (identified slate versus identified slate)	12	47	292

in the previous campaign. The rise of *identified* slates of delegates was even more prevalent: in 1990, 76 percent of the delegates were chosen in this fashion, a rate more than triple that of 1984. Carty terms constituency-level competitions between slates of identified would-be delegates as "trench warfare." In 1984, only 12 percent of the delegates reported involvement in such a competition. By contrast, in 1990 almost half of the delegates emerged from this type of battle.

Although these figures suggest a level of factional organization which far exceeds that of 1984, the data in Table 1 do not necessarily represent a continuum of increasingly complex selection processes. There is no necessary connection between the four elements of the model. For example, some delegates could have been members of identified slates, yet did not ask others to come and support them. However, if we take the case of those delegates who had the particular selection experience involving the greatest organizational complexity (i.e. those who were contested, sought support from others and ran on an identified slate) we obtain further evidence about the extent to which leadership campaigns have become increasingly organized affairs. In 1984, only 14 percent of delegates reported this unique selection experience. In 1990, however, almost one-half of all delegates were selected in such a contest.

On the basis of the 1983 and 1984 surveys, Carty concluded that while leadership conventions are no longer elite-dominated races with a non-competitive delegate selection process, the reports of national leadership campaigns pursuing widespread and highly organized strategies at the constituency level may have been exaggerated.[3] However, just as an important transformation took place between the late 1960s and the conventions of the mid-1980s it is equally clear that significant differences exist between the 1984 Liberal leadership race and the contest which took place just six years later.

Although the extent to which delegateships were contested changed little between the two conventions, the nature of these competitions changed greatly. The constituency delegate selection process is now intimately linked with the national leadership decision. While more than half of the delegates to the 1984 convention were autonomous agents with no prior commitments to particular candidates, in 1990 such individuals were in a distinct minority. Those seeking delegate status also were far more organized in their efforts: between 1984 and 1990, the percentage of delegates who sought support from others increased, while the percentage of delegates who joined others on a slate more than doubled.

Not only did local delegate selection become more linked to the national leadership decision, but those involved were far more organized in their efforts, with more than three-quarters of the delegates being selected as members of identified slates. Writing of the 1983 and 1984 conventions, Carty notes that "party leaderships are not yet won or lost on the basis of constituency level battles between competing slates of supporters."[4] In 1990, however, 47 percent of the constituency delegates were veterans of trench warfare, which translates into almost one-third of all delegates to the convention. Clearly, organization at the constituency level was crucial in the 1990 leadership campaign.

There is also evidence that the size of the meetings in which delegates are chosen has increased. In 1984, 29 percent of the delegates reported being chosen at meetings of less than 100 people and only 8 percent claimed to have been selected at meetings of greater than 500 people.[5] In 1990, the percentage of delegates chosen at meetings of less than 100 fell to 16 percent, while the percentage of those who were chosen at meetings larger than 500 people more than tripled to 26 percent. This increase in meeting size is hardly surprising, given the heightened organization and competitiveness in 1990. Efforts to bring supporters to selection meetings were more widespread and intensive.

How are we to account for the fundamental transformations in the delegate selection process which took place from one convention to the next? It seems likely that the experiences of the 1983 and 1984 conventions played an important role in the changes which took place in 1990. Although reports about the earlier races which stressed the extensive organization at the constituency level, including tactics such as packing, were exaggerated, they appear to have had a profound effect upon party members.

In addition, the mere presence of identified slates in 1983 and 1984, combined with the excessive attention which they received, presumably influenced the leadership candidates' national organizations. The utility of such strategies was self-evident. As a result, organizing at the constituency level became a higher priority than it had been in previous campaigns. In a sense, the prevalence of such slates may have been something of a self-fulfilling prophecy: their perceived importance in 1983 and 1984 led to their actual significance in 1990.

Although a much higher percentage of delegates ran on slates in 1990 than did in 1984, in both years slated delegates pursued different strategies and had different experiences than those who ran on their own. In both campaigns, members of slates were more likely to ask for support from others and were twice as likely to be identified with a particular candidate. In addition, while those on slates in 1984 were four times as likely to be opposed by other slates, slated delegates in 1990 were three times more likely to face such competition than were non-slated delegates. This smaller ratio can be explained by the fact that there simply were a higher percentage of slates in general in the 1990 race.

Similarly, identified delegates in both 1984 and 1990 were more likely to ask for support and were more likely to run as members of slates than those who were not identified. However, while identified delegates in 1984 were more than twice as likely to run on slates than those who were not, in 1990 slightly less than twice as many identified delegates ran on slates as compared to non-identified delegates. Again, this lower ratio reflects the largest percentage of slated delegates overall in 1990. Thus, from a national perspective the selection process in 1990 was more organized and sophisticated than in 1984, but the dynamics of individual local contests were fundamentally quite similar.

Interest Group Penetration of the Leadership Process: the Wappel Case

One of the forces at work which led the Liberal Party to adopt an all-member vote for future leadership conventions was a perception that the delegate selection process could be penetrated by interest groups pushing a narrow agenda. This leads me to ask whether the 1990 contest was characterized by meeting where "instant" party members were enlisted to vote for delegates identified with particular candidates. Did the system leave the party overly vulnerable to those wishing to promote single and special interests?

Of course, a true measure of the extent to which new recruits were brought into the party simply to vote for delegates to the leadership convention would require survey data on all those who voted at the selection meetings and not merely those who became delegates. However, by looking at when delegates joined the party, we can draw some preliminary conclusions about the extent to which new members were brought into the party simply to participate in the selection of the leader. In 1984, slightly more than three-quarters of the constituency delegates had been members of the party for at least five years prior to the convention.[6] By 1990, this percentage had dropped, but two-thirds of the delegates still had been party members for at least five years. Yet, 16 per cent of constituency delegates in 1990 became members of the party during the course of the actual leadership campaign.

These figures may be somewhat deceiving however. It must be understood that under the existing rules, one-third of the constituency delegates in 1990 were required to be youth members (people 30 years of age or younger.) By their very nature, these delegates will have been members of the party for a shorter period of time than others. If we look only at senior constituency delegates, we find that more than three-quarters of them had been members of the party for at least five years prior to the convention and that only 10 per cent of them joined the party during the course of the actual leadership campaign. Thus, while we cannot be sure of the political experience of all those who attended selection meetings, we may conclude that those who actually were selected to go to the convention were, in the main, long-standing members of the party who had not become involved solely because the party was choosing a leader.

The 1990 Liberal leadership campaign provides an excellent opportunity for examining the extent to which the existing process was overly susceptible to single issue or special interest candidacies. Although leadership candidate Tom Wappel frequently denied being a single issue candidate, from the beginning he was identified with the pro-life movement. Wappel's association with this movement did not begin with his leadership bid. The Coalition for Life group had assisted Wappel in his successful attempt to become a Member of Parliament in 1988, including distributing literature which referred to his Progressive Conservative opponent (a pro-choice advocate) as a "child-killer."[7] Throughout his leadership campaign, Wappel received assistance from a group called Liberals for Life, a pro-life faction within the party which possessed its own organizational structure. In Saskatchewan, where Wappel received a higher percentage of delegates than he did in any other province, the Saskatchewan Pro-Life Association used a direct mailing to encourage its members to obtain Liberal Party memberships and attend selection meetings to vote for delegates aligned with Wappel.[8]

By comparing the experience of Wappel supporters with those of other delegates, we can gain some understanding of the way these delegates differed from others as well as how much success largely single-issue candidates might obtain under the system in place in 1990. Delegates who voted for Wappel were slightly more likely than average to ask for support and were 10 per cent more likely to run on slates, with 95 per cent of them being elected in this fashion. In a seeming anomaly, Wappel delegates were slightly less likely to have been identified with a candidate and to have run on identified slates than others. Given the fact that such a high percentage of those who voted for him at the convention ran on slates and that, as we shall see, such a high percentage received assistance from the pro-life movement, it seems likely that some of those who supported Wappel ran on pro-life slates that were not specifically identified with Wappel, but were clearly composed of his supporters.

Table 2 compares the experience of those delegates who voted for Wappel at the convention to those who did not. Three-quarters of the delegates who voted for Wappel received interest group support in their attempt to become delegates, while the rate for the others was only 22 per cent. For both the Wappel and non-Wappel voters the percentage of interest group support was not significantly affected by the delegate's selection strategy.

Table 2: Experience of Wappel Supporters versus Others

	Wappel Voters %	Others %
1. Received interest group assistance	79	22
2. Percentage of identified delegates who received interest group assistance	78	24
3. Percentage of members of identified slates who received interest group assistance	78	26
4. Joined party at least five years before leadership convention	13	69
5. Joined party during leadership campaign	53	15

Wappel supporters tended to have been members of the party for a shorter period of time than others. Only 13 per cent of Wappel voters had been members of the party for at least five years prior to the convention, as compared to 69 per cent of other delegates. Similarly, while more than half of Wappel voters joined the party during the leadership campaign, only 15 per cent of non-Wappel voters became members during this period.

Clearly, Wappel delegates were, on average, less experienced members of the party, were more likely to have joined during the campaign than others and, in addition, received far greater levels of interest group support. Furthermore, this support came disproportionately from one group: the pro-life movement. Almost three-quarters of all Wappel supporters received assistance from pro-life advocates, while 93 per cent of Wappel voters who received interest group assistance received it from this group.

Tom Wappel's candidacy illustrated that under the 1990 system, it was possible for a candidate to attract the attention and support of a special interest group whose members would join the party for the express purpose of electing delegates to the leadership convention. However, it should be remembered that Wappel was able to gain the support of only 7 per cent of the constituency delegates, a total which likely would not have been as high were it not for the ability of the Saskatchewan Pro-Life Association to organize within the framework of a weak Liberal Party in Saskatchewan. While the process may have been open to "hijacking" by single issue groups (especially in areas where party organization was weak) candidates of this sort could not hope to capture the leadership, nor even play the role of "kingmaker." However, if a number of single issue candidates became involved and gained some measure of support, they conceivably could come to have some influence on the eventual outcome...

Conclusions

Commenting on the extent to which both the selection of leadership convention delegates and party nominations were becoming more open and competitive affairs, Carty notes that while it was clear that constituency politics were undergoing a significant transformation, "[h]ow far this process will go, and with what consequences for traditional local party organization, remains to be seen."[9] At this point, we still cannot make any conclusive statements about the actual effects on parties at the constituency level. However, on the basis of the delegate survey data from the 1990 Liberal Convention, we can draw a number of conclusions about the way in which delegates to leadership conventions are chosen.

The difference in the level of competitiveness, openness and organization between the 1984 and 1990 conventions is very striking. While the rate at which delegateships were contested remained fairly constant over the two campaigns, the nature of these contests was altered significantly. While the majority of constituency delegates who travelled to the 1984 convention were autonomous agents not linked to a specific leadership hopeful, in 1990 more than 80 per cent of the delegates were elected as supporters of a particular candidate. Constituency contests were highly organized and were strongly linked to the larger national leadership decision. Fully three-quarters of the delegates in 1990 ran on slates identified with a particular candidate. Further, almost half the delegates emerged from the trench warfare of head- to-head competitions between slates of identified would-be delegates, as opposed to only 12 per cent in 1984. Clearly, the experiences of the 1983 and 1984 leadership campaigns had a profound effect upon party members and the organizational strategies of the leadership candidates. While it might be an overstatement to call these changes revolutionary, it is clear that, unlike 1984, it was vital for candidates to be highly organized at the constituency level. Rather than attempting merely to gain the support of those who already had been selected as delegates, to be successful a candidate had to ensure that his identified supporters were able to compete and win at the grassroots.

Notes

1   Carty, R.K., "Campaigning in the Trenches: The Transformation of Constituency Politics," in George Perlin ed., *Party Democracy in Canada: The Politics of National Party Conventions*, (Scarborough: Prentice-Hall, 1988).

2   The 1990 survey data come from a study done for the Royal Commission on Electoral Reform and Party Financing by Professor George Perlin. Neither the Commission nor Professor Perlin are responsible for my interpretation of the data. The 1988 data comes from Carty, *Campaigning in the Trenches*.

3   *Ibid.*, 85-87.

4   *Ibid.*, 91.

5   *Ibid.*, 89.

6   *Ibid.*, 93.

7   *Vancouver Sun*, January 31, 1990.

8   *The Globe and Mail*, June 21, 1990.

9   Carty, 96.

Royal Commission on Electoral Reform and Party Financing

The Selection of Candidates by Political Parties

Our system of government requires that the prime minister and the cabinet have the support of a majority of members in the House of Commons. In practice, this means that party government is the operative dynamic. Under party government, members of the House of Commons organize themselves as members of parliamentary parties that support or oppose the prime minister and cabinet. This has had a profound influence on the procedures adopted by parties to nominate candidates.

Candidate Selection

Elections to the House of Commons are essentially contests among the candidates of competing political parties. This is recognized in our electoral law, which allows candidates of registered political parties to be identified on the ballot. This recognition is reinforced by the requirement that all such candidates be confirmed officially by the party leader.

The selection of candidates by political parties is one of the most fundamental functions that parties perform. It distinguishes them from all other types of organizations that bring individuals together to promote common political ideas, interests and values. As R.K. Carty and Lynda Erickson put it, "It is through this process of labelling candidates that parties...make their principal contribution to the conduct of electoral democracy and responsible government as it is practised in Canada."

As a result of the parties' constitutional arrangements, the candidate selection process is primarily a function of the local constituency associations. Each constituency association decides not only who will be its candidate, but also when and by what procedures candidates will be selected. In performing this function, local associations are primarily responsible for the degree to which citizens can exercise their constitutional right to be a candidate. Although candidates of smaller or new political parties—and even independent candidates—are occasionally elected to the House of Commons, the vast majority of elections are contests between the candidates of the largest parties. Securing nomination by one of these parties is thus the normal access to electoral politics and membership in the House of Commons.

Historical Development

The development of national political parties in the decades immediately following Confederation stands as one of the most significant accomplishments of Canada's first political leaders.

The success of Sir John A. Macdonald and Sir Wilfrid Laurier was due to their recognition of the need to build their parties both inside and outside Parliament. This was no mean feat; as David Smith has noted, "the centre of gravity of the post-Confederation parties was located in the constituencies." The single-member constituency basis of the electoral system, which predated the emergence of national political parties, combined with what Smith describes as the "intense localism" that characterized political life, required these leaders to build from the ground up.

During the first half-century after Confederation, party adherents met to select their party's candidates whenever this was necessary, but formal party membership did not exist. The formulation of party policy and the selection of the party leader were the prerogatives of the parliamentary party, that is, the caucus of Members of Parliament in each party.

The informal character of the extra-parliamentary party led to candidate selection being remarkably open to local party supporters. In contrast to the practices of their British counterparts, the two national parties did not recruit candidates on a national basis, or exercise national party control over the local nomination of candidates. As a consequence, these two parties also differed from the British parties in that candidates were selected almost exclusively from among local party adherents.

These features of candidate selection were gradually altered in the second decade of this century. Several factors promoted this development. First, the two largest national parties increasingly sought to have candidates in all constituencies. This meant that efforts had to be made in areas where the party was electorally weak, or where the local party was unable or even unwilling to field a candidate. These efforts obviously required a greater role by the national party in recruiting, if not formally selecting candidates.

These efforts were further stimulated by the advent of radio broadcasting as an election campaign instrument, especially as regulated access to this new medium included incentives for parties to nominate as many candidates as possible.

Second, the Liberal Party developed the practice of regional ministers assuming an increasingly interventionist role in recruiting and selecting candidates in the local areas within their informal, but nevertheless real, spheres of influence. Third, the emergence of a third national party, the Co-operative Commonwealth Federation, brought with it centralized control in the candidate selection process, exercised by the provincial councils of this national party over local party associations. This was deemed necessary to prevent "infiltration [by] Communists."

Developments in the national parties themselves were even more significant. In the 1960s, the increasingly active role of national party associations in leadership selection and review, as well as in party policy discussions, resulted in increased competition for appointments as delegates to national party conventions within local party associations. These changes coincided with a greater recognition of political parties in the electoral law. For instance, reforms to federal electoral law in the 1970s allowed registered national political parties to be identified on the ballot next to the names of candidates. This required the national leader of a registered party to endorse the nomination of a local association as the party's official candidate. In addition, reforms to election finance law concerning reimbursement of election expenses further increased the advantages of running complete slates of candidates across the country.

As a consequence, the candidate selection process of the national parties has become more formalized and thus more restricted. As late as 1962, Howard Scarrow could still report that open nomination conventions, in which all interested voters could participate, were still common. However, the practice of open conventions to select candidates were gradually abandoned with the adoption of formal membership requirements. By the 1988 election, almost all local constituency associations of the Progressive Conservative, Liberal and New Democratic parties stipulated that only individuals who held valid party memberships, as defined and prescribed by the local association, could participate in selecting the local party candidate.

This evolution of candidate selection was characterized by increasingly formalized and structured processes at the local level. In part, this was the result of similar developments in national party associations. There is competition within local constituency associations over candidate selection and the selection of delegates to national leadership and policy conventions. This has meant a tightening of the rules of membership and the procedures governing decision making by the membership to ensure that factions or advocacy groups do not control the process, and that a certain degree of fairness prevails.

Local constituency associations in the large national parties have not generally been centres of great activity, however, let alone of intense intra-party competition. In many cases, the local association still finds itself in the position of having to search for a prospective candidate for nomination. And in many local associations, the executive can still exert considerable influence, if not dominance, over the candidate recruitment and selection process without much reaction from the party membership. Finally, incumbent MPs are infrequently challenged for their party's nomination. Thus the local autonomy that has characterized candidate selection has in some large measure been the result of the low degree of competition for party nominations.

Candidate Selection Process in the 1988 Federal General Election

Decentralized candidate selection processes in Canada have resulted in a wide array of procedures and practices. Moreover, less is known about this aspect of party politics than about any other similarly significant dimension of national politics. The tradition of local autonomy has also meant that, in the absence of national objectives, the national parties have no central reporting requirements on local candidate recruitment and selection procedures or practices. On the basis of a survey of the official agents of candidates in the 1988 general election for the three large national parties, we can identify a number of salient features of candidate selection. The representative sample included just under a third of all associations for the three parties.

The survey revealed that just over 80 per cent of the nomination contests for all three parties were completed before the writs were issued. Moreover, constituency associations with incumbent MPs seeking re-election were far more likely to hold early nomination conventions. Post-writ nominations were usually held in constituencies where the political parties were electorally weak. In approximately two-thirds of the constituency associations, the timing of nomination conventions was decided by the local party executive; in one-fifth of the associations the full membership selected the date; and in the remaining cases, party officials other than local executives had to convene a nomination convention because in these constituencies, the party was weak or badly organized.

For the 1988 federal election, each of the three large national parties held 295 nomination meetings, for a total of 885. The level of competition varied considerably within each party, and from province to province. Any measurement of the competitiveness of nomination contests must be assessed against the presence of a large number of uncompetitive contests where the parties were either electorally weak or where incumbent MPs were not challenged for the nomination. Almost two-thirds of the nomination races surveyed were uncontested, including 90 per cent of the incumbents. Two contestants sought the nomination in 20 per cent of the constituency associations, and three or more contestants competed in almost 15 per cent of constituencies. In constituency associations where there was no incumbent, almost 60 per cent of the party nominations were uncontested.

Although the mobilization of party members is essential to a contestant seeking a nomination, the data indicate that, even in competitive nomination races where there were significant increases in paid membership, the turnout rate for new members attending candidate selection meetings averaged less than 50 per cent. "The simple truth is that, in most cases, the majority of party members do not bother to turn out to vote at nomination meetings, even when they are contested." Local membership expanded most rapidly where an incumbent was challenged for the nomination. Even where membership increased for these races, the number of members who actually attended nomination conventions averaged less than two-thirds of the total.

Membership requirements varied considerably among constituencies and parties. Just over half the associations of the three large national parties allowed non-residents of the constituency to vote at nomination conventions. This included a large proportion of Progressive Conservative associations, which in theory were precluded from doing so by the party's national constitution.

Few associations required lengthy membership periods. The majority allowed individuals to vote during the nomination convention if they had held a party membership for between one week and one

Table 1: Media images of party nominations, 1988 (per cent)

The Globe and Mail stories reporting

Contested nominations	66
Conflicts over mobilization	28
Appeals	19
Local-national conflict	10
Ethnic mobilization	5
Nomination expenses	4
Local issue	0
Total stories	93

Source: Carty and Erickson 1991 RC.

Note: All stories in *The Globe and Mail*, 1 June-30 October 1988, that reported nominations.

month. Membership fees varied within and among parties. These minimal membership requirements made it easy for individuals to join the party in order to participate in the candidate selection process.

Half the local constituency associations had formal search committees, including 15 per cent of the associations where an incumbent was seeking re-election. Most associations, however, did not actively seek assistance from national party organizations in recruiting potential nomination contestants.

Less than 15 per cent of local constituency associations in the three large national parties had guidelines on nomination spending limits. Neither the development nor the enforcement of the spending guidelines were initiated by the central party organizations. Rather, various constituency associations used guidelines at their own discretion. Spending in the constituencies with guidelines, however, was not significantly lower than in constituencies without them.

The mobilization of new party members and the high cost of the small number of competitive nomination races received extensive media scrutiny and coverage in the 1988 federal election. As a result, the candidate selection process acquired a high public profile. Newspaper readers and television viewers were left with the impression that the candidate selection process as a whole was subject to widespread abuse and that large amounts of money were being spent by numerous contestants seeking party nomination.

Table 2: Image v. Reality, 1988 (per cent)

Nomination meetings	Press image[a]	Constituency reports[b]
Contested	66	35
Conflicts over recruitment	28	9
Appeals	19	6
Local-national conflict	10	4
Specific issue	0	21

Source: Carty and Erickson 1991 RC.

[a] Press image refers to *The Globe and Mail* reports.
[b] Constituency association survey done by the authors.

Carty and Erickson suggest that media coverage of the candidate selection process in the 1988 federal election focused mostly on a small number of competitive nomination races where large amounts of money were spent and controversial practices were used by candidates to mobilize support. The narrow scope of this coverage contributed to public perceptions that the candidate selection process was marked mostly by high spending and abuse of party membership rules. Carty and Erickson conducted a content analysis of the treatment of candidate selection by *The Globe and Mail*; it is reasonable to suggest that this newspaper's coverage was representative of the other media. The survey of *The Globe and Mail* coverage of the selection process for the four months before the 1988 election was called suggests that its readers were not necessarily given a representative picture of the way in which candidates were nominated (see Table 1). Approximately 66 per cent of the stories carried by *The Globe and Mail* about the candidate selection process concerned contested nominations. This figure contrasts with data from the survey of official agents, which indicates that just over 34 per cent of nominations were contested by two or more candidates (Table 2). A third of *The Globe and Mail* stories reported on internal party conflicts concerning the accreditation and mobilization of new party members; however, the recruitment of new members led to internal party conflicts in only 9 per cent of nomination contests. Further, approximately 20 per cent of *The Globe and Mail*'s news articles concerned the use of internal party appeal mechanisms to challenge membership rules or nomination results. In reality, less than 6 per cent of the nomination contests involved internal party appeals.

This limited but telling examination of *The Globe and Mail* coverage suggests a considerable gap between perceptions of how the candidate selection process functioned in 1988 and actual practices. For example, survey data indicate that only in a small number of highly competitive constituencies was a large amount of money spent by candidates seeking nominations. When supporters were mobilized to become members of a candidate's campaign organization, the average cost was nine times the cost for constituencies where new members were not recruited. An assessment of the candidate selection process must be based on a full understanding of the dynamics and factors shaping the nomination of party candidates, not on inaccurate perceptions of experience. *The Globe and Mail's* coverage misses an essential point: many of the problems associated with the nomination process—the low proportion of women recruited, for example—stem not from the high level of competition in a limited number of constituency associations, but from the large number of uncompetitive, relatively closed nomination contests conducted by local party insiders.

Canadian political parties stand at one end of the continuum between local responsibility and autonomy for candidate selection on the one hand, and party member participation in candidate selection, on the other. There is no public regulation of these processes, and with the exception of the NDP, there is little in the way of national or provincial party control or influence over the procedures used by local party associations. In comparative terms, Canadian parties are highly decentralized and open, with relatively little direction and control from the national level. While this decentralization stems from a longstanding tradition of localism in party affairs and is frequently praised in those terms, the present structure and its results have raised a number of concerns, particularly regarding the competitiveness and openness of the system.

Close to two-thirds of constituency nomination contests are uncompetitive—that is, the nomination is by acclamation. This contributes to what is perceived to be the closed nature of nominations, because it is often assumed that this outcome is the result of decisions by local executives. Opportunities exist to introduce changes to the candidate selection process that will make it more open, more amenable to grassroots participation and more consistent with democratic principle and processes.

Notes

Carty, R.K. & Erickson, Lynda. "Candidate Nomination in Canada's National Political Parties" in H. Bakvis, ed., *Canadian Political Parties: Leaders, Candidates and Organization* vol. 13 (Ottawa: Royal Commission on Electoral Reform and Party Finance: 1991).

Royal Commission on Electoral Reform and Party Financing

Financing Contemporary Party Problems

The capacity of federal political parties to perform their roles as primary political organizations is also related to the state of their finances. Before 1974, the Liberal and Progressive Conservative parties were in most cases able to collect fairly substantial sums to run election campaigns. During non-election years, however, their spending and revenue declined dramatically. For example, the Liberal Party spent $5.5 million on the 1974 election campaign; the Progressive Conservatives spent $4.5 million. During calendar year 1973, however, the Liberals had spent $407,130 and the Progressive Conservatives had spent $900,195. The contrast was less marked in the case of the NDP, which spent only a small fraction of what the two older parties were spending on election campaigns: the NDP spent $353,852 during the 1974 election; its regular budget in 1973 had been around $250,000.

Reviewing the overall impact of the 1974 legislation, which introduced an income tax credit for political contributions, W.T. Stanbury has stated that it "transformed the financing of federal political parties in Canada. Its most important consequence has been to provide all the main parties with vastly larger sums to spend in the years *between* elections." Table 1 provides an overview of the revenue (contributions and other sources of income) and expenditures of the Progressive Conservative, Liberal and New Democratic parties from 1 August 1974 to the end of 1990.

Immediately after the 1974 legislation came into effect, the Liberal Party's revenue exceeded that of the Progressive Conservative Party. The latter benefitted from its early move to solicit funds by direct mail, and by 1978 its revenue had risen to $5.5 million (compared with just over $5 million for the Liberal Party). The financing of the NDP improved considerably during the post-1974 period, and by 1978 the NDP's federally receipted revenues totalled $3.4 million.

As Table 1 indicates, although revenues for these three parties increased during the period up to and including 1983, a different pattern subsequently emerged: revenue for the Progressive Conservatives and NDP continued to rise most years, but the Liberal Party

Table 1: Revenue and Expenditures of the Progressive Conservative, Liberal and New Democratic Parties, 1974-1990

period	Progressive Conservative Party rev	exp	Liberal Party rev	exp	New Democratic Party total rev[a]	federal rev[b]	expc
1974	1,721[d]	1,597[d]	2,217[d]	1,935[d]	1,437[e]	N.A.	1,270[e]
1975	1,203[f]	889[f]			2,580	N.A.	2,570
1976	4,084	3,497	5,823[g]	4,707[g]	2,925	2,281	2,381
1977	3,774	4,233	4,587	4,187	3,525	3,006	3,105
1978	5,465	5,470	5,018	5,283	4,184	3,400	3,514
1979E	8,376	5,184	6,302	2,771	6,020	4,741	4,678
EE		3,845		3,913			2,190
R	794		718		496		
1980E	7,564	4,923	7,457	3,702	6,101	4,921	5,992
EE		4,407		3,846			3,086
R	978		910		677		
1981	6,950	7,542	5,592	5,116	6,003	3,856	6,491
1982	8,521	8,521	6,746	6,781	7,108	4,766	4,871
1983	14,767	13,199	7,736	6,277	8,669	5,972	8,009
1984E	21,979	20,777	11,598	11,999	10,513	7,357	7,407
EE		6,389		6,293			4,731
R	1,438		1,416		1,064		
1985	15,073	11,654	6,163	8,149	10,152	6,464	11,071
1986	15,639	14,141	10,719	11,166	14,639	6,984	15,188
1987	13,058	13,490	8,882	9,274	12,608	6,833	14,012
1988E	25,231	21,124	16,358	10,176	18,754	12,162	14,933
EE		7,922		6,840			7,061
R	1,782		1,539		1,589		
1989	14,521	12,824	6,397	7,115	13,865	7,746	12,507
1990	11,298	10,635	13,778	13,327	15,439	9,043	14,262

Source: Adapted from Stanbury 1991 RC, Tables 3.1 and 3.2.

E = Election year; EE = 'Election expenses' for the party; R = Reimbursement of election expenses by federal government, that is, one-half permitted spending on the electronic media for advertising in 1979 and 1980 and 22.5 per cent of total allowable expenditures in 1984 and 1988.

[a] Before 1980, the chief electoral officer did *not* include provincially receipted revenue in the NDP revenue figure. As of 1976, this revenue has been included here. After 1960, the chief electoral officer's report included as revenue provincially receipted revenue, as well as provincial rebates and subsidies.

[b] Federally receipted contributions plus other income and reimbursement of party 'election expenses'.

[c] Total expenditure for the party including most of its provincial sections (does not include Ontario).

[d] From 1 August 1974 to 31 July 1975.   [e] From 1 August 1974 to 31 December 1974.   [f] From 1 August 1975 to 31 December 1975.   [g] From 1 August 1975 to 31 December 1976.

Table 2: Value of Contributions to the Progressive Conservative Party, by source, 1974-1990 (per cent)

Year	Individuals	Business and commercial organizations	Trade unions	Other[a]
1974-75[b]	45.84	51.83	0.0	2.33
1976	48.89	49.32	0.0	1.80
1977	49.16	48.62	0.01	2.20
1978	49.62	48.95	0.0	1.44
1979E	38.00	59.94	0.01	2.05
1980E	40.24	57.75	0.0	2.01
1981	62.15	37.03	0.0	0.82
1982	63.23	35.67	0.0	1.10
1983	64.54	34.16	0.0	1.29
1984E	47.96	52.04	0.0	0.0
1985	54.05	45.95	0.0	0.0
1986	51.88	48.10	0.01	0.0
1987	47.53	52.47	0.0	0.0
1988E	41.49	58.51	0.01	0.0
1989	49.63	50.30	0.01	0.06
1990	42.42	57.48	0.0	0.09

Source: Calculated from data reported in Stanbury 1991 RC, Table 4.1 and fiscal period returns for 1990.

E = Election year

[a] Includes other organizations and governments.
[b] 1974-75 figures combine 1 August 1974 to 31 July 1975 and 1 August 1975 to 31 December 1975.

---

was able to better its 1983 revenue in only two of the four subsequent non-election years.

A further contrast between the pre- and post-1974 periods lies in the sources of these parties' funding. Before adoption of the *Election Expenses Act*, the Liberal and Progressive Conservative parties were financed by contributions from at most a few hundred corporations, primarily to finance election campaigns. The NDP relied on union contributions and relatively small donations.

Tables 2, 3 and 4 report the proportion of these three parties' total contributions since 1 August 1974 by source. The NDP has consistently obtained the greatest share of federally receipted con-

Table 3: Value of Contributions to the Liberal Party, by source, 1974-1990 (per cent)

Year	Individuals	Business and commercial organizations	Trade unions	Other[a]
1974-75[b]	51.40	46.22	0.03	2.35
1975-76[c]	52.79	45.98	0.01	1.22
1977	44.84	51.80	0.03	3.33
1978	43.97	52.05	0.01	3.97
1979E	22.69	74.24	0.03	3.04
1980E	36.63	60.00	0.03	3.34
1981	41.24	53.10	0.03	5.63
1982	52.34	41.31	0.04	6.30
1983	44.78	48.63	0.04	6.55
1984E	49.09	50.60	0.02	0.28
1985	56.17	43.66	0.02	0.15
1986	54.18	45.63	0.05	0.14
1987	39.31	60.50	0.10	0.09
1988E	35.94	63.96	0.04	0.06
1989	37.72	62.16	0.05	0.07
1990	61.81	37.94	0.03	0.22

Source: Calculated from data reported in Stanbury 1991 RC, Table 5.1 and fiscal period returns for 1990.

E = Election year

[a] Includes other organizations and governments.
[b] From 1 August 1974 to 31 July 1975.
[c] From 1 August 1975 to 31 December 1976.

tributions from individuals: in non-election years (excluding the first five months the legislation was in effect), the proportion averaged 80 per cent; in election years, when the party usually receives a number of large union donations, the share from individuals has averaged 63 per cent.

The Progressive Conservative Party initially obtained less than half the value of its total contributions from individuals, but by 1981 donations from individuals accounted for 62 per cent of the total. Except for the 1984 election year, the proportion remained over 50 per cent until 1987, when it dropped to 47.5 per cent. In 1990, the

Table 4: Value of Contributions to the New Democratic Party, by source, 1974-1990 (per cent)

Year	Individuals	Business and commercial organizations	Trade unions	Other[a]
1974[b]	89.47	0.99	9.30	0.24
1975	80.14	5.56	14.20	0.09
1976	80.33	4.17	15.33	0.16
1977	77.23	6.64	15.25	0.88
1978	78.32	6.34	15.04	0.29
1979E	55.36	3.85	38.47	2.31
1980E	60.64	2.08	36.65	0.63
1981	81.15	3.09	14.57	1.19
1982	83.20	3.18	10.43	3.19
1983	86.99	0.72	11.08	1.21
1984E	63.45	0.79	32.96	2.79
1985	81.71	1.04	15.40	1.85
1986	77.89	2.75	18.14	1.23
1987	77.05	0.76	21.67	0.51
1988E	71.46	2.39	24.76	1.39
1989	83.12	0.75	13.99	2.14
1990	72.60	1.70	14.08	11.62

Source: Calculated from data reported in Stanbury 1991 RC, Table 6.1 and fiscal period returns for 1990.

E = Election year

[a] Includes other organizations and governments.
[b] From 1 August 1974 to 31 December 1974.

party received 42.4 per cent of the value of its contributions from individuals.

The proportion of the Liberal Party's total contributions from individuals has been greater than 50 per cent during four of the eight non-election years since 1980. In 1989, the proportion was 37.7 per cent (lower than any non-election year since 1974). In 1990, 61.8 per cent of the total value of contributions to the Liberal Party were from individuals; however, this includes contributions to candidates and fees paid to the party by delegates who attended the June 1990 leadership convention.

Table 5: Accumulated surplus (or deficit) of the three largest federal parties, 1974-78, 1979, 1980-84, 1985-1990 (thousands of dollars)[a]

Party	1974-78	1979	1980-84	1985-1990
Progressive Conservative	561	241	(3 560)	4 811
Liberal	1 505	336	(2 558)	(2 211)
New Democratic[b]	1 811	(350)	(453)	(1 988)

Source: Adapted from Stanbury 1991 RC.

[a] Nominal dollars.
[b] New Democratic Party as a whole as reported to the CEO after a few minor adjustments.

While year-to-year comparisons are useful, a better index of the parties' ongoing financial health is their accumulated surplus or deficit. Stanbury's analysis is reported in Table 5. During the 1980-1990 period, the Liberal Party ran an accumulated deficit of $4.77 million, while the Progressive Conservatives had an accumulated surplus of $1.25 million. The NDP as a whole ran an accumulated deficit of $2.44 million during the 1980-1990 period. This contrasts with the period between the coming into force of the election expenses legislation and the end of 1979, when all three parties ran a surplus. On this basis, there is room to question how successful one if not two of the largest parties have been in meeting the spending pressures they have faced in recent years—pressures that are particularly strong in the context of running competitive election campaigns. (The Liberal Party's deficit is rooted in the 1984 campaign, when it spent almost $6 million, virtually half its total revenue, including the post-election reimbursement for that year.)

The financing of candidates' campaigns reveals a different situation. Following the 1984 general election, the combined surplus of all candidates was more than $8 million. The comparable figure for the 1988 general election was $9.6 million. The Liberal Party has been able to benefit somewhat from the healthy state of most candidates' election finances. Since the 1979 election, the party has regularly 'taxed' a proportion of candidates' reimbursements. Following the 1988 election, the party collected $2.27 million by obliging the majority of its candidates to pass on 50 per cent of their reimbursements to the federal party. In 1988, the British Columbia section of the NDP required all candidates in the province to remit

Table 6: Number and average size of contributions by individuals to the Progressive Conservative, Liberal and New Democratic parties, 1974-1990[a]

Year	Progressive Conservative Party[b] Number	Average ($)	Liberal Party[c] Number	Average ($)	New Democratic Party Number	Average ($)
1974 (5 mos)	6,423	284	4,117	321	27,910	132
1975	10,341	253	13,373	292	58,889	90
1976	23,409	197	18,261	274	56,142	77
1977	20,339	192	21,063	209	60,169	82
1978	35,615	153	22,350	192	67,133	78
1979E	34,952	170	13,025	170	63,655	80
1980E	32,720	167	17,670	240	62,428	88
1981	48,125	136	24,735	128	56,545	77
1982	52,694	134	27,968	156	66,665	58
1983	99,264	119	33,649	125	65,624	98
1984E	93,199	135	29,056	220	80,027	64
1985	75,117	125	28,545	131	97,364	56
1986	52,786	170	35,369	186	90,487	64
1987	39,320	168	28,972	131	87,927	59
1988E	53,893	199	30,642	163	118,390	69
1989	40,191	170	19,970	119	89,290	67
1990	27,702	161	36,361	196	116,448	50

Source: Adapted from Stanbury 1991 RC, tables 8.2 and 8.3.
E = Election year

[a] In 1989 dollars. The table does not include contributions by individuals to *candidates* in election years.
[b] The original figures for the Progressive Conservative Party were for 1 August 1974 to 31 July 1975 and 1 August 1975 to 31 December 1975. They were recomputed on a pro rata basis to fit the calendar years.
[c] The original figures for the Liberal Party were for 1 August 1974 to 31 July 1975 and 1 August 1975 to 31 December 1976. They were recomputed on a pro rata basis to fit the calendar years.

100 per cent of their reimbursements to help meet its quota for the federal party. Candidates submitted a total of $558,127. Party representatives indicate that through various other arrangements, candidates have shared some of the funds received through reimbursements.

Table 7: Other registered parties: financial activities, 1990

Party	Revenue ($)	Expenses ($)	Number of contributions (N)	Average contribution ($)
Christian Heritage Party	497,956	376,665	9,268	54
Party for Commonwealth of Canada	350,038	406,402	431	108
Communist Party	487,805	471,994	710	465
Confederation of Regions Western Party	159,841	196,057	2,962	54
Green Party	52,928	56,337	389	136
Libertarian Party	57,152	57,530	476	120
Reform Party	2,213,762	1,721,468	23,736	93
Parti Rhinocéros	400	230	2	200
Social Credit Party	22,853	15,466	212	108

Source: Adapted from Canada, Elections Canada 1990.
Note: Total revenue for the Communist, Confederation of Regions Western and Commonwealth of Canada parties consists of total contributions and other revenue, while the other parties listed contributions as their sole source of revenue.

Another perspective on the state of national parties' finances can be gained by examining the number and average size of individual contributions. Table 6 indicates that excluding election years, the number of individuals donating to the three largest parties has declined in recent years. For the Progressive Conservative Party, the peak was in 1983, when a leadership convention was held, with 99,264 contributions from individuals. (The number for 1990—27,702—was less than one-third that number.) Except for 1990, when the party held a leadership convention, the largest number of individuals contributing to the Liberal Party was in 1986—35,369; in 1989, the number was 19,970. The number of individual contributions to the NDP in non-election years was the greatest in 1990—116,448. The number of donations from individuals to other registered parties was much higher in 1989—17,232—than in any other year since the 1974 legislation came into effect; in 1990, that number rose to 37,837. The number of contributions to the Reform Party from individuals was 7,630 in 1989 (its first full year as a registered party) and 23,462 in 1990. The Christian Heritage Party received 7,541 contributions from individuals in 1989 and 9,226 in

Table 8: Number of contributions from individuals to parties and candidates, 1974-1990

Year	PC, Liberal and NDP	Other parties	All parties	All candidates	Total
1974 (5 mos)	34,703	7,796[a]	42,499		42,499
1975	82,603	2,007[b]	84,610		84,610
1976	97,812	11,432	109,244		109,244
1977	101,571	2,754	104,325		104,325
1978	125,098	5,040	130,138		130,138
1979E	111,632	7,701	119,333	67,323	186,656
1980E	112,908	3,865	116,773	70,528	187,301
1981	129,405	1,600	131,005		131,005
1982	147,327	1,538	148,865		148,865
1983	198,537	6,556	205,093	205,093	
1984E	202,282	8,700	210,982	87,456	293,438
1985	201,026	1,622	202,648		202,648
1986	178,642	2,442	181,084		181,084
1987	156,219	2,603	158,822		158,822
1988E	202,925	5,410	208,335	104,807	313,142
1989	149,451	17,232[c]	166,683		166,683
1990	180,511	37,837[d]	218,348		218,348

Source: Stanbury 1991 RC, table 8.1.
E = Election year

a From 1 August 1974 to 31 July 1975.
b From 1 August 1975 to 31 December 1975.
c Includes 7,541 for the Christian Heritage Party (22 October 1988 to 31 December 1989) and 7,630 for the Reform Party. The total number of contributions from individuals to the Confederation of Regions Western Party was not disclosed; the number included here, 265, is based on those contributing $100 or more and so is understated.
d Includes 23,642 contributions to the Reform Party and 9,226 to the Christian Heritage Party.

1990. Further details on the financing of parties other than the Progressive Conservative, Liberal and New Democratic parties in 1990 are found in Table 7.

As indicated in Table 8, the number of individual contributions to candidates has increased at each election since 1979. Table 8 also shows that, when adjusted for inflation, the average size of donations from individuals in recent non-election years has been considerably

Table 9: Public funding programs of political parties and candidates in Canada

Jurisdictions	Candidates: election reimbursements	Parties: election reimbursements	Parties: annual funding	Tax credits
Canada	X	X		X
British Columbia				X
Alberta				X
Saskatchewan	X	X		
Manitoba	X	X		X
Ontario	X	X		X
Quebec	X		X	X
Nova Scotia	X			X
New Brunswick	X		X	X
Prince Edward Island	X		X	X
Newfoundland				

Source: Constantinou 1991 RC, tables 6.1, 6.3 and 6.5-6.8

smaller than during the initial period after the legislation came into effect.

Although the number of individuals making political contributions to federal parties and candidates rose after 1974 (and has certainly been much higher than before adoption of the *Election Expenses Act*), the proportion of Canadians who participate in this way is low. In both the 1984 and 1988 election years, less than 2 per cent of Canadians made a political contribution to a party or candidate, and the rate was no higher in any other year since 1974. Thus, while the base of federal party finance has broadened, only a small fraction of Canadians financially support the federal political process.Public Funding and the Political Contribution Tax Credit

As indicated in Table 9, seven provinces provide direct public funding to parties and/or candidates. All provide election reimbursements to candidates, three provide election reimbursements to parties, and three fund political parties through annual allowances... All provinces except Saskatchewan and Newfoundland provide indirect public funding through a provincial tax credit for political contributions.

The total and per-voter cost of public funding at the federal and provincial levels is presented in Table 10. At the federal level, the cost per voter ($1.03 a year in 1989 dollars) is higher than in

Table 10: Public funding of political parties and candidates in Canada: cost (1989 dollars)

Jurisdictions	Total	Total cost per voter per year
Prince Edward Island	682,038	2.55
New Brunswick	6,195,949	2.47
Manitoba	3,031,310	2.08
Nova Scotia	3,541,638	1.42
Ontario	10,747,033	1.29
British Columbia	2,126,069	1.20
Canada	72,662,758	1.03
Saskatchewan	2,406,893	0.90
Quebec	14,125,769	0.76
Alberta	1,393,351	0.47
Newfoundland	None	None

Source: Constantinou 1991 RC, tables 6.12.
Note: Cost is calculated based on most recent election cycle for which complete data were available.

four provinces, but is considerably lower than in the three maritime provinces and Manitoba, and somewhat below the cost in Ontario ($1.29) and British Columbia ($1.20).

The political contribution tax credit is an incentive to donors rather than a direct grant of public monies. Therefore, it is also essential to measure its costs to the public treasury to assess the behaviour of contributors and to determine how, and if, any modifications should be enacted to improve its effect on the finances of registered parties.

Table 11 reports the number and cost of federal tax credits claimed since 1974. The data indicate that, for the most part, the number of individuals claiming tax credits and the cost of those credits (in foregone revenue) have risen in successive non-election years. Between 1975 (the first full year when the tax credit was in effect) and 1978, the number of individuals claiming the credit nearly doubled (64,547 individuals claimed the credit in the latter year). The number and amounts of credits claimed peaked in 1986, when 117,566 individual taxpayers claimed credits worth $9.93 million; including credits claimed by corporations, the total was $10.77 million. In 1987, the number of individuals claiming credits dropped to 102,824 and the total amount to $8.47 million. Based on prelimi-

Table 11: Federal Income Tax credits for political contributions, 1974-1989

Year	Individuals (N)	Tax Credits: individuals ($)	Corporations (N)	Tax credits: corporations ($)	Tax credits: totals ($)
1974	19,584	1,273,000	N.A.	N.A.	1,273,000
1975	36,227	2,394,000	N.A.	N.A.	2,394,000
1976	48,313	2,800,000	N.A.	465,000	3,265,000
1977	48,027	3,114,000	N.A.	500,000	3,614,000
1978	64,547	3,973,000	N.A.	634,000	4,607,000
1979	92,353	6,111,000	N.A.	1,233,000	7,344,000
1980	95,547	6,378,000	N.A.	1,247,000	7,625,000
1981	77,114	4,910,000	N.A.	538,000	5,448,000
1982	85,941	6,268,000	3,507	567,000	6,835,000
1983	104,599	8,237,000	4,178	762,000	8,999,000
1984	151,308	13,588,000	7,561	1,595,000	15,183,000
1985	109,310	8,624,000	5,995	1,254,000	9,878,000
1986	117,566	9,934,000	3,979	836,000	10,770,000
1987	102,824	7,660,000	3,647	808,000	8,468,000
1988	184,410	17,515,000	5,471	1,333,000	18,848,000
1989	108,740	8,874,000	5,744	1,333,000*	10,207,000
Total	1,446,410	111,653,000	40,082	13,105,000	124,758,000

Source: Data provided by Revenue Canada, Taxation.
N.A. = Data not available.
* Preliminary statistics

nary statistics, the number of individuals claiming the credit rose somewhat in 1989, to 108,740, as did the total cost ($10.21 million).

A similar pattern has developed in election years. The number of individuals claiming the credit has risen at each election, and the number claiming the credit in 1988 (184,410) was nearly double the number in 1979 (92,353). The total cost in credits claimed rose from $7.63 million in 1979 to $18.85 million in 1988.

The tax credit has been successful in broadening the base of party finance, but the number of individuals making political contributions dropped in the late 1980s, and even at its peak, it represented only a small fraction of Canadians. This implies that the tax credit may not be as strong an incentive as some have suggested. In fact, as Table 12 indicates, a significant proportion of individuals do not claim the tax credit for their political contributions, although the percentage of those who do has risen in recent years. Until

Table 12: Number of individuals making political contributions and number claiming the federal income tax credit for political contributions, 1974-1989

Year	Number of individual donors to parties and candidates	Number of individuals claiming tax credits	Number claiming tax credit as a percentage of total donors	Average individual credit*
1974	42,499	19,584	46.1	65
1975	84,610	36,227	42.8	66
1976	109,244	48,313	44.2	58
1977	104,325	48,027	46.0	65
1978	130,138	64,547	49.6	60
1979E	186,656	92,353	49.6	66
1980E	187,301	95,547	51.0	67
1981	131,005	77,114	58.9	64
1982	148,865	85,941	57.7	73
1983	205,093	104,599	51.0	79
1984E	298,438	151,308	50.7	90
1985	202,648	109,310	53.9	79
1986	181,084	117,566	64.9	85
1987	158,822	102,824	64.7	75
1988E	313,142	184,410	58.9	95
1989	166,683	108,740	65.2	82

Source: Stanbury 1991 RC, Table 8.4; 1989 tax credit statistics provided by Revenue Canada, Taxation.
E = Election year
* Nominal dollars

1980, less than 50 per cent of those making contributions claimed the credit. The claim rate subsequently rose, and in 1986, 1987 and 1989 almost two-thirds of those who made contributions claimed the credit. The 1989 claim rate (based on preliminary statistics) was the highest since the tax credit was initiated.

Indirect public funding through the tax credit represents a significant share of federal party finances: the value of tax credits claimed was equal to 29 per cent of the parties' total revenue during the 1985-88 cycle and 30.7 per cent of their total revenue during the 1981-84 cycle...

Table 13: Reimbursements to candidates, federal general elections, 1979-88

Party	1979 (N)	1979 Cost ($)	1980 (N)	1980 Cost ($)	1984 (N)	1984 Cost ($)	1988 (N)	1988 Cost ($)
Progressive Conservative Party	219	2,867,691	215	2,871,029	282	5,117,066	293	6,055,597
Liberal Party	273	3,594,244	275	3,656,074	238	4,081,353	264	4,655,526
New Democratic Party	147	1,670,601	152	1,884,863	140	1,917,095	170	2,839,253
Social Credit Party	29	359,273	8	111,802	–	–	–	7
Reform Party	N.A.	N.A.	N.A.	N.A.	N.A.	N.A.	11	162,122
Christian Heritage Party	N.A.	N.A.	N.A.	N.A.	N.A.	N.A.	–	197
Parti Rhinocéros	–	–	–	–	–	–	–	–
Union populaire	–	–	–	–	N.A.	N.A.	N.A.	N.A.
Libertarian Party	–	–	–	–	–	–	–	97
Marxist-Leninist Party	–	–	–	–	N.A.	N.A.	N.A.	N.A.
Confederation of Regions Western Party	N.A.	N.A.	N.A.	N.A.	3	28,870	–	–
Communist Party	–	–	–	–	–	–	–	–
Green Party	N.A.	N.A.	N.A.	N.A.	–	–	–	–
Party for the Commonwealth of Canada	N.A.	N.A.	N.A.	N.A.	–	7	–	–
Parti nationaliste	N.A.	N.A.	N.A.	N.A.	–	–	N.A.	N.A.
Independent	2	25,972	–	–	1	26,340	1	22,070
Total	670	8,517,781	650	8,523,768	664	11,170,724	739	13,734,568

Source: Canada, Chief Electoral Officer 1979a, 1979b, 1980a, 1980b, 1984a, 1984b, 1988, 1989.
Note: N.A., not applicable—party did not run candidates in year indicated.

Table 14: Reimbursements to political parties, federal general elections, 1979-88

Party	1979	1980	1984	1988
Progressive Conservative Party	793,967	977,835	1,437,512	1,782,391
Liberal Party	718,020	909,923	1,415,921	1,538,972
New Democratic Party	496,350	677,481	1,064,413	1,588,627
Social Credit Party	7,769	1,749	–	–
Christian Heritage Party	N.A.	N.A.	N.A.	48,906
All others	143	268	–	–
Total	2,016,248	2,567,256	3,917,846	4,958,896

Source: Canada, Chief Electoral Officer 1979b, 1980b, 1984b, 1988.
Note: N.A., not applicable—party was not registered in year indicated.

Public Funding of Election Participants

At present, public funding of federal political parties and candidates is provided indirectly through income tax credits and directly through election reimbursements. Both forms of public funding were introduced in 1974, although the rules relating to reimbursements were subsequently amended.

Under the 1974 legislation, registered political parties were reimbursed for 50 per cent of their election expenses on television and radio advertising. In 1983, the rules were changed; since then, all registered parties have been reimbursed 22.5 per cent of their total election expenses provided they have spent at least 10 per cent of their limit. Candidates qualify for reimbursement by meeting the following requirements: they must have been elected or have obtained at least 15 per cent of the valid votes in the constituency; they must also have submitted their post-election report on spending and contributions and the accompanying auditor's report.

The original legislation provided for a reimbursement of the lesser of the candidate's election expenses and the aggregate of the following: the cost of one first-class mailing to each person on the preliminary list of voters, $0.08 for each of the first 25,000 voters on the list, and $0.06 for each additional voter. In 1983 the formula was amended, and qualifying candidates now receive a reimbursement equal to 50 per cent of the sum of their election expenses and personal expenses up to 50 per cent of the spending limit.

Table 15: Federal election reimbursements to parties and candidates, federal general elections, 1979-88

Election	Total reimbursements	Total reimbursements to parties	Total reimbursements to candidates
1979	10,534,029	2,016,248 (19.1%)	8,517,781 (80.9%)
1980	11,091,024	2,567,256 (23.1%)	8,523,768 (76.9%)
1984	15,088,570	2,917,846 (26.0%)	11,170,724 (74.0%)
1988	18,693,464	2,958,896 (26.5%)	13,734,568 (73.5%)

Source: Canada, Chief Electoral Officer 1979b, 1980b, 1984b, 1988.

At the heart of this reimbursement system lies the belief that candidates and parties perform important and necessary functions during elections in a democratic system; it is therefore in the public interest for the state to provide public funds to support these functions. Reimbursement also lessens candidates' and parties' reliance on large donations from a few donors and helps ensure that candidates and parties are able to conduct effective campaigns. Finally, reimbursement lowers the cost of running for office, thereby facilitating access to the system....

The record shows that candidate reimbursement has been almost strictly the privilege of candidates for the Progressive Conservative, Liberal and New Democratic parties, leaving virtually all other party and independent candidates with no public funding at elections (see Table 13). In the four elections since the legislation came into effect, 2404 candidates from the three largest parties were reimbursed, compared with only 51 candidates from other parties and four independent candidates. On no occasion have the candidates of more than one party other than the three largest parties been reimbursed; in 1988, for instance, 11 of the Reform Party's candidates qualified, but not one of the candidates of any other smaller party did so. In the four elections in question, the proportion of candidates not receiving reimbursements has ranged between 53 per cent in 1979 and 57 per cent in 1980. Among those candidates not reimbursed under the present system were several whose electoral support approached, but fell short of, the 15 per cent threshold. In the 1984 and 1988 elections, for example, 226 candidates received more than 10 per cent of the vote but were not reimbursed.

Table 16: Analysis of surpluses reported by candidates, 1988 federal general election

Party	Number of candidates	Number reporting a surplus	Number receiving reimbursement[a]	Candidates reporting a surplus (%)	Total surplus reported[b] ($)	Average surplus reported[c] ($)
Progressive Conservative Party	295	231	230	78	4,639,000	20,080
Liberal Party	294	234	220	80	2,978,000	12,727
New Democratic Party	295	167	143	57	1,740,000	10,421
Reform Party	72	21	11	29	140,000	6,650
Christian Heritage Party	63	31	0	49	104,000	3,368
Confederation of Regions Western Party	52	9	0	17	2,400	262
Communist Party	52	8	0	15	1,800	223
Green Party	68	9	0	13	1,300	143
Libertarian Party	88	8	0	9	1,900	242
Social Credit Party	9	1	0	11	N.A.[d]	81
Parti Rhinocéros	74	0	0	0	–	–
Party for the Commonwealth of Canada	61	0	0	0	–	–
Independent	154	4	0	3	N.A.	63

Source: Stanbury 1991 RC, Table 12.33.

[a] Number of candidates reporting a surplus who *also* received reimbursement.

[b] Surplus = contributions - election expenses - personal expenses - campaign expenses + reimbursement.

[c] Only for those candidates reporting a surplus. Amounts may vary slightly because of rounding.

The pattern can also be seen in the distribution of the money allocated through reimbursement over the past four elections. Of the $41,946,841 allocated to candidate reimbursement since 1979, only $736,449 (1.76 per cent of the total reimbursed) has gone to candidates from other than the three largest parties.

The reimbursements to registered parties tell a similar but more striking story. Since the introduction of the 10 per cent threshold in 1983, only one party other than the three largest parties has qualified for reimbursement: the Christian Heritage Party, in 1988. Under the previous rules, in the 1979 and 1980 elections, the Social Credit Party was the only small party to receive more than $270 in reimbursement payments. Moreover, the Social Credit Party was reimbursed only a total of $9518 following these two elections, compared with the average amount of $762,263 paid out to each of the three largest parties in the same two elections. Over the past four elections, parties other than the Progressive Conservative, Liberal and New Democratic parties together received a total of $58,835 (0.44 per cent of the $13,460,246 paid out) even though they won 3 to 6 per cent of the vote in every election (see Table 14).

The case of the Christian Heritage Party in 1988 clearly illustrates this shortcoming of the present party reimbursement system. In that year, the Christian Heritage Party was reimbursed $48,906, having spent more than 10 per cent of its spending limit. But the Reform Party, which won almost three times as many votes as the Christian Heritage Party and had 11 candidates qualify for reimbursement, received no reimbursement whatsoever because it did not spend more than 10 per cent of its limit. The 10 per cent threshold therefore makes the system of public funding of election participants inaccessible to emerging parties, except those able to spend enough money to reach that threshold.

In short, the present reimbursement system has disproportionately overcompensated the three largest parties and their candidates and undercompensated the smaller parties, their candidates and independent candidates. This is in large part the result of the thresholds, although the fact that reimbursements are based on amounts spent rather than on popular support is also a factor...

The issue of the proportion of election public funding provided to parties on the one hand and to candidates on the other must also be addressed. Over the post-1974 period as a whole, average proportions were 76.3 per cent for candidates and 23.7 per cent for parties. As Table 15 indicates, reimbursements to parties, although the amounts are significant, account for a relatively small share of total direct public funding.

Payments under the present reimbursement system do not reflect the needs of candidates and parties. This is indicated by surpluses from candidates' election campaigns. Following the 1988 election, for instance, the total surpluses of candidates, including reimbursements received, amounted to $9.6 million. More than 75 per cent of Progressive Conservative and Liberal candidates had surpluses after the 1988 election, as did more than half the New Democratic Party candidates (see Table 16). The surpluses averaged $20,080 for Progressive Conservative candidates, $12,727 for Liberal candidates and $10,421 for New Democratic Party candidates. For the 11 candidates who raised more than $100,000 in that election, the surpluses ranged from $38,236 to $96,284.

In this context, it is not surprising that transfers from national parties to candidates' campaigns declined after adoption of the 1974 reforms. The Liberal Party, for example, transferred $2.6 million to its candidates in 1974, but only about $300,000 in the 1979 election and $485,000 in 1988. The Progressive Conservative Party transferred about $1.7 million to candidates in the 1974 election; this dropped to $450,000 in 1979 and totalled $232,000 in the 1988 election. The national parties recognize that candidates generally, given the benefit of the tax credit and the likelihood of reimbursement, have needed less financial assistance since the 1974 legislation. The New Democratic and Liberal parties have 'taxed' some of the surplus funds from candidates' campaigns by requiring that a certain proportion be paid to the federal level, a practice that is bound to accelerate unless a better balance is found in the allocation of public funding through reimbursements.

Notes

Stanbury, W.T. 1991. *Money in Politics: Financing Federal Parties and Candidates in Canada* vol. 1, Ottawa: Royal Commission on Electoral Reform and Party Financing: 1991.

A. Brian Tanguay Canadian Party Ideologies in the Electronic Age

The study of political parties and ideologies in Canada has attracted a great deal of scholarly attention, but produced very little in the way of a general theory. One recent assessment of this particular field of inquiry concluded that it is in disarray, with little agreement on just how important ideology is in Canadian party politics or on the most appropriate research strategies for studying this question (Johnston, 1988, p. 57). By far the dominant view—the textbook version, so to speak—is that the Liberals, Conservatives, and, in some versions, the New Democrats as well lack clearly defined programs and are essentially opportunistic. All three parties manipulate ideas and doctrines in their attempt to win elections, but these ideologies are flags of convenience, adopted as expedients in the struggle for power, and not deeply held world views. Supporters of this interpretation of the Canadian party system disagree over the reasons for this ideological flexibility. According to one school of thought, unprincipled and incoherent politics is simply the price Canadians have to pay in order to preserve national unity (Alford, 1963, pp. 251-261; Siegfried, [1907] 1966, pp. 113-114; Dawson, 1970, pp. 430-433). Another contends, however, that the apparent lack of party ideologies serves to stifle dynamic political debate in this country, thereby contributing to the perpetuation of a social order based on inequality and exploitation (Porter, 1965, pp. 368-379; Taylor, 1970, chap. 1; Brodie and Jenson, 1988, 1989).

There is another, less widespread, interpretation of the ideological basis of the Canadian party system,[1] the proponents of which indignantly deny that the major parties are "vacuous look-alikes" (Wearing, 1988, p. 9; compare Christian & Campbell, 1983, chap. 1). Citing the historical origins of each of the parties, as well as selected speeches and writings of key party figures, the defenders of this view claim that the Liberals, Conservatives and NDP are the institutional embodiments of particular ideologies. Admittedly, the ideological spectrum in this country, because of the peculiar nature of its origins as a "fragment" of European society and its subsequent cultural development, is somewhat narrower than that found in most European countries. Thus there have been no significant, enduring Communist or fascist parties in Canada. As well, each of the three parties represents a coalition of ideologies, rather than unalloyed liberalism, conservatism, or socialism. As a result, Canadian political parties appear to be less ideologically coherent than their European counterparts, but the supporters of this interpretation nonetheless claim that "the history of the leading Canadian political parties has a consistency that can best be understood by recourse to an explanation that assumes that voters, parties and leaders guide their activities by reference to ideas and principles that they inherit from their political tradition" (Christian, 1983, p. 109).

One of the objectives of this paper is to try to make sense of these contradictory interpretations of the Canadian party system. I argue that both perspectives have a certain amount of validity...

But while acknowledging that ideology can still play a significant role at the activist level, even among Canada's notoriously flexible and opportunistic "old-line" parties, this paper shares the prevailing view that clashes of ideas are relatively unimportant in electoral politics at the federal level. Ideologies, to the extent that they have existed at the level of the voter, have always been less crucial in electoral competition than other factors, such as leadership, party "style," and the appeal to material interests, both individual and regional (what falls under the broad rubric of patronage and pork barrelling). This was obviously the case in the post-Confederation period, as André Siegfried astutely observed in his 1907 classic, *The Race Question in Canada*: parties at that time were loose coalitions of local notables, and elections were essentially conflicts between "ins" and "outs" over the control of patronage. The relative unimportance of ideology to the party-in-the-electorate is all the more apparent today, as new patterns of stratification continue to erode the historically low ideological profiles of our major parties. Put simply, the shift to an increasingly services-based economy and the attendant rise of a broad stratum of non-manual workers have encouraged all of the federal parties to reduce the ideological distance separating them from their opponents, as they scramble to win over the burgeoning "middle class" of voters, for whom ideological rigidity is thought (by party leaders and strategists) to be a source of fear and dread...

In the final section of this paper I examine the impact that the new technologies of political marketing have had on the ideological basis of party competition in Canada. In the age of "electronic politics,"[2] the media (especially television), pollsters, consultants, assorted "spin doctors," and political handlers of all stripes combine to erode a party's ideological appeal, replacing it with an increasingly personalized bond between the individual voter and the party leader. The development of these new political technologies has led to the professionalization of party organizations, and encouraged electoral appeals based on personality, style, leadership, and motherhood issues that do not divide or frighten the electorate (so-called valence issues, such as economic growth, prosperity, and social stability, which nobody in his or her right mind is against), and that can be attractively packaged for consumption by a television audience. Recent federal and provincial election campaigns will serve as convenient backdrops against which to sketch the implications of electronic politics for liberal democracy in this country.

Party Organizations and the Uses of Ideology

...If ideologies can serve to mobilize different social groups behind a particular political agenda, then political parties are one of the most important vehicles for this mobilization. This ideological function of political parties is not simple or unidirectional, however: parties do not merely act as passive vessels for the particular demands of a given social group, they also mould ideology to their own organizational ends. As Panebianco has cogently argued, one of the roles historically fulfilled by party organizations has been the "creation and preservation of collective identities through ideology" (1988, p. 268). To use Panebianco's terminology, political parties have used ideology to define their specific "hunting domain," that is,

> the portion of the electorate in which the organization stakes its claims, and with respect to which its organizational identity is defined both "internally" (in its members' eyes) and "externally" (in the eyes of its electorate)...Parties which define themselves as "workers' parties," "catholic parties," etc., for example, delimit electoral territories—workers, catholics—and accordingly establish conflictual and/or cooperative relations with all other organizations that "hunt" in the same territories. (p. 13)

Ideology, in this view, is a tool wielded by political parties to control and shape the loyalties of their most faithful supporters (the *external* function of ideology) and of their members (the *internal* function).

Panebianco stresses the fact that political parties are complex hierarchical organizations, and contends that the function of ideology differs across the various levels of the organization (voters/supporters/members/activists). Among activists, one finds basically two types of individual: those who join the party primarily because of their devotion to the organization's official ideology, whom Panebianco labels "believers," and those who join mainly for the material or psychic (status) benefits that might accrue from participation, whom Panebianco designates "careerists":

> The believers' presence keeps the party from acting exactly like those opportunistic animals described by Downs, ever ready to move from the political left to the right and from the right to the left for a handful of votes.... The careerists constitute the main force behind the factionistic games, are often the human base for the schisms, and represent a potential source of turbulence and threat to the organizational order which the leaders must attempt to neutralize. (1988, p. 27)

Every party will have a different "mix" of believers and careerists, and this has a profound influence on a party's ideological profile. Even the flexible, opportunistic *brokerage* parties[3] in Canada contain varying numbers of "believers" who are attracted to the party by their commitment to what they perceive to be that party's core ideology. In the case of the Liberals and Conservatives (and increasingly, the NDP as well), however, ideology tends to be latent rather than manifest,[4] and its function is overwhelmingly internal rather than external, since the core electorates, or "hunting domains," of these parties have always been much more heterogeneous than those of most European parties. In essence, ideology in "brokerage parties" serves primarily to provide cohesion among their activists rather than to create groups of voters united with one another and with the party on the basis of a common world vision.

Even this diluted form of ideology places limits on the electoral opportunism of a brokerage party: abandoning long-standing principles will take its toll on the party's ideological health, usually in the form of a haemorrhage of the most committed party activists, for whom any apostasy by the leadership is unacceptable. This is precisely what happened recently to the federal Liberal party, which very nearly ripped itself apart in the wake of the decision by John Turner and other party notables to support the Meech Lake Accord, the political handiwork of a Conservative government. For many Liberal activists, their party had been the architect of institutional bilingualism and a number of other policies that had served as a counterpoise to separatist sentiment in Quebec. Acquiescing in the Meech Lake Accord, which would grant Quebec a form of special constitutional status, a move that has been adamantly opposed by federal Liberals since the mid-1960s, was for these activists tantamount to treason. This ideological conflict is one important factor in explaining the organizational travails of the federal Liberal party during Turner's uneasy reign as party leader.

None of this, however, should be taken to mean that ideology outweighs patronage or other more venal motives in the organizational dynamics of the old-line parties. Recent events at the federal level and in some of the provinces confirm the conventional wisdom that patronage is the lubricant of Canadian politics, that "whom you know" counts for more in party politics than "what you know," or what your beliefs happen to be. Several members of the Conservative caucus in Ottawa continue to be plagued by conflicts of interest and other financial scandals, while... the popular Liberal government in Ontario had its image tarnished by the fallout from the Patti Starr affair, in which a number of Liberal cabinet ministers and backbenchers (as well as a few federal Conservative and Liberal MPs) received campaign contributions from a Toronto-based charitable organization, run by Ms Starr... [These instances remind us] that among the activists in the old-line parties in this country, careerists like Patti Starr far outnumber the minority of believers.

Ideologies and Party Politics in Canada: Two Models

Failure to take the structural complexity of party organizations into account explains, at least in part, the dialogue of the deaf that characterizes much of the literature on the ideological make-up of the Canadian party system. The advocates of the ideological interpretation, for instance, focus their attention almost exclusively on the beliefs of party activists and of the leaders themselves. Citing the historical origins and pattern of development of the major parties, supporters of this model argue that the Liberals, Conservatives and NDP (as well as its precursor, the CCF) embody *coalitions* of ideological traditions. The Liberal party includes both business and welfare liberals, the former committed to a relatively unfettered free enterprise economy, the latter to a "mixed" economy and an extensive social welfare system. Both groups, however, are motivated by a primordial concern for individual freedom. The Progressive Conservative Party, Christian and Campbell maintain, is a rather fragile coalition of business liberals and tories ("small-c" conservatives). The tories champion order, hierarchy, deference to authority, and resistance to rapid social change, and unlike the business liberals in the party, they are not averse to state intervention if it is necessary to protect the community against the depradations of modernity. Finally, members of the CCF/NDP—whom Prime Minister Louis St. Laurent sarcastically dubbed "Liberals in a hurry" —include a goodly number of welfare liberals, as well as moderate socialists, the latter drawing their inspiration from the Fabians in Great Britain, the Social Gospel movement, and populism, rather than the revolutionary theories of Karl Marx. The aim of most socialists or social democrats within the CCF/NDP has been to reform, or humanize, the capitalist economic system, not to overthrow it.

A major shortcoming in this approach lies in the fact that the historical evidence cited as proof of the ongoing ideological "dialogue" carried on within each of the major parties is highly selective, and tells us more about the core values of individuals like George Brown, Wilfrid Laurier, Robert Stanfield, and Ed Broadbent than it does about the behaviour of parties at election time or while they are in power. This is patently obvious when the authors are confronted with some of the more egregious examples of electoral opportunism in Canadian political history. Christian and Campbell attempt to explain away Pierre Trudeau's recanting of his opposition to wage and price controls in 1975, for instance, by calling it merely a "movement...within the bounds of liberal ideology" (1983, p. 78). This may be true, but it is neither a very informative observation nor a useful insight into the nature of brokerage politics. Rather than passing off Trudeau's stunning reversal on a crucial matter of economic policy as a minor deviation within liberalism, as Christian and Campbell do, one ought to examine why the Liberal party felt compelled to take such a measure, and whether it had any damaging consequences on organizational unity (did some activists leave in disgust at this sign of crass opportunism?) and on the party's standing in the electorate (did voter cynicism increase to even higher levels after the 1975 flip-flop?)

A slightly different version of the ideological model of the Canadian party system relies on survey data to show that party activists and supporters—those whose identification with a particular party is strong and consistent over time—are much more willing to define their political views and motivations in ideological terms than are "average" voters. These survey data point to significant inter-party differences in activists' attitudes on a range of public policy issues—free trade with the United States, defence policy, social welfare spending, taxation, privatization, and so on. The views of activists and strong supporters are also more consistent than those of average voters.... Blake's survey of delegates to the leadership conventions of the federal Conservative and Liberal parties (in 1983 and 1984 respectively), for instance, showed the Tories to be somewhat more continentalist, in terms of their opposition to controls on foreign investment, than their Liberal counterparts. Tory activists were also more hawkish, more favourably disposed toward privatization of Crown corporations, and less committed to social welfare than were the Liberals. Nevertheless, Black acknowledged that there were marked variations within each party, and the level of ideological constraint among activists (the relationship between attitudes on a whole range of policy questions, from the economy to social welfare and defence) was surprisingly low, though higher than that for the electorate as a whole (1988, pp. 34-48). While there is some evidence to support the "ideological model of interparty differences," therefore, Blake remarks that

> we cannot ignore the brokerage model. Even if we allow for the possibility of increased rank-and-file influence over government policy, given internal party differences it is not clear that either party organization could present a coherent and ideologically consistent program without causing a good deal of internal disagreement. Moreover, it does not appear that the electorate is ready for such a development. (p. 48)

Blake assumes that voters "are not ready" for ideological politics because, again on the basis of existing survey data, they do not appear to perceive the parties as representatives of distinctive political visions, except on the question of language policy and Quebec's place in Confederation (p. 46). Of course, this still begs the question: do the voters view politics in non-ideological terms because they all share the fundamental values, or because the political parties do not present them with distinctive alternatives on important issues?[5] I will return to this point below.

McMenemy has undertaken a comparable study at a different level of analysis, which tends to support Blake's findings. Using election survey data, McMenemy argues that one can distinguish "core partisans" from the bulk of a given party's electoral supporters.

These core partisans have fairly permanent and strong psychological ties to a political party, are more interested in politics than the average voter, and are also more likely to participate in political activities other than voting (attempting to influence others' political views, for instance) (1989, pp. 325-327). According to McMenemy, the "attitudinal profiles" of these core partisans on a series of policy issues—the government's role in the economy, the welfare state, the distribution of wealth, Canada's role in NATO, the rights of organized labour, and so on—tend to be "more sharply delineated or polarized than those of non-core party supporters. This [is] particularly so for the Conservatives and the NDP and less so for the Liberals" (1989, p. 324). Predictably, on most issues NDP and Conservative core partisans occupy the left and right poles respectively, with the Liberals somewhere in the middle (but usually closer to the Tories than to the NDP).

Finally, Ornstein and Stevenson have investigated the political ideologies of state, business, and labour elites in Canada, and concluded, among other things, that there "is a degree of relationship between the elite ideology and party identification that is surprising given the extensive literature on the irrelevance of ideology to elites and the Tweedledum-Tweedledee character of the party system" (1984, pp. 327, 329). The authors show that those in their sample with "left-wing" ideologies, who favour strengthening the rights of labour, redistributing income, and nationalizing key industries, also tend disproportionately to identify with the NDP. On the other hand, those who oppose income redistribution and government intervention in the economy are most often Conservative supporters, with the Liberals gaining the allegiance of a somewhat smaller proportion of right-wingers.

Without disputing any of this evidence, I would nevertheless take issue with Ornstein and Stevenson's assertion that their findings *contradict* the vast literature on the irrelevance of ideology in Canadian party politics. As I argued above, it is entirely possible for activists to hold reasonably coherent ideological positions while the parties themselves appear to the voters as Tweedledum and Tweedledee (or, as some wags would have it, Tweedledumb and Tweedledumber). In this regard, André Siegfried's dissection of the role of parties in Canadian politics, written over eighty years ago, remains devastatingly accurate today. In *The Race Question in Canada*, Siegfried, who is sometimes described as "the Canadian Tocqueville," observed that Canada's two major political parties were chiefly machines for the conquest of power. The Liberal and Conservative parties, he pointed out, had vaguely defined programs—if they had programs at all. Neither of the parties hesitated to steal planks from the other's programs; both often made the same promises to the voters, each party loudly proclaiming that it was the team best able to implement a common objective. As well, the parties tended to behave in much the same way once they were in office. In Canadian politics, Siegfried concluded, "even the most naive can hardly help but see that it is not the party which is at the service of the idea but the idea which is at the service of the party" ([1907] 1966, p. 113).

One consequence of this remarkable ideological flexibility, Siegfried contended, was a lessening of the "clarity of political life" in Canada, in comparison with most European countries at the turn of the century. As well, Siegfried noted that because of the ideological vacuum that existed in Canada, elections tended to turn on questions of crass material interest, collective and individual ([1907] 1966, pp. 112-113). Patronage was the stuff of Canadian politics, not ideas or principles. Yet another consequence of the non-ideological character of Canada's major parties was the dominant role in political life played by the leader: the key to success for a Canadian political party was that it be led "by someone who inspires confidence, and whose mere name is a programme in itself." Like most Anglo-Saxons (and this is true of both the French and English in Canada), Siegfried averred, "Canadians attach themselves rather to the concrete reality than to the abstract principle. They vote as much for the man who symbolizes the policy as for the policy itself" ([1907] 1966, p. 136).

As far as the party-in-the-electorate is concerned, Siegfried's analysis remains remarkably persuasive even today. The nature of leadership may have changed since the days when Macdonald and Laurier virtually embodied their respective parties, but its significance has certainly not diminished. If anything, in an era when new campaign technologies are revolutionizing party politics in Canada and elsewhere, the direct link between the individual voter and the party leader is increasingly important in determining electoral outcomes (Amyot, 1986, pp. 954-955; Carty, 1988, pp. 24-28). Also in keeping with Siegfried's analysis is the electoral behaviour of the two old-line parties: they continue to exhibit a pragmatism that at times borders on ideological incoherence. Thus the spectacle of a Liberal government enacting wage and price controls in October

1975, only sixteen months after an election campaign in which the party had voiced its implacable opposition to this Tory proposal, would have come as no surprise to Siegfried. Nor would he have been nonplussed by the Conservative government's orgy of patronage appointments and the innumerable conflicts of interest that plagued some of its leading ministers between 1984 and 1989, all of which contrasted starkly with Brian Mulroney's impassioned indictment of John Turner's sorry record on patronage during the 1984 campaign. These examples, and a litany of other policy flip-flops, support Siegfried's view that the major parties in Canada are unprincipled and opportunistic.[6]

Many observers argue that it is not only the established parties that are flexible, pragmatic, and opportunistic: this is increasingly the case with Canada's minor parties, such as the NDP. A widespread view among political scientists has always been that these minor parties of protest are responsible for what little policy innovation there is in the Canadian party system, since the two centre parties have been forced to pre-empt challenges on their left or, less commonly, on their right (Thorburn, 1985, pp. 31-35).[7] There is growing agreement, however, that the NDP has been almost completely seduced by the brokerage politics practised by its two older cousins (Brodie, 1989, p. 179). In its concerted attempts to attract the mythical "average voter," the party hierarchy has chosen to downplay those elements of its program—nationalization of a major bank and withdrawal from the NATO alliance, for example—that might make these average voters uneasy. The NDP has also resorted to the politics of leadership with an alacrity altogether unbecoming a party that styles itself the "conscience" of Canadians: witness its 1988 election campaign, structured almost entirely around the reassuring image of its leader, Ed Broadbent.

Two basic explanations of this brokerage style of politics can be found in the literature on Canadian political parties, one that might be labelled the *classical version*, the other the *radical critique*.[8] The first contends that the intellectual incoherence of Canada's major parties is a necessary feature of a polity riven by ethnic, linguistic, religious, and regional cleavages. Siegfried, for instance, argued that the primary task of political leadership in Canada was to conciliate the disparate social groups—Catholics and Protestants, French and English, townspeople and farmers, employers and labourers, central Canadians and those living in the peripheries—that made up a very fractious electorate. Because of the heterogeneous composition of their electorates, Siegfried asserted, each of the major parties was virtually compelled to obfuscate its position on major issues, for to do otherwise would have been to court electoral suicide or inflame social tensions in the country. Periodically, Siegfried noted, an issue such as the rights of French-speaking people or the status of the Catholic Church would force its way onto the political agenda despite the assiduous efforts of the parties, and in this case certain groups of voters (Catholics, French Canadians, and so on) would act in unison, whether they were Liberals or Conservatives, to protect their threatened interest ([1907] 1966, pp. 113-114).

With the few noteworthy exceptions, this view of the Canadian party system has been the standard version disseminated by most textbooks.[9] It tends to be accompanied by the complacent belief that, on the whole, the system works quite well for Canadians—Canadian party politics may be dull as ditchwater, this argument goes, but at least it is relatively stable (Canada as "the peaceable kingdom"). This system is also thought to allow for just the right amount of ideological innovation, when the two old-line parties are forced periodically to respond to the electoral challenge of various protest parties. In the words of one recent assessment of the Canadian party system, it may be "somewhat confused and intellectually incoherent; but since our people are happy, prosperous and at peace, is there any need for more than...minor reforms...?" (Christian, 1988).

The response to this kind of thinking, of course, is that prosperity in Canada is distributed in a grossly unequal fashion, with some disadvantaged and marginalized groups (by no means an insignificant portion of society) receiving few or none of the benefits of economic growth. And whether "our people are happy" or alienated and apathetic depends to a large extent on the observer's theoretical *parti pris*. These are precisely the sorts of criticisms that have been levelled at classical brokerage theory by radical intellectuals such as Porter (1965, chap. 12), Taylor (1970), and Horowitz ([1965] 1979). In their view, the ideological incoherence of the major parties betrays an underlying pro-business bias: in Canadian politics, to paraphrase an old saying, what is good for the Masseys is usually considered to be good for the masses. Alternative visions of politics are simply beyond the pale, as far as the two established parties are concerned, and thus electoral competition between them is a fraud:

> The real function of the two-party system since the Laurier
> era has been to provide a screen behind which the control-

ling business interests pull the strings to manipulate the Punch and Judy who engage in mock combat before the public.... Both parties take for granted that their first duty in office is to assist the triumphant progress of big business in the exploitation of the country's resources. (Underhill, 1960, p. 168)

Questions of class, property, and power are studiously avoided by the established parties, Underhill and other critics charge, and politics thus revolves obsessively around national unity—the need to accommodate refractory ethnic and linguistic groups in the country.

Whether a creative politics centred on issues of class can ever be established in Canada, and how this is to come about, are questions left largely unresolved by the critics of classical brokerage theory. By the late 1950s, for instance, Underhill confessed that he did not have the slightest idea where one might discover some "stimulant" that would shatter Canada's stagnant party system (1960, p. 254). Horowitz, meanwhile, placed his faith in the ongoing process of urbanization, which he felt was creating similar social conditions across all regions of Canada, and therefore laying the groundwork for class politics ([1965] 1979, p. 76). This was a common refrain among those who fully expected Canada to some day come to resemble its European cousins, where the politics of class had gradually displaced divisions based on religion, ethnicity, and territory, or at least so it seemed in the early 1960s (Alford, 1963, pp. 251, 284-286). Horowitz added another wrinkle to this theory, however, by calling for a constitutional accommodation of Quebec nationalism: "if we can attain an approximately final solution of the French-English problem through special status for Quebec, the political energies of each nation will be diverted from the problem of the inter-national relationship to the social and economic problems which exist within each nation" ([1965] 1979, p. 76).

The critiques of brokerage theory first formulated by Porter and Horowitz have formed the basis of an important new theoretical understanding of Canada's party system. For Brodie and Jenson (1988, 1989), political parties do not act as mere transmission belts for the demands of various social groups; they actually shape the definition of politics that prevails in a society at a given time. In this they depart from the more sociological perspective of Siegfried, Dawson, Alford, and even Porter:

Parties provide voters with a definition of politics. In other words, political parties help to shape the interpretation of which aspects of social relations should be considered political, how politics should be conducted, what the boundaries of political discussion most properly may be and which kinds of conflicts can be resolved through the political process. From the vast array of tensions, differences, and inequalities characteristic of any society, parties treat only some as alternatives in the electoral process and thereby influence how the electorate will divide against itself. (Brodie & Jenson, 1988, p. 11).

Historically, Brodie and Jenson argue, the Liberals and Conservatives have sought to define politics in cultural terms, as a division between the dominant ethnic and linguistic groups in Canada. Since both parties draw their electoral support from broadly similar coalitions of classes (both are, in the words of Brodie and Jenson, "bourgeois parties"), a cultural definition of politics is much more congruent with their organizational interests than a definition based on class. Whenever issues based on class differences threaten to erupt onto the political agenda, "the bourgeois parties divert...the challenge by reformulating new conflicts in the old familiar discourse of bicultural conflict or regional differences" (Brodie & Jenson, 1989, p. 39). The NDP, they argue, after a brief and electorally unsuccessful flirtation with class politics (in its previous incarnation as the CCF), has increasingly come to accept the prevailing definition of politics, and to compete with the bourgeois parties on their own terms.

This conceptualization of political parties as "independent variables" that mould the prevailing definition of politics is undeniably an important contribution to our understanding of the Canadian party system. In the particular formulation given it by Brodie and Jenson, however, this model is not without its flaws. This is especially true of the authors' contention that the bourgeois parties in Canada have manipulated the political discourses of religion, regionalism, and biculturalism in order to prevent the emergence of a class-based definition of politics. This seems both to carry the Machiavellianism of the established parties to excessive lengths and to overestimate their ability to determine the content of the political agenda unilaterally. It also downplays the independent importance of religious, regional, linguistic, and cultural differences among Canadians. Lurking behind this view is the tacit assumption that class in capitalist society is the only *real* basis of division and exploitation, and that other cleavages are somehow epiphenomena of class. To argue that the bourgeois parties might benefit from the prevailing cultural definition of politics in Canada, which is perfectly legitimate, is not the same as to claim that these parties actively create or inflame cultural divisions in order to conceal class conflicts. The latter may or may not be true, but I would argue that Brodie and Jenson overestimate the extent to which this type of intentional manipulation has occurred in federal politics. The fact that cultural or linguistic or regional politics has usually taken precedence over class politics at the federal level may have been enormously beneficial to the bourgeois parties in this country, but in most instances they have been the unwitting beneficiaries of this situation...

Electronic Politics and the Waning of Party Ideologies in Canada

One of the most formidable obstacles to the emergence of creative politics in Canada is to be found in the new technologies of political marketing that have fundamentally transformed the nature of election campaigns, and the conduct of government itself, in all liberal democracies. Thirty years ago, when television and most of the other techniques of modern electioneering were in their infancy, Aldous Huxley wrote that the methods then being employed "to merchandise the political candidate as though he were a deodorant, positively guarantee the electorate against hearing the truth about anything" (Huxley, [1958] 1983, p. 93). In the new era of democratic propaganda, Huxley lamented, party programs and principles had become virtually irrelevant; all too often, they were seen by campaign strategists as obstacles to the overriding goal of winning power. The conventions of advertising and public relations had come to dominate political life: they dictated that parties parlay the irrational fears and hopes of individual voters into electoral advantage, mainly by projecting a reassuring or heroic image of their candidates and leaders. To Huxley, politics was no longer a reasoned debate about where society should be headed, as the early liberal and democratic thinkers had insisted it should be. Rather, it seemed to be a form of hucksterism, the art of the soft (and hard) sell. Although Huxley maintained that politics need not ineluctably degenerate into a form of mass consumer manipulation, he was not terribly sanguine about the prospects for the survival of rational democratic debate in modern industrial societies.

A fairly common response to Huxley's *Brave New World Revisited* is to dismiss it as apocalyptic claptrap. After all, everyone knows that Huxley had experimented with psychedelic drugs; perhaps this warped his perspective on democratic politics! And yet Huxley's jeremiad seems all the more prescient in the light of the subsequent revolution in campaign techniques wrought by television, pollsters, consultants, "spin doctors," and political handlers of all stripes. The attempts to manipulate voters have reached a level of sophistication—or brazenness—that might beggar even Huxley's imaginative powers. This is most evident in the peculiar environment of American politics (Paltiel, 1989, pp. 335-339), but no large democracy is immune to this trend.[10] Not even Canada has been spared, as Jeffrey Simpson (1989) has remarked:

> The holy grail of every party [is] the tightly scripted, poll-driven message capable of attracting the largest number of voters. Spontaneity has become every party's sworn enemy. As such, most of what could contribute to a fuller exposition of the party's positions—more television debates, free-time broadcasts, freewheeling media interviews, extensive party platforms—are out of favour. The parties win. The public loses.

Because of the importance of television, polling, and the other tools of political marketing, modern election campaigns in Canada are long on style and hoopla and disconcertingly short on substance. The major parties' fear of spontaneity derives from their horror of committing the one big gaffe that might lose an election. Campaigns are therefore stage-managed (tightly scripted, to use Simpson's apt imagery) by a coterie of media professionals who manufacture political events and happenings that can gain their clients valuable exposure on television and the other electronic media, regardless of what message they are attempting to convey. These staged events, or "medialities" (Ranney, 1983, p. 23), showcase the candidate's personal qualities (voice, appearance, bearing, and so forth) without telling the viewer much at all about his or her political beliefs. And since television is better at communicating images and feelings than dealing with information or analysis (Ranney, 1983, pp. 102-105; Crotty, 1984, pp. 75-89), the parties avoid complex issues and ideological debates, dispensing instead what some journalists refer to derisively as "marshmallow rhetoric" and "white noise"—intellectual pablum that will reassure, or at least not offend, the voters/viewers. The demeaning of political debate in the electronic age has been explained in rather cynical fashion by American pollster Pat Caddell: "Too many good people have been defeated because they tried to substitute substance for style" (quoted in Sabato, 1981, p. 144).

Critics might argue that elections in Canada have always lacked clarity and philosophical depth—after all, Siegfried was lamenting these same things over eighty years ago!—so there is no reason for anyone to get excited about the current trends. This Pollyanna-ish view overlooks the fact that the scope for electoral manipulation is now much greater than ever before, given the singular importance of television in shaping political life. In 1978 two-thirds (67 per cent) of the respondents in a nation-wide American survey stated that they got most of their news about politics from TV; the comparable figure among Canadians in 1987 was 47 per cent (Ranney, 1983, p. 14; McMonagle, 1988, p. A8). About half of the respondents in each country (47 per cent in the United States and 43 per cent in Canada) believed television to be the most accurate and impartial medium, and in the Canadian case, a clear plurality of respondents named TV as the medium most likely to provide an "in-depth analysis" of a political event (35 per cent, versus 27 per cent naming magazines, 23 per cent citing newspapers, and only 6 per cent naming radio). (McMonagle, 1988, p. A8).

This widespread faith in the veracity and analytical depth of television contrasts starkly with the view of most media experts that television's coverage of politics is

> superficial with emphasis on the visual. Television focuses on the obvious. It is not concerned with the extended exploration of policy issues, relative differences in position, or even thorough investigations of an individual's background and previous policy stands. (Crotty, 1984, p. 85)

Anne Rawley Saldich (1979), building on Marshall McLuhan's notion of television as a "cool medium"—one that conveys little information, is "low definition," and therefore requires the audience to complete or fill in the images—has argued that the low definition of television entails a considerable amount of political simplification. As David Halberstam has wryly noted, television telescopes complex issues in order to fulfill its self-imposed mandate of entertaining the audience; information is condensed so much that it is a bit like "printing the *New York Times* on a postage stamp" (quoted in Crotty, 1984, p. 88).

Television also provides the viewing audience with a form of vicarious participation in politics, a sense that they are actively involved in the events taking place on their screen. But this participation, according to both McLuhan and Saldich, is passive, and actually anaesthetizes the viewer's desire for real involvement in politics.

Perhaps the greatest danger posed by the electorate's growing reliance on TV as a source of political information is the viewer's inability to distinguish between "reality" and televised reality (or mediality, to use Ranney's term), between real events and happenings that are staged for the cameras... Frizzell, Pammett and Westell (1989) mention one incident during the 1988 federal election that raises grave doubts about the objectivity and credibility of television as a source of political news. In mid-October, just three weeks into the campaign, CBC broadcaster Peter Mansbridge aired a story claiming that a group of top Liberal strategists were seriously considering dumping John Turner as leader.

> And to illustrate the item, the CBC showed what purported to be a copy of the memo which the strategists had sent to Turner. Taken at face value, it seemed to prove that Mansbridge knew of what he spoke, but in fact it was a fake: the CBC did not have the memo, and after initially claiming that it was a legitimate "graphic representation," [Elly] Alboim [the CBC's bureau chief on Parliament Hill] later conceded that to use it had been a mistake. (p. 82)

By embroidering on the well-known organizational problems within the Liberal Party, and adducing a fake memo as "proof," the CBC had gone beyond its role as reporter and become a manufacturer of the news. Combined with the surprisingly high levels of public confidence in the objectivity of television, this incident and others like it underscore the potential for voter manipulation in the era of electronic politics.

Another reason for concern over the pernicious effects of electronic democracy is that the rise of the new political marketing technologies has spawned a species of party professionals who are little concerned with the niceties of ideological debate. For the extremely influential clique of pollsters and consultants who serve the party leader, ideology, issues, and attempts to inform the electorate necessarily take a back seat to the more compelling task of winning. And the quickest route to an electoral win is usually seen as the bland and cautious campaign that focuses on the supposed leadership qualities of the party's standard-bearer. Nothing is said or done before the party pollsters—latter-day Delphic oracles whose every word, no matter how ambiguous or questionable, is treated as gospel—have determined which way the electoral wind is blowing.

This formula for electoral success has been perfected by, among others, Patrick Kinsella, a former insurance salesman and executive director of the Ontario Conservative Party in the late 1970s.[11] Kinsella, who learned the arts of modern political marketing from the American Republican Party, the pioneers in the field, has served as chief electoral strategist for Premiers Bill Davis and Frank Miller of Ontario, and for the Social Credit government in British Columbia; he also worked on Michael Wilson's bid for the leadership of the federal Conservatives in 1983. According to Kinsella,

> Exploiting the public opinion for your advantage...depends on knowing what it is...by polling and then squeezing it. And putting the screws on and making sure that everyone is going to respond exactly the way you want them to. You may see that as somewhat offensive, because it is government by poll, if you will, and it is to that extent. (quoted in Stephens and Cruikshank, 1985).

During the 1985 provincial election in Ontario, when Frank Miller and the Conservatives enjoyed a seemingly insurmountable lead in the early opinion polls, Kinsella heaped scorn on David Peterson and the Liberals for their technological illiteracy—their failure to exploit the sophisticated polling methodologies that were the keystone of the Tory campaign. Kinsella wondered, "Without polling...how do they know where to go, how do they know what to say?" (quoted in Stephens, 1985).

Kinsella's polls informed him that Ontario's voters were happy and contented with the province's booming economy, and that Miller himself was an enormously popular leader among the electorate, who appreciated his homespun humour and folksy charm. Since Miller was a front-runner in a period of economic prosperity, Kinsella chose to run a cautious campaign and to avoid any controversies that might arise if the parties actually engaged in a debate over policies and issues (and there was one important issue that all three parties were trying desparately to avoid in 1985: the extension of public financing of separate schools to grade thirteen). Thus Miller was "low-bridged," to use the consultant's jargon: his public appearances were limited to forays among the Tory faithful, and the opposition parties' call for a televised debate among the leaders was rejected as too risky.

As the election results in Ontario in 1985 attested, the political consultants are not always successful: Kinsella's efforts to low-bridge his candidate and capitalize on the province's economic prosperity proved ineffective in the face of the voters' outrage over the separate school financing issue. But even in this instance, no real ideological debate took place among the parties (and voters were therefore deprived of effective alternatives on this crucial policy question), since all shared the same basic viewpoint on the question of extending public funding of separate schools to grade thirteen.

In the age of professional, media-dominated election campaigns, voters are likely to be presented with competing ideological visions and clear-cut alternatives on major policy issues only when some unforeseen event upsets the calculations of the political consultants. Such was the case in the 1988 federal election, which *almost* became a referendum on free trade, despite the heroic efforts of the incumbent Conservatives to run a cautious, leader-centred campaign reminiscent of Frank Miller's doomed election bid in 1985. What is remarkable about the 1988 election is that the Conservatives, with a little help from the NDP, conspired to keep the issue of free trade in the background for the first three weeks or so of the campaign—until the televised debates on October 24 and 25 (the writs had been issued on October 1). Campaigning on the unimaginative slogan of "Managing Change," the Tories chose to stress their experience and the quality of their leadership; the early days of the election witnessed a steady stream of TV spots showing the Prime Minister acting prime ministerially and speaking to throngs of excited Conservative supporters. Mulroney himself, in his opening remarks during the French-language debate, pounded home the Tory theme of the 1988 election: "On a besoin d'un chef"—Canadians need a leader. In a recitation of his government's accomplishments, Mulroney buried the free trade pact towards the end of his list, just ahead of Canada's hosting of the Francophone summit!

Like the Tories, the NDP opted for a leader-centred campaign: the party's television advertisements often concluded with the on-camera testimonials of average voters who announced their intention "to vote for Ed Broadbent"—sometimes adding, almost as an afterthought, that they would vote for Ed *and* the NDP team. No mention of socialism or social democracy was made in the party literature, and controversial articles in the party program—withdrawal from NATO and the nationalization of a major bank, for instance—were resolutely ignored (Whitehorn, 1989, pp. 46-47). Incredibly, in the party's election kickoff, Broadbent failed even to mention free trade, partly because internal polls had shown that "the public trusts the party most on social and environmental issues, and least on managing the economy" (McQuaig, 1988). "When it became apparent to even the most myopic of party hucksters that free trade *was* the issue, they seized upon it more for the purpose of dislodging the Liberals" (Whitaker, 1989, pp. 11-12). These monumental strategic errors, which undoubtedly contributed to the Tories' victory, were later assailed by Bob White of the Canadian Auto Workers and Gérard Docquier and Leo Gerard of the United Steelworkers. Organized labour pinned much of the blame for the NDP's abysmal showing (abysmal in terms of the expectations for the party going into the election) on the excessive power concentrated in the hands of the party's top strategists, who ignored or overturned advice from the party grassroots. The NDP gambled heavily on the new political marketing technologies in the 1988 election, and ended up as big losers.

Finally, the Liberals focused most of their energies on opposing free trade, mostly out of desperation, since the opinion polls seemed to have sounded their death knell at the start of the campaign. The party's television ads were blunt and hard-hitting: one featured two men sitting at a table, peering at a map of North America. With pencil in hand, one of them began to erase the boundary separating Canada from the United States—a graphic representation of what the party believed might happen to Canadian sovereignty if the free trade pact went ahead. In the early weeks of the campaign, however, the only news was old news: the media concentrated on John Turner's *faux pas*, and appeared to be setting up a death watch for his leadership. It was only with Turner's surprisingly effective performance in the televised debates, and his impassioned cry that opposition to free trade was the cause of his life, that the media—and the other two parties—began to take the Liberals seriously. From that point on in the campaign, both the Conservatives and the NDP devoted a great deal of their energies and resources to discrediting the Liberals, and Turner in particular. When the election results were finally in, Tory strategists were convinced that "their own negative advertising in the last 10 days of the 1988 campaign ensured victory" (Simpson, 1989), a certain sign that the politics of image and style will continue to have prominence over substantial doctrinal debates for a long time to come.

Conclusion

Canada's major political parties have always been more interested in winning power than in presenting coherent world visions to the electorate, even if there are activists within each of the old-line parties who are strongly committed to a particular ideology. This chapter has shown that the NDP, partly because of changing patterns of stratification in post-war Canada, and partly because of the dictates of electronic politics, has begun to imitate the unprincipled and opportunistic electoral appeals of the Liberals and Conservatives. In contemporary Canadian politics, all three major parties obscure their principles and programs in an attempt to cobble together a winning electoral coalition of heterogeneous social groups. In all three, the corps of hired professional consultants take advantage of the latest technical wizardry in political marketing to construct a highly personalized appeal to individual voters. Ideology therefore appears to matter less and less in party competition. This is not to say, however, that ideology is dead in this country: fundamental conflicts of class, ethnicity, language, and religion (as the issue of separate school funding in the 1985 Ontario provincial election attested) still exist, and constitute the subtext of political life in Canada. At election time, however, there is scarcely a trace of these important issues to be found in the rhetorical candy floss disseminated by each party. It seems that it is only *after* the election that the ideological stakes of the voters' decision become apparent: so it was with free trade, which received nary a mention by the Conservatives in the 1984 election, only to become the key item on their political agenda shortly thereafter. The same is true of the current obsession with the national deficit (which has prompted the government to spend almost three million dollars on an advertising campaign to convince Canadians of the need for Draconian measures to cope with the problem), which received only perfunctory attention in the 1988 campaign.

The implications of the changes described in this chapter are profoundly negative. At a time when the major parties are marketing themselves and their programs (to the extent that they exist) in the same way that the big breweries flog their homogenized and insipid products, it is highly unlikely that any party will run the risk of crafting intelligent policy responses to issues that are now clamouring for attention. When the political parties are unwilling to take a clear stand on pressing issues of public policy—abortion and how to reconcile environmental protection with continued economic growth, to name two obvious ones—growing numbers of voters are likely to seek out alternative institutional mechanisms, such as interest groups and single-issue movements, for the representation of their interests (Galipeau, 1989). Or, what is equally possible, they will lapse into a debilitating apathy and cynicism about politics in general.

If there is to be any change in this style of politics, it is becoming increasingly obvious that the stimulant must come from outside the present party organizations. The 1988 federal election, which otherwise gave little cause for optimism about a resurgence of creative politics in Canada, did provide one small glimmer of hope; the extremely dynamic role played by the underfinanced coalition of social groups opposed to free trade. This may not be much of a toehold on which to establish creative politics in this country, but it seems to be the only one we have.

Notes

1   The primary focus of my analysis is on the federal party system, although I would argue that the trends occurring at this level mirror those taking place in the provinces, with minor variations.

2   In a perceptive article on the historical evolution of Canadian politics at the federal level, Carty (1988) divides this country's political history into three broad periods, each characterized by a distinctive party system: 1. patronage politics (1867-1917), in which parties were coteries of local notables and elections were contests between the "ins" and the "outs" for control of patronage; 2. brokerage politics (1921-1957), in which the parties depended on strong regional chieftains to mollify competing geographical, economic, and ethnic interests; 3. electronic politics (1963-the present), in which parties have become extensions of the leader, and politics has been personalized by the growing reliance on new campaign technologies—the electronic media, pollsters, consultants, and so on. The one constant interwoven through these three periods, according to Carty, is the overriding importance of the party leader in Canadian politics.

3   According to Corry, "[Parties] are brokers of ideas. They are middlemen who select from all the ideas pressing for recognition as public policy

those they think can be shaped to have the widest appeal and, through their party organization, they try to sell a carefully sifted and edited selection of these ideas (their programme) to enough members of the electorate to produce a majority in the legislature" (1951, p. 22). See Dawson (1970, pp. 430-433) for a similar view. Porter notes that Canada's two established parties are "brokers" in another sense: "They arrange deals between different sections of opinion, or interest groups, by working out the necessary compromises." Elections in this kind of political system do not involve a debate between competing world visions; they are merely contests between "one set of brokers and another" (1965, p. 374).

4   According to Panebianco, a party's ideology is manifest if it involves "explicit and coherent objectives"; it is latent if these objectives are "implicit and contradictory" (1988, p. 16). As a political party evolves into a mature organization, there is a natural tendency for manifest ideology to be transformed into latent ideology, no matter how dedicated to its founding principles the party claims to be.

5   This is the important question raised by Brodie and Jenson (1988, 1989) in their pathbreaking work on parties as "independent variables" in politics, which actively shape the definition of the political at a given moment. Parties therefore help to determine what reaches the political agenda, and what remains de-politicized.

6   Two prominent examples from the recent past are the Conservative government's abortive attempt to de-index old age pensions in May, 1985, less than a year after Brian Mulroney had pledged to treat social welfare programs as a "sacred trust," and the same government's dogged pursuit of a free trade agreement with the United States after 1985, though Mulroney himself and other prominent Conservative leaders had previously sneered at the idea of such a pact (Gwyn, 1985, p. 288). For a more complete catalogue of historical examples of the ideological flexibility of the two established parties, see McMenemy (1976, pp. 10-26).

7   The "public service mandarinate" is also considered to be an important source of policy innovation in a system where the major parties "rarely offer clear policy options, and when they do, they may not deliver on their undertakings" (Thorburn, 1985, p. 39).

8   This is obviously a simplification of a complex and diverse literature, but I am examining only the broad explanatory trends here. For a fuller discussion of the varied explanations of Canada's brokerage politics (insofar as the party-in-the-electorate is concerned), see Brodie and Jenson (1989, pp. 29-33) and Thorburn (1985).

9   Dawson, for instance, claims that "what is probably the primary political generalization about Canadian parties [is] that no party can go very far unless it derives support from two or more regional areas in the Dominion, and this leads to the further consequence that a national party

must take as its primary purpose the reconciliation of the widely scattered aims and interests of a number of these areas. It is chiefly for this reason that the party leaders have been compelled to modify their principles and their policies, to favour the neutral shades rather than the highly satisfying—but politically suicidal—brighter colours." (1970, p. 430).

10　Sabato cites a particularly egregious example of this sort of manipulation: in 1978 the Butcher-Forde consulting agency was fined for having recruited a third candidate in a California election contest—even paying the candidate's filing fee!—"in order to increase a client-candidate's chances of winning" (1981, p. 339, note 38.).

11　Kinsella is one of a small but growing number of consultants, pollsters, and lobbyists who offer their services to one of the established parties (others on this list would include Bill Lee, Allan Gregg, Martin Goldfarb, Angus Reid, and, before he moved to the private sector, John Laschinger). In the United States, where thousands of these tacticians ply their trade, the relationship between the new political marketing technologies and party politics is quite well studied (see, in particular, Sabato, 1981). In Canada, where the phenomenon is less visible, there are unfortunately few if any scholarly studies of the new politics.

References

Alford, R.R. (1963). *Party and Society*. Westport, CT: Greenwood.

Amyot, G. (1986). The New Politics. *Queen's Quarterly, 93*, pp. 952-955.

Blake, D. (1988). Division and Cohesion: The Major Parties. In G. Perlin (Ed.), *Party Democracy in Canada* (pp. 32-52). Scarborough: Prentice-Hall.

Brodie, J. (1989). The Free Trade Election. *Studies in Political Economy, 28*, pp. 175-182.

Brodie, J. & Jenson, J. (1988). *Crisis, Challenge and Change: Party and Class in Canada Revisited*. Ottawa: Carleton University Press.

Brodie, J. & Jenson, J. (1989). Piercing the Smokescreen: Brokerage Parties and Class Politics. In A.G. Gagnon & A.B. Tanguay (Eds.), *Canadian Parties in Transition* (pp. 24-44). Scarborough: Nelson.

Carty, R.K. (1988). Three Canadian Party Systems: An Interpretation of the Development of National Politics. In G. Perlin (Ed.), *Party Democracy in Canada* (pp. 15-30). Scarborough: Prentice-Hall.

Christian, W. (1983). Ideology and Politics in Canada. In J.H. Redekop (Ed.), *Approaches to Canadian Politics* (2nd ed.) (pp. 102-131). Scarborough: Prentice-Hall.

Christian, W. (1988, September 17). Dreams and the Reality of How the Canadian Political System Works. *The Globe and Mail*, p. F13.

Christian, W. & Campbell, C. (1983). *Political Parties and Ideologies in Canada* (2nd ed.). Toronto: McGraw-Hill Ryerson.

Corry, J.A. (1951). *Democratic Government and Politics* (2nd ed.). Toronto: University of Toronto Press.

Crotty, W. (1984). *American Parties in Decline* (2nd ed.). Boston: Little, Brown and Co.

Dawson, R.M. (1970). *The Government of Canada* (5th ed.). Toronto: University of Toronto Press.

Frizzell, A., Pammett, J.H., & Westell, A. (1989). *The Canadian General Election of 1988*. Ottawa: Carleton University Press.

Galipeau, C. (1989). Political Parties, Interest Groups, and New Social Movements: Toward New Representations? In A.G. Gagnon & A.B. Tanguay (Eds.), *Canadian Parties in Transition* (pp. 404-426). Scarborough: Nelson.

Gwyn, R. (1985). *The 49th Paradox*. Toronto: Totem Books.

Horowitz, G. ([1965] 1979). Canadian Politics, Mosaics and Identity. In R. Schultz, O.M. Kruhlak, & J.C. Terry (Eds.), *The Canadian Political Process* (3rd ed.), (pp. 73-81). Toronto: Holt, Rinehart and Winston.

Huxley, A. ([1958] 1983). *Brave New World Revisited*. London: Triad/Panther Books.

Johnston, R. (1988). The Ideological Structure of Opinion on Policy. In G. Perlin (Ed.) *Party Democracy in Canada* (pp. 54-70). Scarborough: Prentice-Hall.

McMenemy, J. (1976). Parliamentary Parties. In C. Winn & J. McMenemy (Eds.), *Political Parties in Canada* (pp. 10-28). Toronto: McGraw-Hill Ryerson.

McMenemy, J. (1989). Getting to Know the Parties by the Company We Keep: Local Sources of Party Imagery. In A.G. Gagnon & A.B. Tanguay (Eds.), *Canadian Parties in Transition* (pp. 309-330). Scarborough: Nelson.

McMonagle, D. (1988, January 27). TV Favoured as Source of News, Poll Finds. *The Globe and Mail*, p. A8.

McQuaig, L. (1988, December 9). NDP activists say free trade underplayed by strategists. *The Globe and Mail*, p. A3.

Ornstein, M.D., & Stevenson, H.M. (1984). Ideology and Public Policy in Canada. *British Journal of Political Science, 14*; pp. 313-344.

Paltiel, K.Z. (1989). Political Marketing, Party Finance and the Decline of Canadian Parties. In A.G. Gagnon & A.B. Tanguay (Eds.), *Canadian Parties in Transition* (pp. 332-353). Scarborough: Nelson.

Panebianco, A. (1988). *Political Parties: Organization and Power*. (M. Silver, Trans.). Cambridge: Cambridge University Press.

Porter, J. (1965). *The Vertical Mosaic*. Toronto: University of Toronto Press.

Ranney, A. (1983). *Channels of Power*. New York: Basic Books.

Sabato, L.J. (1981). *The Rise of Political Consultants*. New York: Basic Books.
Saldich, A.R. (1979). *Electronic Democracy*. New York: Praeger.

Siegfried, A. ([1907] 1966). *The Race Question in Canada*. (F. Underhill, Ed.). Toronto: McClelland and Stewart (Carleton Library No. 29).

Simpson, J. (1989, February 28). The 15-Second Tactic. *The Globe and Mail*, p. A6.

Stephens, R. (1985, April 3). Tory Polls Show Miller a Reminder of Good Old Days. *The Globe and Mail*, p. 24.

Stephens, R. and Cruikshank, J. (1985, March 4). Politics by Poll and Squeeze. *The Globe and Mail*, p. 8.

Taylor, C. (1970). *The Pattern of Politics*. Toronto: McClelland and Stewart.

Thorburn, H. (1985). Interpretations of the Canadian Party System. In H. Thorburn (Ed.), *Party Politics in Canada* (5th ed.) (pp. 20-40). Scarborough: Prentice-Hall.

Underhill, F.H. (1960). *In Search of Canadian Liberalism*. Toronto: Macmillan.

Wearing, J. (1988). *Strained Relations*. Toronto: McClelland and Stewart.

Whitaker, R. (1989 March). No Laments for the Nation: Free Trade and the Election of 1988. *Canadian Forum*, pp. 9-13.

Whitehorn, A. (1989). The New Democrats: Dashed Hopes. In A. Frizzell, J.H. Pammett, & A. Westell (Eds.), *The Canadian General Election of 1988*. (pp. 43-53). Ottawa: Carleton University

R. Jeremy Wilson Horserace Journalism and Canadian Election Campaigns

The 1979 and 1980 Canadian election campaigns were marked by an unprecedented amount of self analysis on the part of the nation's political journalists. Newspaper columnists penned assessments of their role in the process,[1] a freelance journalist produced Canada's very own "boys on the bus" account of the working world of campaign reporters,[2] and at least one professor of journalism did running commentary on the coverage.[3] What we might call "cube root" introspection even appeared, with media figures writing about the way they were being written about.[4]

By and large, all of this navel gazing failed to address one fundamental question. Just how are Canadian election campaigns being portrayed to the citizenry? This question is important in several respects. The media's description of the campaign shapes the amount and quality of information acquired by voters while influencing the perceptions of elections held by both the public and the politicians. Since elections are central symbols of our democratic process, the way they are described bears significantly on people's attitudes toward the political system. And because politicians are assiduous students of the way their activities are reported by the press, the coverage influences their images of the campaign, the design of their electoral strategies and their perception of their own political *persona*.

This article assesses the way the English Canadian print and electronic media depicted the 1979 campaign. Observation of the 1980 coverage suggests that our conclusions apply to that campaign as well. The Canadian media, like their American counterparts,[5] tend to portray the campaign as a horserace or game. At election time our political journalists are transformed into what James David Barber has called "electoral bookies."[6] Much of the coverage is analogous to the colour commentary one hears during televised athletic events. It is not just that our journalists rely heavily on the argot of the sporting world. What is more important is their approach. There is endless speculation about how the teams are running, continual analysis of their competitive strengths and weaknesses, and a steady stream of commentary on their strategies. Every move by the parties and politicians is analyzed for its political impact and described in terms of its tactical motives. Headlines such as

Table 1: Story type analysis of newspaper coverage in 1979. Percentage of printed coverage[a] accounted for by stories of different types.

	Star	Globe	Times	Colonist	All Newspaper Coverage
Basic reports from the trail	19.0	20.2	41.3	32.4	25.0
Issue commentaries	21.6	17.3	9.7	17.3	17.6
Other Descriptive	13.6	11.3	9.5	9.7	11.6
Horserace commentaries	37.6	43.4	21.1	31.4	35.9
Mixture	8.2	7.8	18.4	9.2	9.9
	N = 9752 col. cm.[b] in 412 stories	N = 8976 col. cm.[b] in 309 stories	N = 4468 col. cm.[b] in 245 stories	N = 3939 col. cm.[b] in 247 stories	N = 27135 col. cm.[b] in 1213 stories

[a] Pictures and cartoons accounted for additional coverage in the following amounts: 3658 col. cm. in the *Star*, 2618 col. cm. in the *Globe and Mail*, 970 col. cm. in the *Times*, and 675 col. cm. in the *Colonist*. In total there were an additional 7921 col. cms. of pictures and cartoons.

"Make-or-Break Week: Worried Liberals Pull Out Stops," "Lang Fights Uphill Battle in Riding Where Every Issue Counts" and "They're in the Home Stretch: A Dead Heat—Gallup" are common. The coverage is liberally sprinkled with such commentary as the following:

> The shadows now threaten to overwhelm the carefully groomed image. Just as Clark appeared to have gotten over the effects of his world trip—the campaign has been super-efficient and Clark has shown no sign of being tired—doubts are being raised again about his apparent lack of confidence and stiffness.... Party officials bitterly dispute suggestions that they are keeping Clark in a protective cocoon, saying they are just determined to set their own strategy. But behind their remarks lies the unspoken fear of the Big Blun-

Table 2: Textual analysis of newspaper coverage in 1979. Percentage of printed coverage[a] accounted for by "bites" of different types.

	Star	Globe	Times	Colonist	All Newspaper Coverage
Descriptive reports of statements, attacks	17.0	20.2	36.1	30.6	24.7
Editorials on issues	7.0	5.6	9.4	6.1	7.0
Issue analysis	10.5	16.3	4.6	13.3	11.2
Descriptive reports on campaign activity	5.2	3.8	5.5	3.9	4.7
Horserace	41.2	45.2	29.2	29.3	37.5
Miscellaneous descriptive	19.2	8.8	15.2	16.8	14.9
	N = 5600 col. cm.[b] on 12 days	N = 4741 col. cm.[b] on 12 days	N = 4129 col. cm.[b] on 18 days	N = 2916 col. cm.[b] on 18 days	N = 17386 col cm.[b]

[a] Pictures and cartoons accounted for an additional 2378 cm. in the *Star*, 1371 cm. in the *Globe*, 977 cm. in the *Times*, and 465 cm. in the *Colonist* for a total of 5201 col. cm. across the four papers.

der. Political wisdom holds that Clark can win as long as he makes no major mistakes, but it's a strategy that can back-fire.[7]

Until now the tour's pace has been purposely leisurely, with Broadbent's efficient five-person staff picking the policy shots and attempting to "regionalize" the party's three main issue areas: price controls, Canadian development of resources, and medicare.... Broadbent's savvy crew, led by research director Mark Eliesen, is playing the media violin with considerable skill, using well spaced policy statements and an "issue-a-day" approach. Policy announcements will be

Table 3: Network news coverage of the 1979 campaign. Per cent of coverage accounted for by "bites" of different types.

	CBC	CTV	All Television News
Descriptive reports of statements, attacks	31.3	35.8	33.2
Editorials on issues	0.0	1.5	.6
Issue analysis	9.5	1.2	6.1
Descriptive reports on campaign activity	7.7	15.4	10.9
Horserace	49.9	40.4	46.0
Miscellaneous descriptive	1.5	5.7	3.2
	N = 209.5 minutes in 20 broadcasts	N = 144.8 minutes in 22 broadcasts	N = 354.3 minutes in 42 broadcasts

goosed along by six recently completed television commercials in English and French and a $1.2-million ad campaign.... Despite the fast start and pluses afforded by the Election Expenses Act, the effective initial push will inevitably fade as the Liberal and Tory juggernauts clear the carbon from their engines. The NDP has clear problems. Medicare is a fragile issue that could easily be shattered by a well-placed Liberal campaign promise. The ballyhooed support of the Canadian Labour Congress has yet to materialize....[8]

Trudeau's challenge comes on a day when Liberal organizers were making deliberate efforts to change their leader's campaign image.... The children of the St. John New Brunswick boys and girls club helped Pierre Trudeau today. They gave his image makers a chance to lighten what some feel has been a somewhat stodgy and rather traditional looking campaign so far. When Trudeau decided he didn't want to do a T.V. interview this morning they brought him here in the hope that he'd react to counter the rather testy image he's developed....[9]

In order to assess the extent of horserace journalism we examined a sample of the coverage in four daily newspapers, *Maclean's* magazine, and the evening newscasts on CBC and CTV television during the weeks leading up to the May 22, 1979 election. The newspapers were two morning dailies, the Toronto *Globe and Mail* and the Victoria *Daily Colonist*, and two evening dailies, the Victoria *Times* and the Toronto *Star*.

The newspaper coverage was analyzed in two ways. All editorial and news coverage of the campaign appearing on alternate days during the six weeks prior to the 1979 election was categorized by "story type." Coverage appearing on a smaller number of days was examined in more detail with each paragraph or "bite" coded separately. The story type analysis dealt with 80 separate editions of the four papers and over 1,200 stories.[10] Stories were placed in one of the following categories:[11]

1. *Basic report from the campaign trail.* Stories dominated by straight-forward reports of candidates' assertions, promises, and attacks on other candidates, or by descriptions of campaigning, audience reaction and travel itineraries.

2. *Issue commentaries.* Stories featuring analytic or editorial discussion of policy issues, such as those which compare party policies, examine party records, consider the implications or feasibility of promises, give the reaction of experts, or outline relevant experiences with similar policy ideas elsewhere.

3. *Other descriptive.* Stories on electoral mechanics (such as voter enumeration), announcements of meetings, reports of nomination meetings, negotiations on the debate, along with stories on campaign trivia (such as the naming of the new NDP campaign plane).

4. *Horserace commentaries.* Stories dominated by discussion of campaign strategies, use of the media, poll results, candidates' performance, lay of the political land, and party prospects.

5. *Mixture.* Stories not falling into one of the above types.

The horserace commentaries account for more than one-third of all coverage. As Table 1 shows, this is more than twice the amount accounted for by issue commentaries, and almost as much as the combined total for basic campaign reports and other descriptive stories. There is considerable variation between the Toronto papers and their smaller counterparts. A much larger share of the Victoria papers' content was accounted for by basic campaign reports, with smaller proportions of coverage devoted to the horserace aspects of the campaign. In large measure this is due to the fact that the

Victoria dailies were more dependent on stock wire service reports from the leaders' tours, and the fact that their meagre resources had to cover the concurrent federal and provincial campaigns in British Columbia. The greater resources of the large papers had little impact on the priority given to issue commentaries. Instead, these papers poured considerable effort into handicapping constituency races, speculating about strategy and probing the psyche of the voter.

Because about 10 per cent of stories could not be assigned to a story type category, and because many of those categorized as "reports from the trail" contain bits of issue analysis or horserace commentary, we undertook a more detailed textual analysis of content. The categories used in the first part of the analysis were refined. Editorial statements on issues were distinguished from analyses of issue positions. Separate categories were established for straight reports of candidates' rhetoric (claims and attacks), for reports of campaign activity (for example, audience reaction and travel itineraries), and for miscellaneous descriptions (coverage of trivia, nomination results, the mechanics of the electoral system and so on). Stories were broken into "bites" which ranged in length from one sentence to several paragraphs depending on how long a focus was maintained. For example, a story might be divided into a short lead paragraph describing audience reaction to a leader's visit, a section on party prospects in the area, a paragraph reporting the leader's attack on an opponent, and a sentence on the leader's travel itinerary.

The detailed textual analysis was applied to 12 issues of both the *Globe and Mail* and the *Star* and to 18 issues of both the *Times* and *Colonist*.[12] As Table 2 indicates, the results are similar to those found in the story type analysis. Overall, about one-third of coverage fell into the horserace category. Descriptions of candidate statements accounted for about one-quarter. Both of the Toronto papers devoted over 40 per cent of their coverage to the horserace, with the figure for the Victoria papers once again substantially lower.

An even stronger emphasis on the contest is revealed in a parallel analysis of Canada's weekly newsmagazine, *Maclean's*. Region-by-region assessments of party prospects, feature stories on such things as "20 Tell-tale ridings to watch," along with weekly wrap-ups full of references to polls and strategies were the steady diet of the *Maclean's* reader. In all, we estimate that 59.0 per cent of coverage in the seven weeks prior to the election fell into the horserace category. Issue analysis accounted for approximately the same amount of coverage as in the newspapers—about 10 per cent.

Somewhat surprisingly, the horserace approach was only slightly more prevalent on television newscasts than it was in the newspapers. Forty-two CTV and CBC national newscasts were recorded during the seven weeks prior to May 22.[13] This content was coded according to the procedure applied in the textual analysis.[14] As Table 3 shows, horserace commentary accounted for an approximate 46 per cent of the coverage monitored while content in the "claim or attack" category accounted for 33 per cent. The CBC did more issue analysis while the CTV gave more time to straight description of campaign activity and rhetoric.

The Canadian media, then, portray election campaigns in roughly the same way as do their American counterparts. Studies of American coverage using similar measures place between 40 and 60 per cent of all coverage in the horserace category.[15] Our estimates for the 1979 Canadian campaign are similar—commentary on polls, strategies, prospects, and other facets of the contest account for over a third of the newspaper content, nearly half of the television news coverage, and close to 60 per cent of *Maclean's* coverage. If anything, these statistics underestimate the pervasiveness of the horserace style. Our analysis does not capture fully the extent to which reports of issue statements are placed in a "strategic context" by accompanying commentary which cues the audience to respond to the entire item as any other bit of intelligence about campaign tactics. As John Carey says: "The 'strategic frame' suggests, in effect, that to get at the *real* meaning of what a candidate said or did, the viewer should interpret its strategic significance in the campaign."[16]

Even though the space devoted to the horserace is greater than that given to description and analysis of issue positions, the media did supply information about the promises made by leaders. However, a considerable portion of the content in the candidate statements category is of dubious educational value. Reports of campaign rhetoric seem to overemphasize conflict and easily accessible issues like leadership. Issues which arise from campaign events (such as the argument over the leaders' debate) appear to receive more attention than do most policy issues. Reliable judgments concerning bias would, of course, have to be based on careful comparison between the coverage and a full account of what a candidate said. A bias in favour of conflict issues is suggested, however, by the fact that references to candidates' attacks on one another account for about 40 per cent of all the content in the "descriptive report of statements and attacks" category. In addition, the accent is on the most easily understood issues. For example, the themes of leadership and willingness to debate were the most heavily emphasized in reports of attacks on Clark by Trudeau and Broadbent. Accounts of their attacks on these two themes accounted for more than twice the newspaper coverage devoted to their anti-Clark statements on four key policy issues—mortgage deductibility, external affairs (including Jerusalem), Petrocan and energy. Indeed, the Trudeau and Broadbent attacks on Clark's leadership were given more space in the newspaper coverage we sampled than all of their utterances (assertions and attacks) concerning these four issues.

The amount of space and time devoted to editorial or analytical treatment of issues was extremely low. Our definition of issue analysis was not overly stringent. We were not looking for academic tomes, but simply for instances where reporters or commentators offered assessments or comparisons of party positions which would help voters (at least those so inclined) comprehend the issues. For example, we were looking for commentary which considered the costs, implications or feasibility of policy proposals, or examined a candidate's proposals in light of facts about the causes of the problem in question.

What we found was that the reporters and commentators showed no reluctance to step back from the rhetoric to offer their assessments. But over and over we found that those assessments dealt with the impact of policy proposals on the election itself, and not with their social, technological and economic impacts. We found the media ignoring questions like those illustrated above and turning their attention instead to questions such as: How will this promise affect the party's chances of election? How will voters react? How does this proposal reflect the party's electoral strategy?

The media we monitored did contain some good explanatory pieces on various policies. The mortgage deductibility plan, for example, was the object of some excellent analysis. There were some attempts to unravel the Petrocan issue, including a full page treatment in the *Star* which presented background pieces on other state-run oil companies.[17] The print media presented charts with capsule descriptions of party positions set out for easy comparison.[18] CBC television news presented some good analyses of economic questions.[19] Additional examples of policy commentary no doubt appeared on days other than those monitored. Nonetheless, our results suggest that voters had to be quite vigilant to find explanatory treatments of a number of the supposed issues of the campaign. For example, they would have been hard-pressed to find information about which other nations had moved their embassies, or advice about the probable reaction to such a move. It is unlikely that voters emerged from the campaign with a better understanding of Canada's energy problems, or a better grasp of the constraints on the federal government's ability to solve them.

The paucity of issue analysis is only part of the problem. The other part relates to the media's reluctance to treat seriously the analysis which is done. Over the course of the campaign most of the issues receive analytic treatment in at least one of the country's major newspapers. Much of this analysis, however, seems to be forgotten as soon as it appears. It does not become news, it does not influence subsequent stories on the subject, and it does not serve as a basis for a more critical approach to the leaders' rhetoric. It does not generate questions and further commentary which could stimulate public debate, force leaders to defend themselves and, in a snowballing fashion, help to elevate the tone of the campaign.[20]

According to Elihu Katz, "election campaigns, for all their faults, may be the major learning experience of democratic polities."[21] No doubt this potential exists since campaigns are periods of heightened citizen awareness when politicians are in relatively close contact with their constituents. In fact though, in this regard at least, campaigns must be considered a glorious opportunity wasted. Our analysis argues that little educational significance should be attributed to Canadian campaigns as currently designed and depicted. Since they do little to develop or disseminate causal explanations of social and economic problems, it is unlikely that they help voters acquire a better grasp of where to place responsibility for those problems. Since they do little to teach us about the constraints which bind policy makers, campaigns would seem, if anything, to contribute to delusions about the solvability of problems. It is hard to see how they help voters acquire the kind of comprehension which would allow them to appraise more realistically the performance of governments.

Voters seeking information from the media during the campaign will find relatively little which would contribute to informed, issue-oriented choices at the polls. On the other hand, they will hear considerable speculation about how they are expected to react to policy proposals (often before they have had a chance to react), and receive much advice which might help them place their bets in the office pool on the election result. Unfortunately for the would-be punter, the quality of much of the advice is dismal. Amidst all of the talk about bellwether ridings, swing voters, and "soft" support, there is much sloppy analysis and silly speculation. The quality of punditry varies, but for the most part reveals a tendency to make unsubstantiated claims about the mood of the electorate, an unwillingness to acknowledge the limitations of opinion polls, an inability to distinguish between good and bad polls, and an inclination to accept superficial maxims about how electoral outcomes are determined. The boldness of the assertions about the impact of campaign events which pepper the commentaries belies the fact that these assertions are based on nothing more than a few man-in-the-street interviews or talk show calls, and sometimes seem to be pulled out of thin air by reporters who impute their own emotions to the electorate. For example, where was the evidence to support the confident assertions about the electorate's hostile reaction to the prospect of a winter election which we heard within minutes of the Clark government's parliamentary defeat in December 1979?

The fact that reports on polls are usually prefaced with phrases like "only a snapshot" or with renditions of the margin of error caveat might lead one to conclude that criticism concerning the reporting of polls has had some salutary consequences. Unfortunately, after expressing these qualifications, most reporters blithely ignore their implications. We are typically told that a poll indicates that Party X is two points ahead of Party but seldom reminded that, given these results and the customary margin of error, X could be several points ahead or behind. And unfortunately, for every reporter who conscientiously tries to present careful interpretation of poll results there is at least one editor ready to send a cub reporter onto the street or to the telephone to conduct totally worthless straw polls of 75 or 100 voters.

Although there is nothing particularly new about horserace journalism it has increased in prominence over the past twenty or thirty years. No good comparative data exist, but our limited analysis suggests that the shift towards the horserace mode has been quite pronounced. We replicated the story type analysis reported above on a sample of coverage from the Vancouver *Sun* and Victoria *Times* during the 1935 and 1957 federal campaigns. We found that the horserace model of coverage was relatively insignificant in the treatment of these earlier elections, accounting for just 3 per cent of content in 1935 and 9 per cent in 1957.[22] Basic reports from the campaign trail and other descriptive stories were about twice as important as they are now, with newspapers frequently reproducing large segments of leaders' speeches.

How can we account for the contemporary style of election reporting? The best short answer is that we are getting the kind of coverage which the media enterprises think is most saleable and the kind which comes easiest to the political reporters. It reflects the demands of the television news format and the character of jet-age, leader-oriented, made-for-television campaigns. It is a logical product of the training and working conditions of reporters. No doubt it also reflects the prevailing journalistic guild norms.

Television news demands good visuals and short thematic reports which capture the drama of the campaign. Horserace stories meet these demands better than analysis of ideas. And the kind of campaign which television has helped create lends itself nicely to the horserace style. Television wants a campaign which is truly a campaign—there must be attacks and counter-attacks, victories and losses, feints and strategies, generals and lieutenants. The parties have responded. They jet their leaders back and forth across the country, dropping them down here and there to shore up the defences or spur on the locals. They spread the "newsworthy" announcements across the length of the campaign. They provide the media with ready access to coteries of "handlers" who ladle out the behind-the-scenes gossip on expectations, strategies and party polls which is so vital to the formula televised report and weekly backgrounders.

Polls also fit the demands of television. The profusion of polls means that the campaign is punctuated by a series of pseudo-events which are designed to have the feel of hard news. Each poll provides grounds for media gossip before its release, and grist for speculation (how is the leader reacting? how will the strategy shift?) afterwards.

The advent of made-for-television campaigns also has had far-reaching effects on the quality of newspaper coverage. Most importantly, it has meant that the job of reporting and commenting on the campaign has been placed in the hands of the "boys on the bus." The characteristics of this species are well known. They are isolated from the real world, surrounded by distractions, jet-lagged, captive in an environment shaped by an interaction between their fellows and the party functionaries, and dependent on the handlers' manipulative ministrations. With neither the time nor the energy to undertake the research and reflection needed for background pieces on the issues, the typical campaign reporter naturally tends to file easy stories in the style of the television reporter—simple description of the leaders' claims framed by some colour commentary and some speculation about how the campaign is going.

The paucity of policy commentary also reflects the lack of policy expertise and specialization among public affairs correspondents. Although a few have begun (or perhaps it is more appropriate to say, have been allowed) to specialize in such policy areas as energy, most commentary outside of the business pages is done by jack-of-all-trades writers who can hardly be expected to produce lucid pieces on complex matters such as federal-provincial fiscal arrangements or international monetary policy. It can be argued, of course, that the media's job is to report the news and that while they should strive to convey newsworthy analysis done by experts, they should not be expected to do that analysis themselves. This contention leads to an important point. In a sense the characteristics we have observed in election coverage are symptomatic of the underpoliticization of our society. Political debate is often starved for the nourishment which we might expect to be provided by those with expertise. The recent campaigns offer an excellent illustration of the minimal impact of experts—academics, spokesmen for interest groups, and others—on public discourse. The C.D. Howe Institute's analysis of the Conservative mortgage plan in 1979 and the commentary by Mr. Justice Emmett Hall and others on Trudeau's double-tracking idea in 1980 illustrate a fairly rare phenomenon.[23] This is not the place to explore the reasons for this problem. Hypotheses would be suggested by reflection on John Porter's contributions, by consideration of the character of our interest groups and universities, and by examination of the way expertise in some policy areas is monopolized by government and industry. Despite the complexity of the problem, however, improvements might be made if the media would do more to prod those who are in a position to offer informed reaction.

A relatively small shift in priorities would do much to redress the imbalance between junk news and issue analysis in current election coverage. The media industry would have to shift resources away from covering the colour of the campaign. At least some of the boys on the bus would have to become boys in the library. It seems doubtful that the media industry has the will to make these decisions. The kind of coverage we are prescribing would be seen by many as inconsistent with the norms guiding contemporary journalistic practice. As well, such coverage would no doubt be viewed as much more likely to repel readers and viewers than attract them.

While we still await the definitive treatment of the guild norms of Canadian journalism, we can speculate that at least two facets of the normative climate impede improvements. First, the operative standards of excellence seem to have been sired by Theodore White out of "Woodstein." The impression one gets is that good reporting involves digging behind the scenes for the inside dope on the campaign. The good reporter seems to be the one with the best contacts among the handlers, the scoop on the party's secret polls, or the low-down on its financial benefactors, advertising strategies or internal squabbles. The new investigative reporting of the 1970s does not mean investigation of the policies and their consequences. The desideratum is better horserace analysis.

Second, our political journalists seem to adhere to notions of objectivity (or at least neutrality) which discourage analytic treatment of policy proposals. In many cases, treatments of policy and follow-up efforts like those envisaged earlier must necessarily involve criticism of politicians' ideas or attacks on the veracity of their claims. The coverage suggests that many reporters or editors (or both) think that it is not their place to levy such criticism, or at least believe that attacks on one politician should be balanced by attacks on his opponents. Either norm is sure to discourage serious issue analysis.

The canons of objectivity adhered to by the media might be laudable were it not for the fact that a double standard prevails. The same journalists who seem reluctant to attack a leader's ideas show no compunction about offering glib assessments in the horserace vein which may have just as much impact on the voter. The commentators are not at all reticent to pronounce that a leader is performing poorly, that a campaign has lost its momentum, or that a party's strategists have made a serious tactical blunder. Often these judgments are most debatable.

The profitability factor probably provides the most significant barrier against a shift to a different type of coverage. In response to what has been said, the media would no doubt contend that consumers of campaign journalism are being given what they want, and that it is misleading to imply that the audience is thirsting for information which would make the issues understandable. Instead, they would argue, the audience should be seen as composed of political fans—people who follow the campaign for its entertainment value, people who want to be vicariously involved in the game, and people who want to know how their "team" is doing.

Horserace coverage presents some pictures of politics which are not likely to boost faith in the system. A desire to simplify and dramatize a complex process has led the media to overstress the degree to which the result is manipulated. Their portrayal overemphasizes the importance of campaign strategists while underemphasizing the free will and common sense of the electorate. Many pundits seem to find "great men" theories of the campaign irresistible. As a result we see the emergence of myths like that focussing on the role of the "great rainmaker" in the 1974 campaign. Leaders and voters alike tend to be depicted as under the spell of clever backroom boys and wunderkind pollsters. Such portrayals are not totally groundless and clearly no one would want to suggest that the public should be protected from the truth about the tactics being used. At the same time, however, it can be argued that the media present some distorted pictures of the process. The extent to which electoral outcomes can be ordained by Jim Coutts, Keith Davey, Allan Gregg and their ilk has been exaggerated. The fact that these outcomes are the product of thousands of unfathomable decisions has been understated. And while this is not the place to debate whether our politicians are men with ideas and beliefs, we might consider whether the media have not perhaps overdone the tendency to portray politicians as people who never advocate anything for any other reason than that it will win votes.[24]

Whatever its impact on citizen orientations, the media's fascination with the horserace has certainly influenced the character of the modern campaign. It has meant that politicians are faced with a new kind of scrutiny, one which focusses on their campaign's momentum and tactics. As a result, campaign strategists must strive to present themselves as skilled campaigners. They must engage in what John Carey refers to as the "meta-campaign," a secondary campaign designed to convince the media that the primary campaign is cleverly designed and possessed of great momentum.[25] In this regard the party functionaries are probably motivated in part by a desire to win the esteem of their peers among the press. One suspects that they are also persuaded that some voters' judgments about a leader's competence for office are based at least partially on assessments concerning his skill as a campaigner.

The importance of the meta-campaign helps account for certain facets of the recent campaigns which, at first glance at least, seem rather bizarre. For example, there is something strange about the fact that the leaders continue to dash from place to place in an attempt to create "newsworthy" campaign events, even though the television reporters for whom these events are staged frequently begin their reports by pointing out that the purpose of the event was simply to provide a photo-opportunity. There is something Kafkaesque about representatives of the party advertising agencies turning up in the national media to describe how they are "packaging" the leaders in order to neutralize their weaknesses.[26] After all, basic maxims of attitude-change theory surely suggest that the value of a manipulative strategy is negated if the potential "manipulatees" are warned in advance of the intent.

Our puzzlement evaporates once we take into account the meta-campaign argument. It suggests that the parties view the audience (at least part of it) as made up of fans or critics who sit in judgment on the effectiveness of the campaign. Since the audience is perceived in this way it is only natural that the parties conduct a "campaign about the campaign" in an attempt to persuade us of their shrewdness. It may be that parties see two types of audience: first, one which responds at a primary level, that is an audience which can be persuaded by ads and promises *per se*; and second, an audience of political fans who respond at a secondary level as critics of tactics. What is interesting is that the size of the second audience should increase as horserace commentary becomes more pervasive. Perhaps we will soon reach the point where there are no voters of the first type left. Perhaps we will be left with an audience composed entirely of amateur political scientists, all analyzing the strategies, all "distancing" themselves from the process, all assuming that somewhere there are voters who actually do respond on the primary level. Perhaps we will reach the point at which the meta-campaign becomes more important than the campaign.

Horserace journalism has no doubt become a permanent feature of the modern campaign. But does so much of the media's energy need to be applied to speculating on the contest? Must the horserace coverage dwarf that devoted to such things as exposing the implications or feasibility of policy promises, explaining what is at stake, and exploring the causes of the problems under discussion? We think not. Certainly we must acknowledge that the media are in the news business, and not the education business. Certainly, as James David Barber says, we must take as given certain basics of the craft of political journalism, most notably the need for haste and drama.[27]

But our media enterprises have resources sufficient to allow more of their reporters and commentators to approach the campaign's issues in a reflective way. This could be done without seriously depriving that portion of the audience which wants to be vicariously involved in the game. Indeed, a big improvement would be evident if even part of the energy now devoted to handicapping riding contests, conducting straw polls and such exercises was applied to commentary on policy issues. And such a shift in priorities need not necessarily result in uninteresting coverage. As Barber says in urging American campaign journalists to attend more to the candidates' grasp of the situation which will face the winner, the public imagination might well be gripped more firmly by the "drama of revelation" than it is by much of the coverage now offered.[28]

Those who set priorities for the Canadian media presumably need not be reminded that political journalists provide an important link between government and the public. They presumably need no reminder of the responsibilities attached to that position or of the fact that those responsibilities are becoming increasingly critical as the gulf between complex reality and the public's understanding of that reality widens. We have argued, however, that the media do need to be reminded of the ways in which their depiction of election campaigns is contributing to the intellectual barrenness of an experience which should symbolize the vitality of a democracy.

Notes

1   See, for example, Robert Lewis, "Politicians, the Party Lines...and the Press," *Maclean's*, 21 May 1979, pp. 4-9; Allan Fotheringham, "Lobster? Champagne? Doughnuts? Beer? Nothing's too Good for the Boys on the Bus," *Maclean's*, 14 May 1979, p. 56; Jeffrey Simpson, "Campaign Junkie: The Insular Little World of the Election," *Toronto Globe and Mail*, 30 April 1979, pp. 1-2; and Richard Gwyn, "Election Made Trivial by Media Manipulation," *Toronto Star*, 18 May 1979, p. A10.

2   Clive Cocking, *Following the Leaders: A Media Watcher's Diary of Campaign '79* (Toronto: Doubleday Canada, 1980).

3   Murray Goldblatt's pieces in the *Globe and Mail* such as "The Debatable Clout of Punditry's Stars" (9 May 1979, p. 7); and "Record on Issues Still Below Par" (8 February 1980, p. 7).

4   For example, Mary Janigan, "Boys on the Bus Bite Back," *Toronto Star*, 30 April 1979, p. A12; and Alan Fotheringham, "In Which the Scribe Dissects Another Scribe Dissecting," *Maclean's*, 28 January 1980, p. 52.

5   Thomas E. Patterson, *The Mass Media Election: How Americans Choose their President* (New York: Praeger, 1980), chap. 4; John Carey, "How Media

Shape Campaigns," *Journal of Communications, 26* (Spring, 1976), pp. 50-57; and John Russonello and Frank Wolf, "Newspaper Coverage of the 1976 and 1968 Presidential Campaigns," *Journalism Quarterly* (Summer 1979), pp. 360-364, 432.

6   James David Barber, *The Pulse of Politics: Electing Presidents in the Media Age* (New York: Norton, 1980), p. 315.

7   *Toronto Star,* 5 May 1979, p. A3.

8   *Maclean's,* 16 April 1979, p. 18.

9   CBC National Television News, 5 April 1979.

10   We generally took odd numbered days for the *Star* and *Colonist,* and even numbered days for the *Times* and *Globe and Mail.*

11   Here and in subsequent analysis the coding was done by the author. Checks involving both a recording of a sample of stories at a later date, and a second coding of a sample of stories by a "blind" helper produced strong reliability coefficients.

12   For the *Star* and *Globe* two editions per week were selected at random from those considered in the story type analysis. For the *Times* and *Colonist* we took three editions per week because the total amount of coverage per edition was smaller.

13   CBC and CTV broadcasts were taped on alternate evenings. A total of 20 CBC and 22 CTV newscasts were covered. Of the six newscasts that were missed during the seven-week period, five were on weekend evenings. Since the "wrap-ups" and "retrospectives" prevalent on weekends generally contain a high proportion of horserace commentary, the horserace estimates in Table 3 are probably slightly on the conservative side.

14   We should stress that only the audio content was coded, and acknowledge that often (as when the correspondent voices an account of a leader's promises while video footage depicts the leader's progress through a crowd) the audio and visual components may create different impressions.

15   Patterson, *The Mass Media Election*; Carey, "How Media Shape Campaigns"; and Russonello and Wolf, "Newspaper Coverage...".

16   Carey, "How Media Shape Campaigns," p. 55.

17   *Toronto Star,* 20 April 1979, p. A16.

18   For example, *Toronto Globe and Mail,* 17 May 1979, p. 9, and *Maclean's,* 14 May 1979, p. 38, and 9 April 1979, pp. 25-26.

19   For example, treatments of unemployment on April 10 and inflation on April 12.

20   There was a good illustration in the 1980 campaign. Ten days before the election Mary Janigan of the FP News Service wrote an incisive analysis of Clark's rhetoric concerning the Liberal performance on defence policy. Janigan pointed out a number of partial truths and falsehoods among Clark's statements. This piece had no impact on the campaign's

final week. See "Clark rattles Canada's rubber sabre at the Russians," *Vancouver Sun*, 8 February 1980, p. A14.

21 Elihu Katz, "Platforms and Windows: Broadcasting's Role in Election Campaigns," *Journalism Quarterly* XLVIII, 2 (1974), p. 304.

22 This finding is consistent with Patterson's observation that there has been a shift in emphasis towards the horserace in American coverage since the 1940s when the Lazarsfeld and Berelson studies pointed to its presence. See *The Mass Media Election*, pp. 28-30.

23 For example, "You'll Pay for Joe's Home Plan: Economists," *Toronto Star*, 18 April 1979, p. A1, and "Trudeau's Plan to Double-Track CN Rail Line Ill-conceived, Non-sensical, says Professor," *Vancouver Sun*, 18 January 1980, p. A1.

24 Henry Fairlie expresses this point in "Press Against Politics," *The New Republic*, 13 November 1976, p. 14.

25 Carey, "How Media Shape Campaigns," pp. 56-57.

26 One such discussion was carried on CBC radio's Sunday Morning program on April 1, 1979. See also Roy MacGregor, "The Selling of the Candidates," *Maclean's*, 7 May 1979, pp. 45-50; and Richard Gwyn, "No holds barred as election ads plug up the air waves," *Toronto Star*, 28 April 1979, p. C4.

27 Barber, *The Pulse of Politics*, p. 312.

28 *Ibid.*, pp. 315-316.

David C. Walker Pollsters, Consultants, and Party Politics in Canada

Introduction

The relationship between political parties and polling firms is one of the least researched areas of Canadian politics. This is not surprising given the secrecy shrouding the role played by pollsters and the advice they proffer to party strategists and their leaders. Information exchanged under these circumstances is considered by the participants to be most confidential, dealing as it does with the strengths and weaknesses of the party, its policies, images, and leaders. Senator Keith Davey honoured his pollster as the cornerstone of the modern Liberal Party. "The most basic tool in establishing a strategic game plan today is political polling" (Davey, 1986: 175). Polling is very much a part of our political life because of its usefulness to senior party strategists, but its presence is far from welcome in many circles. This chapter will analyze the role of Canadian pollsters in terms of their impact on our political parties.

Critics attack pollsters for a number of reasons: their role in parties subverts rank-and-file attempts to democratize these traditional elitist organizations; their services are somewhat suspect from a methodological and professional perspective; and their data unduly influence the political discourse and the outcome of elections. As the industry was first established in the United States 50 years ago, opponents have investigated the issues there in much greater detail than is the case in this country. Indeed, just as American giants like George Gallup, Lou Harris, and Richard Wirthlin set the pace of Canadian polling, so also Canadian critics are strongly influenced by commentaries from south of the border.

The rise of the pollster has coincided with the rise of the mass media, particularly television, which has had a dramatic impact on North American politics, one which has been very extensively recorded and analyzed elsewhere (Qualter, 1985: 192-224). As politicians have been forced to redefine their relationship with voters through the media, many of the traditional communications processes have been shattered. Canadian society is now highly urbanized, bureaucratized, and industrialized; politicians now reach out to voters through the communications industry in what at first appears to be a very direct relationship. Voters see and hear politicians on television and then respond positively or negatively. In reality, however, the modern political relationship between leaders and voters is indirect and remote, and, as a result, good politicians have a great sense of insecurity about voters. They are always asking themselves what voters are reading, how they are reacting to government, how a better job can be done in communicating, and what Canadians think of their leaders. Since it is impossible for politicians to get to know many people on an individual basis, they rely on others to supply the information and analysis that will make sense of the unknown. Political parties and pollsters are the major brokers between the politician of the 1980s and the voters of the television era.

Political parties have always played the role of power broker by providing national party leaders with policy ideas, workers, funds, professional and personal networks, and campaign experience. In an electoral system that requires an overwhelming amount of work in constituencies covering all corners of the country, political parties have seen themselves as the principal contributors to election victories and have expected, in return, to have a special bond with their leaders. Since democratization of major political, economic, and social institutions is in many ways one of the most dominant themes in the political life of the 1980s, Canadian parties have not been exempt from pressures to be more open and accessible. Samuel Bowles and Herbert Gintis have written that the promise of a more democratic future is based partly on making state power democratically accountable. "It affirms the traditional democratic forms of representative democracy and individual liberty and proposes novel forms of social power independent of the state" (Bowles and Gintis, 1986: 177). These writers argue that the vision of a more democratic society is not limited to the state but involves also the transformation of economic and community institutions.

Pollsters enter this partisan arena at a much different level. Their understanding of the political world is based on analysis of voter attitudes and behavioural patterns and not on contracts with the party's rank and file. Their *modus operandi* is reporting data and offering strategic advice, on the most confidential basis, to corporate and government clients. Their success is based on limiting access to information and maintaining a mystique regarding the collection and analysis of data. Their world is dominated by hierarchical organizations in which it is taken for granted that they negotiate and confide with only a few at the top. The democratization of this world is still a long way off; pollsters often appear to be very comfortable working under these circumstances.

A direct contradiction exists between the activities of the pollster and those of the party. The former builds up trust and respect by dealing in absolute confidences and proving beyond a doubt that information is not being freely circulated. The latter builds its base through friendship networks—challenging closed elites, questioning policies, sharing information, and building alliances. As ideal types, these two political activists have clashed over the past thirty years. Consequently, political parties have undergone appreciable changes since the arrival of the pollster on the Canadian political scene.

Since public opinion polls are not always a neutral factor in national campaigns (Polsby and Wildavsky, 1980), reporting the outcome of polls affects the behaviour of candidates and party leaders by giving them information about the state of an election. When publicly released through the media, polls often create chaos on the campaign trail, if for no other reason than that journalists can easily distort or misinterpret the pollster's "scientific data." "The use of poll results as journalism is the natural outgrowth of the 'precision journalism' movement and has become a vital component of the picture journalists draw of a political campaign" (Stovall and Solomon, 1984: 615). "Horserace" stories are always more easily reported than more substantive issues, particularly by journalists who are on the bus or airplane sharing the leader's hectic campaign schedule. A *New York Times* editor once commented that he had a difficult time remembering how political reporting was done before polls were used. "The response of successful politicians to public opinion is no secret. For years they have been paying for more and more elaborate systems to help in deciding what issues to address and how to approach those issues. With the explosive growth of opinion sampling and the widespread dissemination of that information I wonder if the media and the polls are feeding on each other" (Kovach, 1980: 570).

Pollsters working on the inside, giving information and offering advice, experience no similar ambivalence about their role. They are there to help the politician gain and maintain office. More often than not, however, pollsters play an important public role, either through the publication of their polls or through the many interviews given to the national media. The American pollster, George Gallup, was always quite comfortable with the publication of polls, modestly claiming that "[p]olls constitute the most useful instrument of democracy ever devised" (Wheeler, 1976: 170).

This self-congratulatory tone has frequently been challenged in American politics. Observers have decried the fact that public-opinion polls have come to have a pervasive and often dangerous impact and argue that these polls can actually "determine who runs for political office and, often, who wins. They also influence the tone and context of debate on great national issues" (Wheeler, 1976: 260). Polls create intense feelings among those who read them, those who claim never to read them, and political strategists who see them as one of their major weapons in the struggle for power in a democratic society.

Writers such as Larry J. Sabato have been quite critical of the pollsters' presumption that their work is technically beyond question. "It should be clear," he argued (1981: 68), "that polls are far less 'scientific' and reliable than is commonly believed and that pollsters are not always the *vox populi* the press acclaims." While he has several criticisms, the heart of his concern is that pollsters rarely acknowledge that polling is more of an art than a science. "By the scientist's criterion, polling could never qualify as an experimental discipline because any given poll's results cannot be truly tested and replicated. Every poll is unique, a snapshot of a moment in time" (Sabato, 1981: 87). He concludes (1981: 82) with the sobering thought that "opinion surveys can never substitute for good sense and thoughtful study."

As can be seen from these criticisms, not everyone has been happy with the emergence of pollsters as thinkers and strategists moulding modern political parties. The academic community, as well as rank-and-file party activists, have decried the entry of pollsters directly into the inner sanctums of prime ministers and pretenders to the throne.

Nonetheless, political strategist Keith Davey, renowned as he is for his promotional skills, is quite proud of how he helped transform Martin Goldfarb from a highly successful but private market entrepreneur into a widely-known political adviser, close to the heart of the Liberal Party. Davey has made no apology for introducing the new technology of polling into Canadian politics.

In this chapter we are going to examine just how the major pollsters have changed Canadian politics since the mid-1960s. We will look at the services they provide to political parties and the media, their impact on local campaigns, and the efforts now being made in Ottawa to reform their roles.

Polling Comes to Canada

The public-opinion polling business emerged simultaneously over the past three decades within academic circles as well as in the commercial world. Professor John Meisel's pivotal study recounting the 1957 election and the subsequent landslide election of John Diefenbaker in 1958, marked the Liberal Party's push into a more modern phase of its development (Meisel, 1962: 271-276). One of the new tools in the rebuilding process was to be polling. After John F. Kennedy won his squeaker of a victory over Richard Nixon in 1960 with the help of pollster Lou Harris, Liberal Party reformers brought in American expertise and jumped on the pollster's bandwagon (McCall-Newman, 1982: 48).

Harris was instrumental in helping party strategists understand the perception of Canadians about their leaders and their parties, quite apart from their own "gut reactions." His polling for the 1963 election showed, for example, that Canadians were not overwhelmed by Lester Pearson's international accomplishments, although his close political friends originally thought this was one of his strongest points. As Davey (1986: 45) noted, "there is no secret to winning elections, but too many academic journalists and politicians make it seem complicated.... Far more important, however, is the overall strategic game plan.... Having determined the best issue, then that becomes the issue of the campaign. Polling is extremely useful in making this determination."

During this same period, when Martin Goldfarb was building his market research business in Toronto, he and Keith Davey developed a close working relationship. After the 1963 election, Harris was replaced by Oliver Quayle, another American. When the 1965 election turned into another disaster, Goldfarb gained national prominence as the Liberal pollster. As the "Davey-Coutts gang"—the unflattering description given them in the final months of the Trudeau era—gained control over the central party and the apparatus of the Prime Minister's Office (PMO), Goldfarb established himself as the most visible and controversial Canadian pollster. In fact, until Allan Gregg of Decima Research began in the late 1970s to develop his own profile through his connections with the Progressive Conservative Party, Goldfarb's position was unchallenged.

Polling firms have really only two choices available if they wish to develop a political role for themselves. Pollsters provide information critical to tying public opinion into the political process by polling voters on issue preferences and by asking them about parties, their leaders, and their voting intentions. This information is then either fed directly and privately to political parties, associations, corporations, and governments or delivered to the mass media for publication in national and regional markets.

There are no independent Canadian market-research corporations dealing exclusively in the public-opinion research business, that is, the interviewing of adult Canadians regarding attitudes on leaders, parties, and public policies. There are too few clients capable of paying the full costs of maintaining such polling services. This is the one distinct difference between Canadian and American public-opinion polling; in the United States, the high frequency of state, civic, and Congressional elections (every second year) and the competitive print and television conglomerates lead to an industrial specialization not possible here.

Political soundings are undertaken by market-research companies often as a reflection of the partisan interests of their owners. In some cases, these entrepreneurs have sought out market research to support their interest in politics; Allan Gregg moved from being a researcher in the Progressive Conservative Party to setting up his own firm, which was soon doing party research at the provincial and federal levels. Contract research followed in several government departments and with private clients interested in the same areas of expertise. His political work has been estimated at 15 per cent of Decima's 1985 gross revenue of $10 million, while in 1986 Goldfarb publicly estimated his to be less than that (Fulford, 1985: 30). In other words, all the publicity is derived from a small percentage of the firm's research business which, by its very nature, is carried out in confidence for clients whose identity is rarely known outside the firm. The bread and butter of the polling industry is market research undertaken in the private sector. *Saturday Night* editor Robert Fulford, (1985: 30) described Gregg's work in the following way: "The essence of his business is business. His function is to inform corporate executives of public attitudes and tell them how to use those attitudes or change them. He and his colleagues are social scientists for hire, people who have figured out how to absorb the techniques developed in universities and put them to work in the service of corporate profit."

Association with either the Liberal or Progressive Conservative parties has been an effective strategy for broadening the recognition of three or four firms both within their industry and in the public arenas. Depending on the owner's inclination, the strategy has included granting extensive media interviews and playing the role of political guru by giving the public a taste of what is being whispered in the ears of the powerful. *Globe and Mail* columnist Jeffrey Simpson, in describing Martin Goldfarb, laid bare the jaundiced view many journalists have of pollsters when he commented (1984: 11) that

> his polls for the Liberals, and the interpretations that he gave to them, inspired among the politicians, bureaucrats, journalists and lobbyists of Ottawa the kind of speculation and wonder that primitive hill tribes bestow upon herbal medicines. Goldfarb has come to be perceived as a kind of witch doctor of politics, capable of restoring an ailing party to health or casting curses on the Liberals' political opponents by his almost magical ability to interpret the mood of the country.

The NDP has not nourished a political polling firm in the same manner as the two other major parties, although, in some provinces, they have developed close working relationships, especially where they have formed the government. This can be explained partially by the NDP's weaker financial situation, which, until recently, precluded their buying enormous studies. More importantly, the trade unions have long been suspicious of polls and, within their own organizations, have relied on the mythology of union democracy to legitimize their leadership. In this context, many unions have found it difficult to endorse the concept that a market research company, which normally deals with corporate clients, can, through the magic of polling, understand the working world better than the membership. The labour movement is still careful not to circumvent the traditional communication and decision-making channels of the unions and the NDP. Having noted this internal dilemma, it must also be said that this is changing and that both the NDP and the unions now use small, independent, and lesser-known polling organizations more regularly to gauge public moods.

As a consequence of their relationship with political parties, two major firms, Martin Goldfarb and Associates, connected to the Liberals, and Decima, connected to the Tories, gained national exposure in the 1970s and 1980s and have, among political pundits, taken on a special status that has raised many questions about their roles. In addition to these two firms, three others have positioned themselves outside of Quebec to be part of the political process. Environics is a Toronto-based firm which polls regularly for *The Globe and Mail* in addition to providing public-affairs research services to its corporate and government clients. Its polls cover not only the horserace or voting intention question, but also major public-policy issues such as free trade. In direct competition is Angus Reid Associates, a Winnipeg-based firm which, in 1985, began to sell public-opinion research to Ontario newspapers and in 1986 launched a national service with seven subscribing newspapers. In 1987, Southam News Service began carrying the Reid Poll. The Reid-Southam Poll, featuring questions on a wide range of public-policy issues, competed directly with Environics and the Gallup Poll, the granddaddy of polling organizations whose monthly release of its party-support question has been guaranteed front page headlines across the country. Gallup has been in the business since the Second World War, so its credibility as the benchmark for determining Canadian support for political parties has gone largely unchallenged. While these three polling firms do not have as intimate a relationship with the political parties as do the other two, they are called upon for presentations and for briefings.

Tools of the Trade

Firms provide four types of public affairs research for their clients: custom or specialized survey studies, focus groups, omnibus surveys, and regular public affairs reports. As noted earlier, the Canadian public-affairs business (the usual nomenclature for the political or public-opinion side of the market-research business) has a very limited market place. Some firms, such as Decima, offer both public-opinion research and representational advisory services as their corporate strategy. In this case, Decima's sister company, Public Affairs International, offers clients advice on possible approaches for dealing with provincial and federal authorities. Most firms, however, specialize only in public-opinion research on public-policy issues.

The largest volume of public-affairs research in Canada is purchased by federal government departments requiring information about public attitudes on policies directly controlled by them. Other major purchasers are provincial governments, associations, and private corporations. The size of the market is difficult to estimate because of contract procedures in both the public and private sectors, but a conservative figure would be $20 million annually.

Custom Research: Surveys of National and Targeted Audiences

The relationship between the party in power and those departmental contracts is very important. For the party, operating through the cabinet and the PMO, public attitudes on policy issues are central to the political planning that takes place among senior aides. They are always interested in what research is being commissioned, and what firm is receiving the contract, and who is seeing the results. Since the party's budget and that of the PMO are very limited for national surveys, politicians often see public-opinion research being done by departments and central agencies as being available for political questions of great sensitivity. As a consequence, the polling firm with the strategist and the track record for working closest to the PMO and senior cabinet ministers is likely to gain the most contracts. That research then becomes not only a departmental resource in policy development, refinement, and evaluation, but also a tool in political planning for the government.

Partisan research is frequently undertaken and funded through departments whose research budgets are sufficiently large to incorporate political questions into the interview schedules. A research project such as this is known as "custom" research; that is, it is done solely for the client department and is not intended to be read elsewhere. The costs can range widely, from $25,000 to over $200,000. Typically, a department hires a firm whose ostensible purpose is to research a topic of direct concern to the policy interests of the department. For example, the Department of Agriculture might be interested in levels of public support for federal payments to finance western wheat farmers. In the course of conducting these telephone interviews, the polling firm might also ask questions about party support, popularity of national leaders, and the profile of the minister. The research is funded sufficiently so that these questions can be asked, but the responses are most likely only reported directly to the minister and his staff. Department officials who originally funded the research are not likely to see the political report if, in fact, the data are ever documented in writing.

Since 1983, however, the Access to Information Act has had a great impact on public-opinion research, inasmuch as these publicly-funded reports must be made available to the public on request. Thus, it will be interesting to determine the extent to which these political questions gain wider public circulation than was the case only five years ago.

If a party decides to undertake its own custom research, the survey is not normally tendered out but given to the firm which has the closest working relationship with the leader's office (in the case of the opposition parties) or with the PMO (in the case of the government). For reasons of trust and loyalty, the party, in commissioning its own national survey, is not likely to seek price quotations from more than one or two pollsters, as these are not competitive bid situations. When the survey is being fielded before an election, the most common technique used is the 20-30 minute telephone survey of 1,000-2,000 voters, depending on the accuracy needed.

The PMO during the last years of the Trudeau government (1982-84) changed its strategy from sole-sourcing of public-opinion research to one based on two or three firms undertaking field work without actually competing against each other for any specific assignment. Having only one pollster offering advice made the chief political strategists very vulnerable to criticism about this advice, methodology, interpretation and pricing. By allowing regional firms such as Angus Reid Associates to conduct work in Western Canada, the PMO deflected criticism that they listened only to Martin Goldfarb. Similarly, as everyone was preparing for the changing of the guard with Prime Minister Trudeau's resignation, the alliances within the Liberal Party became more difficult to interpret. Everyone wanted to have some connections with a polling firm, but they were equally wary about getting caught with a pollster whose advice might be valued less by the new incumbent. Because of the jockeying for position, the Liberal Party found itself in 1984 using both Angus Reid Associates and Martin Goldfarb Associates as pollsters during the election, an awkward situation at best.

A firm such as Angus Reid Associates is able to set a questionnaire, pull a sample out of its computer bank, telephone 1,500-1,600 adult Canadians for 15-20 minutes each, enter the data, and analyze the results—all within seven days. The cost for this research would likely be in the range of $50,000-$100,000. Parties also undertake very sophisticated targeted research dealing only with the marginal voting situations that might make the difference between winning and losing an election. For example, the parties do not treat each constituency as being of equal value because some can be won easily, while others will not likely be won barring a major shift in public-opinion. As a consequence, parties tend to monitor only those seats where a relatively modest shift in voter support can win the election. Key groups are identified, and their views on major issues, party preferences, and leadership issues are tabulated and examined closely.

Parties use this type of public-opinion research to identify constituencies that are considered to be "swing" and, during an election, likely to change voting patterns sufficiently to defeat the opposition. These seats can be isolated geographically or they can be targeted because of the types of voters living in these ridings. In the first case, the regional context is important to understand and therefore critical for the pollster to follow. For example, even though most of western Canadian rural areas are safe for Tories, the emergence of right-wing separatist fringe groups might be enough to upset an incumbent.

Tracking a group of like-minded voters across constituencies is a more difficult task from a sampling perspective and incurs much higher costs. Here, an example might be young voters, 18-24, whose attitudes on training, education, and employment programs are important in understanding how they intend to vote. More importantly, since at this age they are also inclined to work hard as campaign volunteers, they are an important consideration in the long-term development of all parties. They are motivated by electoral themes and party track records on these highly salient issues.

Once the election has been called, polling is undertaken on an intensive daily basis across the country with special monitoring of key electoral groups. During the 1984 federal election, phone calls were made each evening and the results presented to party strategists by 10:00 o'clock the next morning. The surveys covered questions about leadership, partisan support, and issues. The purpose of this electoral polling is to measure on a daily basis what impact events of the day might be having on voters' intentions. It helps the campaign strategists decide what has to be responded to and what can be ignored on a day-to-day basis. However, this type of research is very expensive for political parties, who must spend several hundred thousands of dollars during a campaign.

Focus Groups

Custom research can also involve focus groups. Sometimes political parties will define their research program through a series of focus groups which are not unlike an undergraduate seminar group of one-and-a-half to two hours in length, but featuring discussions that are much more directed and probing than normally experienced in a university setting. These audio-taped sessions, often conducted in the presence of party researchers who remain anonymous behind one-way mirrors, allow for the testing of ideas for a research agenda among a group of 12 to 20 randomly-selected voters who either represent a general audience or a more specialized target of particular interest. For example, in the case of the former, a political party might be interested in finding out how Canadians in general think about its priorities for government expenditures in times of public restraint and concern about the high deficit. They might hold focus groups in five or six locations across the country to get a better understanding for the right questions to probe in a national telephone survey. A party might also be interested in learning more about the concerns of urban working-class women who require assistance for daycare or in adapting to new technology in the workplace. In this case, the focus groups would involve only working women—probably those earning less than $30,000 annually and only those in the major metropolitan regions: usually, Montreal, Toronto, Winnipeg, Edmonton/Calgary, and Vancouver are selected.

Omnibus Surveys

In order to minimize polling costs, parties often buy time in monthly omnibus surveys which are a service provided by most firms in the industry. Three to seven organizations buy survey time and thereby cut down on their individual costs. The omnibus technique allows the purchase of three to five minutes of interview time during a national survey, which strategists can then use to track selected issues and leadership problems three or four times a year. Survey time is also sold to corporations, federal departments, and associations. The polling firm acts as a broker among buyers, whose identity is confidential. All clients share in the demographic information, which is one way costs are kept to a minimum. When this service is purchased one to four times annually, clients can follow Canadian perceptions and attitudes on public issues, evaluate their own profiles and images, track their communications strategies, and access public attitudes on issues breaking into public view. The cost for each unit is usually $10,000-$20,000.

Public Affairs Publication

A fourth service provided by the major firms is in-depth analyses of independent public-opinion research. *The Goldfarb Report* is an annual document; *The Reid Report* is issued monthly; and Decima's is a quarterly report, described by Robert Fulford (1985: 30) as, in relation to the size of the Canadian market, "probably the most successful piece of opinion-research publishing in the world." Clients purchase these services for trend analyses and for suggestions on how to interpret these changes. Not all the research is political, but it gives the reader an opportunity to think of new approaches to public problems. In 1986, for example, *The Reid Report* reviewed the following issues, based on a series of 1,600 interviews in national polls and a second tier of interviews with 250 chief executive offices: agriculture, beer advertising, bilingualism, the federal budget, corporate concentration, Crown corporations, education, financial institutions, and health care. Firms use this data as a basis for developing closer working relationships with politicians, who, in turn, find the reports an excellent source for policy ideas and speeches.

The Pollster as Political Strategist

While polls undertaken for the media or through government departments tend to be directed at the general population, custom research by parties is frequently designed to measure attitudinal changes only among those voters whom strategists think might be influenced by specific government/party activity in the period leading up to the next election. The present volatility among Canadian voters seriously affects the prime minister in calling an election. In practical terms, there is a twenty-four month "window" during the last two years of any Parliament—a great opportunity to call for dissolution according to changing attitudes. The prime minister can take advantage of an opponent's miscue, a sudden crisis, or an improving economy. In order to make the right move, however, it is necessary for the prime minister to have up-to-date information about the marginal areas of support, which, indeed, are the only ones to be concerned about come election day. From this perspective politicians and their planners must often have the combined skills of military strategists and market analysts. The political calculations about the available opportunities are done with the help of public opinion research indicating which party the voters are likely to support under what conditions. The intuitive insightfulness of elected politicians is certainly important, but no political planning group can allow the polls to be shrouded in mystery. The political strategy is straightforward. The appeal at election time must be good enough to win over various groups in a majority of constituencies across Canada and so win control over the next Parliament.

Strategists use polling information to trace changes in regional support because these signal more accurately than the simple national figures where the intense battles for voter support will take place. Regional voting patterns differ greatly and tend to coincide with specific media markets. Party strategists, following regional trends, work out plans for a media message which will help them correct whatever problems have been identified at the polls. A good example of this is the Mulroney government's efforts to gain or maintain support of western grain farmers facing a combination of tougher international markets and declining commodity prices. Dissatisfaction with the government was so great by 1987 that long-term Conservative support dating back to the Diefenbaker era was beginning to slip. Announcements of improved government support were made in Winnipeg and Regina on the assumption that the target audience could best be reached through the regional media. Messages are so tailored that political managers know how to command the front page of the Winnipeg *Free Press* or the top item on the evening news by announcing new program funds directly to the target audience.

The pollster is brought in to identify where the effort must be made to win a highly competitive national campaign. Even though there is a great deal of dispute within the polling industry and among politicians about the impact of campaigning on voter preference, the 1984 general election showed that an effective strategy could damage the front-runner. In this example, John Turner's Liberals were thought to have a lead, but a series of errors combined with an unimpressive television debate contributed to their eventual loss to the Conservatives. Polling was used by the parties to track these happenings.

The one figure quoted in the media each month, the Gallup Poll, gives viewers a bottom line answer as to who is ahead. People are asked to answer the hypothetical question, "If an election were held tomorrow, which party would you vote for?" This is an interesting reading and gives Ottawa watchers an opportunity to discuss the ups and downs of governments, opposition parties, and their leaders. However, this information is too sketchy for campaign planners.

Many party leaders, including Pierre Elliott Trudeau and John Turner, have always declined to comment on the release of a poll, realizing that this picture can change dramatically and without warning. Instead, their strategists are looking for the story behind the story, to find what is remaining constant. Pollsters are more than passive researchers; they must have the interpretive skills needed to help politicians formulate election-winning strategies at particular points in time.

The pollster explains to the politician what is happening across the country, in each of the regions, in specific constituencies, and among particular voting groups according to the research findings. The data must be put into the context of party support, leadership, and policy preferences. It then has to be styled into a format which can be effectively used by the politicians in their campaigning and in selling their programs to Canadian voters.

Constituency Politics and the Polls

At the constituency level, public-opinion research is most valuable when used in advance to plan out campaigns based on the weaknesses and strengths of the candidates and their opponents. The three federal campaigns between 1979 and 1984 in the federal constituency of Winnipeg-Fort Garry illustrate this point.

Months before the 1979 campaign, the incumbent, James Richardson, had resigned from the cabinet over policy differences with Prime Minister Trudeau. For a while it was unclear whether or not Richardson would run as an independent in Winnipeg-Fort Garry, a traditional Liberal stronghold. Since his policy differences, principally over bilingualism, were popular among local voters, Richardson was thought to be a strong figure, one who might win as an independent. Senator Keith Davey arranged for a poll to be undertaken by Goldfarb. The poll indicated that Lloyd Axworthy, well-known in his local provincial riding but an unknown factor in the rest of the federal constituency, could win the contest. As the seat was also the one from which the most senior Manitoba cabinet minister was always chosen, the campaign strategy based on this public-opinion research was to move quickly by having the prime minister attend Axworthy's nomination meeting (a manoeuvre designed to discourage other candidates from seeking the nomination), and then to imply in the campaign itself that the candidate was the obvious next cabinet minister. Since the poll showed that voters really thought Liberals would be forming the next government (because of support in the East and despite their own reservations), the campaign focused on having a "local star" in that cabinet. Richardson declined to run as an independent so that the race became a traditional three-party contest.

Near the end of that campaign, with less than a week to go, Senator Davey phoned to report that Goldfarb's final poll for Manitoba did not look good; Lloyd Axworthy was down by seven points and would definitively lose. Consequently, Davey was changing Trudeau's travel plans and moving him to a rally in Edmonton where Goldfarb thought prospects were better, rather than in Winnipeg as originally scheduled. "Sorry guys," Davey signed off, not to be heard from again until Axworthy's victory by a margin of one per cent was broadcast nationally late on election night. The second campaign came shortly later and led to the last Trudeau victory. With the Liberal Party far ahead in the national polls, there was little need to conduct local polls.

One of the most conflict-ridden situations that can arise between a pollster and the local, constituency-based campaign committee stems from the traditional organization's heavy reliance on worker insight and information collected at the door for signs of strengths and weaknesses during the campaign. Resources are routinely reallocated on the basis of this new information. If polling data is used too much, then campaign workers feel quite ignored and sense that their advice is being discounted. This is all counter-productive to a successful election-day operation. The essential job in a local campaign is to identify, count, and bring out to vote those who are supporters and to persuade others to be supporters. As regional media advertising is rarely available to local candidates—mainly because costs are prohibitive—local communication systems based on contact at the door are a major source of success in a competitive race. If the workers sense that the party elite is more concerned with polls than their own views, they will be less motivated to work on election day.

In 1984, the polls played an unusually important role in both the national and local campaigns. After trailing the Conservative Party for months, the Liberals found themselves ahead in the polls, by a wide margin. During the campaign, this lead fell off quickly and featured one of the greatest mid-campaign turnarounds ever measured in Canadian public opinion. The Conservative victory, while consistent with months of their leading the polls, signalled that Canadian opinion is volatile and subject to campaign appeals. Once opinion began to change at the national level and voters became more certain that they were voting Conservative, the national news stories were that the Conservatives were about to sweep the country for the first time since Diefenbaker's 1958 victory. With that interpretation dominating the national media, local newspapers and electronic media looked for regional stories reflecting the same analysis.

With the national poll results showing Liberal fortunes in dramatic decline, the local press naturally became interested in the fate of Manitoba races. The two seats, St. Boniface and Winnipeg-Fort Garry, held by Liberals, were likely to be affected by a Tory sweep. With Axworthy being the high-profile cabinet minister, his seat was the obvious one to watch. During the last two weeks of the campaign, a radio station operated by a Tory campaign manager announced a poll showing Axworthy's Conservative opponent to be ahead and likely to win. The poll was said to be based on interviews conducted in a regional shopping centre outside the constituency. While shopping-centre intercepts are a technique frequently used for testing consumer products, it is a methodology highly suspect for measuring localized political trends. The poll released at 1:00 p.m. was immediately challenged by the Axworthy campaign lawyer with a complaint to the CRTC. The challenge was made for three reasons. First, the evening news and the morning newspapers would be forced to carry both stories—the poll and the challenge—thereby diminishing its potential impact. Second, in a campaign under siege because of national trends, workers and the candidate had to be reassured that the local situation was not the same as the national one. Third, if the credibility of the poll was allowed to go unchallenged, then everyone would agree that the local Liberal candidate was in as much trouble as the national polls indicated. The counterattack effectively forced the media to treat the poll with suspicion and not jump on a bandwagon. Every broadcast that evening featured not only the poll, but also the threatened legal action. Axworthy went on to win by a four per cent margin.

Policing the Polls

Politicians generally decry the use of polls, and it is particularly fashionable to lash out at pollsters for manipulating the system. Politicians who admit to following the polls are characterized as being weak and lacking in leadership. However, despite these protests, politicians are curious and like to know results beforehand, or in more detail than what is provided in media accounts. The relationship can often be a delicate one for all concerned. Ottawa loves gossip, and information about soon-to-be released polls is powerful material. As pollsters generally bring both bad and good news, politicians are quick to question any public-opinion research which is not consistent with the way they would like to see the world. As a consequence, natural conflicts exist between those publishing public-opinion polls and those seeking power, if only because information means power, and damaging information can seriously affect combatants in the struggle for control of government. Yet, the public conflict and disclaimers do not tell the whole story because both politicians and pollsters spend a lot of time communicating behind the scenes, either directly or indirectly.

Pollsters differ as to how they should deal with political parties. It is a seductive relationship, with all the trappings that go with political power. It involves helping to form strategy at the highest levels, giving advice to the most senior bureaucrats and politicians, and appearing in public as the most astute observers of political events. Closeness breeds difficulties, however, since public-opinion research, like any academic research, is based on asking objective questions and offering straightforward analyses.

As part of the June 1986 *White Paper on Election Law Reform*, circulated by the President of the Privy Council and House Leader, Ray Hnatyshyn, the government sought ways of controlling the publication of polls during election periods. Recognizing that, since the early forties, polls had been published at regular intervals, including times of election campaigns, the government referred to widespread concern about the margin of possible error in each poll. Pollsters regularly publish polls which have a margin of error of plus or minus 4 per cent (on samples of approximately 1,000-1,100 adult Canadians—only the Reid Poll and Environics use bigger samples of 1,500-2,000 for a margin of plus or minus 2.5 per cent). During a campaign, this percentage takes on more significance since each point can spell the difference between success and failure. For example, 40 per cent support can actually mean 36 to 44 per cent if the margin of error is plus or minus 4 per cent. For party strategists, 44 per cent means a majority in Parliament; 36 per cent likely means a minority government. This has led to the concern that, at election time in particular, a poorly constructed poll, whether or not it was published in good faith, could be quite destructive. The White Paper recommended that the publication of opinion polls during election campaigns continue to be allowed but that the following information be provided by each poll:

> the name and address of the organization which conducted the inquiry;
> the population polled, the size of the sample, and the percentage of completed interviews;
> the dates of the first and last completed interviews;
> the name and address of the person or organizations who paid for the conduct of an inquiry; and
> a summary description of any normalization procedure used in order to account for the under- or over-representation of some strata of the population in the sample (Canada, 1986: 27).

To date, the government has acted on none of these recommendations.

Conclusion

The academic and journalistic communities have been quite mixed in their opinions of public-opinion polls and their uses by political parties. While Jeffrey Simpson admits that political polling is entering an even more refined state, he doubts whether the polls have been good for the public. He decries the way "the increasing sophistication of polling tempts government to aim specific policies at special-interest groups or small slices of the electorate, since these groups can be monitored more easily than ever before" (Simpson, 1984: 18). Paul Fox (1985-86: 11) admitted begrudgingly that polls are definitely here to stay: "Honest public polling is useful and can be informative. However, perverted and private polls are something else, and we should worry about them."

For the media, polls are here to stay. They serve as an independent and up-to-date source of stories for reporters and are likely to be used to seek out interest groups and political reactions to the moods and ideas of the public. In many respects, this is the easiest part of the dilemma faced by polls. Since it is known that all senior government, political, associational, and corporate leaders have access to public opinion and that they are willing to pay good money to have that information, the only question is why voters should not have access to the same data. It is difficult to understand the alarmists who argue that too many polls are being published. It can be argued on technical grounds that some polls are less valuable than others, but that is no reason for hiding information already available to political and corporate elites.

The more difficult question concerns the use of public-opinion polls by party and government elites who appear to many observers to be following the mob and not showing political leadership. They are said to be changing parties int market organizations devoid of democratic policy discussions. Government by polling implies that immediate popularity outweighs the burden of seeing to it that important but tough new legislation comes into existence. These are very real considerations in a democratic society which depends upon a healthy relationship between its leaders and voters. Where the latter believe that they are being used as pawns in electoral manoeuvres, the political climate turns to indifference and hostility. However, to imagine a situation where politicians are going to become less interested in what Canadians think of them, their careers, and their ideas is to ignore the twentieth century, with its great emphasis on the popularization of knowledge.

Notes

Bowles, S. and Gintis, H. (1986). *Democracy and Capitalism: Property, Community, and the Contradictions of Modern Social Thought.* New York: Basic Books. Canada. (1986). *White Paper on Election Law Reform,* prepared by the Honourable Ray Hnatyshyn. Ottawa.

Davey, K. (1986). *The Rain-maker: A Passion for Politics.* Toronto: Stoddart.

Fox, P. (1985-86). "Public Opinion Polls: Who Gains—Who Loses?" *Canadian Parliamentary Review* (Winter): 10-11.

Fulford, R. (1985). "This Brain for Hire." *Saturday Night* (December): 29-37.

Kovach, B. (1980). "A User's View of the Polls." *Public Opinion Quarterly, 44,* 567-571.

McCall-Newman, C. (1982). *Grits: An Intimate Portrait of the Liberal Party.* Toronto: Macmillan.

Meisel, J. (1962). *The Canadian General Election of 1957.* Toronto: University of Toronto Press.

Polsby, N. and Wildavsky, A. (1980). *Presidential Elections*. (5th ed.). New York: Scribner's.

Qualter, T. (1985). *Opinion Control in the Democracies*. London: Macmillan.

Sabato, L.J. (1981). *The Rise of Political Consultants*. New York: Basic Books.

Simpson, J. (1984). "The Most Influential Private Citizen in Canada." *Saturday Night* (December): 11-18.

Stovall, J. and Solomon, J. (1984). "The Poll as a News Event in the 1980 Presidential Campaign." *Public Opinion Quarterly, 48*, 615-622.

Wheeler, M. (1976). *Lies, Damn Lies, and Statistics: The Manipulation of Public Opinion in America*. New York: Dell.

PART 4   The Three Canadian Party Systems

The four papers in this section reflect upon the experience of party politics in Canada. Each explores the dynamics of party life and competition, as it has been played out over the three party systems, from differing perspectives. Taken together they provide a powerful argument that not only have there been three very distinct party systems, but that the very nature of Canadian government and politics was different in each one. Given that the Canadian experiment has been one of building, in Cartier's words, a "political nationality," it is as if there have been three different Canadas. In each the basic political equations that defined the constitution of public life have differed.

David Smith is concerned with the process of party governance. His theme is that it is not possible to understand Canadian government, or the political development of the nation, without understanding the character of the parties that have dominated it. Smith demonstrates how the very nature of party governance has varied across Canadian history. He charts three distinct periods. First, Macdonald and Laurier practiced a "purposive federalism" whose logic demanded "minute attention to local constituencies." Then, after World War I, that long successful pattern of governance gave way to an "accommodative approach" (called by many regional brokerage) under Prime Ministers King and St. Laurent. Most recently, the last twist in the evolutionary path has led to our contemporary politics which Smith describes as characterized by a "pan-Canadian" approach to party government.

Each of these three systems of party governance made distinct demands of its parties. Though the manifest functions of parties (nominating candidates, contesting elections, and organizing parliamentary life) persisted, their latent functions changed dramatically. In a paper entitled "Three Canadian Party Systems" Carty describes the organization, nature and character of the parties in each of these distinct periods. It illustrates how integrated and stable patterns of party life gave way to quite new constellations when the governing imperatives of the system required it. In turn, the strategies and structures party leaders adopted in building new party systems themselves shaped the patterns of party governance that would characterize the period.

It is the electoral bases of these three systems that concern Richard Johnston and his colleagues. In a brilliant overview of Canadian electoral history they demonstrate how the alignments that structured party competition, and the issues that gave it voice, can best be seen in terms of three distinctive party systems. As they comment, their argument "should be read as a complement to those [of Carty and Smith]." For those who want to explore the evolution of Canadian voting patterns, both across time and political space, Richard Johnston provides a statistically rich analysis in his "Federal and Provincial Voting: Contemporary Patterns and Historical Evolution" in David Elkins and Richard Simeon's *Small Worlds*. Much can be learned even from a careful study of tables 3 and 8 in that essay.

Finally, this section ends with a short paper that seeks to pull many of its themes together. It starts, as much work on Canadian politics must, from the lessons of John Meisel, but goes on to argue that our contemporary party system is not the one so long admired or damned by fans or critics of brokerage politics. It reminds us that, though party names and traditions persist, we would do well not to assume that the essence of the Canadian party system is unchanging. It also reminds us that to understand the nature of government in Canada, and Canada itself, it is necessary to come to grips with the country's peculiar party systems.

David E. Smith   Party Government in Canada

While political parties have scarcely gone unstudied in Canada, their
central role in the operation of national political institutions has, surprisingly, escaped the attention it deserves. Two reasons may be suggested for this oversight. First, parties are informal private organizations which, when they are successful in dominating the House of
Commons, provide for a time the formal public institution which is
government. Except on rare occasions before the 1970s and thereafter
mainly for election expense purposes, national parties have stood outside the law. Consequently, they have not been amenable to external
reform, and Canadians, who by habit and tradition are institutionalists
in their political interests, have left them alone. The nexus between
party and government, which is the heart of Canadian politics, remains unexplored in its details and the reciprocating influence of its
parts has been underestimated.

A second reason for this condition is the blinkered scholarship
which accompanies the prevailing theory of parties. This is the brokerage theory, which is both empirical and prescriptive. It purports
to describe how parties actually practise their art and it defends that
practice. According to this theory, political parties in Canada are
supposed to be agents of consensus, not instruments of choice: they
should include, not exclude. Therefore, the attention of scholars
and critics is focussed on how well or how poorly national parties
accommodate the variety of opinions that characterize modern society. Moreover, the hold of this theory is so strong that where
parties are found to be insufficiently national in their appeal (measured in brokerage theory by the bases of their voting support),
blame is generally attributed to formal political institutions such as
the electoral system, and the utility of the theory itself is not questioned. Avoiding for the time being arguments about the electoral
system's relationship to the party system, the fact remains that the
influence of brokerage theory is to divert attention once more from
what is argued here to be the crucial relationship—the relationship
between national political parties and the development of national
political institutions.

The primary thesis of this paper is that party government, that
is, the system of rule which places a party in government, has determined Canada's political development. It has done this not only

because party government results in a remarkably concentrated form of political power, but also because parties must look outside of Parliament to secure the support necessary for dominance in Parliament. Always then, there are the two dimensions to party government: the intra-parliamentary and the extra-parliamentary. Each requires special abilities from the party leader if he is to succeed in dominating his party. Since Confederation, political parties have had to make choices about how they would seek to secure support. Until the First World War they followed what is described in this paper as a local approach, paying heed to constituency factors but often enveloping their appeal in a national or expansive language. After the war a more accommodative approach was favoured in which emphasis was placed on reconciling group interests. This, in turn, gave way after the Second World War to what might be called a centralist or pan-Canadian approach to seeking support, wherein politics were designed to appeal to individual citizens regardless of their geographic location, religion or class....

Party Government

Canadians live under the misunderstanding that theirs is a young country, when in fact it has enjoyed a comparatively long interrupted constitutional development. The major continental powers of Europe have all experimented with several constitutional structures in the period since Canada was formed as a federation. In none of them can it be said, as it can in Canada, that political parties played an instrumental part in their creation. Nineteenth-century party organization, though incomplete by today's standards, predates modern Canada; it was the rudiments of party which converted colonial forms of rule into responsible government. The achievement of responsible government was the achievement of party government....

The achievement of responsible government conferred on political parties a primacy in the governmental system which can hardly be exaggerated. At the centre there is the "governing party," a telescoped phenomenon between whose parts it is difficult if not impossible to distinguish. Party and government bear on each other: party enhances or limits what government can do; government enhances or limits the ambition of party. The intermingling of party and government and the consequence of that hybrid for Canadian federalism will be discussed below. At this point, the essential feature to note is that party government confers exceptional power on the leader of the legislative party in particular (especially when in government), the legislative members generally, and a handful of notables. This power allows them to exert control over their extra-legislative parties, that is, over the rank and file, and to use them for electoral purposes.

How the inside party determines to use the outside party depends on many factors, such as ideology, electoral calculations and leadership aspirations, but that the party leaders enjoy an advantage which results from a political system that places them at the very centre of government is the hallmark of Canadian politics....

Models of Party Government

Post-Confederation Political Parties

Before 1914, political parties dominated the federal system; the governing parties, Conservatives under Sir John A. Macdonald and Liberals under Sir Wilfrid Laurier, were creating the Canadian nation. After 1918, this paramountcy disappeared in the face of regional revolt and sectional change. In its place, William Lyon Mackenzie King established a form of party and governmental leadership which, in this paper, is labelled as accommodative. That approach directed Canadian politics through the interwar years and then, with declining vigour, until the end of the Louis St. Laurent era. With John Diefenbaker as Prime Minister, the primary goal of intergroup consensus began to give way to a pan-Canadian approach to leadership, an approach that was sympathetic to group interests but even more favourable to a conception of Canada as a nation of individuals. This break with the accommodative model became clearer under Lester Pearson and then guided the leadership of Pierre Trudeau. The details of the evolution follow but before embarking on that discussion it is necessary first to summarize the character of political party leadership in the period between Confederation and the First World War and then to comment on the changes in economic, political and social conditions which preceded and accompanied the disruption of the war and to which the old political parties had to adjust when that conflict had ended.

Political parties played a central role in the territorial expansion of Canada; they made national integration possible because they provided the ligament for a society whose economic and cultural ties were slow to grow. One student of the period has said of the federal government that it was "the single most important energizing agency" in post-Confederation Canada (Stewart, 1980, p. 16). This assertion would seem to conflict with a description of Canada as a weak state model of national consolidation, but there is no inconsistency, for two reasons. First, the growth of the nation in these years was in the West, and in that region there was a deviation from the model in the form of such regionally specific features as a federal department of the interior, federal retention of the Prairies' natural resources and the creation of the North West Mounted Police. A more important reconciling factor lies in the vehicle of that active federal government; it was the Conservative and Liberal parties, the alter egos of their respective federal governments, which were the organizing forces in Canadian society and politics. As Gordon Stewart (1980) noted:

> There was no aristocratic or traditional landed class that still had an influence in public affairs; there was no lingering peasant presence upon which a political movement could be based; there was no rapidly expanding capitalist class deriving wealth and power from industrialization; there was no mass labor movement seeking to form its own party. In these conditions the federal political parties, representing the dominant middle class and particularly the professionals were extraordinarily influential in Canadian society. (p. 15)

Donald Creighton (1955) has noted that the original provinces of Confederation constituted only a fragment of British North America and that, as Sir John A. Macdonald liked to phrase it, "even in the existing union, it would be a long time...before the gristle hardened into bone" (p. 3). As Stewart has brilliantly shown, Macdonald was the first to see that political parties could be the agent of nourishment.[1] And it was he, personally and throughout his career, who used "patronage to build up not merely party loyalty but party structures outside the assembly." The features of the system he created are described in illuminating detail by Stewart, but for the purposes of this discussion, the principal points to note are the following: patronage pervaded the political system; it was systematically followed; and Macdonald played a central role in its conduct. The chief result of this development, which Stewart emphasized was "taken over, as with so much else, by Laurier," was a party system both intensely local in its interests and profoundly personal in its management by the party leader. For Canadian politics, the effect of this approach to party management was to ignore and even resist change that could not be accommodated within the framework of constituency politics. There was "a structural problem in the federal parties" which made it difficult for them to respond to the new forces of urbanization, industrialization and provincialism that became manifest toward the turn of the century. It was an "effective party structure" but not, says Stewart, a "modern" one.

This depiction of Macdonald and Laurier runs counter to their popular image as nation builders. Their achievements in securing and rounding out Confederation would seem to place them alongside the pan-Canadian leaders who, it was suggested earlier, view Canada as a collection of individuals to whom national appeals are made that override divisions of class or religion. There is an ambiguity, then, between the popular perception of these singular leaders as nation-builders and the reality of Macdonald's and Laurier's intense localism in managing politics; party structures should imitate, not conflict with, governmental objectives. The explanation for the poor fit between practice and governmental performance lies in the unique era of expansion following the post-Confederation years.

For Macdonald, "the primacy of the Dominion" was the measure of all things. Therefore, repeal of the Union, in the case of Nova Scotia's discontents, was "not even a matter for discussion"; negotiating "collectively rather than individually" with the unruly provinces in 1887 was out of the question (Creighton, 1955, pp. 3, 473). The role of the Dominion in national affairs was paramount, as demonstrated in settlement of the West, development of eastern industry and construction of a transcontinental railway. The continuing thread of Macdonald's era and of Laurier's, over four decades together, was expansion of territory, of economy, of population. More than anything else, the experience of expansion set Macdonald and Laurier apart from their successors. Great enterprises successfully achieved marked their administrations. It was argued earlier that the goal of expansion more than any other motivated the Fathers of Confederation, for from expansion would come not only economic well-being, but also political breathing space and military security. This was purposive federalism, and while its outward sign might be great enterprises, its inward logic demanded the creation of a party system based on minute attention to local constituencies. Only if the party were built in each constituency, in each new territory added to the Dominion, would the majority be there in Parliament available to the leader to advance his nation-building ambition. Macdonald and Laurier were the creators not only of modern Canada but of modern political parties in Canada. They learned to command the party in Parliament by dominating the party outside Parliament.

The appeals of post-Confederation politics were national, the practices local. Nevertheless, the combination worked and by the opening of the twentieth century, national political parties and national integration through the political parties was achieved. Party competition right across the country was secured for the first time by 1896 (Reid, 1932). However, as already intimated, the party system was based on a society whose foundations were beginning to crumble. The success of the national economic policy and the First World War guaranteed that Canada would not remain the fixed society of local, agricultural communities that the creators of the post-Confederation party system had known. In the West, the arrival of the immigrants created another agricultural society of ethnic communities and gave the original party system a second life, which lasted until the disruption of the grain trade during and after the war. In the Maritimes, where emigration and the tariff undermined the region's industrial base, the society grew more entrenched and more dependent on staples than before, so that the old party system could continue unchallenged by new economic and social forces (Acheson, 1977). At the centre, however, and then in the West, the strains became evident as the premises of post-Confederation politics confronted, but did not yield to, the changes of twentieth-century society.

To the reasons usually cited for this transition (the growing partisanship among provincial farmers coupled with new demands on their governments to act in areas of legislative responsibility allocated to the provinces) should be added one other of long-term import for governing the federation. The homogeneous political elite of 1867 (homogeneous in the sense of having brought Confederation into being and of having nurtured the new national institutions of Parliament, cabinet, the civil service and parties) was no longer ascendant.[2] New provincial elites had been formed and, in some instances, separated from the federal: Saskatchewan's early political leaders were graduates of federal politics. Even in Quebec and Ontario, it had taken at least two decades for provincial elites to secure a hold against Macdonald's centralized federalism.

The First World War accentuated this phenomenon of changing elites by accelerating trends in urbanization and industrialization which were already evident before the conflict and had their most direct and immediate impact in Ontario and, to a lesser extent, in Quebec. Rural and agrarian interests no longer held the unchallenged attention of the federal government, and it was this change in the relative importance of agrarian and non-agrarian interest which W.L. Morton (1950) suggested was an important contributing factor to the rise of Progressives. Neither the tariff nor freight rates explained the farmers' electoral combustion; rather, they saw a future in which agriculture served but did not rule Canada, and they resisted. They also failed.

Agriculture might be declining relative to industry, although a decade and a half later, responding to western farm pressure and in opposition to private traders, the federal government "nationalized" the collection and marketing of wheat. The economic transition, however, did not mean that government was in the pocket of Canadian commerce. In fact, the experience of agriculture following the war was a harbinger of the federal government's later response to demands of other economic and social groups. Ottawa is the political, not the economic or cultural, centre of Canada. While there have been notable exceptions, the most obvious being C.D. Howe's long tenure in the business-related portfolios of the governments of William Lyon Mackenzie King and Louis St. Laurent, the federal government has also experienced difficulties in working with the business community. Unlike the societies of traditional European capitals (or even those of most Canadian provincial capitals), businessmen and politicians do not rub shoulders in Ottawa. A similar separation might have happened but did not in the United States; there an easy movement between public and private sectors occurs. Part of the reason lies in the separation of governmental institutions, the "multiple crack" phenomenon, to use Morton Grodzins' (1967) picturesque phrase, which offers a variety of access to those who approach government.[3] Despite the need for contact, Canada has fewer arrangements for continuing consultation among these groups than exist in most other industrial countries, where the isolation is less acute.[4] It is now clear that the isolation is not limited to agriculture or traditional business matters but extends in other directions as well, including labour questions and science policy (Fish, 1983).[5]

With the end of the wartime emergency, the conflict of demands on government, generated in part by this economic transition, had become a permanent feature of national politics. Demands on government were not new of course, nor was conflict, but they mounted in the 1920s and government set its modern course by responding with regulatory action and shared-cost programs. The Liberals, who after 1921 formed the government most of the time and who for this reason will receive disproportionate attention because of their influence on federal and governmental development, greeted with reluctance this changing attitude toward the role of government. Philosophically, the party and its leader, Mackenzie King, opposed activism and warned repeatedly of the dangers of intervention. This is one reason why it is impossible to find the Liberal Party, as opposed to the Liberal government, reforming its organization to accommodate change. There were other reasons as well. The party first and last was an electoral organization; policy discussion during the long King era was strange, even forbidden, territory for the rank and file. It continued this way until the late 1950s. As well, and this was to become a significant factor once policy did rise to the surface of party consciousness, Anglo-American-style parties congenitally resist manifestations of professionalism. Proponents of professionalism might argue that it strengthens party by providing intellectual resources to debate and helps formulate policy; nonetheless it is invariably held suspect as being a limit on participation and a restraint on political activity (see Blondel, 1963, pp. 128-130; and Fairlie, 1968, chaps. 1 and 2). This was to be the experience of the Liberal Party; during the King and St. Laurent years, professionalism was shunned; during the Pearson and Trudeau years, non-elected managers gained unprecedented influence in Ottawa only to encounter strong opposition from Liberal supporters distant from the capital (Smith, 1981, pp. 62-71, 84-89, 148-149).

To these old and new examples of restriction on Ottawa's contact with the country's geographic hinterland and economic base must be added the cultural isolation of the capital for the French-Canadian Member of Parliament. McMenemy and Winn (1976, p. 75) treat this form of isolation as "as proxy for distance." Nothing has been said so far in this paper about French-English relations and parties, but any discussion of the party tradition in Canada would be remiss and misleading in not stressing its central place and the fundamental role of party from the outset. Territorial incorporation and social inclusion, argued here as primary functions of political parties, have special significance in the context of maintaining Quebec's commitments to Canada.

The Accommodative Approach: The King and St. Laurent Years

From 1920 on, Ottawa began to lose control of organized forces in Canadian life: farmers first, then business and labour, and still later, the provinces. It took the Second World War with the vast powers it conferred to order events (powers and a confidence thus engendered which continued for another dozen years) to restore the federal government to its former dominance. It was in the years between the wars, however, that a revised form of political rule took shape under Mackenzie King, one which checked the disintegration implicit in the events surrounding the conclusion to the First World War. Inheriting a divided party and faced with what still remains the largest electoral revolt in federal political history, King began a record of leadership whose most outstanding characteristic was his success at accommodating the factions and divisions in Canadian society. The test of his political dexterity continued through depression, drought, war and reconstruction: an unprecedented series of challenges to occur in the space of one man's tenure in office as Prime Minister and of such magnitude as to give cause for the expressions of self-pity in his diary. The legion of critics notwithstanding, it was a remarkable achievement and not only for political longevity.

The foregoing is not an apologia for King or his party but a reminder of two facts: the importance of dominant though not necessarily commanding leadership (the electorate is right to grant it so much weight) and the kaleidoscopic demands made on leadership in the second half-century since Confederation. One of King's remarkable skills was his ability to recognize and give rein to the political talent around him, although his biographer (Neatby, 1976) notes that the independence and power his colleagues were given as reward could also limit their influence: "their success as the advocates of the interests of their region made them less acceptable in other parts of the country" (p. 15). Opportunities to hone this skill recurred throughout his leadership as he sought to deflect the depradations of bumptious third parties and pugnacious provincial governments. It is not necessary to describe King's organizational and political triumphs; this has been done with admirable care by Reginald Whitaker (1977). From the perspective of a study of national political parties, the importance of the King years is that the key to party organization, the basic tenet of political life, was federalization. The provincial base of party organization had always been significant, for Liberals and Conservatives alike. During the tenure of Mackenzie King, however, the "decidedly federal nature" of the party became an article of faith and practice, one which profoundly affected political rule in the country and one which equally distinguished King's leadership from that of Macdonald and Laurier in the post-Confederation period.

The linkage was provided by ministers who dominated their regions, such as James G. Gardiner, C.D. Howe, Ernest Lapointe, and Angus MacDonald in the King cabinet; the names alone conjure up associations with strong administration and partisanship. However, "ministerialism" (the term is Whitaker's) did not convert the cabinet into a holding company of provincial chiefs. Always, there was King's insistence on the need for consensus, regardless of time, before decisions were implemented. King's deftness in defusing the Progressive threat in Parliament and in the general elections from 1921 through 1926 took time and patience. Gardiner, then still in Saskatchewan, wanted to meet the farmers' challenge head-on, but King's will prevailed, as it always did on political strategy. The farmers could be accommodated and, later, the interests of labour met, if the party acted judiciously and reasonably. The latter injunction made sense if it were realized that the Liberals should represent, that it was their natural obligation to represent, the interests of farm and labour. King did not see such economic groups, even when organized politically, as the enemy but only as the misguided. His pompous and turgid rhetoric, his platitudes, made him an easy target for ridicule, and his parliamentary opponents often fell into the trap of resorting to that and doing nothing else.

The earlier era of national expansion had passed, but King's sense that the Liberals had a mission to guarantee national unity and social justice provided an integrating force for his government and party which held in check strong and potentially divisive tendencies. Any number of illustrations of this shrewdness could be cited, but King's decision not to contest the Hamilton East by-election in 1931 reveals his skill from several perspectives. Here was a rare instance of central authorities intervening locally to prevent a Liberal nomination. It was King's opinion that if the Liberals stood to one side and allowed the Labour and Conservative candidates to do battle, Labour would win, which it did, and that the Labour candidate, Humphrey Mitchell, could be co-opted into Liberal ranks, which he was, eventually becoming Minister of Labour between 1941 and 1950. As Whitaker (1977) noted:

> The riding lost its traditional Tory cast and has since been a Liberal stronghold, where the party has drawn considerable support from the unionized working class electorate.... The Liberal party thus gained a labour base in a working class constituency which might otherwise have turned to the CCF, and drew in a representative of organized labour to the federal labour ministry. (p. 46)

As Macdonald and Laurier had before him, King excelled as a party leader, but his methods were different. If the earlier Prime Ministers had perfected the uses of patronage to create and hold constituency loyalties, King favoured a position at one remove from such direct involvement. He supported party organization and organizers in their work because it protected him from innumerable local squabbles, but distance had an added advantage. Unlike his predecessors, King throughout his years in office had to calculate in his political strategies the potential of third-party activity. Intimate involvement with constituency matters could only complicate the negotiations and compromises he always sought in order to include rather than exclude interests within the Liberal Party. On the other hand, King maintained a strong belief in his judgment of what was best for the party and would, if need be, interfere in organizational matters. This meant overriding, on occasion, the advice of ministers whose responsibility for Liberal welfare in their respective provinces or regions King normally respected. One example is his disagreements with James G. Gardiner over how to combat the Progressive challenge in the 1920s.

King's concern for the party, however, was paramount, and this awareness, perhaps more than any other factor, accounts for the Liberal Party's multiple successes before and after the Second World War. Ward (1977b) has described how the party established

> acceptable relationships between (among others) the parliamentary and extra-parliamentary wings of the party, between the leader and his supporters, between federal and provincial organizations, and between contributors of campaign funds and those who let government contracts. (p. 43)

King's accommodative tactics, however, did not vanquish all opponents, and it was indicative for future Canadian politics that his chief failures lay in dealing with provincial governments of disparate partisan complexion: in Alberta where the Liberals were a lost cause provincially and federally after 1921, in Quebec where they monopolized federal politics but, by the mid-1930s, faced implacable provincial opposition in the Union Nationale, and in Ontario where the fiercest opponents to the national Liberal Party in elections at either level were the provincial Hepburn Liberals.

Neatby (1976) has written that King "did not realize that regional frustrations were too profound to be resolved by political tactics" (p. 247). It was a curious weakness in a party of such talent and strength, with a leader so attuned to changes in public opinion, although it is true that a regional lieutenant like Gardiner, with roots in the West, remained equally impervious to the tremors of ferment there. Federal government emergency power and its use during the Second World War to deal with defence, external relations and economic production matters, blunted national sensibility to provincial concerns remote from these great questions of state. The imperatives of wartime government also coincided with the recommendations of the Rowell-Sirois Report (Royal Commission on Dominion-Provincial Relations), thus placing a "burden" on the federal civil service which Harold Innis (1940, p. 568) described as "disquieting." Growth of the federal bureaucracy, even when intended to help the provinces, restricted their internal development: money and knowledge might move out from the centre, but it did so at the cost of provincial initiative and responsibility. Innis' reservations about treating the provinces as "static institutions" concerned economic adjustment, but the same could be said of political adjustment, the first major failures of which were evident even under so successful a party leader as Mackenzie King.

The accommodative party of King continued nine more years in power under Louis St. Laurent, but appearance disguised reality in several important respects. Unlike King, who always maintained an interest in party matters (but kept his distance from its conduct in his own mind as well as in public), St. Laurent "never had any genius for organization."[6] At the very time when bureaucracy was growing fastest and party needed tending, interest in it waned. The extra-parliamentary party, which had been Mackenzie King's sounding board, petrified. The cabinet ministers now indeed became the provincial chiefs they had always threatened to become. The centralism of Canadian federalism, let loose during the war years, was given free rein by the detachment of the leader from the affairs of the party. If localism had made the parties of Macdonald and Laurier unresponsive to social change of national proportions, the isolation of the Liberal leadership from constituency opinion in the early 1950s brought about an equivalent rigidity only now as a result of loss of touch with the people. The party leaders turned inward to instruments of government. As Ward (1977b) remarked:

> In that right turn the party virtually merged with the state, so that top civil servants, all appointed, and ministers, all Members of Parliament, became almost indistinguishable from one another. (p. 43)

The interpenetration of party and bureaucracy, which before the First World War had taken place only at the lowest level of the civil service and which had been prohibited by the introduction of the merit principle through the Civil Service Act of 1918 and its regulations, returned after the Second World War in the guise of shared attitudes, if not common membership, at the highest level. Partisan sclerosis ensued though the symptoms of the disease, let alone the fatal prognosis, remained veiled to "the government party" almost to the end.

A second distinction between the King and St. Laurent eras, scarcely developed yet important for the evolution of Canadian political parties, was the articulation during the 1950s of attitudes and policies that might be called pan-Canadian. King had been a nationalist in that he sought to define dominion status and promote Canadian autonomy in peace and war. However, he avoided actions which would disturb relations between groups of Canadians and, particularly on the national question, between English and French Canadians. Only at the end of his period in office was there a suggestion of a new, pan-Canadian approach, in the form of the Canadian Citizenship Act of 1946. Although it was the first legislation of its kind, it was a harbinger of an attitude the St. Laurent government was to reveal on several occasions. Generically, the policies flowing from this approach might be seen as defining or promoting "national status." This, in fact, is how they are grouped in the guide to the St. Laurent papers in the Public Archives of Canada, the bulk of which, relating to this subject, were opened to the public in January 1984. They include, among other matters, discussion of a national anthem, a distinctive flag, the 1949 amendment to the BNA Act included in a new sectioon 91(1), and dropping such customary usages as "dominion" and "royal."

In these circumstances, the government's objective had to be inferred from its actions, since nowhere is there an explicit statement of pan-Canadian attitudes. In other areas, especially the relatively unexplored domain of cultural policy, more concrete evidence of a change in direction from the King years is available. The 1951 Report of the Royal Commission on National Development in the Arts, Letters and Sciences (the Massey Commission) made a strong claim for federal government activity "in the general education of Canadian citizens" and argued that, if Ottawa does not act, "it denies its intellectual and moral purpose, the complete conception of the common good is lost, and Canada, as such, becomes a materialistic society" (p. 8). The St. Laurent government never spoke so boldly on behalf of the federal power, but its actions following the report's recommendations (establishment of university grants, creation of the Canada Council, introduction of a national television system, heightened support for existing cultural agencies) testified to its acceptance of a responsibility to act, at least in the nebulous realm of culture, for all Canadians.

The impact of cultural policy on the self-definition of citizens has yet to be evaluated in Canada. It seems indisputable, however, that the St. Laurent government's decisions in this area of public policy were of immense importance. On the one hand, they promoted on many fronts a Canadian cultural community which before 1950 had one public base, the Canadian Broadcasting Corporation; on the other hand, they stopped the drain to the metropolis of artists who in earlier years had had to abandon their region or culture if they were to find commercial work. Much could be said of the long-term influence of this set of policies on Canadians as individuals and as a people, but for the purposes of this discussion it is enough to end this section of the paper by making two points. First, such national policies would never have been considered by Mackenzie King, partly because it would have been foreign to him to think of federal government playing this kind of educative role and partly because he would have been concerned about their impact on his accommodative approach to politics. Second, these policies were not welcomed in Quebec for the very reasons King would have cited; they interfered with provincial jurisdiction and they demonstrated a federal system which had lost its balance and in which the central government knew no self-restraint.[7]

The Pan-Canadian Approach: Diefenbaker, Pearson and Trudeau

The defeat of the Liberals in 1957 marked the end of the accommodative party identified with Mackenzie King and modified by Louis St. Laurent. John Diefenbaker and the Progressive Conservatives did not bring this skill with them nor did they acquire it in office. Diefenbaker was chosen leader in 1956. In the 20 years before that, the party had had five leaders (R.B. Bennett, R.J. Manion, Arthur Meighen, John Bracken and George Drew), as well as an 18-month period in 1940 and 1941 when there was no leader. Conservative organization reflected the instability that follows rapid changes in leadership and precluded the integration of national, provincial and constituency associations: "Much of the organization," a student of the party wrote on the eve of Diefenbaker's coming to power, "exists almost entirely as 'window dressing' to impress the public" (Williams, 1956, p. 110). Further, abrupt reversals in policy designed to attract or to repel in turn advocates of social welfare and private enterprise aggravated the problem and prevented the creation of a dependable support base among the electorate.

The Diefenbaker administration, especially after the 1958 sweep, appeared set to give stability to a party unfamiliar with that condition. But the forces of regionalism which had percolated and boiled over, even under King, now grew much stronger. It was Diefenbaker's misfortune to preside over the federal government as the Quiet Revolution burst on the scene in Quebec. Whether the federal Liberals, given their old dominance in the province, could have done better at meeting the challenge of Jean Lesage's Quebec Liberals is problematic. What is certain is that under Mr. Diefenbaker, the horde of western MPs in the Progressive Conservative caucus and the handful of Quebec ministers in cabinet proved unsympathetic and unequal to the task. Not for the first time were the costs of the Tory exclusion from Quebec to be paid by a Progressive Conservative government in Ottawa (and perhaps by Canadians across the country). William Hamilton, Postmaster General in that cabinet, later said that "none of [the French-Canadian ministers] approached a few of the outstanding ministers from other provinces" (Stursberg, 1975, p. 198). The front bench was not the only problem in Parliament. On the back benches sat nearly 50 MPs from Quebec whose Tory credentials were their good standing with Maurice Duplessis' Union Nationale, a warranty that expired when both Duplessis and Paul Sauvé, his highly regarded successor, died in 1959. Although there were an unprecedented number of Quebec MPs, there were now, proportionately, even more who were not from Quebec, for the sweep of 1958 had given Diefenbaker the largest majority in Canadian history. He had taken all but five seats in the four western provinces. These, plus the Ontario seats, created an imbalance between government and opposition members in the House and between Quebec and non-Quebec members in caucus that was to plague the new Prime Minister and exacerbate the problems he faced.

One of Mr. Diefenbaker's major difficulties was political abundance; its effect, paradoxically, was to immobilize the executive. Decisions in cabinet occurred infrequently and then after excruciatingly inconclusive debate. The "Chief's" electoral dominance in the West, the uncertain base of the PCs in Quebec and the divisions evident between Toronto and non-Toronto Ontario Tories meant that this cabinet was a far cry from St. Laurent's "corporation" of provincial chieftains. Personal style, too, influences personal leadership, and Mr. Diefenbaker's style was to be that of extreme caution in delegating authority; at the same time, he experienced great (and inevitable) difficulties in coordinating decisions himself.

In the end, it was style, style determined by a personality one colleague (Jacques Flynn in Stursberg, 1975, p. 218) described as "flamboyant," which "started something new in many areas." The "something new" was policies and actions in the period between 1957 and 1963 which deliberately and directly appealed to Canadians as Canadians regardless of where they lived or what language they spoke. Mr. Diefenbaker's concept of his country was not a community of communities but, as he repeatedly avowed, "One Canada." The Bill of Rights, the national development policy (with its vision of the North, its Roads to Resources and National Energy Board), the extension of hospital insurance and the creation of the Royal Commission on Health Services under Mr. Justice Emmett Hall, these and other national policies revealed a pan-Canadian approach to political leadership which, in its explicitness, went far beyond the actions of the St. Laurent government before him.

The explicitness resulted in part from Mr. Diefenbaker's own personal interpretation of his policies. Unlike Mackenzie King's consensual style which avoided direct displays of leadership or St. Laurent's collegial cabinet, Mr. Diefenbaker repeatedly demonstrated that he saw himself as the leader of the people. There were specific party reasons for this: he was leading a party only recently long out of power and riven by division, in particular between progressive Prairie Conservatives and non-radical central-Canadian Conservatives. This was not a new division; it had plagued John Bracken, but Mr. Diefenbaker devised, through his appeals to the people, a new approach to overcoming it. This explanation, by itself, would make his seeking of direct access to the people only a partisan strategy, but it was more than this.

Mr. Diefenbaker was a product of the Prairies and, for whatever combination of personal and societal factors, acutely conscious of ethnicity. He was indeed the first national leader to give evidence of this consciousness: one which struck a responsive chord not only in the "old ethnic" West but also in the "new ethnic" East—especially southern Ontario.[8] As a result, he took pride in his appointment of the first Ukranian to the cabinet (Michael Starr of Oshawa) and the first Indian to the Senate. His sensibility to perceived discrimination and to the need to recognize previously unrecognized groups, thereby including them (for he thought they had not been included before) in the political system, derived from a common conviction that all Canadians were equal and none privileged.

Multiculturalism married to liberal individualism in the leadership of a Progressive Conservative was bound to create intra-party tension and thereby press the leader to look to the electorate to vindicate his interpretation of Canada. The same priorities were also to bring friction with French Canada, especially as the flowering of the Quiet Revolution became manifest. Mr. Diefenbaker's response was of a piece with his response to all groups in Canada. He would recognize them by some distinctive act; among others, in this instance, by introducing simultaneous translation of debates in the House of Commons and appointing the first French Canadian since Confederation to the office of governor general. He vehemently rejected, however, any policy that implied special status in Canada for the province of Quebec or for French Canadians (as he did for any other Canadians). It was over a proposal that the Progressive Conservative Party recognize Canada as composed of *deux nations* that he fought his last battle as leader, right up to the 1967 Progressive Conservative leadership convention (see Churchill, 1983).

Mr. Diefenbaker unequivocally introduced a pan-Canadian approach to leadership in the politics of the country but this approach did not disappear with the end of his Prime Ministership. In fact, the significance of this interregnum in the long period of Liberal rule was that it established an approach to leadership that Lester

Pearson and Pierre Trudeau were to develop further and with distinctive adjustments, especially to accommodate French Canada. As well, they were to experiment, as Diefenbaker did not, with party reorganization to try to make the Liberal Party fit more closely their governments' national, pan-Canadian policies. Mr. Diefenbaker had neither the time nor the inclination to do this. On political matters, as opposed to administrative ones where his ministers acknowledge that he respected their departmental prerogatives, his leadership was markedly personal. "He really believed," said Alister Grosart, national director of the Progressive Conservative Party from 1957 on, "that he was elected, to put it in the corniest terms, the Prime Minister of all the people. He really felt that he had to be very very careful...to make his decisions in the interests of all the people and not for political reasons" (Stursberg, 1975, p. 151).

Quite separate from the electoral or personality dimensions of Mr. Diefenbaker's leadership, but of long-term significance for the development of Canadian political parties, was his relationship to the bureaucracy. The first transition of government in 22 years presented a test for the British-Canadian model of a non-partisan civil service at the ready to serve any parliamentary master. The decision as to how adequately it performed its task is open to interpretation; Mr. Diefenbaker and some of his ministers remained forever suspicious of the bureaucracy's alleged Liberal proclivities, springing less perhaps from outright partisan attachment than from a symbiotic relationship engendered by decades of proximity. The non-elected side of "the government party" continued in office, according to Walter Dinsdale (Stursberg, p. 47), Diefenbaker's Minister of Northern Affairs and Natural Resources, and it proceeded to harass its new political masters: "I was constantly being pursued by certain departmental officials confronting me with crises that I must deal with immediately."[9]

This was only one side of the bureaucracy question. The other was the concern Innis had expressed two decades before, about the bureaucracy's effect on federalism. Diefenbaker had charged the Liberals and their civil servants with being insensitive to regional concerns; his own administration went some way to reverse this trend with policies of regional economic development (for example, the Agricultural and Rural Development Act, northern development, and Atlantic Provinces Adjustment Grants) that harkened back to activities identified with J.G. Gardiner and the PFRA (Prairie Farm Rehabilitation Act). When Mr. Diefenbaker spoke of his close relationship to the people, he had in mind not only pan-Canadian policies like the Bill of Rights, but also these and other countervailing policies which were attempts to reverse the centralism he identified with the Liberals.

The Diefenbaker government collapsed as a result of an issue of high bureaucratic content but traditionally of low concern in domestic politics and of slight structural effect on Canadian political parties. The area was defence and foreign policy. The question which proved to be incendiary was whether Canada should acquire or had agreed to acquire nuclear warheads for missiles placed on Canadian territory. It brought the government into conflict not only with US politicians and their military advisors but with its own advisors, especially in the Department of External Affairs, a department uniquely identified with earlier Liberal policies to foster Dominion autonomy (and therefore in conflict with Mr. Diefenbaker's personal attachment to Anglo-Canadian ties) and more directly the modern creation of the former secretary of state for external affairs and now Liberal leader, Lester Pearson.

The triangle of government, party and bureaucracy which had brought down the Liberal Party after two decades of rule, proved the nemesis of the Progressive Conservative Party in a quarter of that time. The difference between the two events was that with the Liberals the parts had become so interrelated, if not fused, that "the Government party had lost touch with opinion not sponsored by the elites with which it was in daily and intimate contact" (Whitaker, 1977, p. 210); with the Progressive Conservatives, the relationship was never close enough to provide a workable partnership. On the particular question of the nuclear warheads for missiles, Mr. Diefenbaker chose the route dictated by public opinion as he discerned it. Thus, in opposition to the advice of his Minister of Defence, Douglas Harkness, who subsequently resigned from the cabinet, he refused to accept the warheads (Stursberg, 1976, p. 25).

Whether a decision to accept the warheads would have saved the minority government of Mr. Diefenbaker from the disintegration that soon followed the decision to reject them is a matter for conjecture. The party and government were so divided over policies, military and otherwise, and over personalities, principally Mr. Diefenbaker and his leadership, that it seems improbable it would have lasted for long. From the perspective of this paper, the most significant factor in the debate of 1962-63 was Mr. Diefenbaker's dependence in this tumultuous period on his appeal to the people.

The pan-Canadian approach to leadership which, it has been argued, characterized Mr. Diefenbaker's years as Prime Minister, guided him up to his defeat and indeed afterward in his struggle to retain leadership of the Progressive Conservative Party.

The return of the Liberals in 1963 signalled neither a return to accommodative policies as practised by Mackenzie King nor the incorporation of provincial political communities through a minister at the centre, as seen in the St. Laurent cabinet. Instead, what has been described as pan-Canadianism, an attempt to create a Canadian community, became firmly established, first as the policy of the Pearson government and then of the Trudeau government. However, the policies that now appeared challenged the unhyphenated Canadianism of Mr. Diefenbaker. In its place and from the outset of his administration, Mr. Pearson sought to construct a country-wide nationalism based on bilingualism and biculturalism. In a speech in the House of Commons which he later described in his Memoirs as the speech of which he was the "most proud," he depicted Confederation as "a settlement between the two founding races of Canada made on the basis of an acceptable and equal partnership" (Munro and Inglis, 1975, pp. 239, 67-69). Here was the mustard seed of a policy which was to germinate and blossom through royal commission, statute and administrative order over the next two decades and transform Canada's perception of itself.

The old mold of triumphant unilingualism outside of Quebec was to be broken and a new era of cooperative federalism was prophesied. The error of the past, said Mr. Pearson, was the centralist assumptions the federal government had taken from the Rowell-Sirois Commission's report (Munro and Inglis, 1975, p. 238). There was a contradiction here between, on the one hand, advocating a policy which would transcend provincial boundaries and on the other, promising a retreat from interventionist central government. The success of the one undertaking would appear to challenge the other, for stronger, more active provinces would be less amenable to the assertion of federal language policy. This would be particularly the case where the assumptions of that policy had the least validity—in the West. Not only were there few Francophones in the Prairie provinces, there were also proportionately fewer Anglophones than elsewhere. Here, bilingualism and biculturalism ran up against Mr. Diefenbaker's ethnic world.

This paper is not concerned with the history of this policy or with its worth. What is pertinent, however, is that there was such a policy, that it was based on assumptions having little regard for either the West or the East, and that in the West, there was a tradition (embodied in Mr. Diefenbaker) of objecting to perceived special status. Mr. Pearson might say that the days of centralism had ended, but to westerners long sensitive about the question of their economic and political status in Canada, bilingualism and biculturalism betrayed the claim and added a new dimension to an old set of grievances.

Pan-Canadianism was not limited to language, however. Under Mr. Pearson, medicare and the Canada Pension Plan were policies with national content too, for they dealt with social matters and individual concerns that did not coincide with provincial boundaries. The same was true during Mr. Trudeau's years in office; to bilingualism in the early period and medicare restored as an issue of national debate most recently must be added energy, constitutional reform and the Charter of Rights. These have affected all parts of the country because of their individual, regional and national importance and will be discussed further toward the end of this paper.

At this point, it is necessary to turn to the subject of party organization during the Pearson and Trudeau years. Unlike their predecessors in office, both Liberal leaders experimented with party reorganization and in particular, both experimented with party reforms in the 1960s. Participatory democracy, the sophisticated use of polling and public relations agencies, the use of mass media, and the emphasis on the leader (to the detriment of regional chieftains) all reflected the same motivation as their major government policies, which was to speak to Canadians directly, in a national language, and without intermediaries.

The lesson the Liberals drew from their defeats in 1957 and 1958 was that "ministerialism" as practised in the St. Laurent period was at fault and that the party must be "rejuvenated." To this end, two unprecedented experiments in reform ensued: one, to create "pan-Canadian" structures free from provincial entanglements and the other, to promote a "mass membership party" that encouraged individual participation.[10] Each reform was associated with a dominant extra-parliamentary figure, the first with Keith Davey, the national organizer for the period in question (1961-66), the second with Richard Stanbury, party president between 1968 and 1973, and each had a detrimental effect upon relations between Liberals at the centre and those in the regions.

The urbanizing and industrializing trends which the Progressives had resisted a half-century before and whose centralizing efforts Mackenzie King sought always to ameliorate by political means now reached full force in the Liberal Party's reforming zeal. The voice of reform spoke a vocabulary that rang strange in the ears of hinterland Liberals. The primacy granted to rank-and-file participation in policy formulation, the belief that policy should be the product of exchange of opinion and not a balancing of interests, the rejection of patronage as a perversion of principle and a vestige of old-style politics, the commitment to "nationalized" standards (be it in health, welfare or the dairy industry, among others) were all new ideas to the party of King and St. Laurent.[11] The vanguard of change was the Toronto-and-district riding associations; here tradition fell first because demographic and economic change was strongest and here the stakes were greatest once redistribution showed more concern for reflecting population growth than for protecting political fiefdoms. With the Liberals ever dominant in Quebec and the Diefenbaker Conservatives entrenched in the West, the focus of attention shifted.

Electoral strategy alone did not account for the shift either. Technology and increased sophistication in political knowledge also played a part. To overcome the gap in communication with which the end of "ministerialism" presented them, the Liberals resorted to myriad structures and techniques borrowed from abroad (especially from the presidential campaign of John F. Kennedy in the United States), showing particular enthusiasm for public relations agencies and opinion polls whose Canadian offices were in Ontario.[12] Television, too, played an important role. Transmission from Toronto and Montreal had begun in 1952, and a microwave network for instantaneous national programming was in place by 1958. More than radio, television's influence was to centralize; considerations of cost and scarce expertise discouraged multiple production facilities, with a consequent sacrifice of regional perspective. The impact of these changes has only now begun to be evaluated (Siegel, 1983; Fletcher, 1981).[13]

The first set of reforms (between 1961 and 1966), which transferred organizational and electoral matters into the hands of committees whose members were appointed by the federal party leader, were in place for the election of 1963. But neither then nor in 1965 did Mr. Pearson secure the majority he and the federal campaign committee desired. The depressing news came always from the West; in 1963 three seats in the Prairies, in 1965 only one. The second set of reforms, devised to promote participatory democracy, were scarcely in place at the time of the Trudeaumania election (1968), when the Liberals won their first majority in a decade (with 11 out of 45 Prairie seats). By the time of the next election (1972), when the Stanbury reforms were fully operational, the Liberals lost their majority and were back to three Prairie seats.

The centrepiece of the Stanbury reforms was the politicization of government through opening decision making to rank-and-file participation. By so doing, it was believed, the scope of government would expand, for in the language of the period, the political agenda would be defined by the mass and not by the elite. Along with a policy organization of gargantuan proportions, there were a host of innovations in the form of "the political cabinet," a national as well as a provincial advisory council (composed of representatives of caucus, the Prime Minister's Office, Liberal headquarters and regional caucuses) and regional desks in the PMO to inject party considerations into government decision making. The impact of the parts and the whole of this reform enterprise proved disappointing when measured by observable policy emanating from government. That, perhaps, should not have been surprising, for parties are not, in Finer's word, "republics" whose members dictate to their leader (Finer, 1980, p. 180). If not surprising, however, it was nonetheless a premise that underlay Liberal action in these years. It is not necessary to detail its successes and failures; it is enough to note that it was tried. The contrast between the earlier accommodative party of King and St. Laurent and its opposite, a pan-Canadian party under Pearson and Trudeau, illuminates the circuitous journey that Canada's dominant political party had made during five decades of policy and organizational change....

Conclusion: Potential Parties and National Integration

This study has taken as its fundamental premise the centrality of party government (more specifically, party-in-government) in the evolution of Canadian political parties and even in the growth of Canada itself. The claims made here for parties are great; they are agents of territorial and social inclusion, of economic expansion, and of national identification. They are, in fact, "political systems in themselves" with a multitude of functions and a multidimensional life, but most crucially they are, in the hands of their leaders, autonomous institutions (DeVree, 1980, p. 211). Although they may respond to change, they do not only respond; they initiate and determine events as well, and by this power they affect the lives of all Canadians.

The most recent model of party and government leadership is the pan-Canadian, and its structuring influence on the self-perception of Canadians cannot be exaggerated. Consider, for example, the finding that "Liberal voters in the West in 1979 were very likely the people who felt national unity and Quebec relations are major issues" (Pammett, 1981, p. 217). The 25 per cent of the electorate in the West who supported the Liberals then and in 1980 was the subject of anguish among party strategists, who ponder how to increase the number and who attribute its current size to unpopular Liberal policies. However, it is at least worth asking whether in the absence of Liberal language and national unity policies western support would not have gone even lower. Could it not be that this vote represents "restructured" support in response to pan-Canadian policies (rather than a vestigial Liberalism from the days of Mackenzie King) and to a different kind of party leadership?

This paper argues that the brokerage theory of politics offers a poor explanation of Canadian party development. It does not allow for the direct, national approach to leadership which has characterized Canadian politics at least from the time of Lester Pearson and which, as demonstrated above, was evident even during Mr. Diefenbaker's Prime Ministership. A very different attack on the brokerage theory has recently been made by John Wilson (1983, p. 181), who questions whether Canada is a nation at all, in the conventional sense of one whose symbols and perspectives are more national than regional. Instead, he argues that political behaviour federally is a continuation of political behaviour in the provinces. Wilson's argument and that of this paper agree that brokerage theory is in error when it brands Canadian political parties as failures. Wilson rejects the charge because he rejects the assumption that there must be some kind of underlying uniformity in the national party system. This paper accepts that there is an underlying uniformity; indeed, it makes models of party and governmental leadership its centrepiece. However, with Wilson, it seriously questions the validity of the failure charge.

Moreover, it argues that the pan-Canadian approach to leadership, with its reduced sensitivity to provincial communities (the reverse side of its commitment to policies that touch Canadians directly: medicare, the Charter of Rights, the Constitution, energy, language), is a far more useful explanation of the current Canadian political scene than is brokerage theory. In particular, it explains the heightened conflict in federal-provincial relations already mentioned, and which is a cardinal feature of the country's modern politics. Pan-Canadian policies push the provinces into an exaggerated defence of provincial concerns because, unlike the era of Mackenzie King or St. Laurent, whose cabinets were composed of provincial spokesmen, or the period of Macdonald or Laurier, when localism controlled by the leader triumphed, the provinces today see no defenders of their interests at the centre.

That is the source of the demand for institutional change: the belief that the central government does not understand the regions, that it does not hear them. On this, however, the regions are wrong. They do not see the real issue. The governing party can court the regions at any time, just as governing parties did in the past. The truth is that the Liberals under Mr. Trudeau chose not to do so, and the reason was that the governing party held a different view of Canada. Canada, as Mr. Trudeau repeatedly said during the constitutional discussions, was composed of more than its parts.

If this interpretation is accurate, then the question must be asked: how useful will institutional reforms be in changing political behaviour? The question is more easily posed than answered. It is nonetheless worth commenting that in the past parties have shown themselves neither easily subject to control nor predictable in their response to change.

Traditionally, political parties have rested outside the scope of statute law, although this immunity has been breached in the last decade by election expenses legislation. Because parties touch multiple levels of public and private life, the impact of specific reforms is not easily isolated. Certainly, for instance, there is no way of predicting at one election, let alone at several over the space of a decade or a generation, the effect of giving millions of voters preferential choice. Reforms possess the potential to surprise, as the experience with leadership conventions suggests.[14] On the one hand, a convention of delegates, representative perhaps of the party but not society, drawn from across the land and assembled to perform a common act, is an integrating and nationalizing event in the country's politics. On the other hand (which has taken longer to show itself), the contest among the candidates and the search for delegate support can have a disintegrating impact on existing structures. There is reason to believe that contradictory impulses are latent in electoral reform as well.

Although it began with the Liberals in 1919 as a strategy to unite a divided party, the leadership convention before 1968 was more what Bagehot called "dignified," rather than efficient. The 1948 and 1958 conventions approximated a laying-on-of-hands ceremony, with the old leader playing a key part in the convention's choice. Mr. Pearson favoured Mr. Trudeau, but the presence of eight serious candidates and the availability of national television with its multiplier effect on rank-and-file participation immensely changed the character of the undertaking. In this, the Liberals were imitating the Progressive Conservatives, who had chosen Robert Stanfield in 1967 at a convention in which nine serious candidates were present and which followed several years of spectacular intra-party fighting aimed at removing Mr. Diefenbaker. Although the Conservatives had had frequent recourse to conventions to find leaders in the 1930s, '40s and '50s, it was the 1967 meeting and the Liberal convention following close in 1968, that whetted public appetite for leadership debate.

But it did not end there. Biennial party meetings where leadership review might become an issue fed political excitement more regularly than general elections could. Because of extensive television coverage, leadership is no longer a matter of caucus or even intra-party discussion: partisan opponents as well as party members become engaged. With candidates appearing in constituencies across the country, something analogous to James McGregor Burns's (1982) useful concept of a "followership" for each candidate is formed. Significantly, in a country where territory has been so dominant an organizing principle in political life (Bakvis, 1981), it is not territory but ideology, doctrine or policy that is stressed in the quest for delegates who, when assembled, stand as virtual representatives of nationwide bodies of opinion. At its base the convention's weakness is the same as that of the parliamentary parties criticized by the Progressives long ago: the selection process. Rather than using an American-style primary contest to fit an American-modelled institution, delegates, like party candidates, are the choice of limited numbers of local activists whose practices occasionally call for turning a blind eye. The convention's chief weakness and its chief characteristic is the independence of the delegates in casting their votes. An individual secret ballot gives advantage to the new and the fresh; experience in the forum where the leader must work has never determined the convention's choice.

If experience is any guide, the introduction of leadership conventions has increased the power of the leader of the governing party, for it gives him a basis of authority separate from that of the parliamentary caucus. For the major opposition party, the effect has been quite different—institutionalizing intra-party criticism of the leader who has failed to bring the party to power. This effect further protects the governing party's security. The impact of an altered electoral system on party behaviour can only be surmised, but it is not improbable that proportional representation, through the compilation of the lists, could similarly enhance the leader's power. Institutional reforms can have unexpected results, but the Canadian experience is that they reinforce existing models of leadership.

Henry Fairlie has said, with Macaulay, that North American parties are "all sail and no anchor."[15] However, federal Liberal problems in the West or federal Progressive Conservative problems in Quebec have been problems of sail; theories and policies of organization, theories and policies of the economy, theories and policies of nationalism. It is no wonder that leadership preoccupies Canadian politics: appointments rest with it; party organization serves it; and policy reflects it.

The challenge to Canadian parties has been to assert and make firm their claim to be national. At different times and under different leaders, national integration has proceeded by various means; the incorporation of people and territory through local patronage supervised personally by leaders like Macdonald and Laurier; the accommodation at the centre of multiple interests and communities by Mackenzie King and St. Laurent; and the nationalization of individual Canadians into a single community (though of two languages and many cultures) through policies enunciated first by John Diefenbaker and later by Pierre Trudeau. Only in this last model of leadership has there been an attempt to incorporate all the people and all the territory. In the past, Quebec, to a greater extent than elsewhere, had been treated differently and allowed its separate development.

However, the integrative capacity of political leadership committed to a pan-Canadian ideology, but one deprived of a territorial base other than the nation as a whole, is flawed. In the absence of provincial chieftains whose responsibilities once extended from cabinet through province to constituency, and in the absence of leaders who used to superintend constituency party-politics through control of local notables, national parties now find themselves isolated from an electorate which is still distributed among 282 districts. Pan-Canadian appeals are horizontal, the electorate's view of politics vertical. The significant questions are whether pan-Canadianism can be combined with localism and, if that proves possible, whether the combination will produce national parties with greater integrative capacities.

The combination is possible if the structuring effect of the pan-Canadian appeal is extended into the constituency. That, of course, would require a level of debate and a mechanism to regulate it which have never before been present in local politics. As noted earlier in this paper, constituency energies have traditionally been devoted to electoral campaigning and candidate selection. The experience of each of the old parties in recent years is that leadership contests and elections reveal, to a degree, the strata of opinion in each constituency and that the conflict of values represented by the strata create problems of legitimacy when a choice must be made between potential delegates or candidates. The introduction of primaries would be one method of resolving such conflicts, to the benefit of constituency harmony and national party unity. The advantage of pre-election contests within the constituencies would be to bring national appeals, made by electoral aspirants or by contestants for delegate selection to leadership convention, directly before individual party supporters. As it is now, the selection of candidates or convention delegates is made through procedures in constituencies that ignore the choice of values being presented to local supporters and that highlight once again the contestants' personal qualities.

Modern Canadian politics is characterized more by patronage at the top of the party hierarchy than at the bottom. The parties of the post-Confederation and the accommodation periods derived much of their structural consistency from the distribution of local patronage. This is hardly feasible any longer. Local activists are more probably animated by their attachment to a party's pan-Canadian policies—for example, bilingualism. In itself such activist attachment is not sufficient for the party locally or nationally. What is required is the unifying and broadening effect of constituency debate, which would de-emphasize personality while promoting the opportunity to dissent within party ranks and not outside them. Currently, without a local base where local advocates can espouse, debate or oppose pan-Canadian policies, constituency dissent as well as support is muted, and policies appear to be imposed upon the electorate rather than emanating from it.

The Liberals' pan-Canadian policies were designed to incorporate Quebec, but they estranged the West. The Progressive Conservatives' "One Canada" and their "community of communities" succeeded in the latter but failed in the former. In power and with access to appointments and instruments of policy, the Liberals in a quarter-century made no gains in the West. Out of office and without access to the levers that power brings, the Progressive Conservatives were excluded from Quebec for much longer. The two situations, though comparable, are different: given the choice, the Liberals did not trim to win regional support. Instead, through policies of national breadth, they sought to effect fundamental change in constitutional condition and citizen perceptions. Party-in-government has succeeded in aggregating a large and growing number of voters irrespective of place. The political contest has been redefined to set nation ahead of region. Language, energy, and medicare are national issues, although their origins can be traced back to the provinces—namely, Quebec, Alberta and Saskatchewan. Through them, region is drawn into nation even when rejecting pan-Canadian policies, and national integration through debate is achieved.

Notes

1   The remainder of this paragraph is based on Stewart (1980, 1982).

2   There is a great need in the study of Canada's development to look more closely at generations and political change. Societal adaptation is a crucial factor in peaceful territorial expansion. See, for example, Prang (1983).

3   For Canadian contrasts, see Gillies (1981). The mobility in question is particularly important to new governments who seek informed but non-bureaucratic advisors: see Canadian Study of Parliament Group, *Seminar on New Parliament, New Government, Old Public Service: The Changing of the Guard* (Ottawa, October 25, 1979). The ignorance of businessmen about the ways of government has long been a subject for comment by politicians; see Cartwright (1912, p. 340) and the papers of Sen. R.J. Stanbury, vol. 5, in the Public Archives of Canada, especially his 1969 paper on "The Attitudes of Businessmen."

4   See "The MP as Broker: Business/Labour/Government Relations," *Parliamentary Government* 2 (1) (1980), pp. 13-15.

5   In discussing caucus research offices, "one director noted that staff hiring has a strong political requirement. It is difficult to get the best combination of skills when party affiliation is the primary consideration" (Fish, 1983, p. 33).

6   This is the assessment of Brooke Claxton, who first was Minister of Na-

tional Health and Welfare and then Minister of National Defence in the King cabinet and who kept the latter portfolio in the St. Laurent cabinet; see volume 79 of the Claxton papers in the Public Archives of Canada, especially his memorandum on "What should the Liberals do" (undated typescript post-1957).

7   This was the central criticism of the Tremblay report, which appeared in Quebec in 1957; see Kwavnick (1973). For an example of specific criticism of a single program, see "Federal Grants to Universities" in Trudeau (1968).

8   The scope of this paper does not permit consideration of regional contrasts in ethnic demography. Its importance for the development of Canadian political parties after 1950, however, demands investigation. The National Liberal Federation papers in the Public Archives of Canada contain many files related to ethnic organizational matters, for southern Ontario especially. To this writer's knowledge, they have not been used for academic research.

9   Almost 20 years later, another minister in the next Progressive Conservative government had the same complaint about "corridor decisions." See F. MacDonald (1980, p. 30). The now classic statement on bureaucratic cunning is in Crossman (1979, pp. 92, 148).

10   The details of each set of reforms can be found in Smith (1981) and Wearing (1981).

11   At least the reformers believed they were new. Mackenzie King had entered national politics advocating social reform, and party stalwarts like C.G. Power had long argued the need for electoral reform. See Ward (1966).

12   Already there was a prescient remark on this trend, as usual by Innis (1946, p. 85): "The Gallup Poll has possibly made politics more absorbing. But statistics has been particularly dangerous to modern society by strengthening the cult of economics and weakening other social sciences and the humanities."

13   According to Siegel (1983), "The 'modern media' have become agents of denationalization by serving as roadways for foreign, largely American, cultural values."

14   On the subject of conventions, see Courtney (1973).

15   Henry Fairlie, "Letter from Washington," Encounter, January 1973.

Sources

Acheson, T.W. (1977). "The Maritimes and Empire Canada," In Canada and the Burden of Unity, edited by David Jay Bercuson, pp. 87-114. Toronto: Macmillan.

Bakvis, Herman. (1981). Federalism and the Organization of Political Life: Canada in Comparative Perspective. Kingston: Queen's University. Institute for Intergovernmental Relations.

Blondel, J. (1963). *Voters, Parties, and Leaders: The Social Fabric of British Politics.* London: Penguin Books.

Burns, James MacGregor. (1982). *The Vineyard of Liberty.* New York: Knopf.

Cartwright, Sir Richard. (1912). *Reminiscences.* Toronto: William Briggs.

Churchill, Hon. Gordon (1983). Conservative convention, Toronto, September 6-9, 1967. In "'Deux Nations' or One Canada: John Diefenbaker at the 1967 Conservative Convention." *Canadian Historical Review* 64 (4): 597-604.

Courtney, J. (1973). *Selection of National Party Leaders.* Toronto: Macmillan.

Creighton, Donald. (1955). *John A. Macdonald: The Old Chieftain.* Toronto: Macmillan.

Crossman, Richard. (1979). *The Crossman Diaries: Selections from the Diaries of a Cabinet Minister, 1964-1970.* Edited and with an introduction by Anthony Howard. London: Methuen Paperbacks.

DeVrees, Johan K. (1980). "In Pursuit of the Common Weal: A Theory of Emergence and Growth of the Political Party," *Acta Politica* 15: 191-218.

Fairlie, Henry. (1968). *The Life of Politics.* London: Methuen.

Finer, S.E. (1980). *The Changing British Party System, 1945-1979.* Washington, DC: American Enterprise Institute.

Fish, Karen. (1983). *Parliamentarians and Science: A Discussion Paper.* Ottawa: Science Council of Canada.

Fletcher, Frederick J. (1981). *The Newspaper and Public Affairs.* Vol. 7: Royal Commission on Newspapers. Ottawa: Minister of Supply and Services Canada.

Gillies, James. (1981). *Where Business Fails.* Montreal: Institute for Research on Public Policy.

Grodzins, Morton. (1967). "American Political Parties and the American System," In *American Federalism in Perspective*, edited by Aaron Wildavsky, pp. 133-135. Boston: Little, Brown.

Innis, H.A. (1940). "The Rowell-Sirois Report." *Canadian Journal of Economics and Political Science* 6 (November): 562-571.

Innis, H.A. (1946). "On the Economic Significance of Cultural Factors." In *Political Economy in the Modern State*. Chap. 6. Toronto: Ryerson Press.

Kwavnick, David, (ed.). (1973). *The Tremblay Report: Report of the Royal Commission of Inquiry on Constitutional Problems.* Toronto: McClelland and Stewart.

MacDonald, Hon. Flora. (1980). "The Minister and the Mandarins." *Policy Options* 1 (3): 29-31.

McMenemy, John, and Conrad Winn. (1976). *Political Parties in Canada.* Toronto: McGraw-Hill Ryerson.

Morton, W.L. (1950). *The Progressive Party in Canada.* Toronto: University of Toronto Press.

Munro, John A., and Inglis, Alex I., (eds.). (1975). *Mike: The Memoirs of the Right Honourable Lester B. Pearson*, Vol. 3. Toronto: University of Toronto Press.

Neatby, H. Blair. (1976). *William Lyon Mackenzie King: The Prism of Unity, 1932-1939*. Toronto: University of Toronto Press.

Pammett, Jon H. (1981). "Elections." In *Canadian Politics in the 1980s*, edited by Michael S. Whittington and Glen Williams. Toronto: Methuen. pp. 206-220.

Prang, Margaret. (1983). "The Family and Canadian Federalism." Paper presented to Joint CHA-CPSA Session, Learning Societies Meeting, June 1983, Vancouver.

Reid, Escott M. (1932). "The Rise of National Parties in Canada." *Parties and Proceedings of the Canadian Political Science Association* 4. Reprinted in *Party Politics in Canada*, 4th ed., edited by Hugh G. Thorburn, pp. 12-20. Scarborough: Prentice-Hall. 1979.

Siegel, Arthur. (1983). *Politics and the Media in Canada*. Toronto: McGraw-Hill Ryerson.

Smith, David E. (1981). *The Regional Decline of a National Party: Liberals on the Prairies*. Toronto: University of Toronto Press.

Stewart, Gordon. (1980). "Political Patronage under Macdonald and Laurier, 1878-1911." *American Review of Canadian Studies* 10: 3-12.

Stewart, Gordon. (1982). "John A. Macdonald's Greatest Triumph." *Canadian Historical Review* 63 (1): 3-33.

Stursberg, Peter. (1975). *Diefenbaker: Leadership Gained, 1956-1962*. Toronto: University of Toronto Press.

Stursberg, Peter. (1976). *Diefenbaker: Leadership Lost, 1962-1967*. Toronto: University of Toronto Press.

Trudeau, Pierre Elliott. (1968). *Federalism and the French Canadians*. Toronto: Macmillan.

Ward, N. (1966). *A Party Politician: The Memoirs of Chubby Powers*. Toronto: Macmillan.

Ward, N. (1977b). Review of *The Government Party*. *Globe and Mail*, October 22, 1977.

Wearing, Joseph. (1981). *The L-Shaped Party: The Liberal Party of Canada, 1958-1980*. Toronto: McGraw-Hill Ryerson.

Whitaker, Reginald. (1977). *The Government Party: Organizing and Financing the Liberal Party of Canada, 1930-1958*. Toronto: University of Toronto Press.

Williams, John R. (1956). *The Conservative Party of Canada, 1920-1949*. Durham: Duke University Press.

Wilson, John. (1983). "On the Dangers of Bickering in a Federal State: Some Reflections on the Failure of the National Party System." In *Political Support in Canada: The Crisis Years*, edited by Allan Kornberg and Harold D. Clarke, pp. 171-222. Durham: Duke University Press.

R.K. Carty Three Canadian Party Systems

From the beginning, Canadian party politics has been dominated by Conservatives and Liberals. However, there is little about the contemporary parties that their founders would recognize, for virtually all aspects of them have been reshaped. The process of change has not, however, been either smooth or constant. Twice, the long-established practices of party life have been overthrown, leading to the emergence of wholly new patterns of organization and behaviour. An analysis of Canadian political parties must start by recognizing that three quite distinctive party systems have marked the country's political development.

Such sharp changes in the party system are the result of major alterations in the role of political parties in the governing process. While parties have continually played a central part in managing the electoral process and in organizing parliamentary life (including structuring legislative-executive relations), their latent functions emerged when the country's dominant political formula changed. As David Smith recently argued, three different models of party government, each characterized by different approaches to political leadership and the mobilization of support, have informed Canadian experience. Here, the analysis of parties as organizations reveals clearly how each of these "governing approaches" required distinctive party forms to articulate its principal modalities and encompass its primary political relationships.[1]

The paper sketches the three party systems that have existed over the past 120 years, describing and comparing the party types in each and briefly considering the forces and processes that drove the systemic transformations. The periods identified parallel those of Smith's party-in-government model of Canadian politics, supporting the theory of intimate links between political parties and changes in the functional requirements of governing.

Patronage Politics and Caucus Parties (1867-1917)

During the first half-century after Confederation, parties created and dominated Canadian politics. Canada had a small, rural society essentially devoid of aristocrats, large capitalists and organized workers. A professional middle class rooted in parochial communities dominated public life, and government was one of the few institutions (aside from the church) that provided a channel for personal mobility and the opportunity to exercise power. This made elections, which determined who would monopolize government power, high stakes events. Thus, André Siegfried would be led to observe that while "Liberals and Conservatives differ very little really in their opinions on crucial questions, and their conception of power seems almost identical...there [can] be few countries in the world in which elections arouse more fury and enthusiasm than in Canada."[2]

These contests took place within a set of rather fluid, pre-democratic institutional arrangements. The country was expanding from four to nine provinces, and the terms on which it evolved were being contested. The Prime Ministers of the day did not hesitate to take partisan advantage of the political developments. Although open voting and staggered elections ended in the 1870s, governmental control of the electoral administration, blatant gerrymandering, and manipulation of the franchise were regular features of the party battle over most of the period. Corrupt practices flourished and few elections went by without some MPs being unseated for illegal activities. At the same time, party competition was conceived as a series of discrete constituency contests. Acclamations were a persistent, if declining, element of every election, because parties could not always nominate candidates in hopeless situations.

Canada's system of "purposive federalism"[3] and Canadian parties were designed to achieve practical results in governing. For Macdonald, and then Laurier, party-building was simply the necessary political dimension of state-building.[4] The Conservative party emerged as a coherent political entity well before the Liberal opposition because it was in office first and so was able to exploit the prerogatives of power. Patronage was the life-blood of the parties, and partisanship pervaded the state. In his determination to build a lasting political coalition, Macdonald insisted that no government position, from senior bureaucrat or judge down to humble wharfmaster, be given to anyone who had not established a record of service to the party. The entire civil service came to be regarded as a partisan bailiwick, the parties emerged as the principal channel of recruitment for the state, and electoral turnovers quickly led to the replacement of vast numbers of civil servants.[5] In power, the party consumed the state.

As organizations, the national parties were little more than coteries of political notables. The parliamentary caucus was the party;

the Liberal convention in 1893 was the only instance in 50 years of a national gathering of extraparliamentary partisans. Despite national rhetoric, party politics focused on the constituency and the parochial and personal claims of individual voters. Parties were vote-gathering machines. Local partisan associations and their supporters were linked through their MP, or defeated candidate, to the leadership at the centre. This structure put an enormous burden on the party leader because he assumed most of the responsibility for party organization, strategy, tactics, management, finance and policy. There was little room in this sort of party for mass participation and few were concerned with notions of internal democracy.

Elections demanded the full attention and participation of all local partisans. Although practices varied widely, it appears that public conventions were commonly used to nominate candidates. They allowed local associations the prerogative of determining who their standard bearer would be, while limiting the forum in which supporters might participate in party decision-making.

It took time to discipline local political notables so that parties could emerge as genuinely national organizations. Early parliaments contained a large number of "loose fish," and governments could not routinely count on the votes of their supporters. During the first decade after 1867, the incentives of office welded Conservatives from across the country together, while the Liberals remained an ill-matched alliance of regionally based opponents of Macdonald's governing coalition. As late as the fifth general election in 1882, the Liberals "had not yet become the truly national party that the Conservatives had.... Not only was the Liberal leadership still Ontario-oriented, but the issues they stressed often had little attraction outside of Ontario." It would take Laurier's leadership to "[complete] the forging of a loose alliance of provincial parties into a coherent, national organization."[6]

With 95 per cent of the vote between them, the two great parties easily monopolized electoral competition during this first-party system. The record suggests that they were remarkably successful at knitting the country's diverse regions together, for the variation in their vote shares across the provinces was remarkably low.[7] In addition, as one would expect of a territorial system rooted in a politics of patronage, the support base of the party in power was normally even more balanced and geographically representative than that of its opponents.

Partisanship was no cloak to be put on or discarded as the

weather changed, and little distinction was made between party activity in federal or provincial arenas. Men served in both, and rewards could come from either the national or provincial government, depending upon the party's position. As Reid noted in his analysis of the Saskatchewan Liberal machine "It [was] the give and take of patronage that [bound] together in an apparently indissoluble union federal and provincial politics."[8] This union was necessary for politicians in opposition as they had to depend upon colleagues in power at the provincial level to produce the resources necessary to nurture and sustain a party organization. Thus Laurier defeated the Tories in 1896 with the support of several provincial Liberal machines, and was in turn defeated in 1911 when Conservative premiers helped return Borden.

Local party organizations normally operated at both levels of competition, with members of constituency associations treating federal and provincial political activity as indistinguishable (see English for evidence from Ontario).[9] Certainly, party notables treated the system as one, moving from one level to another as opportunity allowed or party need demanded. The best-known instances involved premiers, or their nominees, being drafted into Laurier and Borden's new national governments, but men such as George Ross also moved down into provincial politics. Not surprisingly, the evidence suggests that the electorate responded to these parties by being fairly consistent in its voting behaviour across successive federal and provincial elections.[10]

These two cadre parties revolved around their leaders. This was true both of their organization and their appeal. Siegfried was particularly struck by the extent to which electoral contests in turn-of-the-century Canada revolved around leaders "whose mere name is a programme in itself." They did so because successful leaders personified the party, in parliament and in the country.

Leadership selection was the business of the caucus. It was concerned with finding someone who could direct the party in the daily parliamentary battle, and so sought a leader among its own membership. The process was informal and private, and involved weighing opinions as to who was most suitable. Not all opinions counted equally, for senior members of the caucus would inevitably have more influence than younger men. Out of these discussions one man would emerge as most acceptable, and then be designated leader. The governor-general would be involved in the choice of leader for the party in government, as the leader would become the

Prime Minister. For the party in opposition, the problem would likely be to persuade the favourite to take on the burden his colleagues had assigned him.[11]

The lines of leadership responsibility in this system were clear, for what the caucus had given it could also take away. In both parties there were instances of leaders being forced to give up their position when they lost the confidence of the parliamentary party. This practice allowed for fairly quick transfers without a prolonged, semi-public washing of party laundry. It also enabled a caucus to select a temporary, compromise candidate who could serve until one of the strong men appeared to command wide enough support that he could safely be installed. This was the point of Sir John Abbott's ("I am here very much because I am not particularly obnoxious to anybody") short leadership of the Conservatives in the wake of Macdonald's death. That a governing caucus could twice choose a senator to lead it in the 1890s is a useful reminder of the pre-democratic character of this first-party system's politics.

Naturally enough, those who rose to lead their fellows were men of the party. They had generally served a long parliamentary apprenticeship and their experience in office had demonstrated their leadership and managerial abilities.[12] This was a closed leadership politics because there was no way an outsider, or a man not perceived as broadly representative of the party's ideology, might capture the leadership. The system was also a stabilizing force because, with the support of his caucus, a leader could go on indefinitely—no Conservative or Liberal since has managed to lead his party for as long as Macdonald or Laurier. However, such lengthy service inevitably meant that these came to shape and personify the parties that had raised them to power. Writing of Laurier's leadership, John Dafoe noted: "It is in keeping with the genius of our party system that the leader who begins as the chosen chief of his associates proceeds by stages, if he has the necessary qualities, to a position of dominance; the republic is transformed into an absolute monarchy."[13]

In the absence of any formal or informal extraparliamentary organization, the party leaders had to assume much of the work of building and managing a party machine. Personal attention had to be paid to an endless river of particular requests flowing out of each constituency. One has the impression that the business of patronage overwhelmed their mail. Not the least onerous of a leader's tasks was financing party and electoral activity. In an era characterized by what we would call massive corruption (legislative, administrative and electoral), party politics was inordinately expensive—probably more than it has ever been since. For example, a successful candidate in 1904 might need to spend somewhere between $15,000 and $20,000 to win a riding that had but 8000 voters, at a time when a dollar was equal to a day's pay for a labouring man. This apparently insatiable demand for party money existed even though some public service funds were also directly used in the interests of party-building.

As a consequence, party leaders were driven to recruit relatively well-off local men who had influence in their constituencies and could be expected to help subsidize their own political careers. But at the same time parties were forced to attach themselves to corporate interests (railroads and banks) in Montreal and Toronto that were in a position to supply funds and had some incentive to do so. The result was a series of scandals that plagued parties throughout the period, the most famous being the great Pacific Scandal, which brought Macdonald's government down in 1873. After the turn of the century, western farmers would increasingly come to focus on this eastern money as the symbol of why the system was failing them and demand that parties be reformed.

The practice of leaving important aspects of party finance in the hands of the leader probably had a modest centralizing and disciplining effect at a time when leaders had few other organizational tools at their disposal. There was no control or accountability in the use of party resources, but then there was no national organization or party membership to which the politicians might answer.

The letters of the great party chieftains of this system reveal that they also spent a good deal of time and energy trying to manage and direct the press. All democratic politicians in open societies do so, but in early Canada particularly intimate relationships bound journalism and party together.[14] A great majority of the weekly and daily newspapers, which existed in far greater numbers than they do today, were little more than partisan instruments. Even as late as 1900, the circulation of the party papers exceeded that of the growing independent press. Politicians wanted and expected subservience, not objectivity, from the media.

Parties needed to have their own newspapers in a community to get their message across locally. Where none existed, parties were often driven to help supporters establish a paper. Macdonald himself was involved in starting Conservative papers in Toronto, on three separate occasions, in an attempt to counter the influence the *Globe* gave the Grits. In return, the newspapers and their proprietors received government patronage in the form of advertising and printing contracts. Parties rewarded their friends and punished their enemies. As early as 1876, official lists of papers "deserving" government business were in existence. Journalism came to be one of the common routes into parliament because, in a constituency-based politics, local journalists often came to be important partisan actors.[15]

When party and paper were working well together, three important political tasks were accomplished. First, the party had a communication system that tied its supporters together and kept them informed of its policies and activities. This was vital when no other mechanism existed to link partisans across constituency boundaries. Second, the papers were constant boosters of the party leader and the policies emanating from the caucus. When necessary they could provide an intellectual gloss on party positions, or explain away unpopular or unexpected decisions. Finally, party papers provided an endless critique of the opposition in all its manifestations. As Rutherford concluded: "All in all, a network of newspapers seemed essential to give the party substance, to make it a community of ideas and interests as well as a formidable foe able to compete in the game of politics."[16]

The first-party system was stable, well integrated and predictable. The parties were well suited to the rural social order whose governing institutions they designed and managed. But the practices and institutions of half a century's party competition would be swept away by the administrative reform, social mobilization and political realignment that flowed from World War I. New governing approaches would require new parties.

Brokerage Politics and Ministerialist Parties (1921-1957)

Canadian society was beginning to change in the early years of the twentieth century. It began to urbanize and industrialize, to think in modern and self-consciously national terms, and to fill up: modern Canada's set of complex cross-cutting cleavages was developing. However, it took the war to crystallize and accelerate these forces and to stimulate new styles of governing, and hence quite different kinds of political parties.

Party politicians faced a transformed environment after 1918. The West had quickly emerged as a significant and distinctive political region by a process which began at the turn of the century, but was substantially completed by the end of the second decade. This region's socio-economic base put it fundamentally at odds with the industrial interests of central Canada. The protection of these interests had been entrenched in the National Policy by the two old parties, and therefore western farmers perceived that they would have to change the parties before they could alter government policy. The Progressive movement, which coupled that discontent with rural claims in Ontario and the Maritimes, was thus an attack on the first-party system[17] and it created a degree of political uncertainty in the opening years of the second-party system not unlike that the loose fish had provided Macdonald.

At the same time, the country had just gone through its first electoral realignment. Conscription shifted almost a quarter of Quebec's voters to the Liberals, leaving that party in an almost unassailable position in the country's second largest province and ending the possibility of genuine national party competition. But political élites, especially in English-Canada, were beginning to adopt self-consciously national perspectives. The Unionist experiment brought into active politics a modern political class whose informal networks were tying the society together and who rejected the piecemeal politics of constituency patronage.[18]

Progressives and Unionists alike articulated profound shifts in the political culture. Mirroring and responding to these shifts were two important institutional changes. The first was the acceptance and adoption of democratic electoral arrangements. Provision was made for impartial electoral machinery, attempts to gerrymander the constituency map *en bloc* were abandoned, and politicians implicitly decided to stop manipulating the franchise by adopting universal suffrage. Modern party competition began with the 1921 election.

The second change, civil service reform, constituted a direct blow to the parties. The abolition of widespread patronage deprived the party organizations of the glue that held them together, and which had tightly bound federal and provincial partisan interests. The parties also lost the power to dominate the administrative machinery of the state. This major institutional change ended party life as Canadians had known it for 50 years.

The central task of governing during this second period soon emerged as one of "accommodating the factions and divisions in Canadian society."[19] The country had divided in response to Borden's attempt to establish a national politics. Political cleavages, partially caused by the working of the electoral system were defined in regional terms.[20] This left the parties to operate as regional brokers preoccupied with the delicate balancing act required of nation-building. The Liberals had an inherent advantage in balancing the regions because only they could incorporate Quebec. Mackenzie King's intuitive understanding of what was required allowed him to absorb the West and build a winning cross-region electoral coalition that eventually turned the Liberals into the "Government Party." So successful was their political formula that eventually the state consumed the party.[21]

The focus of party politics in the second system shifted from constituency to region. With a deliberately federal approach to party organization, strong linkages developed between the grass roots and powerful regional bosses. Those men were responsible for the vitality of the party in their regions and, when the party was in power, for articulating regional claims in a way that promoted the emergence of a national consensus. This "ministerialist party"[22] was presided over by a leader who reserved to himself questions of political tactics and timing, and who, standing above his associates, could defend the integrity of the brokerage process.

Parties, as organizations, grew well beyond the confines of the parliamentary caucus during this period. In many ways the real organization was the set of informal political networks trailing down from the regional chiefs, but formal extraparliamentary national party associations were also established to provide some continuity with organizational work and to link partisans together. Central offices were opened in Ottawa but they were meagrely staffed, underfunded and occasionally closed. The politicians were never clear on what they expected of these bodies, other than to help win elections while refraining from voicing their opinions on questions of public policy. Although these national party councils did not play an important role, they did mark a stage in the institutionalization of party life, legitimating the notion that the party belonged to its members, and not just those elected to public office.

The federal character of party organization and the considerably increased geographic variation in party support were evidence of the lower levels of national integration that characterized the brokerage parties of this period. The electoral data also suggest that the parties' capacity to integrate national and provincial politics within individual provinces was coming under strain.[23] But the regionalization of the country's politics was showing up even here: in the Maritimes and Quebec (until the emergence of the Union Nationale) the Liberals and Conservatives continued to structure political competition, while west of the Ottawa River the traditional two-party system lost its grip. Much the same pattern of organizational separation appeared in the career paths of party politicians.[24]

To even casual observers, the changed structure of competition in the second-party system stood in distinct contrast to its predecessor. Gone was nation-wide competition, but also gone with it were the balance between the two historic parties and their once easy mastery of Canadian politics. After their defeat in 1930, the Liberals created an enduring electoral predominance while protest parties established themselves as permanent fixtures. This was an inherently asymmetrical system: only the Liberals could build an organization capable of embracing the regions' diverse interests.

A demand for regional brokerage seemed guaranteed to produce Conservative defeats. That in turn prevented the party from developing a working ministerialist organization, perpetuating its inability to practise party brokerage. The one time they won a majority during the period was in 1930, when the direct personal appeal of the leader, R.B. Bennett, could be used to circumvent the otherwise winning brokerage mode. Although this was recognized as a new and potentially significant development in the nature of party leadership (Chubby Power noted: "Beginning with Bennett, I think it could reasonably be said that the party was his rather than he was of the party"), charisma could not be institutionalized and the party was left in chaos after the leader proved incapable of reconciling all the competing regional claims in his own person. Significantly, the only other time the Conservatives managed to win in the second system was when they duplicated the experience of the early 1930s. Diefenbaker's charisma brought the party to power, only to have his government end in much the same disarray as Bennett's. By then, the system of party brokerage was itself passing.

In almost every election of the period considerable numbers of voters rejected both the Liberals and the Conservatives. Although the vitality of other political movements and parties seemed a regular part of the system, three quite distinct phenomena were involved. First there were the farmers of the Progressive movements in the early 1920s. Essentially, they were the heralds of the politics of regional brokerage springing up in opposition to the old politics of prewar Canada. Their absorption by the Mackenzie King Liberals, in Saskatchewan and Manitoba, defined the character of the second system. Their continuing alienation in Alberta revealed the limits of that politics.

Social Credit represented a second kind of protest party. It expressed the claims and grievances of those who felt their region had been left out of the accommodative package assembled by the Liberals. It was perhaps inevitable that not all interests could be incorporated in an attempt at nation-wide brokerage, and that as a result a regionally based party would arise to exploit the resulting competitive opportunity. Thus it is hardly surprising that Social Credit's national appeal was limited to Alberta, the very province that had resisted Mackenzie King in the 1920s. As a party of protest it did not survive the system that spawned it.

Socialists, in the form of the Co-operative Commonwealth Federation (CCF), constituted the third variety of protest party. It rejected brokerage politics in principle. Believing in an explicitly ideological politics, the CCF sought to reshape both the definition of Canadian party politics and the national political agenda. In fact its appeal was always highly regional, never really crossing the Ottawa River, and it was soon cast as a Western party. The Liberals, demonstrating the same policy flexibility that they had in the 1920s, moved to pre-empt popular CCF positions on welfare and government management of the economy. Unable to establish a national working class constituency in the face of successful Liberal government brokerage, the CCF went into steady decline after World War II, finally ceasing to exist as a separate entity just as the second-party system was ending.

The CCF was committed to democratic politics. Its organization was designed to allow party members, many originally politicized by the Progressives' democratic critique of Canadian practices, an opportunity to discuss and participate in the making of party policy. This participation was certainly far more than either the Liberals or Conservatives permitted their supporters. As the party was never in power nationally, it is impossible to judge whether the caucus would have felt bound to implement policies that party conventions had passed, but there is little doubt that the CCF considered internal party democracy one of its most important distinguishing features.

The one area in which the two major parties responded to the new ethos and became more democratic was their leadership selection process. Party leaders in this second-party system were chosen by national conventions in which the majority of delegates were representatives from local constituency associations. Conventions emerged to ensure that the national leader, who had to stand above all the interests gathered into the party, was chosen by a regionally representative assembly rather than a regionally unbalanced caucus.

The first leadership conventions, attended by about 1200 delegates, were managed affairs in which the party notables played an influential role in determining the outcome. There were rarely many serious candidates. Only once (the first time) did it take more than two ballots to determine a winner, and no extensive pre-convention campaigns were conducted by rival candidates. Although the conventions were relatively closed affairs, the process did allow men who were outside the caucus to stand for and win the party's leadership. As a result, parliamentary service and experience became less important qualities.[25]

The decision by the parliamentary caucuses to allow extraparliamentary conventions to choose party leaders divided authority and responsibility within the parties. How any serious leadership conflict might have been resolved was unclear for, as Mackenzie King is reported to have told his colleagues, a leader not chosen by the caucus was not responsible to it. On the other hand, conventions to choose new leaders were only called into being when a leader himself resigned. The potential contradictions in this bifurcated definition of party never became an issue, given the general weakness and timidity of the extraparliamentary organization throughout the period.

Although it occurred in the context of general organizational quiescence, the move towards a more open, democratic leadership selection process did not lead to more active constituency level parties. Indeed, though the evidence is sketchy, it appears that a vigorous local party life was in decline as even the nomination process came under the sway of established regional party élites.

Problems associated with party finance had bedeviled party leaders all during the first-party system. In an attempt to prevent elected politicians from continually being tainted by money scandals, the tasks associated with the raising and spending of party funds were divorced from other party activity and assigned to a small number of individuals who kept very much to the back rooms and the Senate. On the whole, the relative costs of electoral politics were probably lower during this period than they had been before World War

I, though definite regional differences existed. East of the Ottawa River, traditional (corrupt) electoral practices flourished.

Although all of the parties appear to have been perennially broke, there were vast differences in their relative poverty. The CCF depended on the contributions of its members, and so lived on a shoestring. Conservative fortunes were very uneven.[26] Bennett himself generously funded much of the party's activity during his leadership, while his successor faced a financial boycott from Montreal supporters due to differences over railroad policy. The party became so strapped that it had to close its national office in 1940. The Conservatives began to make a slow financial recovery only after they were returned to power in Ontario and Toronto business interests decided that a stronger national party was necessary to help counter the socialist threat of the CCF.

The Liberals had far fewer financial worries.[27] Being in office gave them access to the private sector, and they took advantage of it. Reversing the usual case of special interests supporting the governing party in order to win influence, Liberal bagmen instituted a system of kickbacks. Government contractors or suppliers were expected to make a contribution to the party that was proportionate to the amount of government business they were doing. These funds were supplemented by monies raised from large national corporations in private appeals. Together they gave the Liberals a comfortable advantage.

All the parties faced a dramatically changed media environment which altered the basic patterns of political communication. The partisan press was dead, killed by new economic realities and the greater appeal of independent and less political newspapers. Unlike their predecessors, these new papers did not take their cues from politicians as to what and how they should report, and they would not carry partisan messages for free. During election periods many papers charged more than normal advertising rates (a political rate often set only after the ad had been placed), knowing that the parties would have very little option but to pay. Radio emerged as an important communication tool during the 1930s, and parliament began to regulate party access to and use of the airwaves. Although several provincial parties were able to exploit the radio to advantage, national party organizations paid it less attention and as late as the 1950s continued to devote the largest part of their media budgets to the press.[28]

Perhaps the most significant change was the growth of advertising, both as an industry and as a profession. It was inevitable that advertising and politics would be drawn to one another from the beginning: politicians wanted help selling their message, especially in the absence of a docile press, and ad men wanted work. The war made the government the largest advertiser in the country, so the stakes were substantial. Thus was born the ad agency-party-government *ménage à trois*: advertisers did party work in exchange for government contracts. Naturally the governing party had a significant advantage and therefore this pattern was most developed by the Liberals. For the last decade of the system, the general secretary of the national party organization was actually an employee of one of the leading agencies, on "loan" to the politicians.

For the most part the advertising professionals' role was technical. They gave advice on how to package and deliver political messages but were not deeply involved in broader questions of party strategy and policy. The impact of these changes seems to have been to force the parties to clarify the message they wanted to communicate to the electorate, and to lift the substance of political debate from a preoccupation with local patronage. Both were prerequisites to the development of national, issue-centred campaigns.

This party system was well-adapted to meeting the brokerage demands of regional accommodation. As organizations, the parties reflected the imperatives of the system, but when it became clear that the brokerage function was being institutionalized in another part of the political system, the stage was set for the emergence of yet a third pattern of party competition.

Electronic Politics and Personal Parties (from 1963 on)

The Diefenbaker revolution and realignment ended four decades of Liberal brokerage. It opened up Canada to a new, modern, national politics. The country had developed an urban, industrialized, educated, plural society stretching across five distinctive political regions. The electorate was growing quickly, forcing the parties to find ways to socialize and incorporate large numbers of new voters. The parties abandoned the pretense that they were merely informal private groups, and during the 1960s began a process that defined their position and rights in parliament and law.[29]

Provincial governments were growing quickly and provincial politicians took the role of principal regional spokesmen, articulating grievances and pressing demands on the national government.

The important political mechanisms for regional accommodation, which had been the life-blood of the parties for 40 years, shifted to the first ministers' conference, and were institutionalized in a complex system of federal-provincial executive relationships. Deprived of the function that had driven them, the parties developed a new style of politics, a new basis for political mobilization.

Parties responded to the new context by shifting the focus of their attention from region to nation, to build an electoral constituency for their policy preferences. This new focus has produced what Smith calls a pan-Canadian style of political leadership and governance.[30] Parties direct their appeal to individual citizens and seek to engage their support for particular definitions of the political agenda and appropriate patterns of public policy. The national parties compete for individual support with one another and with their provincial counterparts.

Dramatic changes in the organization of the two major parties have been produced by the new politics. On one hand, the parties have become more than ever an extension of the leader, a personalized machine to build and sustain a coalition of support for the leader's policies. On the other hand, they have become open, participatory institutions in which the caucus and the extraparliamentary organization often seem to be quite separate, unrelated bodies. These two features have created a continuing internal tension within the parties that has largely focused on leadership issues and personalities.

In order to create a consistent national appeal, party leaders have taken personal control of the campaign machinery across the country. Appointments to all critical party positions are now made from the Leader's office, and if necessary are even made in defiance of powerful regional politicians.[31] This system of appointments guarantees a far more centralized control of electoral strategy, but also makes the party the creature of the leader. Independent regional bosses no longer exist; position and influence are no longer derived from being representative as they are the gift of the leader. The personalization of the entire party organization has an inherent propensity to stimulate the growth of national factions and to transform policy disputes into leadership conflicts.

At the same time, as part of their mobilization strategies, the Liberals and Conservatives have strengthened and institutionalized their extraparliamentary wings. The national party now meets regularly in convention and debates questions of organization, policy and leadership. The national officers it chooses have become increasingly important figures in party life and its committees and agencies are vital parts of the organization. These new structures now constitute a central forum for internal party struggles, and provide party activists with an opportunity to impose their views on the caucuses. By continually bringing together party militants from across the country, these conventions help to establish the parties as national communities of partisans. With the centralization of the electoral machine around the leader has come a significant nationalizing effect within the parties.

Changes in the organization and activities of national political parties have severely strained their ability to integrate politics within the provinces. The result has been the separation, or often formal divorce, of the provincial and federal wings of the same party. As with much in Canadian politics the extent of this internal party disintegration has varied across the regions; it has proceeded furthest in Quebec, while it has been resisted in Atlantic Canada where traditional loyalties and practices still hold the two levels together. On the west coast the two old national parties have simply disappeared from provincial politics, leaving British Columbians to live in "two political worlds."[32]

National electoral competition was reshaped by the realignment of the prairies. As the West deserted the Liberals for the Conservatives and the New Democrats (a development more pronounced at the level of parliamentary seats than of votes), Quebec became the least Tory province for the first time. A system emerged in which there was no genuinely national party, national, that is, in the geographic sense of the term, a definition fostered by the territorially based electoral system. Competition was being structured by parties representing national coalitions of voters not spread evenly across the country. The Liberals sought to align the young, the ethnics, the French-speakers, women, and the urban middle class; the NDP sought to unite trade unionists, the poor, and small farmers. Now that the party system no longer carried the major burden of accommodating regional differences in the governing process, the geographically unbalanced character of the parties' support bases and of party competition was not an inherent threat to the working of the Canadian polity.

Perhaps the clearest evidence of the strength of the new coalitions was the withering of the parties of protest that had been such a visible part of the second-party system. Those parties had come into existence as a response to the workings of brokerage politics. In its absence they no longer had any purpose. The Ralliement des créditistes did disrupt party politics throughout the 1960s, generating the same parliamentary uncertainty that had marked the first decade of each of the two previous party systems, but it was essentially a party in protest against the second system's treatment of its constituency. Like the Progressives of the 1920s, the Créditistes proved to be the harbinger of a new system, but not a part of it.

As the period started, the CCF, with the support of the five-year-old Canadian Labour Congress, transformed itself into the New Democratic Party. The formation of the NDP was a deliberate attempt to escape the regional cast that had settled on the CCF. The provision that trade unions might affiliate themselves was an attempt to tie the party to a distinctive national interest. But the very strength of the party in three of the four Western provinces has made it difficult for its national organization to rise above its provincial roots.

The party has increased its share of the national popular vote to about 20 per cent, but because of the single-member constituency system, it has so far been unable to translate that vote into a proportional share of seats in parliament.

The Liberals managed to dominate the first two decades of this third-party system not only because their continuing pre-eminence in Quebec made it easier for them to establish a winning coalition, but also because the Conservatives' ongoing leadership conflict had a debilitating effect on its capacity to compete.[33] And, as in each of the previous party systems, leadership has been a central dimension of party activity.

Mr. Diefenbaker's leadership of the Conservative party ended badly. A majority in the extraparliamentary party moved to depose the leader against the wishes of the caucus. Although procedures by which the national convention might regularly hold the leader accountable were instituted, this did not resolve the question of where final authority in the party lay. Joe Clark lost his leadership, despite a two-thirds convention vote, when he proved unable to command the loyalty of the caucus. The bifurcation of party between caucus and convention has proved profoundly destabilizing for party leadership, especially when in opposition, and has opened the parties up to being captured and controlled by highly personalized factions.

Leaders are now chosen in large, competitive conventions. In order to maximize their chances, contestants must engage in extensive pre-convention campaigns to have as many of their supporters as possible selected as delegates and to persuade others to vote for them. This requires the creation of a highly personalized national network capable of penetrating and capturing the wider party. Thus leadership contests now force the building of parties within the party on the basis of winner-take-all. As the direction of the parties can then be set by the leaders through their control of the organization, these contests become struggles over the political agenda and the kind of coalition the parties will seek to mobilize.

In leadership contests there is no premium on parliamentary experience. Some might even suggest, on the basis of the Clark, Mulroney and Turner victories, that outsiders offering a fresh, unsullied face have a distinct advantage. Most important is the capacity to build a sophisticated political machine that, using the modern electronic technologies of polling, communicating and constant monitoring, can mobilize a national constituency.

Much the same pattern of open competition is now typical of the constituency nominating process. Surprisingly large numbers of friends and neighbours are being brought to meetings to support particular candidates. The rather wholesale, almost casual recruitment of individuals for a single meeting may be debasing the notion of party membership, but it has stimulated local political participation. In areas of one-party dominance it is providing a real contest for office.

Early in this third-party system, the parties confronted the problem of their own relative poverty and instituted sweeping changes in the laws governing party income and electoral expenses.[34] The net effect of these developments was to make the parties' financial affairs public, to set limits on the amount of money they could spend and to make it much easier for the parties to raise funds from individual citizens. Some of the provisions have accelerated the drift from the print media to television and most of them have made the parties comparatively rich.

Generous tax credits for small political donations have provided the parties with a major opportunity to raise money from their supporters. They have learned to exploit the electronic technology of direct mail which allows them to connect the party centre directly with individual voters. Appeals typically invite individuals to support a particular leader in implementing his vision for the Canadian future. Not only does this reinforce a personalized definition of party, but it also frees the party from dependence on formal members for financial support. Mailing lists need not correspond with membership lists, and may come to be seen as a representation of the real party to which the leadership needs to respond. This technology also makes possible the organized factionalism that is at the heart of the politics of leadership within the parties.

These changes do not discriminate between the parties, so one of the major consequences has been the equalization of resources available to the three national parties. Indeed, in the last years of the Trudeau regime, both the Conservative party and the NDP were able to raise more money than the governing Liberal party. Whether this foreshadows a politics in which the opposition is better financed than the government remains to be seen, though that would certainly represent a major reversal from the earlier systems. A secondary consequence has been the enrichment of constituency associations, many of whom now appear to have more money than they know how to spend. Wealthier constituency associations seem certain to shift some of the traditional internal organizational balances towards increasing local autonomy and weakening party discipline and coherence.

At the same time, the rapid growth in party resources has stimulated the emergence of permanent national headquarters with million-dollar operating budgets. With the establishment of these headquarters has come an increase in the number of professional political technicians who have taken over electoral decision making and campaign management. Instrument of the leadership that appoints it, this new coterie of partisans does not fit easily with the parties' new participatory structures or assertive local associations and so its power is another source of internal conflict.

The character of the third-party system has most obviously been affected by the electronic mobilization of information. As the system started, television was revolutionizing the patterns of communication between party and voter. Television, with its emphasis on personality, and its structural bias towards gathering a national audience, reinforced the imperatives in the system that were producing new forms of party. In this environment the advertising expert evolved from being a technician to being a central advisor and strategist responsible to the leader. As the medium became defined as a potential tool of the opposition, these experts had to learn to manipulate television and use it to communicate a highly personalized image of the party. What was essentially new about television was the technology, and the premium it put on new kinds of skills.

Even more significant than television are the remarkable advances in attitude and opinion polling that have been part of this third system. They now allow for a systematic upward flow of information that permits party politicians to discern with remarkable accuracy what the concerns and interests of the public, or selected publics, are.[35] These are both catered to and manipulated by the image makers: they are rarely ignored. With a scientific reading of public opinion now available to the leadership, the traditional feedback role of party members and even MPs has become superfluous. Therefore, the hired pollster has replaced the newspaper editor of the first system, and the public relations consultant of the second, to become one of the key figures in the entourage of the successful party leader, and in the electronic politics of the third-party system.

By the end of the 1970s, this third system had begun to crystallize. Like its predecessors it appears to have developed a kind of stable equilibrium in which the various aspects of the parties are well-integrated, and which serve the functional requisites of the wider political system.

Three Canadian Party Systems

Seen in terms of three distinctive systems, the changes in Canadian political parties assume a pattern that might not otherwise be obvious. What is striking is not the fact that many aspects of the parties have changed, but that these changes in organization, leadership, finance and communication have twice come together in short periods to form quite new politics.

The first years of each system were marked by considerable electoral and parliamentary fragmentation and uncertainty. Macdonald faced the loose fish, Mackenzie King the Progressives and Pearson the Créditistes, in their struggles to establish new patterns of party organization and electoral politics. The strategies of political mobilization and incorporation each adopted proved to be characteristic of the system of governance that followed. At the same time one can see forces at work in the last years of each of the first two systems, during the Borden and St. Laurent governments, that were signalling the end of the system and the nature of what would follow.

The periods of party system transformation followed considerable social and demographic change in the basic structure of the

Table 1: A Summary of Variations in Canadian Parties during the Three-Party Systems

	I 1867-1917	II 1921-1957	III 1963-
Dominant Politics	patronage (state-building)	brokerage (nation-building)	electronic (agenda-building)
Focus	constituency	region	nation
Parties	caucus	ministerialist	personal

Leadership	caucus choice
	proven
	  parliamentarians
		managed
		  conventions
		known politicians
			open competition
			outsiders

Finance	civil service private capital	kickbacks corporations	public funding mass appeals
Media	party papers editors	independent press/radio P.R. consultants	TV/polling pollsters
Transitions	confederation loose fish	civil service reform 1917/farmers	federal-provincial diplomacy 1958/Créditistes

electorate. Both periods of change helped break old electoral align-ments and patterns of political organization, making it easier for new systems of partisan mobilization to emerge. In both cases, the Liberals were then left best placed to establish and epitomize the new system.

These party systems, so well-adapted to their political environ-ments, persisted only as long as they served the functions for which they had been called into being. They changed when the basic Ca-nadian political formulae changed, for "the heart of Canadian poli-tics" has always been "party government."[36] Whatever other social or ideological changes were altering Canadian society, the first-party system ended when civil service reform deprived the parties of their state-building role; the second-party system ended when the nation-building tasks of regional accommodation were absorbed into the system of federal-provincial diplomacy. This is not to suggest that those tasks were no longer performed. They had been institution-alized in new ways, and in other parts of the political system. The parties continued to play at patronage, and talk of regional interests, but neither drove party competition as they once had.

Canadian parties have reflected the demands imposed by the structure and character of the relationship between the state and society. They have primarily been shaped by the politics of party governance: party system change has flowed from political change, and most directly from changes in the institutional arrangements for governing, within which the political parties have had to operate.

Writing of the first-party system, André Siegfried pointed to the absolute centrality of the leader in all aspects of party activity. The leader was the entire central organization and policy making apparatus as well as the focus of electoral appeal. Although the modalities of party leadership have changed as the politics of Canadian parties shifted focus from constituency to region to nation, party leaders have remained the hub around which the parties revolve. Siegfried would have recognized in the party leaders who gathered powerful regional chieftains around them, or who personalized the party organization to pursue a national agenda, a continuity that wove a distinctive historical experience through the three systems. This continuity makes the issue of leadership selection—how and whom the parties choose—one of the central issues of Canadian politics, and explains why the study of leadership selection provides one of the most fruitful avenues for studying the country's parties and its policies.

Notes

1   D. Smith, "Party Government, Representation and National Integration in Canada," in P. Aucoin, ed., *Party Government and Regional Representation in Canada* (Toronto: University of Toronto Press, 1985).

2   A. Siegfried, *The Race Question in Canada* (Toronto: McClelland and Stewart, 1906, 1966 edition), pp. 114, 117.

3   Smith, "Party Government," p. 82.

4   G. Stewart, "Political Patronage Under Macdonald and Laurier, 1878-1911," *The American Review of Canadian Studies* 10.1 (1980); "John A. Macdonald's Greatest Triumph," *Canadian Historical Review* 63.1 (1982).

5   R.M. Dawson, *The Civil Service of Canada* (London: Oxford University Press, 1929), pp. 73-74, 81-82.

6   J.M. Beck, *Pendulum of Power* (Scarborough: Prentice-Hall Canada, 1968), pp. 43-73.

7   R. Johnston, "Federal and Provincial Voting: Contemporary Patterns and Historical Evolution," in D.J. Elkins and R. Simeon, eds., *Small Worlds: Provinces and Parties in Canadian Political Life* (Toronto: Methuen, 1980).

8   E. Reid, "The Saskatchewan Liberal Machine before 1929," in H.G. Thorburn, ed., *Party Politics in Canada*, 4th ed. (Scarborough: Prentice-Hall Canada, 1979).

9   J. English, *The Decline of Politics: The Conservatives and the Party System 1901-20* (Toronto: University of Toronto Press, 1977).

10   Johnston, "Federal and Provincial Voting."

11   J.C. Courtney, *The Selection of National Party Leaders in Canada* (Toronto: Macmillan of Canada, 1973).

12   Courtney, *ibid.*, pp. 142-143.

13   J.W. Dafoe, *Laurier: A Study in Canadian Politics* (Toronto: McClelland and Stewart, 1922, 1963 edition), p. 83.

14   P. Rutherford, *A Victorian Authority: The Daily Press in Late Nineteenth-Century Canada* (Toronto: University of Toronto Press, 1982).

15   N. Ward, "Patronage and the Press," in K.M. Gibbons and D.C. Rowat, eds., *Political Corruption in Canada* (Toronto: McClelland and Stewart, 1976).

16   Rutherford, *A Victorian Authority*, p. 221.

17   W.L. Morton, *The Progressive Party in Canada* (Toronto: University of Toronto Press, 1950).

18   M. Prang, "Networks and Associations and the Nationalizing of Sentiment in English Canada," in R.K. Carty and W.P. Ward, eds., *National Politics and Community in Canada* (Vancouver: University of British Columbia Press, 1986). English, *The Decline of Politics*.

19   Smith, "Party Government," p. 21.

20   A.C. Cairns, "The Electoral System and the Party System in Canada, 1921-1965," *Canadian Journal of Political Science* 1.1 (1968).

21   R. Whitaker, *The Government Party: Organizing and Financing the Liberal Party of Canada, 1930-58* (Toronto: University of Toronto Press, 1977).

22   Whitaker, *ibid.*, p. xxii.

23   Johnston, "Federal and Provincial Voting."

24   Whitaker, *The Government Party*, Part B.

25   Courtney, *The Selection of National Party Leaders*.

26   J.L. Granatstein, *The Politics of Survival: The Conservative Party of Canada, 1939-1945* (Toronto: University of Toronto Press, 1967).

27   Whitaker, *The Government Party*.

28   Whitaker, *ibid.*

29   J.C. Courtney, "Recognition of Canadian Political Parties in Parliament and Law," *Canadian Journal of Political Science* 11.1 (1978).

30   Smith, "Party Government."

31   J. Wearing, *The L-Shaped Party: The Liberal Party of Canada, 1958-1980* (Toronto: McGraw-Hill Ryerson, 1981), ch. 2.

32 D.E. Blake, *Two Political Worlds: Parties and Voting in British Columbia* (Vancouver: University of British Columbia Press, 1985).

33 G.C. Perlin, *The Tory Syndrome: Leadership Politics in the Progressive Conservative Party* (Montreal: McGill-Queen's University Press, 1980).

34 F.L. Seidle and K.Z. Paltiel, "Party Finance, the Election Expenses Act, and Campaign Spending in 1970 and 1980," in H.R. Penniman, ed., *Canada at the Polls, 1979 and 1980* (Washington, DC: American Enterprise Institute, 1981).

35 R. Graham, *One-Eyed Kings: Promise and Illusion in Canadian Politics* (Toronto: Collins, 1986), pp. 284, 307-308.

36 Smith, "Party Government," p. 2.

Richard Johnston The Electoral Basis of the
Canadian Party Systems,
1878-1984

In most elections between 1878 and 1984, the dominant force was the
Liberal party. This domination persisted through three distinct party
systems. The transition between each system was marked by a Conservative landslide but the government formed by each landslide was
short-lived. Each period in power left the Conservative party worse
off in at least one key particular. One possible reading of electoral
history, then, is that the 1984 landslide was just another occasion for
the Liberal party to regroup and for the Conservatives to alienate yet
another part of the electorate.

But the electoral record admitted an alternative reading. At
each realignment in this century, Liberal support shrank. In the
third system, Liberal governments were narrowly grounded in the
electorate and often weak in parliament. There was, then, no mistaking the trajectory the Liberals were riding. On this reading, 1984
heralded not just a short-lived censure of the natural party of government but a wholly new alignment of electoral forces, ones which
promised to make the Conservatives the dominant party.

At each realignment of the party system at least one important
element in its social base shifted profoundly. Two shifts were especially critical. By 1984 the alignment of groups with a stake in
commercial policy – with tariffs in particular – had rotated 180
degrees: the cleavages of 1878 had been reversed. In 1984 another
group appeared to have rotated 360 degrees: Quebec francophones.
In 1878 this group lay at the heart of the then dominant Conservative coalition. The Liberals supplanted the Conservatives in great
part by detaching Quebec from them. If the Conservative party has
ended the Liberal century, the final step in its doing so was taking
Quebec back.

This essay fleshes out these propositions. Emphasis is on the
mass electorate, on one hand, and the policy and personal appeals
that parties made to that electorate, on the other. We argue that
each transition signalled a change in the party-electorate nexus. The
essay does not dwell on party organization and finance or on how
campaigns were organized. But each of these areas also changed
as one party system yielded to the next. These changes are reviewed
in outline in two other places, Carty (1988) and Smith (1985). Our

Through an error by the editor and publisher, the names of
Richard Johnston's co-authors were omitted at the top of
this page and in the Table of Contents; this piece is by **André
Blais, Henry Brady, Jean Crête**, and Richard Johnston. The
editor and publisher sincerely apologise for this error.

argument should be read as a complement to those pieces.

The Adversaries and The Stakes

The Canadian electorate has been polarized along three basic dimensions, much as other representative democracies are (Lipset and Rokkan, 1967). One dimension, itself really several dimensions, is *ethno-religious*. Electoral cleavages in this realm tend to be peculiar to each country, reflecting the configuration of religious groups and nationalities that happens, often accidentally, to get enclosed by a juridical boundary. The outstanding group for this account is French Canada. The second dimension is *urban-rural*. For the Canadian case, the central cleavage is between export-oriented agriculture and the rest and the issue is commercial policy. The third dimension is *class*. As a practical matter, the operative definition of the class cleavage is the union movement versus the rest. This cleavage too is implicated in the debate over commercial policy. The order in which the cleavages were just enumerated is the order in which they appeared in historical time.

Ethno-religious Divisions

Cultural divisions have persisted from the beginnings of Canadian politics. The main antagonists have been Catholics and Protestants, although the most visible expression of this cleavage has often been linguistic, French versus English. More recently, groups which stand outside the old religious-cum-linguistic division were added to the mix; typically the new groups allied with Catholics and the French.

Only some of the time were the stakes specifically religious or linguistic. Indeed, religion dominated as a policy question only at the Liberal century's beginning: the Liberal party's rise was attended by conflict over the place of the Catholic church in the emergent Canadian nationality. Language policy dominated only towards at its end, in the third party system.[1] Neither religious nor linguistic conflict promised easy returns for any party; indeed, both conflicts divided each party against itself, partly as a reflection of the awkward fit between the geography of group membership and the location of provincial boundaries. The parties sometimes changed their positions on the divisive issues, partly as they sought tactical advantage, partly as their own makeup shifted. Sometimes the parties' leaders colluded to keep the issues off the agenda.

For most of the past century, however, the ethno-religious division has been over something else entirely: over the moral and symbolic claims of the British connection. Down to 1945 (and perhaps 1962), the problem was mainly one of external policy, of how much Canada collectively and Canadians individually owed the Empire. This was not just a disagreement over sentiment. At least until the 1920s, Canada arguably needed the diplomatic weight of the Empire to counter the claims of the United States. But British diplomatic support carried a price; it required Canadian participation in overseas wars, in South Africa and in the First and Second World Wars. What one thought possible, or even desirable, in external relations depended on the price one was willing to pay and thus on how aggressively one was prepared to force the question of the Canadian nationality's essential character. The nationalism of the years before 1920 was commonly linked to imperialism; with resistance to imperialism also went resistance to assertive definitions of the national interest, in either economic or military policy. After 1920, rival versions of nationalism competed. For some, the imperialistic version was still the only realistic one; the continuation of the Empire as a diplomatic unit was deemed essential for the realization of Canada's own goals. For others, imperialism and nationalism seemed antithetical: Canada's interests had to be expressed in their own right, were little served by combining diplomatic forces with the Empire, and, indeed, could often be blocked by conformity to an imperial line. After 1960, nationalism was stripped of its British content; there was no longer an empire for Canada to be a part of.

So long as the British connection was viable, English Canadians were naturally more enthusiastic about both its internal and external aspects than were French Canadians. Within English Canada, Protestants were palpably more sympathetic to the moral claims of the Empire and to the symbolic appeal of a British definition of the polity than were Catholics. Non-Christian groups, Jews at first and later other groups as well, gained demographic weight and tended to side with Catholics. On the place of Canada in the Empire and of the Empire in Canada, the two parties differed profoundly and consistently over the entire period under consideration. The Conservative party championed the British connection. Although not all Conservatives sought a closer integration of Canada into the Empire, almost everyone who sought such integration was perforce a Conservative. The Liberal party resisted the pull of Empire. Not all Liberals opposed the connection; but most of its opponents were forced, sooner or later, into the Liberal camp. As long as questions were defined in terms of the British connection, the various lines of force in the country's ethno-religious structure tended to cumulate and the cleavage that divided Catholics and Protestants, Liberals and Conservatives tended to be wide but simple.

Farmers versus All Others

Farmers producing for the world market found themselves at odds with the major thrust of national commercial policy, protective tariffs. As the prairie West filled up in this century's first decade, export-oriented agriculture gained political weight. In due course, grain producers shifted their attention from tariffs to other targets. In particular, they sought government intervention in key markets, for credit and, most importantly, for the commodities themselves. These demands were pressed all the more strongly as the agricultural sector as a whole shrank relative to the rest of the economy. Farmers producing for domestic consumption also pressed for government intervention.

While the Liberal party may not always have been the farmers' friend, the Conservative party before 1957 was always their foe. The "National Policy" of tariff protection, railway subsidies, and Dominion lands (Mackintosh, 1964) was *their* policy. For Conservatives it derived warrant not just on economic grounds but also as an expression of mutually reinforcing national and imperial interests: creating a transcontinental polity and economy secured an "All Red Route to India". An attack on the National Policy was vulnerable to being styled as an attack on the nationality, at least in its British definition, and as a thinly veiled plot to deliver Canada to the American enemy.

Since 1957, the Conservative party has moved off this position. In part this reflected a profound realignment in its geographic base. Export-oriented farmers shifted into the Conservative coalition. In doing so they helped prepare the way for the 1988 version of the politics of free trade. Also preparing the way was the disappearance of the Empire; Conservatives' evaluation of commercial policy now had to be detached from imperial considerations. As the Conservative party moved away from protectionism, the Liberal party moved toward the Conservatives' former ground and came to share it with the NDP.

The Union Movement

A second economic division has gradually become more important. The growth of the labour movement has injected labour-management issues more centrally into the national agenda. Organized labour roughly trebled its share of the labour force between the onset of World War II and the mid-1950s. The unionized share grew still more over the 1960s and 1970s. Now about 35 percent of the labour force is unionized, not a large share by the standard of many European countries but about twice the unionized share in the United States.

No less important than the growth of the labour movement has been its consolidation, at least in English Canada. The creation of the Canadian Labour Congress in 1956 removed the major barrier to official links between the English Canadian labour movement and a political party (Horowitz, 1968). The link was consummated, after a fashion, in 1961, with the founding of the NDP.

The interplay of these adversaries and stakes defined the temporal boundaries in the history of the party system. The passages which follow identify the factors which dominated each system and which seemed to bear most specifically on each transition between systems. Special attention is paid to ethno-religious factors, mainly but not exclusively as they affected voting in Quebec, and to shifts in commercial policy.

The First Party System

Figures 1 and 2 track Liberal and Conservative shares, respectively, of the national popular vote from 1878 to 1984. The first year of the series, 1878, marked a key institutional boundary for Canadian elections. It was the first election in which a secret ballot was employed and only the second in which virtually all writs were issued on the same day (Qualter, 1970). Figure 3 tracks the combined share for all other parties over the 1878-1984 period. It also isolates the only enduring third party, the Cooperative Commonwealth Federation and its offspring, the New Democratic Party, for 1935-84.

The Liberals became the natural party of government in and after 1896. Their base grew, if rather fitfully, over the 1880s and 1890s and peaked in 1904. Although the Liberals lost office in 1911, their 1911 share exceeded that for every election but one (1887) before 1900. The Conservative record (Figure 2) in the first system largely mirrored the Liberal one. Usually, when the Liberals

Figure 1: National Popular Vote Share, 1878-1984: Liberals

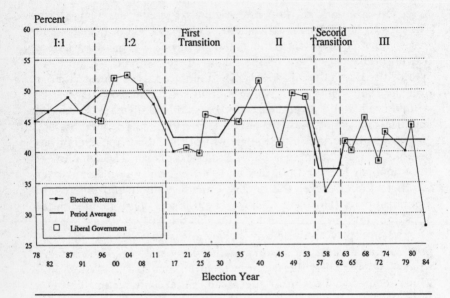

gained, the Conservatives lost and vice versa.

Temporal boundaries in the first system were a bit ambiguous. Popular vote movements in 1880s foreshadowed the system to come. But the full flowering of the changes had to await 1896. Thus the system is split into its Conservative and Liberal periods at that year. The last election fought clearly under first-system rules was the 1911 one. Although the dominance of the two old parties continued, in a manner of speaking, through 1917, the parties which contested the 1917 election were not quite what they had been before: what we record as the Conservative share really belonged to the Unionist coalition, formed by Conservatives and English-speaking Liberals and dedicated to, among other things, conscription for overseas service in the First World War; the Liberal party was reduced to a preponderantly French and Catholic rump.

The sectional foundations of the two 1878-1911 subsystems are contrasted in Figures 4 and 5. Each figure gives Liberal and Conservative vote shares averaged, province by province, over several elections. Provinces are ordered from west to east, to emphasize the party system's geography. Two contrasts dominate the transition between the two subsystems.

Figure 2: National Popular Vote Share, 1878-1984: Conservatives

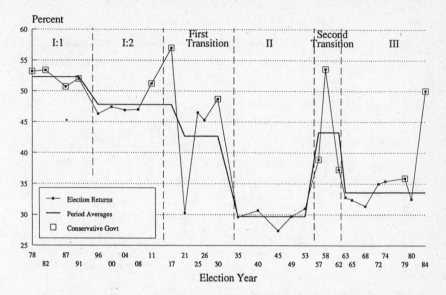

The first is in the place of Quebec, on one hand, and Ontario and Manitoba, on the other. Before 1896, Quebec was in the Conservative camp. After 1896, it was in the Liberal camp. In the popular vote the swing was not dramatic, a net shift of some ten points. In seats, the real currency, the significance of this swing was much greater.

The second contrast is in the sheer number of provinces: it grew, effectively, by three. British Columbia did not really engage in party politics before 1896. And Manitoba's pre-1896 appearance in Figure 4 is something of a courtesy: the province was much more important after 1896. But if Manitoba and British Columbia grew in importance, Alberta and Saskatchewan fairly exploded. They did not acquire provincial status until 1905 and their demographic growth from 1896 to 1911 was nothing short of astounding. By 1911, Saskatchewan was the third most populous province in the dominion.[2] And Saskatchewan, like Alberta, was squarely in the Liberal camp.

How the Liberals supplanted the Conservatives is still a subject for scholarly investigation. The Liberals were clearly on the rise over the 1880s. Their growth was probably a compound of the

Figure 3: National Popular Vote Shares, 1878-1984: Other Parties

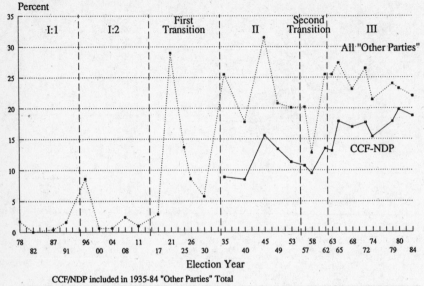

Percent

I:1 | I:2 | First Transition | II | Second Transition | III

All "Other Parties"

CCF-NDP

Election Year

CCF/NDP included in 1935-84 "Other Parties" Total

Conservative government's own senescence, of economic distress, and of careful linguistic and sectarian tactics on the Liberals' part. The Conservative government was old: eighteen uninterrupted years to 1896 and twenty-four of the twenty-nine years after 1867. By the 1890s the Conservative organization was corrupt and rotting. The 1880s and early 1890s were also a period of intense economic distress. The price level in 1896 was well below that of 1873. The country experienced severe net outmigration. In the ethno-religious game, the Liberals held a trump in Quebec: Wilfrid Laurier, the first Catholic francophone to lead a national party.

The dawn of the Liberal era in 1896 was accompanied by a minor party surge (Figure 3) that was rich in anticipation if not in result. Minor-party and independent candidacies in the 1890s reflected agrarian discontent and labour insurgency, in reaction to persistent economic adversity. Disturbances in the Canadian system were, if anything, pale by comparison with American populism in this period and they abated after 1896. But they anticipated later disturbances, including the ones which brought the first system to an end.

Notwithstanding these tensions, the parliamentary character of

Figure 4: The First Party System 1: Conservative Party Dominant, 1878-91

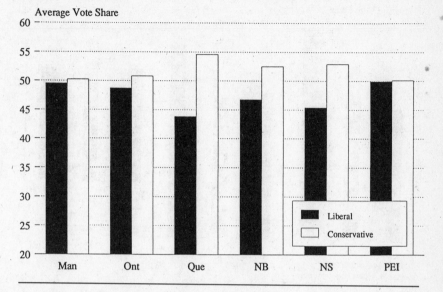

Average Vote Share

Legend:
- ■ Liberal
- □ Conservative

the first system was simple and quite stable. Figure 6 plots seat shares for the two old parties combined and for the winning party. Down to and including 1917 virtually every seat was held by one of the major parties. Governments were always returned with a majority and always by about the same margin.[3] For instance, when the Laurier government fell in 1911 the Borden government which replaced it had almost exactly the same number of seats as the Liberals had won in 1908. In no year did the government utterly swamp the opposition yet in no year was the government's majority razor-thin.

Ethno-religious Divisions

One thread running through the geography of the post-1896 Liberal coalition was religion. Liberals tended to be strong where Catholics were numerous and vice versa. The Liberal base was not just in Quebec but in the heavily Catholic Maritime provinces as well. Ontario, Manitoba, and British Columbia were, conversely, the heartlands of Anglo-Protestant triumphalism. It bears emphasis that this relationship was *not* the product of a close identification of the Liberal party

Figure 5: The First Party System 2: Liberal Party Dominant, 1896-1911

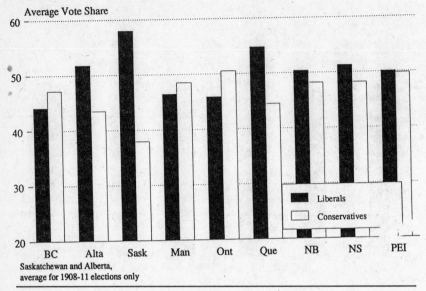

Saskatchewan and Alberta,
average for 1908-11 elections only

with the Catholic project for Church and State – that is, the defence of the separate school system in Manitoba, the extension of separate schools in Ontario and the Northwest Territories (later Saskatchewan and Alberta), and the settlement of the Jesuit Estates in Quebec. Collectively, the Liberal party was ambivalent about the place of Catholicism, just as the Conservative party was. They may have been helped by being out of power in Ottawa for the most critical years.

The issues Liberals were forced to manage once in power tended to be outward looking, to be about Canada's place in the Empire. This allowed a simpler coalitional strategy than the internal questions of Church and State and the growing importance of the outward-looking issues explains much of the post-1896 pattern. Nonetheless, the issues were fraught with peril. For instance, Laurier opposed Canada's participation with Britain in the South African War. But he lost the initiative and Protestant opinion forced his government into an active military role. He determined never to lose the initiative again.[4]

Taking the initiative could also be risky, as the next imperial episode indicated. Pressures mounted in the years before the First World War for Canada to contribute to imperial naval defence.

Laurier resolved to create a Canadian naval service, which would relieve the Royal Navy of responsibility for protecting Canadian waters and yet minimize the risk of overseas complications. Imperialists decried this as too little, as not materially contributing to the real need of countering the German High Seas Fleet. Anti-imperialists opposed the Canadian service as the entering wedge for a deeper imperial commitment.

Commercial Policy

Canadian commercial policy has traditionally been embodied in the National Policy on which the 1878 election was fought. The National Policy was designed to create a transcontinental nation and was the Conservative party's legacy to that nation. The policy traditionally had three elements: railway subsidies, virtually free access to dominion-controlled western lands, and protective tariffs.

The National Policy created its own coalition. A manufacturing sector emerged as a political interest in its own right. For most of the last century, labour and capital saw their interests as allied on the National Policy. Allied with them traditionally have been the railways, for which manufactures from Ontario and Quebec provided the westbound freight. In the earlier period the policy was not merely National; it was also Imperial. Between its enactment in 1879 and its effective repeal in 1988, the National Policy was challenged twice. Each time it survived.

The first challenge came in 1891. In that year, the Liberal party committed itself to "Unrestricted Reciprocity" with the United States. The Conservative party responded with the slogan, "the Old Flag, the Old Policy, the Old Leader" and produced the downturn in the Liberal share which is shown in Figure 1 as braking the trend that ultimately put that party in power.[5]

The Liberal government finally formed in 1896 appeared to have learned its lesson. The principal commercial-policy initiative of its first fourteen years of office was a brilliant tactical coup: imperial preference. By reducing tariffs on British manufactures,[6] the party genuflected toward its free-trade roots. By confining preference to imperial production, it neutralized arguments that the Liberal party was disloyal to the British connection. The timing was brilliant: the policy came into force in 1897, Queen Victoria's Diamond Jubilee year.

These lessons seemed to be forgotten in 1911, the year of the

Figure 6: Seat Share, 1878-1984: Election Returns and Period Averages

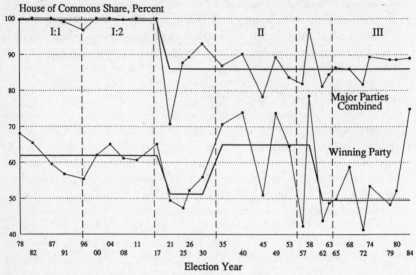

House of Commons Share, Percent

Election Year

second challenge to the National Policy. In 1910, the Laurier government won an agreement for reciprocal free trade in natural products from the Taft administration.[7] Canada enjoyed comparative advantage in most natural products. To wheat, the most important product of all, the agreement was essentially irrelevant; America and Canada were both exporters, principally to the European market. The agreement seemed politically unassailable, in that it left protection for manufacturing essentially untouched. These considerations did not carry the day. The principal argument against the agreement spoke of the "thin edge of the wedge": the agreement was cast as the harbinger of a more comprehensive trade liberalization. The latter threatened the British connection as well as the domestic interests that the National Policy had created. This time the slogan was "No Truck or Trade with the Yankees." The most straightforward lesson of 1911, as of 1891, seemed to be that free trade was electorally too risky.[8]

The First Transition

The 1911 result, although a reverse for the Liberals, was hardly a cataclysm. But it set the stage for a truly profound realignment, which began in 1917 and took until 1935 to be realised fully. In 1917, the Liberals' share dropped to 40.1 percent and barely changed in 1921 and 1925. In these three elections, the party pulled in nearly 10 percentage points less than its average share from 1896 to 1911.

Where 1917 was the year the Liberal share collapsed, 1921 brought retribution to the Conservatives. It was frightful: in 1921, the party lost nearly 27 points, almost half its 1917 share. To be sure, that 1917 share did not fairly represent the pre-1921 Conservative base. But the 1921 result was stunning by almost any standard. Taken against the Conservative average share over the 1896-1911 period, the 1921 vote represented a drop of nearly 17-18 percentage points.[9] The Conservative decline in 1921 was two to three times as large, depending on how one counts, as the Liberal drop in 1917.

The avenging angel was the Progressive party, an agrarian movement. Figure 3 indicates that the combined minor-party vote in that year reached 29 percent, almost all of it for Progressive candidates. The Progressive breakthrough weakened both old parties: the 1921 election brought the first hung Parliament since Confederation, as the Liberals won only 41 percent of the vote (slightly more than in 1917) and 49 percent of the seats. Although the Progressives themselves were destined to disappear, both they and candidates with labour-cum-socialist allegiances anticipated the CCF, a party which was destined to survive.

Figure 7 gives the geography of old-party collapse and third-party insurgency. For clarity, old parties appear above the zero percent line and new parties appear below it. For both old parties, support outside Quebec took on a rough east-west gradient. The Liberals maintained a beachhead in Saskatchewan and the Conservatives one in British Columbia. In Alberta and Manitoba, the Liberals were weaker than both the Conservatives and the new parties. Conservatives were weaker than the new parties in Alberta and Saskatchewan. In each Prairie province new parties controlled either the largest or the second largest share. A new-party bloc was also visible in each of British Columbia and Ontario. In the Atlantic provinces and Quebec, third-party voting was of virtually no significance.

Thanks to their sectional concentration the new parties made a beachhead in parliament. Since 1921, parties other than the Liberals and Conservatives have occupied, on average, 14 percent of the

Figure 7: The First Transition, 1921-30

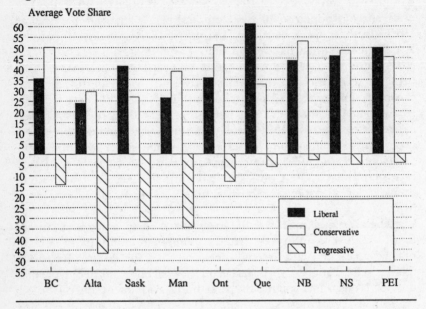

Average Vote Share

seats, according to Figure 6. Although their biggest share came in 1921 and the next three elections saw a restoration of much of the old major-party joint parliamentary share, the third-party presence weakened governments appreciably. Before 1921, the party in government typically controlled just over 60 percent of the House. From 1921 to 1930 the winner's parliamentary share averaged just over 50 percent. From 1921 to 1926 no single party had a majority and neither the 1926 nor the 1930 majorities approached the pre-1917 norm.

Ethno-religious Divisions

The transition between the first and second party systems pushed ethno-religious differences to the limit. This is implicit in the geographic pattern captured by Figure 7. In 1917 the Liberals collapsed outside Quebec; in Quebec they surged. The Conservatives, leading a coalition with English Liberals and calling themselves Unionists, surged outside Quebec but collapsed inside that province. Although Figure 7 concentrates on 1921-30, for the Quebec-rest contrast it also gives a good reading for 1917.

Both the cause and the pattern of the Liberals' collapse outside Quebec was foreshadowed by the geography of prewar party choice. The 1896-1911 regional differences in Figure 5 corresponded closely the most powerful imaginable indicator of 1914-18 commitment to the Empire: the rate of voluntary enlistment. Overseas service was proportionally highest by a wide margin in Manitoba and British Columbia and third highest in Ontario; apart from Quebec, the lowest rates were in the Maritime provinces and Saskatchewan and Alberta.[10] The 1917 crisis was brought on by the Unionist government's desire to go beyond voluntary enlistment, to bring in conscription.

If the 1917 crisis sharpened one element in the pre-war geographic pattern, it shattered the other one. In the first system, the attachment of Alberta and Saskatchewan to the Liberals, like their low Great War enlistment rates, reflected not just ethno-religious considerations but also the dominance of their economies by wheat production. The last election under the old dispensation, 1911, turned in great part on this polarization. But in 1917 the opposition of some Liberals to conscription and the disappearance of the rest into a Conservative-dominated coalition discredited the party for many Prairie Westerners.

One result was an agrarian insurgency, the Progressives. The insurgency picked up threads from 1896. In doing so, it combined two elements of Canadian third-party activity which after 1935 were to be separated. One part was protest against some facet of politics-as-usual; an element in this was distaste with party politics as such, a theme which had surfaced in 1896 and which continues to recur. This distaste for party politics has been a theme in agrarian insurgency in America as well as in Canada.[11] It reflected an individualistic model of society which was congenial to farmers, especially on the wheat-producing frontier, as they saw themselves on the defensive against urbanization and industrialization.

If one part of the Progressives' appeal looked back, the other part foreshadowed issues which were both new and destined to endure. The Progressive movement and the other political tendencies which sprang up in the early 1920s were also outlets for impulses originating in cities and in the ranks of English Canada's intelligentsia. A new cultural nationalism had emerged from the crucible of the Great War. Intellectual leaders in the universities and the Protestant churches had hoped that the war would produce an enlarged sense of citizenship and an end to sectarianism. For this reason

Figure 8: The Second Party System, 1935-53

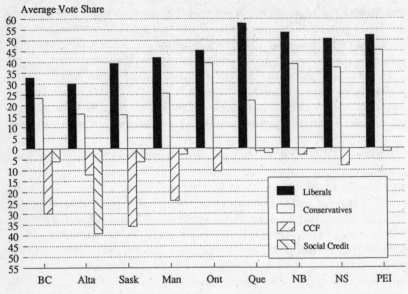

Average Vote Share

many supported the Unionist government; its commitment to conscription seemed consistent with the call to civic duty and it did embrace more than one party. But the government disappointed them and the War purged the intelligentsia's nationalism of much of its overt Britishness and jingoism.[12]

Commercial Policy

On economic policy as well, the Progressive movement embodied both old and new thinking. The old thinking was on the tariff. The 1920s saw an exception which proved the rule that the tariff was too dangerous politically for any party to handle: tariffs on agricultural implements went down. Most tariffs deliver benefits to a concentrated set of producers and impose costs on a dispersed and politically ineffective mass of consumers. Tariffs thus are politically difficult to overturn. But implement tariffs impose costs on a specific producer group. The group in question, farmers, increased their political power dramatically with the postwar Progressive surge. In consequence, implement tariffs went down in 1919, 1922, and 1925. The Progressives' disappearance in the late 1920s facilitated implement (and other) tariff increases in the next decade.

But the Progressive insurgency also led to the articulation of a wholly new agrarian program. The circumstances which produced the Progressive movement challenged the very individualism that seemed to infuse the party's style. During the war demand for wheat had been buoyant; after the war the wheat economy collapsed. Wartime demand coincided with centralized management of the crop; the postwar collapse coincided with the termination of that management system. Farmers drew the obvious moral: centralized management would give them monopoly power and should, thus, supplant the open market. Where in 1911 the central agrarian demand had been for an implicit *reduction* of the government's role in commercial policy, 1921 saw the first focused demand for an *increased* role, in the management of commodity markets.[13] But the late 1920s recovery in the grain market, a major factor in the Progressives' disappearance, made this demand less pressing.

The Second Party System

By 1930 the Progressive impulse was spent and the onset of the Depression led voters to the Conservative party for the first time since 1917. In Quebec, the Conservatives won 45 percent of the vote and 37 percent of the seats – totals commensurate with their performance in Quebec in the first party system. The 1930 election, then, seemed to signal the triumph of the old alignment, a return to the balanced two-party competition of the first system.

Nothing was further from the truth, as 1935 ushered in a new alignment. The old rural-urban cleavage took new forms and a new cleavage, based on class conflict and the experience of the Depression, struggled to emerge. Despite these new forces, the Liberal vote share was hardly touched. The Conservatives, in contrast, met catastrophe: a drop of about 19 points, which left the party at an even lower level than in 1921. This time, the Conservatives did not recover; their 1935 share was virtually identical to the party's average for the next two decades, 29.7 percent, a remarkably feeble share for a system's second major party and official opposition.

The rest of the vote went to third parties, whose collective share rivalled that of 1921. This time, however, the minor-party vote was split three ways. One minor party, the Reconstruction party, attracted votes from a base which was wide but not deep. Reconstruction won only one seat and disappeared in 1940. A second party, Social Credit, had the opposite profile: a narrow base but a deep one, primarily in Alberta. This made it an instant parliamentary presence and helped it survive for the entire span of the second party system. Long-lived though it may have been, Social Credit, like the Progressives, was a vehicle for anti-party sentiment.

The third party was the Cooperative Commonwealth Federation, or CCF. The CCF staked a serious claim from the outset. It articulated a program which combined agrarian, labour, and socialist elements. Protest voting was one factor in the party's early success. But the CCF set out to govern – or at least to affect how other parties governed – and to claim a long-term place in the political order. The CCF did *not* embody antipathy to parties as such, despite its occasional spasm of ritual self-purification.[14] Its members tended to accept that party action is necessary for the achievement of collectivist objectives. By the same token, the CCF was commonly sympathetic with executive prerogatives; executives, after all, actually perform the tasks that social democrats wish upon the state. And CCF MPs tended to be masters of the parliamentary game. If the Progressives were fated to disappear from their internal contradictions, the same could not be said of that part of their legacy that emerged as the CCF.

The geographic basis of the second party system appears in Figure 8. In the five easternmost provinces, continuities with the first party system were obvious. The Liberal party remained strongest in Quebec and retained a comfortable plurality in the maritime provinces. As in the first system, Ontario remained the weak link in the Liberals' eastern chain. In the east, the Conservatives simply mirrored the Liberals. But the Conservative base in each eastern province was markedly lower than in the first system. Where the Liberal advantage in Quebec under the first system had been substantial but reversible, in the second system it verged on hegemonic. Even in the Tories' places of relative strength, Liberals typically returned pluralities.

Conservative first-system weakness in Alberta and Saskatchewan was converted into virtual nonexistence. Even in Manitoba and British Columbia, erstwhile bases for the Conservative party, the tory vote had eroded. The slack was picked up by parties indigenous to the region, heirs to the Progressive movement. The CCF was most important, rivalling the Liberals in Saskatchewan and British Columbia. In Manitoba and Alberta they did only a little worse than the Conservatives. Social Credit was a party almost purely of

Alberta. But in Alberta it was typically won pluralities.

Where the 1921 insurgency produced a hung parliament, its 1935 counterpart produced a smashing victory for the Liberals. This came to typify the second party system. According to Figure 6, the 1935 Liberal seat majority was the largest in Canadian history to that date. The majority only increased in 1940. The government barely survived in 1945 but came back in 1949 with a majority larger than in 1935 and almost as large as in 1940. The majority was cut in 1953 but was still above the pre-1917 norm. No less striking than the parliamentary strength of the government was the feebleness of the official opposition: the average Conservative seat share was only 18.9 percent.

Yet Figure 1 reminds us that the 1935 Liberal share of votes was slightly lower than in 1930. In this too the 1935 outcome set the pattern for the next two decades. Although later elections returned the Liberal vote share to levels akin to those in the 1880s and 1890s, the share never reached the level of the early 1900s. The one-sided Liberal parliamentary majorities which typified the second party system were largely artifacts of the electoral system: as Figure 8 indicates, the Liberals enjoyed pluralities – sometimes quite narrow ones in eight of nine provinces.

Ethno-religious Divisions

Just as the Conservatives overplayed the imperial hand in 1917, they continued to do so over the next several decades. Where the country's mood was isolationist in the 1920s and 1930s and diffidently internationalist in the 1940s and 1950s, the Conservatives continued to emphasize the diplomatic unity of the Empire. For instance, when the report of the 1929 Commonwealth Conference which recommended the outlines of the Statute of Westminster, the legal affirmation of Canada's sovereign status, was presented to the House of Commons, Conservative frontbencher C.H. Cahan summed up the essentially negative reaction of his party: "I am persuaded that it is in the best interests of Canada that the British commonwealth of nations, which is commonly known as the British Empire, should remain a subsisting political unit, and not merely a free association of independent states."[15]

In 1938 Sir Arthur Meighen, sometime Conservative leader, tried to rally English-speaking delegates to that year's leadership convention to a military commitment to the Empire. The failure of the attempt alienated some of the party's traditional supporters even as it reminded others of the continued presence of imperialist tendencies in the party. During the Second World War, Conservatives pressed for a forward policy and called repeatedly for the formation of a National Government, a reminder of 1917. An even more chilling reminder was their call for conscription.[16] Even in the 1950s the party's external affairs spokesman, Howard Green, speaking in opposition to the Canadian role in the Suez crisis that brought Lester Pearson a Nobel Peace Prize, could link nostalgia for the Empire to antipathy to the United States.[17]

Commercial Policy

The biggest story of 1930-5 was economic: the Conservatives had the misfortune of being in power for the worst years of the depression. Their early response to the event was instinctual: a raising of tariff barriers and a renewed emphasis on imperial economic consolidation. Only at the end, with the "Bennett New Deal", did they attempt anything innovative. Few of their enemies were persuaded that this was anything other than a deathbed repentance.[18] Tory times came to be seen as hard times. In this respect 1935 reinforced the lessons of 1896 and 1921. This helps explain the Conservative retreat in the country as a whole. It also helps explain part of the geographic differentiation in that retreat: the Depression hit the grain-exporting Prairie provinces hardest of all.[19] The West thus once again became the heartland of insurgency. This time the insurgents persisted: agrarian politics seemed to have come of age.

The agrarian politics case should not be overstated. The only unequivocally agrarian party was Social Credit, a party which was confined to one province and which had little in the way of a program. The CCF had a broader sectional base because it was not, in the end, much of a farmers' party. Only in Saskatchewan could it claim to represent farmers. Elsewhere, and most notably in its other bastion, British Columbia, the CCF had no agrarian pretensions at all. The claim that the CCF could assert everywhere was to represent the organized working class. To this extent the party represented the emergence of an urban class cleavage. In some ways, the party of farmers, workers, and Canadians of all sorts was still the Liberal party. It was strong in each Eastern province. Even though indigenous parties flourished in the West at the expense of both old parties, the Liberals were still the plurality party in most of the region. As a party in parliament, the Liberals were broadly based.

And the Liberals seemed to have learned the lesson of 1911. After that year no government dared submit free trade with the United States to the electorate for another seventy-seven years. The most venturesome gesture by the Liberals after 1935 was to undo tariff increases made by the Conservatives in 1932. In 1948 the Liberal government contemplated accepting an American offer of complete Reciprocity but recoiled before the electoral implications. For the most part, Canadian governments were prepared to shoulder the political risks of general tariff reduction only in a multilateral context, the General Agreement on Tariffs and Trade (GATT).

At the same time, direct support for farmers was an inadmissible issue. One part of the agrarian program that emerged in the 1920s did get embodied in policy: the Canadian Wheat Board was reinstated in 1935. Governments did spend money on field rehabilitation as well. But beyond this neither party, even the Liberal party, was prepared to go.[20] Both parties seemed to regard direct cash support for the sector as verging on immoral. In effect, they tacitly adopted a gag rule.

Two things emerged in the 1950s to upset this equilibrium. First, the grain export sector was plunged into crisis by an international glut. Second, the Conservative party, almost in spite of itself, chose a leader who understood and sympathized with farmers and other primary producers: John Diefenbaker.

The Second Transition

In 1957, Liberal party's overwhelming majority collapsed. In the popular vote, the Liberals lost eight points from 1953 to 1957. The Conservatives, now led by John Diefenbaker, gained a like amount. Although the Liberals still outpolled the Conservatives by two percentage points in 1957, they won fewer seats and were forced to surrender office. This paved they way for the smashing Conservative victory of 1958: the second largest major-party vote surge, 14.7 points,[21] and the second largest popular vote share, 54 percent,[22] in Canadian electoral history.

Some of this second surge came at Liberals' expense, as that party lost seven more points in 1958. The total drop in Liberal share from 1953 to 1958, fifteen points, was one and a half times as large as their drop from 1911 to 1917. Never before had the Liberal share of the national popular vote fallen below 40 percent.

Figure 9: The Second Transition, 1957-62

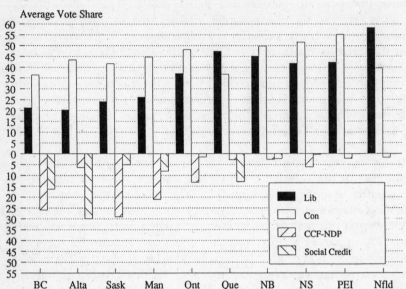

Average Vote Share

BC	Alta	Sask	Man	Ont	Que	NB	NS	PEI	Nfld

Legend:
- Lib
- Con
- CCF-NDP
- Social Credit

The 1958 Liberal share, 34 percent, was not much larger than the average Conservative share had been in its weakest period, 1935-53. If the Liberals suffered, so, according to Figure 3, did the smaller parties. Where virtually all of the Conservatives' 1957 net gain had come from the Liberals, in 1958 over half the gain came from third parties, especially Social Credit.

The geography of the second transition appears in Figure 9. The most striking thing about the Conservatives' transitional geography was its uniformity. Their growth was greatest where they had hitherto been weakest, most notably in the west. This was even true in Quebec, especially in 1958. In that year Mr Diefenbaker assembled a coalition whose sectional makeup was just as diverse as any the Liberals had built in the second party system. The Liberals, for their part, now had a profile like that visited on the Conservatives in the second system: a sharply differentiated one. Now it was the Liberals whose western vote shares were derisory.

Commercial Policy

On commercial policy in particular, John Diefenbaker upped the stakes dramatically. Beginning in 1957-8, the government supported nine commodity prices at 80 percent of their preceding ten-year average; credit facilities were greatly expanded; the Wheat Board began advance payments on the crop; and it sold the crop aggressively.[23] Altogether, direct transfers to Western wheat producers increased more than sevenfold in constant dollars between 1957-8 and 1961-2 and accounted for all the Agriculture department's budget growth. Payments fell back to nil in 1965-6,[24] by which date, significantly, the government was once again Liberal.

Support also went to nonagricultural parts of the primary sector, especially to oil and gas producers. To protect the industry from imports of cheaper oil from Venezuela and the Middle East, the government reserved the bulk of the Ontario market for the high-cost Alberta product. For the first time, Central Canadian consumers were forced to subsidize a western industry which seemed to have no realistic prospect of comparative advantage in the world market.

None of this meant that the Conservative party was about to abandon its commitment to the National Policy and to the ethos which supported it. John Diefenbaker was no more inclined toward closer ties with America than was the man with whose shade he seemed to be in constant contact, Sir John A. Macdonald. A compelling example was his refusal to countenance export of electricity generated on the Columbia River. Instead, Mr Diefenbaker committed his party to protection all around. But the sectional and sectoral reorientation that Mr Diefenbaker had effected, for exquisitely protectionist reasons, prepared his party to abandon the National Policy.

The Third Party System:

The Tory millennium was not to be: the Conservatives proceeded to dissipate most of their gains. Where their 1957-58 popular vote gain was the second largest to that point by any party in Canadian history, their 1958-62 drop of 16.3 points was the third largest.[25] Some of the rest of the 1958 margin was squandered in 1963. For all that, Mr Diefenbaker left his party better off than when he found it. The Conservative vote share from 1963 to 1980 averaged 33.6 percent, about four points higher than the party's average from 1935 to 1953.

The modesty of the Conservatives' net gain from the second

Figure 10: The Third Party System, 1963-80

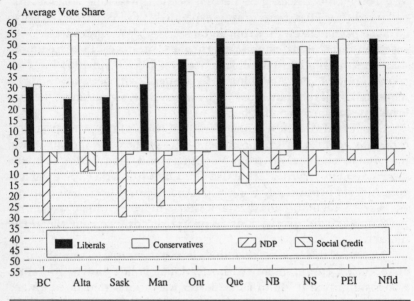

Average Vote Share

Legend: Liberals, Conservatives, NDP, Social Credit

BC Alta Sask Man Ont Que NB NS PEI Nfld

system to the third masked its significance. The Conservative base was not just widened, it was reshaped, as Figure 10 indicates. Now it was the Conservatives who played the ends against the middle: their support was greatest in the maritime and prairie provinces. From 1962 to 1980 the Conservatives were the dominant party in Prince Edward Island and Nova Scotia. Conservative margins there were typically rather narrow, however, and their strength in the region was a legacy as much of Robert Stanfield of Nova Scotia, Tory leader from 1967 to 1976, as of Mr Diefenbaker.

The truly dramatic contrasts with the second party system were in the three prairie provinces. Alberta, Saskatchewan, and Manitoba did not desert the Conservatives in 1962-3. Over the 1962-80 period, Manitoba and Saskatchewan gave the Conservatives only a slightly smaller share than did Nova Scotia and Prince Edward Island.[26] Alberta, which under the first two party systems had been a Conservative graveyard, became by far the most one-sidedly Conservative place in the country.

The Conservative party now often enjoyed pluralities in six provinces: British Columbia (from 1972 on), Alberta, Saskatchewan (especially in the early years), Manitoba, Nova Scotia, and Prince Edward Island. These were, to be sure, provinces of only medium to small weight. But that the Conservatives could return a plurality in any province was a significant shift from the second party system. And the Conservatives remained competitive in Ontario. Thus even though popular vote gains outside Quebec were offset by losses in Quebec and the net shift made to seem small, Conservative vote gains and losses were efficiently distributed and the party made a significant net gain in seats. While in the second system, the Conservatives typically won less than 20 percent of House seats, in the third system their usual seat share was 30 to 35 percent.

The history of the Liberal party in this period was one of recovery, although an exceedingly fitful one. The party's average share over the 1962, 1963, and 1965 elections was 39.7. In the two minority victories of 1963 and 1965 the share barely cleared 40 percent. Only with Pierre Trudeau's accession to leadership did the Liberal popular vote bring the party in range of parliamentary majorities. In Mr Trudeau's five elections the Liberal share averaged 42.3 percent. His very best outing was his first, in which the party pulled in 45.5 percent. Contrast this with Liberal shares before 1957: down to that year there were only four (out of nineteen) elections in which the Liberal share was lower than the party's average share under Mr Trudeau.[27]

As the Liberal base shrank overall, relative to the second party system, so did it contract geographically. As was true in the second party system, Liberal support followed an east-west gradient. But west of Ontario the gradient was now very steep indeed, just as steep as in the 1957-62 transition. The Liberal drop was especially marked in Manitoba and Saskatchewan.[28] In the third system the Liberals held pluralities, typically, in only four provinces: Newfoundland and the three contiguous provinces of New Brunswick, Ontario, and Quebec. In the third party system, the Liberal party made its stand in its traditional core, a zone which might thought of as Catholic Canada. Fortunately for the Liberals, this zone continued to be the country's demographic centre of gravity.

In part, then, the narrowing of the Liberal base complemented the modest broadening of the Conservative one that was Mr Diefenbaker's legacy. But Liberal weakness also reflected the strength of two new-old political forces, one a temporary rival, the other a more serious long-term threat. The short-term problem was Social Credit, the long-term one the NDP.

Social Credit recovered in 1962. But its recovery took place in the very heartland of the Liberal party. Thanks to Quebec, Social Credit's national share grew to 11.7 percent. It edged up a little further in 1963 but then began an inexorable decline. By 1968 Social Credit had, to all intents and purposes, disappeared outside Quebec. By 1980, the party was effectively wiped off the map inside that province. As long as it lasted, Social Credit was a reminder that the Liberal base in Quebec could not be taken for granted. Merely by existing, Social Credit inhibited the Liberal recovery from the 1958 debacle. The weakness of Liberal governments before 1968 was partly a result of the Social Credit presence. The strength (by comparison with 1963-65) of the Liberals under Mr Trudeau was mainly the result Social Credit's marginalization.

The NDP, formed in 1961 out of the remains of the CCF, could not be marginalized. The contrast between the NDP and the CCF is instructive. The CCF's impact was limited; indeed its primary effect may have been to inflate the Liberals' seat share. Apart from the surge in 1945, the party's vote share never got above the low teens. Although 1957 and 1958 were poor years for the CCF, they were not much worse than 1953 had been. The NDP was a significant player from the very beginning of the third system. The 1962 election brought the highest CCF/NDP share, apart from 1945, to that date. The NDP stepped up about another four points in 1965 and stayed at the new level (17-18 percent) until 1972. The 1974 election brought a reverse which was more than made up in 1979, and 1980 brought the party close to the 20 percent level. This was nearly twice the average CCF share. Figure 3 also drives home that the variation in this share was mainly in the form of a gradual positive trend. The NDP share was resilient: not likely to surge much, perhaps, but not likely to decline much either. The NDP reached this eminence in spite of the single-member-plurality electoral system's powerful pressures to the contrary.

The NDP base grew by both broadening and deepening. Figure 10 indicates that in the third party system the NDP was a stronger competitor than the CCF in two provinces, Manitoba and British Columbia, and remained strong in the CCF's bastion, Saskatchewan. By 1980 the NDP had become the Conservatives' main rival in the West.

Although the NDP fills up much more of the space in the West than the CCF did, it is not as peculiarly a party of that region. For the CCF and NDP, the other important shift from the second to the third party system was NDP strength in Ontario. Before 1957 Ontario returned, on average, a smaller CCF share than Alberta did. In the third system, in contrast, Ontario gave the NDP around one vote in five, close to the national average share. And even if this share was only two-thirds of the typical Saskatchewan or British Columbia share, the raw number of votes represented by Ontario was enormous.

The NDP's new-found strength in Ontario (and British Columbia, for that matter) represented the injection of class politics into the third party system. Neither of the old parties could readily displace the NDP's connection to the union movement.[29] At the same time, in spite of the NDP's attempt to stake a pan-regional claim, the party was still concentrated disproportionately in the west. But the new geography meant that the NDP could convert votes into seats. Indeed, now it did so much more efficiently than in the second system.

Thus the third system was characterised by competition that seemed close but, for all that, futile. It was close by comparison with the second system, where only the Liberal party could claim to be a national party. The Liberals won every election hands down and faced only a weak opposition. In the third system, no party was truly national. The Liberal party could no longer command regular pluralities virtually everywhere outside Quebec. But by comparison with the first system, the competition was futile. In both versions of the first system the subordinate party was never far behind. If the third system saw the Conservatives edge closer to the Liberals than they had been in the second system, they were still much further back than the opposition was in the first system. The Conservatives had become the dominant party in English Canada again, but their ability to generate support in Quebec declined in 1962 and diminished still more as the third system matured. The Conservatives thus were still only barely feasible as a single-party government.

Figure 11 brings out the sectional foundations of the impasse. It illustrates the critical role of Quebec in forming governments. In recent decades Quebec seats have constituted about 25 percent of the House. In earlier years the share was closer to 30 percent. If a party could control nearly all of Quebec's seats it would already be halfway to a parliamentary majority. Figure 11 indicates that whenever Quebec Liberals make up 18 percent or more of the House, the Liberals form the government; the one exception to this rule is 1979. As it happens, Quebec seats have tended to come en bloc. The secret for Quebec has not been that all Quebeckers vote

Figure 11: Quebec in the Liberal Coalition

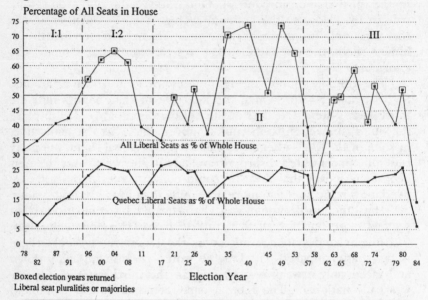

Percentage of All Seats in House

Boxed election years returned
Liberal seat pluralities or majorities

Election Year

the same way. It is true that there have been periods in which
Quebec vote distributions were very skewed and the later years of
the third system happened to be one such period. But the Liberals'
first-system bloc in Quebec was based on quite a narrow popular
majority in the province, as Figure 5 indicated. Modest though the
1882-96 vote swing was, Figure 11 makes clear that it accounted for
almost all of the seat gains the Liberals made in the 1880s and
1890s. Only later did English Canada swing toward the Liberals,
mainly through the addition of western seats to the Liberal total.
For most of this century Quebec seats have gone almost exclusively
to Liberals. This has been so even in the face of fluctuations in
the Liberal vote share in that province. For instance, the Quebec
landslides in and after 1917 did not net the party many more seats
than it had already locked up with the modest majorities of the first
system. Quebec was not always the numerically preponderant element in the Liberal party; in the second system the Liberal coalition
was remarkably broad. But Quebec was the insurance policy: even
when the Liberal party suffered sharp reverses in English Canada,
its Quebec bloc maintained the Liberals as a serious player in the
parliamentary game. In the 1920s, Quebec seats made up a good

half of the Liberal total. This was commonly true once again in the third system.

For the Conservatives to form even a minority government the popular reaction in English Canada against the Liberals had to be extraordinarily intense and a very big fraction of any anti-Liberal swing had to go exclusively to the Tories. But limiting the Conservatives' growth was the NDP. Although the NDP was never feasible in this period as a government, it became steadily more important in a negative sense. It almost always barred the Conservatives' way to pluralities and it often blocked the Liberals from majorities.

Thus, although the Liberals were almost always in government over this period, they were so on a kind of sufferance. Thanks to Conservative renewal and NDP growth, Liberal governments were denied the vote and seat margins typical of earlier periods. Three of their six victories and seven of their roughly twenty years in government were as a minority. Each election in which the Liberals gained votes was followed by an election in which they lost votes (except for the similarly feeble 1963 and 1965 pluralities). No Liberal seat majority was followed by another Liberal majority. As Figure 6 shows, governments in the 1960s and 1970s were even more weakly based than those in the transitional period of the 1920s. What was a symptom of crisis in the 1920s was, in the 1970s, politics as usual.

Ethno-religious Divisions

One element in the geography of the third-system Conservative vote John Diefenbaker's populism. This allowed the Conservative party to preempt the populist impulses that had earlier threatened the two-party alignment. But the legacy, in common with earlier manifestations of populism, was ethnically and religiously narrow.

Before John Diefenbaker, populism and the Conservative party were antithetical. A party of Eastern business could hardly be expected to espouse the interests – not to mention the sentiments – of small producers on the resource frontier. Given this mutual antipathy in economics, a pan-regional coalition could appear only in moments of extreme stress, as happened, for example, in 1917. By 1960, stress was mounting and the situation was ripe for change. By giving resource producers most of what they wanted, Mr Diefenbaker abolished the antipathy in economics at a stroke.

At the same time, the Anglo-Protestant definition of the country was increasingly on the defensive. In the 1920s, notwithstanding the emergence of a new, non-imperialist form of nationalism, most politically active Protestant Canadians agreed that the country was British, somehow. Similarly, even if they might disagree over just how much Canada owed the Empire, none seriously believed that Canada's and the Empire's interests would actually clash. By 1960 this consensus had been shattered. Internally, the country was awakening to its growing diversity and the strongest challenge to the British definition of the country came from Quebec. Externally, the Suez crisis seems to have been a watershed. Many in English Canada were stunned when their government sided with America against Britain and when their Prime Minister, a francophone Catholic, referred pejoratively to Britain and France as "the supermen of Europe".[30]

Practically speaking such pro-British sentiment may have been unsustainable nostalgia. Whereas in 1911 the Empire was a living entity, in the 1950s the influence of its successor, the Commonwealth, was clearly waning, and by the 1970s the old imperialism was only a memory, for many an embarrassing one. But nostalgia did help to broaden the Conservative base, not just in the wake of 1956 but in reaction to Liberal initiatives after 1963. The Conservative party gathered to itself the agrarian and anti-party sentiment that earlier had fuelled third-party movements. Ironically, the Conservatives moved themselves closer to power by preempting the agenda of those who feared power the most and who saw parties as vehicles by which minorities combined to frustrate the wishes of natural majorities.

The Liberal recovery from the debacle of 1958 was engineered by a group of middle class reformers, mainly from Toronto. They moved the party to the left on social and economic policy and tailored its appeal to a more specifically urban clientele. They centralized the party's operations, by creating direct links between the constituencies and the leader and national office; squeezed out were provincial notables, the people who had traditionally been the party's brokers.

The Liberals also grasped the nettle of an issue which was awakening, the place of French Canada in the larger national scheme. For most of the third party system only they succeeded in doing anything creative in relation to French Canada. The Liberals also set out to reshape the symbolism of the polity. The British features of public life were downplayed and emphasis fell instead on ethnic diversity as a value in its own right. Bilingual and multicultural emphases suited the Liberal party's traditional ethnic bases well. But it alienated many others who in earlier years had supported the Liberal party for lack of an alternative.[31]

Commercial Policy

As the party of government, the Liberals made the first post-1963 move. They preempted the Conservatives' traditional control of the nationalist pole. Liberal nationalism advanced on two fronts: an increased commitment to protection for secondary industry and an attack on the primary sector. One front, investment policy, looked to the enemy without. Now it was the Liberals, not the Conservatives, who worried publicly about the weight of (mainly) American investment. As the government, Liberals were in a position to act on the concern, with the establishment in 1974 of the Foreign Investment Review Agency (FIRA), with a mandate to review foreign takeovers of Canadian firms. The other front was internal, pitting energy producers against energy consumers. In the 1960s energy producers were grateful for the protection, in maintained prices and reserved markets, that Mr Diefenbaker had given them. In the 1970s the protection no longer seemed necessary. Indeed the policy instruments created to provide it now were turned against the sector in a bitter struggle over rent created by the oil price increases.[33] This culminated in the National Energy Program (NEP) of 1980, which sought to reduce foreign ownership in the oil and gas sector and to increase the federal government's share of energy rents (Safarian, 1985; James, 1990).

Conservatives opposed all of this. They promised to loosen FIRA regulations and did so once in power. They fought the NEP in Parliament and through their control of the key energy province, Alberta. At one point in 1982 they brought Parliament to a halt. In power, they abrogated the NEP's most objectionable features. But they remained silent on free trade. Protection of manufactures had, after all, been their policy, one of the party's constitutive values. It had derived warrant not just on economic grounds but also as an expression of mutually reinforcing national and imperial interests. An attack on the National Policy had been vulnerable to being styled as an attack on the British definition of the nationality and on the connection which sustained it. But there lay the rub: the Empire had disappeared. Conservatives' evaluation of commercial policy now had to be detached from imperial considerations. The remaining considerations that the party found congenial argued against protection. The party was poised to shift.

The Burden of History

The Liberal party dominated three electoral alignments and was the presumptive party of government for nearly a century, an extraordinary record of longevity. Over the entire period, the Conservative party was the only serious alternative. The Canadian system thus was the only 19th century one, apart from the American party system, to survive into the late twentieth century with its major features more or less intact.

But the Conservative position often seemed tenuous. As parliamentary oppositions go it has been weak. It never came close to victory from 1896 to 1908 and from 1935 to 1953. Between 1963 and 1984 it held power for less than a year. Conservative breakthroughs tended to come only at the punctuation points between party systems. Their success reflected accumulated grievances and their electoral coalitions never were sustainable. Two episodes of power (1911-21 and 1930-5) left them much worse off. Only one (1957-63) left them better off. Even after 1963, the party did not seem poised to form the government.

Although Liberals dominated the entire period, each transition weakened their base. The shrinkage over the first transition ultimately was small and was more than compensated for by the fractionalization of the rest of the popular vote. But it hinted at shifts to come. The second transition had a major impact on the Liberals' base. And in the third system, the Liberal share was typically smaller than the opposition share had been in the first system. The Liberal share was usually just large enough to ensure a parliamentary plurality or majority but not large enough to generate the overwhelming Liberal majorities that had typified the second system.

Each transition brought permanent third-party gains. The key to this permanence was the appearance of a party of the left, first the CCF, later the NDP. The CCF and NDP aside, third party activity was episodic, was often an expression of distaste for the party battle itself and for the grubby compromises of government, and was commonly linked to agrarian discontent.

In the first system, the foundation of Liberal dominance was a combination of Quebec, Catholics outside Quebec, and (towards the end) the two new wheat producing provinces of Alberta and Saskatchewan. The second system was more complex and more polarized. Quebec became more thoroughly Liberal while the Liberal share in the Prairie West shrank modestly. That the Liberals could retreat in the popular vote outside Quebec and yet add to their seats was testimony to the Conservatives' abject weakness: the Tory vote collapsed in both Quebec and the West. The vacuum in the West was filled by new parties, the CCF and Social Credit. The second party system thus brought a sharpening of divisions along the lines which, in a modest way, had controlled choice in the first system: between Catholics (including the French) and Protestants; and between wheat-producing and manufacturing regions. The third system raised electoral polarization to a new level. This polarization produced an endemic parliamentary weakness for all parties. The Liberal party retained and even strengthened its domination of Quebec while the Western part of its coalition evaporated. Its inheritors were the Conservatives and the NDP. Now, no party straddled Canada's traditional cultural and economic boundaries very well. In addition, the third system brought a third cleavage: a union/non-union division. Growth of the NDP was tied in part to the increased importance of this division. When the NDP articulates a class perspective, it must be taken seriously. The same could rarely be said of the CCF.

Confined socially and geographically though they now were, the Liberals could still govern. The provinces in which they remained strong were the demographically dominant ones. If the Liberal base outside Quebec was now more than ever confined to Catholics and to new Canadians, these groups were bigger than ever. The Conservatives dominated the largest (even if shrinking) groups in English Canada. The narrowing of the Liberal base outside Quebec did mean that the party had lost most of its cushion against an electoral reverse. A small popular vote swing would decimate its modest share of seats in English Canada, as happened in 1972 and 1979 (Figure 2-12). But such a decimation would still not give the Conservatives a majority. The Liberals held a trump: Quebec.

References

Allen, Richard. 1971. *The Social Passion: Religion and Social Reform in Canada 1914-28.* Toronto: University of Toronto Press.

Archer, Keith. 1985. "The Failure of the New Democratic Party: Unions, Unionists, and Politics in Canada" *Canadian Journal of Political Science* 18: 353-66.

Berelson, Bernard R., Paul F. Lazarsfeld, and William N. McPhee. 1954. *Voting.*

Chicago: University of Chicago Press.

Berthelet, D. 1985. "Agriculture Canada Policy and Expenditure Patterns 1868-1983." *Canadian Farm Economics* 19: 5-15.

Bliss, J.M. 1968. "The Methodist Church and World War I." *Canadian Historical Review* 49. Reprinted in Carl Berger, ed., Conscription 1917. Toronto: University of Toronto Press, n.d.

Bothwell, Robert, Ian Drummond, and John English. 1981. *Canada Since 1945: Power, Politics, and Provincialism.* Toronto: University of Toronto Press.

Carty, R. Kenneth. 1988. "Three Canadian Party Systems: An Interpretation of the Development of National Politics," in George C. Perlin, ed., *Party Democracy in Canada; The Politics of National Party Conventions.* Scarborough: Prentice-Hall.

Colvin, J.A. 1955. "Sir Wilfrid Laurier and the British Preferential Tariff System." Canadian Historical Association, Report. Reprinted in Carl Berger, ed. *Imperial Relations in the Age of Laurier.* Toronto: University of Toronto Press, 1969, pp. 34-44.

Drummond, Ian M. 1974. *Imperial Economic Policy 1917-1939: Studies in Expansion and Protection.* Toronto: University of Toronto Press.

Ellis, L.E. 1939. *Reciprocity 1911.* New Haven: Yale University Press.

Fowke, V.C. 1957. *The National Policy and the Wheat Economy.* Toronto: University of Toronto Press.

Grant, George. 1965. *Lament for a Nation: The Defeat of Canadian Nationalism.* Toronto: McClelland and Stewart.

Horowitz, Gad. 1968. *Canadian Labour in Politics.* Toronto: University of Toronto Press.

Johnston, Richard and Michael B. Percy. 1980. "Reciprocity, Imperial Sentiment, and Party Politics in the 1911 Election." *Canadian Journal of Political Science* 13: 711-729.

Kent, Tom. 1988. *A Public Purpose: An Experience of Liberal Opposition and Canadian Government.* Montreal: McGill-Queen's University Press.

Lipset, Seymour Martin. 1968. *Agrarian Socialism.* New York: Doubleday.

Lipset, Seymour Martin and Stein Rokkan. 1967. *Party Systems and Voter Alignments.* New York: Free Press.

Mackintosh, W.A. 1964. *The Economic Background of Dominion-Provincial Relations.* Toronto: McClelland and Stewart [Carleton Library Edition].

Marr, William L. and Donald G. Paterson. 1980. *Canada: an Economic History.* Toronto: Macmillan.

Morton, W.L. 1950. *The Progressive Party in Canada* Toronto: University of Toronto Press.

Penlington, Norman. 1965. *Canada and Imperialism 1896-1899.* Toronto: University of Toronto Press.

Robinson, Judith. 1957. *This is on the House.* Toronto: McClelland and Stewart.

Skogstad, Grace. 1987. *The Politics of Agricultural Policy-Making in Canada.* Toronto: University of Toronto Press.

Smith, Denis. 1973. *Gentle Patriot: A Political Biography of Walter Gordon.* Edmonton: Hurtig.

Smith, David E. 1981. *The Regional Decline of a National Party: Liberals on the Prairies.* Toronto: University of Toronto Press.

————. 1985. "Party Government, Representation, and National Integration in Canada'" in Peter Aucoin, ed. *Party Government and Regional Representation in Canada.* Toronto: University of Toronto Press.

Stacey, C.P. 1977. *Canada and the Age of Conflict,* Vol. 1: 1867-1921. Toronto: University of Toronto Press.

————. 1981. *Canada and the Age of Conflict,* Vol. 2: 1921-1948. Toronto: University of Toronto Press.

Waite, Peter B. 1971. *Canada 1874-1896: Arduous Destiny.* Toronto: McClelland and Stewart.

Ward, Norman and David Smith. 1990. *Jimmy Gardiner: Relentless Liberal.* Toronto: University of Toronto Press.

Wearing, Joseph. 1981. *The L-Shaped Party: The Liberal Party of Canada 1958-1980.* Toronto: McGraw-Hill Ryerson.

Wilbur, J.R.H. 1964. "H.H. Stevens and the Reconstruction Party." *Canadian Historical Review* 45. Reprinted in Ramsay Cook, ed. *Politics of Discontent.* Toronto: University of Toronto Press, 1967.

Young, Walter D. 1969. *The Anatomy of a Party: The National* CCF. Toronto: University of Toronto Press.

Notes

1   This generalization, of course, has its exceptions. Two language-community issues which figured prominently in national politics in the early period were the controversy in 1885-6 over the execution of the leader of the Northwest Rebellion, Louis Riel, and the debate over whether French should be an official language in the North-West Territories, which came to a head in 1890.

2   It remained so through the 1941 census.

3   The winner is here defined as the party that won a plurality of seats. Once, in 1925, the plurality winner, the Conservatives, did not form the government. Also plotted for this series is the winner's-share average for each of four periods, 1878-1917, 1921-30, 193558, and 1962-80. Note that the 1962-80 average is projected through 1984.

4   On the South African War, see Stacey (1977) and Penlington (1965). Laurier's position on Canada's entry into World War I and King's handling of the advent of Second World War both showed a preoccupation with the lessons of 1899. On these see, respectively, Stacey (1977) and Stacey (1981).

5   A good capsule account of the 1891 election is Waite (1971), pp. 221-7.

6   The tariff reductions were not, strictly speaking, exclusive to the Empire. The legislation offered reciprocal reductions to any country willing to match them. The United States was not among these as it had just enacted the Dingley tariff. Britain was granted the preference by virtue of its standing policy of free trade. For some Liberals the legislation was appealing as an inducement to American reciprocation. For others the unlikelihood of the latter was a considerable relief. For all, the imperial gloss was no less happy for being something of an accident. See Colvin (1955).

7   On the American side, the incentive for the agreement seems to have been to give a sop to Progressives, who were still smarting from the enactment of the Payne-Aldrich tariff. The classic source on the agreement is Ellis (1939).

8   But see Johnston and Percy (1980).

9   The period-average entry in Figure 2 is calculated for the 1896-1911 period. It did not make sense to include 1917 itself the calculation. It made visual sense, though, to carry the 1896-1911 average through to 1917 to put the 1917 and 1921 results in proper perspective.

10   Stacey (1981), p. 235.

11   Lipset (1968) is a useful review of anti-party tendencies in agrarian politics.

12   See Allen (1971), Bliss (1968), and Morton (1950).

13   Fowke (1957), p. 169ff.

14   Perhaps it would be more correct to say, after Young (1969), that the CCF and NDP, although styling themselves as much movement as party, also accepted, or had influential cadres who accepted, the necessity of being a party.

15   Quoted in Stacey (1981), at p. 119.

16   On the prewar and wartime period, see Granatstein (1967).

17   Bothwell, et al. (1981), p. 145.

18   On early economic policy see Drummond (1974). On the Bennett New Deal see Wilbur (1964).

19   The fall in grain prices was accompanied by drought in much of the region. And recovery was slower in agriculture than elsewhere. See Marr and Paterson (1980), pp. 393-4.

20   See Ward and Smith (1990) for a poignant account of the waning influence of the Minister of Agriculture, Jimmy Gardiner, in the King and St. Laurent cabinets.

21   The 1957-58 swing of + 14.7 points was second only to the + 16.3 gain from 1921 to 1925. Confining our attention to 1958 understates the shift: from 1953 to 1958 the total Conservative surge was 23 points.

22   The largest, at 57 percent, was in 1917. This comparison is unfair to 1958, as Mr Diefenbaker's landslide had no taint of coalition about it.

23   The 1963-4 export volume was 550 million bushels. Never before had Canadian exports exceeded 400 million bushels.

24   Berthelet (1985), p.11. See also Skogstad (1987) and Bothwell, et al., (1981).

25   The largest drop, of 26.7 points, came in 1921. The 1917 Conservative share included returns for Liberal Unionists. The second largest drop, of 19.1 points, was from 1930 to 1935.

26   The full-period average disguises a Conservative slippage in those provinces, however, following Mr Diefenbaker's displacement as leader.

27   These were the elections of 1917, 1921, 1925, and 1945.

28   They dropped in Alberta and British Columbia as well but not by a greater margin than in the rest of English Canada. These had been provinces of chronic Liberal weakness for many decades.

29   The case here needs to made very carefully. The NDP was – and is – not the majority or even the plurality choice among union households. But union households made up a clear majority of NDP supporters and affiliation by a local is an major factor in the NDP share in the corresponding ridings (Archer, 1985).

30   See for instance the acerbic commentary on Suez in Robinson (1957) and in Grant (1965). Bothwell et al. (1981), report a Gallup poll which indicated that a majority of Canadians support˜d the Anglo-French invasion of Egypt.

31   This account of the Liberal transformation is a synthesis of Wearing (1981), Smith (1973), Smith (1981), and Kent (1988).

32   In the 1970s, Canada maintained domestic oil prices below world levels. Eastern Canadian consumption of offshore oil was subsidized by a tax equivalent to the difference between the domestic and world prices levied on exports to the United States from the West, mainly Alberta. This scheme was roughly self-financing as long as Canadian exports and imports were in balance. As the 1970s progressed the trade in oil went out of balance and the fiscal foundations of the policy were undermined.

33   FIRA was renamed Investment Canada. At the renaming the government announced that "Canada [was] open for business."

34   Although the Conservatives' parliamentary share in 1979 was close to a majority, the party's popular vote share was rather smaller than the Liberals'. Indeed, the 1979 Conservative vote, 36 percent, was the smallest for any seat plurality winner in Canadian history.

35   This is not to deny that the NDP has also sought consciously to moderate its appeal. Still, there is no mistaking the direction from which the moderation proceeds.

R.K. Carty On the Road Again: The Stalled Omnibus Revisited

On the road again
Going places that I've never been
Seein' things that I may never see again
I just can't wait to get on the road again

Willie Nelson

"...the rather curious two-plus party system will continue for some time. I expect that minority governments will alternate with those enjoying fairly substantial majorities."

John Meisel 1963

At the end of a striking essay penned amidst the parliamentary confusion that marked the Diefenbaker-Pearson years, John Meisel made what will surely go down as one of the most famous predictions of Canadian political science. Famous because it was so startling, because it exploited an explicitly functionalist model to interpret the impact of ongoing social change on the working of the national party system, and famous because it proved so prescient.

Consider this last point first. In the eight national general elections held in Canada since Meisel predicted that, despite a well established tradition of relatively long periods of one-party rule and stable parliamentar, majorities, a wholly new pattern of government would become the norm, the outcomes were as follows:

1965	Liberal	*minority*
1968	Liberal	MAJORITY
1972	Liberal	*minority*
1974	Liberal	MAJORITY
1979	Conservative	*minority*
1980	Liberal	MAJORITY
1984	Conservative	MAJORITY
1988	Conservative	MAJORITY

Thus, for two decades the Canadian political world unfolded in a quite new way, just as Meisel had said it would. And then when the system finally appeared to revert to the "normality" of successive majority governments, it was the Progressive Conservatives that actually managed it. Given that the Tories had not accomplished that feat since Macdonald's victories a full century earlier, Meisel had been rather less surprising when he had suggested that such a "national comeback [was] unthinkable" unless the party developed new leadership and "extend[ed] its slender foothold in Quebec." Yet that is precisely what the Conservatives had achieved by 1984, and then sustained in the general election of 1988.

What made the prediction so startling was just this idea that the traditional Canadian party and electoral system could no longer be counted on to produce the parliamentary majorities generally assumed necessary to its successful operation. After all Canadians had little experience with minority government, and not much of that was positive. In the aftermath of the 1925 general election a minority parliament led to a constitutional crisis, the King-Byng affair. In the early 1960s Mr. Diefenbaker's disastrous minority government, which had ended with a cabinet revolt, provided the backdrop against which Meisel was writing. The only other minorities, in 1921 and 1957, were seen as transitional peculiarities, not aspects of normal politics. The idea that a whole new kind of parliamentary politics might be developing was unsettling. As Meisel put it, one could only think of the Canadian party system as "on probation."

But if the prediction was startling it was also satisfying. The image of the stalled omnibus seemed to capture the collapse of brokerage politics which conventional wisdom taught was the essence of Canadian party competition. Given that national elections have now delivered three successive majority governments are we to conclude that the party system is working again? Are the historic parties, those "great, nation-wide, easy going omnibus vehicles" which had stalled, now up and running—on the road again? We can start thinking about this by returning to Meisel's analysis of how and why the Canadian party system functioned as it did.

Meisel's Party System

Meisel has never been one to focus on narrow, technical issues. His work is infused with a concern for the big questions: the health of the federation, the state of Canadian democracy, the appropriateness of our public policies, the ability of free citizens to shape their communal existence. In this he has been preoccupied with political parties, and the national party system. For Meisel, parties are the primary institution which tie Canadians together and link them to the state; the condition of the party system may be an indicator of our capacity for democratic government but it is also a reflection of the health of the polity. Thus its functioning has been a recurring theme in his work. In the 1960s his *Stalled Omnibus* essay sought to "probe into the reasons for the current impasse...[and]...the present crisis in Canadian federalism." In the 1970s a paper on the *Decline of Party*, worried about "the declining role of parliament and hence party politics in Canada's political system," and again, at the end of the 1980s, he returned to the problem with an analysis of the *Dysfunctions of Canadian Parties* that sought to map those "activities [of parties] which weaken or undermine the political system."

In the debate over whether ideas, institutions or social forces best explain the pattern and character of party politics Meisel's presumption is that it is the latter. In the *Stalled Omnibus* he staked out his position clearly: "I accept L. Lipson's conclusion that 'parties appear to be the product of their society and are only secondarily the offshoot of governmental institutions'." As important supporting evidence for this perspective he points particularly to Canadian experience: he argues that the two-party party system functioned perfectly well for half a century (1867-1917), and when it failed there were no electoral system or other institutional changes that might convincingly account for its collapse. In this he is suggesting that quite different patterns of party politics, that is different party systems, characterized Canadian politics before and after the period surrounding World War I. This is an important point we shall return to.

For all his acceptance of the primacy of social forces in shaping party politics, Meisel has never been one to downplay the role of politicians or to treat them as mere epiphenomena. It is they who must mediate between social change and political organization and action. In the *Stalled Omnibus* he can be found deploring the "decline in political skill" of Canadian politicians, seeing in this change at least a short-run factor in the parliamentary chaos of the early 1960s. This was a theme Meisel returned to in several papers, in particular his oft cited *Howe, Hubris and '72*. What makes this element of the analysis so important to him is the functional task Meisel assigns the national parties, and by extension the politicians who direct them.

By adopting functionalism as his principal analytic framework Meisel moved beyond describing party competition to ask about the consequences of the party system for the health of the Canadian political community. This led to a preoccupation with the system's 'latent functions' which were too often invisible to other observers. It was precisely this elaboration of the latent functions that brought Meisel to his most perceptive insights. And it is with these latent functions that we must concern ourselves.

In classic analyses of party alignments that rest on a social cleavage model, parties constitute the machinery of political division. Their principal latent function is to articulate the distinctive interests of classes, religious, ethnic or other social groups and to stimulate conflict amongst them. The party system mirrors, but also perpetuates, the salience of particular lines of social cleavage. In John Meisel's Canada, however, the perspective we are given of parties is almost completely reversed, not because social divisions are insufficiently politicized but because the very existence of a common community that can safely be divided is itself at issue.

The *Stalled Omnibus* starts with the proposition that Canada has not much "underlying group cohesion," has not developed much of a "secular political culture," or, to put it more baldly, that "Canadians are hardly a nation." From this we are led to the assertion that "in these circumstances, one of the chief and most important latent functions of the political parties and the party system is to foster and develop a sense of national unity and national being" (p. 370). Thus, rather than articulating and defending the particular interests of their distinctive social constituencies, Canadian parties are driven to obscure the differences and muffle conflicting interests in the name of accommodation and the promotion of a national community. Parties, despite their very nature (and name) are charged with nation-building. The reason for this, Meisel argues, is simple: "parties are among the relatively few genuinely national forces in Canada" (p. 370).

How does the party system do this? The answer is by acting "as a broker of ideas, or of class and regional interests...to create a national consensus" (p. 369). This is, of course, the famous brokerage theory of Canadian politics. It leads us directly to the image of national parties as great omnibus vehicles "whose occupants often have difficulty recognizing their fellow passengers or in understanding why the driver of the bus let them in." It is among the most powerful and compelling images in Canadian politics because it provides a ready account for both the character of Canadian parties—their heterogeneous social bases, and for their characteristic operating code—a relentless search for unthreatening accommodation.

This metaphor assigns the bus driver a key role. Thus it is the party leader who is responsible for assuring the bus travels all the necessary roads and collects sufficient passengers to sustain a coalition capable of governing the country. Of all the bus drivers of this century the rather small grey Mackenzie King was the most successful. His strategy was to fill the Liberal bus, to accept the "regional and cultural particularisms instead of defying them" (Wearing, 1981 citing Neatby). (Presumably it was in this role as bus driver that King complained that Canada was a country with too much geography. After all the voters forced him to travel to five different seats—in Prince Edward Island, Ontario, and Saskatchewan—spread across all three of the English-speaking regions of his Canada.)

The stalled omnibus was thus the party that was no longer capable of operating as national broker. It was no longer capable of gathering within its own confines enough of the differing interests to build a parliamentary majority. Had the driver simply made a terrible error and driven off the road? Meisel's analysis of the decline of the politician's craft suggests that he believed that this was a significant factor, but his social determinism inevitably led him to another conclusion. "The underlying causes for the difficulties experienced by the parties," he wrote, "lie in important changes affecting Canadian society" (p. 378).

There can be little doubt that Canadian society was undergoing marked cultural and rapid demographic change in the years after the Second World War. But of all of them it was the quiet revolution in Quebec that Meisel saw as presenting Canada with its most important political challenge. Most immediately it was the desertion of large numbers of Quebec voters to Social Credit in 1962 that disrupted national party politics, deprived the Liberals of their expected victories in 1963 and 1965, and set in train the series of minority governments. In effect it was the break-up of a solid Quebec that stalled the old Liberal omnibus.

Brokerage politics, if that is what we want to label Mackenzie King style regional coalition building, there may have been. But the Canadian party system since World War I had not been one of brokerage parties. There had only been one party capable of playing that role, and as long as brokerage was the pattern of party governance demanded by the system (Smith, 1985) then only Liberals could

Table 1: Regional Composition of the Electorate (%)

	Atl.	P.Q.	Ont.	Pr.	B.C.
1878	24.1	26.4	48.7		
1900	20.5	25.0	44.9	6.8	2.8
1921	15.0	25.4	36.3	18.2	4.9
1953	13.0	27.4	34.0	17.1	8.3
1988	9.0	26.5	35.5	16.8	11.6

operate a genuine omnibus. The Conservatives were denied this possibility by having excluded themselves from Quebec in 1917 and by being excluded from the prairies in the 1920s (they won 4 and 7 per cent respectively of those regions' seats in the three elections of the 1920s; 2.5 and 7 per cent in three during the 1940s). They were effectively left a party of Ontario. Of the enduring third parties, the CCF rejected brokerage in principle, while Social Credit was simply the national voice of politically isolated Alberta.

So the stalled omnibus was really the stalled Liberal party. Its central brokerage function had been the nation-building task of maintaining an accommodation between English and French-speaking Canada. The Liberals had basically managed it through a political marriage of the prairies (Manitoba and Saskatchewan) with Quebec. And because Quebec had been so central to Liberal hegemony any disruption to its politics naturally threatened the existence of the party system as it had operated since 1921.

But Meisel himself had started the *Stalled Omnibus* with the observation that the party system had "functioned satisfactorily" in the first half century after Confederation. What he did not focus on in his analysis was that there had been a different party system then, one whose "important latent functions" had been different. The system Meisel was concerned with, the politics of party brokerage, was in fact a second, distinctive party system. In retrospect, it now seems clear that it was this second party system that was itself coming to an end. The omnibus was permanently stalled. When the parties got back on the road again they would be different vehicles, going places that they had never been before, and developing a party politics that Canada had never seen before. To elaborate on this we need to put the several Canadian party systems in perspective.

Though characterizations of Canadian parties' socio-economic environment often focus on its fluid changing nature, often over-

Table 2: Government and Opposition

		Vote Gov't	Shares Opp'n	(%) CCF/NDP	National Gov'ts*
I:	1867-1911	51.2	47.1	—	100%
II:	1921-1957	45.7	35.0	11.4	80%
III:	1962-1988	42.0	33.7	17.1	50%

* The proportion of governments winning half the seats in at least half the provinces.

looked are two important underlying shifts in the basic structure of the community. Table 1 reveals the political reality of those fundamental alterations in the regional balances that constrained the party politicians.

For most of the first half century after Confederation Canada was a three region country: Ontario had about half the electorate and the other half was pretty evenly split between Quebec and the maritimes. This was, of course, the basic alignment of interests that had been accommodated at Confederation and in Macdonald's subsequent national policy. In the first decade of the twentieth century the country was transformed by the explosive population growth which filled the prairies. (Its proportion of the electorate would not significantly change after 1911.) The events of the second decade, with its war-time electoral franchise and party coalition in 1917, meant that the political impact of this would not be felt until 1921. But from that point on Canada had a four region political system: Ontario's share of the electorate dropped to a third, Quebec remained stable at a quarter, and the new prairie region surpassed the maritimes which was moving into a long secular decline. Incorporating and accommodating the conflicting interests of the new region proved no easy task under the old political rules and it was for this that Mackenzie King built his Liberal omnibus.

However, by the Diefenbaker interlude British Columbia was pushing into the system as a sizeable and distinctive region in its own right. 1953 marked the first general election in which the province had the third largest number of seats in the House of Commons. Coincidentally, or perhaps not so coincidentally, that was also the time when it was abandoning the national parties in its provincial political system. British Columbians were coming to live in 'two political worlds' which only accentuated its regional peculiarities. Thus, in the years since the omnibus stalled, Canada has operated as a five region country: the relative positions of Ontario, Quebec and the prairies have changed remarkably little since the 1920s but B.C. has outstripped the Atlantic region, itself much changed by the addition of Newfoundland.

As one might expect, these regionally distinct periods in Canadian political development were each marked by different political equations and different patterns of party competition (see also Johnston et al., 1992: ch.2). Something of the consequences for the electoral balance between government and opposition can be seen in Table 2. Let us consider them in turn.

First, The 'Pre-Brokerage' Party System

Meisel was on to an important point when he observed that the party system had "functioned satisfactorily" in the fifty years after Confederation. However it was not because more skillful brokerage politicians managed it better. The demands made on that first party system were quite different and so then were the latent functions it performed in the new three region state.

Early party competition involved a classic two-sided confrontation between government and opposition. In such a situation the government almost inevitably won over half the vote; only once, in 1896, did it fall below that point. With the official opposition monopolizing the anti-government vote elections were relatively close so that the average distance between the two was just over four percentage points. This evenly balanced competition engendered widespread support for majority governments in parliament. In not one of the dozen general elections of the period (1867-1911) did a government fail to command a majority of the seats in at least half the provinces.

As Johnston (1980, table 3) has convincingly demonstrated, this was a geographically very homogeneous party system with patterns of party support that looked more national in character than anything seen since. This despite the fact that the same single-member plurality electoral system that many now hold responsible for so much of the country's political regionalism was in use. Of course the system was still capable of producing its characteristic anomalies. In 1896 the party that formed the government (with a comfortable parliamentary majority) did so despite having won fewer votes than its opposition.

It was during this period that Ontario, with half the national electorate, had the greatest potential to dominate Canadian politics. But that very size made the post-war type of regional politics less salient and allowed relatively homogeneous patterns of two-party competition to emerge. National politics in Ontario were tightly contested though the Conservatives had an edge and won a majority of seats in every general election (with the exception of the Pacific scandal of 1874). This kept them in power for a quarter-century until Laurier and the electoral system (in 1891) were able to shift enough Quebec seats to provide the Liberals with a parliamentary majority. Though Laurier's Liberals never did win more seats in Ontario than their Tory opponents they certainly captured enough constituencies in the province to form genuinely national governments. And it was the local constituency that provided the principal focus for party activity in those years.

The politics of this first system was centred on the parochial interests of small-scale constituencies. Writing about the party politics of the day, Peter Waite (1986: 161) observes: "Not the least part of this process of accommodation was patronage, in all its many variations." In building political coalitions, cementing party loyalties and defining competitive relationships, patronage was the politician's principal tool. They were aided in their political struggles by a rather pragmatic attitude towards the franchise and a happy willingness to fiddle the electoral list or map as partisan need dictated.

Party politics was distributive in the simplest sense, and politicians dealt directly with the "greedy, rapacious, impatient, unforgiving...[and]...alarmingly tenacious" demands of their constituents (Waite, 1986: 162). To succeed parties needed to penetrate and consume the state, filling its every nook and cranny from deputy ministership to Antigonish stationmaster, with partisans. Macdonald and then Laurier dominated because they understood this best and organized their parties on that principle (Stewart, 1986).

A politics of constituency level distribution and log-rolling allows for the careful calculation of the costs and benefits of party activity. And this is what explains the dramatically more homogeneous patterns of support that Johnston reveals existed in this first party system. As if to confirm this portrait of the essence of the system Johnston's data also show that on that measure the governing party, with the most tangible resources to distribute, typically did better than the opposition.

Debating the bounds of the new country Cartier had argued that a shared political nationality might be hoped for, but that a common state could actually be made to work by national parties. Thus the most important latent function performed by this party system was that of state-building. The parties were the agents responsible for establishing a common institutional framework and they did this largely through their management and manipulation of a national public service. This is why when the party-state relationship was suddenly transformed by civil service reform (a euphemism for the abolition of patronage), and the parties' central role as a public employment agency was shifted to another site in the political system, the distinctive parties of this first system were killed.

Second, The 'Brokerage' Party System

Conscription may have buried the old evenly balanced two-party system of national competition in 1917 by burying Conservative chances in Quebec. However it was the eruption of the prairies into the system as an electorally significant region that underlay the new politics. The west's distinctive interests could not have been easily accommodated, even if the politicians had not just been deprived of their traditional tools. Out of the political and parliamentary chaos generated by the first post-war election was to come regional accommodation via the great brokerage party organization that we now associate with the long King-St. Laurent period of Liberal predominance.

Analyses of this second party system often point to the continuing presence of minor parties as evidence that Canadian party politics had changed in important ways. The other side of that same coin was the sharp decline in the vote share garnered by the two major parties. It fell by nearly twenty percentage points. In sharp contrast to the first system only once did the government party manage to capture half the vote: its average level of electoral support was lower than the opposition's during the earlier, first party system. Even more dramatic was the fall in the opposition vote: it fell to an average of only 35 @7 per cent so that the gap between government and opposition more than doubled. This meant that after 1930 the opposition Conservatives were not a serious contender for national office.

Voters in the west no longer divided their votes between the major parties. In virtually every election both Saskatchewan and Alberta were even less Conservative than Quebec. The Tories were not a national force and it was left to the Liberals to form governments by brokering the interests of the prairies and Quebec with what support they could find in the rest of the country (it took the Great Depression to give the Liberals their first Ontario victory, in 1935, since the railway scandal election of 1874). The much increased regional heterogeneity of party support patterns began to undermine the legitimacy of governments as truly national instruments. As if to signal this ominous trend, 20 per cent of the governments formed did not have the support of the majority of MPs from at least half the provinces when they were first elected.

Thus the challenge of governing this new four region Canada was one of "creat[ing] a national consensus on the broad purposes of government and on the general means to achieve them" (Meisel, 1963:369). The latent function required of the party system, but particularly the Liberal party, was now that of nation-building. Whitaker's account, titled *The Government Party*, describes how this was done by building the great omnibus party electoral machine centred on strong and autonomous regional minister-political bosses.

Regional policy accommodation (labeled brokerage) now replaced constituency patronage as the principal tool of the governing party. Mackenzie King demonstrated in the 1920s, and again in the 1940s, how the Liberals were prepared to shift their position to satisfy the politically insistent in order to maintain hold on office. This is why King needed powerful regional figures like Lapointe, Gardiner, Ilsley, or Crerar. They had to be able to accommodate as well as articulate their region's conflicting interests in "the government party's" national policy-making. That process was inevitably both piecemeal and continuous which is why Meisel's analysis rightly gives so much attention to the political skills of those in the party charged with it.

Certainly the minor parties reflected the range of conflicting interests in the country and pointed to the demand for regional brokerage and accommodation. Social Credit was a permanent reminder to the end of the system that Alberta felt excluded from national political life, and the CCF gave evidence that some rejected the very idea of brokerage as a mode of politics. But neither of these parties stalled the omnibus. Indeed they eased its journey by making some vehicle like it necessary and by fragmenting its opposition. When the second system came to a close so too did those parties.

This brokerage, nation-building party system ended when, like the first state-building system, its latent functions were drained away into another part of the political system. That happened when premiers, leaders of provincial governments and their own increasingly independent parties, displaced national cabinet members as the principal spokesmen for their regions. The political brokerage that was still essential to Canadian nation-building now found a home in the evolving system of executive federalism. The impulses of national party competition were largely irrelevant to the politics of federal-provincial diplomacy. By the end of the 1950s Canadian parties were about to be transformed once again.

Third, The 'Post-Brokerage' Party System

Canada changed rapidly in the years after World War II, and by 1965 the politicians were facing an electorate that had grown by almost 50 per cent in just two decades. As Meisel noted, this involved a massive reshaping of the socio-political cast of English-speaking Canada but an even more dramatic transformation of the country's French-speaking community. When this was coupled to the political maturation (in size if not sophistication) of British Columbia as a fifth region, it was evident that the parties would need to find new ways to organize and mobilize political support. The omnibus was not so much stalled as in need of being rebuilt, much as Macdonald and King had been compelled to build new parties at the beginnings of their distinctive eras.

In the new third party system the share of the vote controlled by the government and opposition dropped once again. But with the government party winning only a little more than two votes in five, and the opposition one in three, the gap between the two closed somewhat compared to the second system. The consequence of these two developments taken together was a less stable parliamentary system, the very pattern that Meisel had predicted as the period opened.

The governments that were thrown up by these parliaments were less "national" than ever. Only half of the ten formed from 1962-1988 could count on the support of even fifty percent of the MPs from half of the provinces. Electoral results seemed particularly capricious, for of those governments Trudeau's in 1972 and Mulroney's in 1988 were the least national (by this measure) but the former was a minority and the latter a majority. Aside from the landslide of 1984, the most broadly based of all the governments was actually Clark's (with at least half the MPs from six provinces) but it was returned with fewer votes than its opposition, and the lowest vote in its history (save 1945) in Quebec.

This also reflected the new political equation that had been stimulated by the Diefenbaker-led realignment of the prairies. It now became as Conservative (especially Alberta and Manitoba) as it had been Liberal in the second party system. But with the prairies returning Conservatives, and Quebec Liberals, this meant that for the first time in the country's history the political ground where elections were fought and won was Ontario. Only in 1972, the closest of the contests, did the party that captured the most seats in Ontario not win the election. With both major parties completely shut out of a major region, and the NDP nonexistent east of the Ottawa River, Canada's parties no longer operated as the omnibus regional brokers of old.

In the period since the 1960s, with the flowering of the Canadian version of the welfare state and the managed economy, the dominant style of party governance has been what David Smith (1985) calls pan-Canadianism. This required parties to appeal directly to Canadians as individuals and not simply as members of geographic or linguistic communities. To do so the two large national parties developed centralized, top-down campaign machines, cut the ties to their provincial wings and built organizations based on mass memberships. As parties defined themselves in terms of a national agenda, partisan activists were regularly drawn into both policy and leadership struggles. The electoral constituencies for particular political agendas were not particularly geographically homogeneous but this was now regarded as of little consequence by party-builders like Davey and Stanbury who pioneered the new style Liberal party (Wearing, 1981).

The Conservatives were slower to adapt to the new demands of the system, in part because the long bitter conflict over Diefenbaker's leadership left them divided and fractious. When they did, their response was to adopt the new technologies of opinion polling, television advertising and, most important, direct mail fund-raising to pay for the burgeoning permanent professional organization the party was putting in place. By the early 1980s their organization had leapfrogged the governing Liberals and they had the dominant party machine and a vague bias for an agenda of retrenching the public sector.

Canada's social democrats found this new party system, whose latent function was one of providing competing definitions of the national political agenda, far more hospitable. As the new system emerged they transformed themselves from a party based on an idea to one based on an interest with their marriage to the new national labour congress. The comprehensive reform of the party financing and electoral expense regime, which had been a necessary condition of the evolution of the new national agenda parties (and had made them rich beyond anything they might have conceived of two decades earlier), allowed the New Democrats to compete more or less evenly for the first time. Though the party could not establish itself in the eastern end of the country, by the 1980s its national vote share was virtually double that of the old CCF.

Thus, twenty years after the *Stalled Omnibus*, it appeared as if the parties were back on the road again. They were now defining their bases of support in terms of their conception of the agenda and finding new ways to reach and involve individual voters. This led to an electoral politics that would have horrified Mackenzie King, for it provided the spectacle of Liberal Prime Minister Trudeau telling voters that if they didn't agree with him to go away and vote for someone else. Given that the government party was pursuing a national agenda without national support it seemed inevitable that they would.

The Mulroney Interlude

The electoral results of 1984 constituted a political earthquake. Not only was there a huge explosion but when all the dust settled it appeared that old familiar landmarks had disappeared with the reshaping of the political terrain. When this was followed by a second Conservative majority government in 1988 the curse that had been put on the party system by the *Stalled Omnibus* prediction seemed finally to have been lifted.

Mulroney's Conservative party victory was one of epic proportions. Only twice since the end of the first party system had a government won a larger vote share than the Tories' 50 per cent, and never in Canadian history had the gap between government and opposition party been so great. In the Commons the new government commanded the second largest majority ever. But most striking was the very breadth of the outcome as a truly national result. For the first time ever in Canadian electoral history a government's parliamentary party included a majority of the MPs from every province.

The key to making this possible was the replacement of Clark with Mulroney and the new Conservative leader's ability to recapture Quebec for his party. By doing so he upset the basic political formula that had governed the third party system and he made the Conservative party a genuinely national party for the first time since the conscription crisis of the First World War. The concomitant of this was the prospect that the Liberals might be reduced to a replica of the inter-war Tories.

However the Conservative party victory of 1984 was built on a mirage. The Conservatives had fashioned no clear sense of their own agenda but had rather run against that of the Trudeau Liberals. And an exhausted electorate looking for relief had rather unquestioningly adopted them. While the manifest electoral payoffs proved enormous, the party had failed to perform its most important latent function. This left the system rudderless. More particularly, without a clear sense of its own agenda, the new government was left unable to distinguish between its real supporters and its fair weather friends. The result in the first year was policy drift as the government feared to do anything that might be unpopular with anyone (see Perlin, 1988).

Irony then dictated that in 1988 the Conservative party was forced to run the most issue driven election campaign in generations in defense of its economic agenda, and especially the Free Trade Agreement with the United States. When the dust settled the government commanded a majority of seats in only Alberta and Quebec (with just half in Manitoba and New Brunswick). For the first time since Diefenbaker realigned the electorate, a majority government had been formed without winning more than half of Ontario's seats.

The Liberals began their long climb back from the disaster of 1984 by seeking to recapture groups like immigrants, women, and the economically disadvantaged in the urban areas who had been an important part of the Trudeau coalition. Victories in the 1988 election in Halifax, Montreal, Ottawa, Toronto, Hamilton and Winnipeg suggested they had made some progress. The New Democrats were not able to use the free trade issue to alter the party's base, though their victory in British Columbia did mark the first time they captured a majority of Commons seats in a province other than Saskatchewan.

The Conservative results in 1988 suggested that the party may have unwittingly recreated (or been driven back upon) Mackenzie King's old coalition of the prairies and Quebec. This too was illusionary, for King had to broker competing interests while Mulroney was supposed to be articulating and representing a common agenda. Yet there had never really been any such common interest underlying the Mulroney Conservative party. This has become painfully clear with the rise of the Reform party and the Bloc Qubcois in the only two provinces the Tories managed to control in 1988. Both these parties offer the electorate a clear definition of the public agenda, a central element of which was a radical redefinition of the political community. Their agendas are for different nations.

Putting the parties back on the road again as new vehicles attempting to take more carefully defined groups of passengers to new destinations has been exhilarating but also politically exhausting. The public opinion polls now suggest the probable result will be a major traffic jam, perhaps even a disastrous crash in the next elections. Not having the perspicacity of John Meisel I hesitate to predict. We would do well, however, to remember our past. When Conservative Prime Minister Robert Borden swept to office with a coalition which defined its politics in terms of the national interest (English, 1977, 229) "'National government' became, to too many Canadians, a symbol not of innovation and creativity but of domination by an arrogant majority. Thereafter they would prefer the muddle,...the Union government which divided us most was succeeded by that Prime Minister who would divide us least."

Note

1   This paper was originally prepared for a Conference entitled *Canada's Century* which was held at Queen's during the University's sesquicentennial year in the spring of 1991. It was held to celebrate and honour the contributions of John Meisel. It is hoped that all the papers of that conference will be published together as a feschrift to Professor Meisel. This paper appears in the fall 1992 *Queen's Quarterly*.

References

English, J. (1977). *The Decline of Politics: The Conservatives and the Party System 1901-20* (Toronto: University of Toronto Press).

Johnston, R. (1980). "Federal and Provincial Voting: Contemporary Patterns and Historical Evolution" in D. Elkins & R. Simeon *Small Worlds: Provinces and Parties in Canadian Political Life* (Toronto: Methuen).

Johnston, R., Blais, A., Brady, H., & Crete, J. (1992). *Letting The People Decide* (Montreal: McGill-Queen's University Press).

Meisel, J. (1963). "The Stalled Omnibus: Canadian Parties in the 1960s" *Social Research*, XXX(3).

Meisel, J. (1973). "Howe, Hubris and '72: An Essay on Political Elitism" in *Working Papers on Canadian Politics* (Montreal: McGill-Queen's University Press).

Meisel, J. (1979). "The Decline of Party in Canada" in H.G. Thorburn ed. *Party Politics in Canada* 4th ed. (Prentice-Hall).

Meisel, J. (1991). "Dysfunctions of Canadian Parties: An Exploratory Mapping" in H.G. Thorburn ed. *Party Politics in Canada* 4th ed. (Prentice-Hall).

Perlin, G. (1988). "Opportunity Regained: The Tory Victory in 1984" in H. Penniman ed. *Canada at the Polls, 1984* (Duke University Press).

Smith, D. (1985). "Party, Government, Representation and National Integration in Canada" in P. Aucoin ed. *Party, Government and Regional Representation in Canada* (Toronto: University of Toronto Press).

Stewart, G. (1986). *The Origins of Canadian Politics: A Comparative Approach* (Vancouver: University of British Columbia Press).

Waite, P. (1986). "Becoming Canadians: Ottawa's Relations with Maritimers in the First and Twenty-First Years of Confederation" in R.K. Carty & W.P. Ward eds. *National Politics and Community in Canada* (Vancouver: University of British Columbia Press).

Wearing, J. (1981). *The L-Shaped Party: The Liberal Party of Canada 1958-1980* (McGraw-Hill Ryerson).

Whitaker, R. (1977). *The Government Party: Organizing and Financing the Liberal Party of Canada 1930-58* (Toronto: University of Toronto Press).

Acknowledgements

"Party Politics in Canada," by André Siegfried
From André Siegfried, *The Race Question in Canada*, originally
published in 1907; republished as #29 of the Carleton Library
Series, 1966, McClelland & Stewart. Reprinted by permission of
Carleton University Press.

"Political Patronage Under Macdonald and Laurier 1878-1911,"
by Gordon T. Stewart
From *American Review of Canadian Studies*, X(1), (1980). Reprinted by permission of the author.

"Politics at the Grassroots: Lessons from post-Confederation
Nova Scotia," by P.B. Waite
From P.B.Waite, "Becoming Canadians: Ottawa's Relations with
Maritimers in the First and Twenty-first Years of Confederation"
published in R.K. Carty and W.P. Ward eds., *National Politics and
Community in Canada*: Vancouver: UBC Press: 1986.

"Electoral Management," by H.B. Ames and
"Electoral Management: A Reply to Mr. Ames by a candidate in
the recent elections" from *The Canadian Magazine* vol xxv, 1905

"Party Leadership Selection in the New Dominion," by John C.
Courtney
From John C. Courtney, *The Selection of National Party Leaders in
Canada*: Toronto: MacMillan of Canada: 1973.

"Party Finance Before World War I," by K.Z Paltiel
From *Political Party Financing in Canada*: Toronto: McGraw-Hill
Ryerson: 1970. Reprinted by permission of the Estate of K.Z.
Paltiel.

"The Politician's Dominion: party media relations in early Canada" by Paul Rutherford
From Paul Rutherford, *A Victorian Authority*: Toronto: University
of Toronto Press, 1982

"The End of the Great Party Era" by John English
from John English, *The Decline of Politics*: Toronto: University of
Toronto Press: 1977

"The Government Party" by R. Whitaker
from R. Whitaker, *The Government Party: Organizing and Financing the Liberal Party of Canada 1930-58* Toronto: University of
Toronto Press: 1977)

"The Liberal Party," by Joseph Wearing
From Joseph Wearing, *The L-Shaped Party*, Toronto: McGraw-Hill
Ryerson: 1981.
Reprinted by permission of the author

"The Conservative's National Organization," by John R. Williams
From John R. Williams, *The Conservative Party of Canada 1892-
1949*: Durham, North Carolina: Duke University Press, 1956
"A Party-Movement: The CCF and the rejection of brokerage politics" by Walter Young
from *The Anatomy of a Party*: Toronto: University of Toronto
Press: 1969

"The Coming of Leadership Conventions," by R.K. Carty
From R.K.Carty "Choosing New Party Leaders" in H. Penniman
ed., *Canada at the Polls 1984*: Durham, North Carolina: Duke University Press: 1988.

"Two Liberal Leadership Conventions," by C.G. Power
From C.G.Power, *A Party Politician*: Toronto: MacMillan of Canada: 1966.

"Party Finance in the Second Party System," by E.E. Harrill
Based on the author's PhD thesis at UNC (1958) and this ex-
cerpt from H.G. Thorburn *Party Politics in Canada* 1st ed.:
Toronto: Prentice-Hall: 1963.

"From a Single Medium to a Multimedia Society," by W.C. Soderlund et al
From Soderlund et al, *Media & Elections in Canada*: Toronto:
Holt, Rinehart & Winston: 1984. Reprinted by permission of the
author.

"The Problem of Election Spending," by C.G. Power
From *Maclean's Magazine* Feb. 1, 1949 and this excerpt from
H.G. Thorburn *Party Politics in Canada* 1st ed. Toronto: Prentice-
Hall: 1963.

"Advertising, Parties and Elections: the case of the Liberals" by
R. Whitaker
from *The Government Party: Organizing and Financing the Liberal
Party of Canada 1930-58*, Toronto: University of Toronto Press:
1977.

"The Stalled Omnibus & The Decline of the Party," by John
Meisel
From the author's essays by these names in *Social Research* vol
30, 1963, and H.G. Thorburn *Party Politics in Canada* 5th ed.:
Toronto: Prentice-Hall: 1985)

"Recognition of Canadian Political Parties in Parliament and
Law," by John C. Courtney
From *Canadian Journal of Political Science*, 11, (1), 1978.

"The NDP: A Trade Union Party?" by Keith Archer
From Keith Archer ed., *Prime Ministers and Premiers*: Montreal:
McGill-Queen's University Press: 1990)

"The Cauldron of Leadership: Prime Ministers and Their Par-
ties," by Leslie A. Pal
From Leslie Pal, *Prime Ministers and Premiers*: Toronto: Prentice-
Hall Canada: 1988.

"Joe Wearing's 12 rules for Winning a PC or Liberal Leadership
Contest," by Joseph Wearing
From Joseph Waring *Strained Relations: Canadian Parties and Vot-
ers*: Toronto: McClelland & Stewart: 1988

"Contesting the Leadership at the Grassroots: the Liberals in
1990," by Lawrence Hanson. Reprinted permission of the author

"The Selection of Candidates by Political Parties,"
Royal Commission on Electoral Reform and Party Finance
(from *Reforming Electoral Democracy*, vol. 1, 1991)

"Financing Contemporary Party Politics," Royal Commission on Electoral Reform and Party Finance (from *Reforming Electoral Democracy*, vol. 1, 1991)

"Canadian Party Ideologies in the Electronic Age," by A. Brian Tanguay
From A. Gagnon & J. Bickerton eds., *Canadian Politics*, Peterborough: Broadview Press: 1990.

"Horserace Journalism and Canadian Election Campaigns," by R. Jeremy Wilson
From *Journal of Canadian Studies*, 15(4) 1980-81.

"Pollsters, Consultants and Party Politics in Canada," by David C. Walker, M.P.
From A. Gagnon & B. Tanguay eds., *Canadian Parties in Transition*: Toronto: Nelson Canada: 1989

"Party Politics in Canada," by David E. Smith
Excerpt from "Party Government, Representation and National Integration in Canada" by David E. Smith from *Party Government and Regional Representation in Canada*, edited by Peter Aucoin.

Reprinted by permission of University of Toronto Press in cooperation with the Royal Commission on the Economic Union and Development Prospects for Canada, Ministry of Supply and Services, vol. 36

"Three Canadian Party Systems," by R.K. Carty
From G.C. Perlin ed., *Party Democracy in Canada*: Toronto: Prentice-Hall: 1988.

"The Electoral Basis of the Canadian Party Systems," by Richard Johnston
From Johnson et al, *Letting the People Decide: History Contingency, and the Dynamics of Canadian Elections*: Montreal: McGill-Queen's University Press: 1992

"On the Road Again: the Stalled Omnibus Revisited" by R.K. Carty
Queen's Quarterly, fall 1992

Printed in Canada